Europe Today

Europe Today

A Twenty-first Century Introduction

Fifth Edition

EDITED BY RONALD TIERSKY
AND ERIK JONES

ROWMAN & LITTLEFIELD
Lanham • Boulder • New York • Toronto • Plymouth, UK

Published by Rowman & Littlefield
4501 Forbes Boulevard, Suite 200, Lanham, Maryland 20706
www.rowman.com

10 Thornbury Road, Plymouth PL6 7PP, United Kingdom

British Library Cataloguing in Publication Information Available

Library of Congress Cataloging-in-Publication Data
Europe today : a twenty-first century introduction / edited by Ronald Tiersky and Erik Jones. —
Fifth edition.
     pages cm. — (Europe today)
  Includes bibliographical references and index.
  ISBN 978-1-4422-2109-3 (cloth : alk. paper) — ISBN 978-1-4422-2110-9 (pbk. : alk. paper) —
ISBN 978-1-4422-2111-6 (electronic) 1. European Union countries—Politics and government—
21st century. 2. Europe—Politics and government—21st century. 3. Europe—Forecasting.
I. Tiersky, Ronald, 1944– II. Jones, Erik.
  JN30.E82478 2014
  320.94—dc23
                                                                      2014001481

∞™ The paper used in this publication meets the minimum requirements of American
National Standard for Information Sciences—Permanence of Paper for Printed Library
Materials, ANSI/NISO Z39.48-1992.

Printed in the United States of America

Contents

Preface

A Note to Students

Introductory textbooks are notoriously difficult for professors to write. Success demands from authors not only a mastery of subject matter but also an ability to explain things to beginning students without talking down to them. The job isn't easy.

For your part, you, the student, must be willing to read seriously and to engage the book in good faith. You must be willing to try to imagine what many or most of you have not yet seen, that is, Europe and its vividly different countries and societies. You must begin with nothing more than a willingness to get interested—an intellectual curiosity about the world outside the United States. We can assure you that cosmopolitan knowledge will repay you in ways that you will understand only later. You will discover the empowerment of traveling with your mind. You will, we hope, go to Europe and feel after a day or two that you are not completely a stranger in London, Paris, Berlin, Rome, Stockholm, Warsaw, or even Brussels, home of the often-confusing European Union (EU).

Understanding international politics first requires familiarity with particular countries, so as to possess a sort of foundational stone of knowledge upon which to build a progressively larger view of the world. One must be a specialist before becoming a generalist. You will find several country chapters in this book, but you will find the separate countries again in every European-gauge chapter. Be aware that your job is to hold the two ends of a rope—to know separate countries and to understand the EU as a whole.

As students just arriving on the scene, you have the advantage of naïveté, meaning a relative lack of prejudices and stereotypes. How fortunate you are, we think, not to begin with the heavy baggage of the past! Yet how much you don't know of what you need to know—that is, the past!

A Note to Teachers

In our note to students, we've put teachers on the spot. We've asked students for imagination in addition to information; we're asking the same of teachers. We hope that at the end of your courses, you will feel that this book has done its part by giving you what you need to do an important job.

Some teachers have raised the issue of whether the country chapters or the European-integration chapters should come first. There is no obvious or completely satisfactory answer. At those moments when integration stalls, as in the context of the economic and financial crisis, putting the country chapters first seems best. That is what we have chosen for this edition. Teachers, obviously, can use the book from either direction according to their own inclinations.

Nor should teachers feel obliged to teach entirely "with the book" in order to get the most out of it. Each chapter in some way is an argument rather than a description. Teaching partly against rather than with the author of a chapter can be a powerful pedagogical strategy.

Above all, this fifth edition of *Europe Today* strives to be teacher- as well as student-friendly. We welcome comments about how the book can be improved.

In closing, we should give credit where credit is due. This book would not have been possible without the support of Amherst College, the Johns Hopkins University School of Advanced International Studies (SAIS), and Nuffield College in Oxford. Saskia van Genugten played a vital role in producing the previous edition during the final stages of her doctorate; she has now moved on to greener professional pastures and yet the contribution she made remains significant. This edition has also depended upon the support of an excellent group of research assistants attached to the Bologna Institute for Policy Research at SAIS Europe. Special thanks go to David Attewell for updating much of the supporting material and to Irena Grizelj for formatting the manuscript for submission. Katrina Pirner and Daniel Richards helped assemble the proof corrections and Andrew Whitworth compiled the index. Dea Di Furia and Kathryn Knowles provided invaluable support from start to finish. This project would not have come together when it did without their hard work.

Finally, it's a pleasure once again to thank Susan McEachern, our editor at Rowman & Littlefield, who has been so important in the success of the Europe Today series. She makes a great deal happen and she saves us from many mistakes.

A personal note from Ronald Tiersky: With this fifth edition of *Europe Today*, it seems to me the right time to pass the torch to my coeditor and good friend, Erik Jones. He will be sole editor of future editions of the book. In addition, Erik will be joining me as co–general editor of Rowman & Littlefield's Europe Today series. Great thanks to Erik for all he's done over the years for this book and the series. The project is in very good hands.

Ronald Tiersky and Erik Jones
November 2013

European Union
Statistical Information

Population (million)	507.1 (January 2013)
Area (square miles)	1,707,787
GDP (trillion, PPP)	$16.584 (2012 est.)
GDP per Capita (PPP)	$32,021 (2012 est.)

Performance of Key Political Parties in Parliamentary Elections of June 4–7, 2009*

Group of the European People's Party (Christian-Democrats, EPP)	36%
Group of the Progressive Alliance of Socialists and Democrats in the European Parliament (S&D)	25%
Group of the Alliance of Liberals and Democrats for Europe (ALDE)	11.4%
Group of the Greens/European Free Alliance (GREENS/EFA)	7.5%
European Conservatives and Reformists Group (ECR)	7.3%
Confederal Group of the European United Left – Nordic Green Left (GUE/NGL)	4.8%
Europe of Freedom and Democracy Group (EFD)	4.3%
Nonattached (NA)	3.7%

Main Officeholders: President of the European Parliament: Martin Schulz (Germany), S&D, in office since 2012; President of the European Commission: José Manuel Durão Barroso (Portugal), EPP, in office since 2004, reelected in 2009; Permanent President to the European Council: Herman van Rompuy (Belgium), EPP, in office since 2009; and High Representative for CFSP: Lady Catherine Ashton (Britain), S&D, in office since 2009.

---

*The European Parliament will hold elections as this book goes to press. Those elections will coincide with a turnover of a number of high offices in other institutions including the European Commission and the European Council.

Timeline of Events Leading to the Current State of the European Union

May 1945	End of World War II in Europe.
June 1945	The United Nations is founded.
June 1947	The Marshall Plan (European Recovery Program) is launched.
April 1948	The Organization for European Economic Cooperation (OEEC) is established.
May 1949	The Council of Europe is founded.
April 1951	The Treaty of Paris is signed, which establishes the European Coal and Steel Community (ECSC).
March 1957	The Treaties of Rome are signed, which establish the European Atomic Energy Community (Euratom) and the European Economic Community (EEC). Members of the EEC are France, the Netherlands, Belgium, Luxembourg, Germany, and Italy.
February 1958	The Benelux Economic Union is founded.
July 1958	The Common Agricultural Policy (CAP) is proposed.
December 1960	The OEEC is reorganized into the Organization for Economic Cooperation and Development (OECD).
August 1961	Denmark, Ireland, and the UK apply for EEC membership. (President Charles de Gaulle of France vetoes the British application twice: in January 1963 and November 1967.)
April 1962	Norway applies for EEC membership.
April 1965	The Merger Treaty is signed, which consolidates the institutions created by the Treaty of Paris and the Treaties of Rome.
July 1968	The EEC Customs Union is finalized and the CAP is enacted.
January 1972	EEC negotiations concluded with UK, Denmark, Ireland, and Norway.
September 1972	A national referendum in Norway goes against its membership in the EEC.
January 1973	UK, Denmark, and Ireland join the EEC.
January 1974	Creation of the European Social Fund.
January 1975	Creation of the European Regional Development Fund.
June 1975	Greece applies for EU membership.

March 1977	Portugal applies for EEC membership.
July 1977	Spain applies for EEC membership.
March 1979	The European Monetary System (EMS) established.
June 1979	First direct elections of the European Parliament (EP).
January 1981	Greece joins the EEC.
January 1986	Spain and Portugal join the EEC.
February 1986	The Single European Act is signed in Luxembourg, removing most of the remaining physical, fiscal, and technical barriers to the formation of a European common market. The EEC now referred to as the European Community (EC).
June 1987	Turkey applies for EC membership.
July 1989	Austria applies for EC membership.
December 1989	Turkey's membership application is rejected.
July 1990	Malta and Cyprus apply for EC membership.
October 1990	German reunification brings the former East Germany into the EC.
July 1991	Sweden applies for EC membership.
February 1992	Treaty on European Union (Maastricht Treaty) signed, which expands the process of European integration and creates a timetable for the European Monetary Union (EMU). The EC is now referred to as the European Union (EU).
March 1992	Finland applies for EU membership.
June 1992	Danish voters reject the Maastricht Treaty.
May 1993	Danish voters approve the Maastricht Treaty after certain compromises are inserted into the treaty.
January 1995	Austria, Sweden, and Finland join the EU after their respective national referenda favor membership. A national referendum in Norway rejects EU membership.
October 1997	The Treaty of Amsterdam is signed, which aims, among other things, to equalize tax structures among members of the EU in preparation for the upcoming monetary union.
January 1999	The EMU goes into effect. The eleven EU member states participating are Austria, Belgium, Finland, France, Germany, Ireland, Italy, Luxembourg, the Netherlands, Portugal, and Spain.
May 1999	The Treaty of Amsterdam enters into force.
September 1999	EP approves a new European Commission led by Romano Prodi.
December 1999	A European Council meeting in Helsinki decides to open accession negotiations with Bulgaria, Latvia, Lithuania, Malta, Romania, and the Slovak Republic and to recognize Turkey as a candidate country.
June 2000	A new partnership agreement (2000–2020) between the EU and the African-Caribbean-Pacific (ACP) countries is signed in Cotonou, Benin.
December 2000	The European Council agrees on the Treaty of Nice (to be ratified by all member states). EU leaders formally proclaim the charter of Fundamental Rights of the European Union.

January 2001	Greece joins the euro zone.
February 2001	Regulation adopted establishing the Rapid Reaction Force.
Jan.–Feb. 2002	The euro becomes legal tender and permanently replaces national currencies in EMU countries.
December 2002	The Copenhagen European Council declares that Cyprus, the Czech Republic, Estonia, Hungary, Latvia, Lithuania, Malta, Poland, the Slovak Republic, and Slovenia will become EU members by May 1, 2004.
February 2003	The Treaty of Nice enters into force.
April 2003	The Treaty of Accession (2003) is signed in Athens.
May 2004	Cyprus, the Czech Republic, Estonia, Hungary, Latvia, Lithuania, Malta, Poland, the Slovak Republic, and Slovenia become EU member states.
October 2004	President-designate of the European Commission Jose Manuel Barroso is forced to withdraw his proposal for the other members of the Commission.
October 2004	EU leaders sign the treaty establishing a constitution for Europe.
November 2004	The EP approves the new Commission proposed by Barroso.
February 2005	Spain holds the first referendum on the European Constitution; the Spanish people accept it.
April 2005	The EP gives its approval to the accession of Bulgaria and Romania to the EU by 2007.
May 2005	The French electorate rejects the European Constitution in a national referendum.
June 2005	The Dutch electorate rejects the European Constitution in a national referendum; a "reflection period" on treaty reform initiates.
October 2005	European accession negotiations open with Croatia and Turkey.
January 2007	Bulgaria and Romania become EU member states; Slovenia joins the euro zone.
June 2007	A German EU presidency ends the "reflection period" and relaunches negotiations for a new treaty.
December 2007	The Lisbon Treaty, a slightly slimmed-down alternative to the European Constitution, is signed by the EU heads of state or government. Only Ireland is obliged to ratify by referendum.
January 2008	Cyprus and Malta join the euro zone.
June 2008	The first Irish referendum is held on the Lisbon Treaty: the treaty is rejected.
June 2008	Negotiations for a new EU-Russia agreement are launched at the EU-Russia summit.
July 2008	At the Paris Summit, French President Nicolas Sarkozy launches the Union for the Mediterranean, aimed at revitalizing the Euro-Mediterranean Partnership.
August 2008	Russia and Georgia fight a war over the provinces of South Ossetia and Abkhazia.
January 2009	Slovakia joins the euro zone.

June 2009	EP elections; the European People's Party (EPP) becomes the largest party.
September 2009	Parliament confirms a second term for European Commission President Jose Manuel Barroso.
October 2009	Second Irish referendum on the Lisbon Treaty: the treaty is ratified.
November 2009	Appointments take place for the two newly created EU top jobs in the Lisbon Treaty. Herman van Rompuy is elected EU council president, and Catherine Ashton is elected high representative for foreign affairs and security policy.
December 2009	The Lisbon Treaty enters into force, thereby amending the Maastricht Treaty (TEU).
December 2009	The Greek sovereign debt crisis escalates, leading to a crisis in the euro zone.
May 2010	Member states and the European Central Bank (ECB) agree on the setup of a European Financial Stability Facility (EFSF) to help weaker euro-zone members remain financially stable.
December 2010	The EU approves the 2011 budget, after disagreements between the member states and the EP. Despite national austerity measures, the EU budget will increase 2.9 percent.
January 2011	Estonia joins the euro zone.
February 2011	Euro-zone finance ministers agree to create the European Stability Mechanism, a €500 billion permanent bailout fund for euro-zone member states in financial difficulty.
November 2011	Silvio Berlusconi resigns as prime minister after interest rates on Italian bonds soar to 7.5 percent.
November 2011	The euro zone officially enters a double-dip recession.
March 2012	All EU member states besides the UK and Czech Republic sign the Treaty on Stability, Coordination, and Governance (TSCG), which creates stricter deficit limits and strengthens oversight of national budgets by the EU Commission and politically independent domestic bodies.
March 2012	Serbia granted the status of candidate for EU membership.
July 2012	ECB President Mario Draghi declares the ECB will do "whatever it takes to preserve the euro"; yields on periphery debt stabilize.
August 2012	ECB announces a program to buy bonds of most indebted countries on secondary markets (Outright Monetary Transactions, or OMT).
January 2013	UK Prime Minister David Cameron promises British voters an in-or-out referendum on EU membership by 2017.
March 2013	Depositors in Cyprus forced to help pay bailout costs in first ever "bail-in"; Cyprus invokes emergency capital controls.
May 2013	Kosovo and Serbia sign an EU-mediated agreement to normalize relations and end the partition of North Kosovo, populated mostly by ethnic Serbs.
July 2013	Croatia becomes an EU member state.
January 2014	Latvia joins the euro zone.

Common Acronyms

CAP	Common Agricultural Policy
CEEC	Central and Eastern European Countries
CFSP	Common Foreign and Security Policy
CMEA	Council for Mutual Economic Assistance
COREU	CORespondance EUropéenne
CSCE	Conference on Security and Cooperation in Europe
CSDP	Common Security and Defence Policy
EAPC	Euro-Atlantic Partnership Council
EBRD	European Bank for Reconstruction and Development
EC	European Community
ECB	European Central Bank
ECHR	European Convention on Human Rights *or* European Court of Human Rights
ECJ	European Court of Justice
ECSC	European Coal and Steel Community
EDA	European Defence Agency
EEA	European Economic Area
EEAS	European External Action Service
EEC	European Economic Community
EFTA	European Free Trade Association
EMS	European Monetary System
EMU	Economic and Monetary Union
ENP	European Neighborhood Policy
EP	European Parliament
EPC	European Political Cooperation
EPU	European Political Union
ERM	Exchange Rate Mechanism
ERRF	European Rapid Reaction Force
ESDI	European Security and Defense Identity
ESM	European Stability Mechanism
ESS	European Security Strategy

GATT	General Agreement on Tariffs and Trade
IGC	Intergovernmental Conference
IMF	International Monetary Fund
JHA	Justice and Home Affairs
LTRO	Long Term Refinancing Operations
MNC	Multinational Corporation
NACC	North Atlantic Cooperation Council
NATO	North Atlantic Treaty Organization
OECD	Organization for Economic Cooperation and Development
OEEC	Organization for European Economic Cooperation
OMT	Outright Monetary Transactions
OSCE	Organization for Security and Cooperation in Europe
PFP	Partnership for Peace
SEA	Single European Act
SGP	Stability and Growth Pact
TEU	Treaty on European Union
TSCG	Treaty on Stability, Coordination, and Governance
TTIP	Transatlantic Trade and Investment Partnership
WEU	Western European Union
WTO	World Trade Organization

Illustrations

Boxes

Figures

Tables

Introduction

Ronald Tiersky and Erik Jones

Europe is about more than just the European Union (EU). This is all too easily forgotten. Whenever the EU runs into trouble, commentators are quick to bemoan the weakness of Europe. Such a rush to judgment was particularly evident during the sovereign debt crisis. As the countries that adopted the euro as a common currency struggled to stabilize both their banks and their public finances, much of the world speculated that "Europe" would soon fall apart.

The purpose of this volume is to offer a more meaningful assessment. In small measure, we achieve that goal by providing a snapshot of *Europe Today* that includes a number of different perspectives, both country specific and thematic. To a much larger extent, we show how that picture of Europe fits within a wider context.

This introduction highlights three overarching themes that are important to any interpretation of current events and are related to legitimacy, solidarity, and security. The themes recur in different ways in each of the chapters in the volume. They are also prominent in European media and political discourse. Europe is changing in fundamental ways. Some of these changes have been underway for decades; others are more recent in origin.

To begin, European democracy faces a decline in voter participation, a rise in electoral volatility, the collapse in support for traditional political parties, and a resurgence of popular protest movements. The challenge to democratic legitimacy is not uniform across Europe, and it is not unique to European countries either; evidence of it can be found in other parts of the world, including the United States. Nevertheless, the prospect of any breakdown in European democracy is important because the countries of Europe are so tightly bound together.

The second theme is solidarity both within and among European countries in the face of great difficulties. Solving domestic problems is hard enough, particularly when any solution creates losers as well as winners. European policymakers describe this challenge using a paraphrase of longtime Luxembourg Prime Minister Jean-Claude Juncker: *They know what they need to do; they just don't know how to get reelected once they have done it.* Solving problems that implicate many countries is even harder. Politicians face national electorates that are reluctant to transfer resources across borders even when it would make good economic sense to do so. Instead, they naturally tend to focus attention on their own situations at home. Often, this self-interested outlook only makes matters worse even for them. As the situation continues to deteriorate, voters become even more attached to the national interest and more suspicious of common endeavors. In practice, this means that voters in countries that are relatively well off become less inclined to support those in more difficult circumstances.

Europeans need to work together, both in principle and as a matter of security. There are frontiers to Europe and there are challenges that arise beyond Europe's borders. European policymakers cannot afford to allow problems outside Europe to remain unattended any more than they can isolate themselves from the consequences of global disorder. Nevertheless, European politicians are often reluctant to take responsibility for their external security or even to agree on what constitutes a threat. Those who are willing to pursue an active foreign and security policy are concentrated in a limited number of countries like France, Great Britain, and Poland, whose national interests are not identical to those of Europe as a whole.

Europe can only emerge as a global actor if more leaders in more countries accept the necessity of meeting their responsibilities abroad. Even then, European politicians must marshal the resources to assert their influence. In turn, this means they must strengthen European economic performance, they must work together effectively, and they must build on a solid foundation of popular support. In this sense, European integration is imperative. Integration is also a multilevel endeavor; it must take place within countries as well as between them.

The EU is a step in the right direction, but it is not a comprehensive solution. The EU is still too limited in scope, too fragile economically, and too weak in terms of political and popular support. This is an observation rather than a criticism. Europeans have made unprecedented achievements in healing and uniting the continent they inhabit after the Second World War and beyond the Cold War. Nevertheless, European integration remains a work in progress.

Legitimacy

The challenge to European democracy should not be overstated. In the early- to mid-twentieth century, European democracy faced an existential threat and survived only by force of arms. Today there are few if any voices in Europe arguing for the replacement of democracy with some other system of government. Indeed, it is difficult to imagine the alternative. Fascism and communism continue to draw adherents on the fringes, but it would be hard to find someone who actually aspires to live within a totalitarian dictatorship. Most supporters of political Islam in Europe want to find a place for themselves in democratic society; only a very small number seek to replace secular democracy with some kind of theocratic government based on Islam through violent acts of terror. Hence, the danger is not that Europeans will reject democracy or that some rival power will conquer and replace European democratic governments; it is that European democracy will cease to function adequately due to neglect.

Three examples illustrate the potential impact of such neglect of democracy: Italy, Hungary, and Greece. The Italian political class collapsed in the early 1990s under the weight of corruption and amidst the ideological turmoil that accompanied the end of the Cold War. Within the space of a few years, both the Christian Democrats and the Communists ceased to function as mainstream political movements. The parties that grew up to replace them led a turbulent existence. Meanwhile, voters became increasingly frustrated with their political leadership. They began to change their votes from one contest to another, they stopped voting (which is rare in Italy), and—most recently—they began throwing their support behind Beppe Grillo's Five Star Movement. This process accelerated when center-right Prime Minister Silvio Berlusconi was forced from office in November 2011 at the height of Italy's sovereign debt crisis; it culminated in the February 2013 elections, when Grillo's group captured more than a quarter of the vote, forcing the center-left and center-right into a grand coalition government. That government survives primarily because Italy's politicians cannot imagine a superior alternative.

The situation in Hungary is different. The country is governed by a center-right political movement—Fidesz—that grew up in opposition to communism at the end of the Cold War; its leader, Viktor Orban, was a central figure in the process of democratic transition. During the intervening decades, Orban and Fidesz have fought both the communist and the noncommunist left. Along the way, the center-right movement attracted more right-wing supporters and adopted more nationalist rhetoric. This was evident already in 1998; it became more prominent as the postcommunist left imploded during the run-up to the 2010 parliamentary elections. The result was an overwhelming victory for the center-right that gave Fidesz sufficient parliamentary control to change the national constitution. The reforms that Orban and his ministers have introduced are each defensible in isolation; in combination, however, they threaten to prevent any alternation in power by giving Fidesz control over the key levers of government. Both the EU and other European countries have complained that Orban and his followers are placing too many constraints on Hungarian democracy through their electoral reforms, political appointments, and restriction of press freedom. These international voices have won some important concessions from Fidesz, yet many still perceive a threat to Hungarian democracy.

Then there is the situation in Greece. The problems in Greek public administration go back many decades. However, the crisis started in the spring of 2008, when the European Commission noted problems in Greek fiscal accounting. This caused international investors to start selling their holdings of Greek government bonds. Tensions mounted further the following autumn as the collapse of the American investment bank Lehman Brothers heightened the sense of fear in international markets. Greece's New Democracy government struggled to respond by tightening its accounting procedures and embracing austerity; the opposition Pan-Hellenic Socialist Movement (Pasok) on the center-left won the October 2009 elections by promising to stimulate growth. That promise came to naught as the incoming Pasok government discovered the extent of the country's financial weakness. What followed was a relentless cycle of domestic austerity, international financial pressure, and European bailouts. For Greek voters, two things became obvious: the political elites of the center-right and the center-left were incompetent, and the international community had effectively usurped many of the formal institutions of government. Greek voters went twice to the polls in the spring of 2012. In May, the vote divided almost evenly between New Democracy, Pasok, and Syriza—the latter is a left-wing protest movement that rejects both fiscal austerity and international interference in Greek politics. A number of smaller parties also gained representation and so it was impossible to form a government. In June, the vote share for New Democracy and Syriza increased dramatically. New Democracy won enough seats to form a workable coalition with support from Pasok, but Syriza remains a potent threat to the stability of Greek democracy. A rise in support for the right-wing extremist Golden Dawn movement is even more problematic.

The threats to democracy are not limited to extreme cases or small countries; they are apparent everywhere to a greater or lesser extent. Consider the UK Independence Party (UKIP) in England and the National Front (FN) in France. UKIP exists to protest British membership in the EU and not to subvert British democracy or to undermine the parliament at Westminster. Nevertheless, UKIP is a useful barometer for disaffection with the Conservative, Labour, and Liberal Democratic parties that are the mainstays of British politics. That disaffection is growing. UKIP had its best ever performance in the May 2013 local elections, winning 147 seats on local councils and 23 percent of the popular vote. UKIP's showing in the 2014 elections to the European Parliament is likely to be even stronger. The question is how much this will complicate Conservative Prime Minister David Cameron's plans for the 2015 legislative elections and whether it will shake the Conservative–Liberal Democratic coalition government. The British first-past-the-post electoral system works best with two parties; it can manage with three; but it will struggle to accommodate four political parties while at the same time producing stable governments.

The French National Front is even more challenging. The FN has been around since 1972 under the leadership of Jean-Marie Le Pen and arguably represents an even older tradition on the right of French politics. Now, however, it is gaining support from beyond its historic base. Marine Le Pen assumed leadership of the FN from her father in January 2011, giving the party a more dynamic and youthful appearance. She has retained many of the strong right-wing policy positions, but she is able to deliver them with a softer edge. The result is very attractive for voters from across the political spectrum who seek an alternative to the more mainstream political parties—the center-right Union for a Popular Movement and the center-left Socialist Party. Such voters are also likely to be frightened by globalization and distrustful of the EU. They do not seek to undermine French democracy, but they do want to change the terms of access to French institutions and social benefits. As with UKIP, support for the FN is a good barometer for popular disaffection. What is different in the French case is that the FN has a more realistic chance of gaining some measure of political power and influence.

A final illustration comes from Turkey. Again, the problem is not that powerful actors want to mobilize support against democracy and in favor of some alternative form of government; it is that broad sections of society are frustrated with the functioning of democratic institutions and they disagree about what democracy represents. This frustration has deep roots. Among Prime Minister Recep Tayyip Erdoğan and his supporters, the source of concern is the "deep state," which is the nexus of the army, the judiciary, and the state security apparatus that long assumed responsibility for preserving the legacy of Kemal Mustafa Atatürk in the form of secular state institutions. Erdoğan won three electoral contests (2002, 2007, and 2011), each time with increasing popular support. In 2011, he received 49.9 percent of the votes on a platform of curbing the "deep state," embracing religious pluralism, and promoting conservative values associated with Sunni Islam. He has done this in part while promoting Turkey's European identity and negotiating for Turkish entry into the EU.

To his opponents, however, Erdoğan and his party appear differently. They see his government's reform efforts as an Islamist attack on Turkish national identity, they decry the persecution of military officers and the subversion of legal institutions, they complain loudly about the restraints on press freedom, and they worry that Erdoğan has authoritarian pretensions. The challenge for Erdoğan's opposition has been to organize an effective political campaign.

The situation in Turkey crystallized during the summer of 2013 in a popular protest against the building of a shopping mall on a park near Taksim Square in downtown Istanbul. The protest highlighted the extent of the divisions within the country: west and east, urban and rural, secular and conservative, and so on. It also revealed how cumbersome democratic institutions can be in mediating distributive conflict. The protestors claimed the right to peaceable assembly and freedom of speech; the government pointed to its electoral victories and popular mandate. The government also organized counterdemonstrations to demonstrate the strength of its base. Only belatedly did Erdoğan admit the need to open up direct conversation in order to calm the situation.

The Turkish case is dramatic for those most deeply involved. However, Turkey is not the only place where such conflicts look unmanageable without some reform of democratic institutions. The easiest illustrations are those places where separatist movements are most intractable—like Flanders in Belgium, Scotland in the United Kingdom, and Catalonia in Spain. These are conflicts where a reform of democratic institutions is an essential part of the problem and the solution. Belgium went more than five hundred days without a government after the 2009 national elections; Scotland has just negotiated the right to a referendum on continued membership in the United Kingdom; Catalonia is asserting a right to greater autonomy that the Spanish courts are unwilling to recognize as legitimate. It is hard to anticipate how these conflicts will develop. However, we do not have to see into the future to recognize that democratic institutions are challenged.

Again, it is important not to overstate the case. The consequences of declining support for democratic institutions are more likely to be incremental than revolutionary. Nevertheless, deepening disaffection with democracy will have an impact both at the national level and within the EU. Nationally, governments may find it increasingly difficult to make concessions to "Europe." In a speech on Britain's relationship with Europe, British Prime Minister David Cameron announced his intention to review the balance of competences between European institutions and national governments. He also called for an "in-or-out" referendum to be held before 2017. The pressure from UKIP is an important factor behind those demands. Moreover, Cameron is not alone. The Dutch government has already conducted a competency review under pressure from Geert Wilder's opposition Party of Freedom on the far right; meanwhile, other member states are looking more quietly at how they must comply with Brussels and where they can ignore inconvenient policies or decisions.

Within the EU institutions, European politicians find it challenging to work with explicitly anti-European political actors. UKIP leader Nigel Farage is a Member of the European Parliament (MEP) already; so is Marine Le Pen. These leaders are famous for using their positions to campaign against Europe. The only question is how large their support in the European Parliament will swell on the back of popular dissatisfaction with traditional democratic politics. The result will be a kind of cognitive dissonance that saps support from European integration.

Solidarity

The issue of solidarity is intertwined with challenges to democratic legitimacy. This is clear in the policy preferences of the various antisystem parties from the right and the left. The only issues that Italy's Five Star Movement has in common with Syriza, the FN, UKIP, and other groups like the Sweden Democrats, the True Finns, and the Dutch Party of Freedom are a distrust of the EU, a resentment of interference with national sovereignty, and a resistance to transfers across countries. Antisystem parties like these tend to be "welfare chauvinist" as well: they do not have much tolerance for immigrants—particularly those who come from outside Europe. Hence, they seek to reserve access to welfare benefits for citizens who can establish their national ethnic or cultural heritage.

There is nothing new in the existence of such anti-immigrant sentiment. What is noteworthy is how widespread it has become. It is found in countries with a long tradition for tolerance, like the Netherlands, and in countries that have relatively little contact with immigrants, like Norway, Sweden, and Finland. It is present in liberal countries like Great Britain, in more statist countries like France, and in decentralized countries like Belgium. It is also a potent force in countries that have more experience with emigration than immigration, like Italy and Spain.

The spread of anti-immigrant sentiment is partly a function of more general economic insecurity. It is one thing to embrace immigrants when the economy is growing, work is plentiful, and benefits for the unemployed, the sick, and the elderly are secure. It is quite another matter to compete for resources during a period of weak economic performance, fiscal austerity, and welfare state reform. During the enlargement of the EU to the countries of Central and Eastern Europe in the early 2000s, most European governments sought to restrict the movement of workers from the new member states. The British government was more welcoming. Soon after the crisis started, however, the British government faced a choice about opening its labor markets to workers from Bulgaria and Romania. It joined with those countries that sought to restrict the movement of labor instead of maintaining a more relaxed regime.

On one level, these economic insecurities are about the appropriate balance between equity and efficiency, states and markets. Economists and politicians talk about the need to restore "competitiveness." The implication is that there is some institutional solution to harness creative energies and unlock national assets. Unfortunately, competitiveness is a moving target that Europeans have pursued at least since European Commission President Jacques Delors published a white paper on the subject in 1993.[1] The results have been uneven both across countries and over time. National economies have moved into and out of favor over past decades. The Dutch, the Danes, and the Irish each had their economic miracles. The luster on those miracles has since faded. Meanwhile, the German economy struggled mightily during the 1990s and early 2000s.

The ups and downs in economic performance are only to be expected. There is no magic formula for success, particularly in a context of fast technological change. What is more alarming is when everyone moves in the same direction at the same time—particularly when that direction is negative. During the economic crisis that started in 2007, most countries did poorly. The Irish suffered in particular, but neither the Dutch nor the Danes were spared. Germany was one of the few European countries that could claim to have a consistent competitive advantage. The German government undertook sweeping reforms in the mid-2000s, and the German economy emerged from the downturn of 2008–2009 relatively quickly. That relative success has not banished economic insecurity altogether. Even Germans worry that unfettered immigration could rob them of their virtues. A book on that theme by Thilo Sarazin called *Germany Does Away with Itself* was a bestseller in 2010.

On a deeper level, anti-immigrant sentiment is symptomatic of concern about who will pay the costs of adjustment—not just to a multicultural society, but also to a more flexible economy, more streamlined public benefits, and more sustainable public finances. Recent immigrants draw immediate attention because they are most easily stigmatized or excluded. Nevertheless, welfare chauvinism like that advocated by right-wing extremists is never a comprehensive solution. Indeed, it is often counterproductive because many immigrant groups are net contributors to public finances and welfare state systems. Immigration also relieves pressure from population aging, since immigrants tend to be young rather than elderly. Even assuming away those two qualifications, however, expelling or restricting immigrants has little to offer in macroeconomic terms. To understand why, it is only necessary to consider the magnitude of the problems that most European countries face. Unemployment, and youth unemployment in particular, top the list. Two out of every three Greek persons under the age of twenty-five are out of work and looking for a job; so are one out of every two young Spaniards and two out of every five young Italians. These figures dwarf the population of immigrants in any country. The only way to address unemployment is with comprehensive and lasting reform. The same is true if we substitute population aging or public debt sustainability for unemployment.

Unfortunately, reform is difficult, as Europeans know all too well. As big as the numbers for unemployment are, they are not unprecedented. Many of the countries of southern Europe went through wrenching reforms in the 1980s and 1990s, as did Ireland, Belgium, and the Netherlands. The countries of Central and Eastern Europe went through even more dramatic adjustment processes after the end of the Cold War. Sweden and Finland were similarly challenged, albeit for very different reasons. Meanwhile, Germany had to adapt to unification and the economic collapse of the former German Democratic Republic. Indeed, the shock of unification goes a long way to explain the country's economic weakness at the turn of the twenty-first century.

Such experiences make new reforms harder and not easier. The reason is simple: every benefit cut takes away from someone's income, as does every tax raised to pay down the debt and every job lost in a more flexible labor market. Of course, the goal of reform is to make societies better off in the aggregate. Unavoidably, however, reform creates losers as well as winners. Reform also generates fatigue. Voters grow tired of sacrifice and politicians grow weary of conflict.

That fatigue explains why European electorates tend not to be supportive of one another in the context of the ongoing economic crisis. Those countries that have gone through crisis before believe they have paid their dues and expect others to do so as well. The German case is a good illustration. The Hertz labor market reforms that were introduced in the early 2000s under a center-left coalition of Social Democrats (SPD) and Greens placed a huge burden on the working classes. The Hertz reforms curtailed unemployment benefits and created incentives for unemployed workers to seek lower paying jobs than the ones they used to hold. In effect, this put the cost of getting the unemployed back to work on the unemployed themselves.

Economists can make a strong case for the welfare improvements created by such market incentives, but those arguments did not convince left-wing voters to support the center-left party that initiated the reform process. In 2002, the SPD got just over 20 million votes in single-member districts and 38.5 percent of the proportional vote. Then the SPD split and the most disaffected part fused with a predominantly eastern German postcommunist party to form "The Left" as an antireform alternative. By 2005, the district vote for the SPD had fallen to 18 million and the proportional vote to 34 percent, and by 2009, the SPD garnered just 12 million votes in district contests and 24 percent in the proportional ballot. Not all of these votes went to "The Left"; the split was only one of many problems. What matters is that the voters appear to have abandoned the SPD. The figures for the 2013 elections show only a marginal recovery.

There are many explanations for why support for the SPD fell so far and so fast; reform fatigue is just one of them. Nevertheless, the experience of the SPD is repeated in other countries and so it is possible to suggest that the marginal influence of reform fatigue is significant. The Polish economist Leszek Balcerowicz used to talk about "extraordinary politics" and "normal politics": extraordinary politics is when politicians are free to make reforms because the people believe this will make things better in the future; normal politics is when the losers from any reform effort exact their political price. As Balcerowicz showed when he was finance minister during the Polish transition in the early 1990s, periods of extraordinary politics are very short lived. Many of the Central and Eastern European countries have not yet seen an incumbent government reelected to office; more than a few have gone through a complete overhaul of their system of political parties. This translates into a lack of support for other countries because they cannot see how they would justify taking resources out of the domestic economy to ease another country's adjustment process. They know the price that was paid at home both economically and politically, and would prefer that other countries just get on with it.

The situation is not helped by the suspicion that those countries suffering most in Europe are culturally predisposed to financial mismanagement. This kind of stereotyping is most obvious in the case of Greece, but it also occurs with respect to Italy, Spain,

Portugal, and even Ireland. The crux of the argument is that these countries deserve their fate and so must suffer to achieve redemption.

This stereotyping has three practical implications that show up in terms of tough conditionality on any bailout or conditional credit arrangements, limited enthusiasm in the Northern and Central European countries for common insurance funds or bailout mechanisms, and increased frustration in the Southern and peripheral European countries with European interference in domestic politics. The conditionality is easiest to demonstrate. When Greece, Ireland, Portugal, and Spain sought assistance from their European partners, they were forced to accept to undertake specific reform commitments as a condition for the money they received. In Greece, Ireland, and Portugal, the reform commitments were wide-ranging because the assistance was for public finances; in Spain, the assistance was to shore up the banking system and so the conditions attached were more limited.

Any conditionality is hard to accept because it takes the assignment of winners and losers from the reform process out of the hands of national politicians. It is one thing to navigate adjustment by shielding your friends at the expense of those who would not support you anyway; it is quite another to take from your supporters and opponents alike. Worse, that is precisely the objective. International creditors do not want to see national politicians protect their supporters in what should be a sweeping reform project. Even a more limited reform of the financial system, as in the Spanish case, should be comprehensive and so should take place outside political influence. International creditors are not putting their money at risk to "line the pockets" of political cronies or vested interests.

The problem is that national politicians in distressed countries do not see themselves as clientelistic, corrupt, or incompetent; rather, they see themselves as safeguarding the national interest. For them, it is not a question of demonstrating good faith to international creditors; it is a matter of protecting what is important and promoting common values. Pasok leader George Papandreou saw himself as a patriot and not a villain; so did his successor, Lukas Papademos. Italian Prime Ministers Silvio Berlusconi, Mario Monti, and Enrico Letta regard themselves as patriots as well. So did Spanish Prime Ministers José Zapatero and Mariano Rajoy, and Irish Taoisigh Brian Cowen and Enda Kenny. Not all of these figures have sterling reputations. That is not the point. What matters is that how they are seen inside the country differs greatly from how they are perceived by the outside world.

This contrast in views percolates up through the framework for macroeconomic governance and into new institutions that are supposed to insure against financial disaster. The focus here is usually on Germany, which has become the leading voice in debates about fiscal austerity and which is also the most prominent obstacle to the creation of shared banking resolution funds, common deposit insurance, and mutualized sovereign debt instruments, also known as "eurobonds." The center-right government that German Chancellor Angela Merkel led from 2009 to 2013 staked out clear positions; it wanted all member states to commit themselves to balance their fiscal accounts, it accepted pooling only limited financial resources, and it underscored the importance of having national governments accept responsibility for their domestic economies.

The problem is that austerity is not always the best policy, and shared institutions for underpinning European banks and government finances may be necessary to stabilize the internal European market. Political leaders in the countries most affected by the crisis have raised these concerns repeatedly. Their voice is suspect, however, because they have the most to benefit in the short run from a relaxation of austerity and from more generous and less restrictive bailouts. Therefore, it is important to note that they are not alone in advocating these positions. The International Monetary Fund (IMF) and the administration of President Barack Obama in the United States have made similar arguments; so have both the European Commission and the European Central Bank (ECB). This suggests that some compromise is probably warranted. However, in the absence of solidarity across countries, compromise is hard to achieve.

The balance of power favors the creditor countries and not the debtors. Meanwhile, the IMF, the EC, and the ECB must comply with their mandates no matter what they may think about the wider framework for macroeconomic governance. As a result, the three international institutions—known collectively as the "troika"— are responsible for the enforcement of conditionality in those countries that have received bailouts. The Commission is also responsible for managing the broader framework for macroeconomic policy coordination. In these roles, both the troika and the Commission have become advocates of fiscal austerity and welfare state reform and the hate objects of those political parties like UKIP, Syriza, the FN, and the Italian Five Star Movement that are most suspicious of any interference in domestic politics by outsiders.

This brings the discussion of solidarity full circle. The loss of solidarity at home makes it hard to retain abroad; meanwhile, the loss of solidarity abroad fuels divisions at home. The result is a vicious circle that works against integration at both the European and national levels. Moreover, we have seen this negative interaction before. It was a hallmark of the Great Depression and the period between the two world wars. It emerged again in the 1970s. The result does not have to be disaster. Eventually the cycle abates enough to allow more positive influences to take hold. However, it is a great force for European self-obsession.

Security

Americans are unsurprised when Europeans ignore the outside world. But that is due in part to the narrow focus of attention that Americans have for the instruments of power projection. Robert Kagan wrote a famous essay called "Power and Weakness" in 2002 that captured the essence of this perspective. He explained that when the United States provided military security for Europe during the Cold War, it inadvertently made it easy for Europeans to allow their own military potential to atrophy. The Americans did the heavy lifting, and the Europeans got out of shape. As a consequence, the United States continues to see the world from the perspective of a country that is militarily powerful. The Europeans see the world from a perspective that is militarily weak. This difference in perspective has an influence on both the instruments and the objectives of foreign policy. The United States has great power and so can pursue ambitious purposes. The Europeans have softer instruments and so also more modest aims.

If Kagan's view of the contrast between the United States and Europe is accurate, then it is also unsustainable. The United States is not as powerful as it was in the past and often cannot achieve its national objectives when acting alone. That is the lesson of the wars in Iraq and Afghanistan, where U.S. forces failed to obtain a sustainable peace despite enormous costs in terms of human life and public expenditure. Even armed with the greatest military force the world has ever seen, neither the George W. Bush nor the Obama administrations can claim they got what they wanted in either theater of operations.

Meanwhile, it is hard to see how the Europeans can hold on to modest foreign policy objectives. The world is developing too quickly in too many complex ways. This can be seen in the rise of China and the rapid growth of emerging market economies in Asia, Latin America, and Africa. It can also be seen in the changing dynamics of the transatlantic relationship. These concerns arise time and again in debates about European foreign policy. However, perhaps the best illustration comes from North Africa and the Middle East. That is where changes have occurred since the fourth edition of this book was published that have been most profound for European foreign and security policy.

The collapse of Arab regimes in North Africa and the Middle East ended a long-standing European policy of trading off democratization for stabilization. European governments hoped that by dealing with authoritarian leaders, they would be able to ensure the supply of vital energy supplies and raw materials while at the same time staving off the problem of illegal immigration both from the North African countries and from sub-Saharan Africa. The curious interaction between Italian Prime Minister Silvio Berlusconi and Libyan leader Muammar Gaddafi is a good illustration. Berlusconi went to great lengths to strengthen relations between Italy and Libya in order to benefit from the supply of natural gas and petroleum that the Libyans could offer. Berlusconi also relied on Libyan security authorities to stop sub-Saharan migrants from trying to cross illegally into Tunisia in order to set sail for the Italian island of Lampedusa. Gaddafi's authoritarian rule and eccentric behavior seemed not to matter. Indeed, many Italian politicians viewed him as better than the possible alternatives.

Berlusconi and Gaddafi were a strange pairing but not a unique one. French President Nicolas Sarkozy was close to Tunisian President Zine El Abadine Ben Ali for similar reasons. Successive French governments have also tolerated military leaders in Algeria who promised to hold off the threat of political Islam, and they had good relations with Syrian leader Bashar al-Assad. Most importantly, virtually everyone in Europe learned to live with Egyptian leader Hosni Mubarak. Egypt under Mubarak was a central player in the European neighborhood policy and a key recipient of European foreign aid and development assistance.

European leaders were caught by surprise when popular unrest in Tunisia sparked a wave of protest that toppled that country's political leadership before spreading across North Africa and into the Middle East. Many countries were able to resist this democratization movement, but Egypt underwent a revolution shortly before first Libya and then Syria descended into civil war. Europe's politicians were ill prepared to deal with the fast pace of transition—as were politicians elsewhere, particularly in the United States. It was not long, however, before the implications became apparent and so did the need for an effective response.

The term "implications" is intentionally clinical here. On normative grounds, European governments should have embraced the democratization of North African and Middle Eastern countries wholeheartedly because "democratization" meant drafting constitutions that looked more like those in Europe than anywhere else in the world, the United States included. The goal of democratization was not problematic. The unintended consequences were. Here it is useful to focus on four elements: the pressure of illegal migration, the security of energy supplies and raw materials, the prospect of humanitarian disaster, and the threat of militant Islamic extremists.

The pressure of migration was a result of both the loss of control over national borders and the economic chaos that results from revolutionary transition. The forces of order in countries like Tunisia, Libya, and Egypt had enough to do to retain power before the revolution and to stabilize civilian life once the change in political leadership had taken place. Controlling the flow of migrants into Europe fell very low on the priority list. For Europeans, the effects were seen almost immediately. The island of Lampedusa began receiving migrants in large numbers early in 2011. However, the Berlusconi government did not want to bring those illegal immigrants onto the mainland for processing for fear that this would only accelerate the movement. Very quickly, Lampedusa was overwhelmed and so the Berlusconi government looked for ways to release the pressure. Once they did so by bringing some of the migrants to Italy, however, they provoked a crisis in relations with France because migrants leaving Tunisia are more likely to speak French than Italian.

The resulting conflict between the Berlusconi government in Italy and the Sarkozy government in France threatened to bring down the whole framework for borderless movement across the EU. The French wanted to reintroduce border controls; the Italians wanted help dealing with the problem of illegal immigration. The solution was at best a stopgap measure with some powers restored to France and some assistance promised to Italy. It remains unclear whether this stopgap will hold under pressure from significant migration out of Egypt.

The confluence of energy security and humanitarian disaster can be seen in the case of Libya. The popular uprising in Libya was relatively slow to materialize because Gaddafi had sufficient resources from the sale of gas and oil to buy the loyalty of the population. However, Gaddafi's support came more from the west of the country than from the eastern part. This imbalance made it possible for the opposition to concentrate into a critical mass in the eastern capital of Benghazi. When Gaddafi threatened to wipe out his opponents, European leaders faced the prospect of humanitarian disaster. They also worried about the disruption of oil and gas supplies. The reactions differed from one country to the next. France and Great Britain advocated intervention; Italy hoped to achieve a negotiated solution. Ultimately, the French and the British succeeded in persuading the Obama administration to join them by pointing to Gaddafi's imminent and brutal repression of the Libyan opposition.

The Libyan intervention showed that some Europeans were willing to use military force to achieve their foreign policy objectives. It also showed the limitations of European capabilities and consensus in security matters. While the Obama administration sought to limit the United States' involvement in the conflict, they quickly discovered that U.S. forces would have to play a substantial role. The result was to make the Obama administration more reluctant to support European-led military interventions. Hence, when the French called for further military action to stop the threat of Islamist extremists in Mali, the United States offered support but played a more modest role.

These illustrations are also important to understand the situation in Syria. The civil war that has developed there is of much more immediate relevance to Europe than to the United States. Conflict in Syria threatens to ignite a further wave of illegal immigration in the form of refugees from the conflict and displaced persons on both the Jordanian and Turkish borders. Conflict in Syria also promises a humanitarian disaster that only intensifies as the violence drags on. Syria has become a new training ground for Islamic extremists. And it is a source of instability for the wider Middle East, which in turn jeopardizes European energy resources. In other words, the conflict in Syria is not something that the Europeans can easily ignore. It is also not something that the Obama administration is eager to tackle alone or in partnership with just one or two European countries.

The only good option is for Europeans to come up with a common strategy toward the region. That strategy will have to involve Russia and Turkey as well. Even a united EU cannot achieve its objectives by acting alone. This is a daunting requirement. The EU member states are deeply divided about how best to deal with Russia and Turkey; they are divided about how best to deal with the Middle East and Syria as well. Nevertheless, it is hard to see a superior alternative. The United States cannot provide order in the Middle East. Meanwhile, the countries of Europe cannot afford for the Middle East to fall into chaos—because they cannot escape from the pressure of illegal migration, they cannot safeguard their energy requirements, they cannot stand by as humanitarian disaster unfolds, and they cannot insulate themselves from the threat of terrorism. The Europeans may have been able to accept "weakness" during the Cold War, but that is no longer an option. The potential costs of European weakness are even more unsettling if we broaden the scope of security and foreign policy concerns beyond the Mediterranean basin.

The developments in Ukraine offer a reminder of the volatility beyond the European Union. The political unrest that began in November 2013 catalyzed around Ukraine's relationship with the EU. Ukrainian President Viktor Yanukovych chose not to sign an association agreement with the European Union and opted for closer relations with Russia instead. A number of groups—primarily, though not exclusively, from western Ukraine—took to the streets in opposition. As the protests wore on, the focus gradually shifted from relations with Europe to the legitimacy of the Yanukovych regime. Yanukovych offered belated concessions but opposition leaders demanded he resign. Events culminated when the Ukrainian president fled the capital, Kiev. The protesters greeted this as an abdication; Yanukovych denounced it as a coup.

Russian President Vladimir Putin supported Yanukovych, although he made it clear that Yanukovych was unlikely to reverse the facts on the ground. Instead, Putin ordered the Russian military to secure the Crimea, a peninsula that juts into the Black Sea and is home to Russia's most important warm water naval base. Putin also instructed his military to mass along the Ukrainian border as he denounced what he claimed were violations of the human rights of Ukraine's ethnic Russian minority—which happens to predominate in the eastern regions of the country, including the Crimea.

The European response to this move was hesitant and divided. Meanwhile, Putin created some "facts on the ground" of his own. He organized a snap referendum within the Crimea to support its independence and subsequent annexation to Russia, and he passed legislation through the Russian parliament to approve the absorption of Crimea into the Russian federation. The European response to this move was more forceful, but they faced a fait accompli. If the EU's ambition was to prevent the division of Ukraine, it was unsuccessful. Subsequently, all eyes turned to NATO to see whether the same fate could await Latvia and Estonia—two Baltic states with significant Russian minorities of their own.

Integration

Building a comprehensive solution for European security will not be simple. Constructing the EU was not simple either. The first step is to shore up the legitimacy of European democracies and the institutions of the EU. The second is to find some way to share the burdens of adjustment to a fast-changing world. The third is to accept that Europe extends beyond the EU, and so integration must include more significant actors like Turkey and perhaps someday even Russia. The fourth is to get everyone in this wider Europe to agree to a common vision for world order and to act together in the service of that objective. The blueprint is clear enough. The implementation is what is going to be difficult. However, this would not be the first time that Europe reordered the world in its own image.

Note

1. Commission of the European Communities, *Growth, Competitiveness, Employment: The Challenges and Ways Forward into the 21st Century*, white paper, http://europa.eu/documentation/official-docs/white-papers/pdf/growth_wp_com_93_700_parts_a_b.pdf (accessed January 8, 2014).

PART ONE

COUNTRY STUDIES

CHAPTER 1

France

THE HOLLANDE PRESIDENCY: PROMISES AND PITFALLS

Gabriel Goodliffe

France

Population (million):	65.6
Area in Square Miles:	212,934
Population Density in Square Miles:	308
GDP (in billion dollars, 2013):	$2,291
GDP per Capita (PPP, 2013):	$36,100
Joined EC/EU:	January 1, 1958

Performance of Key Political Parties in Parliamentary Elections of June 2012

Greens	5.5%
Radical Party of the Left	1.7%
National Front (FN)	13.6%
Socialist Party (PS)	29.4%
Democratic Movement (MoDem)	1.8%
Union for a Popular Movement (UMP)	27.12%
New Centre (NC)	2.2%

Main Officeholders: President: François Hollande, PS (2012); and Prime Minister: Jean-Marc Ayrault, PS (2012)

Never in the history of the Fifth Republic has a sitting French president's popularity fallen so far so quickly. From a 65 percent approval rating following his election in May 2012, François Hollande's popularity has collapsed to 24 percent a short twelve months later—a low unprecedented for any Fifth Republic president, including his unpopular predecessor, Nicolas Sarkozy.[1] What makes this precipitous—and, some would say, calamitous—decline all the more noteworthy is that Hollande's election had come as a great relief to many in France and abroad. Hollande's victory marked only the second time in the history of the Fifth Republic that a candidate from the Socialist Party (PS) had been elected president, eighteen years since François Mitterrand's departure in 1995.

The purpose of this chapter is to assess the trajectory of the Hollande presidency and to flesh out the departures and continuities it presents within the longer run of French political development. In particular, it will evaluate the new president's leadership and policies against those of his predecessor, Nicolas Sarkozy. The chapter has three main sections. The first section outlines the economic challenge. The second looks at politics and society. The third brings in France's relations with the outside world. Each section provides sufficient historical context to facilitate an understanding of more recent events.

The Economic Challenge

Since 1970, France's average unemployment rate has hovered at around 8 percent and frequently topped 10 percent from the mid-1980s onward (compared to a median unemployment rate of 4–5 percent in the United States for that period). As we saw, these figures have worsened with the onset of the global economic and European sovereign debt crises. Certain groups have been particularly hard hit, with joblessness among the young plateauing at around 20 percent since the mid-1980s and reaching 28 percent for immigrant youth. To make matters worse, a substantial proportion of existing jobs are government subsidized, meaning that they would not exist at all without the state's largesse.

This persistently high unemployment rate is attributable in part to the unresponsiveness of the French labor market to changing economic circumstances due to the rigidity of labor laws—many extending back half a century—which focus on protecting existing jobs rather than spurring economic and hence job growth. At the same time, the cost burdens placed on French firms in order to pay for government-mandated fringe benefits make it more expensive for firms to hire new workers, while a high minimum wage exceeds the productivity of workers, thereby reducing the number of full-time minimum-wage jobs. In turn, long-paying and generous unemployment benefits lessen the incentive for the unemployed to seek new jobs. Finally, the labor market's rigidity is exacerbated by the traditional French resistance to moving to a new city or region for work or switching professions midcareer, as well as the growing incompatibility between the technical skills demanded by companies in the modern economy and those developed by students in the general university system.

As a result, a surprising number of good jobs remain unfilled in the private sector for lack of qualified candidates.

The labor laws protecting employees from dismissal, the wage growth to stimulate consumption, the generous welfare and social security regimes, and the statist-corporatist arrangements to oversee these institutions that were introduced during the *Trente Glorieuses* (the thirty boom years following World War II) when France was a relatively self-enclosed economy shielded from international competition were ill adapted to an increasingly integrated global economy subject to intensifying trade competition and international capital flows. As French firms became less and less competitive and were forced to lay off growing numbers of workers, French society grew increasingly divided between "insiders" (the shrinking core of workers whose jobs remain protected and who continue to enjoy the benefits of the Fordist welfare state) and "outsiders" (the growing number of unemployed or underemployed workers, particularly among the young and unskilled, excluded from the system and exposed to worsening professional and socioeconomic uncertainty as a result). These developments fed a narrative, particularly within French conservative circles (not to mention among many American academics), that France needs to "modernize" its economic and social system in order to give its economy the requisite flexibility to cope with globalization.

THE END OF STATE PLANNING AND THE REFORM OF THE WELFARE STATE

The roots of this globalization challenge can be traced back to the 1970s. That was when France experienced mass unemployment for the first time in the postwar period combined with spiraling inflation. The causes were to be found in the two oil price shocks and the growth of unregulated international capital flows. The Socialist-Communist coalition that came to power following François Mitterrand's election in 1981 attempted to overcome economic stagnation by stimulating consumption through a dual strategy of reflation and statist economic management. However, the failure of this strategy to achieve growth forced the government to accept the abandonment of economic planning (*déplanification*) combined with the introduction of a more paternalist social management. This was the course that was adopted by the Right when it took control over the government (but not the presidency) in 1986–1988 and 1993–1995, and then was alternately pursued by governments of the Right and the Left throughout Jacques Chirac's presidency. (Table 1.1 provides a chronology of the political leadership of the French Fifth Republic.)

During the first two years of Mitterrand's presidency, the Socialist-Communist government pursued a sweeping reflationary program that amounted to a 12 percent increase in government spending in real terms. This stimulus program was accompanied by the most comprehensive nationalization campaign since the end of the Second World War, and the resumption of industrial policies, including setting production targets for a large contingent of industries as well as a "national champions" policy that called for small and medium-sized enterprises (SMEs) to be fused into larger, often state-controlled firms. This return to state-directed economic management, or

Table 1.1   Political Leadership of the French Fifth Republic

President	Prime Minister
Charles De Gaulle (I)* (1959–1966)	Michel Debré (1959–1962) Georges Pompidou (1962–1966)
Charles De Gaulle (II)** (1966–1969)	Georges Pompidou (1966–1968) Maurice Couve de Murville (1968–1969)
Georges Pompidou (1969–1974)	Jacques Chaban-Delmas (1969–1972) Pierre Messmer (1972–1974)
Valéry Giscard d'Estaing (1974–1981)	Jacques Chirac (I) (1974–1976) Raymond Barre (1976–1981)
François Mitterrand (I) (1981–1988)	Pierre Mauroy (1981–1984) Laurent Fabius (1984–1986) **Jacques Chirac (II)*** (1986–1988)**
François Mitterrand (II) (1988–1995)	Michel Rocard (1988–1991) Édith Cresson (1991–1992) Pierre Bérégovoy (1992–1993) **Édouard Balladur*** (1993–1995)**
Jacques Chirac (I) (1995–2002)	Alain Juppé (1995–1997) **Lionel Jospin*** (1997–2002)**
Jacques Chirac (II) (2002–2007)****	Jean-Pierre Raffarin (2002–2005) Dominique de Villepin (2005–2007)
Nicolas Sarkozy (2007–2012)	François Fillon (2007–2012)
François Hollande (2012–2017)	Jean-Marc Ayrault (2012–2013) Manuel Valls (2013–?)

*Elected by members of parliament to a seven-year mandate; **first directly elected mandate; ***cohabitation: prime minister and president are from different parties; ****first five-year presidential mandate.

dirigisme, was accompanied by a series of unemployment reduction measures that would become a staple of French economic policy in subsequent years, including reducing the work week from 40 to 39 hours, extending paid vacations from four to five weeks, making older workers eligible for early retirement, and subsidizing firms to hire younger workers. In addition, a slew of policies were promulgated to placate the political base of the Socialist-Communist coalition, principally industrial workers and civil servants, including reforms giving workers a greater say in running their firms and reinforcing their collective-bargaining rights, as well as redistributive policies that benefited the poor as well as the fast-growing population of retirees. Last but not least, the government raised taxes on capital owners and businesses in order to pay for these benefits, notably by instituting the highest capital gains tax in the industrialized world, which triggered massive capital flight from France to more investor-friendly markets.

The failure of reflation and nationalization to return the economy to a path of growth, however, forced the Socialist government to reappraise its policies and reverse course. In a radical turnabout, it embarked on a more comprehensive liberalization program than had hitherto been attempted. The proximate causes for this shift were the spiraling inflation and gaping budget and trade deficits that had been generated by the increase in government spending, combined with the contraction of demand for French goods due to the global economic slowdown. These conditions in turn wrought unsustainable pressure on the French franc, triggering a run that jeopardized its participation in the European Monetary System.

In March 1983, the government was forced to implement a harsh austerity program in order to rein in inflation and relieve pressure on the franc. Under the stewardship of Finance Minister Jacques Delors, a series of strict price and wage controls, compulsory savings measures, and, most significantly, painful spending cuts was enacted to stabilize the public deficit. These measures were intensified under Delors' successor, Pierre Bérégovoy, who in turn did away with wage indexation and reduced price controls. As a corollary to this austerity package, Bérégovoy also introduced the *franc fort* (strong franc) policy that sought to maintain the franc at a higher exchange parity with the German mark (or deutschmark), thereby forcing French firms to lower their costs so as to remain internationally competitive. This "competitive disinflation" implied severely tightening the money supply and markedly raising interest rates in order to buttress the franc and reduce inflation by curbing investment.

This combination of budgetary austerity and monetary rigueur allowed France to achieve one of the lowest inflation rates in Western Europe while initiating a period of steady balance-of-trade surpluses. However, by choking investment and depressing consumer demand, the new policy caused, in the words of one observer, "damage to the economy . . . so severe and persistent" that growth was effectively strangled and unemployment shot up to 10 percent.[2] At the same time, these restrictive macroeconomic policies were accompanied by microeconomic reforms that aimed to enhance the flexibility of the economy by disengaging the state from the marketplace. This disengagement, overseen by the new Finance Minister and subsequent Prime Minister Laurent Fabius (1984–1986), meant eliminating state outlays to nationalized industries, exposing public enterprises to market competition, and lifting state restrictions on closures or layoffs within them. In the private sector, meanwhile, the state abandoned efforts to steer industry toward planning targets, while restrictions on firing workers and raising capital were lifted in exchange for firms no longer receiving government assistance. In turn, price controls were fully eliminated in 1986, a measure that forced public and private firms to become more competitive in order to remain economically viable.

The *déplanification* and deregulation campaign launched by the Fabius government was expanded by the second Chirac ministry of 1986–1988 and finalized by governments of both the Left and the Right in the early 1990s. These governments reversed the nationalizations undertaken between 1982 and 1984 and returned most public firms to private ownership. In addition, beginning with the ministry of Michel Rocard (1988–1991), a raft of measures was introduced to promote the growth of SMEs as the agents of the country's economic revival, including state subsidies and performance-conditioned loans to help them modernize their production and upgrade their product lines.

The implementation of these microeconomic reforms did much to rationalize the structure and liberalize the operation of the French economy. The elimination of subsidies to public and private enterprises resulted in a large number of bankruptcies, financial deregulation spurred greater firm reliance on financial markets, and labor market deregulation enhanced wage flexibility and reduced production costs, increasing firm profits. Revealing the "decontrol" of the French economy relative to the selective *dirigisme* (state economic management) of the 1970s and the Socialist étatisme (statism) of the early 1980s, these reforms marked a profound shift away from the direct management of public and private enterprises by the state toward its essential disengagement from the economy.

However, this retreat from *dirigisme* did not spell the end of state intervention in all its forms, but instead marked its displacement to the realm of social policy. It is no small paradox that despite the abandonment of planning and the decline of state intervention in the economy, overall government spending continued to increase. The end of the neo-Keynesian experiment in the early 1980s and the ensuing process of *déplanification* saw the share of public expenditure rise from 42.6 percent of GDP in 1983 to 46 percent in 1999. This upsurge in government expenditure was almost wholly attributable to the growth of the welfare state in order to attenuate the social dislocations caused by the retreat from *dirigisme* and economic liberalization. First, the growth in welfare spending underwrote labor market programs designed to dampen the rise in unemployment triggered by economic restructuring and the deflationary policies that accompanied it—mostly early retirement programs intended to allow firms to pare down their workforces without provoking a new increase in unemployment.

By the early 1990s, given their failure to reduce unemployment, successive Socialist and center-right governments supplemented these early retirement programs with various work subsidy measures and business-friendly tax incentives to encourage low-wage hires, particularly among young workers. In turn, in the second half of the 1990s, these were followed by two further initiatives introduced by the government of Socialist Party leader Lionel Jospin, including subsidies for nonprofit and public sector organizations to encourage youth hires and, most famously, the Aubry Law—named after Jospin's labor minister, Martine Aubry—which reduced the work week from 39 to 35 hours. Overall, the number of workers affected by these labor reduction measures increased from 1.2 million in 1984 to 3 million in 1999. Adding this figure to the approximately 2 million unemployed, this meant that by the close of the twentieth century, France had one of the lowest labor force participation rates—particularly among the youngest and oldest workers—and the shortest average duration of employment in the industrialized world.

As the 1990s drew to a close, a retrenchment of the welfare state became an increasingly urgent priority. Domestically, the ballooning social security obligations imposed on French firms in order to fund this welfare expansion hurt their cost competitiveness and impeded their ability to hire more workers. Externally, the growth in welfare spending threatened France's position within the Stability and Growth Pact. In 2003, the country was placed on notice by the European Commission because it exceeded the 3 percent limit for excessive government deficits. Thus, political elites finally accepted the need to shrink the French welfare state, notably through reductions in benefits, pension reform, and cuts to the public sector.

Beginning with the Jospin government and especially under the succeeding governments of Jean-Pierre Raffarin (2002–2005) and Dominique de Villepin (2005–2007), there were concerted attempts to reduce both government expenditures and tax obligations on firms, specifically by cutting welfare benefits for certain categories of the population such as the long-term unemployed, and peeling back social security taxes for employers. These were accompanied by a series of cost-cutting reforms of the health system that achieved savings by increasing personal deductibles and reducing the number of services that could be reimbursed by the state. In turn, the Jospin government drew up plans to reduce corporate and income taxes, including for the highest income brackets, in order to encourage savings and investment. These measures were intensified by the Raffarin and Villepin governments, which, in addition to reducing inheritance taxes and the rate on the highest earners, cut corporate tax rates and worked to shift the burden of social security taxes away from firms and toward employees.

Finally, the cost burden attaching to the payment of welfare benefits was further diminished through the decentralization of income supports to the poor in 2004 and the replacement of the *Revenu Mensuel d'Insertion* (Monthly Integration Benefit), which had been introduced in 1988 to protect the long-term unemployed from falling into poverty, by a less generous *Revenu de Solidarité Active* (Professional Solidarity Benefit) designed to serve as a complement to poorly paid short-term or part-time work. These retrenchment measures continued to be accompanied by various proposals to encourage employment, notably among affected groups such as the young, through activist policies exempting firms from having to pay social security taxes on certain types of jobs.

SARKOZY'S ECONOMIC "RUPTURE" AND HOLLANDE'S PROMISE

These retrenchment strategies were continued and expanded following Nicolas Sarkozy's election in 2007; the new government standardized civil service pensions with those in the private sector by making a full pension for both categories of workers contingent on paying into the social security system for forty-one years. In turn, after initially attempting to shrink the public sector through natural attrition (one in two public sector posts were to be eliminated upon their occupants' retirement), it proposed to cut the public sector by 30,000 posts in 2008 and again in 2010. The impetus behind such cuts continued to grow in the wake of the 2008 financial crisis and ensuing economic recession, which saw a dramatic increase in the budget deficit (which reached 7.7 percent of GDP at the end of 2010) as a result of falling tax receipts and renewed welfare spending. Accordingly, the budget for 2011 called for reducing the public sector by 31,638 posts, principally in education, in addition to eliminating 62,000 posts in 2012 (and 97,000 through 2013) through the nonreplacement of retiring public sector workers (*fonctionnaires*).[3]

Last but not least, deepening the strategy of retrenchment engaged by the Jospin, Raffarin, and Villepin governments, the François Fillon government (2007–2012) also sought to diminish the economic costs attaching to the welfare state while enacting substantial cuts in social spending. On the one hand, it attempted to shift the burden of social security financing away from firms toward consumers by offsetting a reduction in the share of the payroll tax levied on employers with an increase in the value-added tax—the so-called *TVA sociale*. On the other, it built on social spending reductions by increasing individual health care liabilities as well as by reducing unemployment benefits for those who refused to take a job. Finally, the Fillon government complemented these retrenchment measures with policies to stimulate saving and encourage people to work more. Most notably, it exempted employers and employees from social security taxes on overtime work, while further reducing corporate and income tax rates—particularly on the highest brackets—and cutting the "wealth tax" in an effort to create a supply-side "confidence shock."[4]

The 2008–2009 financial crash and the subsequent European sovereign debt crisis failed to deflect the course of these policies. After the passage of a timid and short-lived stimulus package at the end of 2008 and 2009, the Sarkozy government resumed its course of public sector and welfare state retrenchment.[5] This strategy gained particular urgency in the midst of the ongoing European sovereign debt crisis as financial markets lost confidence in the country's ability to service its debt, culminating in the downgrading of its AAA credit rating in January 2012. In December 2010, the government pushed through a pension system reform that standardized public sector pensions with those in the private sector by making retirement benefits for both categories of workers contingent on paying into the social security system for forty-one years. In turn, in August 2011, it introduced an austerity budget that sought to reduce government expenditures by €1 billion in 2011 and another €11 billion in 2012. This plan was revised in November 2011 to take account of falling growth projections, calling for €65 billion in budget cuts by 2016, including €7 billion in 2012 and €11.6 billion in 2013, the overall objective being to achieve €100 billion in savings and balance the budget by 2016. Since these cuts would accelerate the course of public sector retrenchment and welfare reform, they were bound to disproportionately impact those worst affected by the economic and social crisis.

In this respect, despite his commitment to initiate a reflationary policy in order to restart growth and reduce unemployment, François Hollande has stipulated that he intends to respect the budgetary rules of the Stability and Growth Pact and to balance the budget by 2017. Initially, the Hollande presidency banked on a 75 percent marginal tax on annual incomes above €1 million as well as higher tax receipts made possible by increased economic activity in order to achieve this aim. However, faced with the prospects of slower growth than that which underpinned their budget projections as well as unexpectedly stiff resistance elicited by the 75 percent tax plan, the president and his team have been forced to opt for more orthodox retrenchment policies. In order to bring the budget deficit back to 3 percent of GDP by the end of 2013, the government unveiled a severe austerity plan that included €24 billion of additional taxes as well as further spending cuts of €10 billion.[6] As the plan unfolded during the course of that year, the International Monetary Fund began to question whether the Hollande government was pushing matters too far.[7] On the revenue side, after being initially repealed by the incoming government, the *TVA sociale* has been reintroduced as a means of both funding social security while lowering hiring costs for employers. Meanwhile, on the expenditure side, a number of hitherto taboo measures are being explored by the government in order to lessen its budgetary burden. These include means-testing family benefits, breaking the link between pension benefits and inflation, lengthening contribution periods for pension rights, and eliminating the duplication of public sector jobs—often building on policies that were introduced by the Fillon government under the previous administration.[8]

In turn, in order to enhance the country's economic competitiveness, the Hollande administration has introduced a number of measures that were intended to enhance labor market flexibility. The goal was to increase efficiency while at the same time promoting broader concerns for welfare in terms of social and income security as well as the even distribution of the burdens of the economic crisis in the name of social solidarity.[9] Two of these measures consisted of employment subsidy programs, principally targeting younger workers. The first scheme, *emploi avenir*, is to reduce youth unemployment among the unskilled; it offered three-year contracts to people between the ages of sixteen and twenty-five who come from officially designated "disadvantaged" areas, with the state paying 75 percent of the wage and employers 25 percent. Scheduled to cover 150,000 jobs over the course of Hollande's term, the measure is expensive; it is estimated to cost €5 billion per year to fill the yearly job quota, plus €2.3 billion over five years to implement. The second scheme, *contrats generation*, aims to reduce youth unemployment while maintaining older workers in their jobs by phasing in retirement for the latter, so they can mentor young employees hired on permanent contracts. Firm participation would be secured through a system of tax penalties and financial inducements in order to encourage larger firms to set targets for both hiring young people on an open-ended basis while preserving their older workers.

The third measure, the "secure employment pathways" (*sécurisation de l'emploi*) program, seeks to balance the imperatives of employment security and firm competitiveness by improving social security and training rights, human resources management, and skills and employment planning, while helping business to adapt to downturns and regulating layoffs. An agreement that was concluded between employer and union representatives, the Growth and Competitiveness Pact, granted employers greater leeway to lay off employees while affording them greater workplace "flexibility," particularly in times of crisis. In exchange, employers were forced to accept restrictions on the use of very short-term contracts and new obligations for training young and part-time workers.

Contrary to critiques that portray these reforms as inconsequential, it could be argued that France has liberalized its economy substantially since the mid-1980s. Though such liberalization has occurred in piecemeal fashion and has not unfolded as quickly as some critics have called for, such was perhaps the best outcome that could be expected in a country as prone to social conflict and upheaval. Likewise, though this process has been accompanied by unacceptably high unemployment and worsening social inequality, it is far from certain that more rapid or radical liberalization would have produced a superior outcome. In this connection, Britain and the United States, despite achieving lower unemployment, continue to display dramatically higher levels of income and wealth inequality than France, which suggests that merely providing people with jobs is not in itself a guarantee against poverty and its attendant social blights.

By the same token, it is important not to minimize the social costs attaching to this process of liberal reform. Even if reform was necessary to make the French economy more competitive, the price exacted in terms of unemployment, inequality, and falling living standards of those who have been hurt along the way should not be underestimated. These costs have fueled a general fear and rejection of globalization, the sociopolitical manifestations of which will be examined in the "Politics and Society" section.

Politics and Society

Income inequality has increased markedly in France, and the living standards of certain groups—notably, industrial workers but also a growing proportion of service sector employees—have eroded substantially since the early 1980s and the beginning of economic reform halfway through François Mitterrand's first term. Correspondingly, the corporative and partisan organizations that traditionally defended these groups, notably the trade unions and Communist Party (PCF), have been severely weakened or collapsed over this period. For better or worse, this has been blamed—chiefly but not only by people on the Left—on an American and European Union (EU)-led process of liberal economic globalization whose goal is to maximize returns to corporate leaders and the holders of capital at the expense of wage earners and stakeholders. According to these critics, advanced social democracies like France are being forced to dismantle their welfare states so as to satiate the greed of increasingly mobile financial and corporate actors who have been empowered by this process. In turn, the socioeconomic fears linked to the decline of formerly dominant producer groups dovetail with broader anxieties that, as a result of globalization's homogenizing effects, France is losing its cultural distinctiveness and identity. For a growing number of people, the disorienting impact of globalization is putting into question what it means to be French by eroding the structural and symbolic foundations of France itself.

SAFEGUARDING *LA FRANCE PROFONDE*

The first of these foundations is the notion of *La France profonde* and the ensuing conception of rural rootedness held by French people to subtend their collective identity. Despite having experienced rapid urbanization following World War II, the French remain strongly attached to their country's rural past. This past is predicated on the concept of *terroir*, which refers to the distinctive rural microregions or *pays*, often no larger than a town or village and its environs, which endow France with the richness and diversity of its countryside, as well as its craft and culinary cultures, folk traditions, and historical memory.

Politically, this attachment to the *terroir* can be traced to the Jacobin Republican belief, born at the Revolution and disseminated during the Third Republic (1875–1940), in the universal accession of the people to small-scale property in the form of a farm or small artisanal business as the key to preserving the Republican order. This accounts for the sectoral dominance of the agricultural and artisanal sectors during the Third and Fourth Republics and explains why France still boasts more artisans and small shopkeepers as a proportion of its population than any other advanced industrial country, with the possible exception of Italy. Symbolically, these microregions have a special resonance for native-born French people because they represent the historical and cultural repository from whence their families issued and to which—either in old age or, if they are lucky, at the weekend—they can hope to return.

The strength of this local identification translates into occasional demands for cultural and, in some cases, political autonomy or independence. The most obvious contemporary example is in Corsica, where an irredentist organization, the Corsican National Liberation Front (FLNC), and the various splinter groups that issued from it have engaged in acts of vandalism, extortion, and attacks on the symbols and representatives of the French state—the most spectacular being the assassination of the island's prefect, Claude Érignac, in 1998. However, this is far from the only case, with autonomist or independence movements also active, though not to the same extremes, in Alsace, Brittany, Languedoc-Roussillon, and the French Basque country.

Partly in an effort to recognize the specificity of these different regions and to preempt future demands for autonomy or independence, the French state has sought, since the 1980s, to decentralize its competencies, particularly in matters of infrastructure, technological investment, and fiscal and welfare policy. The state has also officially recognized regional cultures and languages and promoted their teaching, particularly in primary school. However, the inherent tension posed by these initiatives between granting greater autonomy to the regions and maintaining the central authority of the state was underscored when the Constitutional Council—the highest authority on legislative matters—struck down a law granting special autonomous status to Corsica in January 2002. Accordingly, tensions between the state and local or regional collectivities are likely to persist, especially as the particularistic identities bound up in the latter are inflamed with the advances of globalization.

Not surprisingly, these transformations have provoked a strong backlash against globalization in France. Jose Bové provides the most recognizable face of the antiglobalization movement. An activist and author who once served a prison sentence for ransacking a McDonald's restaurant and now a European Parliamentary representative for the Europe Écologie party, Bové has been a long-standing presence at antiglobalization protests against institutions like the International Monetary Fund and the World Trade Organization as well as at the "alter-globalization" meetings organized each year to coincide with the World Economic Forum assembling global political and business leaders in Davos, Switzerland. Bové is something of a folk hero in France, where he acts as the self-appointed defender of the products of the *terroir* against the homogenization and debasement of food products by the global agro and food industries. In this capacity, he has led the opposition to the importation of hormone-treated beef and the use of genetically modified organisms in Europe, citing how the outsized profits made possible by these technologies outweigh the health and environmental hazards they pose for the multinational corporations and international organizations that promote their use.

Bové strikes a chord among the French even though farmers represent a dwindling proportion of the country's demographic and productive base. Although less than 4 percent of the population today earns a living from the land as opposed to 20 percent in 1970, French people continue to defend farmers' economic interests, notably in the form of the EU's Common Agricultural Policy (CAP), even if this means having to pay higher food prices and impoverishing small farmers in developing countries. On one level, this appeal is reflected in the disproportionate power that continues to be wielded by the rural sector within the country's political institutions and among its political leaders. This is most evident in the Senate, whose members are elected by officials from the country's 36,000 communes, the overwhelming majority of which are rural.

On another level, popular sympathy for the plight of French farmers derives from the conception of *ruralité* or rootedness in the countryside that casts agricultural workers as custodians of the French countryside who are charged with safeguarding its natural beauty and cultural specificity. This romanticized view of farmers is largely mythical, of course, since big agro-industrial interests today dominate the country's agricultural production. However, it resonates with the rurally based representation that French people have of themselves.

The history of the CAP highlights the extent to which the French state has been willing to play the protectionist card and interfere in the internal management of firms if this is deemed to be in the national interest. For example, appealing to the imperative of "economic patriotism," in the summer of 2005 the Villepin government facilitated the merger of the publicly traded Suez SA with the state-controlled GDF in order to prevent the potential takeover of GDF by the Italian firm Enel. In turn, the 2008 global financial crisis and ensuing global economic downturn intensified Sarkozy's protectionist and interventionist instincts. In December 2008, his administration announced a €26 billion stimulus package to support sectors that were particularly hard hit by the crisis, including the banking, auto, and construction sectors, as well as called for the adoption of EU-level trade protections.[10]

Throughout the 2012 campaign and during his first year in office, Hollande pledged to expand his predecessor's interventionist initiatives so as to mitigate the impact on French firms of the worsening European economic crisis and, more broadly, to shield them from the effects of global competition. This commitment resonated with another key theme that he sounded during the campaign: that he would do more to protect French jobs than his predecessor. It was not long after his election that Hollande's interventionist pledge would be tested, with a number of major French manufacturers announcing plans to lay off significant parts of their workforces and reduce their operations in response to the crisis, including PSA (Peugeot-Citroën), Arcelor-Mittal, Sanofi, Doux, Goodyear, and Air France.

IMMIGRATION AND IDENTITY IN THE AGE OF GLOBALIZATION

If the economic and cultural transformations occasioned by globalization provide the general context fueling fears over the loss of France's cultural identity and specificity, no single issue has more vividly crystallized these fears than immigration. This is understandable since the debate over immigration brings into play a second great pillar of French identity and self-definition: the Republican model of citizenship constructed around the twin principles of *laïcité* ("secularness") and equality under the law. Inherited from the Revolution and shaped by the Catholic-Republican culture wars that dominated the early decades of the Third Republic, this model strives in theory to assimilate foreigners and their French-born children into the national community, no matter what their country of origin or their ethnic or religious background, in the name of the Republican ideal of civic equality.

The growth of a large immigrant population of non-European descent in France has sorely tested the limits of this republican model of citizenship, and is increasingly seen in some quarters as posing a threat to the civic identity of the nation. These shortcomings are highlighted by the negative indicators reflecting the exclusion of these immigrants from the country's economic and social life. These are especially dire for immigrants from North and sub-Saharan Africa, who suffer from unusually high rates of unemployment, poverty, and educational failure. Members of these groups are often concentrated in government-subsidized housing projects (*cités*) situated on the fringes of French cities and towns, which are bereft of public services, civil society organizations, and economic opportunities. Such conditions contribute to periodic explosions of unrest in these areas—the most spectacular instance of which was the month-long wave of rioting that swept the country in November 2005—which serve to further criminalize immigrants in the eyes of their co-citizens.

Such developments have raised doubts about the viability of the Republican model. There are those who argue that the Republican model has failed to live up to its ideal of equality for all, condemning certain categories of immigrants to de facto underclass status within French society. For these critics, official appeals to Republicanism have become a pretext for inaction that releases politicians and the broader society from the obligation to address the profound structural inequities and social injustices that are faced by many immigrants in France. The answer, they aver, is to replace the universalist model of Republican integration with a multicultural one in which communal differences are officially recognized and in which the state takes action to remedy the discriminations to which certain immigrant groups are subjected in the aim of facilitating their integration into the society. Not surprisingly, these critics hold up the United States and the United Kingdom as successful examples of this multicultural model of integration and argue that France would be well served to recast its integration policies along similar lines.

Conversely, there are those who argue that the predominantly Islamic character of France's immigrant population places an unmanageable strain on the capacity of the Republican model to integrate what they consider to be an irreducibly alien and inassimilable religious minority. According to these critics, the hegemonic political as well as spiritual ambitions of Islam, as well as the inability of its practitioners to distinguish between the public and private spheres, render the Republican model inoperable. The debates over the wearing of the headscarf in public schools and of the burqa in the street crystallized for them the cultural intractability of Islam and the incapacity of the Republican model to integrate its denizens, instead marking the emergence of a de facto "communitarianism" in the midst of secular French society.

The debate over the wearing of the headscarf in public schools first gained prominence in the late 1980s. Those who opposed it claimed that the headscarf was an overt religious symbol that, when worn in an official public space such as a public school, constituted an affront to the Republican principle of *laïcité*. Meanwhile, those who supported the right to wear it claimed that it was not incompatible with *laïcité*, but instead that banning it was an attack on an individual's right to practice her religion. The government reaction was initially confused, with the Constitutional Council defending in 1989 the right of Muslim girls to wear the headscarf in schools "unless it threatened [their] orderly functioning," followed by a decree in 1994 that sought to differentiate between "discreet" versus "ostentatious" symbols, without distinguishing into which category the headscarf fell. The expulsion and ensuing cases involving around 100 Muslim girls for wearing the headscarf in public schools under this decree, as well as continuing demonstrations and counterdemonstrations on both sides, forced the government to take an unequivocal stand, resulting in a law in March 2004 banning the wearing of overt religious symbols, including headscarves, yarmulkes, and large crosses, in state schools.

This debate over the wearing of religious symbols in public places was reignited in the summer of 2010, when the Fillon government passed a law banning the wearing of the burqa (a robelike garment covering the eyes and hands of the woman, which is in use in Afghanistan) and niqab (the burqa's equivalent in the Arab world) in any public space, whether official or not. Notwithstanding the enforcement difficulties it posed and the fact that it would only concern about 1,900 out of 1.5 to 2 million Muslim women in France, the law's advocates saw it as necessary to defend the principle of *laïcité* against the encroachments of fundamentalist Islam on a secular society.[11] And even though the overwhelming majority of Muslims in France are against their use, the mere presence of the burqa and niqab in France, no matter how infinitesimal, attested for these critics to the fundamental incompatibility of Islam with the secular values of the Republic and the insuperable difficulty of integrating Muslims into French society.

Yet, in actual fact, the French situation is not so dire. In the first place, the Republican model has functioned much better than its critics give it credit for given the size of the immigrant communities concerned and the short time period the society has had to integrate them. Indeed, a few basic indicators show that despite everything, integration of these immigrants is progressing. The overwhelming majority of them almost exclusively speak French in their daily lives. Mixed marriages among these immigrants and their children, in particular those from the Maghreb, are rising fast, while birthrates among women from these groups approximate the national norm. Likewise, the attitudes of immigrants in general and Muslims in particular suggest that they have internalized the values of universalism and tolerance associated with Republican citizenship. At the same time, Muslim immigrants are adopting strategies similar to those employed by previous immigrant groups in order to maximize their political leverage vis-à-vis the state and its agents as a means to speed their assimilation. In this capacity, civil society groups have been active at both the local and national levels in organizing immigrants and trying to articulate their concerns and demands to politicians and officials.[12] The fact that these immigrants are resorting to time-proven strategies that facilitated the integration of previous groups into French society should be seen as encouraging testimony to the viability of the Republican model.

At the same time, private actors such as firms and *grandes écoles* like Sciences Po in Paris have reached out to minorities in order to diversify their workforces and student bodies. The most explicit moves in this direction were the creation of the High Authority for the Struggle against Discrimination and for Equality (HALDE) in 2004 and the promulgation of the Charter on the Equality of Chances in 2005 in order to improve the access of at-risk youth to higher education. In short, the French Republican model has shown itself to be much more adaptive to the situation of immigrants than multiculturalist critics would admit, even though more remains to be done in order to advance their integration into French society.

The real problem in this regard appears to reside less in the Republican model itself than in the general recalcitrance of the French to make Republicanism a reality. The social context for the November 2005 riots as well as smaller subsequent episodes of urban unrest is particularly illustrative in this regard. Unemployment among youth of immigrant descent living in the *cités* is often as high as 40 percent, testifying not only to the country's subpar economic performance but also to the deep-seated racism confronted by immigrants and their children in the labor market. This social discrimination reflects negative popular stereotypes associated with these populations, many of which date back to colonial times. Moreover, it is magnified by official racism on the part of civil servants and the police who are often implicated in racial profiling and even violence against immigrants. The detonator of the November 2005 riots was the death of two teenagers of Tunisian and Malian descent who were electrocuted while trying to hide from the police in an electric power substation. Likewise, the wave of unrest that swept the eastern city of Grenoble in July 2010 followed the police shooting of a suspect of Algerian descent who was being sought following a bank robbery. More recently, a night of rioting in the suburbs of the northern city of Amiens in August 2012 was precipitated by the rumors of the death of a young man from that *banlieue* from wounds he had received in a motorcycle accident he suffered while being chased by the police.

The consistent loyalty displayed by Muslim leaders to the French state confirms the insignificance of religion as a factor explaining the failure of Muslim immigrants to integrate into French society. This is true particularly in the context of conflicts opposing the Islamic world and the West. Despite the often painful claims placed on their Muslim identity during the Gulf Wars of 1990–1991 and 2003, the wave of Islamic terrorism that swept France during the Algerian Civil War in 1995–1996, and the second Intifada that began in September 2002, the vast majority of French Muslims harbored no intention of endangering their right to peaceful residence in their adopted country. Indeed, their self-restraint highlighted the same desire that paradoxically underlay the violent demonstrations of immigrant youth: that Muslims in France want to be absorbed on equal terms within the broader society.

The impediments to such a program remain numerous, with politicians on both the Left and the Right attempting to thread the needle between improving the life chances of immigrants in French society, on the one hand, while trying to address broader societal fears tying immigration to sociostructural problems such as unemployment, crime, and declining social services, on the other. Perhaps most worrying, integration efforts have been rendered more difficult by the economic crisis that began in 2009, with unemployment hitting immigrant youth from the *banlieues* hardest, while cuts in social services disproportionately affected the residents of the so-called *zones sensibles*. According to a government observatory, in 751 such "sensitive urban zones" the poverty rate increased from 30.5 percent in 2006 to 36.1 percent in 2010, as compared with from 11.9 percent to 12.6 percent in the rest of the country.[13]

HOLLANDE'S IMMIGRATION POLICY: SARKOZY LITE?

Nicolas Sarkozy's election was particularly instructive with respect to the immigration and integration issues, not least because it perpetuated the schizophrenic character of previous attempts to address these problems. On the one hand, Sarkozy actively promoted integrative policies that recognized the need for affirmative action in order to improve the situation for immigrant youth. He did so by naming ministers from immigrant backgrounds to his cabinet and by pushing for more diversity in the civil service and television sectors. Similarly, his government attempted to broaden the affirmative action mechanisms called for in the Charter of Equality by facilitating the access of members of poor minorities to better schooling and higher education.

On the other hand, Sarkozy also displayed a troubling willingness to exploit the immigration issue and pander to the xenophobia of the electorate for political gain. Since his election had in large part depended on siphoning off a substantial number of votes from the National Front (FN), his various "hardline" pronouncements on immigration could be interpreted as part of a strategy to win over these voters and keep them electorally on his side. Already as interior minister, his reference to the November 2005 rioters as "scum" and subsequent call for the *cités* to be cleaned out with a fire hose (*au Kärcher*) raised eyebrows in many quarters. In turn, a number of initiatives undertaken by his administration created doubts about Sarkozy's commitment to the goal of integration, since they singled out immigrants for discriminatory treatment. Plans to establish a Ministry of Immigration and National Identity, institute DNA testing as a precondition for reuniting immigrant families, and encourage "selective" immigration were viewed as racist by immigrant groups.

The ambiguities of Sarkozy's approach to immigration were best exemplified by the "debate on national identity" launched by his government in 2008. At one level, such a debate could be seen as salutary since it facilitated an open discussion of the status of immigrants within French society and yielded a positive agenda for facilitating their integration within it. However, it also had a negative effect by explicitly tying the issues of national identity and immigration. In this way the debate served to radicalize those who, particularly on the Far Right, were opposed to regularizing the status of Muslim immigrants within French society. It also provoked a communitarian backlash among French Muslims and brought them to reject the Republican model of integration in favor of asserting their own religious and ethnic particularism. Hence, Sarkozy's hardening of immigration policy and opening of this debate on national identity impeded the flexibility of the Republican model in assimilating Muslim immigrants while allowing them to assert their cultural and religious specificity under the formal framework of equality.

The accession to power of a Socialist administration appeared to herald substantial changes in immigration policy. Culturally and ideologically, the Left in general and PS specifically have been more welcoming of immigrants than have been parties of the Right; socioeconomically, the Left formerly put in place welfarist and pro-employment policies in order to improve the living conditions of immigrants, in particular youths of immigrant backgrounds living in the *banlieues*. By the same token, Manuel Valls, François Hollande's minister of the interior, has sought to revise the stricter naturalization criteria that had been introduced by his predecessor under Sarkozy—criteria that included toughening language qualification requirements and having candidates for naturalization sign a "charter of rights and duties of the citizen," while loosening the entry restrictions placed on immigrants from other Schengen member countries.

However, Hollande and his ministers have not sought to repeal the most controversial piece of legislation that was enacted under Sarkozy's administration, namely, the law prohibiting the burqa in public spaces. The maintenance of this law is intended not just to deflect criticism from the Right on the immigration issue, but also to find favor with those who maintain a strong commitment to *laïcité* on the Left. Likewise, the present government, with Valls in the lead, sought to hold on to the "tough-on-crime" image cultivated by its predecessor in the name of shoring up "Republican authority." This has included offering unequivocal support to the muscular police repression of rioters at Amiens in August 2012, and stepping up the dismantlement—begun under Sarkozy—of illegal Roma encampments throughout the country and deporting the latter to their countries of origin (a policy that contravenes the EU's free movement of peoples clause). Finally, Hollande's interior minister has gone on record to oppose the new president's pledge to allow foreigners to vote in local elections on the grounds that this could retard or impede the process of integrating immigrants in French society.

In short, Valls conceives of his role as "rehabilitating" the function of "first cop of France" (*premier flic de France*), which he accused Sarkozy of having "killed." Designed in part to blunt criticism from the Right and extreme Right, which had successfully portrayed previous Socialist governments—notably that of Lionel Jospin—as "soft on crime," the effective linkage established by the Hollande administration between immigration and crime and its largely repressive approach to resolving the problem underscore yet another area of continuity between its own policy agenda and that of the preceding administration—a continuity seemingly belied by Hollande's divergent discourses and promises during the campaign.

FRENCH POLITICS IN THE AGE OF GLOBALIZATION

The challenges posed by immigration and globalization, and the difficulties of the French state in dealing with them, highlight the incapacity of the French political establishment to address the principal issues of concern to French voters. The result is an increasingly fragmented party system, on the one hand, and governmental blockage or one-party rule, on the other.

This fragmentation can be seen in the erosion of the bipolar pattern of party competition that had developed in the 1970s, opposing an alliance of the PS and PCF on the Left to the UDF and RPR on the Right. The most obvious beneficiary of this trend has been the National Front, but this splintering occurred on the Left as well, with the emergence of smaller parties to the left of the *PS* that occupied the space opened up by the collapse of the Communist Party. These include the Greens, the Revolutionary Communist League (LCR), the New Anti-Capitalist Party (NPA), Workers Struggle (LO), and, most recently, the Left Party (PdG). This fragmentation reached its apogee in the first round of the 2002 presidential election. With the electoral field dispersed among a record sixteen candidates, enough votes were siphoned off from Socialist Party candidate Lionel Jospin to result in his elimination and the accession of the National Front's Jean-Marie Le Pen to the second-round runoff.

The hybrid presidential-parliamentary system instituted by General Charles de Gaulle at the Fifth Republic's inception has proved increasingly dysfunctional in the age of globalization. This system reinforces the power of the executive at the expense of the legislature where, except on the most controversial pieces of legislation, the opposition fulfills basically a ceremonial function. When the prime minister comes from the same party as the president, the National Assembly's role is essentially to rubberstamp the initiatives of the president, with little real debate or amendment. At the same time, as voters grew increasingly dissatisfied with the policy records of sitting governments, instances of *cohabitation* where the president and the prime minister come from different parties grew increasingly frequent beginning in the 1980s. Characterized by intense policy rivalry between the president and prime minister, these periods of *cohabitation* often resulted in political stalemate and paralysis, contributing to the delegitimization of the country's political institutions among the electorate.

In turn, these institutional failings have become coupled in the public mind with the staleness and mediocrity of the nation's political elite. Until Sarkozy's election, France's political leaders, notably Jacques Chirac and François Mitterrand, had begun their careers half a century earlier, if not more. These men had been the faces of French politics for over three decades, and those who served under them represented an equally long-standing clique of professional politicians and party notables. The sense of permanence attaching to the political class was reinforced by their exclusive backgrounds, reflecting the fact that the country's political and economic elites almost all issue from highly selective schools (*grandes écoles*) such as the École Polytechnique and the ÉNA (National School of Administration). In their preparation for the task of steering the state bureaucracy and the country's leading firms, these future leaders developed tightknit social and professional networks that facilitated their movement between the highest positions in the public and private sectors. To French voters, this exclusive and incestuous elite appears as at best out of touch, and at worst corrupt.

This impression has been reinforced by the numerous political and financial scandals that have embroiled leading French politicians over the years. The country has seen a former minister of the interior, Charles Pasqua, jailed for his role in facilitating illegal arms sales to Angola in 1995; the alleged involvement of former Prime Minister Dominique de Villepin in forging bank account statements implicating his political rival, Nicolas Sarkozy, in the receipt of kickbacks in the 1991 sale of frigates to Taiwan; and the charging of former President Jacques Chirac—a first in the history of Fifth Republic—on charges of corruption during his tenure as mayor of Paris during the 1980s and 1990s.

The Sarkozy administration was also far from free of scandal. In the fall of 2009, he was accused of nepotism for promoting his son Jean, who was only twenty-three at the time, for the job of running the organism charged with overseeing the business quarter of La Défense just outside Paris, despite his lack of managerial experience. More damaging was the scandal linking Eric Woerth, one of Sarkozy's closest aides and the cabinet minister charged with pushing through the 2010 pension reforms, to the Bettencourt affair, the dynastic court case surrounding Liliane Bettencourt, France's richest woman and heiress to the L'Oréal cosmetics empire, in an illegal party-financing scandal. Though Woerth was quickly jettisoned, allegations of misdoing have continued to swirl around the former president.

Given this distrust of the political establishment, it is not surprising that significant protest parties have emerged on both the Far Right and the Far Left since the 1980s, the most significant by far being the National Front. The FN brings together former Vichy sympathizers, neo-fascists, Catholic fundamentalists, and dissidents from the mainstream Right. It first broke through on the national political scene in the mid-1980s and then went from strength to strength, its charismatic leader Jean-Marie Le Pen reaching the second round of the 2002 presidential election and winning 18 percent of the vote. The manifestation of an exclusivist nationalist and authoritarian tradition whose roots can be traced back to the late nineteenth century, the FN has made the fight against immigration and linking it to France's current social and economic ills the cornerstone of its political message.

For many observers, the 2007 presidential election marked a critical setback for the National Front. Its poor score—10.4 percent, its worst result since its electoral breakthrough in the mid-1980s—combined with its lack of a clear successor to the eighty-two-year-old Le Pen perhaps signaled the start of its definitive decline. However, the party's strong performance in the March 2010 regional elections and local elections a year later, combined with the appointment of Marine Le Pen as successor to her father, laid the foundations for the party's spectacular resurrection.

Recasting the FN's anti-immigrant and anti-EU message as part of a broader critique of globalization that resonates with voters of both the Right and the Left, particularly from the industrial and clerical working classes, Marine Le Pen has steered her party from electoral success to electoral success, establishing herself as the new kingmaker of French politics. This was confirmed in the 2012 presidential election in which her party won a record number of votes and garnered 17.9 percent in the first round of voting—breaking the record set by her father a decade before. This pattern continued in the June 2012 parliamentary elections, with the FN winning two seats in Parliament for the first time since 1988 and improving its electoral performance from an average of 4.7 percent in the first round in 2007 to 13.6 percent in 2012. Having already asserted itself as the driving force in shaping the French political debate, with its message recalibrated to harness the anxieties of the victims of the ongoing economic crisis, the FN under Marine Le Pen is emerging into a legitimate contender for political power.[14] This populist upsurge poses critical challenges and dangers for Hollande's presidency.

HOLLANDE—STRIVING TO BE "NORMAL" IN ABNORMAL TIMES

If François Hollande is today the most unpopular president in the history of the Fifth Republic, it is worth remembering that this was not always the case. As we saw, his election was received with relief in many quarters, marking a respite from the unceasing agitation and constant about-faces of the Sarkozy presidency. After the hectic and seemingly, at times, incoherent policy style of the preceding administration, the French welcomed the return to a more measured pace and approach to governance, characterized by greater reflection, caution, and gravitas. In a word, they welcomed the advent of a "normal" presidency by historical standards with which Sarkozy had emphatically tried to break during the course of his term.

Yet, there was an underside to this resumption of political normalcy. The partisan fragmentation that has plagued the French political system since the 1980s returned with a vengeance and the Hollande administration found itself confronted with social conflict and political division from the outset. Most worryingly for Hollande, this conflict pits the Socialist Party elite against his electoral base, thereby raising concerns about the long-term viability of the current government. Hollande was elected with the backing of a hard-left electorate that has grown progressively disenchanted with his perceived diffidence and inaction in the face of the economic and unemployment crisis. More broadly, such a division raises the question of the political status of working-class voters who are disappointed with the administration's inability to protect their jobs and social *acquis* and so are growing increasingly amenable to populist alternatives to protect them.

Similar divisions also exist on the center-right. The Union for a Popular Movement (UMP) has seen a damaging split between the party's social Gaullist wing, which is more closely identified with the statist and Christian Democratic traditions of the French Right, and its neoliberal and increasingly nationalist wing. This intraparty division, which first emerged during Sarkozy's term of office, came to the fore following the 2012 election in a primary campaign to decide who would lead the UMP after Sarkozy's putative retirement. The tension between these two currents came to a head in November 2012 when François Fillon, as leader of the social Gaullists, and Jean-François Copé, as head of the liberal nativists, both claimed victory in the UMP's primary to determine its new leader. Each blamed the other of cheating and other irregularities, with Copé finally claiming his interim leadership of the UMP on a permanent basis, while Fillon threatened to launch an independent parliamentary group and candidacy, and thereby split the party. Senior party leaders scrambled to mediate these differences in order to keep the UMP together, forcing the candidates to agree to a new primary election in October 2013—a date that has come and gone without such an election being held. Reflecting its indefinite postponement, there is no guarantee that such a vote will put to rest the divisions that arose in the fall of 2012, reflecting the contrary pull of ideological and policy differences within the UMP as well as personal rivalries within the party leadership.

Last but not least, the Hollande administration has itself not been immune from scandal. Indeed, perhaps the most damaging blow it has suffered in the course of its first year was the admission by the minister of the budget, Jerôme Cahuzac—after repeated denials before the National Assembly—that he possessed a secret bank account in Switzerland in which he had hidden €600,000 beyond the reach of the French taxman. In turn, he is alleged to have deposited a further €14.4 million in other secret foreign accounts, much of this money said to be proceeds from his consultancy work for large pharmaceutical interests.

The political damage has been incalculable. For many, particularly among lower-class voters, the scandal confirmed the hypocritical image of a government of caviar-eating elites out of touch with their concerns and preoccupied with feathering its own nest. More broadly, it dealt a blow to Hollande's aspiration to clean up French politics after the scandals of the Sarkozy years and to impose "transparency" in government, instead discrediting his own government's integrity and even casting into doubt its legitimacy.

Disillusionment with politicians is not the only problem. Hollande also confronts a recalcitrant electorate that, though it understands the need to liberalize the economy and reform the welfare state in the age of globalization, wants the state to continue to protect it. More than anything, it is this historically ingrained dependence on the French state that makes substantial reforms so difficult to achieve.

The problem is structural; the state sector still accounts for roughly a quarter of full-time jobs in the country. Attempts to cut this sector, let alone eliminate or reduce the privileges attaching to it, incur the wrath of the trade unions—the public sector representing the one area where these remain strong—who are well placed to paralyze the country's public and transport services and bring the economy to a halt. The most spectacular instance of such protests took place in the fall and winter of 1995, following the Alain Juppé government's attempt to push through comprehensive pension reform. Month-long strikes resulted in the proposal being withdrawn and the government collapsing, which forced Jacques Chirac to call fresh parliamentary elections that brought a Socialist majority to power five years before the end of Chirac's seven-year mandate.

Fifteen years later, similarly widespread demonstrations met the Fillon government's plans to cut the public sector by one-third and align civil servants' pensions with those of private sector workers, bringing between 1.2 and 3.5 million protestors into the streets of French cities in October 2010. Such strikes are likely to recur as the Jean-Marc Ayrault government, in yet another violation of Hollande's campaign pledge to restore the retirement age to 60, seeks to raise the latter by extending social contributions from 41.5 to 44 years, effectively entrenching the pension reforms that Sarkozy had forced through and that the PS had unanimously condemned while in opposition.

Firms also depend on the state's largesse. Thus, responding to fallout from the global financial crisis, in October 2008 the Sarkozy administration injected €3 billion into Dexia Bank, a leading lender to municipalities, to save it from bankruptcy. It also orchestrated a merger between the Caisse d'Épargne and the Banque Populaire—at a cost of €5 billion—to keep them from going under following Lehman Brothers' collapse. Likewise, in December 2008, the Sarkozy administration lent the Renault and Peugeot-Citroën automobile groups €7.8 billion in exchange for maintaining their operations in France and agreeing not to lay off workers or outsource jobs. Finally, as part of an Estates General of Industry convened from November 2009 to March 2010, Sarkozy announced over €1 billion in ad hoc aid to keep firms from closing their operations, arguing that "France must keep its factories; France must keep its instruments of production." As part of this commitment, Sarkozy even stipulated, in a seeming return to 1970s-style indicative planning, specific production and performance targets.[15]

François Hollande has perpetuated such interventionist initiatives in order to mitigate the impact on French firms and jobs of the worsening European economic crisis as well as to shield them from the impacts of intensifying global competition. This policy has been most prominently tested during his first year in office by the PSA case, which involved the standoff between the government and the PSA automaker (formerly Peugeot-Citroën) following the government's rejection of the company's plans to shed 11,000 jobs countrywide and close its factory at Aulnay-sous-Bois (3,000 jobs) near Paris. However, once PSA's management returned to the negotiating table, the government did not interfere in the process of elaborating and approving its "social plan" to make these layoffs effective. PSA's works committee, including labor and management representatives, signed off on the plan on April 29, 2013, despite the ongoing strike called by the Aulnay workers since February.[16] Thus, despite registering its initial opposition to the closure, the Hollande administration effectively failed to prevent PSA from offshoring its production and shedding jobs in France.

Just as the state under Sarkozy proved powerless to prevent the dismantling of former French national champions (Alsthom), the offshoring of productive operations (Alsthom and Airbus), or the foreign takeover of French firms (Pechiney and Arcelor), so Hollande's experience has highlighted the limited capacity of state intervention to protect production and safeguard jobs in the face of international competition.

Accordingly, it is not surprising that, when confronted by the gap between politicians' assertions of the state's protective capacity and global economic realities, more and more French people feel frustrated by the state's inability to shield them from the forces of globalization, let alone turn them to their advantage.

Foreign Policy

With the predominance assumed by the economic slowdown and the European debt crisis, foreign policy took a back seat to domestic policy during Hollande's 2012 election campaign. But, as in the area of domestic policy, there are also more continuities than meet the eye between the foreign policy course adopted by François Hollande and that pursued by his predecessor.

Before analyzing these continuities, however, it is first necessary to say something about France's postwar foreign policy persona and, specifically, the legacy of General Charles de Gaulle. At the center of General de Gaulle's conception of French foreign policy was the imperative of making France "count" as a world power by striving to maintain its "independence, sovereignty, and *grandeur*." This implied an assertive discourse that was marked by a willingness to break with the United States or European allies as a means of reaffirming France's global role. Likewise, the Gaullist assertion of French independence was also manifest in spectacular acts of diplomacy, such as the veto of the UK's EEC accession bids in 1963 and 1967, France's pullout from NATO integrated military command in 1966, and de Gaulle's Phnom Penh speech denouncing the American war in Vietnam later the same year. At the same time, de Gaulle's foreign policy aimed to establish France as an indispensable intermediary between the Eastern and Western blocs, on the one hand, and the developed and developing worlds, on the other. By playing such a role, he believed, France would be able to recapture the global prestige it had enjoyed prior to the defeat of 1940 and thus punch above its weight as a middle power.

With different styles, we find a similar assertion of the imperatives of French independence and *grandeur* among de Gaulle's successors. Georges Pompidou, though he finally acceded to the UK's admission to the EEC, also indulged in sometimes virulent criticism of the United States (as in response to the arming of Israel during the Yom Kippur War of 1973). Valéry Giscard-d'Estaing irritated Washington by characterizing the Soviet invasion of Afghanistan in 1979 as an act of self-defense and refusing to boycott the Moscow Olympics in 1980. François Mitterrand, while accommodating U.S. strategic aims by accepting the installation of Pershing and Cruise missiles in Europe; supporting Chad in its war against Libya, a Soviet ally; and participating in the U.S.-led coalition to expel Iraqi troops from Kuwait, was also determined to act on his own on certain issues. Thus he resisted U.S. and UK pressures to rescind energy contracts with the USSR and called, alongside German Chancellor Helmut Kohl, for the pursuit of an independent European Common Foreign and Security Policy. Finally, Jacques Chirac's two terms as president were characterized by a mix of foreign policy activism combined with independent policies vis-à-vis the United States. His hardening of the French line against Serbia in 1995 and decision to resume French nuclear testing in the South Pacific were examples of his activism, while his threat to veto a UN Security Council resolution authorizing a U.S.-led invasion of Iraq in 2003 was the most dramatic instance of independence.

Finally, despite his Atlanticist reputation and desire to repair the damage wrought on Franco-American relations by his predecessor, Nicolas Sarkozy remained staunchly Gaullist in terms of both the underlying beliefs and actual initiatives that characterized his foreign policy. He posited a multipolar world in which France, through the EU, rightfully exercised its diplomatic, security, and economic influence in order not only to defend the national interest but also to secure the country's independence, influence, and *grandeur*.

Alongside this traditional commitment to independence, French foreign policy has been focused since the Second World War on three geographically defined areas or "circles" of activity: the Atlantic or Western Alliance, Europe, and the French-speaking countries (*francophonie*) incorporating France's former colonies, particularly in North and sub-Saharan Africa and the Arab world. French foreign policy in these three areas has been remarkably consistent.

In the Atlantic area, relations between France and the U.S.-led Western Alliance have been characterized by mutual wariness and support. Relations hit a new low in the run-up to the Iraq war in 2003, marking the first time that France had openly and actively opposed the United States in an international crisis. However, even in the wake of this episode, the two countries continued to work together behind the scenes and cooperated on issues of vital interest to both, such as the fight against global terrorist networks. This mixed relationship is best summed up in former Foreign Minister Hubert Védrine's quip that the two countries remain "friends, allies, [but] non-aligned."

This tension was evident under Sarkozy who, despite his rhetoric, did not substantially move French foreign policy in a more Atlanticist direction, whether on Israel-Palestine; on Iran, where there was only a slight hardening of France's position compared to the Chirac years; or on Afghanistan, where after a slight initial increase in French troop commitments to the NATO coalition following his election, Sarkozy quickly began to wind down French involvement in the face of mounting military difficulties and the growing unpopularity of the Afghan war at home. Even Sarkozy's much-publicized decision to return France to NATO integrated command in 2009 was prefigured by Chirac's failed attempt to do so in the mid-1990s.

In short, the Atlanticist hype aside, these foreign policy choices suggest that, much like his predecessors, Sarkozy viewed the world in terms of an emerging multipolar dispensation, which the United States and the West more generally will find increasingly difficult to control. Much like de Gaulle before him, in such a world Sarkozy believed that France had a crucial role to play in reaching out to and bridging divides with other states, regions, and cultures. Such was the thinking behind his proposals to establish a Union of the Mediterranean between "Latin" Europe and North Africa, his "AREVA" diplomacy promoting the development of civilian nuclear energy in Arab countries, and his advocacy of enlarging the G-8 into a G-13 and increasing the number of permanent members of the UN Security Council.

At the European level, French policy has been consistent since the Élysée Treaty of 1963, which attempted to cement the economic rapprochement with West Germany under the auspices of French foreign policy leadership. This policy reflected the belief that European economic and political integration could only be advanced on the basis of cooperation between France and Germany—the famous "Franco-German engine." However, this conviction was tempered by the recognition that only through cooperation with London could Europe assume an independent military capability under Franco-British leadership.

Under Sarkozy and with the onset of the European debt crisis, the erosion of French power within Europe became as evident as ever. Indeed, the independent and leading role that he had fashioned for himself at the start of his term—through proposals such as the creation of a Union of the Mediterranean without consulting Berlin, or his call for an "economic (read: French-led) government" of Europe to counter Germany's dictation of policy on the euro—was in striking contrast to the clearly subordinate role his administration assumed vis-à-vis the German government during the last two years of his term. Reflecting the growing disjuncture in economic performance between Europe's and the euro zone's two core powers, no one was fooled into thinking that the Franco-German tandem was a partnership of equals.

Outwardly at least, it is perhaps at the level of *francophonie* that things have changed the most. Although France still ascribes great importance to what goes on in Algiers, Rabat, or Tunis, it no longer enjoys the influence to shape policy in these places that it once did. Likewise, though France continues to maintain a military presence in sub-Saharan Africa, this presence is much less significant than before. Finally, although French leaders continue to dream of influencing developments in the Middle East, particularly in resolving the Israeli-Palestinian conflict, they harbor no illusion about their lack of leverage to do so.

This declining influence in the region was emphatically underscored by France's confused and contradictory reaction to the Arab Spring and, in particular, the unconditional support it lent to Tunisian strongman Zine El Abidine Ben Ali in the face of mounting popular pressure for his ouster. And despite the Sarkozy administration's policy reversal to assist the uprisings—first by helping to negotiate Ben Ali's departure from power and then militarily intervening on the side of the Libyan rebels to speed the overthrow of Muammar Gaddafi, France's ability to put its stamp on events in the region, rather than simply reacting to them, appears as circumscribed as ever.

The central dilemma facing contemporary French diplomacy has less to do with defining its foreign policy aims than with how to go about fulfilling them. Despite boasting the third largest diplomatic corps in the world after the United States and China, broader structural and cultural changes in the global system have diminished France's influence. Signs of this loss of stature can be seen at a number of levels: the ascendancy of English as the undisputed *lingua franca* of diplomacy as well as business; the hegemony, even following the financial and economic crises of 2008–2009, of liberal economic ideas; and the continued American economic and political dominance combined with the emergence of new world powers such as China and India. More than ever before, these developments are forcing French policymakers to confront the reality of their country's relative decline in a globalized world.

The challenge of decline is not new, of course. Mitterrand was the first to try to negotiate the transition from a bipolar to a plural global system complicated by the tension between America's unipolar pretensions and the emergence of a multipolar order in which France would be reduced to the rank of a middling power. Likewise, Chirac made it a priority to prepare French diplomacy for the challenges posed by the "horizontal" supranational forces shaping the contemporary international system, and hence to move beyond the bilateral focus of interstate relations inherited from the Cold War. Still, the question of France's place in the world is especially urgent today because it poses the challenge of how it is to negotiate its post–Cold War decline while minimizing its loss of influence and prestige.

HOLLANDE'S FOREIGN POLICY: A BREAK WITH THE PAST?

Where does François Hollande's foreign policy fit in terms of this attempt to compensate for France's loss of influence in an increasingly plural and globalized world? How is it to be assessed in respect to the Gaullist heritage that informed the foreign policies of his predecessors, particularly that of Nicolas Sarkozy? An examination of the principal "circles" of French diplomacy identified above makes it possible to identify the areas of continuity and discontinuity that characterize Hollande's approach to international affairs.

During the election campaign, Hollande took care to send reassuring signals to the American government, announcing that he would continue the policies of his predecessor on Iran and Syria as well as in regard to NATO. Similarly, the incoming administration minimized the potential negative fallout by opting for transparency and consistency on issues where Hollande harbored disagreements with the United States, so that the Obama administration would not be caught unawares by French policy decisions. This was true particularly in terms of hastening the departure of French troops from Afghanistan (a decision first announced by Sarkozy in early 2012) and regarding U.S. plans on antimissile defense (on grounds of cost as well as concerns that it threatened to nullify the effectiveness of France's nuclear deterrent). Such an approach contrasted with the impulsive and at times erratic character of Sarkozy's foreign policy, which often appeared to be driven by political expedience rather than consistency of alliance solidarity.

However, it is as a function of the international economic context, and notably their common diagnosis of and solutions to the European sovereign debt crisis, that Hollande's policies may end up coinciding more with those of the current U.S. administration than did those of his predecessor. Indeed, whereas Sarkozy had been forced to hew to the deflationary economic policy espoused by German Chancellor Angela Merkel to address the European debt crisis, Hollande has advocated an alternative, countercyclical reflationary policy in order to kick-start growth as the precondition for reducing the unsustainable sovereign debts plaguing the peripheral euro-zone member states. This line dovetailed with the economic policy priorities—not to mention reelection considerations—of the Obama administration, with stabilization of the European economic situation a key to the United States' own economic prospects. Hence, Obama gave his approval to Hollande's pledge to renegotiate the European budgetary pact and to introduce a continent-wide investment and stimulus program as a means to restart growth in Europe at the G20 summit in Cancún, Mexico, in June 2012.

In short, due largely to external (economic) circumstances as well as a shift in style of foreign policymaking, Hollande stands to reinforce and deepen the positive state of cooperation with the United States that was initiated under Sarkozy. As Justin Vaïsse has observed, it thus may be only a matter of time before Sarkozy *l'américain* is forgotten and replaced by Hollande *l'américain*.[17]

Perhaps the most obvious outward break of Hollande's foreign policy with that of Sarkozy is in regard to France's relations with Europe, specifically with respect to economic governance on the European sovereign debt crisis. Such a call for European economic government on the part of France was not new, of course. The first iteration of this concept was exposed in the Delors Commission's 1993 white paper on "Growth, Competitiveness and Employment," which defended the principles of "social cohesion" and "social solidarity" as the basis for the EU's economic prosperity.[18] "Economic government" meant having the Bundesbank followed by the European Central Bank address the imperatives of economic growth and employment rather than exclusively focus on maintaining price stability.

In order to achieve these aims, French proposals called for EU-level stimulus and investment programs to boost short-term demand while enhancing long-term productivity, as well as "selective" protectionist measures in order to shield European firms from the pressures of globalization. Jacques Chirac reiterated these proposals prior to the 1995 presidential elections when he campaigned to loosen the Maastricht criteria as a precondition for healing the "social fracture" in France. The Jospin government did so as well in the late 1990s as the country prepared for Economic and Monetary Union. Even Nicolas Sarkozy called for a European economic government to mitigate the impact of the global financial crisis in the fall of 2008.

Yet, as in these prior cases, Hollande's entreaty fell on deaf ears in Berlin. In particular, Germany refused any effective measure to relax or weaken the conditions of the European budgetary pact, thus confirming the EU in its present deflationary course based on slashing government spending and raising taxes in order to overcome the European debt crisis. This became the source of a growing rift between Paris and Berlin, causing many commentators to observe that Franco-German relations had reached a new nadir since the launch of the European project some sixty years ago. More than a contest of power over who should rule Europe, this rift reflected two very different, indeed incompatible, visions of the economy and society.

In the end, reflecting France's waning economic and, consequently, political influence within the EU, and taxed with policy immobilism by both the Left and the Right at home, Hollande effected his own policy U-turn. He shifted from affirming reflation and investment spending during the campaign and his first months in office to embracing austerity and retrenchment at the start of the second year of his term. The most obvious sign of this shift came in October 2012 with his government's approval and the Socialist-led majority's passage of the European fiscal compact that Hollande had denounced during the campaign.

The political consequences of this shift could be significant. Hollande has bitterly disappointed his left-wing base, which may compromise the capacity of his administration to rule, let alone win reelection. Perhaps even more consequentially, this policy shift may serve to confirm the arguments advanced by populists on the far Right and

Left—that Hollande's government is fundamentally no different from that of its predecessor in its commitment to the neoliberal project animating European integration, and that it holds closer to heart the interests of the Brussels technocratic elite and the globalized corporate interests they defend than those of the average French citizen. Likewise, this policy turn could be interpreted as suggesting that when push comes to shove, Hollande's government will do Berlin's bidding rather than fulfill its campaign pledges to the latter.

In practice, of course, Hollande had little choice but to adopt the austerity policies dictated by Germany or risk being blamed for jeopardizing monetary integration and, by extension, the European project as a whole. This situation testifies to France's declining power within Europe, not only as a function of Germany's new assertiveness within the EU but also as a result of successive EU enlargements to include increasingly politically and culturally diverse states.

Finally, Hollande's foreign policy presents significant continuities with that of his predecessor in respect to *la francophonie*. One can see a resumption or intensification of Sarkozy's policy course in a number of areas and particularly in respect to France's former colonial dependencies. For example, Hollande has been determined to take a hard line on Syria, with France taking the lead among the Western powers in officially recognizing the Syrian opposition and calling for it to form an alternative government to the Assad regime. France also pushed the EU to lift the arms embargo so as to facilitate the armament of the rebel forces. Likewise, Hollande has continued the sanctions regime imposed by his predecessor on Iran, calculating that the sanctions are more likely to result in a diplomatic solution for the Iran nuclear issue and thereby diminish the likelihood of American and Israeli strikes against Iran and hence the outbreak of a new war in the region. As for the Israel-Palestine conflict, the Hollande administration has pursued the more "balanced" (i.e., less pro-Arab) approach that was put in place by his predecessor, working within the EU and in collaboration with the United States and France's other partners in the UN Security Council to restart the peace process.

Even Hollande's most spectacular foreign policy initiative, his sending of 4,000 French soldiers to the former colony of Mali to prevent the sitting government from being toppled by an alliance of Tuareg separatists (Mouvement national pour la liberation de l'Azawad [MNLA]) from the North and al-Qaeda-affiliated Islamist forces (Al Qaida au Maghreb Islamique [AQMI]) from both within and without the country presents definite continuities with the foreign policy activism of his predecessor. First, there is an obvious parallel between Hollande's intervention in Mali and that orchestrated by Sarkozy in Libya—though, in the Libyan case, support for the rebels was limited to air strikes and logistical support. Second, at a political level, though they achieved their immediate aims—in Libya, the overthrow of Gaddafi, and in Mali, that of preventing MNLA and AQMI forces from taking the capital city of Bamako and then dislodging the jihadists from their northern redoubts—the domestic political benefits of these respective interventions have been meager.

Both the Libyan and Malian interventions have served to underscore France's current military insufficiencies, putting into question the country's capacity to project force to a degree commensurate with its ambitions in the region. In particular, both interventions have highlighted the shortfall in the country's logistical capabilities, particularly in the area of military transport, as well as its glaring lack of advanced military and reconnaissance technologies. In Mali, for example, the French have only been able to deploy two aerial surveillance drones in theater, and have been almost wholly dependent on the United States for logistics and surveillance support. Thus, this experience underscores the importance of sharing the responsibilities and costs for developing new military technologies and capacities with France's European partners, particularly Great Britain.

Even more daunting perhaps are the economic and political development challenges faced by France in Libya and Mali, making development assistance to hasten the processes of disarmament, demobilization, and reintegration of rebels in both countries that much more crucial. In both places, these processes are likely to be complicated by ethnic and religious conflicts and the economic- and resource-based disputes—particularly over land—on which these are superimposed. Likewise, the need to support and facilitate sustainable political transitions in both countries, by affording adequate representation to key ethnic and social players as well as establishing institutional mechanisms that will ensure the emergence of stable regimes within them, is also essential.[19]

In short, the limitations of French power that became obvious after the Cold War are making it increasingly difficult for the country to live up to its self-image as a global power, even in areas where it formerly held sway. In turn, this loss of power underscores the fact that the foreign policy challenge facing Hollande remains fundamentally the same as that which confronted his predecessors: France needs to redefine its foreign policy in the context of an increasingly multipolar and integrated international system, without relinquishing the balancing capacity that had allowed it to punch above its weight for most of the postwar period.

Conclusion

François Hollande's agenda of breaking with the policies of Nicolas Sarkozy has been unsuccessful. Contrary to the promises he issued during the campaign, whether in the domestic or the international arena, particularly regarding Europe and Germany, Hollande has ended up embracing many of the same policies that were enacted by his predecessor. Consequently, Hollande is likely to run up against the same deep-seated structural and cultural impediments that moderated or deflected the sweeping changes that Sarkozy had announced at the start of his presidential term. On domestic policy, anxieties over globalization, the survival of the welfare state, and the spread of a "savage" liberal capitalism forced Sarkozy to embrace the path of slow and piecemeal reform espoused by previous presidents. Viewed in this light, Hollande's economic reforms are also likely to face staunch opposition. On the foreign policy front, the reality of the erosion of French influence since the end of the Cold War has translated under Hollande into the same neo-Gaullist policy that was pursued by Sarkozy of trying to count in the world. This has been the new president's course whether in France's traditional spheres of influence such as Europe, Africa, and the Middle East, or in areas where its influence has been more circumscribed historically, such as within the Western Alliance.

These structural and cultural impediments to change mean that Hollande's reform program, much like that of Sarkozy before him, is likely to be modest. By the same token, it is also likely to cause considerable disillusionment and disaffection among his supporters, possibly casting into doubt the survival of his majority and jeopardizing his chances of reelection. The May 2014 European elections should be instructive, particularly since these will serve as a referendum on the government's performance and on the austerity policies and structural reforms that it has been forced to enact by the EU and Germany.

The one area in which Hollande presents a notable difference is in terms of his governing style. Whereas Sarkozy appeared manic and impulsive, Hollande gives the impression of calm deliberation. Likewise, where Sarkozy was often accused of micromanaging issues—particularly on economic and social policy—that should have been the rightful preserve of his prime minister, Hollande has sought to restore his prime minister as the proper steward of domestic policy. Finally, whereas Sarkozy strove to adopt the trappings of forceful and voluntaristic leadership in the Bonapartist mold, Hollande seeks to appear a humble and sanguine figure with whom the average French voter can identify.

Hollande's distinctiveness may turn out to be a weakness. The same qualities that were seen as positive by voters during the campaign are ill adapted to the requirements of governance, particularly in the face of economic and social crisis; appearing laid-back and deliberate is easily taken for indecisiveness. Thus, following a TV address on March 28, 2013, in which he sought to halt his slide in the opinion polls and limit the fallout from the Cahuzac affair, Hollande's formula of disposing of a "box of tools" to deal with the economic crisis was cruelly lampooned in the press, which compared him to a hapless plumber attempting to forestall a tsunami. In this respect, Hollande contrasts unfavorably with Angela Merkel who, whatever one may think of her policies, exudes firmness, determination, and control.

Thus, whereas Sarkozy's hyperactive style cost him in terms of governing popularity and effectiveness, Hollande's unassuming and cautious style appears to have produced a similar disillusionment among voters, albeit for different reasons. As one French commentator observed, this points to a fundamental contradiction in the way the French perceive leadership, particularly among their presidents: "They defy all kinds of authorities and yet at the same time they crave authority. We have killed our kings and yet we are looking for a king."[20]

Beyond the world of popular perception, Hollande finds himself caught between a "hard" interventionist Left that wants him to embrace a more activist economic policy, even at the risk of alienating Germany and jeopardizing European economic governance, versus a "social liberal" or pro-market center-left that is committed to adhering to the present course of austerity and budgetary retrenchment. This tension has yielded paralysis in terms of economic and social policy, so that policymaking under Hollande has been shifted—much as in the United States—toward essentially legislating cultural or lifestyle issues such as gay marriage. The fundamental questions of how to maximize the nation's prosperity and distribute its proceeds (i.e., of who gets what and why) are now, it seems, off the table. This can only play to the advantage of those political actors who, currently encamped on the populist fringes, are alone in advocating a more activist economic program.

   Combined with the negative impact of the recession, this sense of indecisiveness has weakened Hollande's political position. Only a year after his election, the new president finds himself embattled and there are serious doubts as to whether he will be reelected. Although there is still time for him to turn things around before 2017, the window of opportunity to make good on his reform program, let alone pull France out of recession, is closing fast. In this sense, it is not just Hollande's reform agenda but also his very political survival that hang in the balance.

Notes

1. "François Hollande: Presidency through Ambiguity," *Economist*, May 25, 2013, 53.
2. Tim Smith, *France in Crisis: Welfare, Inequality, and Globalization since 1980* (Cambridge UK: Cambridge University Press, 2004), 102–3.
3. AFP and Reuters, "Les principales mesures du projet de loi des finances pour 2011," *Le Monde*, September 29, 2010, http://www.lemonde.fr/economie/article/2010/09/29/les-principales-mesures-du-projet-de-loi-de-finances-pour-2011_1417551_3234.html (accessed January 31, 2014).
4. Jean-Marie Monnier, "Politique fiscale. Une mise en perspective," in *L'état de la France 2009–2010*, ed. E. Lau (Paris: La Découverte, 2010), 182.
5. Cf. Jonah Levy, "The Return of the State? French Economic Policy under Nicolas Sarkozy," paper presented at the annual meeting of the American Political Science Association, Washington, DC, September 2–5, 2010; and Liêm Hoang-Ngoc, "La Sarkonomics entre promesses électorales et crise économique. Bilan d'étape fin 2008," *Modern and Contemporary France* 17, no. 4 (2009): 423–34.
6. See Jacques Fayette, "Economic Issues in the French 2012 Elections," paper presented at the conference "La France de François Hollande," Johns Hopkins University School of Advanced International Studies, Bologna, Italy, October 13, 2012, 18.
7. Ambrose Evans Pritchard, "IMF Warns France on Austerity Overkill," *The Telegraph*, September 13, 2013.
8. "France's Economy: Austerity Stakes," *Economist*, March 2, 2013, 52.
9. For a full explanation of the measures enumerated below, see Susan Milner, "The Party's Over? Early Employment Dilemmas of the Hollande Presidency," paper presented at the annual conference of the Political Studies Association, Cardiff, UK, March 25–27, 2013.
10. The actual size and impact of this program, which depended in large part on bringing forward the expenditure of moneys that had already been allocated to infrastructure and industrial spending in subsequent fiscal years, have been brought into question. See Hoang-Ngoc, "La Sarkonomics entre promesses électorales et crise économique," 423–34.
11. See John Lichfield, "France's Highest Legal Authority Removes Last Obstacle to Ban on Burqa," *The Independent*, October 11, 2010, http://www.independent.co.uk/news/world/europe/frances-highest-legal-authority-removes-last-obstacle-to-ban-on-burka-2101002.html (accessed January 20, 2014).

12. Cf. Rémy Leveau, "Change and Continuity in French Islam," in *New European Identity and Citizenship*, ed. R. Leveau, K. Mohsen-Finan, and C. Wihtol de Wenden (Aldershot, UK: Ashgate, 2002), 91–99.

13. See "Les banlieues, premières victimes de la crise," *Le Monde*, November 15, 2012, http://www.lemonde.fr/societe/article/2012/11/15/les-banlieues-premieres-victimes-de-la -crise_ 1791604_3224.html (accessed January 20, 2014).

14. See Hervé Algalarrondo, "Les Leçons d'une Partielle: Le Jeu de l'Oise," *Le Nouvel Observateur*, March 28, 2013, 49.

15. Levy, "The Return of the State?" 18–19.

16. "Plan social à PSA: feu vert au comité d'entreprise," *Le Monde*, April 29, 2013, http:// www.lemonde.fr/economie/article/2013/04/29/psa-derniere-etape-avant-la-mise-en-oeuvre -du-plan-social_3167975_3234.html (accessed January 20, 2014).

17. "Franco-American Relations after the Election of François Hollande," *Fondation Robert Schuman: European Issues*, no. 241 (May 22, 2012): 5.

18. Commission of the European Communities, *Growth, Competitiveness, Employment: The Challenges and Ways Forward into the 21st Century*, white paper, http://europa.eu/ documentation/official-docs/white-papers/pdf/growth_wp_com_93_700_parts_a_b.pdf (accessed January 8, 2014).

19. Jean-François Bayart, "Mali: le choix raisonné de la France," *Le Monde*, January 22, 2013, http://www.lemonde.fr/idees/article/2013/01/22/mali-le-choix-raisonne-de-la -france_1820680_3232.html (accessed January 20, 2014).

20. Quoted in Julian Coman, "François Hollande: From Mr. Normal to Mr. Weak," *Guardian*, April 27, 2013, http://www.guardian.co.uk/world/2013/apr/28/francois-hollande -mr-normal-mr-weak (accessed January 20, 2014).

Suggested Readings

Culpepper, Pepper, and Peter Hall. *Changing France: The Politics That Markets Make*. New York: Palgrave Macmillan, 2006.

Goodliffe, Gabriel. *The Resurgence of the Radical Right in France: From Boulangisme to the Front National*. New York: Cambridge University Press, 2012.

Goodliffe, Gabriel, and Riccardo Brizzi, eds. *France after 2012*. New York: Berghahn Books, 2014.

Laurence, Jonathan, and Justin Vaïsse. *Integrating Islam: Political and Religious Challenges in Contemporary France*. Washington, DC: Brookings Institution Press, 2006.

Nord, Philip. *France's New Deal: From the Thirties to the Postwar Era*. Princeton, NJ: Princeton University Press, 2010.

Weil, Patrick. *How to Be French*; trans. C. Porter. Durham, NC: Duke University Press, 2008.

CHAPTER 2

Great Britain

FROM NEW LABOUR TO NEW POLITICS?

Kate Alexander Shaw and Jonathan Hopkin

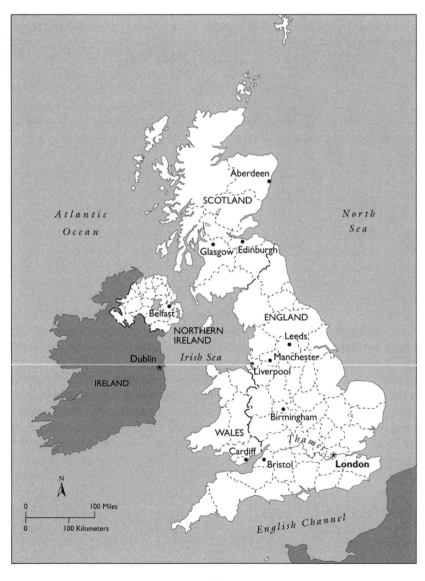

United Kingdom

Population (million):	63.7
Area in Square Miles:	94,548
Population Density in Square Miles:	674
GDP (in billion dollars, 2012):	$2,375
GDP per Capita (PPP, 2012):	$37,500
Joined EC/EU:	January 1, 1973

Performance of Key Political Parties in Parliamentary Elections of May 2010

Conservative and Unionist Party	36.1% (306 seats)
Democratic Unionist Party (DUP)	0.6% (8 seats)
Labour Party	29.0% (258 seats)
Liberal Democrats	23.0% (57 seats)
Party of Wales (Plaid Cymru)	0.6% (3 seats)
Scottish National Party (SNP)	1.7% (6 seats)
Sinn Fein	0.6 % (5 seats)
UK Independence Party (UKIP)	3.1% (0 seats)
Ulster Unionist Party (UUP)	0.3% (0 seats)

Main Officeholders: Prime Minister: David Cameron, Conservative (2010); Head of State: Queen Elizabeth II

On May 6, 2010, Britain went to the polls to take part in one of the most uncertain elections for decades. The ruling Labour Party, having won a third general election in a row five years earlier, was desperately battling to avoid a crushing defeat under its new leader, Gordon Brown, the former chancellor of the exchequer (treasury minister) under Tony Blair. The Conservative Party, under its young, fresh-faced leader David Cameron, hoped to exploit the unpopularity of the Labour government to win the keys to Number 10 Downing Street. But opinion polls suggested, unusually for the United Kingdom, that there was a strong chance that no party would win an overall majority in the House of Commons, the main chamber of the British Parliament. The centrist Liberal Democrats, led by another ambitious young politician, Nick Clegg, hoped that such a "hung parliament" would turn his party into kingmaker, allowing the Liberals to enter government for the first time in eighty years. In most British elections, the winner is declared just a few hours after the polling stations close, but such was the tightness of this election that the outcome was still not clear at daybreak on May 7.

What followed was an entirely new situation in contemporary UK politics. The Labour Prime Minister Gordon Brown had suffered a humiliating defeat, his party shedding almost a million votes and ninety-one parliamentary seats, registering one of Labour's worst electoral performances in its history. Yet instead of driving to Buckingham Palace the following day to offer his resignation, as is the convention for a defeated prime minister, Brown stayed put in Downing Street. As the chancellor of the exchequer (based at Number 11) and then prime minister (Number 10), Brown had been resident in Downing Street for thirteen years, and hostile newspapers accused him of "squatting" in the prime ministerial quarters. However, Brown's delayed resignation was consistent with constitutional practice: the sitting prime minister does not resign until his or her successor can command majority support in Parliament, and David Cameron's Conservatives had 306 seats, twenty short of an overall majority. The impasse was only resolved when, after five days of negotiations, Cameron reached an agreement with Liberal Democrat leader Clegg to form a coalition government, the first multiparty administration in Britain since the Second World War.

The 2010 election marked the end of a thirteen-year period in which British politics had been dominated by Tony Blair's Labour Party. On May 1, 1997, almost two decades of continuous Conservative governments had come to an end with a landslide election victory for Labour. This was a remarkable achievement for the party's youthful leader Blair, who remolded the party to his image, even to the point of informally renaming it "New Labour" and promising that the rebranded party offered a "New Britain." Blair's Labour Party went on to win two further elections: another landslide in 2001, and a third, narrower victory in 2005, making him the most successful Labour leader ever. But by 2005, Blair was increasingly embattled, haunted by his decision to join George W. Bush in his unpopular invasion of Iraq, and constantly pressured to leave office by his ambitious deputy Gordon Brown. He resigned in the summer of 2007, but Brown very quickly came under pressure as the lurking financial crisis and other political difficulties exposed his weaknesses as a political leader.

Labour's defeat was therefore the end of an era, and a chance to take stock of the achievements and failures of the "New Labour" project. With a parliamentary majority even bigger than those enjoyed by Margaret Thatcher in her heyday of the 1980s, and an initially benign economic climate, the Labour government had an unprecedented opportunity to make its mark on British society and politics. So, has New Labour made a "New Britain"? With Labour's exit from office, it has now become possible to provide an answer to this question. This chapter will seek to draw a balance sheet on the Blair administration's achievements and failures by analyzing the transformations brought about by a historically unprecedented period of left-of-center political dominance.

In doing so, this chapter will also assess another historic transformation: the birth, or more accurately rebirth, of multiparty politics in Britain. For only the second time since the war, the British electorate defeated the governing party without providing the party of opposition with a ruling majority. The formation of a coalition government in 2010 signaled a dramatic shift in the nature of British politics. This chapter will trace the origins of the shift and tentatively assess the priorities and achievements of the coalition government so far. It will look at three broad areas: the British economy and the impact of the financial crisis of 2007–2010; the important changes made to the British Constitution since 1997, including the implications of multiparty politics for the UK political system; and Britain's foreign policy under the leadership of Blair, Brown, and Cameron. The discussion will focus on recent developments over the past fifteen years or so, but in doing so will also provide a general overview of the main trends and developments in contemporary British politics, and the historical context that has shaped them.

The British Economy: From Boom to Bust

The politics of Britain's economy in the last two decades can be divided into two distinct phases: before and after the crisis. The full implications for the UK of the global economic downturn are still unfolding, but its political ramifications were felt almost immediately, as a decade of apparent prosperity under Labour gave way to recession and, shortly afterward, a change of government. Both before the crash and since, Britain's leaders have been engaged in a struggle for economic credibility, recognizing that the economy is, as ever, an election-deciding issue.

WINNING CREDIBILITY: NEW LABOUR'S ECONOMIC STRATEGY

In many respects, 1997 was a good time for Labour to win an election. From a short-term perspective, the British economy was in good shape by historical standards. After the pound's devaluation and dramatic exit from the European Exchange Rate Mechanism (ERM) in September 1992, the British economy very quickly began to emerge from the deep recession that had begun in 1990. By 1997, unemployment had been falling continuously for five years, but without sparking inflation. Britain appeared to be on the road to recovering from its postwar history of macroeconomic instability. Labour had hoped to win power in 1992, when an election was held in the middle of a recession and the Conservatives appeared weak and divided. However, in retrospect, Labour was fortunate to have lost the 1992 election: the Conservatives were left to sort out the ERM crisis, and when Labour finally won, they inherited a healthy economy.

Tony Blair's priority as Labour leader was to win credibility for his party as competent managers of the economy, perceiving that this would be critical if Labour were to attract the middle-income voters it needed for an electoral majority. Moreover, it had become clear that a growing share of Labour's traditional working-class supporters felt that the Conservatives, with their stress on property ownership and low personal taxation, offered greater opportunities for improving their living standards. In order to win an election, Labour needed to convince such people that the party was on their side. Labour's manifesto for the 1997 election sought to do precisely that. Labour would be fiscally responsible, promising to follow clear fiscal rules to keep government borrowing low. There would be no increase in income tax rates, and the party would effectively freeze public spending for the first two years in office. At the same time, Labour promised to increase investment in key areas of the public sector, particularly in the health service and education systems. This greater spending would be paid for by a one-off "windfall" tax on the excessive profits of utility companies privatized by the Conservatives, and through a program aimed at slashing long-term unemployment and its related social costs.

As well as winning over wavering Conservative voters, Labour also had to make new friends in the business community. In a world of globalized capital flows, the financial services industry based in London had become indisputably the key strategic sector of the British economy, and the Conservatives had traditionally been the party closest to the City's interests. Labour's leaders felt that any lack of confidence in the new Labour government among City institutions could lead to capital flight and currency instability, which would derail their plans; courting City elites was therefore a priority from the start.

First, Labour sought to address its reputation for fiscal irresponsibility. By signing up to the previous Conservative administration's budgetary plans for the first two years of the new Parliament, Labour was committing itself to a tough approach to public spending; after all, the Conservatives were expecting to lose and felt free to make unrealistically restrictive plans about how much the government would need to spend. By sticking to these heroically frugal plans, Labour aimed to show the financial and business elite that it could be trusted to keep government borrowing low. It reinforced this approach with a so-called golden rule—a commitment that the government would not borrow to fund current spending over the business cycle—and a further commitment to keep total government debt below 40 percent of gross domestic product. These policies were followed so strictly that the Labour government managed to run a budget surplus for every year of the 1997–2001 Parliament.[1]

A second fundamental reform was not trailed before the election. In his first act after being named chancellor of the exchequer, Gordon Brown announced that the new government would no longer set interest rates, which would become the responsibility of the UK's central bank, the Bank of England. By putting monetary policy at arm's length, Labour hoped to enhance its credibility as a responsible manager of the UK macroeconomy. This policy also quickly appeared vindicated, as interest rates and inflation both dropped to historically low levels within Labour's first term of office. Remarkably for recent British economic history, unemployment also continued to fall without sparking price increases. The immediate success of these policy decisions was a boost to Labour's fortunes. First, they vindicated one of Labour's most prominent messages in their political campaigns—that they would put an end to the "boom and bust" of the Thatcher period and lay the foundations for more stable economic growth. Second, the success in reducing both inflation and unemployment at the same time allowed Brown to follow a cautious economic policy without having to demand too many sacrifices of Labour's traditional supporters.

By granting independence to the Bank of England and committing itself to tough fiscal rules, Labour was signing up to the reigning economic orthodoxy of the 1990s. Significantly, Blair and Brown were also enthusiastic about a further plank of this orthodoxy: financial market deregulation. Unlike in monetary policy, New Labour did not embark on major reforms in the regulation of financial services, largely because a series of deregulatory measures had already been adopted by the Thatcher governments in the 1980s, removing a range of restrictions on financial activity and promoting a modernization and rapid expansion of the financial sector. The so-called Big Bang of 1986—which removed some key regulations and established electronic trading in the London Stock Exchange—brought a surge in capital flows to the City of London and a boom in lending to British consumers. Also in 1986, the Thatcher government passed the Building Societies Act, deregulating the usually small mutual financial institutions that financed most housing purchases in the UK. The majority of building societies converted to banks owned by shareholders as a direct result of this legislation and adopted more expansionary lending practices. This led to a rapid increase in property prices, followed by an equally rapid collapse of the property market in the early 1990s.

These changes to the financial sector, along with most other reforms promoted by the Thatcher governments, were strongly opposed by the Labour Party at the time, but by the mid-1990s, Labour had begun to adopt a much less confrontational strategy under Tony Blair. Blair's centrist orientation had two clear consequences for Labour's attitude to finance (see box 2.1). First, Labour became very anxious to court middle-class voters who, notwithstanding the collapse of property prices, were supportive of many aspects of the Thatcherite economic program. Second, Labour was desperate to win over the City of London by reassuring powerful figures in the banking world that Labour would not only protect and nurture the financial sector but also promote its expansion as a motor of economic growth. One of Blair's key allies, the then–Business Secretary Peter Mandelson, famously stated that "we are intensely relaxed about people getting filthy rich, as long as they pay their taxes." Such thinking was informed by the "third way" advocated by Blairite sociologist Anthony Giddens, who argued that progressive politics needed to move "beyond left and right."[2] In practice, this meant that once in power, Labour would maintain the deregulatory approach to the financial sector pioneered by the Conservatives. The housing market reached its bottom in 1995–1996 and had entered another rapidly expansionary phase once Labour was elected in 1997. This time, the rise in the housing market was bolstered by trends in the world economy, in particular the spectacu-

Box 2.1 From "Old" to "New" Labour: The End of Socialism?

Clause IV of the Labour Party constitution approved in 1918:

> To secure for the workers by hand or by brain the full fruits of their industry and the most equitable distribution thereof that may be possible upon the basis of the common ownership of the means of production, distribution and exchange, and the best obtainable system of popular administration and control of each industry or service.

Excerpt from Tony Blair's first speech to the Labour Party conference as leader, October 4, 1994:

> Market forces cannot educate us or equip us for this world of rapid technological and economic change. We must do it together. . . .
>   That is our insight: A belief in society. Working together. Solidarity. Cooperation. Partnership. These are our words. This is my socialism. And we should stop apologizing for using the word.
>   It is not the socialism of Marx or state control. It is rooted in a straight forward view of society. In the understanding that the individual does best in a strong and decent community of people with principles and standards and common aims and values.
>   We are the Party of the individual because we are the Party of community. Our task is to apply those values to the modern world.
>   It will change the traditional dividing lines between right and left. And it calls for a new politics.

> (*Source*: http://www.australianpolitics.com/uk/labour/941004blair-new-labour-speech.shtml)

The "New" Clause IV approved by the Labour Party conference in 1995:

> The Labour Party is a democratic socialist party. It believes that by the strength of our common endeavor we achieve more than we achieve alone, so as to create for each of us the means to realize our true potential and for all of us a community in which power, wealth and opportunity are in the hands of the many, not the few. Where the rights we enjoy reflect the duties we owe. And where we live together, freely, in a spirit of solidarity, tolerance and respect.

lar housing boom in the United States and the associated innovations in the financial sector. Securitization of residential housing mortgages—in which banks lent money for housing purchases but then sold the debt to investors—was also adopted by British banks, and the City of London became a major center for hedge funds dealing in a range of sophisticated and risky financial products.

GROWING THE STATE: PUBLIC SPENDING AND REDISTRIBUTION

Of course, Labour's success in managing the macroeconomy was hardly enough to satisfy the party's core left-wing supporters, who demanded action to reduce poverty and achieve a more equitable distribution of wealth. So, in addition to adopting an orthodox approach to monetary and fiscal matters, the government also proposed other, more traditionally social democratic policies. The high levels of poverty among British pensioners were addressed by introducing a "minimum income guarantee" for the elderly, providing increased state pensions for those without private pension entitlements. The New Deal program, financed by a windfall tax on privatized utility companies, provided assistance to the long-term unemployed to encourage them back into the labor market. This formed part of a series of measures called Welfare to Work, aimed at increasing employment as a way of reducing poverty without increasing the burden on the welfare state. Labour Chancellor Gordon Brown had identified low wages for unskilled workers as a "poverty trap"—many of the unemployed could not easily earn enough to move out of welfare. The government attacked this problem by establishing a minimum wage and by providing tax credits for low earners with family responsibilities, topping up low wages to encourage work over welfare. Although some observers remain skeptical about the specific impact of the New Deal on employment, the Labour government was able to point to a continued decline in joblessness through its first term in office as proof of its success.[3]

Falling unemployment and healthy tax revenues allowed Labour, after a cautious start, to increase public spending in a number of areas, most notably health care and education. Despite the Thatcher and Major governments' commitment to a larger private market in health and education services, the vast majority of British citizens remained reliant on state provision in these two areas. Moreover, opinion polls had long shown that voters demanded higher spending on these services, and that many of them even claimed to be willing to pay higher taxes to achieve this. As regards spending, there is little question that Labour has met this demand for greater resources. Education spending, for example, rose from £38 billion in 1997 to £73 billion in 2006, a spectacular increase in times of low inflation. Health spending, in turn, grew even faster, from £33 billion in 1997 to £96 billion in 2006.[4] Visible evidence of this greater largesse could be found in the new school and hospital buildings that sprang up around the country in the years after 2000. Evidence of increased performance in the delivery of services has been more controversial, however. Official government targets for cutting medical waiting times and achieving better school exam results have been met, but public skepticism over the effective improvement in services abounded. For some Labour opponents, the prioritization of public health and education over private consumption had simply increased the pay of public sector workers without any clear productivity gains. Labour, meanwhile, argued vigorously that the increased spending was an overdue corrective to years of underinvestment in public services during the Major-Thatcher period.

The growth of government spending was the "big story" of Labour's second term as far as domestic politics were concerned. Much political debate therefore revolved around the question of how to pay for this higher spending. This question could be elided for some time thanks to the buoyant budgetary position built up during Labour's first term of office. However, as soon as the economic cycle began to turn downward, budget surpluses quickly turned to deficits in 2003 and by 2005 had breached the euro area's 3 percent limit. The problem of how to pay for higher spending was met in a combination of ways. First, Labour was obliged to allow some slippage in the observance of its own fiscal rules, which required budgets to balance over the economic

cycle. In 2005, Brown's Treasury recalculated the dates of the economic cycle in order to make the rules easier to meet, allowing higher borrowing to continue. Second,
Labour responded by raising taxes. Although Brown stuck to Labour's promise not
to increase income tax rates, he did increase revenues through fiscal drag, and he also
increased the British payroll tax—National Insurance—for high-end wage earners.
Third, the government's budgetary position was helped by the consistent economic
growth enjoyed from the mid-1990s, which reduced the costs of unemployment and
brought increased tax receipts from property sales and consumption. In short, Labour
seemed to have pulled off a difficult balancing act by significantly increasing public
spending without a dramatic increase in personal taxation.

THE TRAIN HITS THE BUFFERS: GORDON BROWN
AND THE FINANCIAL CRISIS

In June 2007, Tony Blair finally left Number 10 Downing Street, handing it over to
Gordon Brown, who had been pressuring him to resign for several years. Although
reluctant to leave, Blair could point to several achievements in the fields of economic
and social policy in his decade as prime minister. Most obviously, Labour had presided over one of the longest periods of uninterrupted economic growth in British
history, with high levels of employment, historically low inflation, and an average
growth rate of 2.5 percent between 1997 and 2007, well above trend. However, just
two months later, the first unmistakable signs of economic collapse could be detected.
A small regional bank, Northern Rock, requested liquidity support from the Bank of
England, a clear sign of financial difficulty. The immediate response was panic: the
bank's shares collapsed, and depositors rushed to withdraw their savings, leading to
scenes reminiscent of *Mary Poppins* as desperate account holders queued in the streets
outside Northern Rock branches. This was the first run on a bank in the UK since the
nineteenth century, a huge embarrassment for a country whose economy had revolved
around the financial sector in recent decades. By the second quarter of 2008, Britain
had entered what was proving to be its longest recession since the 1930s.

The run on Northern Rock and its subsequent rescue by the government were defining moments in the recent economic and political history of the UK. Although the
financial crisis was obviously not solely a British problem—the Northern Rock bank
run began on September 15, 2007, but on the same date a year later Lehman Brothers' insolvency provoked a world financial meltdown—it has had particularly powerful
consequences, both economic and political, in the UK. It also made the defeat of the
Labour government in the 2010 general election almost inevitable. The financial crisis
plunged Britain into recession, destroying Gordon Brown's oft-repeated claim that
New Labour had put an "end to boom and bust." But the crisis also exposed two key
weaknesses at the heart of New Labour's economic strategy: its closeness to the City of
London and its enthusiasm for public spending.

New Labour's charm offensive in the mid-1990s had succeeded in convincing the
City that a Labour government would be competent custodians of the economy and
friendly to the interests of the financial sector. However, this success came at a price,

as Labour's embrace of financial deregulation allowed the financial sector to expand lending to households and companies at unprecedented rates, generating a credit-fueled consumer boom. UK consumers borrowed to buy houses, cars, holidays, and even everyday purchases. The influx of credit into the housing market led to a rapid rise in house prices, to which consumers responded by increasing their borrowing, including extracting equity from their homes to finance other spending. This borrowing fueled economic growth, which enhanced consumer confidence and encouraged further increases in indebtedness. In 2006, UK household debt exceeded £1 trillion, comfortably higher than annual GDP. Meanwhile, the City of London enjoyed spectacular growth in its revenues, with the financial sector growing to the extent that total financial assets in the UK amounted to 440 percent of GDP in 2006 (from 100 percent in 1980). Much of that growth was achieved by using unprecedented amounts of leverage, as banks borrowed to turbo-charge their returns. Financial sector debt soon dwarfed borrowing by either households or the government, totaling more than 200 percent of UK GDP in 2011.[5]

The growth of finance undoubtedly contributed to Britain's comparatively strong economic performance between the mid-1990s and the mid-2000s and generated unexpectedly high tax revenues, allowing Labour to expand public spending rapidly. Ironically, the financial boom had the curious outcome of allowing Blair and Brown, alone among center-left politicians in recent European history, to significantly expand the role of the state in the economy. Public spending increased substantially, from £315.9 billion in 1996–1997, the last year of Conservative government, to £550 billion in 2006–2007, a real-terms increase of 37 percent. Although tax rates and borrowing paid for part of this growth, a significant part of the expansion was made possible by the buoyant tax revenues from the booming financial sector, in particular the overheated housing market. When the financial sector entered a catastrophic crisis in the autumn of 2008, a huge shortfall in the government's budget opened up with frightening speed, with the UK Treasury reporting a double-digit budget deficit for both 2009 and 2010.

The financial meltdown after 2007 undermined nearly all of the policy successes claimed by Gordon Brown and New Labour over their decade in power. The "light-touch" regulation of finance had allowed an asset price bubble to develop that destabilized the whole economy, and Blair and Brown had apparently not noticed that banks had built balance sheets that left them dangerously exposed to any turbulence in the financial markets. Moreover, the Labour governments had built up public spending to levels that quickly became unsustainable when the credit-fueled growth of consumption ceased, having assumed that rising revenues from the financial and property sectors would continue indefinitely. The end of the boom produced a triple whammy of falling tax receipts, increased spending through the "automatic stabilizers" (such as the benefits including income support for the unemployed), and prior commitments to expansive spending plans, which together left the UK with one of the biggest fiscal deficits in the world.

Gordon Brown's direct responsibility for the economy over a thirteen-year period, first as chancellor of the exchequer, then as prime minister, left him politically accountable for the disaster. Labour's expansion of public spending, which had been a major part of their appeal during the boom years of the 1990s and early 2000s, became an object of criticism after the crash, for example when it became clear that much of the employment growth during that period had been driven by new jobs in the expanding public sector. The Conservative opposition attacked Brown as a "credit card Prime Minister" and New Labour's economic record went from being an electoral asset to a serious liability.

COALITION ECONOMICS: DEFICIT REDUCTION ABOVE ALL

In the 2010 election, the British voters deserted Labour in sufficient numbers to relieve the party of its parliamentary majority, bringing Brown's short premiership to an end. However, if Labour undeniably lost the election, it was not clear if anyone else had actually won it. The Conservatives had played their cards relatively close to the chest during the campaign, preferring to let Labour lose the election than to advance an economic policy alternative that would be unpopular or open to attack; while they promised to control public spending, few concrete proposals were advanced beyond a fresh round of "efficiencies" in central government itself. Indeed, even though tackling public debts was the headline priority, the Conservatives made commitments to protect certain popular or symbolically important parts of Labour's spending program, notably health funding, international aid, and some pensioner entitlements. Their Liberal Democrat partners had meanwhile adopted a centrist line on public spending, and their economic spokesman Vince Cable was both popular with the public and relatively left-wing on economic matters, arguing that the banks, having been publicly bailed out, should be made "the servants, not the masters of the economy."[6]

The coalition agreement between the two parties made clear that the new government's overriding priority, and a prior condition for its other policy aims, would be tackling "our record debts." The focus on debt reduction has specifically applied to public debt, with household and financial sector indebtedness being largely excluded from a narrative that makes reducing the fiscal deficit the coalition's number one economic priority. To that end, Conservative Chancellor George Osborne has implemented a wide-ranging program of spending cuts across local and central government budgets. The government also moved to reform, and ultimately reduce, certain welfare programs, including, for the first time, introducing an income threshold for eligibility for child benefit, a small but symbolically potent withdrawal of one of the remnants of Britain's universal welfare state, aimed at signaling that the middle and upper classes would share some of the brunt of the cuts. Other changes, however, will fall on the poorest households, including the delinking of benefits and inflation, and moves to cap housing benefits, the costs of which had risen with the buoyant housing market and remained high. Alongside the cuts there have been attempts at public service reform, from sweeping changes to school curriculums, an overhaul of police pay and conditions, and a controversial new system of eligibility assessments, conducted by private firms, for the incapacity benefit available to people who cannot work due to ill health or disability.

On the tax side, the national sales tax (the value-added tax) was increased in 2011, and a new 50 percent top rate of income tax on earnings over £150,000, which had introduced by Labour weeks before the election in 2010, was maintained by the coalition for three years before being made permanent at the lower rate of 45 percent in 2013. Overall, however, deficit reduction has been pursued mainly via spending cuts.

The coalition has sought to brace its commitment to fiscal austerity by reforming key institutions, conscious of the previous government's difficulty in adhering to fiscal rules of its own devising. Just as Labour had sought to remove inflationary temptations by delegating monetary policy to an independent Bank of England, the coalition has sought to constrain fiscal policy by delegating forecasting of the economy and public finances to a new, formally independent Office for Budget Responsibility (OBR). While tax and spending decisions remain with the Treasury, the presence of an arm's-length forecaster is intended to reduce the government's ability to select favorable assumptions in making its fiscal plans, or to redefine the economic cycle to accommodate its spending plans. By early 2013, the OBR was reporting that the government had made some progress toward reducing the headline deficit, which was down by a quarter over the three years to 2012. However, weak growth in the British economy has frustrated the attempt to bring down public borrowing, with disappointing tax receipts and stalled GDP making it difficult to reduce the deficit relative to the size of the economy, forcing the government to abandon its aim of eliminating the structural deficit by 2015. International observers, including the International Monetary Fund, have suggested that Osborne should consider relaxing the pace of the planned cuts, and bring forward plans to invest in key infrastructure, or risk prolonging what is already the weakest recovery in Britain's recent history.

Britain's commitment to fiscal austerity can be understood in relation to both domestic and international contexts. At home, the Conservatives have traditionally been the party of lower taxes and smaller government, with the current generation of members of Parliament (MPs) having largely come of age during the Thatcher era. It is perhaps not surprising that a Conservative government would look to roll back some of Labour's increased public spending, nor that they would generally favor a smaller and less redistributive role for the state. The fact that the Conservatives have been able to pursue such cuts whilst in coalition with the Liberal Democrats is more surprising, and perhaps electorally dangerous for the Lib Dems. Internationally, Britain's austerity policies are part of a wider European retrenchment of welfare states following the banking crisis and subsequent sovereign debt crises. The UK has, of course, retained its own currency, allowing Britain to offset the impact of fiscal austerity to some extent by keeping interest rates low, and using "quantitative easing" (effectively, the supply of new money into the economy) to try to stimulate growth via new lending to businesses and households. In practice, the effectiveness of those measures has been open to question, but there is no doubt the UK has avoided some of the pain inflicted on euro-zone countries without access to monetary levers.

Britain's economic prospects remain underwhelming. The economy has been in technical recession twice since 2009, and even the official forecasts suggest that a substantive recovery is not likely for several years, and not before the next election. Long-standing fault lines, including the UK's overdependence on financial services, and the concentration of economic activity in London and the southeast of England, are as present as ever. Despite this, Cameron and Osborne have stuck firmly to the position that fiscal consolidation is necessary and that no "plan B" is available.

The British Constitution: A Modern Democracy?

The last two decades have been a significant time for the British state, and while the most substantive changes in that period occurred under Labour, the coalition period has also opened up, though not resolved, some very large questions about the future shape of Britain's constitutional settlement.

Although epitaphs for the New Labour administration have mostly focused on its economic and social successes and failures, and the consequences of Tony Blair's foreign policy choices, the period since 1997 has also seen major constitutional innovation. The Third Way thinking that formed the basis of Tony Blair's governing strategy was not solely concerned with governing the economy and managing the social consequences of economic change. The Third Way also contemplated addressing the workings of democracy itself in order to make the political system more open, transparent, and effective. Labour had developed a coherent and powerful critique of the failings of British democracy, which it saw as excessively centralized and elitist, governed by an unaccountable metropolitan elite. The 1997 Labour manifesto therefore proposed a number of reforms in a bid to modernize and open up the UK political system, and these reforms have been described by some as the most radical in decades. However, perhaps the most important change was ushered in by the election result of 2010, which gave Britain a coalition government and brought an end to half a century of alternation between the two main political parties. This section provides an overview of the nature of the British constitution and assesses the implications of recent developments in the working of the UK political system.

THE BACKGROUND: THE UNITED KINGDOM'S "WESTMINSTER MODEL"

The United Kingdom is often described as the oldest democracy in the world. With the Magna Carta of 1215, the English king became subject to legal constraints long before most other monarchs, and the House of Commons—the lower house of the British Parliament—is the oldest legislative institution in the world, sitting continuously in the Palace of Westminster in central London since 1547. Unlike in many other countries, in Britain there has been no specific founding moment at which a democratic system became established. Instead, British democracy was the result of a centuries-long process whereby political power gradually passed from the monarch to the Parliament, and the British Parliament itself won democratic legitimacy by progressively expanding voting rights until—with votes for women—universal suffrage was finally attained in 1928. This conventional interpretation of a smooth transition from absolute monarchy to full democracy, of course, glosses over the political violence and social conflict that have marked several periods of British history, such as the religious tensions sparked by the Protestant Reformation in the sixteenth century, the civil war of 1642–1649, and the working-class mobilization of the nineteenth and early twentieth centuries, not to mention the frequently changing borders of the British state. However, it does accurately reflect the remarkable institutional continuity the UK has enjoyed since at least the late seventeenth century, with a stable parliamentary monarchy that has managed to avoid the violent revolutions and foreign invasions suffered by many of its European neighbors.

This remarkable history has left the UK with a rather anomalous constitutional system. To begin with, Britain does not even have a written constitution: there is no single text codifying and recording the rules regulating the political system. Instead, the British constitution, such as it exists, consists of a mixture of legislation and conventions, many of which are only written down in academic texts. As a result, "much of the substance of the contemporary constitution remains shrouded in uncertainty,"[7] something that in normal times matters little, but becomes more important at times of political flux, such as the 2010 election. Second, a number of features of Britain's "constitution" appear out of date and inappropriate for a modern, twenty-first-century democracy. For example, although the monarchy appears for the most part to play a purely symbolic role in British politics, a number of powers exercised by the British government, including the decision to engage British troops in combat, formally belong to the monarch through the so-called Royal Prerogative. This reflects the British political elite's reluctance to address the thorny issue of the constitution, rather than any particular enthusiasm for extending the powers of the queen. The anachronistic and sometimes dysfunctional nature of the British system of government can be best understood in terms of the British elite's preference for working around the constitution rather than openly and systematically updating it.[8]

This peculiar approach to defining the way government works has some advantages. The British constitution is inherently very flexible. When laws regulating the broader political system become obsolete, they can easily be changed. One of the defining principles of the British political system is "parliamentary sovereignty," which means that no Parliament can bind future Parliaments, and that legislation is not subject to judicial review. This gives the Parliament of the day unlimited freedom to legislate on any matter with a simple majority vote, making reform of the political system much more straightforward than in other democracies, where constitutional reforms usually require enhanced majorities, and often popular referenda too. Parliamentary sovereignty explains in part why British governments have often preferred to leave the constitution alone: as long as a government enjoys a parliamentary majority, there are relatively few limits to its freedom of action.

This flexibility is also a problem. Because there are few constitutional restraints on a parliamentary majority, a strong-willed government with sufficient parliamentary support can force through unpopular measures relatively easily. Moreover, through the Royal Prerogative, many powers once belonging to the monarchy are now exercised by the head of the government, the prime minister, in the monarch's name. These powers, such as government appointments, are not subject to any consultation with Parliament and imply a greater concentration of power around the head of the executive than is usual in parliamentary democracies. Parliamentary sovereignty, of course, also means that the executive is ultimately dependent on the majority support of the House of Commons in order to continue governing. British prime ministers, unlike U.S. presidents, can be forced to step down at short notice by a majority vote of censure, known as a "vote of no confidence." But provided the prime minister retains the support of a parliamentary majority, there are few limits on his or her power, since Parliament can pass any law and there is no higher judicial power to review legislation.

In practice, therefore, the British parliamentary system has tended to create strong governments subject to few checks and balances. British political parties tend to be fairly cohesive, and individual MPs are usually heavily dependent on their party's support in their efforts to win reelection. As a result, governing majorities in Parliament are mostly disciplined in their support for the executive in general and the prime minister (who is also party leader) in particular. Moreover, members of the House of Commons are elected in small, single-member constituencies, which leads to a heavy overrepresentation of the winning party. Governments often enjoy very large majorities in the Commons that make their parliamentary positions almost unassailable. The upper house of Parliament, the House of Lords, is traditionally an unelected body of nobility and party appointees, and it therefore lacks the political legitimacy to challenge the power of the government. The House of Lords can return legislation to the Commons for redrafting, but ultimately it must acquiesce in passing the legislation without amendment if the Commons stands firm. Until 1999, the House of Lords had a built-in Conservative majority due to the predominance of hereditary peers (nobles) and tended only to use its delaying powers against Labour governments. The Blair government abolished the voting rights of hereditary peers in 1999, leaving only ninety-two in place, with the remainder of the Lords consisting of retired party politicians and prominent members of civil society, all appointed by government. However, the Lords still lack the democratic legitimacy to challenge the government, leaving the UK without any effective separation of lawmaking powers.

The successive governments headed by Margaret Thatcher in the 1980s, for many of Thatcher's opponents, epitomized the abuse of executive power made possible by the UK's constitutional vagueness and the distortions of its electoral system. With a little over 40 percent of the vote but a comfortable majority in the House of Commons, the Conservative administration forced a number of controversial and divisive measures through Parliament in the face of great popular unrest. Thatcher's own robust style was criticized as authoritarian, as she refused to consult with interest groups and trade unions, and even rode roughshod over Conservative opponents within her own government. In response, demands for constitutional reform grew, with the Electoral Reform Society arguing for the House of Commons to be elected by proportional representation, while a group named Charter 88 campaigned for a wholesale updating of Britain's constitutional arrangements, including the democratization of the House of Lords and greater transparency in government.

Ironically, Thatcher's political demise was a timely reminder that parliamentary sovereignty was not a blank check for the prime minister. Faced with an economic crisis and growing unpopularity over the reform of local taxes and her European policy, opposition mounted to Thatcher's leadership within the Conservative Party itself. At the end of 1990, a rival challenged Thatcher to a leadership election; although she won the election, the number of votes against her signaled that a substantial portion of her parliamentary party wanted a new leader. Persuaded by her own ministers that she was in an unsustainable position, she resigned, only three years after winning her third general election. But her long period in office, and Labour's own disillusionment at its inability to defeat Thatcher at the polls, had entrenched demand for constitutional change within the opposition party. When Tony Blair led Labour to victory in 1997, a reform of the British system of government was a key part of the party's program.

DECENTRALIZING BRITAIN: DEVOLUTION AND NORTHERN IRELAND

The most urgent item on Labour's reform agenda was "devolution"—the creation of new tiers of government in Scotland, Wales, and Northern Ireland, all part of the United Kingdom but culturally and politically distinct from England, where the bulk (around 85 percent) of the British population lives. Devolution addressed one of the most potent critiques of the British system of government: its intense centralization of power around the capital city, London, where the executive, civil service, and Parliament are based. Decentralization—bringing government closer to the people—was a prominent feature of Blair's Third Way discourse, and it appeared to offer a response to citizens' growing sense of detachment from the political elite. Labour had long pushed for greater decentralization of power, unsuccessfully proposing devolution to Scotland and Wales in its previous period of government in the 1970s. Reviving this project in the 1990s was consistent with both Labour tradition and the New Labour image.

Understanding the devolution issue requires an understanding of the rather complex history of the United Kingdom.[9] It was argued earlier that the British state has enjoyed remarkable institutional continuity in the past three centuries, but the same cannot be said for the UK's borders. The core of the British state, England, has a long history as a unified nation, dating on some accounts from the tenth century. The history of Britain, however, is marked by a process of expansion and then partial retreat. Wales was definitively annexed by England under King Henry VIII in 1536, and Scotland was absorbed into the British state by the Act of Union in 1707. The island of Ireland, long dominated by its larger neighbor, was integrated into the United Kingdom in 1800. This political unity of the British Isles did not last long. Discontent among the majority Catholic population of Ireland developed into a political movement for Irish independence, and the "Irish question" dominated British political life toward the end of the nineteenth century and the beginning of the twentieth. Faced with constant unrest, the London Parliament decided in 1921 to pull out of most of Ireland, but it retained six counties with a large Protestant population (mostly descendants of Scottish settlers) in the north of the country. This act, known as "partition," allowed for the creation of an independent Irish Republic in the south, while the north remained part of the United Kingdom. Northern Ireland was governed by its own Parliament, based at Stormont Castle outside Belfast, which was dominated by

Unionists—mostly Protestant supporters of the union with Britain. This arrangement was relatively stable until the 1960s, when the growing Catholic population of Ulster—largely of Irish Nationalist sympathies—began to protest against discrimination and denial of political rights. This movement, initially a peaceful protest, turned to violence as the Unionist-dominated security forces adopted a repressive line, and the British Army was sent over to restore order. After thirteen Catholic protesters were shot by British troops on Bloody Sunday (1973), the situation developed into open conflict between Nationalist paramilitaries (the Irish Republican Army [IRA]) fighting for a united Ireland, Unionist paramilitaries defending the status quo, and the British Army, which quickly became identified with the Unionist side. Two decades of sectarian violence followed, including terrorist attacks in London and other British cities.[10]

The situation in Scotland and Wales was very different. Although both countries had a distinctive national identity, expressed through culture, language, and political movements, Scottish and Welsh nationalisms were almost exclusively nonviolent. Political nationalism in the two countries had emerged with some force in the 1974 election, where both the Scottish National Party and Plaid Cymru (the Party of Wales) made spectacular electoral gains, winning substantial parliamentary representation at Westminster. Although the Labour government of the late 1970s failed to push through devolution, Scottish and Welsh nationalism grew in strength in the 1980s and 1990s. This was in part a response to Margaret Thatcher's virulent English nationalism, and in part the result of Scotland and Wales suffering disproportionately from the economic changes resulting from her free-market reforms. Governed by an increasingly unpopular Conservative Party, despite voting overwhelmingly for the Labour opposition, both Scotland and Wales saw big increases in support for more self-government, and Labour adopted devolution as one of its priorities once elected.

Although devolution to Scotland, Wales, and Northern Ireland may have appeared to form part of a coherent package of constitutional reform, there was a clear difference between the Scottish and Welsh situations, on the one hand, and Northern Ireland, on the other.[11] In Scotland and Wales, Labour was keen to shore up its support base by delivering decentralized government. In Northern Ireland, the aim was to resolve a historic problem facing the British state, taking advantage of the shift in mood in Irish nationalism, which was increasingly favorable to a negotiated solution. By dealing with these very different issues simultaneously, Labour could also attempt to defuse the Northern Ireland situation by pointing to the peaceful nature of territorial reform in the rest of the United Kingdom.

THE GOOD FRIDAY AGREEMENT

Although Tony Blair's government could claim credit for addressing the Northern Ireland problem, it also enjoyed favorable circumstances. Under his Conservative predecessor, John Major, the IRA had sent clear signals of a change in strategy, calling a cease-fire in 1994 that held for two years. The Major government was unable to take advantage of the opportunity, in part because of opposition to negotiations among hardline sectors of the Conservative Party, and in part because his weak government frequently sought the support of Unionist MPs in the House of Commons to pass legislation. Shortly after the 1997 election, the IRA called a new cease-fire, and after several months of negotiations, agreement was reached between the Unionist and Nationalist leaderships in Northern Ireland, and between the British and Irish governments, with the U.S. administration playing an important mediating role.

The basis of this agreement was that the Northern Ireland Unionists would share power with Nationalists in a new Northern Ireland Assembly and executive, rather than being governed directly from London, which most Unionists preferred. In return, the Nationalists accepted the "principle of consent"—in other words, that Northern Ireland would remain part of the United Kingdom until a majority of its population decided otherwise. Given the Unionists' majority status in the "Six Counties," this locked the province into the UK for the foreseeable future, a major concession for the IRA, which is dedicated to the creation of a united, independent Ireland. The Irish Republic, as part of the deal, removed its territorial claim on the Six Counties from its constitution. All of this was directed at reassuring the Protestant majority in the north that they would not be swallowed up into a united Ireland as a result of the agreement. Just as importantly, the agreement included a commitment, albeit vaguely worded, from the IRA to disarm and definitively renounce violence, while the British government undertook to reduce significantly its military presence in Northern Ireland.

The power-sharing agreement meant that the Nationalist community would gain a substantial role in the government of Northern Ireland, a role denied them under direct rule from Westminster. The Northern Ireland Assembly was to be elected by proportional representation in order to ensure that each community was adequately represented. Moreover, its procedures were to be based on "cross-community consent": Assembly members would have to declare their "community identity"—Unionist, Nationalist, or "other"—and important decisions would require the support of either a majority of the community, or a 60 percent majority with at least 40 percent support in each community. This innovative arrangement forced the two sides into a close working relationship if the province was to be governed effectively, encouraging political leaders to overcome the suspicions of the previous decades. The outcome of the agreement remained uncertain even as the Blair government moved into its third term in 2005. On the positive side, an effective cease-fire of all the major paramilitary organizations had remained in place ever since the agreement, a remarkable achievement given the levels of bloodshed of the previous quarter century. Moreover, historical enemies had indeed been involved in joint decision making, with Nationalist leaders for the first time taking on significant executive powers. On the negative side, the newly devolved institutions had to be suspended four times and direct rule reestablished, due to the difficulties involved in verifying the IRA's adherence to the commitment to dismantle its paramilitary structure. In February 2010, further negotiations between Unionist and Nationalist politicians in Northern Ireland, alongside the governments of the UK and Ireland, agreed terms for the devolution of policing and justice powers from London to Belfast, administered by a cabinet minister from the nonaligned Alliance Party. The agreement has huge practical and symbolic implications in a place where the British Army had been deployed as recently as 2007, and represented a further milestone in the "normalization" of politics in Northern Ireland.

Devolved government in Northern Ireland has not meant a simple end to all the old problems; the Assembly was suspended and direct control from London reinstated between 2002 and 2007, and tensions continue to flare periodically, as in early 2013 when sectarian riots broke out in Belfast over the flying of a Union flag over city hall. There have also been incidences of violence, particularly targeting members of the police and prison services. Nevertheless, although the future of the agreement cannot be taken for granted, the achievement of almost two decades of effective peace has changed, perhaps irreversibly, the political atmosphere in Northern Ireland.

DEVOLUTION TO SCOTLAND AND WALES

Compared with resolving such a difficult issue as Northern Ireland, the creation of decentralized government institutions in Scotland and Wales appeared rather straightforward. Unlike Northern Ireland, where a majority of the population was at the very least skeptical, and in part openly hostile, to devolution, in Scotland and Wales there was broad support for institutions of self-government. Moreover, in the Scottish case, all the major parties, with the exception of the Conservatives, had been working together to plan devolution for some time. The vast majority of the Scottish political class was therefore broadly in agreement on the path to follow, and the Labour Party in Scotland, itself closely aligned with the national leadership in London, was an enthusiastic proponent. A referendum held in Scotland in September 1997, only four months after the Blair government was elected, showed overwhelming support for devolution, with 74 percent of Scots voting in favor.

The Scotland Act of 1998 established a Scottish Parliament in Edinburgh, which would elect a Scottish executive responsible for a range of policy areas, including education, health care, transport, and local government. The Parliament, elected by proportional representation, has legislative powers and can pass laws on any issue except those "reserved" to Westminster, the most important of which are foreign and defense policy, monetary and fiscal policy, and social security. The Government of Wales Act of 1998 established devolved government for Wales, but with more limited powers. Only a bare majority (50.3 percent) voted in favor of devolution in the Welsh referendum, and the project came within a handful of votes of failing at the first hurdle. The Welsh Assembly, elected on similar principles to the Scottish Parliament, was granted only secondary legislative powers, meaning that it could only develop the detailed implementation of legislation emanating from the Westminster Parliament, rather than making laws of its own. These secondary powers related to similar areas as those devolved to Scotland: mainly education and health. Unlike Scotland, which had minor tax-raising powers, Wales was entirely dependent on the central government in London for its budget.

Devolution made an immediate political impact in these two territories. The first step toward devolution was the election of representatives to sit in the new institutions, and the elections in Scotland and Wales in 1999 suggested a major change in the workings of British politics. Most significantly, the elections took place under a form of proportional representation, making it difficult for Labour—the dominant party in both territories—to win sufficient support to govern alone, and making coalition government almost an inevitability. In Wales, the party fell just short of a majority, forcing it to rely on the support first of the centrist Liberal Democrats, and then that of the nationalist Plaid Cymru. In Scotland, Labour was far short of a majority, and therefore it formed a coalition government with the Liberal Democrats. Coalition government and initially frequent changes of executive leadership marked a departure from the patterns of government stability observed in Westminster.

Devolution, as might be expected, also led to Scotland and Wales adopting different policies from those followed in England. In Scotland, policy differences were partly the result of coalition government: although the Scottish Labour Party was close to the UK party leadership, the demands of coalition government with the Liberal Democrats led to policy decisions that were at odds with those taken at Westminster. The most notable examples of this were over university tuition fees, which were raised in England under Westminster legislation, but were turned into a form of "graduate tax" on the future earnings of university graduates in Scotland. More dramatically, in 2007, after two terms of Labour-Liberal coalitions, the Scottish Parliament elections gave a narrow victory to the Scottish Nationalists (SNP), who became the largest party in the assembly (albeit by the tiniest of margins). Although the SNP leader Alex Salmond was unable to piece together a majority and had to form a minority administration, it was still a hugely symbolic development for the Scottish executive to be in the hands of a party that openly advocates Scottish independence.

Although devolution did not immediately bring about dramatic change, it opened up the possibility for the two countries to express their distinctiveness through their own institutions and through different patterns of policymaking. The popularity of the devolved institutions in their territories is relatively high, and even the initially unenthusiastic Welsh ultimately warmed to devolution, demanding powers comparable to those enjoyed by the Scottish Parliament. A 2011 referendum saw all but one Welsh county vote in favor of allowing the National Assembly for Wales to exercise its legislative powers without seeking the permission of the UK Parliament. This was a technocratic change in some respects, removing a layer of bureaucracy rather than expanding the areas in which the Welsh Assembly can make laws. Nonetheless, it illustrated the Welsh public's willingness to consolidate their devolved government and its independence from London.

The return to power of the Conservatives at the UK level has changed the tenor of public debate around devolution in important ways. The Conservatives' electoral presence in Scotland and Wales is very small; in 2010 they won just one of Scotland's fifty-nine constituencies, and eight of forty in Wales. Both countries contain industrial and mining areas that suffered under the Conservative government of the 1980s, and in each nation the political center is somewhere to the left of that in England, with the main nationalist parties adopting broadly left-wing policy positions. While the presence of the Liberal Democrats in the UK government might attenuate the coalition's perceived Englishness to a degree, the government's austerity policies, combined with David Cameron's background as an Old Etonian (along with several cabinet members), has further reinforced its unpopularity with large parts of the Scottish and Welsh electorate, and the sense of distance between the devolved nations and the Conservative-led UK government.

So far, the most dramatic outcome of that political polarization has been the announcement that, in 2014, the people of Scotland will vote in a referendum on whether Scotland should leave the United Kingdom and become an independent nation-state. In May 2011, the SNP won a landslide victory in the Scottish parliamentary elections, increasing their vote by 13 percent and converting a minority administration into a powerful majority government, a stunning result in a body elected by proportional representation. The result was at least partly a consequence of the collapse in support for the Liberal Democrats, deeply unpopular at the time for having formed a coalition with the Conservatives. Nonetheless the main beneficiaries of that change were the SNP, whose charismatic leader, Alex Salmond, was quick to capitalize by putting pressure on Westminster to agree to terms for a vote on independence. Within months, David Cameron had granted the Scottish Parliament the legal power to call a referendum, but insisted that the question would be simply "in or out." Salmond had initially wanted to offer the voters a middle-way option of near-total devolution whilst remaining within the UK (so-called devo max), but any such deal will remain off the table until after 2014. While current polling points to a "no" result in the independence referendum, with further devolution appearing more palatable to Scottish voters than full independence, the possibility remains that Britain could soon undergo a seismic constitutional change.

THE NEW POLITICS?

Although devolution and Northern Ireland had by far the highest profile, the Blair government also introduced other significant reforms to the British system of government. The coalition's policy on the constitution has been more mixed, reflecting the different stances of the coalition partners: the Conservatives are by definition skeptical of change, while the Liberal Democrats regard constitutional reform as a touchstone issue for their party.

In 1997, Labour's election manifesto included commitments to both House of Lords reform and a major reform of the House of Commons, the central pillar of the British system of government. Most radically, Blair promised an inquiry into the possibility of a reform of the electoral system for the Commons, followed by a referendum on a proposed reform. The inquiry, headed by former Labour Chancellor Roy Jenkins, did take place and recommended a form of proportional representation similar to that used in the Federal Republic of Germany.[12] However, this report was simply ignored, and no referendum was held. This outcome was perhaps predictable in light of the enormous difficulties involved in persuading members of an elected institution to change the system that elected them. The Blair government did introduce some changes to modernize the working practices of the Commons, including more family-friendly hours. But the basic workings of the Commons and its role in the constitution remained essentially the same.

The 2010 election, however, threatened to change this. First of all, the 2010 poll saw the departure of one of the most discredited Parliaments in recent history. In 2009, the conservative newspaper the *Daily Telegraph* revealed details of expense claims made by sitting MPs, mostly related to the allowance that members receive for the costs of maintaining a second residence in London. The newspaper reported various examples of abuse of the system, with MPs often claiming very large sums to buy expensive items of furniture, and in some embarrassing cases using public money to pay for items such as tree felling, toothbrushes, lightbulbs, and, in perhaps the most memorable case, a floating house for ducks. Uncovered at the height of Britain's economic downturn under an increasingly unpopular prime minister, the effect of these revelations was explosive, particularly for the governing Labour Party (although many Conservatives and others were affected, too). In addition to further weakening an already fatally damaged government, the scandal fueled demands for a departure from past practices and a (vaguely defined) "new" approach to politics.

The main beneficiaries of this public mood were the new Conservative leader David Cameron and, particularly, the Liberal Democrat leader Nick Clegg. Gordon Brown, aged fifty-eight and with two and a half decades in frontline politics behind him, was unable to dissociate himself from the excesses of his fellow MPs, despite having a relatively clean bill of health in regard to his own expenses. His opposition rivals, both aged forty-three in the election year, belonged to a different generation. Clegg, in particular, sought to present himself as a representative of the "new politics," offering a break with the two-party system of the past and a new coalitional approach to democratic politics. Clegg was a relative unknown to the British public before the election campaign began, but he made a huge impact in the televised debates held between the three main party leaders, briefly boosting the Liberal Democrats to a polling lead. Although the ultimate vote share won by the Liberal Democrats was disappointingly only a marginal improvement on the 2005 result, the failure of the Conservatives to win an outright majority placed Clegg's centrist party in a commanding position.

The "hung parliament" resulting from the 2010 election left open several possibilities. First, the Conservatives could have formed a minority government, seeking support from other parties for individual pieces of legislation. This option was feasible given that the party was only a few seats short of a majority in the House of Commons, but it had the disadvantage that it would necessitate constant bargaining with minor parties. Second, the Conservatives could form a coalition with the Liberal Democrats, which would provide the new administration with an ample majority, but it would force major policy concessions from both sides given the important political differences between the two parties. Finally, a Labour–Liberal Democrat coalition could have formed a government with support from the Scottish and Welsh nationalist parties. This coalition would have been plausible given the common ground between these parties on many issues, but it was effectively impossible given Nick Clegg's stated refusal to work with sitting Prime Minister Gordon Brown. The result, after several days of negotiations, was Gordon Brown's resignation and an invitation to Buckingham Palace for Conservative leader David Cameron, who by reaching an agreement with Nick Clegg had secured sufficient parliamentary support to form a government. The tradition of two-party politics and single-party governments had suffered a brusque interruption.

In theory, the Liberal Democrats' position as kingmakers in the coalition talks should have given them a strong platform from which to pursue constitutional reform. It was certainly their intention to do so. The coalition agreement included the extraordinary statement that "the Government believes that our political system is broken" and promised a referendum on changing Britain's electoral system from "first past the post" (voters pick one candidate; the winner has the most votes regardless of overall vote share) to an "alternative vote" (AV) system. The proposed change was not well explained to the public, but would have instituted a system in which voters rank candidates in order of preference; unless a candidate has 50 percent of first-preference votes, the lowest ranked candidate is eliminated and their second preferences are transferred to other candidates. The process of elimination and preference transfers continues until the leading candidate passes the 50 percent hurdle.

The Liberal Democrats' performance at general elections has historically been weakened by the fact that their voters are spread around the country, not locally concentrated enough to deliver victories in many constituencies at general elections; as such they have tended to favor some form of proportional representation. The alternative vote is a long way from proportionality, but the Liberals were persuaded to advocate it as a modest first step toward electoral reform. The referendum on whether to introduce the alternative vote took place alongside local government elections in May 2011, but Britons' disillusionment with politics did not convert into support for the proposed voting reform, and two-thirds of voters said "no" to AV amid low turnout and some public bewilderment about what was being proposed and why. The result was a humiliating failure for Nick Clegg, whose personal popularity had plummeted since the 2010 election, and meant that one of the flagship Liberal Democrat policies in the coalition agreement had proved a dead end.

Lib Dem plans to reform the House of Lords into a smaller, mostly elected chamber also foundered on opposition from mainly Conservative MPs. Some constitutional reform has gone ahead: the House of Commons will now serve fixed terms of five years, removing the sitting prime minister's right to recommend that the queen dissolve Parliament, which had effectively allowed incumbents to choose the timing of general elections. April 2013 also saw the end of male primogeniture in the British monarchy, after the laws of royal succession were amended to allow female heirs to succeed to the throne even if they have younger brothers. However, the story of constitutional reform under the coalition government has mostly been one of thwarted Liberal proposals and the preservation of the status quo.

Britain in the World: Which Side of the Atlantic?

The last fifteen years have been a controversial time for British foreign policy. In the 1990s, the most pressing problem facing the United Kingdom in international affairs appeared to be its relationship with the European Union, marked by tensions and misunderstandings in the final years of the Thatcher-Major era. Over the following decade or so, a very different set of problems were posed, with the consequences of the September 11 attacks and the resultant changes to U.S. foreign policy. Although foreign and European policies were far from most voters' minds when Labour was elected to government in 1997, the 2000s have been dominated by Britain's international role, particularly its relationship with the United States and, increasingly, its ties to the European Union and the crisis-hit euro zone.

THE BACKGROUND: ATLANTICISM AND EURO-SKEPTICISM[13]

At the end of World War II, the United Kingdom found itself in a contradictory position. On the one hand, it still retained a vast overseas empire, and by virtue of its successful defense of its borders against the Nazi military threat, it was able to take its place at the postwar negotiations between the great powers at Yalta. On the other hand, Britain was exhausted by a conflict that had confirmed the extraordinary military and political weight of the two new superpowers, the United States and the Soviet Union. Britain's status was now clearly that of a "second-rate" world power, while its colonial interests were threatened by economic limitations and the growth of independence movements in various parts of the empire. It is often said that postwar British foreign policy has revolved around "managing decline"—retreating from colonial commitments and recalibrating its international role in recognition of its diminished resources. But this process of managing decline has thrown up a major dilemma. The UK, as a founder member of NATO boasting a "special relationship" with the United States, has seen a close transatlantic alliance as the key to maximizing its influence in the world. But this closeness to the United States, reinforced by a shared language and historical ties, has frequently been viewed with suspicion by Britain's partners in Western Europe, who are determined to enhance integration between the European democracies, in part to counterbalance U.S. power. British governments since the war have been pulled in different directions by the global perspective inherited from the country's imperial past, and by the European imperative dictated by its geographical position and commercial priorities.

Britain's complex relationship with the rest of Europe began with the historic decision not to participate in the first phase of the process of European integration. Preoccupied with maintaining ties to the former colonies in the Commonwealth, and hoping to "punch above its weight" through the transatlantic "special relationship," the UK stayed out of the European Economic Community (EEC) established in 1957 by the Treaty of Rome. Very quickly, British foreign-policy makers changed their minds, applying for membership in 1963, but the French President Charles de Gaulle, suspicious of Britain's closeness to the United States, vetoed the application. When the UK finally entered the EEC in 1973, the organization's essential characteristics were already entrenched, and the close alliance between the two largest founder members, France and West Germany, left Britain in a marginal position. Britain's ambiguous position was also illustrated by its close military cooperation with the United States and the presence of significant U.S. military installations on British soil.[13]

The essential tension between Atlanticism and Europeanism came to a head during the 1980s under the premiership of Margaret Thatcher (see box 2.2). Thatcher was an instinctive Atlanticist, a great admirer of the United States and its economic dynamism, and supportive of the United States' tough approach to

Box 2.2 Awkward Partners: Conservative Prime Ministers on Europe

"Willing and active cooperation between independent sovereign states is the best way to build a successful European Community.

"To try to suppress nationhood and concentrate power at the center of a European conglomerate would be highly damaging and would jeopardize the objectives we seek to achieve.

"Europe will be stronger precisely because it has France as France, Spain as Spain, Britain as Britain, each with its own customs, traditions and identity. It would be folly to try to fit them into some sort of identikit European personality. . . .

"I am the first to say that on many great issues the countries of Europe should try to speak with a single voice. I want to see us work more closely on the things we can do better together than alone. Europe is stronger when we do so, whether it be in trade, in defence, or in our relations with the rest of the world.

"But working more closely together does not require power to be centralised in Brussels or decisions to be taken by an appointed bureaucracy. . . .

"Certainly we want to see Europe more united and with a greater sense of common purpose. But it must be in a way which preserves the different traditions, Parliamentary powers and sense of national pride in one's own country; for these have been the source of Europe's vitality through the centuries."

—Excerpt from Margaret Thatcher's speech to the College of Europe, Bruges, September 20, 1988

(*Source*: http://www.brugesgroup.com/mediacentre/index.live?article=92)

"The EU must be able to act with the speed and flexibility of a network, not the cumbersome rigidity of a bloc.

"We must not be weighed down by an insistence on a one size fits all approach which implies that all countries want the same level of integration. The fact is that they don't and we shouldn't assert that they do. . . .

"We believe in a flexible union of free member states who share treaties and institutions and pursue together the ideal of co-operation. To represent and promote the values of European civilisation in the world. To advance our shared interests by using our collective power to open markets. And to build a strong economic base across the whole of Europe. . . . This vision of flexibility and co-operation is not the same as those who want to build an ever closer political union—but it is just as valid. . . .

"There is not, in my view, a single European demos. It is national parliaments, which are, and will remain, the true source of real democratic legitimacy and accountability in the EU. It is to the Bundestag that Angela Merkel has to answer. It is through the Greek Parliament that Antonis Samaras has to pass his Government's austerity measures. It is to the British Parliament that I must account on the EU budget negotiations, or on the safeguarding of our place in the single market.

"Those are the Parliaments which instil proper respect—even fear—into national leaders. We need to recognise that in the way the EU does business."

—Excerpts from David Cameron's speech on Britain and Europe, delivered at the offices of Bloomberg, London, January 23, 2013

(*Source*: https://www.gov.uk/government/speeches/eu-speech-at-bloomberg)

communism and the Soviet Union. Conversely, Thatcher was suspicious of France and Germany and had little patience for the intricate negotiations that characterized European policymaking. Although a strong supporter of the European Community's deregulatory drive to create a Single European Market by 1992, she was generally unsympathetic to further integration. Her close personal friendship with Ronald Reagan, and poor relations with European leaders such as Mitterrand and Kohl, pushed her into increasingly Euro-skeptical attitudes at a time when other member states were planning to share sovereignty over an increasing range of policy areas, including monetary policy and home and foreign affairs. The situation came to a head in 1990, when Thatcher marked her clear opposition to proposals made by European Commission President Jacques Delors in the House of Commons, declaring "No, no, no" to his vision of Europe.

Although Thatcher was forced out of office shortly afterward, the situation under John Major improved little, and anti-European Conservative MPs forced Major to adopt a tough line toward the other member states. At one stage, this went so far as to order British representatives to "boycott" all European decision-making processes, in protest against the European ban on British beef during the "mad cow disease" crisis. By the mid-1990s, British relations with its European partners were at a low point, and one of Tony Blair's key promises during the 1997 election campaign was to place Britain "at the heart of Europe." This new pro-European policy included the controversial proposal for Britain to join the new euro currency agreed at the Maastricht summit of 1991.

BLAIR'S EUROPEAN POLICY

Tony Blair's relations with the other European Union (EU) member states got off to a promising start, in part because of the relief felt among other European leaders at no longer having to deal with an instinctively hostile Conservative administration. The honeymoon period in UK-Europe relations was extended because of the election of a number of center-left governments in the EU toward the end of the 1990s. Center-left leaders were eager to associate themselves with a leader who had won the 1997 election so decisively and was enjoying high levels of popularity in his own country. This led to the attempt by Blair and the German Social Democrat leader Gerhard Schröder to develop a close working relationship around Third Way principles, the German party having adopted a similar slogan, the "Neue Mitte" (New Center). However, the apparent conservatism of many of Blair's public statements, and the UK's refusal to commit to joining the euro zone, put a damper on cooperation.

The euro, launched in 1999, was a difficult issue for the Labour government to address. Opinion polls suggested that the British public was overwhelmingly opposed to membership, and the UK's relatively virtuous economic performance in the second half of the 1990s did little to predispose Euro-skeptic Britons toward a currency dominated by apparently sluggish economies such as those in France, Germany, and Italy. Blair appeared strongly committed to membership, while his chancellor, the key figure in determining economic policymaking, was unenthusiastic. A wait-and-see approach was therefore adopted, with the government expressing its intention to join the euro "in principle," but only making a final decision in view of a complex set of five "economic tests" announced in 1997. These tests—such as "Would joining the euro promote higher growth, stability, and a lasting increase in jobs?"—were sufficiently ambiguous to allow the government to make a decision on the grounds of short-term realpolitik, and Britain stayed out.

Britain's decision not to join the euro now appears in many respects a lucky escape. Britain's ability to cope with the financial crisis would undoubtedly have been constrained if monetary policymaking had been removed to the European Central Bank, whereas retaining its own currency has enabled Britain to offset its fiscal austerity somewhat by adopting relatively expansive monetary policies. Within the euro, moves such as quantitative easing (or the purchasing of financial assets by central banks in order to increase the volume of liquidity in circulation) would have been more difficult to contemplate for reasons of both substance and process, given the ECB's narrow mandate to control inflation at all costs, and the complexity of decision making in the "troika" institutions. The downside, of course, is that by remaining outside the euro, Britain has only limited scope to influence policy in the "Eurogroup," whose finance ministers meet separately from the rest of the European Council. The relationship between that group and the rest of the EU's decision-making processes remains a vexed question, and while Britain will not be joining the euro zone in the foreseeable future, it retains an interest in influencing policy in its near neighbors and most important trading partners.

Although Britain stayed out of the euro, the Blair government did engage with European policymaking in other ways, most significantly by arguing strongly for structural reforms to liberalize European economies.[14] This pressure on relatively more regulated economies such as France and Germany to adopt an "Anglo-Saxon" model of economic governance was not always popular in European capitals and reminded some Europeans a little too much of the overbearing style of his Conservative predecessors. However, Blair won sufficient support among some other reform-minded governments to launch the so-called Lisbon agenda for economic reform at the European Council in the Portuguese capital in 2000. The aim of the Lisbon process, rather optimistically, was to turn the European Union into the world's foremost knowledge economy within ten years, an aim that a decade later appears laughable. However, the Lisbon objective did amount to a coherent plan for reform, combining liberalization of markets with an emphasis on innovation and technology on the one hand, and sustainability and social justice on the other. Although the process has not been taken as seriously as Blair had hoped, it certainly amounted to an important constructive British intervention in the debate on Europe's future.

More difficult for the Labour government was the constitutional issue arising from the expansion of the EU eastward in 2004. Faced with a further ten member states, the EU's institutions clearly needed updating and reforming, but the proposal to combine this updating with the writing of a European constitution created a serious dilemma for the UK. Britain's tendency toward Euro-skepticism, added to its tradition of constitutional ambiguity and flexibility, made a European constitution an unwelcome proposal and placed Labour in an uncomfortable position. Blair wanted to play an active, constructive role in the debate, but he was wary of how the constitutional issue would play at home and thus he committed the government to holding a popular referendum. Although by most accounts Labour were successful in defending what the government perceived as UK interests in the proposed constitutional text, opinion polls continued to show unremitting hostility. Fortunately for Blair and his government, the "no" votes cast in the French and Dutch referenda in 2005 made the constitutional project unviable, allowing Britain to suspend its referendum and wait for the issue to disappear.

FINANCIAL CRISIS AND THE RETURN OF EURO-SKEPTICISM

If economic liberalization and constitutional treaties had seemed like intractable issues, they pale into normal politics compared with the aftermath of financial crisis in Europe and, especially, the euro zone. Britain's role in Europe's postcrisis politics has been ambivalent as usual, with the UK torn between its traditional wariness of Brussels-led policymaking and its huge commercial and political interest in a stable European recovery. The coalition between the Conservatives, still a hotly Euro-skeptic party, and the pro-Europe Liberal Democrats (whose leader Nick Clegg had served in the European Parliament before becoming an MP) only adds to the tension.

David Cameron's policy on Europe makes him by some distance the most Euro-skeptic prime minister since Thatcher; for example, he withdrew his party from the center-right European People's Party grouping in the European Parliament because of its federalist leanings. Yet Cameron appears a moderate by comparison with many of his own MPs, whose already powerful skepticism has been reinforced by the crisis in the euro nations. Cameron also faces an electoral threat from the UK Independence Party (UKIP), which runs on an anti-EU platform and has succeeded in splitting the conservative vote in large parts of England, including some traditionally safe Tory areas. Cameron's response has been to simultaneously reopen the question of Britain's EU membership, and seek to postpone a confrontation on the issue. In January 2013 he made a landmark speech arguing that the EU faced a crisis of both competitiveness and democratic accountability, and promised to negotiate for "fundamental, far reaching" (though unspecified) reform. Cameron further pledged that if reelected with a majority, his government would hold a referendum by 2017 on Britain remaining in the EU under the newly agreed terms. Cameron has said he will campaign in favor of staying in Europe, provided those terms are acceptable, but has conspicuously declined to say what his position will be if his hoped-for reforms do not materialize. The proposed referendum pushes the Europe question into the next Parliament and so attempts to defuse it in the short term, but in the process Cameron may have set the ground for a much larger battle in the coming years.

FOREIGN AND SECURITY POLICY: TONY BLAIR AND THE "WAR ON TERROR"

The last decade in British foreign policy has been fundamentally shaped by Tony Blair's decision to align Britain wholeheartedly with George W. Bush's "war on terror." The invasion of Iraq in 2003 became the most significant foreign policy decision, and perhaps the defining moment of Blair's premiership. The ongoing deployment of British troops in Afghanistan and the legacy of the Iraq conflict ensure that the shockwaves of the Blair era continue to influence the foreign policy choices of the coalition today (see box 2.3).

Although Blair had quickly succeeded in overcoming much of the negative legacy of Euro-skepticism bequeathed by the Conservatives, his relationship with the other European member states was to run into trouble as a result of the dramatic events of

---

Box 2.3 British Intervention in Iraq and Syria

"Saddam Hussein's regime is despicable, he is developing weapons of mass destruction, and we cannot leave him doing so unchecked. He is a threat to his own people and to the region and, if allowed to develop these weapons, a threat to us also. Doing nothing is not an option."

—Tony Blair to the House of Commons, April 10, 2002

"[Saddam's] weapons of mass destruction program is active, detailed and growing. The policy of containment is not working. The weapons of mass destruction program is not shut down. It is up and running. . . . The intelligence picture . . . concludes that Iraq has chemical and biological weapons, that Saddam has continued to produce them, that he has existing and active military plans for the use of chemical and biological weapons, which could be activated within 45 minutes, including against his own Shia population; and that he is actively trying to acquire nuclear weapons capability."

—Tony Blair to the House of Commons, September 24, 2002

"We expected, and I expected to find actual usable, chemical or biological weapons after we entered Iraq. But I have to accept, as the months have passed, it seems increasingly clear that at the time of invasion, Saddam did not have stockpiles of chemical or biological weapons ready to deploy."

—Tony Blair to the House of Commons, July 14, 2004

"After the Iraq war a lot of work was done in Whitehall to try to put into place systems so that we didn't rush into print or rush into a speech when information like this came to light. . . . So I choose my words carefully, but what I see does look very much like a war crime is being committed in our world, at this time, by the Syrian government. . . .

"We should be clear that this is not about putting British boots on the ground . . . but what is at issue is trying to work more closely with our allies—not just the Americans and the French but the Gulf allies too—to work with the [Syrian] opposition, to shape them, to train them, to mentor them, to help them, so that we put the maximum amount of pressure on the regime and we bring about the change that is required. But it also requires change at the top, it requires Russia, China, others on the Security Council to work together."

—David Cameron speaking to the BBC, April 26, 2013

Sources: Blair quotes at http://news.bbc.co.uk/1/hi/uk_politics/2847197.stm; http://news.bbc.co.uk/1/hi/uk_politics/2955632.stm; http://news.bbc.co.uk/1/hi/uk_politics/3893987.stm; and http://www.publications.parliament.uk/pa/pahansard.htm. Cameron interview available as a video clip at http://www.bbc.co.uk/news/uk-politics-22316517.

September 11, 2001. The response to the challenge of al-Qaeda terrorism drove a wedge between the United States and the most important continental European powers, Germany and France, and Britain's difficult position as the transatlantic "bridge" was placed under acute strain by these developments.

Blair's emergence as an ambitious and activist world leader surprised many, as the Labour leader appeared to pay little attention to foreign affairs before his election in 1997.[15] Very quickly, however, he developed a distinctive approach to foreign affairs that contrasted with the flexible pragmatism that had marked British policy toward international affairs in the postwar period. The Blair government soon found itself involved in military action, first cooperating with the United States in air strikes on Iraq in 1998, and then playing a visible role in the U.S.-led intervention in the Kosovo region of Serbia, where alleged ethnic cleansing was practiced against the Albanian majority population. Indeed, during the Kosovo conflict, Blair made a major statement on foreign affairs in Chicago, in which he laid out an agenda for active commitment on the part of Western powers to intervene against dictatorships and use military action on humanitarian grounds. This speech demonstrates that the choices that Blair made after September 11 were actually consistent with his thinking almost from the very beginning of his premiership. The British intervention in Kosovo was facilitated by Blair's close relationship with Bill Clinton, an enthusiast of Third Way thinking and fellow alumnus of Oxford University. What surprised many was Blair's keenness to continue such a close relationship with Clinton's successor, George W. Bush, a very different kind of political figure who appeared to have little in common with the British prime minister.

In the aftermath of September 11, Blair was quick to line up behind the U.S. administration in its response to the atrocities. The British government participated in the attack on Afghanistan, but perhaps most significantly, it also backed the shift in strategy announced by the Bush administration soon after, which opened up the possibility of preemptive military action against potential threats to U.S. security. The Afghanistan operation received almost unanimous backing from shocked European governments, but the next phase of the U.S. "war on terror," military intervention in Iraq, divided the European powers to an unprecedented degree. Although opposition to the invasion of Iraq was weaker in Britain than in countries such as France, Italy, and Spain, public opinion could be described as at best skeptical, and there was deep unease within the Labour Party toward the plan. In these circumstances, Blair was able to exploit the powerful constitutional position of a British prime minister to push ahead with support for, and full participation in, the Iraq operation. Despite losing two members of his cabinet, who resigned in protest, and facing substantial parliamentary opposition from a large number of Labour MPs, Blair pressed ahead. The consequences were far reaching.

As far as European politics were concerned, the Iraq issue divided the UK from the other major European actors on the international stage, with both France and Germany vehemently opposed. Blair was therefore forced to line up with conservative governments in Spain and Italy in supporting the Bush administration. This had consequences for Britain's European policy, with the initial attempts to form alliances with friendly center-left governments in France, and particularly Germany, being definitively shelved. The Lisbon agenda for economic reform was also tainted by association, as Blair's closeness to Bush on foreign policy discredited his center-left credentials on socioeconomic issues. More broadly, British influence over European politics was affected by the increasing perception, especially in the founding member states of the European Community, that Britain was a mere proxy for U.S. power.

The consequences for Blair's domestic standing were, if anything, far more serious. Determined to roll back U.S. unilateralism, Blair was instrumental in persuading Colin Powell to seek a UN mandate for the invasion of Iraq, regarding suspicions that Saddam Hussein was developing weapons of mass destruction (WMDs) as the most effective rationale for a UN resolution. This move was insufficient to win broad international backing for the war, but it did force Blair into exaggerating the available evidence of the WMD threat in a government document used to win over the British foreign policy community. The misleading suggestion that Iraq could launch WMDs in forty-five minutes had devastating consequences for Blair's political credibility when, after the invasion, no such capacity could be found.

The political damage suffered by the Labour government over Iraq is difficult to calculate accurately, but it appears substantial. First, even before the war, massive demonstrations took place around Europe, with the turnout of up to 2 million protestors in London constituting perhaps the largest public protest in British history. Second, the war caused deep upset in Britain's large Muslim population. British Muslims, who are mostly of Pakistani or Bangladeshi origins and tend to be concentrated in the less prosperous areas of Britain's largest cities, have traditionally been strong supporters of the Labour Party, perceived as the most effective defender of ethnic minority rights. However, the Iraq war and its aftermath undermined this long-standing relationship. Muslim unease with Labour policy was exploited by George Galloway, a former dissident Labour MP expelled from the party for his close relations with the Saddam Hussein regime. Galloway founded a party called Respect, which mobilized around the Iraq issue and was able to win a seat in 2005, defeating a Labour MP in one of Labour's safest London constituencies. Many Muslims also abstained or supported the Liberal Democrats, who had opposed the war. The Iraq issue undoubtedly cost Labour in the 2005 election, which saw its majority cut in half and its vote share decline to just 35 percent.

Blair's decision to back Bush's war in Iraq, and subsequent pro-U.S. positions over Israel and Palestine, including the Israeli attack on Lebanon in 2006, became the defining features of British foreign policy in the first decade of the twenty-first century. Any British prime minister would have been placed in a difficult position by world events after September 11, 2001, given the UK's historically close relationship with the United States and ambiguous relationship with the rest of the European Union. But Blair took a big risk in identifying himself so closely and so publicly with the Bush administration, which became extremely unpopular in British and European public opinion. It is difficult to escape the conclusion that the Blair premiership will be remembered more for its foreign policy choices than for anything else.

Foreign policy under Blair's successors has had a far lower profile both internationally and domestically. Gordon Brown had little interest in foreign policy and sought to focus on the economy and social issues, withdrawing British troops from

Iraq but with little fanfare. Brown maintained a British presence in Afghanistan, which proved an increasingly unpopular war by the end of his premiership, due to the apparent lack of progress and significant British casualties. The coalition's approach to foreign and defense policy must also be set in the context of straitened economic times. Britain's armed forces have not been spared the effects of fiscal austerity. On the contrary, they have been cut significantly. It seems that the new government's willingness to engage in military action abroad has also been conditioned by the experience of the Blair years: while Britain was supportive of military intervention by NATO to topple the Muammar Gaddafi regime in Libya in 2011, unilateral action, or participation in another "coalition of the willing" outside the auspices of international bodies, would have been politically dangerous. As a result the UK pressed hard for a resolution in the UN Security Council, and authorized air support for the Libyan rebels only once opposition from Russia and China had been mollified.

In Syria, the British government has been critical of the UN Security Council's "division" and consequent inaction, but has been reticent to act except in providing humanitarian support. Emerging evidence of the possible use of chemical weapons by the Bashar al-Assad regime has led to a hardening of rhetoric by British and American leaders, and more vocal commitments to support and train the Syrian opposition, but direct military intervention remains ruled out. As of early 2014, this puts the coalition government in broad alignment with the Obama administration, but it is by no means certain that should the United States harden its position on Syria, or on Iran, the British government would be as quick to follow as in 2003. Indeed, when David Cameron went to Parliament for support in countering Syria's use of chemical weapons, he faced an unprecedented backbench rebellion.

Britain's coalition era has coincided with a change in the tenor of the so-called special relationship with the United States. Whereas Blair and Clinton had been natural bedfellows on the center-left, and Blair had cemented an equally, though more surprisingly, strong alliance with the Bush administration, under President Obama relations between Britain and the United States have been cordial but perhaps less close than in the past. In the decades following the Second World War, close ties between the transatlantic allies were taken for granted, but the current generation of leaders is more removed from that era, perhaps removing the assumption that Britain should be first among equals in America's foreign relations. While the UK remains an important diplomatic ally of the United States, President Obama's foreign policy has reflected the new geopolitics of the twenty-first century, with the United States becoming more proactive in cultivating links to China and the Arab world and less focused on its ties to Europe. Britain's history as the colonial power in Kenya until 1963, within the lifetime of President Obama and of his Kenyan father, may also have a bearing on the current administration's view of Britain's role in the world. The coalition government, meanwhile, has been preoccupied by domestic concerns, dealing with recession at home and crisis in its near neighbors, perhaps rendering transatlantic diplomacy a less urgent priority for a while. Whether this signals a post-Iraq period of reflection, or a longer term cooling in the special relationship, remains to be seen.

Conclusion

The 2010 election marked the end of an era: a thirteen-year period in which the Labour Party, for the first time in its history, was able to maintain a parliamentary majority for three whole legislatures. This feat, which had eluded every Labour Party leader before 1994, was testament to the remarkable political abilities of Tony Blair, who led the party to victory in three successive elections. Blair's government could be seen as one of the most successful in recent British history, combining economic expansion with strong public investment in popular services such as education and health care, and largely popular constitutional reforms. However, the financial crisis of 2007–2008 and the deep recession that followed it blotted Labour's record. The financial collapse revealed that the British economy's problems had not, after all, been solved: the prosperity of the early 2000s was to an extent the product of a financial bubble that has wrought terrible economic destruction, and the collapse in economic output opened up a gaping budget deficit that exposed the limits of Labour's expansion of the public sector. The new Conservative–Liberal Democrat coalition has set about reducing the deficit by slashing government programs, reversing much of the socioeconomic project Labour had painstakingly constructed. Labour's crushing defeat in the 2010 election reflected popular disillusionment with the whole New Labour project.

The 2010 election may prove to be the end of an era in a much more fundamental way. For the first time since the Second World War, no British political party was able to form a government alone, and the centrist Liberal Democrats, excluded from government for the best part of eighty years, found themselves once again in power. This marks a significant change in British politics, which has revolved around a two-party system for decades, and which has little recent experience with the kind of coalition government common in continental Europe. Yet the novelty of coalition government has been absorbed by the UK political system with surprising ease, and through 2013 there was little obvious visible change in the way in which government and Parliament operate. The Liberal Democrats have taken up a backseat role in the administration, providing reliable support to a government in which Prime Minister David Cameron appears to wield much the same powers as his predecessors who had won parliamentary majorities. Moreover, the Liberal Democrats' plans for constitutional reform have made little headway, with their prized goal of electoral reform more distant than ever.

The results of the next elections, expected in 2015, will be crucial in determining how much of a lasting change the experience of coalition government will represent. Opinion polls since 2010 have placed Labour, under its new leader Ed Miliband, in the lead, but most commentators hold the view that Labour will struggle to obtain a single-party majority in the next election. The Conservatives under David Cameron are performing even less impressively in the polls, and the UK's poor economic performance up to 2014 makes an outright Conservative victory appear equally unlikely. So although a return to two-party politics is not impossible, the secular trend is toward greater fragmentation of voter choice and a decline in the strength of the traditional parties. If this trend continues, the British political system will need to change to accommodate the end of the "old politics."

Notes

1. Carl Emmerson et al., *The Government's Fiscal Rules*, Institute of Fiscal Studies Briefing Note 16, http://www.ifs.org.uk/bns/bn16.pdf#search=%22public%20borrowing%22 (accessed January 22, 2014).

2. Anthony Giddens, *The Third Way* (Cambridge: Polity Press, 1998).

3. Andrew Glyn and Stewart Wood, "New Labour's Economic Policy," in *Social Democracy in Neoliberal Times*, ed. Andrew Glyn (Oxford: Oxford University Press, 2001), ch. 8.

4. Jonathan Hopkin and Daniel Wincott, "New Labour, Economic Reform, and the European Social Model," *British Journal of Politics and International Relations* 8, no. 1 (January 2006): 50–68.

5. H. Thompson, "UK Debt in Comparative Perspective: The Pernicious Legacy of Financial Sector Debt," *British Journal of Politics and International Relations* 14, no. 3 (2013): 476–92.

6. Vince Cable, speech to Liberal Democrat Party Conference, September 21, 2009.

7. Hilaire Barnett, *Britain Unwrapped: Government and Constitution Explained* (London: Penguin, 2002), 52.

8. For a powerful denunciation of the risks inherent in this constitutional vagueness, see F. F. Ridley, "There Is No British Constitution: A Dangerous Case of the Emperor's Clothes," *Parliamentary Affairs* 41, no. 3 (July 1988): 340–61.

9. For an extensive discussion of the history of the "territorial question" in modern British politics, see Vernon Bogdanor, *Devolution in the United Kingdom* (Oxford: Oxford University Press, 1998).

10. For an extensive account of the "Irish question," see John McGarry and Brendan O'Leary, eds., *The Northern Ireland Conflict* (Oxford: Oxford University Press, 2005).

11. Charlie Jeffery, "Devolution and the Lopsided State," in *Developments in British Politics 8*, ed. Patrick Dunleavy, Richard Heffernan, Philip Cowley, and Colin Hay (Basingstoke: Palgrave, 2006), 138–58.

12. "Jenkins Commission" (Independent Commission on the Voting System), report presented to Parliament by the secretary of State for the Home Department by command of Her Majesty, October 1998, http://www.archive.official-documents.co.uk/document/cm40/4090/4090.htm (accessed January 22, 2014).

13. See Stephen George, *An Awkward Partner: Britain in the European Community* (Oxford: Oxford University Press, 1998).

14. See Jonathan Hopkin and Daniel Wincott, "New Labour, Economic Reform and the European Social Model," *British Journal of Politics and International Relations* 8, no. 1 (January 2006): 50–68.

15. For an analysis of Blair's foreign policy thinking, see Michael Cox and Tim Oliver, "Security Policy in an Insecure World," in Dunleavy, Heffernan, Cowley, and Hay, *Developments in British Politics 8*, 174–92.

Suggested Readings

Bogdanor, Vernon. *The New British Constitution*. Oxford: Hart, 2009.

Denver, David, Christopher Carman, and Robert Johns. *Elections and Voters in Britain*, 3rd ed. Basingstoke: Palgrave, 2012.

Gaskarth, Jamie. *British Foreign Policy*. Cambridge: Polity Press, 2013.

Geddes, Andrew. *Britain and the European Union*. Basingstoke: Palgrave, 2013.

Heffernan, Richard, Philip Cowley, and Colin Hay, eds. *Developments in British Politics 9*. Basingstoke: Palgrave, 2011.

Jenkins, Simon. *Thatcher & Sons: A Revolution in Three Acts*. London: Penguin, 2007.

McKittrick, David, and David McVea. *Making Sense of the Troubles: A History of the Northern Ireland Conflict*. London: Penguin, 2012.

Rawnsley, Andrew. *The End of the Party: The Rise and Fall of New Labour*. London: Penguin, 2010.

Seldon, Anthony, ed. *Blair's Britain, 1997–2007*. Cambridge: Cambridge University Press, 2008.

Seldon, Anthony, and Guy Lodge. *Brown at 10*. London: Biteback Publishing, 2011.

WEBSITES

Richard Kimber's Political Science Resources: http://www.psr.keele.ac.uk/area/uk.htm

Constitution Unit, University College London: http://www.ucl.ac.uk/constitution-unit/

Webpage of the prime minister: http://www.number-10.gov.uk/output/Page1.asp

UK Parliament: http://www.parliament.uk

BBC British Politics Pages: http://news.bbc.co.uk/1/hi/uk-- politics/default.stm

Hansard Society: http://www.hansardsociety.org.uk/

Conservative Party: http://www.conservatives.com

Labour Party: http://www.labour.org.uk/home

CHAPTER 3

Germany

CHALLENGES AND PARADOXES

Helga A. Welsh

Germany

Population (million):	80.8
Area in Square Miles:	137,830
Population Density in Square Miles:	595
GDP (in billion dollars, 2013):	$3,025
GDP per capita (PPP, 2013):	$39,700
Joined EC/EU:	January 1, 1958

Performance of Key Political Parties in Parliamentary Elections of September 22, 2013

Christian Democratic Union (CDU)	34.1%
Christian Social Union (CSU)	7.4%
Alliance 90/The Greens	8.4%
The Left (Die Linke)	8.6%
Social Democratic Party (SPD)	25.7%

Main Officeholders: Chancellor: Angela Merkel, CDU/CSU (2005); and President: Joachim Gauch, no party affiliation (2012–)

The euro crisis has catapulted a reluctant Germany once again to the center of European politics. This development was both accidental and paradoxical: accidental because it was not planned or desired by Germany or its European partners; paradoxical because the creation of the euro was intended to curtail Germany's power but instead propelled it. Critique of Germany's handling of the crisis has come from many corners, some decrying the lack of leadership and others lamenting its heavy imprint on European rescue packages.

The euro crisis is only the latest in a series of developments since the end of the Cold War that have elevated Germany's international status. Unification made it the most populous country in the European Union (EU) and was expected to make it more "normal"—a country like others. It created economic difficulties, but Germany has emerged once again as the European economic powerhouse. Internationally, after the fall of communism in 1989–1990 in Europe, the anticipated peace dividend did not materialize, and Germany was called upon to participate in fights against terrorism and ethnic and interstate conflict. However, foreign and security policy remains constrained by institutional and cultural barriers that evolved as part of the post–World War II settlement and are deeply rooted in the public and the policy establishment.

The unification of East and West Germany in 1990 and the subsequent move of the capital from Bonn to Berlin are widely perceived as important watersheds, warranting the addition of the adjective *new* to describe the result. Not surprisingly, the Berlin Republic registers both continuity with, and change from, the Bonn Republic (1949–1990). A long-missing sense of normality has returned to German domestic politics. The 2013 election season was limited to the summer months, and, with low unemployment and a rebounding economy, the public mood was tranquil. As in most countries, domestic issues were front and center, with particular attention given to the growing gap between rich and poor and advancing social justice. From 2010 to 2012, the euro rescue packages and the future of the EU aroused heated debates, but in 2013, the atmosphere shifted as a result of calmer financial markets and issue saturation. Pundits were more interested in coalition arithmetic that would determine whether Chancellor Angela Merkel could begin a third term in office in the fall. Her popularity was bolstered by her handling of the euro crisis, and the CDU/CSU (the Christian Democratic Union and the Christian Social Union)[1] received a decisive plurality of votes. In sharp contrast, incumbent leaders of other European countries were soundly defeated in recent years. But the elections also delivered some surprising news. The Free Democratic Party of Germany (FDP), Angela Merkel's coalition partner from 2009 to 2013, failed to master the 5 percent threshold level for entry into parliament, complicating coalition building.

In this chapter, the central roles of history and memory inform an analysis of the fundamentals of German politics and policymaking, demonstrating how continuity has meshed with change. It will focus on political parties and elites, elections and coalition governments, the federal system, and the connection between negotiation democracy and policy change before turning to key aspects of foreign and security policy and the challenges that Germany faces in this realm.

History's Legacy: A Tumultuous Century

History is a combination of evidence and interpretation that allows both under-standing and illusion. A country's history is particularly difficult to master when, as in Germany's case, the path toward a securely anchored liberal democracy was tortuous and marked by major ruptures. In one short century (1914–1991), to use Eric Hobsbawm's term, Germans experienced the collapse of three forms of dicta-torship and one democratic political system. The first major transformation came in 1918–1919. As a result of defeat in World War I and the collapse of the Second Reich (1871–1918), an authoritarian monarchy was overturned and replaced with the democratic parliamentary system of the Weimar Republic. Its beginnings were inauspicious, associated with defeat and humiliation, widespread political violence, and severe economic and social problems. The constitution's optimistic assumptions about the balance of power among president, chancellor, and parliament were sorely tested by extreme party fragmentation and polarization, and economic deterioration after 1928 added to the sense of instability. Democracy was shallowly rooted in both the public and elites and rather quickly abandoned. The National Socialist Party, one of many marginal radical groups in 1928 (when it attained 2.6 percent of the vote), received 37.8 percent in the 1932 elections. Once in power, Adolf Hitler ruthlessly and with amazing speed consolidated his leadership. Nazi Germany unleashed World War II to fulfill Hitler's geopolitical goal of building a "Thousand-Year Reich." Ger-many invaded most of Europe; Nazism's racist claim of "Aryan" superiority and anti-Semitic, homophobic, anticommunist, and eugenic views led to the murder, torture, and enslavement of millions of people across Europe and totalitarian rule at home.

By May 1945, Germans were confronted with utter defeat; to signify both an end and a new beginning, this moment is often referred to as "Zero Hour." Time had not stopped; on the contrary, the past would shape German political institutions, policies, and political culture, yet the future was uncertain and open to different scenarios. The country's division into two states was central to, and an early by-product of, the emerg-ing Cold War between East and West. Out of the ashes, in May 1949, the Federal Republic of Germany was created in the western part. The sleepy town of Bonn was chosen as the temporary capital and seat of government; similarly, the constitution was named the Basic Law to emphasize its transitory character, yet a stable democracy evolved. Soviet and eastern German communists founded the German Democratic Republic (GDR) in October 1949, where, under Soviet tutelage, a communist dic-tatorship took hold. With the hope of eventual reunification and from a position of strength, western allies and western Germans sought to secure democracy and to buffer against Soviet expansion. The West promulgated the Federal Republic as the official successor state of the defeated Germany; international recognition of the GDR was denied until the 1970s. The building of the Berlin Wall in August 1961 eliminated the last escape valve for eastern Germans; the ensuing diplomatic ice age between the two German states melted only gradually in the 1970s and 1980s.

Initially, both German states—supported by their respective allies—pursued unification. In response to West German Chancellor Willy Brandt's 1969 pronounce-ment that there are two states but one German nation, eastern leaders developed a policy of strict demarcation and separate identity. For them, unification was no longer on the agenda. In the West, the practicality of unification as a policy goal was increasingly questioned. However, while apparently stable, the communist regime slowly regressed; in 1989, it suddenly collapsed. The promise of unification, kept alive in West Germany as a constitutional prerogative, finally and unexpectedly became reality after four decades of separation.

Article 23 of the Basic Law expeditiously allowed the former GDR to join the constitutional framework of the Federal Republic in October 1990. The more cumbersome approach of renegotiating a new constitution, based on Article 146, was never seriously considered. Unification was a jump into cold water, and its consequences have played out in many ways. Germans in east and west live in a democratic society whose fundamental beliefs are accepted, but "the growing together of what belongs together," to use the words of former Chancellor Willy Brandt, took longer than anticipated. Nevertheless, within two decades, unification became a historical date commemorated on the Day of Germany Unity (October 3) and special anniversaries.

A DIFFICULT FATHERLAND

The past may have made Germany, in the words of poet C. K. Williams, a symbolic nation;[2] Germans are usually defined not by what they are but what they represent. Germany is admired for its cultural and scientific achievements and reviled for horrible crimes. The first eighty years of its history as a nation-state were, in many ways, defined by authoritarianism, militarism, and nationalism.

The lessons of the Weimar Republic's democratic breakdown and the Nazis' smashing of constitutional parliamentary government influenced later politics. "Bonn is not Weimar"—the determination not to repeat the instability that led to Hitler's dictatorship informed the writing of the West German Constitution, the creation of its political parties, and its economic system after World War II. These steps aimed to avoid the mistakes of the past by defending democracy and establishing political, economic, and social conditions that would provide security for individuals and the country as a whole.

The horrors inflicted by the Third Reich forced Germans toward a critical and open confrontation with their past. This process started in 1945 as part of Allied de-Nazification and democratization programs, but after the onset of the Cold War in 1947, swift political and economic consolidation took precedence over historical contemplation. The future seemed more important then, but the past would not go away. Challenged by a new generation, the hushing and muffling of German involvement and collusion with Hitler's regime were shattered in the late 1950s and early 1960s, and, step by step, a historical consciousness emerged that informs the public discourse to this day. No interpretation of German history can avoid confronting the horrors of Auschwitz. The legacy of the concentration camps has pervaded debates ranging from abortion and political asylum to reparations for Nazi victims and foreign military involvement. It explains the heightened sensitivity at home and abroad to right-wing activities. With the beginning of the twenty-first century, after a long silence, Germans also began once again to discuss their own suffering during and after World War II, including expulsions from their homes, mass rape, and the death and destruction wreaked by Allied bombing. After the fall of communism, how to address questions of justice and historical recollection in dealing with victims and perpetrators of the disposed communist regime added another layer of complexity. Having to cope with the legacy of two dictatorships within a relatively short time has made Germany something of a model for societies facing similar challenges. Policies to advance an open confrontation with the past include reconciliation with neighbors; an active memory culture using museums, memorials, and commemorative dates; the centrality of history in the public discourse, political education, and the media; the establishment of far-ranging restitution and compensation schemes; and institutional safeguards against a recurrence of dictatorship.

Predictably, how the past should be remembered often sparks heated debates but, in the end, elicits broad consensus in practical political matters. Although the discourse largely takes place among political and cultural elites, many of its arguments are reflected in newsprint, novels, popular movies, and television documentaries and trickle down into the collective consciousness. Germany has joined the many Western European countries setting memories of the Holocaust quite literally "in stone."[3] The new capital of Berlin is home to the Jewish Museum and, after many years of controversy regarding its design and designation, the Holocaust Memorial, officially named the Monument to the Murdered Jews of Europe. Berlin has also become the center of revival for Jewish culture in Germany. At the beginning of the 1930s, about 600,000 Jews lived in Germany; by 1950, the number had dwindled to 15,000, but it rose to 25,000 by 1989. Largely due to the influx of Jews from the former Soviet Union after 1990, their number has increased to more than 200,000, of which slightly more than 100,000 are organized in the Jewish communities (*Jüdische Gemeinden*). The large influx of Russian Jews has made the German community the third-largest in Europe and has presented the unique challenge of integrating the newcomers.[4]

The fall of communism ended Germany's division into two separate states, granted the country full sovereignty, and rendered obsolete its role as the front line between hostile ideological camps. Nevertheless, its history remains a cornerstone of the political discourse, even as new generations balance the responsibilities and constraints it imposes with national consciousness and pride.[5] For Germans, as British commentator Roger Boyen points out, history and memory are never easy (see box 3.1).

Governance and Policymaking

Germany's political system is commonly called a party democracy or party state. Functions and organizational principles for political parties are explicitly set out in Article 21 of the Basic Law, but the extent of party influence goes far beyond representing the will of the people in the legislature and executive. Over the years, party representatives have become an integral part of federal, *Land* (state), and even public institutions, such as the public television stations; the staffing of leadership positions in many sectors of public life is characterized by power sharing among them.

Box 3.1   The Nervousness about Facing the Positive Aspects of German History

Roger Boyes (2009)

It is a big anniversary year for Germany. Sixty years since the Berlin airlift and the signing of the constitution, the *Grundgesetz*. And, of course, 20 years since the crumbling of the Berlin Wall, the collapse of communism, and the reunification of the country. So Germany should be celebrating a party all year long, right? Wrong.

The country is agonizing, yet again, over how it should show its joy. Dare I say, "*Typisch deutsch*" (typically German)? The Berlin airlift commemorations, I must admit, went relatively well: thousands of Berliners ate *Wurst* and potato salad in Tempelhof Airport; and old pilots, American and British, returned and reminisced with old Berliners. True, there was grumbling—this was Berlin, after all, the European capital of grumbling—about the closing of Tempelhof Airport. But the Senate may yet rescue its reputation with the older generation by shifting the impressive Allied Museum—with its detailed history of the airlift—to some of the empty buildings in the former airport. So far, so good; a *Volksfest* (fair) was exactly what was required for this anniversary. And the local authorities knew what to do because this was about the history of West Berlin and about the transatlantic relationship, about hardship and the heroism of foreigners.

How to Create a Credible Storyline for the Country

The problem starts as soon as one tries to dream up ways of celebrating something abstract—like the *Grundgesetz*. How do you have a *Volksfest* about a document drawn up by politicians and lawyers, with almost no emotional resonance? The anniversary of the *Grundgesetz* is, of course, simply a way of marking the birth of the Bundesrepublik. But if you talk to Germans who lived through these years, you find out that they were moved by economic development rather than the sudden arrival of political freedoms, rights, and duties. "I believe we are more concerned with economic myths, the economic miracle, the D-Mark," says political scientist Herfried Münkler. "The *Grundgesetz* did not play such a big role in the collective memory of the Germans." . . . The question, then, in the sixtieth year of the Federal Republic, is how to create a narrative, a credible storyline for the country. . . .

Reluctance to Identify German Heroes

Now, let's be clear about this: Germans know how to party. People in England are still talking about the carnival mood during the 2006 World Cup, when fans literally danced in the streets. Until the German flags were carefully rolled away, everyone talked about a "relaxed patriotism." Now we are back with more customary tense, nail-biting, lip-chewing, look-over-your-shoulder, are-we-doing-anything-wrong patriotism. Part of the challenge, it seems to me, is the reluctance to identify German heroes who can be used as role models and focal points for celebration. . . .

(continued)

Box 3.1   *(Continued)*

Lack of a Clear Historical Concept

It is this timidity, the nervousness about facing the positive aspects of German history, that so baffles foreigners. A competition was recently launched to find a monument to mark German unity. It is supposed to be unveiled on November 9, 2009, and the competition was thrown open to everybody. Good! No fewer than 532 proposals were submitted. Even better! But then the nineteen-man jury, overwhelmed by the numbers and by the lack of clarity, decided that none of the designs was good enough. . . . The reason for this debacle was not so much the poor quality—some designs could certainly have been developed into something more interesting—but rather the lack of a clear historical concept. Germany's new monument was supposed to be a "freedom and unity monument," taking in the spirit of past centuries but looking positively to the future. Yet freedom and unity have not always gone together. Bismarck united Germany through war and the crushing of domestic critics; Hitler too led a unified Germany. I talked to British architects about this dilemma, about how to fuse, in a single design, complex and competing versions of history. Their solution was simple: accept that ordinary East German people made a major contribution to German unification by abandoning their fear and taking to the streets. . . .

The irony is that Germany is very good at celebrating its victims. The underground library to mark the Nazi book burning is widely regarded as an enrichment of Berlin. Peter Eisenman's Holocaust memorial remains impressive. Naturally, these constructions also took time and political wrangling. But that was understandable: the designers had to take into account the sensibilities of the victims. The Freedom and Unity monument should not be bound by these inhibitions. It should simply be a brave and interesting tribute to German heroism. Why is this so difficult for Germany?

Source: Copyright Goethe-Institut e. V., Online-Redaktion (May 2009; http://www.goethe.de/ges/mol/typ/en4608276.htm).

Through its rulings, the Federal Constitutional Court has reinforced the central role of political parties and given meaning to the principle of "militant democracy" by banning two of them. In the early days of the Federal Republic, one party on the right, the Socialist Reich Party, and one party on the left, the Communist Party of Germany, were declared illegal on the basis of their antidemocratic ideologies. Since then, attitudes have relaxed, trusting that the electorate will reject extremism, but not to the point of abandoning precautions. The Federal Office for the Protection of the Constitution monitors extremist groups to the left and right; most controversial is the observation of some members of the Left Party. The surveillance of the right-wing National Democratic Party of Germany (NPD) arouses less controversy; attempts to ban it come up routinely but so far have been rebuffed. Shunned and criticized by the media and all major political players and hampered by infighting and lack of strong leadership, the NPD has not been able to elevate its voice to the national level but occasionally has reared its head in *Land* and some municipal constituencies.

As for all parliamentary systems, the head of government—called "chancellor" in Austria and Germany and "prime minister" in other countries—is responsible to, and dependent on, his or her party. In Germany, the head of government is a member of parliament, elected from its ranks, and can be removed by a positive vote of no confidence; that is, a chancellor can only be voted out of office if, at the same time, the members of parliament can agree on the successor. In replacing chancellors, political parties, not the electorate, are the prime movers and shakers. Only Helmut Kohl's sixteen-year tenure ended with a clear verdict at the voting booth in 1998; in all other cases, the parties' political maneuvering determined the coalition partners that were able to form a new government. In Germany, the president, who acts as head of state, is chosen by an electoral college. The duties are largely ceremonial, but presidents have used their "soft power" effectively to address questions of national significance, such as the reform gridlock or disenchantment with politics.

A woman leading a major party and becoming head of government did cause a few headlines in 2005 but no waves; in the 2009 and 2013 elections, Angela Merkel was the undisputed leader of the CDU and remains very popular among the German public, receiving support from a cross-section of voters. Women in German politics have come a long way; the first female cabinet minister was only appointed in 1961, and practice limited women to one or two government positions and "soft" areas, such as health, family, and youth, until the end of the 1980s. Now, routinely, more than 30 percent of the members of the federal legislature are women, and women occupy leadership positions in parties and interest groups. Such success in the political arena still contrasts sharply with the dearth of female CEOs or board members of major companies and the relative scarcity of female university professors.

As in other democracies, the background of the political elite does not reflect that of the population at large. A university degree has become the norm, and lawyers dominate; the halls of power hardly reflect the ethnic diversity of an increasingly multicultural society. East Germans are proportionally represented in the Bundestag but stunningly underrepresented in leadership positions, Merkel's chancellorship and Joachim Gauck's presidency notwithstanding. Merkel has carefully avoided making her eastern roots a matter of political significance; she once remarked that U.S. citizens seem more interested in her background than western Germans.[6]

Beyond her upbringing in communist East Germany, Merkel defies the image of most political leaders. She holds a doctorate in physics and became politically active only in the final days of the GDR as a member of one of the newly emerging parties. When her party dissolved, she joined the CDU; her career under the tutelage of then-Chancellor Helmut Kohl involved different posts in the cabinet and the party leadership. In 1998 she became general secretary and in 2000 chair of the CDU. Her scientific background is often cited to explain her systematic approach to, and mastering of, complex policy issues as well as her nonideological approach to politics. Critics see the latter as reluctance to commit to clear policy positions; supporters see it as a desirable pragmatism committed to getting things done. Under her leadership, the concept of chancellor democracy has been revived. It traces its roots to the first West German chancellor, Konrad Adenauer, and is regularly evoked when the head of government enjoys a high level of prestige, heads his or her party, and takes the lead in foreign affairs, sidelining the foreign minister. Decision making during the euro crisis elevated Merkel's profile, supported by institutional changes in the wake of the Lisbon Treaty, as foreign ministers no longer take part in European Council meetings.

ELECTIONS AND COALITION GOVERNMENTS

The need to form coalition governments at the national and *Land* levels is a recurring feature of German politics. In national politics, only once, in 1957, was one party, the CDU/CSU, able to garner a majority of the votes, and even then it entered a coalition. In Germany, coalition governments most often form when one major party aligns with a minor party or parties to achieve a majority in the parliament. Under such arrangements, the profile and political clout of smaller parties is elevated. Formal coalition agreements have become the norm; they outline policy priorities and procedural issues for a four-year term.

Given the centrality of political parties, the gradual shift from the "frozen" three-party system of the postwar era to one that regularly grants four to five parties entry into national and regional parliaments has affected coalition arithmetic as well as resource and power allocation, a process that is still unfolding. In the 1970s, the CDU/CSU and Social Democratic Party of Germany (SPD) garnered over 90 percent of the ballots; by 2005, just below 70 percent; in 2009, 66.8 percent; and, in 2013, 67.2 percent. The national elections mirror voting behavior at the *Land* level; party identification has declined, resulting in greater volatility in electoral outcomes. Though still high compared to the United States and many other democracies, voter turnout in the 2013 national elections only slightly increased to 71.5 from its all-time low of 70.8 percent in 2009 (see table 3.1).

The CDU/CSU and SPD vie for voters at the center of the political spectrum and portray themselves as catchall and social welfare parties; that is, parties with wide appeal. After World War II, the CDU/CSU and SPD represented clear ideological choices and strategies ranging from economic to military policy. For many years, SPD strength was based on mass membership, whereas the CDU/CSU seemed to have a built-in electoral majority. By the mid-1970s, the ideological positions of the major

Table 3.1   2013 Parliamentary Elections (total number of seats: 630)

Party	Second Vote	No. of Seats	Difference between 2013 and 2009 (in percentages)
CDU/CSU	41.5	255	+7.7
SPD	25.7	192	+2.7
Left Party	8.6	64	−3.3
Alliance '90/The Greens	8.4	63	−2.3
FDP	4.8	0	−9.8
AfD	4.7	0	+4.7
Other	6.3	0	+0.3

Note: Germany uses a personalized proportional representation voting system. Each person casts two votes. The first elects one representative from a district, similar to the single-member district vote in the United States. The number of seats in the *Bundestag*, however, is determined by a vote for a party list (second vote). Only parties that receive at least 5 percent of valid votes or three constituency mandates can be represented in the federal diet. Voter turnout in the 2012 election was 71.5 percent, slightly up from 70.8 percent in 2009.

(*Source*: Der Bundeswahlleiter, *Vorläufiges amtliches Ergebnis der Bundestagswahl 2013*, http://www.bundeswahl leiter.de/de/bundestagswahlen/BTW_BUND_13/presse/w13032_Vorlaeufiges_amtliches_Ergebnis.html)

parties had converged in many areas, including foreign and security policy. Coupled with ubiquitous media coverage and the open-ended nature of coalition building, the incremental narrowing of the ideological gap has elevated the role of personalities in elections and encouraged pragmatism over programmatic rigidity.

For most of the postwar period in West Germany, the FDP, rooted in classic European liberalism, had the luxury of choosing its coalition partner; a small party acted as the power broker. Traditionally, the FDP favored alliance with the CDU/CSU, although from 1969 to 1982 it aligned with the SPD. Its fall from power in the 2013 election was steep. In 2009 it had reached an all-time high of 14.6 percent; in 2013 it shrunk to 4.8 percent, prompting the resignation of its leadership and soul searching. Since the 1980s, the Greens (officially, Alliance 90/The Greens after 1993) have brought "new politics" issues, such as gender, environment, peace, and grassroots participation, to the forefront. Ever since the Red-Green coalition of 1998–2005, the Green Party is seen as the SPD's most likely coalition partner. It too experienced a harsh awakening when the 2013 election results were tallied as it had fallen from 10.7 to 8.4 percent and its leadership promptly quit.

Following the fall of the Berlin Wall in November 1989, the former ruling Socialist Unity Party in East Germany changed program and leadership; it renamed itself the Party of Democratic Socialism (PDS). Its considerable electoral success was restricted to the eastern part of the country until disillusioned members of the SPD and trade unionists in the West founded their own party, Labor and Social Justice. The two forged an electoral alliance in 2005 and in 2007 merged to form the Left Party. This marriage of political expedience aligned western and eastern voters to earn 8.7 percent of the national vote in 2005, 11.9 percent in 2009, and 8.6 percent in 2013. Its appeal has weakened somewhat due to factional infighting, often along East-West lines. The improved economic climate in Germany diminished its pull; the SPD also shifted its electoral platform to attract disgruntled voters on the left of the political spectrum.

In the 2013 elections, the FDP and the Left Party in particular were negatively affected by the upstart success of the Alternative for Germany (AfD) party, which garnered a surprising 4.7 percent of the vote. It fell short of the required 5 percent for entry into parliament but drew support from a wide spectrum of disgruntled voters, many of whom decided at the last moment to switch their allegiance. As a protest party, it advocates a particular strand of Euro-skepticism, supporting European integration per se but under new rules that allow, among others, the "orderly dissolution" of the euro currency.

The shifting electoral landscape indicates declining party identification but also a divided electorate (see table 3.2). Some favor comprehensive policy changes associated with the globalization of the economy, the growing needs of a knowledge society, and the challenges associated with demographic change. Others feel that recent political moves have led to an unacceptable weakening of the social safety net and social decline for many. Politicians are challenged to introduce changes that are effective yet socially fair. This dilemma affects the people's or catchall parties, the CDU/CSU and SPD, while the FDP and the Left Party, for example, use it to present distinct versions of the neoliberal versus socialist policy positions.

Table 3.2   Federal Elections, Coalition Governments, and Chancellors (1949–2013)

Election Year	Coalition Parties	Chancellor
1949	CDU/CSU, FDP, and DP (German Party)	Konrad Adenauer (CDU)
1953	CDU/CSU, FDP, DP, and GB/ BHE (All-German Bloc/Federation of Expellees and Displaced Persons)	Konrad Adenauer (CDU)
1957	CDU/CSU and DP	Konrad Adenauer (CDU)
1961	CDU/CSU and FDP	Konrad Adenauer (CDU) October 1963: Ludwig Erhard (CDU)
1965	CDU/CSU and FDP December 1966: CDU/CSU and SPD	Ludwig Erhard (CDU) Kurt Georg Kiesinger (CDU)
1969	SPD and FDP	Willy Brandt (SPD)
1972	SPD and FDP	Willy Brandt (SPD) May 1974: Helmut Schmidt (SPD)
1976	SPD and FDP	Helmut Schmidt (SPD)
1980	SPD and FDP September 1982: SPD October 1982: CDU/CSU and FDP	Helmut Schmidt (SPD) Helmut Schmidt (SPD) Helmut Kohl (CDU)
1983	CDU/CSU and FDP	Helmut Kohl (CDU)
1987	CDU/CSU and FDP	Helmut Kohl (CDU)
1990	CDU/CSU and FDP	Helmut Kohl (CDU)
1994	CDU/CSU and FDP	Helmut Kohl (CDU)
1998	SPD and Alliance '90/The Greens	Gerhard Schröder (SPD)
2002	SPD and Alliance '90/The Greens	Gerhard Schröder (SPD)
2005	CDU/CSU and SPD	Angela Merkel (CDU)
2009	CDU/CSU and FDP	Angela Merkel (CDU)
2013	Not yet determined	Angela Merkel (CDU)

Source: Adapted from Forschungsgruppe Wahlen e.V., *Bundestagswahl. Eine Analyse der Wahl vom 22. September 2012*, Berichte der Forschungsgruppe Wahlen e.V., 138, October (Mannheim: Forschungsgruppe Wahlen, October 2013), 72.

Traditional coalition patterns, which favored the combination of either the CDU/CSU or SPD with a smaller party, often no longer work (see table 3.2). Should the CDU/CSU and SPD form grand coalitions, reach out to new coalition partners, and/or align with two smaller parties instead of just one to garner sufficient votes?

The resounding success of the CDU/CSU in September 2013, its best result since 1990, was a personal triumph for Angela Merkel, although the party was short five seats of an absolute majority. Before the elections, the CDU/CSU and FDP vowed to renew their alliance, despite the fact that they had found little common ground in the last four years; the SPD and The Greens made similar commitments on the center-left. Both the CDU/CSU and SPD ruled out coalition with the Left Party at the national level. Public opinion and many in the political establishment still reject a coalition among the SPD, The Greens, and the Left Party. Many in the SPD do not want to elevate the status of the Left Party, a major competitor for votes, or give it credibility by including it in a coalition government. Some of its western members are considered "traitors" who left the SPD to join a new party that later merged with the PDS. Particularly in the western part of the country, suspicion against what many consider a "postcommunist" party lingers, but in the eastern part of the country, it remains a formidable force.

A minority government composed of the CDU/CSU only was ruled out, which left only two options: a grand coalition, that is, a government led by the two major parties (the CDU/CSU and SPD), or a coalition between the CDU/CSU and the Greens. Arithmetic is just one factor; programmatic proximity and personal chemistry among the party leaders also figure prominently when coalitions are forged. Difficult negotiations were predicted in both scenarios, but another grand coalition was seen as most likely. It arouses different reactions by pundits but was favored by the public. Supporters emphasize that such coalitions can overcome political hurdles to move the policy agenda from initiation to implementation since they garner sufficient votes in the Federal Parliament and the Federal Council (Bundesrat). Critics lament that in such a political arrangement, meaningful parliamentary opposition is limited to minor parties with no power to seriously challenge policy proposals. Others focus on whether such extreme majority coalitions can deliver promised policy changes. Far from innovative, they argue, grand coalitions promote policies that please the least common denominator since party competition continues; the partners have to uphold their programmatic distinctiveness to avoid alienating their voters. Critics and advocates agree that success is not guaranteed. It has to be supported by political will, and leadership is crucial. They also agree that grand coalitions should only be enacted for limited periods in times of duress.

In 2005, the only viable solution turned out to be a grand coalition government. It was not a novelty; a similar and, as regards policy outcomes, largely successful arrangement existed once before between 1966 and 1969. The grand coalition between 2005 and 2009 deserves similar credit. By and large, it kept partisan bickering in check and got things done. In contrast to the first grand coalition government, democratic principles were not devaluated, as opposition parties were stronger compared to the 1960s, and Germany's democracy was established.

The German political system has no primaries; the parties select candidates. Campaigns are generally limited to a few weeks, but the staggering of elections—*Land* and municipal elections often take place between national elections—puts pressure on politicians. When voters cast their ballots in *Land* elections, local and national concerns intermingle, and parties can rebound, stabilize, or fail, with consequences for national politics as the distribution of seats in the Federal Council fluctuates directly with electoral fortunes at the *Land* level (see the "The Federal System" section). In recent years, *Land* coalitions have tested uncharted waters with novel coalition formations, often involving the Green Party. Minority governments do not have a stable parliamentary majority but have to vie for votes from other parties to pass legislation; this practice is rare in Germany and is viewed with suspicion.

THE FEDERAL SYSTEM

The capital of Berlin has reemerged as a cultural and scientific hub. New traffic patterns reconnect it with the world; new architectural venues, including the Reichstag, the seat of the German parliament, have received accolades for innovative design. A major international tourist destination, its special flair was summed up by the principal conductor of its Philharmonic Orchestra, Englishman Sir Simon Rattle, as "60 percent Germany, 38 percent New York, and the rest Wild West."[7] Its increasingly prominent role notwithstanding, federalism engenders competition with other major cities, such as Cologne, Frankfurt, Hamburg, Leipzig, and Munich (see box 3.2). The sharing of competencies and power contrasts with the situation in unitary states, such as the United Kingdom and France, where London and Paris clearly dominate national cultural, economic, and financial life.

Box 3.2   Berlin: City on the Move

Claudia Wahjudi (2005)

Viewed from the eleventh floor of a block of flats in the middle of the city, Berlin presents itself from its best side—in elegant gray. The plain of stone, asphalt, plaster, concrete, granite, steel, and glass extends as far as the horizon, interspersed with the green of parks and the red brick of old factories. Rising up in the center, there are little towers, curved or straight, and a few skyscrapers, some functionally rectangular, others with the sharp angles familiar from computer games. Colors and forms tell of the discontinuities of the city's history: from industrialization, which suddenly made the little residence city a metropolis, to the pomp of the German Empire and the social reforms of the Weimar Republic; from the megalomania of the National Socialists to the bombs and firestorms of the Second World War; from the division of the city into an Eastern European half and a Western European half to the building boom that followed the fall of the Wall. But now you can only sense where the Wall, Berlin's most famous structure, once stood: somewhere over there between the round roof of the Sony Center and the new glass cupola of the Reichstag Building, the seat of the German parliament. . . .

Every time a political system collapses in Germany, its stone witnesses are disposed of in Berlin as an example to others. A practice that is not always free of contradictions. Some people would even like to have a section of the almost completely demolished Wall back: when a private museum recently built a mock-up, locals and tourists flocked to see it.

There is always building, demolition, and rebuilding going on. The various currents of German society compete for visible representation in the capital, which in just 100 years has seen five German states and the end of the Second World War in Europe. Now it is like a patchwork quilt full of holes that someone is supposed to be mending. . . .

Berlin is a city of opposites. It has glittering new government buildings, embassies, shopping malls, and sport arenas, but a few meters away plaster is peeling from a municipal building and cars are bouncing through potholes. The Love Parade, the famous street procession held to the sound of techno beats, was conceived in Berlin, which also hosts a Carnival of the Cultures, Christopher Street Day celebrations, the annual Berlinale film festival, and a Biennale for contemporary art. The 2006 football World Cup final will kick off in its Olympic Stadium. The city has nineteen universities and higher education institutions, three opera houses, and about 300 galleries; you will hear Turkish, English, Polish, and Russian being spoken, and some days more than 120 bands and orchestras perform there. Yet, to the amazement of guests from other major cities, Berlin seems pleasantly empty: such wide pavements, so much sky, so few traffic jams—it is almost as restful as a holiday resort.

Source: Copyright Goethe-Institut, Online-Redaktion: http://goethe.de/ges/sur/dos/ber/en1543951.htm.

Historically, regionalism has been strong in Germany, and the impact of the regions and their state governments is manifest in, among other things, the *Länder*'s leadership role in asserting regional rights vis-à-vis the EU, the training and recruitment of national leaders through state offices, the division of labor between the federal government and the individual *Länder*, the reciprocal influence of *Land* and national elections, and the eminent role of the Federal Council in policymaking. The authors of the Basic Law institutionalized *Land* participation and multiple checks and balances in policymaking. Decentralization is based on a complex division of power; the interests of the initially eleven and, after unification, sixteen *Länder* are represented in the Federal Council. Depending on the size of its population, each *Land* varies in its electoral weight from three to six votes. State governments select their representatives and instruct them how to vote; thus, each *Land* casts its vote as a unit. The interconnectedness of the federal and state levels has reinforced multilevel bargaining in policymaking.

Divided majorities in the Bundestag and Bundesrat became more frequent after 1972, and the passage of many bills could be blocked or subjected to lengthy negotiations. A reform of the federal system was deemed essential to get efficient decision making back on track. Discussed for decades, and elaborated over more than two years in a special commission, the 2006 federal system reform has been the most comprehensive constitutional reform since the founding of the Federal Republic in 1949. It involved numerous changes in the Basic Law, the German Constitution, and federal laws.

One major goal of the reform was to clearly demarcate the responsibilities between the federal and regional governments. New boundaries were supposed to increase transparency and to reduce the number of bills requiring approval by the Federal Council. In exchange for a reduction in Federal Council power—the body of the *Land* governments—the *Länder* gained more responsibility for certain policy areas, such as education and civil service. In 2009, a second federalism reform went into effect, setting new constitutional limits on debt borrowing by the federal government and the *Länder*, and outlining new strategies for modernizing public administration. However, asymmetries in population and, in particular, economic power and enduring center-periphery networks make delineating power exceedingly difficult. Despite major constitutional changes, the long-term political implications for policymaking remain unclear.

German federalism is built on sharing the fiscal burden. To reduce economic inequities, funds are transferred from richer to poorer states. Although givers and takers have changed during the life of the Federal Republic, most of the West is more prosperous than the East, and, due to shifts in employment and industrial patterns, the South (in particular, Baden Württemberg and Bavaria) is now economically better off than the North (e.g., Mecklenburg-Western Pomerania and Schleswig-Holstein). Until 1994, uniformity (*Einheitlichkeit*) of living conditions in the different parts of Germany had been the constitutionally prescribed goal, but, as part of constitutional reform in the aftermath of German unification, the term was replaced with equivalence (*Gleichwertigkeit*), alluding to comparable but not equal living conditions. The superimposition of the East-West divide on the existing North-South gap has added new levels of competition and conflict over the distribution of funds. Today, in the political struggle for influence, who is rich and who is poor matters more than ever.

NEGOTIATION DEMOCRACY AND POLICYMAKING

In all democratic settings, politics is the art of getting things done. It requires bargaining and compromise. In the German "negotiation democracy," a complex system of checks, balances, and conflict-solving mechanisms has emerged. Some features of consensual decision making were intentional; others evolved through cultural preference and political stipulation. Multilevel policymaking combines features of majority government based on competition with power-sharing characteristics, that is, consensus seeking through bargaining, and granting autonomy and veto power to important political actors.

Negotiation democracy takes multiple forms; many are tied to the particulars of German federalism, which combines power sharing with strong centralizing tendencies and operates in a political culture in which comparable norms and living standards across the federation are highly valued. Frequent and successful use of the mediation committee, which is composed of 32 members of the Bundestag and Bundesrat (both bodies are represented in equal number), points to the critical role of negotiation in Germany's political system. The procedures to appoint judges to the highest federal courts, including the Federal Constitutional Court, are shared by the major political parties and emphasize cooperation. Veto players encompass powerful interest groups, notably the labor unions and employers' associations, but they, along with other groups, are often drawn into expert commissions. Informal politics, relying on long-standing networks across party aisles and groups, is a crucial feature of German politics. Such methods secure high levels of acceptance once new policies are formed but also tend to slow down or even block policymaking processes. The challenges associated with such a system became starkly evident in the 1990s.

The German penchant for joining words and coining new ones is well known, and a new "word of the year" is chosen by a jury of experts that captures a national issue of major significance. Some fade away, while others become part of the vocabulary. Pressure for change in the areas of taxes, health care, pensions, the labor market, and immigration built up in the 1980s but boiled over in the 1990s. Decision-making overload, political haggling, and resistance seemed to make reforms impossible. Hence, in 1997 the term *Reformstau* (literally, "reform stall" but meaning something closer to a traffic jam) was born.

Economic globalization, accelerating competition, the outsourcing of jobs, the spread of information technologies, and the migration of ideas and people have had profound effects on all Western economies. The forging of a closer union among the member states of the EU has also exerted pressure for change. Benchmarking—that is, performance comparison within the EU and the Organization for the Economic Development (OECD)—has become the norm. In an environment of shrinking and aging populations, low economic growth rates, and competition for resources, including knowledge and education, Germans were asked to change their ways. Such a task is not easily accomplished under the best of circumstances, but potential reform dynamics were initially absorbed and blocked by the consequences and the costs of merging East and West Germany in the 1990s.

Like most Europeans, many Germans turn to the government to address problems that affect their well-being. While direct state intervention is circumscribed, governmental institutions play important roles as mediators and set the legal framework for semipublic institutions, such as the Federal Agency for Labor. Economic and social systems, including the social welfare system, rely on a highly regulatory culture and transfer payments. These systems evolved after World War II and won out over competing ideas of socialism and pure capitalism. Germans prioritized economic and social stability. A high level of employment and social protection, extensive participatory rights for workers, collective bargaining, and close cooperation between labor unions and employer associations, both of which were given privileged access to, and roles in, managing the economy, became central to the "model" Germany. Praised as a social market economy, for many years this model worked extremely well.

Calls for leadership and decisive action to advance reforms increased after the 2002 election. In March 2003, Chancellor Gerhard Schröder announced a comprehensive policy program, Agenda 2010, to reform the welfare system and labor market policies. However, associated cuts in social benefits aroused strong opposition, especially within the left wing of Schröder's party, the SPD, leading to widespread protests and the creation of a new party, the Labor and Social Justice Party, which later merged with the PDS to form the Left Party. The grand coalition (2005–2009) followed up on numerous reform proposals that had been batted back and forth in parliament and many rounds of informal talks. The lengthy reform impasse has disappeared: in recent years, new policies have been instituted regarding taxes, pensions, immigration, family allowances, child care, health care, the labor market, education, and the federal system, to name the most important. Ten years after the passage of the reform package Agenda 2010, many hailed it as an important foundation for Germany's economic renewal, while others emphasized the negative consequences of clipping the social welfare net. This discourse highlights the importance of social justice and solidarity but also reveals important cleavages in preferred policies and implementation.

Reform capacity is linked to economic performance. Germany competes for the role of world export champion, dueling with the United States and, more recently, China for the top spot. Some tax rates have decreased. Relative to economic output, unit labor costs have fallen; labor unions and their workers have shown wage restraint; and work contracts have become more flexible. Unemployment numbers have declined, but regional variations are pronounced, and they are still higher in the East than the West. For many years, it was fashionable to portray a "sickly" German economy; average economic growth between 1995 and 2009 was a paltry 1 percent, including the worst recession since the end of World War II. In 2010 and 2011, with economic growth rates of 4.2 and 3 percent, respectively, recovery glimmered on the horizon, and although growth slowed in 2012 to 0.7 %, Germany's economy has rebounded and unemployment rates have dropped to levels not seen since unification.

Problem areas remain: low fertility rates and an aging population not only exert pressures on pension and healthcare systems but also expose the need for continued immigration. New immigration and integration acts went into effect, but the practice of allowing immigrants to settle in Germany remains restricted; immigration policies are emotionally charged and hampered by mental and bureaucratic obstacles. Recalibrating the education system from early child care to higher education is bounded by resource issues and political barriers. The ambitious change in energy policy with its shift from conventional power, in particular nuclear power, to renewable energy faces formidable challenges. Inequality has grown, and regional differences have become more pronounced. Keeping the German economic engine tuned is an ongoing task and relies heavily (some say too heavily) on export growth.

Foreign and Security Policy: Redefining Germany's Role in the World

In no other policy area is the collective memory of Germany's past more persistent and relevant than foreign and security policy. After World War II, membership in international organizations provided an opportunity to reenter world affairs and to fend off potentially resurgent nationalism. The history of the Federal Republic reflects a network of international cooperation.[8] The Western allies' aspiration to control (West) Germany, while simultaneously integrating it with the international community of democratic nations, contributed to the creation of the North Atlantic Treaty Organization (NATO) in 1949, and, after a heated domestic debate regarding remilitarization, Germany joined in 1955. The notion that NATO was formed to keep the Americans in Western Europe, the Russians out, and the Germans down captured prevailing concerns. (West) Germany's membership in the European Coal and Steel Community (1952) proved pivotal in the process of European integration; while containing its power, it also granted it a chance to emerge as one of its leaders.

Prior to unification, Germany was widely considered an economic giant but, owing to its limited international role, a political dwarf. In 1990, the end of the Cold War allowed it to regain full sovereignty and to unify East and West. Power—the ability to influence others to act in ways they otherwise would not—can be measured in terms of population, economic, and military strengths. Unified Germany, with its 80.8 million people, clearly surpasses France (65.8 million) and the United Kingdom (63.7 million) in population. Measured in GDP, it is by far the largest economy in Europe and the fourth-largest in the world, trailing the United States, the People's Republic of China, and Japan. It features prominently in weapons export, and is often involved in international conflict resolution efforts, although it does not hold a seat on the United Nations Security Council. Its military is intentionally weak in certain areas. To this day, Germany renounces possession of nuclear, biological, and chemical weapons and long-range combat aircraft and missiles. It has no general staff apart from NATO troops; its troop strength is down to around 220,000 soldiers, with further cuts on the horizon. Its defense expenditures remain low in comparison to those of France and the United Kingdom.

Power projection also depends on how a country is perceived by its international environment, which is the result of expectations built on, and influenced by, long memories and is conditioned by change. Finally, to what extent power is translated into influence also depends on the willingness to use economic and other resources, the preferences of domestic and international actors, and more intangible considerations, such as bargaining skills and institutional constraints and possibilities.

In the first decade of the twenty-first century, Germany was no longer called a "political dwarf" or even a "reluctant power" but the "central power in Europe," the "leading European power," a "global economic power," a "permanently reformed civilian power," and a "reemerging military power."[9] Beverly Crawford argued that "Germany has become a 'regional hegemon' in Europe and one of the 'great powers' on the international stage." She referred to Germany as a "normative power," relying on civilian power and multilateralism; power remains tied to downplaying power.[10] Placed in an environment where power is at times still measured in traditional terms, such a strategy has been praised as worth emulating or criticized as bypassing international responsibilities and burden sharing.

Major coordinates of German foreign and security policy remain steady, but the environment in which they are rooted has changed substantially. They still rely on broad consensus among the major political parties, with the partial exception of the Left Party. An important pillar of German foreign relations has always rested on trade relations; after all, the economy depends on exports and regularly features large trade surpluses. A shift to greater engagement with emerging markets is particularly evident in trade relations with China, now fifth in importance behind France, the United States, the United Kingdom, and the Netherlands. Strong mutual economic interests, if not dependencies, govern relations between Russia and Germany. Germany is Russia's second-largest trading partner behind China, while Russia is a significant source of German oil and gas imports.

The sections below discuss core aspects of German foreign and security policy in greater detail, showing both continuity and shifts. Although the emphasis on multilateral decision making—that is, a team approach to solving international problems within the parameters of international organizations, such as the EU, NATO, and the UN—prevails, Germany's stance is no longer reflexive when its interests are challenged. The strategic triangle of Berlin-Paris-Washington remains the fulcrum of German foreign policy, but the relative weight and proximity of the relationships are evolving. European integration remains the bedrock of German foreign policy, yet redefining its position in tandem with other European partners seems inevitable.

GERMANY AND EUROPE

To explain the support for European integration, aspects of history, political structure, policy style, and political culture must be considered. After World War II, "Project Europe" provided an avenue for peace, economic prosperity, and international recognition. German supporters of European integration also saw membership as a way to assure reconciliation and lasting peace with rival and former enemy France. The German Constitution explicitly authorizes the federation to "transfer sovereign powers to intergovernmental institutions," including a mutual collective security system and the EU. Political elites recognized the interconnectedness of national and European politics; German and European interests were seen as compatible, if not identical. Commitment to Europe also reflected a strong attachment to multilateralism as an idea and a means to pursue national interests.

Germany's complementary institutional structure has also been cited as facilitating its pro-European attitude. The highly decentralized political system, coalition governments, and the principle of delegation to semipublic institutions have made the interaction with European institutions, in the words of one observer, a "warm bath" instead of the "cold shower" that many British elites and citizens may feel.[11] Similarly, a bureaucratic culture of rules and regulations is part of both European and German policymaking. Finally, the lengthy negotiation and bargaining that aim at achieving consensus are key elements of both German and European policymaking. In other words, German politicians are at ease with the institutional and policymaking environment of the EU.

Institutional features may also partially explain why a reluctant or negative attitude toward European integration has remained a "dark matter" in German politics. Charles Lees argues that through the expression of reservations about EU policies and the election of small right-wing parties with an anti-European agenda, the *Länder* have given "soft Euro-skepticism" a limited outlet; it could be articulated and contained at the same time. The adoption of an anti-European attitude by parties on the far right may have discredited Euro-skepticism "by association."[12] The AfD, formed in April 2013, also struggles with this dilemma. Despite pockets of Euroskeptic attitudes, cross-party consensus in the EU's favor has remained high. Rescue packages led to intense exchanges in the German parliament, revealing fissures within parties, but a firm majority of deputies approved them. In several rulings, first challenging the Lisbon Treaty and later in complaints against the permanent euro bailout fund, the European Stability Mechanism, and the Fiscal Compact, the Federal Constitutional Court reaffirmed Germany's strong ties to Europe while affirming compliance with the German Constitution, but strengthened the powers of the Bundestag in regard to European legislation.

In the last sixty years, European integration has extended from economic areas to include, among others, foreign and defense policies, justice and home affairs, research, education, culture, and the environment. It has significantly changed the dynamics among EU member states; the Europeanization of its members' national politics has evolved as a major trend. Germany's share of members in the European Parliament is higher than that of other member countries, but its votes in the much more important Council of Ministers have remained equal to those of other "large" countries. Still, Germany's crucial role in shaping European integration is undisputed. For example, it has played a crucial role in framing and implementing European foreign and military initiatives in the Balkans. It set the tone and pushed for expansion of the EU into Central and Eastern Europe. It is the primary net contributor to the EU budget and the newly negotiated Eurozone European Stability Mechanism. In particular, it has been very successful in dictating the conditions under which countries can join the European currency system and how the euro is managed.

Chancellor Helmut Kohl (1982–1998) considered German and European unity as two sides of the same coin; the promotion of European integration through close Franco-German relations was central to his European policy. Chancellor Gerhard Schröder (1998–2005) came to power with little foreign policy experience, yet he paved the way for a self-confident foreign policy style that paid greater attention to national concerns. Angela Merkel (2005–) started her chancellorship on a high note. During the December 2005 council summit meeting, she successfully brokered a compromise on the long-standing issue of the EU budget, earning accolades at home and abroad. She took a leading role in salvaging important aspects of the Constitutional Treaty during her EU presidency in spring 2007, but her managing of the euro crisis earned her the nickname "Mrs. No."

Various crises have accompanied the European integration project from the beginning, so the crisis narrative is not novel. The euro crisis has elements in common with others that have challenged progress toward European integration: gloomy prognoses about the future of the project capture the headlines but, in the end, are mastered by policy adjustments and new institutions. It also has unique characteristics. For example, it followed battles over the ratification of new EU treaties and an expansion into Central and Eastern Europe that taxed European institutions and the public. Crisis remedies raised important questions about further intrusion on national sovereignty and the decision-making powers left to national parliaments. Finally, although the euro was supposed to boost European identity, when the latest crisis hit it also exposed old stereotypes. German media invoked images of lazy southern Europeans, while Chancellor Merkel and Finance Minister Wolfgang Schäuble were depicted in Hitler moustaches or SS uniforms in many southern European countries.

Even before the euro crisis, Jacques Delors, French EU Commission president from 1985 to 1994, joined the chorus of experts asserting that the EU climate had changed. The partial renationalization of European politics, according to Delors, owed its origins to domestic pressures created by globalization and generational change. Addressing French concerns that German leaders had lost their drive for greater European integration, he remarked that today "Germans must be convinced . . . that Europe is their future."[13] More recently, U.S. scholar David P. Calleo termed Germany's attitude toward the European project an "alarming disaffection."[14] What has happened?

German citizens support European integration, though somewhat less enthusiastically than their leaders; most see advantages and disadvantages. Like other member states, a more sober attitude toward the integration project has emerged over the last two decades. German citizens predominantly associate EU membership with the common currency, free movement of people, cultural variety, peace, and greater world participation. They widely endorse common security measures, defense policy, and foreign policy. Divisive topics include EU enlargement, but nothing was more opposed by the German electorate than the introduction of the euro. A few months before euro coins and banknotes were officially introduced in January 2002, only 45 percent of western Germans and 27 percent of eastern Germans considered replacing the mark a good thing. For the political elites, giving up the "sacred cow" of the national currency was unambiguously the price of unification: Germany had to sacrifice its lead financial role in Europe to compensate for its increased population and status. Neither one of the major political parties veered from completing the project. Germans were also promised that the euro would not entail transfers of funds from the financially stable euro-zone members to the troubled ones.

Enter the euro crisis. Chancellor Merkel's government openly resisted rescue packages for debt-ridden Greece and loan guarantees for countries under similar default pressures, but in the end, Germany took a major part in stabilizing the euro zone financially. Merkel was harshly criticized abroad for indecision that delayed much-needed actions and for forcing countries to implement strict austerity measures. This narrative attributed her hesitancy to domestic imperatives: she was setting the stage for German commitment against domestic resistance, prioritizing national interests. Viewed through a German lens, her policy choices successfully stymied Euro-skepticism and cultivated economic and political stability at home. The euro rescue packages were vital but also difficult to sell to a home audience that reluctantly gave up its beloved German mark. In spring 2013, public attitudes toward the euro were again positive after they had tumbled in 2012. Her handling of public debt and public consumption also adhered to economic philosophies cherished in German economic circles, even if they clashed with those of other Western governments, including the United States, that favored stimulus over austerity. The cautious pattern of incremental decision making was in line with German preferences and tradition and is a hallmark of Angela Merkel's policy style. The reluctance to take charge in the crisis also reflected the institutional and cultural constraints characteristic of German policymaking in general.

In the past, Germany's European vocation made it unique among EU member states, but during the euro crisis, signs mounted that its atypical role might no longer hold. Normality for Germany was "abnormal" for others;[15] when it acted like everyone else by putting national interests first—or no longer automatically equating national interests with European interests—it deviated from its established role as problem solver and mediator. This new approach, coupled with actions in other international arenas, raised questions about its willingness to usurp leadership and all the attendant responsibilities. An enlightened leadership, it was argued, would renounce introspective behavior and grant more attention to the interests of its European partners.[16]

Of course, Europe has not been led by Germany alone; the success of European integration has been based on shared leadership, although none more important than the Franco-German alliance. Since the beginning of European integration, France and Germany set the timing according to which it moved or stalled. Franco-German relations still stand as a model of reconciliation; after three German invasions of France between 1870 and 1940 alone, military conflict between the two has become unthinkable. They remain each other's most important trading partners, and thousands of educational exchanges and partnerships between towns and villages reinforce bonds at the grassroots level, acting as a cushion when leaders disagree.

The relationship between the two countries is closely watched, and over the years, observers have emphasized either ties that bind or degrees of separation. International developments since German unification have favored a more influential Germany and weakened the special position of France. France's national identity is closely tied to its prominent role in European and world affairs; thus, a shift in the balance of power between the two nations is an important reference point for French politicians. Cordial and close relations between French and German leaders covered up recurring bilateral conflicts of interest, reinforced by different policy styles, preferences, and leadership. Chancellors and French presidents, after election, routinely visit each other on their first official state visits abroad, emphasizing the special relationship in a symbolic gesture. The close friendships between Konrad Adenauer and Charles de Gaulle, Helmut Schmidt and Valéry Giscard d'Estaing, and Helmut Kohl and François Mitterrand are legendary but have not been replicated lately. The relationship between Angela Merkel and Nicolas Sarkozy was rocky but bound by reason and mutual interest. Current President François Hollande's leadership malaise and the weak performance of the economy have undermined France's role abroad. Germany misses the partner it relied upon, and both countries agree on their mutual dependence. The European engine still needs France and Germany to power it.

British Euro-skepticism, although hardly novel, ratcheted up under Prime Minister David Cameron, largely canceling out the United Kingdom as a partner in crisis mediation. Spain has serious domestic policy concerns. European leadership has fallen by default to Germany, and it has embraced the responsibility reluctantly. Ulrike Guérot and Mark Leonard rightly suggest that not only Germany must adjust its role in Europe; all member states "need to go through the same process of reinvention that Germany's elite have embarked upon, and design a new approach to Europe which can secure their national interests at a time when Germany has lost its romantic attachment to Europe."[17] This counsel will take time as well as vision and leadership, which are currently in short supply.

TRANSATLANTIC RELATIONS

After the EU, the relationship with the United States is the second pillar of German foreign policy. Integration with Europe and close cooperation with the United States have always been interrelated as part of Germany's strong commitment to Western alliances. With the advent of a European foreign and defense policy, they have become even more intertwined. In foreign and security policy, Germany sees itself as the carrier of both national and European interests.

During the Cold War, Western Europe in general and West Germany in particular benefited greatly from U.S. support in military, economic, and political matters. U.S. leadership was crucial in bringing about German unification when the opportunity arose in 1989–1990. The network of cultural, economic, and political exchanges is dense and has reached a level that is normally reserved for countries that are members of regional integration schemes, such as the EU. With record speed, the occupation power turned into a trusted friend and ally. Americans came to expect German leaders to emphasize friendship and appreciation and to criticize, if at all, subtly and behind closed doors.

The distinct downturn in relations during the debate about how to deal with Iraq in 2002 and 2003 led to intense soul searching among German elites and the public.

To be sure, with joint responsibilities and tasks come competition, and conflicts had emerged in the past as well, yet the level of disharmony and distrust evident during the Iraqi conflict revealed a new and different climate. The adage "All politics is local" may explain Chancellor Schröder's outspoken anti–Iraq War rhetoric during the 2002 electoral campaign. It led to tense, emotional exchanges between him and U.S. President George W. Bush. But soon the policy establishments on both sides of the Atlantic worked diligently at "normalization."

Foreign policy is a matter of pursuing national interests in interaction with other countries. It cannot ignore the importance of personal relationships and the policy styles of politicians at the helm. While good chemistry between leaders of different countries is no guarantee for the successful pursuit of interests, it can promote closer consultation and a cordial climate of cooperation. A significant step was taken with the election of Angela Merkel, which coincided with greater efforts by the Bush administration to consult with European leaders on matters of international concern. The 2008 election of Barack Obama to the U.S. presidency brought transatlantic relations back on track, as his policy style and major initiatives—for example, his support for multilateral strategies, nuclear disarmament, and environmental concerns—conform to German preferences. Approval ratings for U.S. foreign policy jumped from a low of 30 percent in 2007 to 64 percent in 2009 and only declined by 1 percent in 2010; that President Obama "would do the right thing in world affairs" was believed by about 90 percent of Germans surveyed in the 2010 Pew Global Attitudes Project.[18]

Obama euphoria has waned, but he still would have garnered about 90 percent of the German vote in the 2012 U.S. elections; all political parties welcomed his reelection. The normalization of transatlantic relations is not a return to the previous status quo. The roles of both Germany and the United States have changed significantly since the end of the Cold War. The discourse is friendly and frank; in the new global international environment, transatlantic relations still matter greatly but clearly less so in the post–Cold War era. U.S. leaders continue to push Germany (and Europe) to share a greater part of the burden in security matters around the world (see box 3.3). The perceived shift in U.S. foreign policy focus to Asia and troop reductions in Germany concern German politicians, who look for reassuring signs of the old, trusted alliances. The proposed Trans-Atlantic Trade and Investment Pact (TTIP) between the EU and the United States promises economic benefits for both sides, but the devil is in the details, and the timeline for completion is ambitious.

CIVILIAN POWER AND SECURITY POLICY

Nowhere is the change in Germany's international role more apparent than in its security policy. Until the 1990s, checkbook diplomacy was the preferred way to show international solidarity and responsibility. Based on Article 87a of the Basic Law, Germany shied away from direct involvement in military conflict in "out-of-area" operations and instead provided financial assistance to defray the costs. However, first the Gulf War in 1990–1991, then the conflicts in the former Yugoslavia, rendered this position increasingly untenable. Pressure mounted on the Kohl government to engage

Box 3.3   Speech by Federal Chancellor Angela Merkel before the U.S. Congress, November 3, 2009

I would like to thank you for the great honor and privilege to address you today, shortly before the 20th anniversary of the fall of the Berlin Wall.

I am the second German Chancellor on whom this honor has been bestowed. The first was Konrad Adenauer when he addressed both Houses of Congress in 1957, albeit one after the other.

Our lives could not have been more different. In 1957 I was just a small child of three years. I lived with my parents in Brandenburg, a region that belonged to the German Democratic Republic (GDR), the part of Germany that was not free. My father was a Protestant pastor. My mother, who had studied English and Latin to become a teacher, was not allowed to work in her chosen profession in the GDR.

In 1957 Konrad Adenauer was already 81 years old. He had lived through the German Empire, the First World War, the Weimar Republic and the Second World War. The National Socialists ousted him from his position as mayor of the city of Cologne. After the war, he was among the men and women who helped build up the free, democratic Federal Republic of Germany.

Nothing is more symbolic of the Federal Republic of Germany than its constitution, the Basic Law, or "Grundgesetz." It was adopted exactly 60 years ago. Article 1 of the Grundgesetz proclaims, and I quote, "Human dignity shall be inviolable." This short, simple sentence—"Human dignity shall be inviolable"—was the answer to the catastrophe that was the Second World War, to the murder of six million Jews in the Holocaust, to the hate, destruction and annihilation that Germany brought upon Europe and the world.

November 9th is just a few days away. It was on November 9, 1989, that the Berlin Wall fell and it was also on November 9 in 1938 that an indelible mark was branded into Germany's memory and Europe's history. On that day the National Socialists destroyed synagogues, setting them on fire, and murdered countless people. It was the beginning of what led to the break with civilization, the Shoah. I cannot stand before you today without remembering the victims of this day and of the Shoah.

. . .

Not even in my wildest dreams could I have imagined, twenty years ago before the Wall fell, that this would happen. It was beyond imagination then to even think about traveling to the United States of America let alone standing here today.

The land of unlimited opportunity—for a long time it was impossible for me to reach. The Wall, barbed wire and the order to shoot those who tried to leave limited my access to the free world. So I had to create my own picture of the United States from films and books, some of which were smuggled in from the West by relatives.

What did I see and what did I read? What was I passionate about?

I was passionate about the American dream—the opportunity for everyone to be successful, to make it in life through their own personal effort.

I, like many other teenagers, was passionate about a certain brand of jeans that were not available in the GDR and which my aunt in West Germany regularly sent to me.

I was passionate about the vast American landscape which seemed to breathe the very spirit of freedom and independence. Immediately in 1990 my husband and I traveled for the first time in our lives to America, to California. We will never forget our first glimpse of the Pacific Ocean. It was simply gorgeous.

(continued)

Box 3.3 (Continued)

I was passionate about all of these things and much more, even though until 1989 America was simply out of reach for me. And then, on November 9, 1989, the Berlin Wall came down. The border that for decades had divided a nation into two worlds was now open.

And that is why for me today is, first of all, the time to say thank you.

. . .

Where there was once only a dark wall, a door suddenly opened and we all walked through it: onto the streets, into the churches, across the borders. Everyone was given the chance to build something new, to make a difference, to venture a new beginning. I also started anew. I left my job as a physicist at the Academy of Sciences in East Berlin behind me and went into politics. Because I finally had the chance to make a difference. Because I had the impression that now it was possible to change things. It was possible for me to do something.

. . .

Ladies and gentlemen, it is true that America and Europe have had their share of disagreements. One may feel the other is sometimes too hesitant and fearful, or from the opposite perspective, too headstrong and pushy. And nevertheless, I am deeply convinced that there is no better partner for Europe than America and no better partner for America than Europe. Because what brings Europeans and Americans together and keeps them together is not just a shared history. What brings and keeps Europeans and Americans together are not just shared interests and the common global challenges that all regions of the world face. That alone would not be sufficient to explain the very special partnership between Europe and America and make it last. It is more than that. That which brings Europeans and Americans closer together and keeps them close is a common basis of shared values. It is a common idea of the individual and his inviolable dignity. It is a common understanding of freedom in responsibility. This is what we stand for in the unique transatlantic partnership and in the community of shared values that is NATO. This is what fills "Partnership in Leadership" with life, ladies and gentlemen.

. . .

I am convinced that, just as we found the strength in the 20th century to tear down a wall made of barbed wire and concrete, today we have the strength to overcome the walls of the 21st century, walls in our minds, walls of short-sighted self-interest, walls between the present and the future.

Ladies and gentlemen, my confidence is inspired by a very special sound—that of the Freedom Bell in the Schöneberg Town Hall in Berlin. Since 1950 a copy of the original American Liberty Bell has hung there. A gift from American citizens, it is a symbol of the promise of freedom, a promise that has been fulfilled. On October 3, 1990, the Freedom Bell rang to mark the reunification of Germany, the greatest moment of joy for the German people. On September 13, 2001, two days after 9/11, it tolled again, to mark America's darkest hour.

The Freedom Bell in Berlin is, like the Liberty Bell in Philadelphia, a symbol which reminds us that freedom does not come about of itself. It must be struggled for and then defended anew every day of our lives. In this endeavor Germany and Europe will also in future remain strong and dependable partners for America. That I promise you. Thank you very much.

Source: Copyright REGIERUNGonline: The Press and Information Office of the Federal Government.

members of the armed forces in humanitarian and crisis management. The Federal Constitutional Court's 1994 ruling on Article 87a opened the door for out-of-area military deployment, provided that it was part of multilateral operations and had the blessing of the United Nations and the approval of the Bundestag. Burning villages and ethnic cleansing in Bosnia-Herzegovina and Kosovo catalyzed a moral policy of "never again" (Auschwitz) and reinforced the prevailing notion of "never alone." In particular, the Green Party has its roots in the peace movement. Joschka Fischer, the respected foreign minister in both cabinets under Chancellor Gerhard Schröder, used his personal and his party's pacifist credentials to legitimize greater engagement in foreign and security policy. Pacifism and antifascism provided the basis for a new self-confidence. Many have argued that the acceptance of Germany's increased role in foreign and security policy at home and abroad owes much to the Red-Green leadership of confirmed pacifists.

In 1999, the postwar taboo on German military involvement was broken when the German Air Force engaged in the Kosovo conflict. Since then, Germany has rapidly widened the scope of its military operations. In 1998, about 2,000 soldiers were engaged in humanitarian and peacekeeping operations abroad. At the beginning of the twenty-first century, the number had risen to over 8,000, making Germany one of the major sources of international troops. In mid-2013, about 6,600 German soldiers were deployed in Africa, Asia, and Europe. Germany's military mission has shifted from territorial defense to crisis management and international conflict prevention, including the fight against terrorism. Its widening military engagement has been accompanied by ongoing reform of the armed forces, including the switch to a professional army, yet the desire to cut military spending both drives and hampers it.

In line with its security policy, military activities are pursued within the framework of international organizations: NATO, the EU, the UN, and the Organization for Security and Cooperation in Europe. Of the countries that contributed troops to the Afghan battlefield, Germany supplied the third-largest contingent. Often criticized abroad, they have been employed in the safer northern part of the country, where war casualties are lower. Defending German security interests in the "Hindu Kush," taking up the phrase by former Defense Minister Peter Struck (SPD) to rationalize German involvement in the Afghan conflict, remained a difficult sell for all governments. While a cross-party consensus to support German involvement held, excepting the Left Party, the German government, like many other governments involved in the Afghan war, was under pressure to set a timetable for withdrawal. Troop reductions are to be completed by the end of 2014; in 2015, about eight hundred soldiers will take their place to support NATO's ongoing mission.

The shift to a more engaged foreign and security policy remains incomplete and hesitant. For example, in the March 2011 UN Security Council vote authorizing actions to protect civilians against Libya's Gaddafi regime, Germany abstained. This vote was received with consternation, if not shock, abroad but was also criticized by policy experts at home. Not only did Germany side with Russia and China, but also the abstention contradicted the established German principles of multilateralism (to act with its major allies), endorsement of UN interventions, and commitment to humanitarian actions. In a nutshell, the Libya decision exposed a conundrum for German policymakers: how can they fulfill international obligations when the public at home is averse to risk and military engagement? In recent crises from Syria to Mali, Germany has pursued a cautious, largely noninterventionist approach, reinforcing its image as a military lightweight in the body of an economic heavyweight, and restricting itself to geo-economic but not geopolitical power.[19]

The New Germany

In the long view of history, the period of separation into a communist-governed eastern Germany and a democratic western Germany turned out to be a mere interlude, and German politics is most often analyzed as the continuous development of the Federal Republic of Germany. At first, radical transformation of the former GDR seemed the price of continuity in the West. One part of the country was to change according to the parameters set by the other. However, the sense of continuity was deceiving; new transitions, as I suggest here, seized the unified Germany, affecting policies, institutions, and identity.

In domestic affairs, much has changed since unification more than twenty years ago. Federalism is alive but also altered due to the addition of the former East Germany. The changing party landscape is the result of declining party identification and shifting voter preferences. The combined forces of globalization, Europeanization, and unification ratcheted up pressure for policy adjustments and, with some delay, have unleashed forces for policy change. Looking back on the history of the Federal Republic, institutional and policy changes have been marked by a distinct preference for piecemeal approaches and consensual conflict-solving mechanisms rather than radical transformations. This tradition continues; most reforms have been incremental and, with few exceptions, refrain from altering basic structures dramatically. Nevertheless, the sum of the small steps can amount to "subterranean shifts";[20] reforming the reforms is an ongoing process.

Taking stock of more than twenty years of unification is an exercise in weighing pros and cons; assessments vary depending on the criteria and the benchmarks used. If we are primarily interested in economic and political convergence between East and West and the tearing down of mental barriers, then we must concede that unity between East and West has not been accomplished. However, if we shift the focus and ask whether democratic stability has been maintained; economic transformation, painful as it was, completed; and progress made toward integrating the two parts of the country, then the balance is more impressive. Most importantly, there is no desire to turn back the wheel of history to the period before 1989; in survey after survey, an overwhelming majority of Germans endorse unification.

The euro crisis preoccupied leaders, exposing the unsettled nature of German influence, particularly when viewing its European policy within the framework of its foreign and security policy. "Despite the upheavals of the past two decades," the *Economist* wrote in 2011, "Germany's dilemma has not changed: Even with its waxing economic power, it is too small to wield global influence alone. Yet, within Europe it is too big to act freely without provoking resistance."[21] Polish Foreign Minister Radek

Sikorski remarked, "I fear German power less than I am beginning to fear German inactivity."[22] The uneasy combination of more assertiveness and lack of international vision or strategy has prompted criticism abroad and at home. Anti-German rhetoric accompanied street protests and media accounts in many of the southern European countries, demonstrating the shallowness of European identity and how the past can be put to use. Not long after observers credited Germany with "competent normalcy" or "muted normalcy,"[23] the euro crisis may have reopened the "German question" in new and unanticipated ways.

Notes

Except for a later addition of some election coverage and the September 2013 results, this chapter was updated in April 2013.

1. Various Christian-based political groups organized in 1945, but party consolidation across zones of occupation soon led to the emergence of the Christian Democratic Union (CDU). Political leaders of the Christian Social Union (CSU) in Bavaria decided to remain separate; the anomaly of two conservative parties, with many programmatic similarities but divided by region, persists. The CDU is the main center-right party in all parts of Germany except Bavaria; its so-called sister party, the CSU, exists only as a Bavarian regional party. This chapter treats the two as one since they almost always act in unison at the federal level, occasional tensions notwithstanding.

2. C. K. Williams, "Das symbolische Volk der Täter," *Die Zeit* 46 (2002): http://www.zeit .de/2002/46/Symbol (accessed January 11, 2014).

3. Tony Judt, *Postwar: A History of Europe since 1945* (New York: Penguin Press, 2005), 826.

4. For more detail, see Jeffrey M. Peck, *Being Jewish in the New Germany* (New Brunswick, NJ: Rutgers University Press, 2006).

5. For a very readable account of Germany's road to normality, see Steve Crawshaw, *Easier Fatherland: Germany and the Twenty-First Century* (London: Continuum, 2004).

6. "Es ist noch viel Arbeit zu erledigen" (interview with Angela Merkel), *Süddeutsche Zeitung*, September 11, 2009, http://www.sueddeutsche.de/politik/972/487380/text/print.html (accessed January 11, 2014).

7. Quoted in *Deutschland Magazine* 6, no. 4 (special issue on Berlin) (2007).

8. Beate Kohler-Koch, "Europäisierung: Plädoyer für eine Horizonterweiterung," in *Deutschland zwischen Europäisierung und Selbstbehauptung*, ed. Michèle Knodt and Beate Kohler-Koch (Frankfurt: Campus Verlag, 2000), 11.

9. The list is partially taken from Gunther Hellmann, "Precarious Power: Germany at the Dawn of the Twenty-First Century," in *Germany's New Foreign Policy: Decision-Making in an Interdependent World*, ed. Wolf-Dieter Eberwein and Karl Kaiser (New York: Palgrave, 2001), 293.

10. Beverly Crawford, "The Normative Power of a Normal State: Power and Revolutionary Vision in Germany's Post-Wall Foreign Policy," *German Politics and Society* 28, no. 2 (Summer 2010): 169–70.

11. Simon J. Bulmer, "Shaping the Rules? The Constitutive Politics of the European Union and German Power," in *Tamed Power: Germany in Europe*, ed. Peter J. Katzenstein (Ithaca: Cornell University Press, 1997), 50.

12. Charles Lees, "'Dark Matter': Institutional Constraints and the Failure of Party-Based Euroscepticism in Germany," *Political Studies* 50, no. 2 (2002): 244–67.

13. Jacques Delors et al., "Heute muss man die Deutschen von Europa überzeugen. Ein Gespräch mit Jacques Delors," *Leviathan* 38 (2010): 1–21 (my translation).

14. David P. Calleo, "Germany's Alarming Disaffection," *Current History* 112, no. 752 (March 2013): 114–17.

15. See Hanns W. Maull, "Deutsche Außenpolitik: Orientierungslos," *Zeitschrift für Politikwissenschaft* 21, no. 1 (2011): 113.

16. See Christoph Schönberger, "Hegemon wider Willen. Zur Stellung Deutschlands in der Europäischen Union," *Merkur. Zeitschrift für europäisches Denken* 66, no. 1 (January 2012): 8; see also the sequel by the same author, "Nochmals: Die deutsche Hegemonie," *Merkur. Zeitschrift für europäisches Denken* 67, no. 1 (January 2013): 25–33.

17. Ulrike Guérot and Mark Leonard, *The New German Question: How Europe Can Get the Germany It Needs*, Policy Brief 30, April (London: European Council on Foreign Relations, 2011), 10.

18. Pew Research, "Obama More Popular Abroad than at Home, Global Image of U.S. Continues to Benefit," Nation Pew Global Attitudes Survey, June 17, 2010, http://pew research.org/pubs/1630/obama-more-popular-abroad-global-american-image-benefit-22 -nation-global-survey (accessed January 11, 2014).

19. Hans Kundnani, "Paradoxon Deutschland. Eine geoökonomische Macht in der Zwickmühle," *Internationale Politik* 6 (November–December 2011): 62–67.

20. Perry Anderson, "A New Germany?" *New Left Review* 57 (May–June 2009): 5–40.

21. "German Foreign Policy: The Unadventurous Eagle," *Economist*, May 14, 2011, 64.

22. Cited in "Germany and the Euro: Don't Make Us Führer," *Economist*, April 13, 2013, 53.

23. Konrad H. Jarausch, "The Federal Republic at Sixty: Popular Myths, Actual Accomplishments and Competing Interpretations," *German Politics and Society* 28, no. 1 (Spring 2010), 25; and "A Muted Normalcy," in "Older and Wiser: A Special Report on Germany," *Economist*, March 13, 2010, 15–16.

Suggested Readings

Anderson, Jeffrey J., and Eric Langenbacher, eds. *From the Bonn to the Berlin Republic: Germany at the Twentieth Anniversary of Unification*. New York: Berghahn, 2010.

Bulmer, Simon et al., eds. *Rethinking Germany and Europe: Democracy and Diplomacy in a Semi-Sovereign State*. Houndsmill, Basingstoke: Palgrave Macmillan, 2010.

Crawford, Beverly. *Power and German Foreign Policy: Embedded Hegemony in Europe*. Houndsmill, Basingstoke: Palgrave Macmillan, 2007.

Crawshaw, Steve. *Easier Fatherland: Germany and the Twenty-First Century*. London: Continuum, 2004.

German Historical Institute. *German History in Documents and Images*. http://www.ghi-dc .org (accessed January 11, 2014) (a collection of primary source materials documenting Germany's political, social, and cultural history from 1500 to the present).

Jarausch, Konrad H., ed. *United Germany: Debating Processes and Prospects*. New York: Berghahn, 2013.

Peck, Jeffrey M. *Being Jewish in the New Germany*. New Brunswick, NJ: Rutgers University Press, 2006.

Ritter, Gerhard. *The Price of German Unity: Reunification and the Crisis of the Welfare State.* Oxford: Oxford University Press, 2011.

Sarotte, Mary Elise. *1989: The Struggle to Create Post–Cold War Europe.* Princeton, NJ: Princeton University Press, 2009.

Wittlinger, Ruth. *German National Identity in the Twenty-First Century: A Different Republic after All?* Basingstoke: Palgrave Macmillan, 2010.

Zelikow, Philip, and Condoleezza Rice. *Germany United and Europe Transformed: A Study in Statecraft.* Cambridge, MA: MIT University Press, 1995.

SPECIALIZED SCHOLARLY JOURNALS AND THEIR PUBLISHERS

German Politics (Taylor & Francis)
German Politics and Society (Berghahn)
IP Journal (German Council on Foreign Relations)

CHAPTER 4

Italy

STILL THE AGE OF BERLUSCONI?

Gianfranco Baldini

Italy

Population (million):	59.4
Area in Square Miles:	116,320
Population Density in Square Miles:	511
GDP (in billion dollars, 2012):	$1,863
GDP per Capita (PPP, 2012):	$30,600
Joined EC/EU:	January 1, 1958

Performance of Key Political Parties in Parliamentary Elections of February 24–25, 2013

Coalition Pier Luigi Bersani:	29.5%
Democratic Party	25.4%
Left Ecology Freedom	3.2%
Coalition Silvio Berlusconi:	29.2%
People of Liberty:	21.6%
Northern League (LN)	4.1%
Five Star Movement	25.6%
Coalition Mario Monti:	10.6%
Civic Choice	8.3%
Union of the Centre	1.8%

Main Officeholders: Prime Minister: Matteo Renzi, Democratic Party; and Head of State: Giorgio Napolitano, DS (2013)

Seen from the United States, Italian politics has always been problematic. Government instability, corruption, Mafia, scandals, lack of trust (or "amoral familism")—these are among the words most frequently associated with Italian politics during the so-called First Republic (1946–1992). Things did not change much after 1992, despite the collapse of the old party system. Over the last twenty years, Italian politics has been dominated by the controversial figure of Silvio Berlusconi. Since his first electoral victory in 1994, he was prime minister three times for a total of almost a decade, thus becoming the longest serving head of government in postwar Italian history. Berlusconi's dominance in Italian politics has been so consistent that in 2013 he has been able to "win by losing" the general elections. In November 2011, market pressures—and a deteriorated international credibility—led to Berlusconi's resignation as prime minister. After being pushed in third position by a very thin center-left victory, and by the Beppe Grillo's Five Star Movement (M5S) breakthrough, Berlusconi managed to get most out of a predictable defeat. Indeed, the birth of the grand-coalition government in the spring of 2013, led by Enrico Letta, testifies to Berlusconi's capacity to survive as a key protagonist, even after losing more than 40 percent of his votes when compared to 2008.

Because of the peculiarities mentioned above, Italy has often been treated as a "special case" of liberal democracy, thereby emphasizing the political system's many anomalies.[1] This chapter explains why Italy has been a "troubled democracy" ever since its birth as a republic in 1946, and to some extent a problematic polity ever since the foundation of the modern Italian state in 1861. As debates on Italian politics are still dominated by discussions about a transition to a new—second or third, depending on the perspectives adopted—republic, this chapter will take a somewhat longer historical view than the other country studies in this volume.

The Weight of the Past

The most important thing to understand about modern Italy is how much baggage it carries from the past 150 years. Certain influences have emerged at each of the many stages of its development. And, like country houses or furniture, they have been passed down from one generation to the next. The following are particularly important: weak governments, unstable majorities, clientelism, low perceptions of legitimacy, poor social capital, and a ubiquitous North-South dichotomy.

Italy was born as a state in 1861, after the Kingdom of Sardinia (which was based in Piedmont) managed to unify a territory that had been plagued by rivalries and fragmentation for centuries. The Savoy monarchy led an elitist annexation of the ten existing kingdoms. The result was unsuccessful in centralizing authority, and Italian governments were weak ever since state unification.

The Italian state inherited its basic institutional structure from the Kingdom of Sardinia: the Albertine Statute (1848) set up a parliamentary monarchy that was replaced exactly a century later by the Italian Constitution (1948). Prime ministers were constrained on the one side by the powers of the monarchy (the king alone had executive power, which meant he alone could appoint and dismiss ministers) and on the other side by scrutiny provided by parliament.

At the parliamentary level, political affiliations were weak. As a result, many deputies of both left and right used to switch sides to pave the way for the succession of the different governments. This practice—called *trasformismo*—meant that coalitions were unstable and yet no real political alternation took place. In other words, governments were weak but political leaders were also unaccountable to the electorate. This practice had enduring consequences for the development of the political system.

At the societal level, relations between political elites and the electorate were mainly conducted on the basis of clientelistic exchanges, meaning that "deputies were bribed into supporting the government by the uninhibited use of patronage, both for themselves (honours, cabinet posts) and for their constituencies (railways, bridges, government contracts). It required delicate balancing of personal and local interests, and led to numerous changes of government as cabinets were reshuffled and new interest satisfied."[2]

In such a context, "left" and "right" were empty labels. Meanwhile, elected officials tended to develop unhealthy relationships with the civil servants who controlled access to state resources. For example, various Liberal notables managed to control their own constituencies thanks to the help they got from the prefects, the "local guardians" of the state power. Italy was very fragmented, poor, and illiterate, and its political institutions were mainly framed in order to govern a backward society from the center: more local government autonomy would have probably meant the breakup of the polity. Moreover, Italy's early politicians were well aware of the fragile nature of the Italian state. Hence, they incorporated the use of prefects to extend the power of the central government and so bind the country together in administrative terms. In effect, they inadvertently created the institutions for centralized patronage as well.[3]

If elites were aware of the fragility of the state, the masses were aware of its intrusiveness. The process of state building never managed to gain full popular consent—let alone mass enthusiasm. In fact, the masses often saw unification as an imposition: the *Risorgimento* (or, more colloquially, the process of Italian unification) was never a popular phenomenon and was later viewed with suspicion by both Catholics and Communists—who constituted the two most important political groups until the collapse of the First Republic in 1992. This skepticism was linked to conflicting loyalties vis-à-vis the new Italian polity, mainly coming from the Catholic electorate and the southern regions. When Italy was born as a state, the papacy (based in the Vatican, in Rome) did not want to give up its powers; the *non expedit* (1868) meant that Catholics should not take part in politics (being "neither elector nor elected"). Although it was progressively relaxed, the *non expedit* was finally abrogated only in 1919, the year after the first Catholic party, Don Luigi Sturzo's Italian Popular Party (PPI), came into being. This process was particularly problematic in the South, where higher levels of religious practice were complemented by a violent struggle against the state-building process: brigandage was among the most powerful manifestations of hostility toward unification, to such an extent that it has frequently been likened to a civil war.

In such a context, it is not surprising that the democratization process was both contested and only partially successful. Although Massimo D'Azeglio's famous phrase "We have made Italy, now we must make Italians" has become one of the most cited clichés on Italy, the saying bears more than a grain of truth: making Italians proved to be much more complicated than making Italian institutions. Social inequality and fragmentation were extensive. By the turn of the nineteenth century, Italy had the highest rates of illiteracy in Western Europe, and the second-highest percentage of employees in the primary (or agricultural) sector; almost forty years after unification, truancy among school-aged children still reached 80 percent in some southern areas.[4]

Moreover, late extension of the franchise (near-universal voting rights or "suffrage" for men was introduced only in 1913) meant that all main political parties were weak and had extraparliamentary origins. The Catholics were an obvious example, because of their roots in the institutions of the Church, but this was true also for nonreligious ideological groups such as the Socialists and the Republicans. The extraparliamentary origins of the major political parties had important implications for the post–World War I period. The Liberals, who had always governed during the late nineteenth and early twentieth centuries, lacked a strong institutional structure. The other main political parties were marginally better organized and yet only gained access to seats in parliament when proportional representation (PR) was introduced in 1919.

After PR was introduced, the other parties gained more influence over parliament. However, contrary to the experience in many other Western European countries, this change did not lead to democratization as expressed in terms of an abiding and widespread commitment of the electorate to the maintenance of democratic principles. Just a few years after incorporating the masses into the political process through the extension of voting rights, the Italian democratic system was still unprepared to face the combined pressures of a deep economic crisis, revanchist sentiments coming out of the First World War, and a radical mobilization of the workforce.[5] Weak and divided parties were unable to govern such convulsive processes, and their divisions gave way to the rise of Fascism.

The actual experience of Fascism is less important to our understanding of the current situation than the impact this experience had on Italian political attitudes and economic institutions. The Fascist regime left crucial legacies to the (second and more successful) democratization process that took place in the years that surrounded the birth of Italy as a republic in 1946. On the political side, the main legacy was to be found in the peculiar path that led to the fall of Fascism and the subsequent armistice. Indeed, the final two years of the war affected "the whole organism of the Italian state, almost causing—in reality and, most importantly, in the imagination—its virtual disappearance."[6] Hence, the parties that emerged at the end of the Second World War did not share a common idea of the Italian nation; rather, what bound them together was their opposition to Fascism. By implication, popular perceptions of the legitimacy of the Italian state remained weak, and the points of difference both between and within the political parties remained significant. For example, the left-wing Resistance movement that emerged during the Second World War was affected by deep ideological divisions between its predominant radical component (led by the Italian Communist Party [PCI]) and a minority moderate one. Although the PCI soon developed more pragmatic positions on many issues, it remained committed to the belief that democracy is just a provisional step in the long march toward socialism.[7] The different visions held by the political parties involved in building a new post–World War II Italy—coupled with the enduring weakness of state legitimacy—meant that Italian democratization was difficult, even when compared to those other southern European countries that also experienced authoritarian regimes.

As far as the economy is concerned, Italy inherited from Fascism the second-largest public sector in Europe after the Soviet Union (USSR). Large, publicly owned holding companies created in the 1930s, such as the Industrial Reconstruction Institute (IRI) for industry and Istituto Mobiliare Italiano (IMI) for banking, were not dismantled after the war. Such institutions constituted a whole new arena for unhealthy relations to develop between elected officials and appointed civil servants—this time controlling industries rather than regions. As such, they became critical targets for partisan control.

Finally, it is important to consider the structure of life outside the Italian state—or what is called "civil society." Social institutions and the way they function exert a powerful influence on the attitudes and behavior of ordinary people. Some institutions have a very positive influence; others are more negative. Italy had both sorts. As a consequence, social capital, defined by Robert Putnam as "the features of social organization, such as trust, norms, and networks, that can improve the efficiency of society by facilitating coordinated actions," developed very differently in the North and South of the country.[8] In his study of Italian democracy, Putnam contends that different levels of social capital in different parts of the country gave rise to very different sorts of political outcomes. Though controversial, Robert Putnam's thesis underlines the deep-rooted historical reasons for the difference between Italy's North and South.

Putnam's overarching thesis is controversial, and yet few doubt that a wide array of social attitudes and structures is necessary to explain the North-South divide. Underdeveloped, opposed to unification, and resistant to what they perceived as the invaders coming from the North, the South was to provide the greatest socioeconomic challenges to the Italian political and economic system throughout its 150-year existence. As of 2013, some southern regions still display record-high levels of unemployment and poverty, also as a consequence of an ineffective use of European structural funds. Moreover, the South never completely reconciled with state authority: hence the great success of monarchical parties for as long as two decades after the birth of the Republic, and the success of criminal organizations (like the Sicilian Mafia) that still hamper the legitimacy of state institutions in vast areas of the country. The fact that the South has become, after the political crisis of the 1990s, the most volatile area when election time comes adds further significance to this question.

The Many Pathologies of the Italian First Republic

The defining characteristics of the Italian state during the first decades after unification were the distinguishing features of the First Italian Republic as well. Between the birth of the Republic (1946) and the fall of the Berlin Wall (1989), Italian politics was marked by significant continuities with the prewar regimes. Little or no alternation between left and right took place. Governments were weak because they were affected by many constraints aimed at avoiding the resurgence of Fascism. Consensual rules were built in order to tame radicalization. All this, together with the legacies of *trasformismo* and the increasing public resources available with the "economic miracle" of the 1960s, meant that the pathologies mentioned at the outset of this chapter came to affect Italian politics even more pervasively once democratization finally got hold.

Changes in government were limited to a restricted alternation between partners of the predominant Christian party (the Christian Democrats [DC]), which was *always* in government and which, until 1981, *always* selected the (many) prime ministers from among its ranks (see table 4.1). Meanwhile, the political system included antisystem parties ranging from the PCI on the left to the neo-Fascist Italian Social Movement (MSI) on the extreme right. This meant that the DC faced opposition on both sides of the left-right political spectrum seeking to challenge its hegemonic control over the center. It also meant that the ideological distance (or polarization) between left and right was great and that competition for votes was centrifugal and so kept the ideologies apart. Hence, Italy was a textbook case of what Italian political scientist Giovanni Sartori described as "polarized pluralism"—pluralist because of the many political movements it included, and yet polarized because these movements actively opposed each other as well as the governing majority and so resisted consensus.[9]

The polarization worked within as well as between the left and right of the political spectrum. The left camp was divided between the Socialists (the Italian Socialist party [PSI]) and PCI (see box 4.1). Until it condemned the USSR's invasion of Hungary in 1956, the PSI was still an orthodox Marxist party. On the extreme right, the MSI had to contend with the Monarchists. As a consequence, the first general elections in the Republic saw the antisystem (or antidemocratic) forces win almost as many seats as the pro-democracy moderates. These divisions had a regional dimension to them as well. Data from the 1946 referendum on the form of state (Monarchical or Republican) reveal that behind an overall 54.3 percent in favor of the Republic, as many as 85 percent of the voters supported change in the northern Trento Province, contrasted with as few as 23.5 percent in southern Campania. Finally, there was the overarching context of the Cold War. After Prime Minister Alcide De Gasperi's visit to the United States in 1947, the PCI was permanently excluded from government—a pattern only partly mitigated by the party's presence in the local government of important towns in the so-called Red Area (such as Florence and Bologna) and, after the late birth of regional institutions in 1970, at the leadership of regional governments in this same area. This Cold War dimension quickly permeated the whole structure of political competition with the result that a communist-anticommunist cleavage soon overshadowed the more traditional left-right dimension. This can be seen by looking at the very polarized 1948 elections, in which the DC and the Popular Front (a coalition of the PCI and PSI) fought a harsh battle that featured apocalyptic propaganda.

The institutions of the First Republic took shape before this freezing of political alternatives. As mentioned earlier, the consensus underpinning these new institutions was dominated by (and limited to) the fear of Fascism and the desire to prevent the reemergence of a tyrant like Benito Mussolini. Hence the Constitution of the Italian Republic included a panoply of liberal mechanisms (such as a broad array of entrenched civil and social rights, a president of the Republic with significant powers, and an independent judiciary) aimed at constraining the executive in favor of the strengthening the role of parliament. Similar checks and balances operated

Table 4.1 Italy's First Republic National Election (votes [v] and seats [s] for main parties, 1946–1992)

	Left Others[a]	PCI	Radicals and Greens[b]	PSI[c]	PSDI	DC	PRI	PLI	MSI	Mon/LN[d]	Others
1946 (v)	—	18.9		20.7	—	35.2	4.4	6.8	—	8.0	6.0
1946 (s)	—	18.7		20.7	—	37.2	4.1	7.4	—	8.3	3.6
1948 (v)	—		31.0		7.1	48.5	2.5	—	2.0	6.6	2.4
1948 (s)	—		31.9		5.7	53.1	1.6	—	1.0	5.7	0.9
1953 (v)	—	22.6		12.7	4.5	40.1	1.6	3.0	5.8	6.8	2.8
1953 (s)	—	24.2		12.7	3.2	44.6	0.8	2.2	4.9	6.8	0.5
1958 (v)	—	22.7		14.2	4.6	42.4	1.4	3.5	4.8	4.9	1.6
1958 (s)	—	23.5		14.1	3.7	45.8	1.3	2.9	4.0	4.2	0.5
1963 (v)	—	25.3		13.8	6.1	38.3	1.4	7.0	5.1	1.7	1.3
1963 (s)	—	26.3		13.8	5.2	41.3	1.0	6.2	4.3	1.3	0.6
1968 (v)	4.4	26.9		14.5		39.1	2.0	5.8	4.4	1.3	1.5
1968 (s)	3.7	28.1		14.4		42.2	1.4	4.9	3.8	1.0	0.5
1972 (v)	1.9	27.2		9.6	5.1	38.7	2.9	3.9	8.7	—	2.1
1972 (s)	0.0	28.4		9.7	4.6	42.2	2.4	3.2	8.9	—	0.6
1976 (v)	1.5	34.4	1.1	9.6	3.4	38.7	3.1	1.3	6.1	—	0.8
1976 (s)	1.0	36.0	0.6	9.0	2.4	41.7	2.2	0.8	5.6	—	0.6
1979 (v)	1.4	30.4	3.4	9.8	3.8	38.3	3.0	1.9	5.3	—	2.6
1979 (s)	1.0	31.9	2.9	9.8	3.2	41.6	2.5	1.4	4.8	—	1.0
1983 (v)	1.5	29.9	2.2	11.4	4.1	32.9	5.1	2.9	6.8	—	3.2
1983 (s)	1.1	31.4	1.7	11.6	3.7	35.7	4.6	2.5	6.7	—	1.0
1987 (v)	1.7	26.6	5.1	14.3	3.0	34.3	3.7	2.1	5.9	0.5	3.0
1987 (s)	1.3	28.1	4.1	14.9	2.7	37.1	3.3	1.7	5.6	0.2	1.0
1992 (v)	5.6	16.1 PDS	5.9	13.6	2.7	29.7	4.4	2.9	5.4	8.7	5.1
1992 (s)	5.6	17.0	5.6	14.6	2.5	32.7	4.3	2.7	5.4	8.7	1.0

[a] Sin = Various minor left-wing parties, including the Italian Socialist Party of Proletarian Unity in 1968; Proletarian Democracy in 1976, 1983, and 1987; the Proletarian Unity Party in 1979; and the Communist Refoundation Party in 1992.

[b] R/V = Radicals until 1983. 1987: Greens + Radicals (separate parties); 1992: same parties plus the Network (la Rete).

[c] 1968 PSU, where PSI and PSDI had merged.

[d] 1948: Uomo Qualunque; 1948–1968: Monarchists, different labels; as of 1987: Lega lombarda/Lega Nord.

Source: Istituto Cattaneo.

Box 4.1   Chronology of Main Events Triggering the Crisis of the First Republic

1. *November 1989*: Fall of the Berlin Wall. This event took the PCI by surprise. Party leader Achille Occhetto announced a change in party brand just a few days after the wall fell. But this left the activists puzzled as to where the newly branded Democratic Party of the Left (the PDS, born in 1991) were going, triggering a split of Re-founded Communists and significant electoral backlashes in 1992.
2. *May 1990 regional elections*: Umberto Bossi's Lombard League, to be merged in the Northern League the following year, becomes the second most voted party in Lombardy, the richest and most populated Italian region.
3. *June 1991*: Referendum on single preference vote. Despite invitations from both governing parties to boycott the poll (especially PSI party leader Bettino Craxi, who suggested that voters should go to the beaches instead of voting) and the Northern League not to go to the polls, 65% of Italians do go, and 91% of the voters approve change. By cutting "exchange vote" practices by the different chiefs of party factions, the referendum was meant to be a proxy for a change toward majoritarianism, and popular pressure for reform mounted significantly as a consequence of the referendum's success.
4. *February 1992*: This arguably was the month that sowed the seeds of change in an unprecedented manner. In Maastricht, Giulio Andreotti signs the new Treaty. A week after, the Milanese PSI Mario Chiesa is arrested in Milan: it is the first of a long series of arrests in the judicial investigations of *Mani pulite*, "clean hands," which will decapitate the governing parties.

---

within the parliament as well as in the form of three broad procedural principles. First, the parliament provided a "parity norm" protecting the relative positions of all political actors based on both their proportional representation of the electorate and very consensual rules of procedure. Second, the parliament placed both the upper and lower chambers (the Senate and the Chamber of Deputies) on equal footing in a form of balanced bicameralism that remains unique among advanced industrial democracies. Third, the parliamentary structures were built on a broader logic of "institutional polycentrism" that creates many different and at times even countervailing positions of power and influence. As a result, the PCI was able to play an active role in Italian political life at the national level despite the fact that it was perpetually excluded from participation in the government.[10]

The combination of antifascism and bitter polarization explains why the institutions created during the democratization process became so entrenched. Institutions designed to prevent the emergence of a single powerful political force made it easy for multiple competing parties to protect themselves and so resist destruction. This was particularly the case for the electoral system—a very inclusive form of proportional representation—which, despite being written in statute and so not being part of the actual constitution, soon became part and parcel with the Italian First Republic. Of course, the DC had an interest in changing this situation given its hegemonic control of the political center. The problem was that it did not have the power to do so when acting alone. Once the DC failed to nail down its parliamentary majority with a change in the electoral formula in the 1953 elections,[11] all political parties developed vested interests in maintaining PR as the status quo. Indeed, PR soon developed as the best guarantee for sharing the spoils in government—which all of the main parties but the PCI and MSI were to enter—as well as gaining access to seats in parliament and control over regional or local executives for the PCI.

The DC may have failed to reshape the electoral arena to ensure a permanent majority, but it nevertheless managed to get a strong hold on the economy. This colonization of state resources by the DC operated first through the holding companies left over from Fascism and then reached its peak in the 1950s, with the creation of ENI (Ente Nazionale Idrocarburi—the state-controlled energy conglomerate) and the Cassa per il mezzogiorno (a development aid agency for the South), and the Ministry of State's participation, which the party always kept for itself until the 1980s. At the same time, the DC was able to influence and exploit interest groups and public administration at its own service. This meant that the governing parties (meaning the DC and its ever-widening circle of allies) were eager to hold a strict control over appointments. Nevertheless, because the lack of alternation weakened lines of accountability, the governing parties maintained a more tenuous control over policymaking (which was often dictated by long-term civil servants).

Political parties controlled the institutions of the First Republic and they also managed to dominate civil society.[12] In part, this was due to the role of the parties as agents of political socialization. In their polarized and clientelistic competition with one another, the parties failed to play any integrative role across society as a whole and thus jeopardized the development of social capital and the recognition of civic responsibilities.[13] Party system stability—and the "unstable stability" format that came to be associated with Italian governments more generally—was also built on very stable patterns of electoral behavior, whose determinants were not easily captured by traditional cleavages such as class or religion.

In fact, territory was very important at least for two of the three categories of voting identified in the mid-1970s as the bases of party voters' linkages: belonging, exchange, and opinion.[14] In some parts of the country, for example, partisan identification was socially embedded in regional subcultures. This social embeddedness was most obvious in the areas where the two main parties—DC and PCI—managed to aggregate and mediate interests by exploiting cooperative social networks and high levels of social capital. The DC predominated in the Northeast with Trentino-Alto Adige, Friuli-Venezia Giulia, and Veneto; the PCI controlled the Center-North with Emilia-Romagna, Tuscany, and Umbria, as well as the northern province of Marche. In this way, a "vote of belonging" to the subculture of the region also reflected the voter's long-standing affective loyalty to the party concerned (estimated to be typical of a majority of voters still at the end of the 1980s).

Elsewhere in the country, local ties hindered the politicization of the center-periphery cleavage. This was particularly important in Sicily and across the South. Hence the few existing regionalist parties developed in the rich northern areas of Valle d'Aosta or Alto Adige and in Sardinia, even though Sardinian nationalism had never been a problem. Meanwhile, the South developed as a crucial basin for the DC vote as well as an area where "exchange" voting—meaning votes cast in return for the satisfaction of a need or in return for the meeting of a particular interest—was more developed. By contrast, "opinion" voting, where voters cast their ballots based on a pragmatic evaluation of the competing party platforms, was much less in evidence.

The postelectoral nature of Italian governments was broadly consistent with these patterns of electoral choice. Instead of being determined by results at the polls, the composition of Italian governments soon came to be dictated by factional agreements within the DC or between the DC and its allies. This factional dominance over government composition was only reinforced once PR was introduced as the internal rule in DC party congresses in the early 1960s. The result was a degenerative pathology of spoils divisions among the different *capi-corrente* (chiefs of factions), who numbered twelve at the peak of the factionalization process in the early 1980s. With a system frozen along stable partisan lines and the PCI permanently excluded from power, the first unanticipated election took place only in 1972. Despite Italy's reputation for weak and changeable governments, all previous parliaments had been able to complete their full legislative terms.[15]

Foreign Policy: The Least of the Great Powers

The combination of polarization and an absence of left-right alternation affected Italy's international status as well as its political performance throughout the First Republic. Italy has traditionally been described as "the least of the great powers" or "the largest of the smaller powers."[16] This reputation is not for wont of ambition. Because of its geographical location, Italy always cultivated a Mediterranean vocation. Italy also laid claim to an early Atlantic affiliation. Nevertheless, the facts that Italy was always changing its alliances during the wars, that the Iron Curtain had its southwestern-most border in Trieste (where Italy contended with Yugoslavia), and that Italy hosted the largest Communist Party in Western Europe all meant that the United States never regarded Italy as an easy or reliable ally. Moreover, any American suspicion of Italy was more than reciprocated by Italians looking at the United States. Anti-Americanism was strong not just inside the two antisystem forces, PCI and MSI, but also in the PSI—at least until Hungary's invasion in 1956—and, throughout the First Republic, inside a sizable component of the Catholic world, including the leadership of the DC itself.

Italy was among the founding signatory countries of both the NATO and European Economic Community (EEC) treaties (the latter having been launched in Messina in 1955 and signed in Rome in 1957). However, neither choice was uncontentious. In the 1950s, some DC leaders such as Giuseppe Dossetti and Giorgio La Pira were hostile to NATO membership (and President of the Republic Giovanni Gronchi arguably culti-vated "micro-Gaullist" aspirations at the turn of the 1960s), not to mention the more natural hostility displayed by the PCI until the 1970s. Indeed, when PCI party leader Enrico Berlinguer, on the eve of his party's best ever electoral result, declared that he felt safe under the NATO umbrella (1976), hostility within the PCI toward Europe had already been significantly reduced. Of course, European integration was somewhat easier to accept than NATO because of the spread of Euro-communism in the 1970s—not to mention the fact that one of Europe's founding fathers, Altiero Spinelli, was elected as an independent on the PCI ticket in the first European elections of 1979.

Outside the domain of the communists, attitudes to Europe were also mixed. De Gasperi was a convinced Europeanist, as were most of the members of his centrist governments. For its part, public opinion was distant but positive about EEC membership. Nevertheless, much of the political class was only lukewarm. For them, "Brussels was considered a sort of exile from the delicious intrigues and power-brokering of Montecitorio" (the location of the lower House of Parliament in Rome).[17] Suffice it to mention here the fact that the first Italian to be nominated president of the European Commission, the Christian Democrat Franco Maria Malfatti, in 1970, left his post after less than two years in order to take part in the Italian general elections of 1972.

Despite the mixed emotions shared between Italy and the United States, Italy has long been an American semiprotectorate. The country was protected in its strategic affiliation with NATO during the Cold War, but was also a democracy that enjoyed full sovereignty (and that despite frequent claims that Italian sovereignty was actually still limited).[18] So if protection meant interference in domestic affairs, this did not affect day-to-day politics in the Italo-American relationship. Indeed, both sides were quickly able to overcome significant moments of tension. Hence, U.S. administrations accepted the PSI's entry into government in the early 1960s. By the same token, the Sigonella incident (1985), when PSI party leader and Prime Minister Bettino Craxi refused the request of U.S. President Ronald Reagan to extradite the hijackers of the cruise ship *Achille Lauro*, should not be read as a sign of anti-Americanism. Rather, it was part of an attempt to raise Italian international status above its low profile. This episode, at the same time, was just part of a patchwork of Italian ambiguities—from Enrico Mattei's ENI Middle East policy in the late 1950s to the convention that saw for many years the cohabitation of pro-Israeli and pro-Palestine politicians balancing Italian foreign policy in the Ministries of Foreign Affairs and the Ministry of Defense or vice versa.

Therefore, one can argue that during the Cold War, Italy was at the same time firmly located on the Western side, and perceived as a kind of unfaithful ally, to be watched carefully for its delicate geopolitical position, the underlying strength of anti-American sentiments inside both predominant Italian political cultures (Catholic and Marxist), and some recurrent anomalies such as those mentioned above. At the same time, one can argue that both NATO and the EEC, together with the Vatican just a few hundred meters from the loci of power—the office of the prime minister (Palazzo Chigi), the houses of parliament (Montecitorio and Palazzo Madama), and the office of the president (Quirinale)—framed Italian political life during the First Republic. Once the First Republic was over, former President of the Republic Francesco Cossiga articulated this point at its best: "[During the First Republic] we had compulsory constraints: our military policy was based on NATO, our economic policy was that of to the EEC, our ideology was that of the Church. At most we could take some break, thanks to the strategic security guaranteed from the outside."[19]

To sum up, the First Republic was a dysfunctional system. Political parties dominated the public sphere by exploiting the weakness of the state to their own benefit. This colonization of state institutions by political parties had particularly negative consequences in the South, where distrust vis-à-vis the state was traditionally higher, and where clienteles were built upon state-dependent beneficiaries like public officials and state-subsidized businesses, to such an extent that borders between local control of the "exchange vote" and highly successful criminal organizations such as the Sicilian Mafia, Campania's Camorra, and Calabria's 'Ndrangheta became more and more blurred. Lack of alternation meant also that parties did not compete on substantive programmatic issues. This, combined with the factionalized control over government composition—and therefore the substantial lack of direct accountability to the voter—meant that parties in government could use public resources without restraint, thus fueling public debt. Rather, competition was often centered on micropolicies, such as those linked to patronage and the control of preference voting. Indeed, while preference voting gave the appearance of creating more direct popular influence on the political process, it actually became the main mechanism through which party factions could prosper and cultivate their slice of the cake.

Toward a Second Republic?

In the early 1990s, Italy underwent one of the most dramatic transitions that any Western European democracy has experienced in the last sixty years, with the exception of France in 1958. Indeed, at its height there was speculation as to whether Italian democracy had the capacity to survive. The crisis was all the more dramatic because it came after the decade during which the five-party formula (*pentapartito*) saw the extension of *partitocrazia* (or party dominance over state institutions and resources) to its greatest extent. Meanwhile, the political parties ignored both important signs of popular discontent and a burgeoning public debt (that would soon reach 100 percent of the country's gross domestic product [GDP]).[20] They also ignored a series of crucial events that set the stage for the transformation of the system. (See box 4.1.)

And yet, more than twenty years later, many of the problems that brought down the First Republic (and that weakened the Italian state throughout its existence) remain unresolved. It is undeniable that Italy has made great strides in the struggle against criminal organizations, that an increase in the apparent stability of the government has come about, and that progress has been made in many other sectors as well. Nevertheless, international agencies such as Transparency International or Freedom House, in their 2013 reports, still express concern about the level of corruption (and specifically about Berlusconi's conflicts of interest).[21] Meanwhile, major newspapers and magazines like the *Financial Times*, the *New York Times*, and the *Economist* editorialize about the poor state of Italian democracy. Why did the removal of the political class (an impressive 44 percent turnover in parliamentary participation took place in 1994) that had been responsible for perpetuating many of the pathologies of the First Republic not usher in a period of more "normal" politics? Why did the reform of electoral institutions fail to foster a stable pattern of left-right competition based on normal alternation of the political parties in power? And why did the exposure of corruption at all levels of government not pave the way for a brand-new and more legitimate political system based on transparency and accountability to take its place?

Several intertwined factors are necessary to consider in understanding why it is still difficult to talk today of a "Second Republic." Of these, three deserve particular attention: the nature of the transition, the incomplete process of institutional reform, and the shortcomings of both coalitions, represented on one side by the nearly total dominance of Berlusconi and on the other side by the chronic incapacity of the center-left to build a credible alternative.

European pressures significantly helped Italy to build up a more solid economy. As early as 1987, for example, Italians were able to celebrate the fact that their economy had overtaken that of the United Kingdom in size. The United Kingdom has long since regained its position, and yet there are important measures where the Italian economy performs better.[22] That said, the transition was more about politics than about economics, and it was driven by domestic rather than European forces. In that context, the changes that were wrought were ambivalent. Hence, while the judicial inquiries of 1992–1993 were mainly driven by the noble aims of tackling unbearable levels of corruption, they also significantly contributed to the reinforcement of antipolitical attitudes within the electorate that would never completely disappear in the following years.

The point here is not that the judicial inquiries should not have taken place. No one can seriously deny the need to put a halt to the endemic system of corruption built during the First Republic. Rather, it is to suggest that they had unintended political consequences as well as intended ones. The depoliticization (or, better put, disillusionment) of the electorate was one consequence; the politicization of the judiciary was another. Once the trials started to be televised and some prosecutors made exaggerated use of instruments such as preventive incarceration, the stage was set for the activity of the magistrates to be politicized even further by a master of communication like then–media magnate Berlusconi. After entering politics by firmly supporting the judges' initiatives—and unsuccessfully courting one of the most famous of them, Antonio Di Pietro, who later went on to build his own personal party on the center-left camp (Italy of Values)—Berlusconi was able to use his own media empire to turn public opinion against the judges. He was also able to deflect public attention away from the spread of corruption, which was to remain very high throughout the following years.[23] Finally, once his own media empire was made the subject of judicial enquiries, Berlusconi was able to denounce these judicial actions as politically motivated as well. Of course, Berlusconi was not the author of this whole state of affairs. The politicization of the judiciary and the spread of corruption after the fall of the First Republic were also consequences of a lack of intervention by successive governments, which did nothing to shore up the very precarious state of the Italian justice system.[24] Nevertheless, Berlusconi was certainly a willing protagonist.

In other words, judicial investigations, while contributing decisively to the collapse of the old party system, also contributed to the rise of a populist mood that created the best conditions for Berlusconi's rise and success. The point to note, however, is that Berlusconi was not alone. He was well positioned, particularly given his domination over the media, which ably captured and led the cultural change toward consumerism that had already spread since the 1980s. But he also depended upon allies. Berlusconi's populist campaign complemented the Northern League's (LN) federalist message against the centralized control of the national government in Rome over the regions and against the use of public resources (including tax revenues raised in the

North) to subsidize the South. Berlusconi was also able to grant legitimacy to right-wing sentiments that had long been confined to a neo-Fascist ghetto. While Umberto Bossi's LN clearly benefited from the collapse of the DC, as the geography of its vote strikingly confirms, Gianfranco Fini's MSI, later renamed the National Alliance (AN), needed Berlusconi's support to escape what remained of the anti-Fascist consensus.[25] Berlusconi, Bossi, and Fini were all players who grew to prominence after the fall of the First Republic (and arguably because of it). This was an undeniable change in Italian politics. Nevertheless, the fact that these same three leaders managed to lead their own personal political parties for more than two decades—Berlusconi having held on the longest—suggests the emergence of new, unintended, and problematic patterns.

Party System Change, and Electoral and Institutional Reforms

Italy is the only European democracy to have voted with three significantly different electoral systems since the end of the Cold War. Yet discussions on electoral reform are a hardy perennial in Italian political debate. Why is this the case? The answer can be found in the ineffectiveness of successive reforms to the electoral system. It can also be found in the absence of complementary rules regarding parliamentary group affiliations and party finances.

Both electoral reforms, which took place in 1993 and 2005, were driven by partisan aims. At the time of the first reform, political parties were experiencing the harshest moments of the judicial investigations. In the space of a few months, governing parties were decapitated and more than half of the members of parliament (MPs) were investigated. They also faced the outcome of a popular referendum in April 1993 on the abolition of PR, which showed the extent of support for such a change. Nevertheless, they managed not to lose complete control of the electoral reform process. Instead of moving toward a single-round first-past-the-post system like that used in the United Kingdom, or a two-round plurality system like that used in France, they set up a mixed-member majoritarian (MMM) system, which worked through various and very intricate devices to mitigate the majoritarian effect of the single-member districts.

The choice was not obvious. Arguably, either a first-past-the-post system or a two-round plurality system would have done away with the country's tradition for polarized pluralism by forcing the parties into a more clearly bipolar left-right division. Not only would this simplify choices for the voters, but also it would ensure some alternation between government and opposition as well. An MMM system had no such clear-cut implications. In that sense, adoption of an MMM system conflicted with the referendum movement that, albeit divided between proponents of single- and double-round options, had attracted significant support in its campaign for a change in electoral institutions that could drive Italy closer to other large-state patterns of party system simplification and bipolar alternation.

This victory of the parties over the reform movement is all the more surprising given that while almost all political parties of the First Republic disappeared in 1992, the old

Communist left suddenly found its position improved. The party changed names from the PCI to the Democratic Party of the Left (PDS) just before the judicial earthquake (in 1991 rather than 1992). Moreover, since the old PCI had not been involved in government outside a few regions, it was correspondingly less involved in the judicial investigations into corruption in office. Hence, at the end of 1993, the new PDS could face the prospect of an easy win in the forthcoming 1994 elections, to be fought under the new electoral law.[26] It is at this point that Berlusconi "entered the field" of Italian politics with his Forza Italia (Go Italy), and swept the board (see box 4.2).

In fact, Berlusconi's first victory was built on heterogeneous alliances in different parts of the country. In the North, Berlusconi relied on the Northern League; in the South, he depended upon the MSI. Indeed, his dependence upon the support of these groups was such that the government he formed lasted less than seven months, as a consequence of the Northern League's defection. In turn, this made it possible for the center-left to achieve victory in the following 1996 elections, with Romano Prodi's Olive Tree coalition. Once again, however, the coalition depended upon the goodwill of smaller parties and, as a consequence, the Prodi government lasted only two years. At the end of the Prodi government, the Italian political system moved even further from the majoritarian bipolar ideal. For the first—and, so far, the only—time in Italian history, a government fell on a lost-confidence vote, and a new executive was formed mainly thanks to the defections of some centrist MPs elected in 1996 as part of the center-right. Massimo D'Alema became prime minister in a new PDS-dominated government, not as an expression of alternation but in a new form of *trasformismo* for a new age.

Box 4.2   Berlusconi: A Very Peculiar Politician

Berlusconi is no average kind of politician. As of 2013, he is the seventh richest man in Italy. His personal fortune includes assets in the fields of television, newspapers, publishing, cinema, finance, banking, insurance, and sport. Indeed, he became known to the public in the 1980s, when he took over AC Milan, making it one of the most successful football teams in Europe. Craxi's support was instrumental in assuring his televisions could compete against public TV: in 1984, the so-called Berlusconi decree overcame the Constitutional Court ban on Berlusconi's private broadcasting that was broadcasting at the national level rather than by using local frequencies, as the law prescribed at the time. "Dear Bettino, my warmest thanks for what you did. I know it's not been easy and that you've had to spend all your authority and credibility to get this through," said Berlusconi, quoted in G. D'Avanzo, *Il Psi, il governo, Tangentopoli: ecco le carte dell'archivio Craxi,* "La Repubblica," December 6, 2007. In 1990 the Mammì law effectively sanctioned what was to become the Berlusconi's owned Mediaset and public RAI's TV duopoly. Since the latter has always been politicized, once Berlusconi entered Palazzo Chigi this meant that most of the media were biased in his favor. Berlusconi's judicial problems included a number of inquiries on embezzlement, tax evasion, false accounting, bribery of judges, and corruption. Some trials were dropped because of time limits, for other crimes he was acquitted, and while he was sometimes convicted, such convictions were often overturned. In 2013, Berlusconi's conviction on a charge of tax evasion was upheld by the highest Italian court and so he was forced to relinquish his seat in the Italian Senate. Berlusconi's influence in Italian politics continues nonetheless.

This episode marked a significant departure from the spirit, if not the letter, of the 1993 electoral law. Although it is not uncommon for a British or French government to change without elections when one prime minister agrees (or accepts) to stand down as the leader of a party so that another can take his or her place—as with Margaret Thatcher and John Major in 1990 or Tony Blair and Gordon Brown in 2007—D'Alema's replacement of Prodi was nothing of the sort. Although they belonged to the same coalition, D'Alema controlled a political party and Prodi, arguably, did not. More important, the contest between them had less to do with who was strong within the coalition and much to do with who could be convinced to cross the aisle. In that sense, the change in government was an attempt to restore the primacy of parties over coalitions, as well as a gamble on the idea that a new political center could be created that could monopolize the representation of the Catholic electorate. With hindsight, this political maneuver inadvertently delayed the formation of a party that could effectively compete against Berlusconi. The quest for a new hegemonic center drew attention away from the necessity to merge the remnants of the Catholic and Communist cultures in a united party of the center-left and instead perpetuated a climate within which Catholics and Communists continue to wrestle with one another for control.

Therefore, the first two elections with the new system saw the repetition of patterns commonly associated with the First Republic: average cabinet duration was only slightly longer (see table 4.2), *trasformismo* continued to be practiced, and the party system remained fragmented. In addition, the failure of two further referenda in 1999 and 2000 fostered the idea that electoral reform had failed in rationalizing the political system along a pattern of party system simplification and bipolar alternation.[27] Worse, it may even have fueled the (underlying) idea that it would be better to switch back to PR. This is essentially what happened in the electoral reform of 2005—although, this being Italy, it happened in a very peculiar way.

Before briefly sketching out the many faults of the 2005 electoral law, it is important to explain how the electoral system used in the 1994, 1996, and 2001 elections diluted the pressure to create a simplified bipolar party system. From a strict majoritarian perspective, the MMM law clearly had many flaws. Among them, the use of cross-party endorsements of candidacies within coalitions inside the single-member districts had the effect of fostering, instead of curbing, a fragmentation of the party system. All small parties had to do is convince the rest of the coalition of their essential worth and then rely on cross-endorsements from their coalition partners to ensure that they held onto a negotiated number of safe seats on the center-left or center-right. Indeed, this practice was carried out to such an extent that a new all-Italian category of "fragmented bipolarism" has been invented to describe the new party system that was the result.[28]

Moreover, this new fragmented bipolar system behaved somewhat differently from the polarized pluralism of the First Republic, during which each party made up its own parliamentary group. Indeed, and oddly given the expressed desire of the electorate to create incentives for simplification, the rules regulating party groups in parliament were not reformed from the First Republic to the Second. Hence, while parties forged coalitions during elections, they operated as free agents once in parliament. This effectively created two different party systems: one operating at the electoral level,

Table 4.2 Coalition Governance and Governments in Italy (1948–2014)

Legislative Term	Types and Phases of Coalition	Number of Governments	Average Duration of Governments (Days)	Prime Ministers*
I (1948–1953)	Centrism (golden age) DC, PSDI, PLI, and PRI	3	613	De Gasperi
II (1953–1958)	Centrism (crisis, new stabilization)	6	278	De Gasperi, Pella, Fanfani, Scelba, Segni, Zoli
III (1958–1963)	Centrism (new crisis). Preparation of Center-Left	5	341	Fanfani, Segni, Tambroni, Fanfani
IV (1963–1968)	Center-Left (golden age: PSI enters)	4	431	Leone, Moro
V (1968–1972)	Center-Left (crisis and new stabilization)	6	204	Leone, Rumor, Colombo, Andreotti
VI (1972–1976)	Center-Left (final crisis)	5	256	Andreotti, Rumor, Moro
VII (1976–1979)	National Solidarity	3	308	Andreotti
VIII (1979–1983)	Preparation of Five-Party formula (DC, PSI, PRI, PSDI, and PLI)	6	203	Cossiga, Forlani, Spadolini (PRI), Fanfani
IX (1983–1987)	Five-party (golden age)	3	429	Craxi (PSI), Fanfani
X (1987–1992)	Five-party (renegotiation, new stabilization, and new crisis)	4	405	Goria, De Mita, Andreotti
XI (1992–1994)	End of five-party formula and technocratic government	2	280	Amato (PSI), Ciampi (technocrat)
XII (1994–1996)	Center-Right attempt and technocratic government	2	311	Berlusconi, Dini (technocrat)
XIII (1996–2001)	Center-Left	4	450	Prodi; D'Alema, Amato
XIV (2001–2006)	Center-Right	2	1,092	Berlusconi
XV (2006–2008)	Center-Left	1	722	Prodi
XVI (2008–2013)	Center-Right and technocratic government	2	842	Berlusconi, Monti
XVII (2013–)	Grand coalition	2		Letta, Renzi

* Until 1992: all DC members unless otherwise indicated.

Source: Adapted and updated from Maurizio Cotta and Luca Verzichelli, *Political Institutions in Italy* (Oxford: Oxford University Press, 2007), 111–12.

which could appear simplified at first sight, and a different, much more fragmented one operating in parliament. Moreover, party finance regulation was reformed in the opposite direction—in such a way as to facilitate party proliferation by progressively lowering the thresholds for access to reimbursements and refunds. Indeed, party finance regulations make it so easy to gain support that even parties outside parliament, and indeed in some case barely existing, manage to get funds from the state.[29]

The 2005 reform, in turn, did not affect these two crucial elements—the independence of parties once in parliament and in terms of party finances. Almost fifteen years after the beginning of efforts to promote a bipolar political arena, popular interest in using electoral rules to help engineer a more simplified party system had faded. Hence, the way was clear for parties to reform the system to their own advantage: the center-right decided to act after the defeat in the 2005 regional elections and when facing increasingly negative opinion polls in anticipation of the 2006 general election. The law drafted by the center-right government extended the principle of an "adjusted-bonus" form of proportional representation to the national level (55 percent of seats to the first list or coalition). This principle already operated at all the lower territorial levels of government (meaning for the election of the regional, provincial, and municipal councils) in order to provide a seat bonus to the winning list or coalition (subject to complicated thresholds) in order to ensure that the winning group received a workable majority.[30] The main effect was to create two catchall coalitions, one on the center-right and one on the center-left (see figure 4.1). In this context, the return of Romano Prodi in 2006 at the head of a center-left government was mainly due to an anti-Berlusconi appeal rather than to the presence of a coherent coalition capable of governing for a full term.

Arguably, the 2005 electoral reform contained provisions that greatly strengthened the control of the political parties over the whole of the system. Among these, the most important was the introduction of blocked lists through which the party leadership can determine who is likely to receive a seat in parliament and who is not. As an instrument for creating discipline within the party, such lists clearly reinforce the lines of authority from the top down. It is small wonder, therefore, that they have become the object of some of the harshest protests from antipolitics movement such as satirist Beppe Grillo's M5S (Five-Star Movement). Of course, blocked lists are not unique to Italy and can be found in the electoral laws of other countries such as Spain. Nevertheless, in the Italian case, blocked lists meant that parties regained complete freedom of choice in the candidate selection process. In turn, they used this freedom to return "professional" party politicians to their seats in parliament in a very auto-referential pattern.

More generally, the inertia against reforming rules on party finance and parliamentary groups comes from the very nature of party-political competition. As Luciano Bardi explains, it emerges from

> the need of parties to maintain their individual identities and positions between elections so that they can negotiate candidatures for the next elections with coalition partners and, if need be, with the other side—producing individual party behavior that can be very damaging for coalition unity and, in the case of majority parties, for government stability. Such behavior is very difficult to eradicate as it can give strategically well-placed

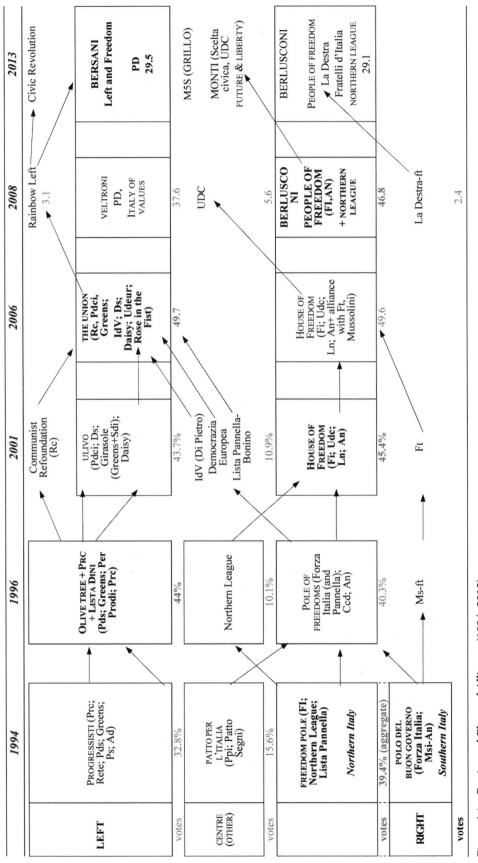

Figure 4.1   Parties and Electoral Alliances (1994–2013)

parties a dual advantage: a bonus in terms of seats in the electoral party system and another in the form of committee and cabinet positions in the parliamentary/governmental system.[31]

In other words, the rules for party organization and electoral competition are mutually reinforcing, and the effects of that reinforcement can be seen in the behavior and preferences of those politicians who must take responsibility for any future reform.

There is a way out of this negative equilibrium. At the end of 2007, the prospects for party system change increased as a consequence of the initiative of the former mayor of Rome, Walter Veltroni. Veltroni became the leader of the newly founded (and much-awaited) Democratic Party (PD) toward the end of 2007. This party brought together the two main center-left parties, the Left Democrats (DS) and the more centrist Daisy (Margherita). Unfortunately, however, the formation of the Democratic Party had the unintended consequence of undermining the already precarious coalition supporting the Prodi government. The election of Veltroni as the first Democratic Party leader weakened and delegitimated Prodi's leadership of the ruling coalition government. And, on the other side of the political spectrum, it triggered an analogous streamlining process among the parties of the center-right, which led to the formation of the People of Freedom Party by Berlusconi (later reluctantly joined by Fini).

The consequences were mixed. Prodi's government fell in 2008, which led to early parliamentary elections. Nevertheless, those elections did bring about a significant simplification of the Italian party system. The radical left was out of parliament; the Union of Center (UDC) barely entered, and Berlusconi had a strong majority and a two-party coalition. Given that this occurred under extremely unfavorable electoral institutions, should we conclude that Italy has finally arrived at a stable bipolar arrangement?

The answer is clearly "no." On November 2011, market pressures led to Berlusconi's resignation. This experience was different from that in other countries. While in 2011–2012, the economic crisis triggered early elections in Greece, Spain, and Portugal, Italy faced government turnover without elections. This unelected turnover was made possible by the constitution: given the presence of a new parliamentary majority, President Napolitano strongly supported Berlusconi's replacement as prime minister by Mario Monti in November 2011. Although Monti could enjoy a substantial majority in parliament (both the PdL and the PD, with the UDC and the newly founded Fini's Future and Liberty Party as his most faithful supporters), parties did not give up on their preferences on institutional reforms, which proved impossible to achieve, starting from a reform of the electoral law. This meant that Monti's attempt to rescue Italy was only partly successful. He established both economic and policy credibility abroad, but he failed to restore confidence at home in a discredited political elite.[32]

The damage to popular confidence was considerable. The Italian political class had been hit by frequent scandals relating to both abuses of power and excessive privilege. As a result, they were widely depicted as a "caste," or a closed circle of self-serving elites. The self-reinforcing nature of the electoral law only made matters worse. Professional politicians would not give up on their partisan preferences and so resisted any effort at electoral reform. As a result, Italy went to the polls in 2013 for the third election under the 2005 electoral system.[33]

Don't Count Your Chickens before They Hatch: Italian Politics after the 2013 Elections

The story of the 2013 Italian elections (both the general and the presidential elections, which took place respectively in February and April) needs to be told as it exposes three critical—and still unsolved—dilemmas for Italian politics: the incomplete nature of Italian institutional change, the PD's uncertain status as a party of government on the center-left, and the possible emergence of the conditions for overcoming the political cleavage focusing on Silvio Berlusconi, with the formation and subsequent preservation of the grand-coalition government led by Enrico Letta.

Why were two elections necessary to form a government? Two main reasons stand out. The first was the indecisive result of the general election (which took place on February 24–25), with a hung parliament and no majority in the Senate. The second relates to the "institutional traffic jam" that followed the parliamentary elections, with the incumbent President of the Republic about to stand down, and hence deprived of the powers to dissolve parliament and call new elections.

For a long time, Italian elections used to have many winners and no loser. The combination of a proportional electoral law and the Cold War cleavage meant that the decisiveness of elections in bringing about government turnover was very low. And yet, although new electoral rules contributed to the "fragmented bipolar" competition of the decade that ran from 1996 to 2006, political parties never recovered from the crisis of the 1990s, remaining fragile and mutable: the longest running party in the Italian parliament (the LN) is just over twenty years old. That is unique in Western Europe.

After Berlusconi was succeeded by Monti in 2011, he was also hit by a number of scandals related to a string of allegations and legal proceedings. Hence, most analysts expected his era to be over. Many opinion polls in 2012 showed the PdL crumbling below the 20 percent threshold. Instead, what emerged in the February 2013 elections was yet another example of Berlusconi's resilience. The electoral result took most by surprise. Although the M5S's rise was predicted by many surveys, nobody—not even Grillo himself—was prepared to see the movement threatening to overtake the Democratic Party (PD) in terms of electoral support.

Even if a tripolar Italy took most observers by surprise, however, the center-left's poor result was not entirely unpredictable. One of the key problems in the center-left coalition opposing Berlusconi has been their lack of unity and the frequent alternation of coalitional leaders. (By contrast, Berlusconi's leadership on the center-right has been unrivaled since 1994.) The center-left's response has been to look for ways to strengthen the democratic legitimacy of their candidate. Ever since Prodi first proposed the use of primary elections in 2005, such contests have become the normal means for coalitional leadership candidate selection (and later for the PD itself).

Primaries have not always fostered unity. After Veltroni had resigned in the aftermath of the 2008 defeat, the PD's new leader, former minister Pierluigi Bersani, faced an internal challenger. Matteo Renzi, the young (born in 1975) mayor of Florence, quickly rose to prominence thanks to a crusade to promote generational renewal in a party still dominated by the "cold-fusion dynamic" of post-DC and postcommunist leaders, all trained to politics during the First Republic. The anti-establishment climate that dominated Italian politics in 2011–2012, with many political scandals, boosted the popularity of both the "scrapper," as Renzi was nicknamed, and especially Beppe Grillo. Renzi lost the primaries to Bersani, who then had to fight against the tide in preserving a 10 percent quota for parliamentary candidates who would not be selected via primaries (while, in all other parties, the decision on who could stand was just left to the leaders), and campaigned rather poorly. Although Bersani had won easily to Renzi (61 to 39 percent) in the primaries' runoff, there is consistent evidence in opinion polls that testifies to Renzi's capacity to attract votes beyond his camp, as well as to effectively counter Grillo's challenge (see table 4.3).

Hence, the center-left's poor result can be seen as a consequence of three main factors. The first is the resilience of Berlusconi's core vote. The PdL's share of the electorate stabilized at around 25 percent, which represents a recovery of 5–7 percentage points from public opinion polling taken in late 2012. This rebound is due in no small measure to Berlusconi's skill as a campaigner. The second factor pulling down the center-left was the disillusion of many who had voted for Renzi in the primaries. They remained bitter that their candidate lost what they viewed as an unfair primary contest. The third factor was the draining of many left votes from the M5S (which also affected the center-right), as confirmed by research on vote flows in twelve Italian towns.[34]

Table 4.4 helps in interpreting the meaning of the 2013 elections. The main indicators show many signs of a return to a very uncertain and volatile party system. The jump in disproportionality (as measured by the Gallagher index) was due to the very close race between the two main coalitions (three forces when one includes the M5S, a result that made the seat bonus obtained by the winning coalition all the more impressive). Turnout also was at its lowest level ever. The rise of an antipolitical climate was a key factor, although the timing of elections could also have played a role (never had Italian elections been held in winter before). Finally, volatility skyrocketed at almost 40 percent, putting Italy behind only the May 2012 Greek elections from a post-WWII Western European perspective.

The last two columns of table 4.4 highlight the many-party system's ambiguities: both the effective number of electoral parties—an index on fragmentation—and the two-party vote tell us that the change from 2008 has been important. Then, Berlusconi's PdL and Veltroni's PD made their political debut by gaining as much as 71 percent of the votes between them (almost reaching the 1976 record high for two-party support of 73 percent), apparently forging a bipolar competition, with just a few minor parties left outside their respective coalitions. But the scene after February 2013 has looked very different. And this was not due to the centrist initiative by Monti, who was strongly supported in Europe for his austerity policies and yet very unsuccessful.[35]

Table 4.3 Results of General Elections, 2013 and 2008 (Chamber and Senate)

Chamber of Deputies	2013 Votes	%	Seats	Senate	Votes	%	Seats
Partito Democratico (PD)	8,932,615	25.5	297	PD	8,674,893	27.5	113
SEL (Left, Ecology, Liberty)	1,106,784	3.1	37	SEL	912,308	2.9	7
Democratic Centre	167,072	0.5	6	Dem Centre	163,373	0.5	—
Südtiroler Volkspartei (SVP)	146,804	0.4	5	SVP	127,656	0.4	3
Total coalition Bersani	**10,353,275**	**29.5**	**345**	**Total coalition Bersani**	**9,878,230**	**31.3**	**123**
Movimento 5 Stelle M5S	**8,784,499**	**25.1**	**109**	**M5S**	**7,375,412**	**23.4**	**54**
Civic Choice for Monti with Italy	2,824,065	**8.3**	**39**				
Unione di centro (UDC)	608,210	1.8	**8**				
Futuro e libertà (FLI)	159,332	0.5	—				
Total coalition Monti	**3,772,281**	**10.8**	**47**	**Mario Monti coalition**	**2,974,888**	**9.4**	**19**
Il Popolo della libertà (PDL)	7,478,796	21.4	98		6,965,639	22.1	98
Northern League (LN)	1,390,014	4.1	18		1,328,624	4.2	17
Brothers of Italy	665,830	2	9		590,083	1.9	—
Others	534,034	2			742,887	2.3	
Total coalition Berlusconi	**9,922,850**	**29.1**	**125**	**Total coalition Berlusconi**	**9,627,233**	**30.6**	**115**
Rivoluzione Civile (Ingroia)	781,098	**2.2**	—	Total coalition—Ingroia	550,007	1.7	—
Fare per Fermare il Declino (Giannino)	390,917	**1.1**	—	Total coalition—Giannino	278,404	1.1	—
Others	693,635	1.7	3	Others	809,963	1.8	1
Total	**34,002,524**		**629***	**Total**	**31,494,137**		**314***

2008

Parties	Votes	%	Seats	Parties	Votes	%	Seats
PD	12,092,998	33.2	211		11,042,325	33.7	116
Di Pietro IDV	1,593,675	4.4	28		1,414,118	4.3	14
Total coalition Veltroni	**13,686,673**	**37.6**	**239**	**Total coalition Veltroni**	**12,456,443**	**38**	**130**
PDL	13,628,865	37.4	272		12,510,306	38.2	141
Lega Nord	3,024,522	8.3	60		2,642,167	8.1	25
Mov. Aut. All. per il Sud	410,487	1.1	8		355,076	1.1	2
Total coalition Berlusconi	**17,063,874**	**46.8**	**340**	**Total coalition Berlusconi**	**15,507,549**	**47.3**	**168**
UDC	**2,050,319**	**5.6**	**36**	**Udc**	**1,866,294**	**5.7**	**3**
SVP	147,666	0.4	2	SVP	247,528	0.8	4
Aut. Lib. Democratie	23,311	0.1	1	Vallée d'Aoste	29,186	0.1	1
Sinistra Arcobaleno	1,124,418	3.1	—	Sinistra Arcobaleno	1,053,154	3.2	—
La Destra—Fiamma Tricolore	885,229	2.4	—	La Destra—Fiamma Tricolore	687,211	2.1	—
PS	355,581	1	—				
Others (no seats)	208,394	2.9	—	Others (no seats)	284,428	3.7	—
Total	**35,545,465**	**100**	**630**	**Total**	**32,131,783**	**100**	**315**

*Does nor include Valle d'Aosta, one seat for each Chamber won by regionalist party in single-member constituency.

Source: Own compilation on official data.

Table 4.4 The 2013 Italian Elections from a Long-Term Perspective (Chamber of Deputies)

Period (Number of Elections)	Electoral Law	Disproportionality	Turnout	Volatility	Effective Number of Electoral Parties	Two-party Vote
1976–1992 (5)	PR	2.6	89.8	9.1	4.6	61.1
1994–2001 (3)	Mixed-member majoritarian (MMM)	8.3	83.5	25.4	6.9	42.6
2006–2008 (2)	PR with majority bonus	4.6	80.8	9.6	4.6	63.0
2013	PR with majority bonus	17.3	75.2	39.0	5.3	50.1

Source: Own update on Luciano Bardi, "Electoral Change and Its Impact on the Party System in Italy," *West European Politics* 30, no. 4 (2007): 711–32.

Bipolarism has not been much affected by a centripetal challenge, but by a "beyond left and right" discourse, skillfully manipulated by Beppe Grillo. Beppe Grillo's success deserves further explanation. The former comedian played a key role in the campaign (and beyond). Although not himself a candidate, for months Grillo imposed his agenda by being omnipresent on TV discussions while refusing to take part in any debate. Rather, he toured the country (visiting seventy-seven cities) with his Tsunami Tour, a name that sums up very effectively the tone and aims of his initiative, culminating at the end of a campaign meeting in Rome with the "surrender" cry to politicians in the *palazzo*: "Surrender! Give yourselves up! You are surrounded!"

Grillo's success has many components; some are common to other European countries, and some are more peculiarly Italian. In a recent volume, Matthew Flinders underlines some important challenges that democracies are facing today.[36] These result from a complex interplay between the spread of consumerism in politics, the fears on which the media focus, the emphasis on the rights (to the detriment of the duties) of citizens, and the obsessive monitoring of the private lives of politicians. All this has contributed to widen the gap between citizens' expectations and what politics—especially in a democracy—can actually deliver. What other European country better exemplifies these dynamics than Italy? To be fair, the Italian political class's discredit is greatly self-inflicted, and the amount of scandals makes any elaboration on this point superfluous.

However, what is more interesting to see is how Grillo's success is built on the channeling of a reservoir of political anger and anti-establishment attitudes that spreads across all of Italy. In such a context, it is not surprising that the physiological gap between expectations and achievements (in a country that wanted to reform politics with a judges' revolution at the start of the 1990s and that ranks below only Greece, Bulgaria, and Romania among the EU's most corrupted countries, according to Transparency International) is subject to periodical outbursts. The M5S builds its discourse on the combination of elements that were present in the previous three big waves of Italian anti-establishment movements.

The first inspiration for Grillo's repertoire comes from Guglielmo Giannini's Uomo Qualunque (Common Man), a flash populist-libertarian movement that attracted many votes—especially in the South—in the late 1940s. This movement depicted all parties as equal, and fascism and democracy as alike, all aiming at squeezing the poor citizen inside a vise (which became the party's symbol). Giannini oversimplified politics, claiming a good *ragioniere* (an accountant) should ideally be in charge.

Giannini's language was irreverent as much as Grillo's. His movement was short lived, but many of the attitudes that inspired it have never disappeared. Many of the social movements of 1968 created problems for the more mainstream Italian political parties that have never been fully addressed. As different as they were, Marxist, anarco-libertarian, and dissenting Catholic groups shared a key challenge to the process of political (and trade union) delegation. Contrary to what happened in other European countries, only a few tiny movements got institutionalized, while some others chose violent means, so much so that the 1970s for Italy meant a decade of violence (on a dynamics that, again, had no parallels in Europe). The continuing challenge to the mainstream was evident in the political crisis of the early 1990s.

The collapse of the First Republic and the rise of Silvio Berlusconi rested in large measure on a widespread disgust with the ruling class. That sentiment has not dissipated as a result of Berlusconi's political leadership, and he continues to rail against the traditional elites of the left. The difference for Grillo is that he can point fingers at all parts of the political spectrum.

The expectations gap analyzed by Flinders has reached in Italy yet another moment of explosion, and possibly the most dramatic one. The M5S voters share, in different combinations, distrust and dissatisfaction toward politics but also the hyperpolitical attitudes of 1968, with their refusal of political delegation, their love for deliberative democracy procedures, and their postmaterialist baggage (the environment, and fights against high-speed train lines and waste incinerators, are key local battles in which the movement got hold) all mixed up in a rather complex blend. While most other parties are postideological, the M5S also talks to a nostalgic electorate, or to the alienated citizens who grew up in a postideological Second Republic only seen in its failures (of which indeed there are many), and along the almost predominant pro- versus anti-Berlusconi cleavage. When the two main alternatives are the heirs of the PCI and DC (from which the core of the PD leadership comes) and an entrepreneur who famously "descended" into politics with the promise of a Thatcher-style revolution (while achieving almost nothing of this, raising taxes, and mainly looking after his business), is it really surprising to find dissatisfied voters of both camps joining a new movement, self-proclaimed a nonparty just to mark its distance from those who have governed so far?

The rejection of political delegation in favor of direct democracy (and "monitory democracy") and distrust vis-à-vis the political system complement each other, providing mobilization resources and a convenient channelling for protest voting.[37] But there is also a critical element in the M5S's success, which is the combination of an external—and therefore unaccountable—charismatic leadership and the use of the Internet not just as a means of political action but also as almost the only veritable source of political legitimation.

The relevance of the M5S's challenge became all the more clear in the aftermath of the general election, when Bersani was left with no majority in the Senate. Bersani tried and failed to negotiate a workable coalition and had to give up on his attempt to form a government. The most important obstacle for Bersani was the unwillingness of the M5S to compromise in its desire to dominate the coalition or trigger new elections.

This is where the presidential elections of April 2013 become important. Since 1992, presidential powers have become more significant, especially with regard to crucial decisions on government turnover and parliament dissolution.[38] Moreover, in a climate of growing political dissatisfaction, all opinion polls show how the president of the Republic remains the only figure able to stand above the discredited political forces. Napolitano, who is now eighty-eight years old and was elected president by a center-left majority in 2006, had many times declared that he would not be available for a second term, an option not ruled out by the Constitution, but never tried before.

Presidential elections have never been a straightforward game. The president of the Italian Republic is elected by an electoral college composed of the members of parliament, plus a selected delegation from the Italian regions. A two-thirds qualified majority in the first three rounds of ballots usually makes quick elections rather unlikely. The only two exceptions (i.e., an election at the first round) came when there was an agreement between the main parties; this occurred in 1985 with Francesco Cossiga, and in 1999 with Carlo Azeglio Ciampi.

Having seen that the dialogue with Grillo could not work, Bersani turned to Berlusconi for support in selecting a possible consensual figure for the Quirinale. In turn, Berlusconi duly gave Bersani a list, from which Bersani first picked former president of the Senate, and PD member, Franco Marini. The trouble with Marini was that he was a candidate who could have (maybe) worked in the previous legislature. A former leader of the main Catholic trade union, CISL, Marini as leader of the post-DC Italian Popular Party (PPI) in 1997–1999 had been rather reluctant to join forces with the former communists of the PDS-DS. On this position, he was matched in the latter party by D'Alema, who had ousted Prodi in 1998, also thanks to Marini's support.

The result was indecisive. Many members of the center-left refused to support Marini, and so Bersani could not get him elected on the initial ballots. Hence, Bersani looked to Romano Prodi as a candidate who could rally the support of the center-left. However, this proved illusory. A group of defectors withheld their support from Prodi, who subsequently withdrew his name from the ballot. The fact that both Marini and Prodi were shot down by members of the center-left is just another example of a disjointed institutional set: old candidates playing with old rules but with a new electorate, the new MPs. And this dramatically exposed the problematic nature of the PD project. Bersani's nominations of Marini and Prodi, although apparently approved by acclamation in two different party meetings, revealed that the PD is still dominated by archrivalries.

Meanwhile, the M5S poured salt in the wound by proposing Stefano Rodotà, a well-known constitutional expert and former president of the center-left former Communist Party. Rodotà was controversial because he chose not to become a PD member, because he saw himself to the left of the Democratic Party. Grillo used this to drive a wedge between the two main branches of the center-left by claiming that if Rodotà were to be elected president of the Republic, Bersani could try again to form a coalition government with the support of the M5S. Such a prospect could not be stomached by a consistent part of the PD. Not only did they dislike Rodotà's hard-left positions, but also they saw that Grillo's offer was a trap intended to put the PD at the mercy of the M5S.

All Berlusconi had to do as the presidential elections unfolded was wait. Once the center-left demonstrated its inability to field a candidate, he could join Bersani and Monti in "begging" Napolitano to solve this rather chaotic institutional traffic jam. Napolitano was also the PdL's favorite candidate as everybody knew how determined he was to have a bipartisan majority that included both the PdL on the center-right and the PD on the center-left. Such a grand coalition would provide the political stability necessary to implement long-awaited institutional reforms, starting with a new electoral law but also including a redesign of the two houses of the Italian parliament, and a speeding up of the parliamentary process. A grand coalition would also help to insulate Italy from the dangers of an economic downfall.

Conclusion: Still the Age of Berlusconi?

The result was the formation of a new executive led by Enrico Letta, the PD's former deputy leader, in the first grand-coalition government in Italy. The key challenge for Letta was to set the conditions to exit from the Berlusconi era. Berlusconi's dominance over the center-right and his splintering of the center-left mean that the future of the political system depends in many ways on the future of the man himself. Indeed, the PDL practically does not exist as a party beyond Berlusconi's personal will, his personal wealth, and his proprietary control. Because of his strong divisive potential, Berlusconi could not directly become a minister in Letta's government. According to the *Economist*, he was, together with Grillo, the winner of the 2013 general elections. The fact that the fate of the grand coalition is so dependent on the actions and the will of these two "winners," who are respectively out of government and out of parliament, still testifies to the anomalies of Italian politics.

All this means that despite the great juncture experienced by Italian politics at the start of the 1990s, Italian problems should be understood as a result of the combination of ineffective political institutions and a profound lack of civic culture and social capital, as much as was the case fifty years ago—if not one hundred and fifty.[39] Economic progress and—more recently—party system change have not done much to improve the overall state of the country. In every election but those of 2008, when the global economic crisis started to emerge, Berlusconi had promised a liberal revolution: to free enterprises from a baroque fiscal system, to foster public investment in infrastructures, and to invest in advanced technology. Yet, not much has been done to overcome the structural weaknesses of the Italian economy, and long-term burdens such as its shadow economy still hamper any effective improvement.[40]

As in many other countries, Italian changes and continuities blend in an often inextricable way. Governments now tend to be stronger, although still affected by difficult coalition patterns and incessant parliamentary maneuvering. Italy's political crisis of the early 1990s reflected a cultural failure to develop institutions resting on universalistic values, above all those of efficiency and transparency in public life. The disintegration of this system has brought about new protagonists, but also a rather peculiar blend of old problems (a weak identification in the institutions, a weak civic culture, and the enduring strength of the North-South divide) and new divisions, to the extent that today the political transition that started as long as twenty years ago still remains incomplete. One can only hope that once Berlusconi stands aside, the clock of politics does not turn back to 1993.

Notes

1. See Fabio Luca Cavazza and Stephen R. Graubard, eds., *Il caso italiano* (Milan: Rizzoli, 1974); and Tommaso Padoa Schioppa and Stephen R. Graubard, eds., *Il caso italiano 2: dove sta andando il nostro paese?* (Milan: Rizzoli, 2001); both were first published as special issues of the American journal *Daedalus*.

2. David Hine, *Governing Italy: The Politics of Bargained Pluralism* (Oxford: Oxford University Press, 1993), 15.

3. Prefectures are a typical French (Napoleonic) institution that Italy inherited from Piedmont. The prefects who control them represent the authority of the centralized state at the local level. These prefects were a key element in the state structure that Italy adopted at unification. Moreover, they were kept with only incremental changes (i.e., regional elective institutions introduced after World War II) until a federalization process started in the mid-1990s. A recent study on the rise of the Italian and German states, while confirming that the federal option was not dismissed as impossible at the outset, plausibly argues that the Italian pre-unitary states lacked the sufficient infrastructural capacity to build a federation similar to the one that Prussia was about to create in Germany. See Daniel Ziblatt, *Structuring the State: The Formation of Italy and Germany and the Puzzle of Federalism* (Princeton, NJ: Princeton University Press, 2006); but see also Carlo Tullio Altan, "Except for Piedmont, Lombardy, Emilia-Romagna and Tuscany, at the Time No Other Italian Region Was Prepared to Be Governed with an Anglo Saxon Self-Government System," in *La nostra Italia, Clientelismo, Trasformismo e Ribellismo dall'Unità al 2000* (Milan: Egea, 2000), 47.

4. See Stefano Bartolini, *The Political Mobilization of the European Left, 1860–1980* (Cambridge: Cambridge University Press, 2000), 132 and 195, respectively. Italy also displayed a high level of economic inequality (as it still does to this day), a factor often considered critical in democratization processes.

5. In other words, and borrowing Stein Rokkan's terminology, the threshold of representation was significantly lowered too soon after the threshold of incorporation (i.e., the extension of suffrage) had been passed, thus decisively jeopardizing the democratization process.

6. Ernesto Galli della Loggia, *La morte della patria* (Rome: Laterza, 1996), 4–5.

7. The PCI was a Janus-faced party. The official face, well after the death of its leader Palmiro Togliatti in 1964, held Moscow as a key reference point. A pragmatic face is apparent when one looks at the fact that, under the same leadership of Togliatti, the party approved almost three-fourths of the laws passed by parliament in the first four legislative terms.

8. Robert D. Putnam et al., *Making Democracy Work: Civic Traditions in Modern Italy* (Princeton, NJ: Princeton University Press, 1993), 167.

9. See Giovanni Sartori, *Parties and Party Systems* (Colchester, UK: ECPR Press, 2005).

10. See Maurizio Cotta and Luca Verzichelli, *Political Institutions in Italy* (Oxford: Oxford University Press, 2007), 144 and 149.

11. The reform was aimed at fostering DC's governing coalitions and soon was dubbed a "swindle" (*legge truffa*) by the main oppositions as it prescribed a consistent majority bonus (64.4% of the seats in the Chamber of Deputies to be assigned to the party or coalition securing 50% of the vote). The left's campaign was successful as it played on the memories of the 1923 Acerbo law, which gave 60% of the seats to the Fascist Party. That device, however, was different, as the seat bonus was awarded to the list gaining a plurality of votes; see Gianfranco Baldini, "The Different Trajectories of Italian Electoral Reforms," *West European Politics* 34, nos. 3–4 (2011): 644–63.

12. Leonardo Morlino, *Democracy between Consolidation and Crisis: Parties, Groups, and Citizens in Southern Europe* (Oxford: Oxford University Press, 1998).

13. See James G. March and Johan P. Olsen, *Rediscovering Institutions: The Organizational Basis of Politics* (New York: Free Press, 1989); and, for an application of these concepts to Italy, Roberto Cartocci, *Mappe del Tesoro. Atlante del Capitale sociale in Italia* (Bologna: Il Mulino, 2007).

14. Arturo Parisi and Gianfranco Pasquino, "Changes in Italian Electoral Behaviour: The Relationships between Parties and Voters," *West European Politics* 2, no. 3 (1979): 6–30.

15. Incidentally, 1972 was the first year when a paradigmatic figure such as Giulio Andreotti first became prime minister. Andreotti was to lead seven governments, being also always a minister from 1948 to 1992 (and, of course, sitting in every parliament until his death in 2013—being elected for the first time at the age of 27, in 1946). Governments were formed and dismissed by partisan (and/or factional) agreements in smoke-filled rooms, and ratified in parliament. Factionalism also brought about the very Italian species of *governi balneari* (literally, "beach government," to last less than a summer).

16. See Carlo Maria Santoro, *La politica estera di una media Potenza* (Bologna: Il Mulino, 1991); and F. Andreatta, "Italian Foreign Policy: Domestic Politics, International Requirements and the European Dimension," *Journal of European Integration* 30, no. 1 (special issue: *The Future of European Foreign Policy*, ed. E. Jones and S. van Genugten) (2008): 169–81.

17. See Paul Ginsborg, *Italy and Its Discontents, 1980–2001* (London: Penguin Books, 2001), 240.

18. See Lucio Caracciolo, "L'Italia alla ricerca di se stessa," in *Storia d'Italia, vol. 6. L'Italia contemporanea*, ed. Giovanni Sabbatucci and Vittorio Vidotto (Rome: Laterza, 1999), 541–604.

19. Caracciolo, "L'Italia," 545.

20. Signs of growing popular discontent included a sharp decrease in interest in politics; the success of anti-establishment movements and parties (such as the Greens and the Radicals); the increasing recourse to referenda, after the 1974 referendum on divorce had for the first time shown that parties were losing voters' confidence; and the increasing popular dissatisfaction vis-à-vis the performance of Italian democracy, as documented by several Eurobarometer surveys.

21. Italy was ranked 63 out of 180 countries surveyed in Transparency International's 2009 Corruption Perceptions Index, the second-lowest rating for Western Europe.

22. One might argue that the Italian economy, despite high levels of unemployment, reacted well to the crisis that began in 2008. See Erik Jones, "Italy and the Euro in the Global Economic Crisis," *The International Spectator* 44, no. 4 (2009): 93–103. This also meant that in the commonly used PIGS acronym, indicating the weak European (all-Mediterranean) economies of Portugal, Italy, Greece, and Spain, recently Italy has often been replaced by Ireland.

23. Arguably, corruption levels also remained high because, despite the removal of some facilitating factors such as lack of alternation or some reforms on public administration transparency, it "has been shown to be—and presumably still is—a *system*, not the mere aggregation of many dispersed, isolated illegal acts. It has become a market, which, as in the case of every functioning market, has developed internal rules and codes of behaviour—a *regulated*, in which the exercise of public authority in many crucial areas—public contracting procedures, licensing, urban planning, etc.—is governed by the laws of supply and demand"; Alberto Vannucci, "The Controversial Legacy of 'Mani Pulite': A Critical Analysis of Italian Corruption and Anti-Corruption Policies," *Bulletin of Italian Politics* 1, no. 2 (2009): 244.

24. In a comparison made in 2009 between the fifteen member states of the European Union (i.e., before the "Great Enlargement"), data show that in Italy it takes 450 days to evict a tenant who has not paid rent: a staggering 426 days more than in Holland, a country characterized by one of the highest levels of judicial efficiency in the world, but even 83 days more than in Austria, home to the second least efficient judiciary system in the EU. The picture is even direr if one seeks an injunction for a bounced check: in Italy, it takes an average of 415 days (i.e., 115 days more than the second-slowest country of the EU, Portugal, and 395 days more than the most efficient country of the EU, Belgium). See Justin Frosini, "The Same Old Film: The Never-Ending Woes of Italy's Justice System," in *Italian Politics*, vol. 25, ed. Marco Giuliani and Erik Jones (New York: Berghahn Books, 2010).

25. See Ilvo Diamanti, *Mappe dell'Italia politica* (Bologna: Il Mulino, 2008); and Piero Ignazi, *Il polo escluso* (Bologna: Il Mulino, 1989).

26. As local elections had shown in the spring and autumn of 1993, the DC and PSI, as well as the minor forces of the *pentapartito*, were all gone by the end of the year.

27. Many party leaders (of both coalitions, including Berlusconi himself) continued to pursue particularistic aims and did not support the two referenda, a fact that was instrumental in their defeat due to lack of a 50 percent quorum.

28. Roberto D'Alimonte, "Italy: A Case of Fragmented Bipolarism," in *The Politics of Electoral Systems*, ed. Michael Gallagher and Paul Mitchell (Oxford: Oxford University Press, 2005), 253–77.

29. Maria Chiara Pacini, "Public Funding of Political Parties in Italy," *Modern Italy* 14, no. 2 (2009): 183–202.

30. For a detailed explanation, see Gianfranco Baldini and Adriano Pappalardo, *Elections, Electoral Systems and Volatile Voters* (Basingstoke: Palgrave, 2009), 71.

31. Luciano Bardi, "Electoral Change and Its Impact on the Party System in Italy," *West European Politics* 30, no. 4 (2007): 711–32.

32. See Jonathan Hopkin, "A Slow Fuse: Italy and the EU Debt Crisis," *The International Spectator* 47, no. 4 (December 2012): 35–48.

33. See Sergio Rizzo and Gian Antonio Stella, *La Casta. Come i politici italiani sono diventati intoccabili* (Milan: Rizzoli, 2007).

34. See Filippo Tronconi, "Da dove arrivano i voti del M5S?" *Il Mulino* 2 (2013): 356–63.

35. I deal with these aspects more in depth in Gianfranco Baldini, "Don't Count Your Chickens before They Are Hatched: The 2013 Italian General and Presidential Election," *South European Society and Politics* (2013): doi:10.1080/13608746.2013.860269.

36. See Matthew Flinders, *Defending Politics. Why Democracy Matters in the XXIst Century* (Oxford: Oxford University Press, 2012).

37. See John Keane, "Monitory Democracy?" in *The Future of Representative Politics*, ed. S. Alonso et al. (Cambridge, Cambridge University Press, 2011), 212–35.

38. See Gianfranco Pasquino, "Italian Presidents and Their Accordion: Pre-1992 and Post-1994," *Parliamentary Affairs* 65, no. 4 (2012): 845–60.

39. See Edward C. Banfield, *The Moral Basis of a Backward Society* (New York: Free Press, 1967 [1958]); and Gabriel A. Almond and Sidney Verba, *The Civic Culture: Political Attitudes and Democracy in Five Nations* (London: Sage, 1989 [1965]), where Italian culture was defined as "parochial." See also R. Vivarelli, *Italia 1861* (Bologna: Il Mulino, 2013).

40. Italy is twenty-second out of twenty-five OECD countries in the size of its shadow economy, with an increase from 21.2 percent of GNP in 1996 to 23.1 percent in 2006; see Friedrich Schneider and Andreas Buehn, *Shadow Economies and Corruption All over the World: Revised Estimates for 120 Countries*, 2009, 28, http://www.economics-ejournal.org/economics/journalarticles/2007-9 (accessed January 11, 2014).

CHAPTER 5

Scandinavia

STILL THE MIDDLE WAY?

Eric S. Einhorn

Scandinavia

Norway

Population (million):	5.0
Area in Square Miles:	125,050
Population Density in Square Miles:	40
GDP (in billion dollars, 2012):	$281.7
GDP per Capita (PPP, 2012):	$55,900
Not a Member of EC/EU; joined European Economic Area	1992

Performance of Key Political Parties in Parliamentary Elections of September 9, 2013

Centre (agrarian) Party (SP)	5.5%
Christian People's Party (KrF)	5.6%
Conservative Party (H)	26.8%
Labour Party (DNA)	30.8%
Left Party (V)	5.2%
Progress Party (FrP)	16.3%
Socialist Left Party (SV)	4.1%

Main Officeholders: Prime Minister: Erna Solberg, H (2013); and Head of State: King Harald V

Sweden

Population (million):	9.6
Area in Square Miles:	173,730
Population Density in Square Miles:	55
GDP (in billion dollars, 2012):	$399.4
GDP per Capita (PPP, 2012):	$41,900
Joined EC/EU	January 1, 1995

Performance of Key Political Parties in Parliamentary Elections of September 19, 2010

Centre (agrarian) Party (C)	6.6%
Christian Democrats (KD)	5.6%
Green Party (MP)	7.3%
Left Party (V)	5.6%
Liberal People's Party (FP)	7.1%
Moderates (M)	30.1%
Social Democrats (SD)	30.6%
Sweden Democrats (SD)	5.7%

Main Officeholders: Prime Minister: Fredrik Reinfeldt, M (2010, 2006); and Head of State: King Carl XVI Gustaf

Denmark

Population (million):	5.6
Area in Square Miles:	16,637
Population Density in Square Miles:	337
GDP (in billion dollars, 2012):	$213.6
GDP per Capita (PPP, 2012):	$38,300
Joined EC/EU	January 1, 1973

Performance of Key Political Parties in Parliamentary Elections of September 15, 2011

Danish People's Party (DF)	12.3%
Unity List-The Red Greens (ERG)	6.7%
Conservative People's Party (KF)	4.9%
Radical Liberal (RV)	9.5%
Social Democracy in Denmark (SD)	24.8%
Socialist People's Party (SF)	9.2%
Liberal (agrarian) Party of Denmark (VDLP)	26.7%
Liberal Alliance (LA)	2.8%

Main Officeholders: Prime Minister: Helle Thorning-Schmidt, SD (2009); and Head of State: Queen Margrethe II

Finland

Population (million):	5.4
Area in Square Miles:	130,560
Population Density in Square Miles:	41
GDP (in billion dollars, 2012):	$200.7
GDP per Capita (PPP, 2012):	$37,000
Joined EC/EU	January 1, 1995

Performance of Key Political Parties in Parliamentary Elections of April 17, 2011

Christian Democrats (KD)	4.0%
Finnish Centre [agrarian] Party (Kesk)	15.8%
Finnish Social Democratic Party (SD)	19.1%
Green Party (Vihr)	7.3%
Left Wing Alliance (Vas)	8.1%
Conservative Party (Kok)	20.4%
Swedish People's Party (RKP/SFP)	4.3%
True Finns Party (PS)	19.1%

Main Officeholders: President: Tarja Kaarina Halonen, SD (2000); and Prime Minister: Jyrki Katainen (2010)

The Scandinavian "middle way" first attracted international attention in the 1930s at the depths of the Great Depression, coinciding with an era when the fragile foundations of democracy were crumbling across Europe. Industrial capitalism based on "free markets," as well as the still-shallow roots of political democracy, was threatened by a rising fascist tide on the right and a brutal but, for many on the left, attractive communist model in the Soviet Union. President Franklin D. Roosevelt's 1933 perception of "a third of the nation, ill-clothed, ill-fed, and ill-housed" described most of the industrialized world. Out of this chaos came a unique welfare-state model in Denmark, Norway, and Sweden, offering a "middle way" between these extremes. It developed over time and out of an accumulation of experience. But if you have to pick a "birthday," January 30, 1933, is our choice.

Copenhagen was cold and foggy in its midwinter gloom. The political and economic situation was as bleak as the weather. Fully 40 percent of Danish wage earners—two out of five—were out of work in this gray third winter of the Great Depression.

The Danish Employers Federation had announced that it would lock out all union members still working on February 1 to enforce its demand on the unions for a 20 percent wage reduction. Farm mortgage foreclosures, following a general collapse of agricultural prices, cast a long shadow in the countryside. The Danish Social Democratic prime minister, Thorvald Stauning—a former cigar worker who had led the government briefly in the 1920s and formed another government with the center-left Radical Liberals in 1929 on the eve of the Depression—called an extraordinary Sunday-morning parliamentary session. The agenda was legislation to extend the national labor contract under which the unions worked, thus to stave off economic disaster. Behind closed doors, the government negotiated with the Agrarians and Radical Liberals to provide the necessary votes on the bill's third reading the following day. When an acceptable compromise could not be reached, Prime Minister Stauning invited the negotiators home for what turned out to be a historic bargaining session.

The agreement that emerged in the predawn hours of January 30 in Stauning's modest apartment in a city-owned housing block on Kanslergade called for four major actions:

1. an extension of the existing labor agreements without wage reductions,
2. a massive public works program to put the unemployed back to work and to provide winter relief for their families,
3. a devaluation of the currency to stimulate farm exports and agricultural price supports to stabilize farm incomes, and
4. a fundamental restructuring of the Danish patchwork of social insurance and poverty relief measures into a comprehensive program.

The exhausted cabinet members and Agrarian Liberal Party leadership announced the agreement to parliament and struggled through Monday evening to finish putting the deal together. Without realizing it, these Danish politicians were founding what would become known as the Scandinavian middle way.

This was, however, not the only portentous political event of January 30. South of the Danish border that same Monday, the German president, Paul von Hindenburg, facing the Weimar Republic's collapse into economic depression and political extremism, summoned a controversial, untried party leader to form a new government. The recipient of von Hindenburg's confidence was Adolf Hitler.

The Meaning of the Middle Way

Hitler's Third Reich engulfed Europe in flames during the next decade, but it finally collapsed under its own aggressive and self-destructive impulses. The hard-won Danish "Kanslergade Compromise," by contrast, set the pattern for the modern Scandinavian welfare states that have far outlasted Nazism and Stalinist Communism. As Western countries struggle with the protracted "Great Recession" after 2008, it is useful to recall these events.

The Kanslergade Compromise called for wide-ranging state intervention to manage the market economy. The government became involved in setting wages and agricultural prices, establishing credit and exchange policy, and putting the unemployed back to work. It created a comprehensive economic security net for the unemployed and for all those out of the labor market. And, as a compromise between Social Democrats, Radical Liberals, and Agrarians, it broadened and cemented the center of the political spectrum.

In a way, events in Germany that day changed the very complexion of democratic politics in Scandinavia. Before Hitler's assumption of power, the Scandinavian Social Democrats—by far the largest party in Denmark, Norway, and Sweden—could reasonably strive to win a majority on their own to enact a socialist program, with the political polarization that would ensue. In Finland, the Social Democrats had emerged from a civil war in a tie with the Agrarians for the largest percentage of the vote. But with Hitler's rise to power in the Weimar Republic, the handwriting was on the wall: compromise among democratic parties was vital.

As Hitler consolidated his power by crushing the German Social Democrats, the Communist Party, and the independent trade unions, in Sweden a new Social Democratic government quickly followed the Danish example by agreeing with center parties on minimum farm prices and a public works program to create jobs for the unemployed. The Norwegian Labor Party struck a similar deal with its Agrarian Party in 1935.

A compromise across the dividing line between socialist and "bourgeois" parties was initially a kind of defeat for the Scandinavian socialist and Social Democratic parties because it postponed indefinitely the achievement of true socialism. But cooperation did solidify democratic politics in a situation that threatened the very existence of social democracy.

Thereafter, Scandinavian compromise became much more than a tactic; it became a virtue in itself because it solidified a broad national consensus around an inclusive democratic society. The Social Democratic welfare state, interventionist and protective of the people, became a surrogate for socialism. Its principle was to achieve redistribution and broadly shared prosperity through compromises acceptable to the nonsocialist center parties. Moreover, compromise worked: state intervention in the collapsing market economy began to stabilize farm income, put the unemployed back to work, reduced conflict in the labor market, and offered hope to the Scandinavian peoples in despair over the Depression and the threat of German aggression. Over the ensuing decades, such compromises would become the hallmark of effective parliamentary democracy throughout much of Europe and beyond.

Right and left faced off despite the Nazi threat in countries such as France. But in Scandinavia, a "national democratic compromise" started building what Swedish Social Democratic Prime Minister Per Albin Hansson called "the people's home": a society that took care of all its citizens.

This Scandinavian model—an interventionist state managing the market economy toward a combination of growth, full employment, and large-scale welfare programs supported by agreement between employers and unions—was widely followed subsequently in Western Europe. In fact, it was the precursor of the Western European "postwar Keynesian consensus" after World War II. In the 1930s, the U.S. journalist Marquis Childs (*Sweden: The Middle Way*, 1936) dubbed the Scandinavian accord "the middle way," meaning a middle or third way between "savage" capitalism—that is, the failed capitalism of the Depression era in the West—and Stalinist Communism, the totalitarian regime then reigning in Russia.

After the war, the Scandinavian democracies continued to constitute a middle way in the Cold War ideological and geopolitical conflict, in both domestic and foreign policy terms. For many in the West (including the United States), the Scandinavian middle way was extremely attractive. For example, a leading U.S. journalist, William L. Shirer, in *The Challenge of Scandinavia* (1955), updated Childs' account to describe the region's blend of capitalism with a social conscience; private production would support full employment and an expanding social welfare network, and it would reduce social and economic inequalities.

In domestic policy, Denmark, Norway, and Sweden built advanced capitalist market economies in which the state played both a regulatory and a redistributive role. Under predominantly Social Democratic governments, the state's role for a generation was far greater than in almost all of the other Western, capitalist democracies, although policy innovations in Scandinavia often set the pattern for policies elsewhere on the Continent ten or twenty years later.

During the Cold War, the Scandinavians sought a middle way in foreign policy as well. Although strong supporters of the United Nations, they recognized quickly its limitations. Efforts to fashion a Scandinavian defense union that would provide a viable military foundation for neutrality broke down in 1949, and on Scandinavia's western fringes, Denmark, Norway, and Iceland joined the North Atlantic Treaty Organization (NATO), although they often seemed reluctant members. Finland, which had fought World War II on the German side, signed a separate peace agreement with the Soviet Union in 1944; its neutrality was guaranteed by treaty. Sweden continued to pursue a neutrality policy that had kept it out of war since 1815. Defense strategists wrote of a "Nordic balance," in which Swedish neutrality between NATO in the West and the Soviet Bloc in the East guaranteed Finnish neutrality and independence vis-à-vis the Soviet Union and permitted Denmark and Norway to pursue a strategy of lowering tensions on the northern flank of NATO by refusing to allow foreign troops or nuclear weapons on their territory.

In international economic affairs, there was balance as well. Denmark reluctantly joined the European Community (now the European Union [EU]) when Britain did in 1973; the Norwegians, even more disinclined, voted narrowly against joining Europe. Sweden and Finland held that joining the European Community would compromise their neutrality. All four distinguished themselves by supporting international cooperation that reached across the dividing lines between East and West and between north and south.

Finland developed differently between World War I and World War II—primarily because of the bitter civil war between the "Whites" and the "Reds" in 1917–1918 that the conservative Whites won. Yet in the post–World War II period, Finland came increasingly to resemble the rest of the Scandinavian area in the realm of domestic politics, as it caught up in terms of industrialization, welfare, and living standards. Even its peculiar international position gradually assumed a more Scandinavian "balance."

All this changed at the end of the 1980s. With the end of Soviet dominance of Eastern Europe and the collapse of the USSR itself in 1991, the Scandinavian countries found their middle way questioned anew. What was it a middle way between?

The middle way that had served the Scandinavian countries so well domestically and internationally from the 1930s into the 1980s became confused amid economic crises and globalization, along with political discord at home. Sweden and Finland opted for EU membership and closer ties to Europe in 1995. The middle way's extensive public services, high taxes, and state regulation of the market economy were challenged as well by international economic integration and the growing predominance of free-market thinking. New interest groups and social changes, including new roles for women, an aging population, and significant non-European immigration, challenged the consensus. Then came the current economic turmoil.

The rest of this chapter analyzes the rise and fall of the Scandinavian model in domestic politics, in European integration policy, and in foreign policy generally.

A SOCIAL LABORATORY

The Nordic countries are idiosyncratic in many ways. They are small in terms of population (see the data on this chapter's opening page). With the exception of Iceland (which has 320,000 inhabitants), they are roughly comparable to medium-sized U.S. states. When compared to other members of the European Union, Sweden is about the size of Greece or Portugal; Ireland and Luxembourg are smaller than Denmark and Finland.

Denmark, Iceland, Norway, and Sweden share common roots ethnically, linguistically, and culturally; and Finland—despite its distinct ethnic and linguistic origins—shares a common Nordic history and religion with them. Further, Denmark, Iceland, Norway, and Sweden also were distinguished by remarkable internal ethnic, racial, religious, and linguistic homogeneity. This aspect of Scandinavian societies, more than any other, made the development of the solidaristic Scandinavian model possible.

Until they began to receive a substantial flow of immigrants in the 1960s, more than 90 percent of the population of each country shared the same cultural, linguistic, and racial roots. About 95 percent of the population was Lutheran and belonged to the state church. As a consequence, politics and policy in all three countries focused for decades to a unique degree on economic and class issues rather than the religious, linguistic, and ethnic conflicts that often dominate other societies. However, a generation of immigration, much of it from non-European countries, has literally changed the face of Denmark, Norway, and Sweden. Today, more than one in ten Swedish residents is born abroad. For the first time in more than a century, "ethnic" and immigration issues have become a source of political conflict.

Historically, Finland has been substantially more divided domestically than its Scandinavian neighbors. The legacy of Swedish settlement and rule until 1809 and of Russian rule from 1809 to 1917 left a significant Swedish-speaking population on the southwest coast of Finland and a small Russian Orthodox religious minority. Moreover, as mentioned, Finland was torn by a bitter civil war in 1917–1918 between the Reds and Whites. The former were radical socialists who sought to emulate Lenin's Bolshevik Revolution; the latter were a coalition of primarily antiradical nationalists. The Finnish Whites, backed by German troops, won the war and interned their opponents in concentration camps for a number of years. Half a century later, the way Finns voted in national elections was still closely tied to which side of the civil war their grandfathers had fought on. Unlike Denmark, Norway, and Sweden—where the communists played a major role only immediately after World War I and World War II—the Finnish labor movement was split down the middle between communists and Social Democrats, by the civil war and its aftermath. This division prevented the Social Democratic dominance in Finland that Denmark, Norway, and Sweden witnessed in the 1930s.

Geopolitical proximity to "big brother" Russia shaped the Finns' national political agenda. Finland by itself fought a brave but doomed war against Russia in the winter of 1939–1940. Then, after Germany invaded the Soviet Union in June 1941, Finland reentered the war on the German side, exiting with a separate peace treaty in 1944. Russia held a major naval base on Finnish soil covering the approaches to Helsinki until 1956.

In the postwar period, the decline in the Swedish minority through assimilation and emigration to Sweden has diminished traditional ethnic and linguistic divisions, and memories of the Finnish civil war have faded. Migration into Finland has been much less than that seen in most Western European countries. And, of course, Finland's dangerous situation vis-à-vis Russia changed dramatically with the Soviet Union's collapse. In the last thirty years, Finnish politics has converged increasingly with the general Scandinavian Social Democratic model.[1]

DOMESTIC POLITICS: HOW DIFFERENT IS SCANDINAVIA?

Its location on the geographical fringe of Europe has meant that the Scandinavian countries have escaped some European developments entirely, while lagging behind on others. Throughout most of the nineteenth century, the Scandinavians trailed Western Europe in both industrial and political development. Industrialization came late, beginning only in about 1855 in Denmark, 1890 in Sweden, and 1905 in Norway—a full century after England, Germany, Belgium, and France. Viewing nineteenth-century European political development in terms of three central themes—constitutionalism, nationalism, and democracy—the Scandinavians lagged behind in all but the first, with Sweden's strong state and well-established constitutional traditions and Norway's 1814 Constitution remaining the oldest written European constitution still in force. Nationalism first became a major impulse in Denmark following its confrontations with German nationalism along its southern boundary after 1848 and the loss of Denmark's German duchies in 1864.[2] Norway enjoyed a national cultural revival in the 1880s, and its confrontation with Sweden over full independence in 1905 sharpened national feelings in both countries. Political democracy (parliamentary supremacy) came even more slowly: in 1884 in Norway, 1901 in Denmark, and 1917 in Sweden and Finland.

Late development in these spheres meant that the economic basis for liberalism developed late. The agrarian and labor movements, which began in Scandinavia as elsewhere in Europe in the latter half of the nineteenth century, swept through the countryside and the new industrial towns like a prairie fire. Organizing in a virtual vacuum, the "popular movements" of family farmers and industrial workers built their own economic and political organizations, which claimed the high ground of an egalitarian response to industrialization and political democracy. Thanks to the high literacy levels encouraged by Lutheranism and by state educational policies in the eighteenth and early nineteenth centuries, the democratic popular movements were led from below, and the tie between the leaders and the led remains close even today.[3]

Even as the Scandinavians lagged behind Europe in many areas in the eighteenth and nineteenth centuries, they led in one: the strong state. The Swedes developed in the sixteenth and seventeenth centuries what was probably the most modern state in Europe in terms of its capacity to govern, and Swedish military prowess from the Thirty Years' War through Charles XII's misadventures in Russia reflected both the state's strength and the success of state-sponsored development of military industries. By the time of the establishment of modern political organizations and democratic institutions in the last part of the nineteenth century, the Scandinavians had a well-established tradition of a strong state and a professional civil service. The right saw the strong state as good in itself; the left, as a tool for reform.

These three factors—relative isolation, powerful popular movements, and a strong state—created the conditions for the Scandinavian middle way in the twentieth century.

SOCIAL DEMOCRACY AND EUROPEAN DEVELOPMENT: SUCCESS, THEN CRISIS

More than any other single factor, what set Scandinavian politics and policy apart was the predominant role played by the "popular movements"—farmers and labor—that represented the economically disenfranchised. Organizing from below in a virtual political vacuum in the latter half of the nineteenth century, farm and labor organizations swept the countryside, towns, and cities in an evangelical wave. In addition to the creation of the agrarian and labor parties, which came to be the great bearers of the democratic tradition, they created an immense economic and cultural infrastructure, including producer and consumer cooperatives, colleges, sports clubs, newspapers and publishing houses, theaters, and much else.

Both agrarian and labor movements shared certain central values. These included egalitarianism, a belief in democracy, and a strong commitment to building their own institutions. Allied in the struggle for political democracy, farmers and workers had much that united them even when ideology—private property versus socialization of the means of production—divided them. It is not inconsequential that the Danish Social Democrats adopted land reform and support for small farmers as their agrarian policy in the 1890s, much to the chagrin of the more orthodox German Social Democrats who were otherwise the Danes' mentors.

This massive political organization preceded the establishment of parliamentary democracy everywhere except Norway, where it coincided with the democratic breakthrough. Because numbers had not counted previously in politics, the conservatives had never taken the trouble to organize. Consequently, they found themselves playing catch-up after the agrarian 'radicals' and labor movement's ideas had already won adherents from their tenants in the countryside and servants in the cities.

Scandinavian popular movements were most remarkable in the degree to which they drew their leadership from the ranks of the movement itself, rather than from the educated elite. The liberal agrarian parties were led predominantly by farmers, and the labor parties by workers—not lawyers, teachers, civil servants, or priests.[4] This kept them honest. Government for the people works best when it is by the people and of the people.

The combination of democracy from below—of leaders sprung from and tied to the organizations of those they lead—with relative ethnic and religious homogeneity, overarching agreement on basic values, and relatively small communities, offers powerful drivers for a cohesive, solidaristic welfare state based, as one turn-of-the-twentieth-century trade union tract put it, on the principle of "reciprocal obligation or mutual responsibility."

Despite such advantages, nineteenth-century Scandinavia was a poor, class-ridden, and static region, as reflected in the waves of immigration to North America that also contributed to rapid social changes. Millions of Swedes and Norwegians, as well as many Danes and Finns, simply left for new opportunities. At first this removed considerable political and economic pressure, but later it stimulated interest in social, economic, and political reforms even among national conservatives. Knowledge of better economic opportunities abroad and the success of democratic government in North America and later Britain encouraged domestic reformers in both the labor and agrarian movements. Nationalists recoiled at the loss of youthful and energetic citizens.

Out of these conflicts emerged a civil society of the strongest sort. Citizens in the popular movements connected in a myriad of voluntary associations that mediated between them and the state and also provided direct economic, cultural, and social benefits. Organizing successfully around these associations, popular movements ultimately also captured state power. In the last fifty years, the welfare, educational, and regulatory functions of the popular-movement organizations were transferred to public administration, and many of the social and cultural functions previously provided by the popular-movement organizations were taken over by local and national government and provided by public employees instead of movement members. This generalized those social services to all the people, but it removed them from control from below. This also left the popular movements—especially the Social Democratic labor movement—dependent on control of the state to achieve their objectives.

The existence of a strong state and the tradition of an honest and professional civil service offered the mechanism for building a more egalitarian society. Principles of Keynesian economics advocating job-creating public programs were independently developed by Scandinavian economists during the Depression. Cautiously applied, they offered a route to use the state to improve the performance of capitalist market economies. The combination of the two provided the means to solve the classic problem of industrial capitalism—great and pervasive poverty amid great wealth—without revolution, by a lasting commitment to spread growth more equally than the existing distribution of wealth and income. That commitment lay at the core of the Kanslergade Compromise and the subsequent, similar national compromises in Norway and Sweden. It was driven forward politically by the Social Democrats with what proved to be a virtually unparalleled grasp on power in democratic elections.

Within the lifetime of a single generation, this commitment transformed Scandinavia from a region of great poverty—characterized by the immigrants' "flight to America"—into societies of widely shared affluence. The image of "the fortified poorhouse," as the title of Zeth Höglund's book characterized Sweden in 1913, gave way to Per Albin Hansson's view of Sweden as "the people's home" (*Folkhemmet*) in the 1930s, as class struggle gave way to national construction under social democratic government. By the 1960s, Sweden and Norway, which had been among the poorest European countries some fifty years earlier, were among the most affluent. The slums and poverty were gone.

The Scandinavian success relied on the use of the state to achieve broad economic goals, and that rested on the assumption that the nation-state was the relevant unit for economic policy. That certainly was true following the collapse of the international trading system in the 1930s, which was anomalous given Scandinavia's long global trading history. It was equally true in the reconstruction after World War II. But by the 1960s and 1970s, as growing national affluence transformed the lives of the working class, the Scandinavian countries once again became fully enmeshed in an interdependent global trading system. This development accelerated prosperity but brought vulnerability to the oil crises of the 1970s and the ever more invasive global business cycles after 1990.[5]

Political Democracy Scandinavian Style

Denmark, Norway, and Sweden share a great deal in terms of political structures and political actors. Finland is different historically, but it has converged on the other three countries in the postwar period.[6] Much of what they have in common stems from their similarities in terms of cohesion, as discussed earlier. Some of it stems from their close ties in the Nordic Council and various European organizations, which facilitates the diffusion of political ideas. The Scandinavian labor movements and the Social Democratic parties have interacted especially closely over the years.

POLITICAL INSTITUTIONS

All four countries are parliamentary democracies based on proportional representation. All are clearly democratic in the sense that regular competitive elections determine who holds political office and what policies are made. All are parliamentary systems in the sense that parliament—the legislative body—is the most important branch of government.

Denmark, Norway, and Sweden are pure parliamentary systems. The legislative majority selects the executive (the prime minister and the cabinet) and can force the executive out by a "vote of no confidence." In both cases, parliament is the ultimate arbiter of the constitutionality of its own legislation, although a variety of checks are imposed on parliamentary abuses of power, as we will discuss in this chapter. Courts rarely review the constitutionality of parliamentary legislation, as the U.S. Supreme Court does, but their membership in the EU has injected substantial portions of EU law into their national legal systems with increasing controversy. EU courts review national legislation and policies, and national courts enforce European laws. Norway is unique in Europe, as its Constitution, dating back to 1814, prevents calling early elections, which is otherwise a standard characteristic of parliamentary government.

Finland has a mixed presidential-parliamentary form of government, not unlike that of France in the Fifth Republic. The president, who heads the executive branch, is directly elected by a popular vote (prior to 1994, Finnish law provided for indirect election) for a six-year term. The president directs foreign policy, commands the armed forces, and can dissolve parliament. A new constitution entered into force in 2000, clarifying and strengthening the primacy of the prime minister and the cabinet, which are selected by the parliament. Together the executive cabinet, led by the prime minister, and parliament share primary responsibility for domestic and EU affairs. Parliament can force the cabinet from office by a vote of no confidence. In practice, this division has made the prime minister the most important actor of the executive branch in terms of policymaking, but there certainly were times during the Cold War when the president's role overshadowed that of his prime minister. There is no national judicial review of the constitutionality of legislation, but again national courts frequently enforce the supremacy of EU law.

Despite the multiparty system—today, seven to ten or more parties are represented in the national parliaments—and the rarity of single-party majorities, the Scandinavians have had stable and effective government because they practice what Dankwart Rustow called "the politics of compromise" in his 1955 classic study of that name.[7] Scandinavian government is coalition government, sometimes through multiparty governments and at other times through bargains worked out in parliament between a minority government and other parties whose agreement has been attained on an issue-by-issue basis.

Although Denmark and Sweden maintained an upper house of parliament until 1953 and 1970, respectively, all four now elect a unicameral—single-house—parliament. Until 2009, the Norwegian parliament (Stortinget) divided into two bodies to consider certain types of legislation, but now all proceedings take place in a single chamber. In all parliaments, much of the detailed legislative and oversight work and most of the necessary multiparty compromises are worked out in standing committees. There are usually parliamentary committees for each governmental ministry, plus some with special competency (constitutional affairs or relations with the European Union). Parties are represented on committees in proportion to their overall strength, but coalitions are usually required for any significant actions. Many committee proceedings are closed, precisely to encourage interparty compromises, but public hearings have become more common. Thanks to the Internet and TV, parliamentary processes now enjoy much greater media coverage.

In all four countries, a proportional representation system is used in electing parliament as well as local councils. Thus, all parties of significant size are represented in parliament with approximately the same proportion of seats as they have support among voters. Although proportional representation was introduced in an existing multiparty system and stabilized it for a number of decades, as new lines of division—including those over the European Union, the environment, and immigration—have come to the fore in recent years, this election system has permitted growing fragmentation in parliament.

Denmark, Norway, and Sweden remain constitutional monarchies. Scandinavian monarchs took office within constitutional limits (Karl Johan in Sweden in 1809 and Norway in 1815; and Haakon VII in Norway in 1905) or accepted these limits with relative grace (Frederik VII in Denmark in 1849). They proved more resistant to yielding the power to choose the prime minister to the elected parliamentary majority (1884 in Norway, 1901 in Denmark, and 1917 in Sweden), but here, too, they bowed to the winds of change. Although the governmental power of the Scandinavian monarchs is virtually nil today, they remain important symbols of national unity, above the lines of party or division by interest. In times of crisis, this symbolic role has had real political significance.

In Finland, the president has the symbolic role played by the monarchs, as well as a more practical role in foreign policy. Although elected with a partisan affiliation, the Finnish president stands above party lines while in office. For more than fifty years (1939–1991), the presidents assumed a special role in managing relations with the Soviet Union. This also enhanced presidential internal political powers.

All four countries have unitary, rather than federal, governments in the sense that all sovereignty resides in the national government, and the powers of the provinces and other subunits of government are derived from the national government. However, Finland provides far-reaching local autonomy for the Swedish-speaking Åland Islands, and Denmark provides even greater autonomy for Greenland and the Faeroe Islands, which have been granted the status of near independence. The Faeroes never joined the European Community, and Greenland, which acquired autonomy in 1979, quickly used its independence to withdraw from the European Community—the only territory to date to do so. In the past decade, both have grown increasingly impatient with their ties to Denmark, but with no substitute in sight for the large budgetary subsidies that are sent from Copenhagen, the status quo will continue for a while longer.

Although power is clearly concentrated in the hands of the national government, many governmental services have been delegated to municipal and county government. Thus, most social services, including education, medical care, hospitals, and services for children, families, and the elderly, are provided by municipalities. Indeed, a higher proportion of governmental spending occurs at the local level in Scandinavia than at the state and local levels in the United States. Thus, within unitary states, the Scandinavians have thoroughly decentralized the provision of governmental services.

In order to make this decentralization effective, Denmark, Norway, and Sweden undertook similar consolidations of local government in the late 1960s and early 1970s. The consequence was to cut the number of local governments by half in Norway, three-fourths in Sweden, and four-fifths in Denmark. Denmark further consolidated local and regional government in 2007. In Finland, a similar consolidation was blocked, and the number of local administrations was reduced only by about one-sixth in this period. Generally speaking, these reforms were successful in establishing the capacity to expand social services in smaller towns and rural areas, but they undercut the relationship between citizens and their government in rural districts. Although access to elected officials remains high in Scandinavia by comparison to most other democracies, it is much diminished in comparison to the past.

Local and regional governments enjoy substantial taxing powers, but their dependence on budgetary transfers from the central government and the standardization of social, educational, and other local services have constrained their autonomy. In Denmark, for example, fourteen counties were consolidated into five "regions" with responsibility primarily limited to health care, but a similar proposal in Norway was withdrawn. One striking aspect of Scandinavian politics is the degree to which government and the civil service are seen as national resources. This is a result of a convergence of causes. Scandinavian conservatives have traditionally supported a strong state as an instrument of national development. Popular movements, including especially the Social Democratic labor movement, have seen the government as a mechanism for extending their egalitarian goals to the entire society. Significant antigovernment or antistate movements have always been few. Despite some libertarians on the right and anarchists on the left, the distrust of government seen across the political spectrum in the United States has generally been absent in Scandinavia. Furthermore, Scandinavian public administration generally has been deserving of citizen respect: its bureaucrats have been professional, efficient, and honest.

However, that popular belief in the benevolence of public administration does not extend to the transnational public policy dimension. The European Union's multitudinous rules and regulations frequently strike most Scandinavians as downright arcane. For example, the European Union promulgated measures regulating the size of strawberries and the curvature of cucumbers shortly before the 1992 Danish referendum on the Maastricht Treaty; an effort to harmonize the dimensions of condoms, however, foundered on Italian opposition. One acerbic Danish placard during this referendum put it succinctly: "If you think there are already enough idiots running your life, vote no!" As EU regulations become targets for public ridicule and additional policy responsibilities shift from national capitals to distant EU institutions, the problem of the "democratic deficit" will become more acute.

POLITICAL ACTORS

Scandinavian democracy historically has been based on strong, disciplined, mass-membership parties, which organize hundreds of thousands of voters as dues-paying party members. Parties had structured political competition at the local as well as the national levels. They provided channels for recruiting political leaders; the career pattern was to start by running for the local municipal council. Municipal office or parliament followed for those who proved themselves. Regular local party meetings ensured close contacts between the elected officials and their party constituency. Because the parties offered different policy choices in the election campaigns, they allowed citizens a means to control not just the people in government but also the policies of government. Problematic for democratic participation has been an accelerating decline in party memberships. Social Democratic parties, which no longer automatically enroll union members, account for much of this decline, but all traditional parties have been hit.

The parties have been complemented by equally strong interest groups that organize workers, farmers, and employers. These groups, which we will look at, have typically been closely linked to individual parties. The unions have traditionally been Social Democratic (except in Finland, where they were hotly contested by the Communists), the farmer organizations have been the mainstays of the agrarian parties, and the employers have typically had a looser association with the Conservatives. Unlike many Western countries, Scandinavian labor unions have maintained their remarkably high memberships (often over 80 percent of blue- and white-collar employees). While most are rather passive members, organized labor remains a strong political actor.

PARTIES AND PARTY SYSTEMS

From the origins of parliamentary democracy at the turn of the twentieth century to the 1970s, the predominant pattern in all four countries was the five- or six-party system. On the right was the Conservative Party, which had been late to organize a mass base because it had wielded the levers of power on behalf of the elites and propertied classes before the democratic breakthrough. In the center were the nineteenth-century proponents of democracy: the Liberals and the Agrarians. To the left of center were the Social Democrats, their junior allies in the nineteenth-century push for democracy. The Social Democrats outgrew the coalition by the mid-1920s and typically polled about 40 to 45 percent of the vote from the 1930s through the 1970s. On the extreme left were the radical socialists—Communists from the 1920s through the late 1950s—and the Socialist People's Parties, which displaced the Communists in the late 1950s and early 1960s in Denmark and Norway. The remaining communists in Sweden and Finland became increasingly independent of the Soviet Union after 1960 and evolved into "radical socialist" parties by the 1980s.

There were also some variants on this general theme, especially in the center of the political spectrum. The accommodating proportional representation system allowed small parties to gain parliamentary seats on issues such as prohibition, land taxation, and cultural distinctions. The Finns had a Swedish People's Party to represent the Swedish-speaking minority. The Norwegians supported a strong Christian People's Party, which was culturally and religiously conservative but centrist in economic terms. It gradually grew into a major force in Norwegian politics. Over the past forty years, similar parties have appeared in the other Nordic countries.

Since the 1920s, the voters have been roughly split between the parties of the right and center (the "bourgeois parties"), on the one hand, and the left (the "labor" or "socialist" parties), on the other. Until recently, those with bourgeois leanings divided their votes among three or four parties of approximately equal size, while the Social Democrats typically captured the lion's share of the labor vote—40 to 45 percent of the total—with the Communists/Socialist People's Party getting 5 to 10 percent. Numerically, this gave the Social Democrats an obvious edge. Furthermore, because of the deep historical division during the struggle for parliamentary democracy between the Conservatives on the one hand and the Agrarians and Liberals on the other through the 1930s, the Social Democrats were able to form coalitions with the parties of the center once they put state socialism on the back burner after 1933.

Thus, the Social Democrats achieved a degree of hegemony in Denmark, Norway, and Sweden that was unparalleled in democratic elections. Social Democrats led the government of Denmark from 1929 to 1968, with only two breaks totaling four years (and two more during the German occupation); of Norway from 1935 to 1965, with a break of two weeks in 1963 and of five years during the German occupation; and of Sweden from 1932 to 1976, with a break of only a couple of months in the summer of 1936. They were able to use these extraordinary periods in government to reshape society by building an exceptionally strong public sector.

Finland constituted something of an exception. The Finnish labor vote (and trade unions as well) was roughly evenly split between the Communist Party and the Social Democrats, and they were direct political competitors. Consequently, the fulcrum of Finnish party politics was in the center, especially with the well-led agrarian Center Party. After 1960, the Communist-led electoral alliance vote declined, and it has taken a course similar to that of the radical socialists in the other countries and has been integrated into the parliamentary give-and-take.

The culmination of this period of Social Democratic construction of the Scandinavian welfare state was the reforms of the late 1960s and early 1970s, which expanded social services into rural areas and raised income replacement rates for the unemployed, sick, injured, and disabled from 40 to 50 percent of their market income to 70 to 90 percent of the average wage. These reforms came on line just about the time the oil price shock of 1973–1974 set off a period of economic adjustment and economic globalization throughout the West. Social democratic ideas and their carefully constructed tools of public economic management, as we will discuss, offered fewer answers in a global economy.

This relatively stable party system changed dramatically in the 1970s and 1980s. New protest parties arose on the right in protest against high taxes, growing immigrant populations, and the fact that the bourgeois parties that finally took governmental power in the late 1960s and 1970s administered the Social Democratic system rather than abolishing it; these were the so-called Progress Parties in Denmark and Norway and the short-lived New Democracy Party and later the Sweden Democrats in Sweden. Finland had somewhat similar but until recently weaker protest parties, including the Rural Party (now known as the "True Finns"). There was further subdivision in the center. Denmark saw the development of a Christian People's Party and a Center Democrat split from the right wing of the Social Democrats, but both declined in the 1990s. In Sweden, the Christian Democrats also broke into parliament. Environmentalist parties won seats in both Sweden and Finland, and the Danes and Norwegians both sent a few members to parliament from groups to the left of the Socialist People's Parties.

The consequence was that the relatively stable five- or six-party model of the 1920–1970 period has given way to a seven- or eight-party model in which several center parties and a protest party on the right seem to be a permanent part of the parliamentary constellation today. The Scandinavian Christian Democrats have more of a "Sermon on the Mount" orientation than the rightist orientation of U.S. fundamentalists. Although socially conservative (especially on the issues of abortion, drugs, pornography, and alcohol), they are strong supporters of the welfare state, foreign aid, and restrained materialism. They show a remarkable streak of religious tolerance as well: although Christian Democratic voters are overwhelmingly devout, evangelical Lutherans, the Danish party was led for some years by a Catholic, and the Swedish party included a prominent immigrant Jewish physician among its leaders and members of parliament. (They have not, however, taken ecumenicalism to the point of inclusion of Muslims.) Consequently, they have accommodated themselves easily to the give-and-take of parliamentary compromise.

The protest parties of the populist right have been less accommodating, and they were initially kept outside the patterns of parliamentary coalitions. Driven originally by opposition to taxes and bureaucracy, they have in recent years become increasingly strident in their opposition to immigrants, particularly those racially or culturally distinguishable, such as Africans, Asians, and Muslims. For a long time, they were "heard" but not "listened to." This began to change in the late 1990s as their electoral advances made them too large to be ignored. Nonsocialist governments in Norway and most recently in Denmark have counted on parliamentary votes from the "New Right." In local government, the pattern is similar; once radical parties draw 10 to 20 percent of the vote, their political influence grows. The rise of the Sweden Democrats and the True Finns since 2000 continues the trend. All of these parties are "populist-nationalist" on immigration, cultural, and European issues, but are strong supporters of the Nordic welfare states.

Although the division of the voters between the blocs long remained relatively even, there has been an increasing tilt to the right, especially when the rightist protest parties gained a growing share of working-class votes. Further, the Social Democrats were weakened by seepage of voters to their left, especially over the issue of European Community membership in the 1970s in Denmark and Norway, and European Union membership in 1994 in Sweden. For the current division of parliamentary seats among the parties, see table 5.1.

Table 5.1   Party Parliament Strength in September 2013

Country/Party	Seats
Denmark	179
Social Democrats*	45
Liberals	47
Danish People's	22
Conservatives	8
Socialist People's	15
Radical Liberals*	17
Liberal Alliance	9
Leftists	12
Greenland and Faeroe Islands	4
Finland	200
Social Democrats*	42
Center (agrarian)	44
Conservatives*	50
Left Alliance*	14
Swedish People's*	9
Greens*	10
Christian Democrats*	6
True Finns	39
Norway	169
Labor (Social Democrats)	55
Conservatives	48
Progress	29
Socialist Left	7
Christian People's	10
Center (agrarian)	10
Liberals	9
Greens	1
Sweden	349
Social Democrats	112
Moderates (conservatives)*	107
Liberals*	24
Christian Democrats*	19
Leftists	19
Center (agrarian)*	23
Greens	25
Sweden Democrats	20

* In government as of February 2014.

The cumulative loss of Social Democratic votes since the 1980s has been 5 to 20 percentage points compared to the 1940s–1970s; even with proportional representation, this produces a significant shift in the parliamentary balance. The half-century of Social Democratic hegemony that began during the 1930s Depression has ended. However, despite increased party fragmentation, the loss of part of their voting base, and a certain poverty of ideas, the Social Democrats remained the largest party in parliament in Denmark (until 2001), Norway, and Sweden. The Finnish Social Democrats have also been the largest parliamentary party for most of the post-1945 period. The Social Democrats have ceased to be the normal party of government, but they are perfectly capable of savaging governments of the right that try to cut the welfare state. Just as the nonsocialist parties have largely accepted the universal welfare state, Social Democrats have followed many neoliberal (free market) doctrines over the past quarter century, not always to their advantage.

One of the major consequences of the fragmented party system and declining Social Democratic hegemony has been the growing prevalence of minority cabinets. If we split the post–World War II period at the 1972 mark—the Danish and Norwegian European Community referenda—the Danes managed majority governments for 25 percent of the period prior to 1972 and 2 percent of the period since. The Norwegians had majority governments for 80 percent of the pre-1972 period and 20 percent of the period since. The Swedes mustered majority governments for 40 percent of the first period and only 15 percent of the most recent period. Finland remains committed to broad majority coalitions, which have accounted for nearly all its governments over the past thirty years. While one might think that this would produce political paralysis, the governments seem to function about as effectively as in the past.

There are three reasons for this. The first is the value, already discussed, placed on compromise, which makes minority government much less frustrating than it otherwise would be. The second is that various "radical" and "protest" parties on the political left and, more tentatively, on the right have become substantially less radical and more interested in participating in shaping legislation through compromise; Social Democratic minority governments can turn to their left as well as to the center for votes, while nonsocialists look to their right. The third is that, by and large, Scandinavian governments of the last twenty years have only undertaken major domestic reforms with broad parliamentary support extending well beyond the governing coalition.

INTEREST GROUPS

The Scandinavian countries are the most thoroughly organized in the world. Practically everybody belongs to his or her economic interest organization. Manufacturers, shopkeepers, renters, farmers, workers, and students are all organized. Around two-thirds of all wage and salaried workers are union members, and farmer and employer organizational percentages are equally impressive.[8] Schoolchildren, university students, priests, and military personnel each have their usually well-ordered group.

As this list suggests, Scandinavian interest organizations are divided primarily along economic lines. This mirrors the lines of political division in these societies. Moreover, the larger of the interest organizations, including both the trade union federation and the employers' organization, are sufficiently inclusive that they have to take broader, societal interests into consideration. Furthermore, until the 1980s they were highly centralized: labor agreements were negotiated nationally between the national employers' organization and the national trade union organization. Recently, collective bargaining has been decentralized by economic sector (e.g., the metal industry and public sector employees). In practice, unions and employers keep a close eye across the labor market, and contract provisions tend to move across it in similar directions. Thus, areas of conflict and cooperation spread across the economy and have immediate societal consequences.

As a result, the Scandinavian countries remain models of a peculiar kind of Social Democratic corporatism, in which interest organizations as a matter of course are integrated in making and implementing public policy. Some prefer to call the process "the negotiated economy." Interest organizations have highly professional staff and are constantly involved in governmental commissions for designing policy, including the Swedish "remiss" system of formal consultation on major initiatives with all relevant interest organizations. It remains a process of interest representation very different from Washington lobbying, but such consultations have declined over the past two decades. Governments are now more inclined to take initiatives without corporatist negotiation.

Not only are Scandinavian interest organizations involved in drafting policy, but also they implement it. Consider the national labor agreement, for example, in the years that a single overarching national contract for the private sector is negotiated: the unions and the employers, with the government as a third party, hammer out the contract, since the contract essentially determines wage formation for the period. The primary aim of the government, in terms of management of the economy, is to ensure that wage increases are noninflationary.

The practice of corporatism is eased by the small scale of the national political class in the Scandinavian countries. One faces the same people across the table. Working together becomes second nature. Economic globalization, neoliberalism, and perhaps European integration have created stress for this cozy but flexible structure. Structural economic changes, the relative decline of the industrial sector, and the rise in small enterprises also challenge the Scandinavian corporatist model. However, the current international interest in the Scandinavian "flexicurity" (flexible labor markets, active public retraining, and generous social security systems) shows that corporatism has not been static.

RESTRAINING THE GOVERNORS

The concentration of power in unicameral parliaments and the presence of strong, disciplined parties not only permit effective and responsive policymaking but also raise the specter of majority tyranny. What prevents a unified parliamentary majority from running roughshod over all opposition? What prevents systematic abuses of citizen rights? In the United States, the system of government has been carefully designed to avert majority tyranny by the division of powers between the three branches of government—legislative, executive, and judicial—and between the federal and state governments. The court system is engaged in a continual review of governmental acts. The Scandinavians do not have those mechanical checks and balances built into their government institutions. They have developed a different set of checks on abuse of power and majority tyranny.

First, the ombudsman—a Scandinavian concept that has entered the English language and U.S. practice—serves as a standing, independent check on abuses of executive power. This position was created in the Swedish Constitution of 1809 as a parliamentary restraint on abuse of royal executive power; today, it serves as a more general check on abuses throughout the executive branch. The Swedish ombudsman is elected by parliament for a four-year term and is empowered both to respond to formal citizen complaints and to initiate investigations on, for example, the basis of press reports. In recent years, the Swedish ombudsman has handled about three thousand cases a year; about 90 percent are citizen initiated. Less prominent but even older is the institution of the chancellor of justice (*Justitiekanslern*), created in 1713 by King Charles XII. In March 2006, the chancellor's office pressured Foreign Minister Freivalds to resign after she lied about her efforts to censor an anti-Muslim website. The modern media are also watchdogs: just after the change of government in Sweden in October 2006, two new conservative ministers were forced to resign when the press revealed unpaid taxes and radio and TV license fees.

The Finns added an ombudsman in 1919 at the birth of the republic that was based on the Swedish model. The Danes added a parliamentary ombudsman in the Constitution of 1953, and the Norwegians established a similar office in 1962. The formal powers of ombudsmen are amplified by a strong tradition of parliamentary inquiry (both questions to the government and committee hearings) and investigative journalism.

Second, voter referenda have increasingly checked parliamentary majorities. This is most formalized in Denmark, which has held nineteen referenda since 1915; Denmark is second only to Switzerland in direct citizen votes on key legislation, but there are no "initiatives" (citizen-proposed legislation). All constitutional changes go to a citizen vote (after having been approved by two sessions of parliament with an intervening election), any legislation except finance and tax measures can be sent to a vote by one-third of parliament, and any surrender of national sovereignty can be sent to a vote by one-sixth of parliament. Such provisions strengthen the hands of the minority vis-à-vis the majority, but they have been used only once, in 1963. While Finland and Norway lack a constitutional sanction for binding referenda (and Sweden limits it to constitutional changes), governments have always abided by voter decision except in the case of the Swedish referendum concerning which side of the road they should drive on (in 1955, despite the government's recommendation and common sense, Swedes voted to continue driving on the left; in 1967, the government shifted without a referendum). Increasingly, highly divisive issues such as nuclear power (Sweden, 1980); European Community and European Union membership (Denmark, 1972; Norway, 1972 and 1994; and Sweden and Finland, 1994); and further EU integration (Denmark, 1986, 1992, 1993, 1998, and 2000; and Sweden, 2003) have been decided by the people directly.

Third, two aspects of Scandinavian political culture tend to check parliamentary majorities. One is that facts count in Scandinavian politics. The policy debate, in both the media and the parliament, is couched in empirical terms. Demagoguery discredits the user, except, possibly, on the immigration issue. The other is that a value is placed on broader compromise. All recent governments have been formal or informal coalitions. Moreover, parties involved in compromises will not reverse the policy when they are in government. But another part is the concept that legislation passed by narrow majorities is less legitimate than that passed by broad majorities. Thus there is a tendency to seek broader majorities than are necessary simply to pass legislation.

Finally, as mentioned earlier, Scandinavian corporatism provides an open door in policymaking. Major legislative initiatives are generally preceded by governmental commissions that involve not only the political parties but also all the relevant interest groups. Trade unions, employers, and farmers' organizations are involved in practically all of these, and more specialized interest organizations take part in commissions in their spheres of interest. Such political transparency is reinforced by an active and diverse media and is supplemented nowadays by the Internet. If, however, Scandinavian corporatism continues to recede, for example in response to EU directives, these democratic safeguards will weaken.

The Welfare State and Economic Stability

The Scandinavian responses to the economic crises of the 1930s marked a sea change in the role of the state. The old "night watchman state" provided national defense, justice, police protection, roads, and elementary education. The new "welfare state" was to regulate the market economy to ensure full employment and growth and to provide social and economic security for those out of the labor market because of old age, sickness, unemployment, and disability and for families whose market income was small and number of children large.[9] This is what political scientists have come to call the "postwar consensus," but in Scandinavia it started before World War II, driven primarily by the predominant popular movements with more of an egalitarian perspective.

Scandinavian welfare states, like those in Europe generally, are not for the poor alone. They are a method of providing universal social services and economic security for the middle class as well as the working class and the marginalized poor. Despite the recent increases in using private providers, practically all social welfare expenses are in the public sector. This includes family allowances, day care and after-school care, unemployment, health care, maternity and sick pay, pensions, disability, housing subsidies, and social assistance. In the United States, by contrast, a number of these, including medical and dental care, maternity and sick pay, and the bulk of our pensions, are handled privately through employers. Unlike the U.S. provision of these services, which varies tremendously between occupational groups and among employers, Scandinavians universally receive about the same benefits.

In the postwar period, Scandinavian governments worked to achieve broadly shared affluence by two mechanisms. First, they sought to manage the economy to limit cyclical unemployment and to bring up the standards of the worst off in the labor market by channeling capital investment and labor from the least efficient firms to the most efficient firms. The trade unions' "solidaristic wage policy" was the most effective mechanism for this purpose. Over time, it raised the wages of the unskilled relative to the skilled and of women relative to men at the same time as it increased the overall efficiency of the economy.

Second, they sought to spread the dividends of economic growth more equitably than the existing market system distributed income and wealth. Those outside the labor market or in low-income groups gained, but no one lost absolutely. As a result, the policy enjoyed widespread political support, and social expenditures expanded rapidly.

Between 1960 and 1974, social spending as a share of GDP nearly doubled in the Scandinavian countries. The growth really was a product of substantial improvements in the social security net that included raising income replacement ratios for the unemployed and the disabled, raising pension levels, and expanding some social services from urban areas to include rural areas. With unemployment at a minimal 2 percent level, it cost little to raise the income replacement ratio to 80 or even 90 percent of market wages. All this occurred during a period of prolonged economic growth and, generally speaking, shared the affluence of those in the labor market with those outside and those in the labor market who had low-income families and numerous children (see table 5.2).

By contrast, the decades after 1974 were characterized by the two oil crises, the unpredicted combination of economic stagnation and inflation ("stagflation"), recurring financial crises, and the new challenges of globalization in Scandinavia as in most Western economies. In Denmark, new social expenditures from the end of the good years finished coming on line, and there was also a rapid expansion of countercyclical social expenditures because of the bad times that saw unemployment rise from the frictional level of about 2 percent to 8 percent. Sweden continued to grow the national economy and hold down unemployment by expanding the public sector; this kept unemployment at 3 percent and restrained social spending for countercyclical programs, but it pushed some economic problems forward. Norway, blessed with North Sea oil, initially escaped the hard times. Finland's economy benefited from continuing modernization and substantial trade with Soviet Russia and other Eastern European states until 1990.

Rising social expenditures in a low-growth economy began to squeeze the tax base, private consumption, and capital investment. Increasingly since the 1970s, the Scandinavian countries have struggled with maintaining economic balance. Generous unemployment benefits protected living standards when the economy turned bad, but how long can you sustain using 4 to 5 percent of GDP for that purpose? Denmark did so for two decades (1975–1995), but the cost forced unemployment policy reforms that, like Sweden's long-standing policy, emphasized "activation"—emergency

Table 5.2   Public Social Security Transfers as a Percentage of GDP (1960–2011, average for period)[a]

	1960–1973	1980–1989	1990–1999	2009–2011
Denmark	9.5	17.1	19.1	16.9
Finland	6.6	13.9	20.3	18.2
Norway	10.3	12.7	15.9	13.7
Sweden	10.0	18.3	20.9	14.8
EU-15 average	11.4	16.5	17.3	17.5[c]
United States	6.4	11.0	12.6[b]	15.4

[a]Benefits in cash or vouchers.
[b]Average from 1990 to 1996.
[c]Euro area.

Source: Organization for Economic Cooperation and Development (OECD), *Historical Statistics, 1960–97, Historical Statistics, 1970–99,* and *OECD in Figures 2009* (Paris: OECD, 1999, 2000); and OECD, *National Accounts at a Glance 2013,* http://dx.doi.org/10.1787/888932762121 (accessed January 30, 2014).

employment or training—rather than passive support. Rising income tax levels yielded increasing tax avoidance strategies until tax reform broadened the tax base by reducing deductions and bringing down marginal rates in the 1980s and early 1990s. All of the Scandinavians except the oil-rich Norwegians repeatedly sought to trim welfare programs at the margins. But despite their best efforts to hold down costs, the secular trends pushing costs up combined with growth in unemployment (particularly long-term unemployment) continued to push spending and taxes up. Governmental expenditures rose roughly 15 percent of GDP between 1974 and 1996 in all Nordic countries except Norway (unchanged thanks to petroleum-fueled prosperity). Structural economic changes finally reversed this negative trend after 1995, and social expenditures declined as unemployment fell and economic growth accelerated until the onset of the global economic crisis in 2008. The Scandinavian states once again face the challenge of effective adjustment to the global economy.

While the welfare state was being constructed—from the 1930s through the early 1970s—increased expenditures were closely correlated with real gains in living standards. Unemployment compensation was enhanced, maternity and paternity leaves were introduced, pensions went up, housing was improved, day-care centers were built, and so on. In recent years, however, expenditures have continued to rise without such clear improvements in welfare.

Today, the cost of social programs is being pushed up in Scandinavia by three other forces: demography, technology, and rising take-up rates. Aging populations—and Scandinavians top the list internationally in terms of life expectancy—require longer pensions and more services. To deal with the former, national pension-funding reforms have raised pension savings and cut unfunded liabilities. The latter is more troublesome. Improved (and expensive) medical technology continues to drive the costs of the health-care system higher; despite the comprehensive and efficient national health systems in the four countries, a health-care cost crisis looms. And take-up rates for social programs have continued to rise among the young, who shape their behavior to conform to the mold of the social-benefit system. The result is that increasing expenditures do not necessarily increase welfare. Medical technology certainly extends life, but much of the costs of that new technology are incurred in the last few months of life, when the quality of life is low.

The costs of Scandinavian social programs burden national economic competitiveness, but strong public sectors can also be a competitive advantage. Global capital mobility means that investment in high-wage areas, such as the Nordic countries, will lag unless productivity (and applied research), or currency devaluations, maintain competitiveness. Fortunately, innovative firms, rising education levels and labor force skills, and cost containment in both the public and private sectors have been successful over the past decade. Some Scandinavian policies, such as the active labor market policy and the solidaristic wage policy, address the competitiveness issue directly. Others, such as national health insurance, spread medical costs generally across society, rather than burdening particular employers.[10] The economic protections provided to families through the social welfare system encourage employees to accept technological innovation. The term "flexicurity"—a flexible economy resting on a secure social security system—still describes twenty-first-century Scandinavia.

A different—and troubling—issue in Scandinavia is the rapid increase in a no-
ticeable immigrant population. Today about 6 percent of the population of Sweden,
Denmark, and Norway carry foreign passports, as do 3 percent of the population of
Finland, and the percentage of the foreign born is higher, especially in Sweden, where
more than 15 percent were born somewhere else.[11] They and their immediate descendants are now citizens, but integration into the social mainstream has been very uneven. To a considerable extent, support for the solidaristic social welfare system rested
on the fact that those who benefited and those who paid were very similar. They spoke
the same language, worshiped in the same church (at least at Christmas), shared the
same culture, and looked very much alike. Under these circumstances, solidarity was
easy. It is far from clear that the same solidarity will pertain as immigrant populations
grow. Successful integration of non–Western European immigrants has so far eluded
the Nordic countries. The result has been higher social costs and the rise of explicitly
anti-immigration parties throughout Scandinavia (see box 5.1).

In the long run, Scandinavian prosperity in the global economy depends on
sustaining the currently successful pattern of high wages and high performance. That
requires action in Brussels and Frankfurt, where full employment has not been part of
the prevailing ideology of the European Union especially since 2008. It also requires
both anchoring domestic and attracting foreign capital. Pension and tax reforms have
encouraged a high rate of savings, bringing mass private investment (under professional management) even to Sweden, which in the past has prospered with perhaps
the most concentrated ownership of any capitalist country under Social Democratic
economic management (see box 5.2).

The past thirty years have been a watershed. The great Social Democratic project—the comprehensive welfare state supported by state economic intervention to
manage the market economy—was completed forty years ago and enjoyed broad
consensus. Various governments of the center-right and center-left could administer
this system, but there was no new, equivalent central thrust for reform as the postwar
consensus came under increasing pressure. Accelerating demographic changes—an aging and increasingly "multicultural" population—as well as relentless changes in the
European Union and in the global economy ensure that the pressure will continue.
Damage from the 2008 "Great Recession" was initially less severe in the Scandinavian
countries (except Iceland) than elsewhere in Europe, but the prolonged period of economic stagnation in Europe (and beyond) has taken its toll on these export-dependent
economies. Few in Scandinavia fault the welfare state for the latest crisis, but social
policy must adjust to the new realities. The current challenge is whether and how the
Scandinavian model can continue to adjust to domestic change and economic globalization while retaining its comprehensive, solidaristic, and humane structure.

The Roads to Europe

Europe, including Scandinavia, faced four vital questions in the wake of World War
II. Two continental conflicts within a quarter century had threatened to extinguish
European civilization. Armed struggle for control of Europe could not be allowed

Box 5.1   Cartoons and Immigrants: No Laughing Matter

Early in 2006, Denmark faced one of its worst foreign policy crises since World War II. The country's largest newspaper, the liberal *Jyllands-Posten*, published the previous September a dozen caricatures of the Prophet Muhammad, or other drawings about contemporary Danish perceptions of Islam. For some religious Muslims, any portrayal of their holiest prophet is sacrilegious, and the humorous, derogatory, or satirical drawings offended many, including some non-Muslims. The editors and Danish politicians failed to understand the potential for harm. Initial reactions were slow, but several radical Islamist activists were not content to let the issue fade. Traveling through the Middle East, they complained to several Arab governments about the intolerable insult directed at their faith. To embellish the case, several especially insulting pictures—neither drawn nor published in Denmark—were added to the "collection." Within days, Arab and foreign media spread the "news" and riots erupted in dozens of cities throughout the Muslim world. Danish embassies were attacked and in some cases destroyed (usually with the passive assistance of the "protecting" local government). Danish firms and products faced widespread boycotts. Other Scandinavian and European papers published the caricatures in support of the right to publish freely. Soon talk of a "clash of civilizations" and the threats to freedom filled the debate. Recurring threats to the cartoonists and publishers have continued.

Underlying this crisis is the challenge of integrating tens of thousands of recent immigrants into the once homogeneous Scandinavian countries. Accommodating differences has always been a challenge to societies, even when the migrants came from distant Scandinavian regions: Finns moving to Sweden in 1950s and 1960s or Greenlanders moving to Denmark a decade later often received less than enthusiastic welcomes. The real challenge was adjusting to non-European immigrants who were a trickle in the 1960s but became the majority of immigrants twenty years later. Now even Scandinavian-born children of the immigrants face significant lags in educational and vocational progress. Some social housing estates have largely immigrant populations with "natives" fleeing the surrounding areas and schools. Violence and crime have compounded the problem, including the urban riots in several Swedish cities in the spring of 2013.

Sweden and Iceland have relied on the labor market supplemented by language and other support to promote integration. When immigrants work and become self-supporting, they are more likely to adjust to the culture. Denmark faced its largest wave of immigrants and refugees during a time of high unemployment and tended to support the new residents through generous social benefits. It was not a successful program, and over the past decade the emphasis has been on rapid movement into the labor market, compulsory language and cultural instruction, and reduced social benefits. Norway and Finland have tended more toward the Danish model. In Norway and Denmark and more recently Finland and Sweden, xenophobic populist parties have attracted growing political support from voters who fear and distrust the new multiethnic society in which they live. Such parties are also anti–European Union (EU), not least because of the EU's free migration provisions. In response, the mainstream political parties have shed their reluctance to discuss the problem and have reaffirmed the supremacy of traditional Scandinavian values, particularly against violence and in favor of women's rights.

More positively, moderates among the immigrant groups have entered the political process through the traditional political parties and are represented from city councils to national parliaments and government cabinets. A willingness to discuss the problems openly—still a challenge in Sweden—but respectfully may have received a boost from the "cartoon crisis," but the immigration and cultural diversity issues will figure prominently in Scandinavian politics for many years to come.

Note: For a scholarly and balanced study of the "cartoon crisis," see Jytte Klausen, *The Cartoons That Shook the World* (New Haven, CT: Yale University Press, 2009). On immigration, see Grete Brockmann and Anniken Hagelund, eds., *Immigration Policy and the Scandinavian Welfare State 1945–2010* (New York: Palgrave Macmillan, 2012).

to occur again. At issue was, first, whether cooperation should be regional or global. A closely related second question was whether states should seek to build intensive integrated communities with like-minded states or whether cooperation should be restrained so as to include the largest number of participating countries (so-called depth-versus-breadth or deepening-versus-widening arguments). Third, should collaboration focus narrowly on specific economic or other policy problems (i.e., functional issues), or should it seek broad federal arrangements in which states would yield sovereignty over a range of policy matters? Finally, should this new international regime reinforce intergovernmental cooperation or should it carefully construct new international organizations with supranational responsibilities?

The Scandinavian states responded individually to these questions, but with some commonalities. Isolation had failed between 1939 and 1945. The collapse of world trade in the 1930s had hurt their economies. Sweden had narrowly preserved its traditional neutrality during World War II, but only by accommodating the dominant belligerents. Denmark, Norway, and Finland had been invaded and found traditional nonalignment and neutrality largely discredited at the end of war. All had supported the League of Nations after World War I, only to see ruthless power politics and fanatical nationalism return. After 1945 they hoped that the emerging United Nations organization would allow them to preserve their independence while participating in the global community and a revitalized collective security system. Finland's position as a defeated power made its position especially precarious. Hardliners in the Soviet Union believed that Finland had been a willing ally of Nazi Germany; instead, Finland's "continuation war" against the Soviet Union had been retaliation for Stalin's attack on Finland in 1939 (which had been encouraged by the Nazi-Soviet pact of August 1939 that established spheres of domination over Eastern Europe).

Scandinavia sought security and prosperity through broad European cooperation. All wished to avoid new divisions despite the obvious differences between the Western democracies and Stalin's Soviet Union. The term applied to this policy of reconciliation and constructive diplomacy was "bridge building." Bridges are built over chasms; the Scandinavian states recognized the fundamental conflicts that threatened the postwar order.

It is useful to view Scandinavian foreign policies from four perspectives: Nordic, European, Atlantic, and global. Such geopolitical shorthand is, admittedly, not precise, especially given the many changes since the Cold War.

Box 5.2   Why Do the Scandinavian Welfare States Survive?

One mystery to Americans is how political support for the Scandinavian welfare states survives when ordinary working people have to pay 50 to 60 percent of their earnings in income and other taxes. When their taxes come due, why don't they rise up in anger and overthrow the government? After all, American taxpayers have rebelled at far lower rates.

The answer is, first, that the Scandinavian welfare states rest on the principle of *solidarity*. By contrast, welfare programs in the United States rest on the principle of social insurance (e.g., Social Security, Medicare, workers' compensation, and unemployment insurance) or altruism (charity to the poor). The limit of social insurance is that we agree to insure ourselves against only those risks that we cannot afford, and altruism is even more circumscribed, limited to keeping the bodies and souls of the poor together. But solidarity—defined as "reciprocal responsibility and mutual obligation"—has permitted the Scandinavians to build far more elaborate structures of mutual support on a consensual basis.

Second, Scandinavian welfare measures are generally *universal* in scope, rather than means tested. Thus, both transfer payments (such as pensions, sick pay, maternity pay, and family allowances) and social services (such as medical and dental care, home assistance for the elderly, free education through college, and day care and after-school care for children) are available to everyone in the category, whether they are poor, working class, or middle class. Transfer payments are usually taxed, so that wealthier recipients keep a smaller share than the truly needy. Fees for some social services, such as day care, also rise with income. But generally speaking, everyone is in the same system and receives the same benefits. Every year, almost every family receives some benefits. As a witty phrase describes the situation, "The richest 90 percent help support the poorest 90 percent."

Such universal programs are costly. Scandinavian public spending on social security transfer payments is 20 percent to 40 percent higher than elsewhere in Europe and the United States.[1] Rising take-up rates for social services such as day care and after-school care have continued to push up social welfare spending despite the financial constraints on public sector spending. More disturbing, the self-restraint of the older generation about utilizing the welfare net is giving way to a culture of "entitlement" among the younger generation. Thus, in Denmark, for example, statistics indicate that the young are sicker than the old, even taking into account legitimate reasons, such as taking care of ill children. Sweden, one of the healthiest nations in the world, had more people on sick leave than most wealthy countries until recent reforms.

Still, universal public provision of social services generally provides a higher standard and is cheaper than provision through employer-funded, private insurance schemes. The classic case is medical care, which is both far more costly (by about 70 percent) in the United States as a proportion of gross domestic product and less adequately distributed than in Scandinavia. Consequently, the Scandinavian countries' health statistics (infant mortality, lifespan, etc.) beat the United States by a wide margin. Likewise the "top 1 percent" in Scandinavia earn three or four times the median income, and not ten or more times as in the United States. Typical middle-class living standards are very similar to the American level, while low-income groups in Scandinavia have a substantially higher living standard than in the United States: after-tax, after-benefit poverty rates in Scandinavia are only about a quarter of the American rate.

Everyone pays, but everyone also benefits.

---

1. Accounting definitions make exact comparison difficult. Overall social expenditures in Germany, Belgium, and the Netherlands are roughly comparable to those in Scandinavia, with France not far behind. See William Adema and Maxime Ladaique, "How Expensive Is the Welfare State? Gross and Net Indicators in the OECD Social Expenditure Database (SOCX)," OECD Social, Employment and Migration Working Papers No. 92 (Paris: OECD, 2009).

The Nordic perspective reflects history and culture, but it also implies deliberate choices. We have mentioned the common roots of the Scandinavian states, which are traceable to a loose dynastic entity known as the Kalmar Union (1397–1523).[12] The next four hundred years saw frequent and often bitter rivalry in the Nordic region until the current five independent states emerged in the twentieth century. Sweden and Denmark competed for hegemony throughout the Baltic: first against the Hanseatic League and later against the emerging Slavic powers of Poland-Lithuania and finally Russia. The dominance of Russia from the eighteenth century onward, and later the growth of German power, forced the Scandinavians into an increasingly defensive position. Not until the collapse of the Soviet Union and its sphere of influence after 1990 would the Nordic states take a proactive role (now based on cooperation) in the Baltic.

Yet even as nationalism was shaping five distinct sovereign countries, there were calls for regional cooperation. They followed two lines: a romantic "pan-Scandinavianism" that argued for a federation of the increasingly democratic societies of the north, and pragmatic functional proposals covering a range of public policies common to the industrializing economies of the five states. Although "Scandinavianism" ended historic rivalries, it did not prevent the further division of the region into the five modern nations. The practical policy approach proved most fruitful, starting with a monetary union at the end of the nineteenth century (which collapsed during World War I), an "interparliamentary union" in 1907, and regular meetings between political leaders.

After World War II, the more ambitious goals of advocates for Nordic integration repeatedly ran into two obstacles. First, the interests of the Scandinavian countries were often different and not infrequently competitive. This strengthened historical and nationalist desires in Norway, Finland, and Iceland to maintain full independence from the older Scandinavian states. Second, outside political and economic ties outweighed Scandinavian alternatives. This would be seen most dramatically in security policy after 1948, when Denmark, Norway, and Iceland chose the Atlantic alliance led by the United States; Finland accommodated its foreign relations within the narrow limits demanded by the Soviet Union; and Sweden reaffirmed its historical and successful nonalignment.

Later, economic cooperation followed a similar path, with broader European opportunities outweighing the potential of narrower Nordic proposals. Although intra-Scandinavian trade expanded significantly after 1950, access to European and global markets remained the higher priority. Despite these setbacks, in 1952 the Nordic countries established the Nordic Council—essentially an extension of the interparliamentary union—that would coordinate legislation and encourage Nordic initiatives whenever consensus could be reached. Underlying the development of Nordic policy cooperation was the primacy of Social Democratic and Labor parties during much of the 1945 to 1975 period. Even in Iceland and Finland, where this was not the case, centrist governments adopted much of the Social Democratic agenda on labor, social, and economic issues. This paved the way for regional cooperation.

Nordic cooperation continues on three levels—parliamentary, ministerial, and nongovernmental—but most efforts are now channeled through larger regional entities, especially the European Union. The annual meetings of parliamentary delegations from the five countries (plus the three autonomous regions: Åland, Greenland,

and the Faeroes) encourage pragmatic cooperation and foster personal contacts across the region as well as a comparative perspective on policy issues. Ministerial contacts are more intense and continuous. In addition, there are regular ministerial "summits"—routinized since 1971 through the Nordic Council of Ministers—which bring together the top political and administrative people for detailed discussions and planning. A common Nordic political culture that emphasizes consensus, fact finding, pragmatism, and responsibility helps this process. Common positions on European and international questions can multiply the weight of these small states. Finally, there are the various nongovernmental organizations in the educational, cultural, and scientific area that bring Scandinavians together on specific projects and interests. Again, this invigorates Nordic cooperation at the grass roots but also mobilizes important interests in support of these activities.

"Europe" in the form of "Western Europe" was at first a Cold War concept, but it increasingly gained real political and economic significance. The Nordic countries chose not to be part of the evolving European community that started with the Brussels Pact of 1948, the Schuman Plan of 1950 for a coal and steel community, and especially the Treaty of Rome in 1957, which sparked the development of a European common market. Yet all but Finland participated in the European Recovery Program (the Marshall Plan) and became part of looser institutional structures that were also favored by Great Britain. Likewise, Denmark and Norway found that NATO membership brought them closer to the Western European democracies and expedited reconciliation with the Federal Republic of Germany. By the 1960s, relationships with expanding Western European institutions (notably the Common Market) became a permanent issue on the Scandinavian political agenda.

The Atlantic dimension overlaps considerably with the European, but it has three distinctive facets. After 1940, the Scandinavian states developed sustained and intensive relations with the United States (and to a lesser extent Canada), with which they had previously had important ethnic ties but no intensive diplomatic history. Further, the Atlantic dimension brought particularly the three Scandinavian NATO members into a much wider community in Europe (especially with the Mediterranean NATO members). Finally, it evolved into a broader Western community exemplified by the Organization for Economic Cooperation and Development (OECD), which emerged in 1960 out of the narrower Marshall Plan structure. Even after the end of the Cold War, the Scandinavian states have sought to keep the United States immersed in European affairs and have encouraged NATO's enlargement eastward. Interestingly, neither Sweden nor Finland sought NATO membership after 1990 but were satisfied with the Partnership for Peace and with the slowly emerging foreign and security cooperation in the European Union and with NATO when authorized by the UN.

Relations with Eastern Europe and the former parts of the Soviet Union represent the legacy of the Cold War, which also dominated Scandinavia for more than forty years. For the past two centuries, Scandinavia's relations with Eastern Europe have been distant, and Russia was most often seen as a threat. After a period of bridge building between 1944 and 1948, the Scandinavian countries chose different options to cope with the East-West struggle. Common to each was a desire to maintain relatively low tensions in the Nordic region and to develop autonomous

Nordic relations. Since 1990, Scandinavia's "Eastern question" has become far more complex. At present, three developments have emerged from the former Eastern bloc. First is the renewed independence of the Baltic states of Estonia, Latvia, and Lithuania. The Scandinavian countries have greeted this unexpected development with sustained economic and political involvement. Second, Russia's instability and uncertain steps toward democracy represent a continuing challenge for the Nordic states. The norm had been an authoritarian, powerful, but often conservative Russia. Finally, as the expanding EU encompasses Central and Eastern Europe, the Nordic countries must adjust to changing institutional and political arrangements while maintaining their influence and independence.

Finally, there is a global perspective that includes Scandinavia's historic commitment to the United Nations and other forms of international cooperation. Scandinavian military units have played a role in many UN peacekeeping missions. The Nordic countries have global economic interests and collectively represent a substantial global economic power. They are among the most generous and steadfast contributors to international economic assistance efforts and often champion the less developed countries in international organizations. Yet they are far from major actors whose decisions can affect global affairs. Here, too, a strategy of bridge building can be constructive, as illustrated by the role of Norway and its late foreign minister, Johann Jørgen Holst, in facilitating the 1993 Israeli-Palestinian Oslo Accords. Scandinavian diplomats continue to pursue "peacemaking," despite frequent frustration.

NORDIC BALANCE

After 1945 the Nordic countries placed their trust initially in the new United Nations and its promise of "collective security" and broad global cooperation. The disappointments of the 1930s were balanced by the lessons of appeasement and the leadership promised by the United States, along with hopes for Soviet cooperation in the postwar order. As a defeated power, Finland was initially denied membership in the United Nations until 1955, but the other four Nordic nations were in from the start. Scandinavians could see that their best foreign policy option was continuing great-power cooperation in the United Nations, and it was here that bridge-building efforts between the emerging Cold War blocs were focused. The appointment of Norwegian statesman Trygve Lie as the first secretary general of the United Nations (1946–1953) augured well for Scandinavian engagement, and he was followed by Swedish diplomat Dag Hammarskjöld (1953–1961), who expanded the writ of the secretary general. Swedish diplomat Folke Bernadotte pursued peace in the Middle East until his assassination in 1948.

Although the Scandinavian states were reluctant to give up on their bridge-building role, they recognized that by 1948, the East-West divide was a reality. Isolated neutrality had failed in 1940, but for Finland normalizing relations with the Soviet Union was the highest priority. A treaty of "friendship, cooperation, and mutual assistance" was negotiated and became the basis of the next forty years of Finnish-Soviet relations. It required Finland to obtain Moscow's approval for political and economic ties with the West and basically gave Moscow a so-called *droit de regard* (veto right) to scrutinize Finnish foreign policy and in practice, for more than twenty years, Soviet veto power over certain Finnish politicians. Crucially, however, it did not end Finland's recovering parliamentary democracy and capitalist economy.

Neither the United States nor Great Britain focused on Scandinavia after 1945. The United States had northern strategic concerns, but these were mainly the air bases in Iceland and, to a lesser extent, Greenland. Both were essential for U.S. military operations in Europe, and their strategic importance would grow significantly during the Cold War. While Finnish options were sharply limited, the other Scandinavian states agreed to reassess their collective security in 1948–1949. Isolated neutrality was discredited in Denmark and Norway, and even the Swedes seemed willing to consider a regional security arrangement.

The effort to create a nonaligned Scandinavian Defense Union failed basically because Norway sought closer ties with the emerging Western defense alliance that evolved into NATO. As one Norwegian politician put it, "We want to be defended, not liberated." Western (in practice, U.S.) military assistance would be directed at the broader alliance and not at peripheral blocs, and without such assistance, Scandinavian military potential would remain at a level characterized by one contemporary observer as a "0+0+0=0" equation. After Norway's choice, Sweden was uninterested in a bilateral arrangement, and Denmark followed Norway into the North Atlantic Treaty Organization in April 1949. Sweden would preserve its nonalignment in peace and hope for neutrality in war.

For the next forty years, this arrangement prevailed with only marginal adjustments. Norway became initially the most enthusiastic Scandinavian NATO member, although the Norwegians adopted a policy of nonprovocation toward the Soviet Union, with which they shared a border in the far north. Denmark also refused to allow permanent foreign bases on its territory in time of peace, although NATO staff and periodic military exercises were accommodated. Denmark also accepted U.S. bases in Greenland without inquiring too closely about their military activities. Norway made a substantial effort to build up its armed forces; in Denmark, defense expenditures were controversial. Nevertheless, both countries developed and maintained military forces and alliance ties that were without historical precedent.

Sweden's nonalignment initially stimulated a considerable defense effort. Swedes believed that their successful neutrality during World War II came from achieving enough military strength to make invasion too costly. That became their defense policy in the Cold War, although we now know that Sweden cooperated secretly with NATO in the 1950s and 1960s in coordinating a defense against the Soviet Union.

By the 1960s, Nordic foreign policies had established patterns that, with occasional variations, were maintained until the end of the Cold War in 1990. Each Nordic country had, of course, its own interests and priorities. Despite the lack of a formal common Nordic foreign policy, each country has assessed the impact its foreign policy might have on an overall "Nordic balance." In addition, as the Norwegian analyst Arne O. Brundtland and others noted, each Nordic country generally has assumed that the success of one Nordic country's foreign policy would benefit the entire region and minimize regional tensions. Nordic regional cooperation avoided defense and security policy, although a de facto Nordic bloc emerged in the 1960s in the United Nations and other international organizations. Nordic political leaders continued their tradition of regular informal consultation on issues of common interest.

The Nordic balance remained deliberately vague and flexible throughout the Cold War. All sought to reinforce the reality that northern Europe was not the main axis of East-West tensions. Despite the different Nordic responses to the Cold War, each country sought to combine credible national security, conflict avoidance with the Soviet Union, and cautious steps toward relaxation of tensions between East and West. From the outset, few Scandinavians believed that the Soviet Union had a timetable for war with the West. War was more likely to occur because of miscalculation or the escalation of conflicts outside of Europe. Hence a policy of "reassurance" and conflict resolution won broad support, although there were genuine arguments about how to carry it out. This was not a policy of "appeasement"; Nordic criticism of Soviet human rights violations and imperialism in Eastern Europe became louder through the 1970s and 1980s. As noted earlier, both the Nordic and global dimensions of foreign policy allowed considerable diplomatic opportunities. Not all were successful, but such negotiations would at least communicate to the superpowers (especially the USSR) that the Nordic countries believed in "peaceful coexistence" combined with full respect for national independence.

While successfully restraining most Cold War tensions in their region, the Nordic countries never succeeded in creating a region truly distinct from the larger European context. In the security sphere, they had insufficient power; in economic matters, their ties to Europe remained supreme. By 1961, however, the dynamic Common Market was a serious issue in Scandinavia. West Germany had become again a vital market for the Scandinavian states, soon surpassing Britain. As security issues waned, economic questions demanded difficult choices: first between competing blocs and models (the European Economic Community [EEC] versus the looser European Free Trade Association [EFTA]), and then over the extent of integration and its political consequences.

Scandinavia and the European Union

In 1989–1991, Scandinavians, along with Europeans and Americans, watched with amazement as forty years of East-West competition ended, a dozen Marxist-Leninist regimes collapsed, and the Soviet Union split into its component republics. More proactively, the Nordic states gave diplomatic and economic support to the emerging independence movements in the Baltic republics (Estonia, Latvia, and Lithuania), which had been forcibly annexed by the Soviet Union fifty years earlier. As in 1918–1920 and 1945–1949, Nordic leaders had to rethink their international position and foreign policy priorities. The challenge would be to balance traditional interests and perspectives with the new opportunities and threats of a changed world. The Nordic balance soon became the "Northern Dimension" to the European Union.[13]

Scandinavia, as noted earlier, remained on the periphery of the European integration project for nearly twenty-five years after World War II. Three factors have repeatedly deterred the Scandinavian states from aggressively pursuing European integration and unity. First was the alternative attraction of Nordic economic cooperation. Although initial attempts to form a Nordic customs union in the 1950s failed, the project was resurrected in new versions until 1970, when Denmark and Norway declared definitively for the European alternative. However, only Denmark joined the EEC in 1973, while Norwegian voters rejected membership and Sweden and Finland never applied. Denmark would preserve its Nordic links and would even promote regional interests in Brussels, but the limits of Nordic cooperation seemed clear. Second, the ultimate goal of a united Europe enjoyed only modest support among the political leadership and the public in these small states, historically unaligned and mistrustful of larger neighbors. Third, with broader free-trade ambitions, the Nordic countries have resisted having to choose sides in economic communities. Until 1973, Britain and Germany belonged to different European trading blocs, while the attractions of global trade (especially with North America and Japan, and even with socialist countries such as the Soviet Union, China, and Eastern Europe) deterred commitment to the European project.

The Scandinavian states favored European cooperation over unity. Cooperation aimed at removing barriers to free trade and investment as well as policy collaboration in areas of common concerns (e.g., the environment, refugees, human rights, and defense) have come to be regarded as "Europe à la carte." States can pick and choose the collection of projects in which they will participate. The alternative they resisted was more grandiose: a "United States of Europe" with genuinely federal institutions that would move significant portions of public policy into a European entity. National governments would still have residual powers through the principle of "subsidiarity," but like other federal systems, the whole would be more than the sum of its parts. Ancient cultures and states would be unlikely to disappear or become mere provinces, but the four-hundred-year tradition of state sovereignty largely would be ended in principle as well as in practice. This second vision has little support in Scandinavia and has met much vigorous resistance.

ECONOMIC COOPERATION

As trading states, the Scandinavian countries have long been wary of economic isolationism. All suffered from the economic nationalism and mercantilism of the interwar period. In response, domestic protectionism gained a foothold in the agricultural and other primary economic sectors.

The Scandinavian countries did not participate significantly in any of the meetings between 1955 and 1957 that led to the Rome Treaty establishing the EEC. Likewise, they had not been involved in the precursors of the Schuman Plan and the European Coal and Steel Community of 1952. The broader trade bloc did raise concerns, especially in Denmark and Sweden, which had important economic ties to the rapidly growing West German economy. British refusal to consider participation, and its establishment of an alternative European Free Trade Association (EFTA) in 1959 confirmed the division of Europe into "sixes and sevens." Generally the Scandinavians favored free trade for industrial goods and international services (e.g., shipping), but only Denmark accepted similar liberalization for the agricultural sector. None of them believed that the integration of all economic sectors, as had begun with the European

Coal and Steel Community, was relevant for their economic situation. This distinction between free trade and harmonization would continue.

By 1961, it was clear that the EEC would progress and that the EFTA would be less significant. The ambiguous British decision to apply for EEC membership forced the Scandinavian countries to reconsider their position. French president Charles de Gaulle delayed British entry for a decade, but when in 1969 the issue again became germane, it was clear that the EEC was an economic and political success and that there would be no other significant European alternative. As the European option again appeared promising, the Nordic countries (now including Finland) commenced negotiations on a wider Nordic economic community that would possibly lead to a common Nordic entry into the EEC. This possibility threatened Finland's special regard for Soviet sensibilities, but Sweden too was concerned about its "nonaligned" status (a point already raised in 1963). In short, whenever a wider European option became promising, the Nordic countries found that they each had different perspectives.

The result would be four Scandinavian roads to Europe, with Denmark's entry into the EEC in 1973, Sweden and Finland in 1995, and Norway's two failed entry attempts in 1972 and 1994. Just to complicate matters, the two Danish autonomous North Atlantic territories of Greenland and the Faeroe Islands remained outside of the EEC, with Greenland actually withdrawing in 1982. Following its severe financial crisis in 2008–2009, Iceland commenced negotiations for entry into the EU but by 2013 progress had stalled.

It is notable that joining Europe has been a divisive issue in domestic politics everywhere, even including Finland, where the European Union seemed to offer guarantees against renewed Russian pressure in the future. The referenda results in table 5.3 suggest just how disputed this key decision in fact was. Ironically, the strength of domestic opposition has not slowed Danish integration into European structures in those areas approved by the voters; Denmark has typically ranked among the top countries in the European Union in actually adapting national legislation and

Table 5.3   European Community and European Union Referenda (%)

	Denmark						Norway		Sweden		Finland
	1972	1986	1992	1993	1998	2000	1972	1994	1994	2003	1994
Yes	63.3	56.2	49.3	56.7	55.1	46.8	46.5	47.8	52.3	41.8	57.0
No	36.7	43.8	50.7	43.5	44.9	53.2	53.5	52.2	46.8	56.1	43.0
Turnout	90.1	75.4	83.1	86.5	74.8	86.7	79.2	88.8	82.4	81.2	70.8

Note: The referenda were as follows:

Denmark 1972: joining the EC
1986: EC single market
1992: Maastricht Treaty
1993: Edinburgh agreement modifying Maastricht Treaty
1998: Amsterdam Treaty
2000: adopting the euro
Norway 1972 and 1994, Sweden 1994, and Finland 1994: joining the EC/EU
Sweden 2003: common European currency

Sources: Danish Folketinget, http://www.ft.dk; Nordic Council, *Norden i Tal, 2002*; and Swedish Riksdag, http://www.riksdagen.se.

regulation to fit European requirements. As late entrants, Sweden and Finland had to accept the developing European Union in 1995, including its extensive rules and regulation (the so-called *acquis communautaire*). The ongoing EU debates and, in the case of Denmark, repeated referenda on Europe disrupted the normal patterns of partisan allegiance in domestic politics.

RELUCTANT EUROPEANS

The European integration project has evolved significantly over the past twenty years, starting with the Maastricht Treaty of 1991 (as amended in Edinburgh [1992] and further in Amsterdam [1997] and Nice [2001]) and the unsuccessful constitutional treaty (2004) to the Lisbon Treaty (2007), but the Nordic countries remain skeptical participants. Norway and Iceland are linked through the agreement on a European Economic Area (EEA), which was negotiated in 1990, took effect in 1993, and essentially gives these countries access to the Single European Market in all areas excepting agriculture, natural resources, and other issues of vital national interest, but they have no direct influence on the development of the European Union.

Denmark and Sweden are full members but with "opt-outs" or reservations. Both have rejected monetary union, although their economies are among the strongest in the EU. Denmark's currency has been closely tied to the German mark and now the euro since 1982. They have been cautious about harmonization of police and judicial affairs and participation in key elements of the common foreign and security policy. Every significant change in European policy has sparked a bitter fight in Denmark and resulting national referenda. The 1997 Amsterdam revision of the union treaty was approved by the Danish voters, but in September 2000 they rejected the euro as their national currency. The Danish government accepted the Nice Treaty of 2001, which prepared the EU for a significant expansion to include Eastern and southern European states. Although domestic opponents of the EU have railed against opening the union to hordes of poor Eastern Europeans, others see the expansion as postponing "federalism" for an indefinite period. Anti-EU parties (on the extreme right and left) are well represented in parliament, and a quarter of the delegates elected by the Danes to the European Parliament are anti-EU activists. After the EU constitutional treaty was killed by French and Dutch voters in 2005, Denmark and possibly Sweden and Finland avoided referenda. The Lisbon Treaty has been deemed a "consolidation" of previous treaties and not a further surrender of sovereignty. Although a parliamentary majority in Denmark supports closer EU ties, public skepticism and the EU's current challenges have prolonged the status quo.

Norway has debated the EU issue for more than forty years, and twice its voters vetoed membership that had been approved by wide parliamentary majorities. As elsewhere in the region, Norwegian Euro-skeptics have bundled political, cultural, and economic issues into their program, but economic factors seem most salient. Although the 1972 rejection predated Norway's current petroleum-fueled prosperity, the continuing boost of oil and gas exports has shielded the country from most of the economic strains of the past thirty years. Most oil revenues are now shunted into a massive "Government Pension Fund–International," which invests globally and whose assets approached $775 billion in fall 2013. Protection of Norway's heavily subsidized agricultural sector and regionally significant coastal fisheries has also been a factor weighing against membership.

Sweden and Finland became EU members in 1995 after vigorous national debates and referenda. As new members they were forced to swallow the whole EU system, but not without protest and regret. Their EU parliamentary delegations have strong anti-EU contingents, and opinion at home is no less skeptical of the EU project than that of the doubting Danes. Neither is firmly committed to a common European security policy or to federalism. Like the Danes, they have encouraged eastward expansion, especially to the Baltic states and Poland. During their EU presidencies, they have pushed the social and labor agenda as well as budgetary and administrative reforms of EU institutions. Only Finland has fully joined the Economic and Monetary Union, with the euro replacing the Finnish markka as the national currency in 2002, while Sweden rejected the common currency in 2003.

Today the Scandinavian countries still see the EU mainly in pragmatic economic terms. They have been especially cautious about expanded cooperation on foreign and security policy matters despite the turmoil in the Balkans after 1990, the "war on terrorism" after September 2001, and a host of continuing crises in Africa, the Middle East, and elsewhere that suggest that world politics is not only the global economy. They accepted without significant debate the expansion of the EU to include twelve central, Mediterranean, and Eastern European countries, including the Baltic states and near-neighbor Poland, but they maintain various restrictions on labor migration.

All of the Nordic countries supported the U.S. response to the terrorist attack of 9/11. Danish, Finnish, Norwegian, and Swedish troops serve with the UN-sanctioned but NATO-led International Security Assistance Force in Afghanistan. Indeed, Denmark has suffered significant casualties in relation to its size and military contribution to the Afghan campaigns. The center-right Danish government gave wholehearted support in 2003 to military action against the Saddam Hussein regime and provided a military contingent for the occupation, while the Swedes, Finns, and Norwegians were critical of the U.S. and British response. It was yet another reminder of the different national perspectives across Scandinavia. The differences were purely governmental; public opinion throughout Scandinavia became increasingly critical of the Bush administration's unilateral interventions. Likewise, the election of Barack Obama in 2008 improved the image of the United States throughout Scandinavia. This was reflected by President Obama's Nobel Peace Prize in 2009, which was awarded by the Norwegian Nobel Committee (with some debate across the region and beyond and furious denunciations by American rightists). Its 2010 award to Chinese political dissident and prisoner Liu Xiao elicited similar hysterics from the Chinese government.

For the Scandinavian Social Democrats in particular, the European Union and economic globalization more generally pose some ironic dilemmas. Although they have always been rhetorically internationalist—and have lived up to the rhetoric in development aid and in direct support for foreign trade unions and labor parties in the Third World and Eastern Europe—their success at home has been premised on the relevance of the nation-state as the unit for making economic policy. The generous and humane provisions of the social democratic welfare states in Scandinavia yielded a truly decent society for all, but they were dependent on strong, carefully managed economies and full employment. It is far from clear that those are at the top of the European Union's economic agenda. If the welfare state was the surrogate for socialism for the Scandinavian Social Democrats from the 1930s through the 1980s, what is to be the surrogate for the welfare state?

HARD TIMES

The so-called Great Recession following the financial crisis of 2008–2009 has challenged the Scandinavian "model" yet again. The impact of the crisis varied from quite mild in petro-Norway to more severe in Sweden and Denmark and harsh in Finland and Iceland. Compared to southern Europe, the Scandinavian economies, except Iceland, avoided disasters because of cautious fiscal policies during the good years (international debt was low or declining until 2008) and successful interventions to shore up financial and export sectors. Unemployment has risen everywhere, but once again the social policies together with countercyclical economic policies have protected average citizens and mitigated the decline. The fact remains that the export-oriented Nordic economies are now deeply embedded with the European and global economy. Recovery depends in large part on the actions of other countries. Interdependence is not new in Scandinavia.

Except for Norway, unemployment is about 40–50% higher than during the pre-recession period, but temporary job and training programs have buffered the economy. Flexible currency exchange rates in Norway, Sweden, and Iceland have restored export competitiveness. Finland and Denmark lack this tool, as the former has fully joined the European Monetary Union while the latter keeps its currency rigidly pegged to the euro. No doubt these experiences will affect future international and EU economic relations.

The habits of nonalignment and independence of all Nordic states, along with their still vigorous sense of nationhood and self-confidence, color their view of Europe and the world. They are also a factor in the continuing debate about non-European immigration and the challenges of multiculturalism. Once again, a Nordic "middle way" has emerged toward the regional and global challenges of the new century. Scandinavians are pragmatic skeptics, seeking "just enough Europeanization" to respond to economic, social, and political challenges. As successful states and just societies, they see no need to bury themselves in a federal Europe. The successful reform and reinvigoration of the "Scandinavian model" after 1990 gave them renewed confidence at home and relevance for larger EU countries seeking new ideas. But they are not isolationists; the past century taught them that their fates are intimately tied to their continent and to global developments. The Nordic EU bloc of three is likely to support a reformed "social Europe" in which the principles of "Subsidiarity" and pragmatism will make the Scandinavians more comfortable in the European home. Maintaining domestic economic and social solidarity during hard times remains a common priority, but commitments to the ever wider EU are tougher. Through reforms and innovation—such as "flexicurity" and welfare state "recalibration"—the Scandinavian countries still challenge their European neighbors and the wider world to do better.

Notes

This chapter draws heavily on earlier versions that were written with the late Professor John A. Logue of Kent State University, with whom I was privileged to collaborate until his untimely death in December 2009.

1. For an excellent survey of Scandinavian history, see T. K. Derry, *A History of Scandinavia: Norway, Sweden, Denmark, Finland, and Iceland* (Minneapolis: University of Minnesota Press, 1979); more concise and up-to-date are Byron J. Nordstrom, *Scandinavia since 1500* (Minneapolis: University of Minnesota Press, 2000); and Mary Hilson, *The Nordic Model: Scandinavia since 1945* (London: Reaktion Books, 2008).

2. Until the war of 1864, the German-speaking duchies of Schleswig, Holstein, and Lauenburg were part of the Danish realm under an exceedingly complex constitutional arrangement. Schleswig had a substantial Danish population that was denied rights under German rule between 1864 and 1918. Following the German defeat in 1918, the Allies supervised a referendum that returned the northern third of Schleswig (Slesvig) to Denmark. Since 1920, the Danish-German border has been fixed, and since the 1950s, the two nationalities have seen greatly improved local relations.

3. Denmark and Norway were under the same monarch from 1380 to 1814. Starting in 1737 in rural Norway, the country was the first in the world to institute universal, compulsory education, culminating in the Danish Education Act of 1814. Sweden followed with a similar law in 1842. By the second half of the nineteenth century, literacy was nearly universal in Scandinavia, and secondary and adult education was advanced by the "folk colleges" and workers' education movements.

4. An exception was K. Hjalmar Branting (1860–1925), one of the founders of the Swedish Social Democratic Workers Party. Branting was of middle-class academic background and university educated, and he was a school chum of the future king. A tireless reformer, he set the Swedish Social Democrats on a moderate path to power. In 1920, he became Europe's first democratically elected Social Democratic prime minister.

5. There are many excellent studies of the global economy. See especially Robert O. Keohane and Joseph S. Nye, *Power and Interdependence*, 3rd ed. (Boston: Addison-Wesley, 2000); and, for the smaller European states, Peter J. Katzenstein, *Small States in World Markets: Industrial Policy in Europe* (Ithaca, NY: Cornell University Press, 1985).

6. There is a rich literature on Scandinavian political institutions and political actors. For good surveys with copious bibliographies, see Olof Petersson, *The Government and Politics of the Nordic Countries* (Stockholm: Fritzes, 1994); Eric S. Einhorn and John Logue, "Can Welfare States Be Sustained in a Global Economy? Lessons from Scandinavia," *Political Science Quarterly* 125, no. 1 (Spring 2010): 1–29; and Eric S. Einhorn and John Logue, *Modern Welfare States: Scandinavian Politics and Policy in the Global Age* (New York: Praeger, 2003).

7. D. Rustow, *The Politics of Compromise: A Study of Parties and Cabinet Government in Sweden* (Princeton, NJ: Princeton University Press, 1955).

8. Recent labor union membership was 54.5% in Norway, 67.6% in Sweden, 68.8% in Denmark, and 69.9% in Finland as contrasted with 11.3% in the United States. Two decades earlier, union membership approached 90% in Scandinavia. See Organization for Economic Cooperation and Development, "StatExtracts: Trade Union Density," http://stats.oecd.org/Index.aspx?DataSetCode=UN_DEN (accessed January 15, 2014).

9. For a more comprehensive discussion of the Scandinavian welfare programs and their impact, see Einhorn and Logue, *Modern Welfare States*, chs. 6–10.

10. Economic policy issues in the Nordic countries are discussed in detail in the economic surveys published every year or two by the Organization of Economic Cooperation and Development as *Economic Surveys: Denmark*, and the like. Sweden's economic problems and especially its welfare have received much international attention in the 1990s. The harshest critique may be found in the writings of Assar Lindbeck, most recently in "The Swedish Experiment," *Journal of Economic Literature* 35 (September 1997): 1273–319. A more technical and less pessimistic survey is Richard B. Freeman, Robert Topel, and Brigitta Swedenborg, *The Welfare State in Transition: Reforming the Swedish Model* (Chicago: University of Chicago Press, 1997). Both the *Financial Times* and the *Economist* regularly survey the Nordic economies, the latter most recently in February 2013.

11. The Nordic countries vary in how they define "immigrants." Including naturalized citizens and second-generation populations inflates the numbers (to about 10–11% of the population in Denmark and Norway in 2010), but it does reflect the socioeconomic challenges of migration. These numbers include Nordic and Western European immigrants, who are generally not controversial.

12. At the end of the fourteenth century, all three Scandinavian crowns passed to Danish Queen Margrethe I. In 1397, this union was formalized by a treaty drafted in Kalmar, Sweden. Although the Kalmar Union survived until 1523, it was constantly challenged. Norway remained united with Denmark until 1814 and then with Sweden until 1905. Iceland was part of the Danish realm until 1944. The Swedish province of Finland became a Russian Grand Duchy in 1809 and declared its independence in 1917.

13. A concise summary of the Nordic region during the Cold War may be found in "The Nordic Region: Changing Perspectives in International Relations," *The Annals of the American Academy of Political and Social Science* 512 (special issue, ed. Martin O. Heisler) (November 1990); and in the books by Stephen J. Blank, *Finnish Security and European Security Policy* (Carlisle Barracks, PA: U.S. Army War College, 1996); and by Don Snidal and Arne Brundtland, *Nordic-Baltic Security* (Washington, DC: Center for Strategic and International Studies, 1993). For the more recent period see Hilson, *The Nordic Model*; and Christine Ingebritsen, *Scandinavia in World Politics* (Boulder, CO: Rowman & Littlefield, 2006).

Suggested Readings

Brochmann, Grete, and Anniken Hagelund, eds. *Immigration Policy and the Scandinavian Welfare State 1945–2010*. New York: Palgrave Macmillan, 2012.

Derry, T. K. *A History of Scandinavia: Norway, Sweden, Denmark, Finland, and Iceland*. Minneapolis: University of Minnesota Press, 1979.

Einhorn, Eric S., and John Logue. "Can Welfare States Be Sustained in a Global Economy? Lessons from Scandinavia." *Political Science Quarterly* 125, no. 1 (Spring 2010): 1–29.

Einhorn, Eric S., and John Logue. *Modern Welfare States: Scandinavian Politics and Policy in the Global Age*. New York: Praeger, 2003.

Heidar, Knut, ed. *Nordic Politics: Comparative Perspectives*. Oslo: Universitetsforlaget, 2004.

Hilson, Mary. *The Nordic Model: Scandinavia since 1945*. London: Reaktion Books, 2008.

Ingebritsen, Christine. *The Nordic States and European Union: From Economic Interdependence to Political Integration*. Ithaca, NY: Cornell University Press, 1998.

Ingebritsen, Christine. *Scandinavia in World Politics*. Boulder, CO: Rowman & Littlefield, 2006.

Nordstrom, Byron J. *Scandinavia since 1500*. Minneapolis: University of Minnesota Press, 2000.

Petersson, Olof. *The Government and Politics of the Nordic Countries*. Stockholm: Fritzes, 1994.

Sejersted, Francis. *The Age of Social Democracy; Norway and Sweden in the Twentieth Century*. Princeton, NJ: Princeton University Press, 2011.

Strøm, Kaare, and Torbjörn Bergman, eds. *Madisonian Turn: Political Parties and Parliamentary Democracy in Nordic Europe*. Ann Arbor: University of Michigan Press, 2011.

Thakur, Subhash, et al. *Sweden's Welfare State: Can the Bumblebee Keep Flying?* Washington, DC: International Monetary Fund, 2003.

CHAPTER 6

Spain

AFTER THE FIESTA

Sebastián Royo

Spain

Population (million):	46.0
Area in Square Miles:	194,982
Population Density in Square Miles:	236
GDP (in billion dollars, 2012):	$1,434
GDP per Capita (PPP, 2012):	$31,100
Joined EC/EU	1986

Performance of Key Political Parties in Parliamentary Elections of November 20, 2011

Amaiur	1.4%
Basque Nationalist Party (PNV)	1.3%
Convergence and Union (CiU)	4.2%
People's Party (PP)	44.6%
Republican Left of Catalonia	1.1%
Spanish Socialist Workers' Party (DNA)	28.8%
United Left-The Greens (IU-LV)	6.9%
Union, Progress, and Democracy (UPyD)	4.7%

Main Officeholders: Prime Minister: Mariano Rajoy, PP (2011); and Head of State: King Juan Carlos I

The overall pattern of Spanish history has been described, crudely, as a graph shaped like an upside-down version of the letter "V." That is, the graph rises—bumpily at times, through 600 years under the Romans, 700 years under or partly under the Moors, and a century of empire building—to the peak of Spanish power in the sixteenth century. After that, the history of the nation goes downhill until the 1970s. A vast empire was gradually lost, leaving Spain poor and powerless. And there was much political instability: Spain suffered forty-three coup d'états between 1814 and 1923, a horrendous civil war between 1936 and 1939, followed by thirty-six years of dictatorship under Generalísimo Francisco Franco.[1]

After Franco's death in 1975, the graph turned upward again. King Juan Carlos, Franco's heir, oversaw the return of democracy to the country. A negotiated transition period, which has been labeled as a model for other countries, paved the way for the elaboration of a new constitution, followed by the first free elections in almost forty years. These developments were followed by the progressive return of Spain to the international arena—where they have been relatively isolated during the dictatorship. The following decade also witnessed the Socialist Party being elected to actual power in 1982, bringing a new aura of modernity to the country. The 1980s also witnessed Spain's integration into NATO (1982) and the European Community (1986). The following two and a half decades were a period of phenomenal growth and modernization.

Indeed, before the global crisis that hit Spain in the spring of 2008, the country had become one of Europe's most successful economies.[2] While other European countries had been stuck in the mud, Spain performed much better at reforming its welfare systems and labor markets, as well as improving flexibility and lowering unemployment. Over the decade and a half that preceded the 2008 global financial crisis, the Spanish economy has been able to break with the historical pattern of boom and bust, and the country's economic performance was nothing short of remarkable. Yet all this came to a halt when the global financial crisis hit Spain in 2008. As a result, Spain is suffering one of the worst crises since the 1940s.

Following the transition to democracy and the country's European integration, Spain was, prior to the 2008 crisis, a model country. But then the dream was shattered and the country's economy imploded after 2008. How did this happen? Policy choices and the structure of decision making, the role of organized interest rates, the structure of the state, and institutional degeneration all played important roles in explaining the severity of the economic crisis in Spain. The country was, as of 2013, facing a triple crisis: financial, fiscal, and competitiveness. This chapter seeks to provide an overview of the country's evolution since the transition to democracy, and to explain its economic collapse after 2008.

The first section of the chapter outlines the country's transition to democracy. The second section describes the process and consequences of European integration. The third section sketches the main features of the Spanish growth model, and the challenges that it faced. The fourth section describes the scale of the shock it underwent from 2008 onward, and analyzes the triple crisis in financial, fiscal, and competitiveness performance.

The Democratic Transition (1975–1982)

Spain had remained under the rule of Francisco Franco, the dictator, for about forty years (1936–1975).[3] He kept control of the political machinery almost unchallenged. On November 22, 1975, two days after Generalísimo Franco passed away, Juan Carlos de Borbon, the designated successor, was proclaimed king. This development initiated the democratization process. The foundations for real democracy were laid through legal reform. The existence of solid institutions permitted the regime to initiate political reform from within as well as to accommodate pressures from below and from the international community.

King Juan Carlos and President Adolfo Suárez were successful in negotiating with the opposition and convincing them to accept their plan of reform from above. Several factors fostered the convergence among the competing political forces: (1) Francoist regime factions did not have the cohesion or strategy to take leadership in government, and internal struggles, consequently, weakened their position; (2) the armed forces had been relegated to a secondary role throughout the final years of Francoist rule; and (3) pressures from governments and political forces from the international community sought a truly democratic outcome in Spain. The lack of strength of the various parties involved to impose their will, joined to a commitment for democracy from King Juan Carlos I, carved out a space for accords that permitted political pluralism to flourish. The fear of a return to civil war discouraged rupture, bringing parties and interest groups together to the negotiating table.

The negotiation among democratic institutions was first implicit and tentative and became gradually more explicit. In this regard, pressure from the working class was fundamental to a negotiated transition. Labor mobilization contributed to the achievement of the goals set by the Left—legalization of political parties and labor unions, amnesties, and elections with democratic guarantees—and forced the Right to break definitively with Francoism and its institutions. Although at first the government defended the interest of the ruling elites, the final agreement granted demands from the opposition, particularly the legalization of the two main political parties of the Left, the Partido Socialista Obrero Español (PSOE, or the Spanish Socialist Party) and the Partido Comunista Español (PCE, or the Spanish Communist Party); the formation of a new centrist party under Suárez' leadership, the Unión de Centro Democrático (UCD, or the Democratic Center Union); the self-dissolution of the Francoist Courts, and the convocation of direct elections. A popular referendum endorsed and legitimized the reform plan.

The emergence of a democratic regime in Spain resulted in the surfacing of over 150 political parties. The first electoral contest, which took place in 1977, clarified the political spectrum. From 1972 until late 1982, the party system was dominated by two moderate political parties—the conservative UCD and the socialist PSOE. The UCD won the 1977 elections with 34 percent of the vote, and the PSOE finished second with 29 percent of the popular vote. Other political parties such as the rightist Alianza Popular (AP, or the Popular Alliance) and the communist PCE gained seats in Parliament. The regional nationalist parties, the Partido Democrático de Cataluña (PDC, or the Catalan Democrats), later Convergencia i Unió (CiU, or the Union and

Convergence), and the Partido Nacionalista Vasco (PNV, or the Basque Nationalist Party) also achieved representation. The newly elected Parliament wrote a new constitution that was approved in a popular referendum in December 1978. In the 1979 general elections, the UCD won again with 35.1 percent of the votes and the PSOE finished second with 30.5 percent.

All these developments took place amid one of the worst economic recessions experienced in Spain since the 1950s. The second oil crisis, the lack of competitiveness of the Spanish economy, a wage explosion, and the international economic crisis resulted in a sharp increase in unemployment (14.6 percent by 1981), and inflation (15.2 percent by 1981).

The weakness of the UCD government, which lacked a sufficient majority in Parliament, prevented it from taking the necessary measures to tackle the economic crisis. The 1981 failed coup d'état became a grave reminder of the shaky foundations of the new regime. The intensity of the economic crisis, coupled with the Basque terrorist problem and the rejection of the new regime by a minority of hardliners, instigated the coup leaders. The majority of the Spanish Army, however, rejected it and the coup failed.

The following year, the PSOE won the 1982 general elections with almost 10 million votes (48.4 percent) and achieved an overwhelming majority in Parliament. These elections signaled the restructuring of the party system. The UCD disappeared as a consequence of internal struggles that culminated in a disastrous electoral performance, and the rightist AP (later named Partido Popular [PP, or the Popular Party]) emerged as the main opposition party. The Socialists remained in power for the next thirteen years, winning three further elections in 1986, 1989, and 1993. The PP defeated the Socialists in the 1996 elections. Table 6.1 summarizes these electoral results.

European Integration

The success of the democratic transitions in the second half of the 1970s paved the way for full membership in the European Community (EC).[4] For Spain and its EC partners, this momentous and long-awaited development had profound consequences and set in motion complex processes of adjustment.[5]

There was no dispute that Spain belonged to Europe. This was not just a geographical fact. Spain shared its traditions, culture, religion, and intellectual values with the rest of Europe. Moreover, it had historically contributed to the Christian Occidental conceptions of humankind and society dominant in Europe. Without Spain, European identity would only be a reflection of an incomplete body. Spain belongs to Europe. Its entry into the European Community was a reaffirmation of that fact.

The Schuman plan was issued in 1950, and Spain was left out because the project was restricted to the democratic regimes in Europe. However, the Spanish government followed the European integration process very closely, and created a commission in the Foreign Ministry especially devoted to it. During the 1950s it seemed clear to the government that the country should not be left out of these integrationist movements, but due to the precarious economic situation of the country, the rapprochement was

Table 6.1   Electoral Results (1977–2011)

Year	Party in Government		Main Opposition Parties	
1977	UCD	34.0%	PSOE	29.9%
			PCE	9.2%
1979	UCD	35.1%	PSOE	30.5%
			PCE	10.8%
1982	PSOE	48.4%	AP	26.18%
			CDS*	9.7%
			PCE	4.13%
			CiU	3.7%
			PNV	1.9%
1986	PSOE	44.3%	AP	26.2%
			CDS	9.3%
			IU**	4.61%
			CiU	5.0%
			PNV	1.5%
1989	PSOE	39.6%	AP	25.8%
			CDS	7.9%
			IU	9.1%
			CiU	5.0%
			PNV	1.2%
1993	PSOE	38.7%	PP	34.8%
			IU	9.6%
			CiU	5.0%
			PNV	1.2%
1996	PP	38.8%	PSOE	37.5%
			IU	5.4%
			CiU	4.1%
			PNV	1.5%
2000	PP	44.5%	PSOE	37.7%
			IU	4.9%
			CiU	4.6%
			PNV	1.3%
2004	PSOE	42.59%	PP	37.5%
			IU	10.6%
			CiU	3.2%
			ERC	2.5%
2008	PSOE	43.8%	PP	39.9%
			IU	3.7%
			CiU	3.0%
			PNV	1.1%
2011	PP	44.8%	PSOE	28.7%
			IU	6.9%
			UPyD	4.7%
			CiU	4.1%

*Centrist part, now disbanded.

**A coalition of Leftist parties, including the Communist Party (PCE), named Izquierda Unida.

Source: Ministerio del Interior, http://www.infoelectoral.mir.es/min/ (accessed January 30, 2014).

very slow. During the late 1950s, there was a controversy in Spain surrounding the convenience for the country of joining the Europe of the Six (the EC) or the Seven (the European Free Trade Association [EFTA]).

It soon became clear that the Treaty of Rome was better suited for Spain's interests. Since Spanish's agricultural exports were critical for the country's economy, the fact that the EC had set the creation of a common agricultural policy as one of its main objectives, whereas EFTA left agriculture aside, convinced Spanish authorities about the benefits of the EC. Furthermore, the commercial volume of Spain with the EC was 50 percent higher than the one with EFTA countries. Finally, at the beginning of the 1960s, Spanish external trade was characterized by a chronic imbalance between a rigid export supply and an increasing import demand. A preferential trade agreement with the EC would offer the country the incentive of enlarging some markets that were very important for Spanish exports, while at the same time contributing toward the acceleration of a series of structural reforms needed at that time.[6]

On February 14, 1962, the Spanish foreign minister sent a letter to Walter Hallstein, president of the Commission of the European Community, asking for the opening of negotiations with the objective of examining the possible accession of Spain to the Community. The request, however, received a cool reception from the Commission, which only acknowledged the reception of the letter. From the outside, several organizations pressured the Community to reject the Spanish request. In 1962, the Confederation of European Unions sent a letter to Mr. Hallstein pressuring for a rebuff. Several European newspapers joined in the campaign against Spain's request. "The EC has to say no to Spain," stated the Netherlands' newspaper *Nieuwe Rotterdamsche Courant*, "until the spirit of democracy and liberty are present in the country." The Congress of the European Federalist Movement meeting in Lyon at that time approved a resolution in which it rejected the possibility of any agreement between Spain and the EC. The Socialist Group on the European Parliament also said no to the Spanish request. Finally, the Congress of the European Movement, meeting in Munich in June 1962 with the participation of a Spanish delegation, approved another resolution in which it was stated that only democratic countries could join the European Community—the Spanish representatives in this Congress were later punished with jail time for their participation.[7]

On June 6, 1964, the Council authorized the Commission to open conversations to "examine the economic problems that the EC causes to Spain, and to look for the appropriate solutions." After eight years of negotiations, on June 29, 1970, the Spanish government reached an agreement with the EC. This agreement established a preferential system with the objective of eliminating the barriers to the commercial exchanges between Spain and the Community. The agreement lasted only for six years.[8] Following Franco's death, on July 22, 1977, the first democratic Parliament was born after the June 15 general election. A few days later, on July 28, Spain presented a formal membership request to the European Economic Community.

Formal negotiations began in February 1979. The prospect of Spain's membership filled many EC members with dread. As a result, enlargement negotiations proved to be slow and protracted. The EC, particularly the French, had misgivings about southern enlargement that were focused more on Spain than on Portugal. Agriculture, textiles, fisheries, and the free movement of labor proved to be the most contentious issues throughout the negotiations. While the French and Italian governments wanted to protect domestic growers, the German, British, and Dutch governments supported the Spanish accession.

Fisheries were also a very controversial issue. Since Spain's fishing fleet was larger than the entire EC fleet combined, there was also strong interest in limiting the access of the Spanish fleet to the Common Fisheries Policy. Negotiations progressed throughout 1981 and 1982 over a wide range of less controversial issues, including capital movement, regional policy, transport, and services.

François Mitterrand's victory in the 1981 French presidential election did not change France's opposition to enlargement. The new French government sought an acceptable arrangement for Mediterranean agriculture. The Spanish membership application was strengthened in the early 1980s by the formation of a stable government. The overwhelming victory of the Spanish Socialist Party, led by its young and charismatic leader Felipe González, in the October 1982 general election gave new impetus to the enlargement process. He was a passionate Europhile, and one of his primary political objectives was to bring his country into the EC. He embarked on a series of visits to EC capitals to make the case for Iberian accession. In the domestic front, he implemented ambitious economic agendas to modernize the outdated economic and social structures of the country. Indeed, the new Socialist government left aside demand-oriented policies and embarked on a supply-oriented restructuring endeavor that sought to address the imbalances in Spanish economic institutions. He also used his personal contacts and ideological affinity with his European counterparts to make the case for his country's accession.

The July 1984 Fountainbleu summit resolved the standing EC budgetary issues; set January 1, 1986, as the agreed date for Spain (and Portugal) to enter the EC; and called for an end to negotiations by September 30, 1984. This date proved too ambitious. In December 1984, the European Council reached an agreement on fruits, fish, wine, and vegetables that was accepted by the Spanish government. The formation of a new European Commission in Brussels led by the energetic and influential Jacques Delors in January 1985 gave a final impetus to the negotiations. Spain (and Portugal) joined the EC on January 1, 1986.

Clearly, accession set in motion a complex and multifaceted process of adjustment. Entry to the EC brought many economic advantages to Spain, which has benefited extensively from the European Union's (EU) "structural and cohesion funds," which have been used to improve the physical infrastructure and capital stock of the country. These funds have contributed significantly to reducing regional disparities and fostering convergence within the European Union. At the same time, they have played a prominent role in developing the factors that improve the competitiveness and determine the potential growth of the least developed regions. Finally, Spanish trade with the Community has expanded dramatically over the last two decades, and foreign investment has flooded into the country.

One of the beneficial consequences of these developments has been a reduction in the economic differentials that separated Spain from the European average. For instance, since 1986 Spain's average per capita income has grown to 95 percent of the

EU average. The culmination of this process was the (largely unexpected) participation of the country as an original founder of the euro as a single currency in 1999.

The process of integration, however, has also brought significant costs in terms of economic adjustment, loss of sovereignty, and cultural homogenization. European integration has had, and will continue to have for the foreseeable future, a profound effect on Spanish society. It has had an impact on issues such as national identity, the sustainability of welfare institutions, and the adjustment of political and economic structures. Under the terms of the accession agreement signed in 1985, Spain had to undertake significant steps to align its legislation on industrial, agriculture, economic, and financial policies to that of the European Community. These accession agreements also established significant transition periods to cushion the negative effects of integration. This process meant that Spain had to phase in tariffs and prices, and approve tax changes (including the establishment of a value-added tax) that the rest of the Community had already put in place. It also involved, in a second phase, the removal of technical barriers to trade. Finally, Spain also had to adapt to successive European treaties, including fulfilling the criteria of the Single European Act and the Maastricht Treaty that led to the creation of the euro. These requirements brought significant adjustment costs to the Spanish economy.

Overall, the path toward "convergence" has been (and will be in the foreseeable future, particularly given the ongoing euro-zone crisis) long and winding. Over the last two and a half decades, Spanish governments have been forced to reform their financial, labor, pension, and welfare systems. They also have had to privatize most public companies to more efficiently enforce the laws to stop unemployment fraud—which is still rampant—and to cut excessive bureaucracy. All of these measures led to social problems because the unions did not accept these reforms easily. Some of these processes remain unfinished.

On balance, however, Spain has benefited immensely from accession. Since the last century, the obsession of Spanish reformists has been to make up the lost ground with modernized Europe. EU membership has been a critical step in this direction.[9]

The Miraculous Decade

European integration was instrumental in the modernization of the country.[10] Indeed, before the global crisis that hit Spain in the spring of 2008, the country had become one of Europe's most successful economies (see table 6.2). Propped up by low interest rates and immigration, Spain was (in 2008) in its fourteenth year of uninterrupted growth, and it was benefiting from the longest cycle of continuing expansion of the Spanish economy in modern history (only Ireland in the euro zone has a better record), which contributed to the narrowing of per capita GDP with the EU. Indeed, in 20 years per capita income grew 20 points, one point per year, to reach close to 90 percent of the EU-15 average. With the EU-25, Spain already reached the average in 2008. The country grew on average 1.4 percentage points more than the EU between 1996 and 2007.

Unemployment fell from 20 percent in the mid-1990s to 7.95 percent in the first half of 2007 (the lowest level since 1978), as Spain became the second country in the

Table 6.2 The Boom Years (2000–2008)

SPAIN	Units	Scale	2000	2001	2002	2003	2004	2005	2006	2007	2008
GDP constant prices	National currency	Billions (euros)	546.9	566.8	582.2	600.2	619.8	642.2	668.0	691.8	697.7
GDP constant prices	Annual % change		5.1	3.7	2.7	3.1	3.3	3.6	4.0	3.6	0.9
GDP per capita, constant prices	National currency	Units	13.6	13.9	14.1	14.3	14.5	14.8	15.2	15.4	15.3
Output gap in % of potential GDP	% of potential GDP		1.9	1.5	0.3	0.1	0.5	1.4	2.9	3.9	3.1
GDP based on purchasing-power parity (PPP) share of world total	%		2.2	2.2	2.2	2.2	2.1	2.1	2.1	2.1	2.0
Inflation, average consumer prices	Annual % change		3.5	2.8	3.6	3.1	3.1	3.4	3.6	2.8	4.1
Unemployment rate	% of total labor force		13.9	10.6	11.5	11.5	11.0	9.2	8.5	8.3	11.3
Employment	Persons	Millions (euros)	16.4	16.9	17.3	17.9	18.5	19.3	20.0	20.6	20.5
General government balance	National currency	Billions (euros)	-6.2	-4.4	-3.3	-1.6	-2.9	8.8	19.9	23.3	-41.9
General government balance	% of GDP		-1.0	-0.6	-0.5	-0.2	-0.3	1.0	2.0	2.2	-3.8
Current account balance	% of GDP		-4.0	-3.9	-3.3	-3.5	-5.3	-7.4	-9.0	-10.0	-9.6

Source: International Monetary Fund, *World Economic Outlook Database*, October (Washington, DC: IMF, 2009).

EU (after Germany, which has a much larger economy) to create the most jobs (an average of 600,000 per year over the last decade). In 2006 the Spanish economy grew a spectacular 3.9 percent, and it grew 3.8 percent in 2007. As we have seen, economic growth contributed to per capita income growth and employment. Indeed, the performance of the labor market was spectacular: between 1997 and 2007, 33 percent of all the total employment created in the EU-15 was created in Spain. In 2006 the active population increased by 3.5 percent, the highest in the EU (led by new immigrants and the incorporation of women in the labor market, which increased from 59 percent in 1995 to 72 percent in 2006); and 772,000 new jobs were created.

The economic success extended to Spanish companies, which expanded beyond their traditional frontiers.[11] In 2006 they spent a total of €140 billion on domestic and overseas acquisitions, putting the country third behind the United Kingdom and France. Of this, €80 billion were to buy companies abroad (compared with the €65 billion spent by German companies). In 2006 Spanish foreign direct investment (FDI) abroad increased 113 percent, reaching €71.5 billion (or the equivalent of 7.3 percent of GDP, compared with 3.7 percent in 2005).[12] In 2006 Iberdrola, an electricity supplier, purchased Scottish Power for $22.5 billion to create Europe's third-largest utility; Banco Santander, Spain's largest bank, purchased Britain's Abbey National Bank for $24 billion; Ferrovial, a family construction group, concluded a takeover of the British BAA (which operates the three main airports of the United Kingdom) for £10 billion; and Telefonica bought O2, the UK mobile phone company. Indeed, 2006 was a banner year for Spanish firms: 72 percent of them increased their production and 75.1 percent their profits, 55.4 percent hired new employees, and 77.6 percent increased their investments.[13]

The country's transformation was not only economic but also social. The Spanish became more optimistic and self-confident (i.e., a Harris poll showed that they were more confident of their economic future than their European and American counterparts, and a poll by the Center for Sociological Analysis showed that 80 percent were satisfied or very satisfied with their economic situation). Spain became "different" again, and according to public opinion polls it had become the most popular country to work for Europeans.[14] Between 2000 and 2007, some 5 million immigrants (645,000 in 2004 and 500,000 in 2006) settled in Spain (8.7 percent of the population compared with 3.7 percent in the EU-15), making the country the biggest recipient of immigrants in the EU (they represented 10 percent of the contributors to Spain's Social Security system). This is a radical departure for a country that used to be a net exporter of people, and more so because it has been able to absorb these immigrants without falling prey (at least so far) to the social tensions that have plagued other European countries (although there have been isolated incidents of racial violence).[15] These immigrants contributed significantly to the economic success of the country in that decade because they boosted the aggregate performance of the economy: they raised the supply of labor, increased demand as they spent money, moderated wages, put downward pressure on inflation, boosted output, allowed the labor market to avoid labor shortages, contributed to consumption, and increased more flexibility in the economy with their mobility and willingness to take on low-paid jobs in sectors such as construction and agriculture, in which the Spanish were no longer interested.[16]

Indeed, an important factor in the per capita convergence surge after 2000 was the substantive revision of the Spanish GDP data as a result of changes in the National Accounts from 1995 to 2000. These changes represented an increase in GPD per capita of 4 percent in real terms (the equivalent of Slovakia's GDP). This dramatic change was the result of the significant growth of the Spanish population since 1998 as a result of the surge in immigration (e.g., in 2003 the population grew 2.1 percent). The key factor in this acceleration of convergence, given the negative behavior of productivity (if productivity had grown at the EU average, Spain would have surpassed in 2007 the EU per capita average by 3 points), was the important increase in the participation rate, which was the result of the reduction in unemployment, and the increase in the activity rate (the proportion of people of working age who have a job or are actively seeking one) that followed the incorporation of female workers into the labor market and immigration growth. Indeed, between 2000 and 2004, the immigrant population multiplied threefold.

As a matter of fact, most of the 772,000 new jobs created in Spain in 2006 went to immigrants (about 60 percent). Their motivation to work hard also opened the way for productivity improvements (which in 2006 experienced the largest increase since 1997, with a 0.8 percent hike). It is estimated that the contribution of immigrants to GDP was 0.8 percentage points annually in the four years to 2007. [17] Immigration represented more than 50 percent of employment growth and 78.6 percent of the demographic growth (as a result, Spain led the demographic growth of the European countries between 1995 and 2005 with a demographic advance of 10.7 percent compared with the EU-15 average of 4.8 percent).[18] They also contributed to the huge increase in employment, which was one of the key reasons for the impressive economic expansion. Indeed, between 1988 and 2006, employment contributed 3 percentage points to the 3.5 percent annual rise in Spain's potential GDP (see table 6.2).[19]

THE BASIS FOR SUCCESS

What made this transformation possible? The modernization of the Spanish economy in the last two and half decades has been intimately connected to the country's integration in the European Union. Indeed, European integration was a catalyst for the final conversion of the Spanish economy into a modern Western-type economy. Yet, membership was not the only reason for this development. The economic liberalization, trade integration, and modernization of the Spanish economy started in the 1950s and 1960s, and Spain became increasingly prosperous over the two decades prior to EU accession. However, one of the key consequences of its entry into Europe has been that it consolidated and deepened that development processes, and it has accelerated the modernization of the country's economy. EU membership facilitated the micro- and macroeconomic reforms that successive Spanish governments undertook throughout the 1980s and 1990s. Spain has also benefited extensively from European funds: approximately €150,000 million from agricultural, regional development, training, and cohesion programs.

Moreover, European Monetary Union (EMU) membership has also been very positive for the country: it has contributed to macroeconomic stability, it has imposed fiscal discipline and central bank independence, and it has lowered dramatically the cost of capital. One of the key benefits was the dramatic reduction in short-term and long-term nominal interest rates: from 13.3 percent and 11.7 percent in 1992, to 3.0 percent and 4.7 percent in 1999, and to 2.2 percent and 3.4 percent in 2005, respectively. The lower costs of capital led to an important surge in investment from families (in housing and consumer goods) and businesses (in employment and capital goods). Indeed, EMU membership (and the Stability Pact) has provided the country with unprecedented stability because it has forced successive governments to consolidate responsible economic policies, which have led to greater credibility and the improvement of the ratings of Spain's public debt (and, consequently, to lower financing costs).

Another important factor to account for the country's economic success was the remarkable economic policy stability that followed the economic crisis of 1992–1993. Indeed, there have been few economic policy shifts throughout the 1990s and early 2000s, despite changes in government. Between 1993 and 2009, there were only two ministers of finance, Pedro Solbes (1993–1996 and 2004–2009) and Rodrigo Rato (1996–2004); and the country only had three prime ministers (Felipe González, José María Aznar, and José Luís Rodríguez Zapatero). This pattern was further reinforced by the ideological cohesiveness of the political parties in government and the strong control that party leaders exercise over the members of the Cabinet and the Parliament deputies.

In addition, this stability was reinforced by the shared (and rare) agreement among Conservative and Socialist leaders regarding fiscal consolidation (the balanced-budget objective was established by law by the Popular Party), as well as the need to hold firm in the application of restrictive fiscal policies and the achievement of budgetary surpluses: as a result, a 7 percent budget deficit in 1993 became a 2.2 percent surplus in 2007, and public debt decreased from 68 percent of GDP in 1998 to 36.2 percent in 2007.

Finally, other factors that contributed to this success include Spain's limited corruption and the fact that politics are fairly clean and relatively open, that Spain has a flexible economy, and the success of Spanish multinational corporations: there were eight firms in the *Financial Times* list of the world's largest multinationals in 2000, and 14 in 2008.[20]

THE CHALLENGES

However, this economic success was marred by some glaring deficiencies that came to the fore in 2008 when the global financial crisis hit the country, because it was largely a "miracle" based on bricks and mortar.[21] The foundations of economic growth were fragile because the country has low productivity growth (productivity contributed only 0.5 percentage points to potential GDP between 1998 and 2006) and deteriorating external competitiveness.[22] Over the decade that preceded the 2008 crisis, Spain did not address its fundamental challenge, its declining productivity, which only grew an average of 0.3 percent during that decade (0.7 percent in 2006), one whole point below the EU average, placing Spain at the bottom of the EU and ahead of only Italy and Greece (the productivity of a Spanish worker is the equivalent of 75 percent of a U.S. one). The most productive activities (energy, industry, and financial services) contribute only 11 percent of GDP growth.[23]

Moreover, growth was largely based on low-intensity economic sectors, such as services and construction, which are not exposed to international competition. In 2006 most of the new jobs were created in low-productivity sectors such as construction (33 percent), services associated with housing such as sales and rentals (15 percent), and tourism and domestic services (30 percent). These sectors represented 75 percent of all the new jobs created in Spain in 2006 (new manufacturing jobs, in contrast, represented only 5 percent). The labor temporary rate reached 33.3 percent in 2007, and inflation was a recurrent problem (it closed 2006 with a 2.7 percent increase, but the average for that year was 3.6 percent); thus, the inflation differential with the EU (almost one point) has not decreased, which reduces the competitiveness of Spanish products abroad (and, consequently, Spanish companies are losing market share abroad).[24]

In addition, family indebtedness reached a record 115 percent of disposable income in 2006, and the construction and housing sectors accounted for 18.5 percent of GDP (twice the Eurozone average). House prices rose by 150 percent since 1998, and the average price of a square meter of residential property went up from €700 in 1997 to €2,000 at the end of 2006, even though the housing stock had doubled. Many wondered whether this bubble was sustainable.[25] The crisis that started in 2008 confirmed the worst fears.

Between 40 and 60 percent of the benefits of the largest Spanish companies came from abroad. Yet, in the years prior to the crisis, this figure has decreased by approximately 10 percentage points, and there has been a decline in FDI of all types in the country, falling from a peak of €38.3 billion in 2000 to €16.6 billion in 2005.[26] The current account deficit reached 8.9 percent of GDP in 2006 and over 10 percent in 2007, which made Spain the country with the largest deficit in absolute terms (€86,026 million), behind only the United States; imports were 25 percent higher than exports, and Spanish companies were losing market share in the world. And the prospects are not very bright. The trade deficit reached 9.5 percent in 2008.[27]

While there is overall consensus that the country needed to improve its education system and invest in research and development (R&D) to lift productivity, modernize the public sector, and make the labor market more stable (i.e., reduce the temporary rate) and flexible, the government did not take the necessary actions to address these problems. Spain spends only half of what the Organization of European Cooperation and Development (OECD) spends on average on education, it lags most of Europe on investment in R&D, and it was ranked twenty-ninth by the UN Conference on Trade and Development (UNCTAD) as an attractive location for research and development. Finally, other observers note that Spain was failing to do more to integrate its immigrant population, and social divisions were beginning to emerge.[28]

By the summer of 2008, the effects of the crisis were evident, and since then the country has suffered one of the worst recessions in history, with unemployment reaching over 27 percent in 2012, and more than 6 million people unemployed. This collapse was not wholly unexpected. The global liquidity freeze and the surge in commodities, food, and energy prices brought to the fore the unbalances in the Spanish economy: the record current account deficit, persisting inflation, low productivity growth, dwindling competitiveness, increasing unitary labor costs, excess consumption, and low savings had all set the ground for the current devastating economic crisis.[29]

After the Fiesta: The Global Crisis Hits Spain

The imbalances in the Spanish economy became obvious in 2007–2008 when the real estate market bubble burst and the international financial crisis hit Spain (see table 6.3). In just a few months, the "debt-fired dream of endless consumption" turned into a nightmare. By the summer of 2013, Spain faced the worst economic recession in half a century. According to government statistics, 2009 was the worst year since there has been reliable data: GDP fell 3.7 percent, unemployment reached over 4 million people, and the public deficit reached a record 11.4 percent of GDP (up from 3.4 percent in 2008). Consumer confidence was shattered, the implosion of the housing sector reached historic proportions and threatened to extend for several years, and the manufacturing sector was also suffering.

Initially, the Zapatero government was reluctant to recognize the crisis, which was becoming evident as early as the summer of 2007, because of electoral considerations: the country had general elections in March 2008. And after the election, the Zapatero government was afraid to admit that it had not been entirely truthful during the campaign. While this pattern has been quite common in other European countries, in

Table 6.3   The Economic Crisis (2008–2013)

Subject Descriptor	Units	2007	2008	2009	2010	2011	2012*	2013*
Gross domestic product (GDP), constant prices	% change	3.5	0.9	–3.8	–0.3	0.4	–1.4	–1.6
Output gap in % of potential GDP	% potential GDP	3.8	2.3	–2.8	–3.4	–3.2	–4.5	–5.4
Total investment	% GDP	31.0	29.1	24.0	22.8	21.5	19.6	18.1
Inflation, average consumer prices	% change	2.8	4.1	–0.2	2.0	3.1	2.4	1.9
Unemployment rate	% total labor force	8.3	11.3	18	20.1	21.7	25	27
General government structural balance	% potential GDP	–1.1	–5.4	–9.5	–8.0	–7.8	–5.7	–4.5
General government net debt	% GDP	26.7	30.8	42.5	49.8	57.5	71.9	79.1
Current account balance	% GDP	–1.0	–9.6	–4.8	–4.5	–3.7	–1.1	1.1

*Estimates.

Source: International Monetary Fund, *World Economic Outlook Database*, April (Washington, DC: IMF, 2013).

Spain the increasing evidence that the model based on construction was already show-ing symptoms of exhaustion in 2007 compounded it. Yet, the Spanish government refused to recognize not only that the international crisis was affecting the country but also that in Spain the crisis would be aggravated by the very high levels of private indebtedness. As late as August 17, 2007, Finance Minister Solbes predicted that "the crisis would have a relative small effect" on the Spanish economy.

When it became impossible to deny what was evident, the government's initial reluctance to recognize and address the crisis was replaced by frenetic activism. The Zapatero government introduced a succession of plans and measures to try to confront the economic crisis, and specifically to address the surge of unemployment.[30]

The sharp deterioration of the labor market was caused by the economic crisis and the collapse of the real estate sector, and it was aggravated by a demographic growth pattern based on migratory inflows of labor: in 2007 there were 3.1 million immi-grants in the country, of whom 2.7 million were employed and 374,000 unemployed. In 2008 the number of immigrants increased by almost 400,000, to 3.5 million (repre-senting 55 percent of the growth in the active population), but 580,000 of them were unemployed (and 2.9 million employed), an increase of 200,000. In the construction sector alone, unemployment increased 170 percent between the summers of 2007 and 2008. Meanwhile, the manufacturing and service sectors (also battered by the global crisis, lower consumption, and lack of international competitiveness) proved unable to incorporate these workers.

The pace of deterioration caught policymakers by surprise. The Zapatero gov-ernment prepared budgets for 2008 and 2009 that were utterly unrealistic in the face of rapidly changing economic circumstances. As a result, things continued to worsen over the next four years. The most significant decline was in consumer con-fidence, which was hammered by the financial convulsions, the dramatic increase in unemployment, and the scarcity of credit. As a result, household consumption, which represented 56 percent of GDP, fell 1 percent in the last quarter of 2009 for the first time in the last 15 years. According to the Bank of Spain, this decline in household consumption was even more important in contributing to the recession than the deceleration of residential investment, which had fallen 20 percent, driven down by worsening financial conditions, uncertainties, and the drop in residential prices. In the end, government actions had a limited effect on stemming this hemor-rhage, and their efficacy was inadequate.

The impact of the global economic crisis has been felt well beyond the economic and financial realms. The crisis also had severe political consequences. Spain followed in the path of many other European countries (including Ireland, Portugal, Greece, and France) that saw their governments suffer the wrath of their voters and be voted out of office.

The Socialist Party (PSOE) was reelected in a general election on March 9, 2008 (see table 6.1). Soon thereafter, economic conditions deteriorated sharply and the government's popularity declined rapidly. Between March 2008 and March 2012, there were a number of electoral contests in Spain at the local, regional, national, and European levels. At the national and European levels, the one common pattern was the outcome: the defeat of the Socialist Party and the victory of the Popular Party

(PP). And at the regional and local levels, the Socialists suffered historical losses, losing control of regional government that they ruled for decades (notably, Castilla-La Mancha and Extremadura), and even losing the election for the first time in one of its historical strongholds, Andalusia (although they were able to reach a coalition with a smaller leftist party to stay in power).

Spain's economic crisis was mainly due to a mismanaged financial sector, which by overlending freely to property developers and mortgages contributed to a real estate property bubble. This bubble contributed to hide the fundamental structural problems of the Spanish economy outlined in the previous section, and had an effect on policy choices because no government was willing to burst the bubble and risk suffering the wrath of voters. Furthermore, cheap credit also had inflationary effects that contributed to competitiveness losses and record balance-of-payment deficits. Therefore, three dimensions of the crisis (financial, fiscal, and competitiveness) are interlinked in their origins. The crisis exposed the underbelly of the financial sector and showed that many banks (particularly the *cajas*) not only were suffering liquidity problems but also risked insolvency, which led to the EU financial bailout of June 2012. The bailout had onerous conditions attached and it limited national economic autonomy.[31]

Now we turn to the elements of domestic policy that underline the triple crisis in financial, fiscal, and competitiveness performance.[32]

The Triple Crisis

THE FISCAL CRISIS

One of the most common misinterpretations regarding the crisis in southern Europe is attributing it to mismanaged public finances. Many policymakers across Europe still insist that the crisis was caused by irresponsible public borrowing, and this, in turn, has led to misguided solutions. In fact, with very few exceptions, notably Greece, that interpretation is incorrect. In Spain, the current crisis did not originate with mismanaged public finances. On the contrary, as late as 2011, Spain's debt ratio was still well below the average for countries that adopted the euro as a common currency: while Spain stood at less than 60 percent of GDP, Greece stood at 160.8 percent, Italy at 120 percent, Portugal at 106.8 percent, Ireland at 105 percent, Belgium at 98.5 percent, and France at 86 percent.

Prior to 2007, Spain seemed to be in an enviable fiscal position, even when compared with Germany.[33] Spain ran a budget surplus in 2005, 2006, and 2007. It was only when the crisis hit the country and the real estate market collapsed that the fiscal position deteriorated markedly and the country experienced huge deficits.

The problem in Spain was the giant inflow of capital from the rest of Europe; the consequence was rapid growth and significant inflation. In fact, the fiscal deficit was a result, not a cause, of Spain's problems: when the global financial crisis hit Spain and the real estate bubble burst, unemployment soared, and the budget went into deep deficit, caused partly by depressed revenues and partly by emergency spending to limit human costs. The government responded to the crisis with a massive €8 billion public works stimulus. This decision, combined with a dramatic fall in revenue, blew a hole in government accounts, resulting in a large deficit.

The conditions for the crisis in Spain were created by the excessive lending and borrowing of the private sector rather than the government. In other words, the problem was private debt and not public debt. Spain experienced a problem of ever-growing private sector indebtedness, which was compounded by the reckless investments and loans of banks (including the overleveraged ones), and aggravated by competitiveness and current account imbalances. In Spain, the debt of the private sector (households and nonfinancial corporations) was 227.3 percent of GDP at the end of 2010; total debt increased from 337 percent of GDP in 2008 to 363 percent in mid-2011.

Though Spain entered the crisis in a relatively sound fiscal position, that position was not sound enough to withstand the effects of the crisis. The country's fiscal position deteriorated sharply—collapsing by more than 13 percent of GDP in just two years. Looking at the deficit figures with the benefit of hindsight, it could be argued that Spain's structural or cyclically adjusted deficit was much higher than its actual deficit. The fast pace of economic growth before the crisis inflated government revenues and lowered social expenditures in a way that masked the vulnerability hidden in Spanish fiscal accounts. The problem is that it is very difficult to know the structural position of a country. The only way in which Spain could have prevented the deficit disaster that followed would have been to run massive fiscal surpluses of 10 percent or higher during the years prior to the crisis in order to generate a positive net asset position of at least 20 percent of GDP.[34] This, for obvious reasons, would not have been politically feasible.

THE LOSS OF COMPETITIVENESS

There is also another way to look at the problem. Many economists argue that the underlying problem in the euro area is the exchange rate system itself, namely, the fact that European countries locked themselves into an initial exchange rate. This decision meant, in fact, that they believed that their economies would converge in productivity (which would mean that the Spaniards would, in effect, become more like the Germans). If convergence was not possible, the alternative would be for people to move to higher productivity countries, thereby increasing their productivity levels by working in factories and offices there. Time has shown that both expectations were unrealistic and, in fact, the opposite happened. The gap between German and Spanish (including other peripheral-country) productivity increased, rather than decreasing, over the past decade and, as a result, Germany developed a large surplus on its current account; Spain and the other periphery countries had large current account deficits that were financed by capital inflows.[35]

Adoption of the euro as a common currency fostered a false sense of security among private investors. During the years of euphoria following the start of Europe's economic and monetary union and prior to the onset of the financial crisis, private capital flowed freely into Spain and, as a result, the country ran current account deficits of close to 10 percent of GDP. In turn, these deficits helped finance large excesses of spending over income in the private sector. The result did not have to be negative. These capital inflows could have helped Spain (and the other peripheral countries) invest, become more productive, and "catch up" with Germany. Unfortunately, in the case of Spain, they largely led to a massive bubble in the property market, consumption, and unsustainable levels of borrowing. The bursting of that bubble contracted the country's real economy, and it brought down the banks that gambled on loans to real estate developers and construction companies.

At the same time, the economic boom also generated large losses in external competitiveness that Spain failed to address. Successive Spanish governments also missed the opportunity to reform institutions in their labor and product markets. As a result, costs and prices increased, which in turn led to a loss of competitiveness and large trade deficits. This unsustainable situation came to the fore when the financial shocks that followed the collapse of Lehman Brothers in the fall of 2007 brought "sudden stops" in lending across the world, leading to a collapse in private borrowing and spending, and a wave of fiscal crisis.

THE FINANCIAL CRISIS

A third problem has to do with the banks. This problem was slow to develop. Between 2008 and 2010 the Spanish financial system, despite all its problems, was still one of the least affected by the crisis in Europe. During that period, of the forty financial institutions that received direct assistance from Brussels, none was from Spain. In December 2010, Moody's ranked the Spanish banking system as the third strongest of the euro zone, only behind Finland and France, above the Netherlands and Germany, and well ahead of Portugal, Ireland, and Greece. Finally, Santander and BBVA had shown new strength with profits of €4.4 billion and €2.8 billion, respectively, during the first half of 2010. Spanish regulators had put in place regulatory and supervisory frameworks, which initially shielded the Spanish financial system from the direct effects of the global financial crisis. Indeed, the Bank of Spain had imposed a regulatory framework that required higher provisioning, which provided cushions to Spanish banks to initially absorb the losses caused by the onset of the global financial crisis.

Nevertheless, this success proved short lived. In the summer of 2012, Spanish financial institutions seemed to be on the brink of collapse and the crisis of the sector forced the European Union in June 2012 to devise an emergency €100 billion rescue plan for the Spanish banking sector. When the crisis intensified, the financial system was not able to escape its dramatic effects. By September 2012, the problem with toxic real estate assets forced the government to intervene and nationalize eight financial institutions. Altogether, by May 9, 2012, the reorganization of the banking sector involved €115 billion in public resources.

There are a number of factors that help account for the deteriorating performance of the Spanish banks after 2009. The first is the direct effect of the economic crisis. The deterioration in economic conditions had a severe impact on the bank balance sheets. The deep recession and record-high unemployment triggering successive waves of loan losses in the Spanish mortgage market coupled with a rising share of nonperforming loans. Like many other countries such as the United States, Spain had a huge property bubble that burst. Land prices increased 500 percent in Spain between 1997 and 2007, the largest increase among the OECD countries. As a result, the collapse of the real estate sector had a profound effect on banks: five years after the crisis started, the quality of Spanish banking assets continued to plummet. The Bank of Spain classified €180 billion as troubled assets at the end of 2011, and banks are sitting on €656 billion worth of mortgages, of which 2.8 percent are classified as nonperforming.

A second factor is concern over the country's sovereign debt. As mentioned before, the crisis in Spain did not originate with mismanaged public finances. The crisis has largely been a problem of ever-growing private sector debt, compounded by reckless bank investments and loans, particularly from the *cajas*, as well as aggravated by competitiveness and current account imbalances. To place the problem in perspective, the gross household debt increased dramatically in the decade prior to the crisis, and by 2009 it was 20 percentage points higher than the euro-zone average (86 percent of GDP versus 66 percent). And the austerity policies implemented since May 2010 have aggravated the fiscal position of the country. The ratio of Spain's debt to its economy was 36 percent before the crisis and is expected to reach 84 percent by 2013 (and this is even based on optimistic growth assumptions). In sum, Spain seemed to have fallen into the "doom loop" that had already afflicted Greece and Portugal and led to their bailout. The sustainability of the Spanish government debt is affecting Spanish banks (including BBVA and Santander) because they have been some of the biggest buyers of government debt in the wake of the ECB long-term refinancing operation liquidity infusions (the percentage of government bond owned by domestic banks reached 30 percent in mid-2012).

Spanish banks are also suffering the consequences of their dependence on wholesale funding for liquidity since the crisis started, and, in particular, their dependence on international wholesale financing, as 40 percent of their balance depends on funding from international markets, particularly from the ECB. Borrowing from the ECB reached €82 billion in 2012, and Spanish banks have increased their ECB borrowings by more than six times since June 2011, to the highest level in absolute terms among euro-area banking systems as of April 2012.

The crisis also exposed weaknesses in the policy and regulatory framework. The most evident sign of failure has been the fact that the country has already adopted five financial reforms in three years, and it has implemented three rounds of bank mergers. The results of these reforms have been questionable at best. The fact that Spain had five reforms in less than three years, instead of one that really fixed the problem, says it all. They have been largely perceived as "too little and too late," and they failed to sway investors' confidence in the Spanish financial sector.

Finally, the current financial crisis can also be blamed on the actions (and inactions) of the Bank of Spain. At the beginning of the crisis, the Bank of Spain's policies were all praised and were taken as a model by other countries. Time, however, has tempered that praise and the Bank of Spain is now criticized for its actions and decisions (or lack thereof) during the crisis. Spanish central bankers chose the path of least resistance: alerting about the risks but failing to act decisively.

Conclusion

The crisis has largely been a problem of ever-growing private sector debt, compounded by reckless bank investments and loans, particularly from the *cajas*, as well as aggravated by competitiveness and current account imbalances. In the end, the crisis has exposed the weaknesses of the country's economic model. Indeed, despite the previous two decades' significant progress and achievements, the Spanish economy still faces serious competitive and fiscal challenges. Unfortunately, the economic success of the country prior to the crisis fostered a sense of complacency, which allowed for a delay in the adoption of the necessary structural reforms. And this was not a surprise; some economists had noted that the Spanish economy was living on borrowed time. Indeed, despite all the significant progress, Spain still had considerable ground to cover to catch up with the richer EU countries and to improve the competitiveness of its economy. Given the existing income and productivity differentials with the richer EU countries, Spain will have to continue and deepen the reform process.

The sudden collapse of the Spanish economy came as a shock. In retrospect, however, it should not have been such a surprise. The policy choices taken during the previous decade led to an unsustainable bubble in private sector borrowing that was bound to burst. Moreover, the institutional degeneration that led to systemic corruption and contributed to the implosion of parts of the financial sector made the crisis almost unavoidable.

Much of Spain's growth during the 2000s was based on the domestic sector and particularly on an unsustainable reliance on construction. Tax incentives favored developers, property owners, and bankers. In addition, the particular regulation of the *cajas* proved fatally flawed, and led to a form of crony capitalism Spanish style, in which they invested massively in the construction sector in search of rapid growth and larger market share. These decisions proved fatal once the real estate bubble burst, and they led to the nationalization of several *cajas*, including Bankia, and the financial bailout from the European Union.

Membership in the European single currency was not the panacea that everyone expected it to be. Adoption of the euro led to a sharp reduction in real interest rates that contributed to the credit boom and the real estate bubble. However, it also altered economic governance decisions. Successive Spanish governments largely ignored the implications of EMU membership, and failed to implement the necessary structural reforms to ensure the sustainability of fiscal policies and to control unitary labor costs. These decisions led to a continuing erosion of competitiveness (and a record current account deficit), and a huge fiscal deficit when the country was hit by the global financial crisis.

The experience of the country shows that EU and EMU membership have not led to the implementation of the structural reforms necessary to address these challenges. On the contrary, EMU contributed to the economic boom, thus facilitating the postponement of necessary economic reforms. This challenge, however, is not a problem of European institutions, but of national policies. Indeed, the process of economic reforms has to be a domestic process led by domestic actors willing to carry them out.

The Spanish case serves as an important reminder that in the context of a monetary union, countries only control fiscal policies and relative labor costs. Spain proved to be weak at both. It failed to develop an appropriate adjustment strategy to succeed within the single currency, and it ignored the imperative that domestic policy choices have to be consistent with the international constraints imposed by euro membership. On the contrary, in Spain domestic policies and the imperatives of participating in a multinational currency union stood in uneasy relationship to one another. The crisis was the tipping point that brought this inconsistency to the fore, which led to the worst economic crisis in modern Spanish history.

Notes

1. "After the Fiesta," *Economist*, April 25–May 1, 1992, 60.

2. This article draws upon S. Royo, *From Social Democracy to Neoliberalism* (New York: St. Martin's Press, 2000); S. Royo, *Varieties of Capitalism in Spain* (New York: Palgrave, 2008); and S. Royo, *Lessons from the Economic Crises in Spain* (New York: Palgrave, 2013).

3. This section borrows from Royo, *From Social Democracy to Neoliberalism*.

4. This section borrows from S. Royo and P. C. Manuel, *Spain and Portugal in the European Union* (London: Frank Cass, 2003).

5. The terms "the European Community" (EC) and "the European Union" (EU) are used indistinctly to refer to the European integration process and institutions throughout the chapter. Similarly, "Europe" is here always used to refer to the countries that are members of the European Union, either before or after the Maastricht Treaty.

6. I. Fernández Guerrero, A. González, and C. Suarez Burguet, "Spanish External Trade and EEC Preferences," in *European Integration and the Iberian Economies*, ed. G. N. Yannopoulos (New York: St. Martin's Press, 1989), 145.

7. V. Pou Serradell, *España y la Europe Comunitaria* [Spain and the European Community] (Navarra: EUNSA, 1973), 112–15.

8. R. Tamames, *Guía del Mercado Común Europeo: España en la Europe de los Doce* [Guide of the European Common Market: Spain in the Europe of the Twelve] (Madrid: Alianza Editorial, 1989), 168.

9. See Royo and Manuel, *Spain and Portugal in the European Union*.

10. This section borrows from Royo, *Varieties of Capitalism in Spain*.

11. M. Guillén, *The Rise of Spanish Multinationals* (New York: Cambridge University Press, 2005).

12. Emilio Ontiveros, "Redimensionamiento Transfronterizo," *El País*, July 15, 2007.

13. Deloitte's "Barometro de Empresas," from "Un año de grandes resultados," *El País*, January 14, 2006.

14. According to the *Financial Times*, 17 percent of those polled selected Spain as the country where they would prefer to work, ahead of the United Kingdom (15 percent) and France (11 percent). See "España vuelve a ser diferente," *El País*, February 19, 2007; and *Financial Times*, February 19, 2007.

15. Calativa provides a detailed analysis of the immigration experience in Spain and exposes the tensions associated with this development. She also highlights the shortcomings of governments' actions in regard to integration, and the impact of lack of integration on exclusion, criminalization, and radicalization. See K. Calavita, *Immigrants at the Margins* (New York: Cambridge University Press, 2005).

16. "Immigrants Boost British and Spanish Economies," *Financial Times*, February 20, 2007, 3.

17. Guillermo de la Dehesa, "La Próxima Recesión," *El País*, January 21, 2007.

18. "La Economía española creció en la última década gracias a la aportación de los inmigrantes," *El País*, August 28, 2006.

19. See Martin Wolf, "Pain Will Follow Years of Economic Gain," *Financial Times*, March 29, 2007.

20. According to the latest data (2013) from the *World Bank Governance Indicators*, http://info.worldbank.org/governance/wgi/index.aspx#home (accessed January 15, 2014), Spain was ranked in the 82nd–100th country percentile ranks in control of corruption, government effectiveness, regulatory quality, rule of law, and voice and accountability.

21. According to Martinez-Mongay and Maza Lasierra, "The outstanding economic performance of Spain in EMU would be the result of a series of lucky shocks, including a large and persistent credit impulse and strong immigration, underpinned by some right policy choices. In the absence of new positive shocks, the resilience of the Spanish economy to the financial crisis might be weaker than that exhibited in the early 2000s. The credit impulse has ended, fiscal consolidation has stopped, and the competitiveness gains of the nineties have gone long ago." See C. Martinez-Mongay and L. A. Maza Lasierra, "Competitiveness and Growth in the EU," *Economic Papers* 355 (January 2009): 1–42.

22. "Fears of Recession as Spain Basks in Economic Bonanza," *Financial Times*, June 8, 2006.

23. "Los expertos piden cambios en la política de I+D," *El País*, December 18, 2006.

24. Angel Laborda, "El comercio en 2006," *El País*, March 11, 2007, 20.

25. Wolfgang Munchau, "Spain, Ireland and Threats to the Property Boom," *Financial Times*, March 19, 2007; and "Spain Shudders as Ill Winds Batter US Mortgages," *Financial Times*, March 21, 2007.

26. "Spanish Muscle Abroad Contrast with Weakling Status among Investors," *Financial Times*, December 11, 2006.

27. "La Comisión Europea advierte a España de los riesgos de su baja competitividad," *El País*, February 4, 2007.

28. "Zapatero Accentuates Positives in Economy, but Spain Has Other Problems," *Financial Times,* April 16, 2007, 4.

29. See Royo, *Lessons from the Economic Crises in Spain*.

30. See Royo, *Lessons from the Economic Crises in Spain*.

31. S. Dellepiane and N. Hardiman, "Governing the Irish Economy," UCD Geary Institute Discussion Series Papers, Geary WP2011/03, February (Dublin: University College Dublin, 2011).

32. This section borrows from Royo, *Lessons from the Economic Crises in Spain*.

33. See Martin Wolf's blog, "What Was Spain Supposed to Have Done?" June 25, 2012, http://blogs.ft.com/martin-wolf-exchange/2012/06/25/what-was-spain-supposed-to-have-done (accessed January 15, 2014).

34. From Wolf, "What Was Spain Supposed to Have Done?"

35. Simon Johnson's blog, "The End of the Euro: What's Austerity Got to Do with It?" June 21, 2012, http://baselinescenario.com/2012/06/21/the-end-of-the-euro-whats-austerity-got-to-do-with-it/ (accessed January 15, 2014).

Suggested Readings

Encarnación, O. *Spanish Politics: Democracy after Dictatorship*. New York: Polity, 2008.

Guillén, M. *The Rise of Spanish Multinationals*. New York: Cambridge University Press, 2005.

Gunther, R., and J. R. Montero. *The Politics of Spain*. New York: Cambridge University Press, 2009.

Magone, J. *Contemporary Spanish Politics*. New York: Routledge, 2008.

Royo, S. *From Social Democracy to Neoliberalism*. New York: St. Martin's Press, 2000.

Royo, S. *Lessons from the Economic Crises in Spain*. New York: Palgrave, 2013.

Royo, S. *Varieties of Capitalism in Spain*. New York: Palgrave, 2008.

Royo, S., and P. C. Manuel. *Spain and Portugal in the European Union*. London: Frank Cass, 2003.

CHAPTER 7

Russia

EUROPEAN OR NOT?

Bruce Parrott and Serhiy Kudelia

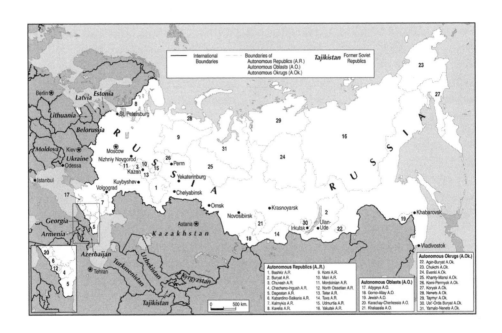

Russian Federation

Population (million):	142.5
Area in Square Miles:	6,592,819
Population Density in Square Miles:	22
GDP (in billion dollars, 2012):	$2,555
GDP per Capita (PPP, 2012):	$18,000
Joined EC/EU:	n/a

Performance of Key Political Parties in Parliamentary Elections of December 4, 2011

United Russia (ER)	49.3%
Communist Party of the Russian Federation (KPRF)	19.2%
Liberal Democratic Party of Russia (LDPR)	11.7%
Russian Democratic Party "Yabloko" (RDP)	3.4%
A Fair Russia (SR)	13.2%

Main Officeholders: President: Vladimir Putin, ER (2012); and Prime Minister: Dmitri Medvedev, ER (2012)

Is Russia part of Europe? For almost three centuries, observers have debated this question, and their answers have been shaped by the specific conditions in Europe as well as in Russia. During the eighteenth-century era of enlightened absolutism, Russia's dominant elites regarded it as part of Europe, and prominent Europeans agreed. Near the start of the eighteenth century, Peter the Great, one of the most important monarchs in Russian history, traveled extensively in Europe and based his sweeping administrative and economic reforms on the models he found there. A half century later, Voltaire, a leading thinker of the French Enlightenment, wrote an admiring history of Tsarist Russia and corresponded with Catherine the Great, another of Russia's modernizing autocrats.[1] Russia's acquisition of a colonial empire outside Europe strengthened its resemblance to other European imperial states. In the case of countries such as Britain and France, these empires lay overseas. In the Tsarist case, the empire grew primarily through overland expansion into adjacent territories such as the Caucasus and Central Asia. Despite this difference, the tsars regarded their empire building as a manifestation of their country's "civilizing" European role, and so did many European observers.

However, several changes during the nineteenth and twentieth centuries raised new questions about Russia's relationship to Europe. First, the spread of heterodox political ideas in Europe aroused Russian anxiety and ambivalence about links with the West. Although the tsars wanted to strengthen Russia through closer economic relations with Europe, they feared that nineteenth-century Europe's increasingly volatile mixture of democratic, nationalist, and Marxist ideas would infect Tsarist society. Fear of such infection nourished the mid-nineteenth-century debate between the Westernizers, a group of political and cultural figures who believed that Russia should emulate trends in the West, and the Slavophiles, a cultural and political group that believed Russia should follow a distinctive non-Western path of development.

In a certain sense, Tsarist fears of ideological infection from Europe came true when the communists seized power in Russia under Lenin's leadership near the end of World War I. However, Lenin and his successors did not intend to remake Russia along conventional Western lines. They sought to transform it according to a communist vision that existed only in the realm of Marxist social theory. They viewed Europe as a theater for communist revolution rather than a model to be imitated, and they expected that communism would ultimately spread to all of Europe and beyond. In other words, they believed that the noncommunist world would increasingly be modeled on the Soviet Union, not the other way around.

Rather than bridge the differences between Russia and Europe at large, the victory of a communist vanguard in Russia deepened them. For seven decades, Russia, as the geographic and demographic core of the Soviet state, was the focus of the Marxist-Leninist drive to create a novel communist order. Launched under the ruthless tyranny of Joseph Stalin, this all-out drive for socioeconomic transformation not only created the world's first planned industrial economy but also killed millions of Soviet citizens through the violent collectivization of agriculture, the creation of a vast network of prison labor camps, and blood purges that decimated the ranks of the Soviet elite itself.

The communist system profoundly altered Russia's social and economic structure, but it did not spread to Europe—at least not to the Western European countries beyond the reach of Stalin's army at the end of World War II. Instead, Western Europe, anchored by the strategic power of the United States, gradually evolved toward a common liberal order antithetical to communism. Due partly to the exhausting effects of World War II, the major European states were also steadily compelled to give up their colonial empires—one of the main features they had earlier shared with Tsarist Russia. In contrast to the USSR, the states of Western Europe no longer had the global ambitions and global reach they had previously possessed.

Toward the end of the twentieth century, the prospects for a new convergence between Europe and Russia improved dramatically. In the mid-1980s, Mikhail Gorbachev, the last Soviet leader, introduced unprecedented internal changes designed to humanize the repressive Soviet political order. These sweeping changes ultimately triggered the collapse of Soviet communism and reversed the vectors of international influence that Soviet officials had long tried to promote. After taking power in Russia and helping enact the final dissolution of the Soviet Union, President Boris Yeltsin and his political allies launched a campaign to make Russia a "normal" state based on liberal-democratic and capitalist principles borrowed from the West. In contrast to a long line of Soviet leaders, they sought to rejoin Europe rather than remake it. However, the workability of their program for Westernizing the country was untested. Moreover, it was unclear whether Russia was ready to disavow the USSR's global role and operate as a regional European power.

The hallmark of this monumental effort to transform Russia has been acute uncertainty for elites and ordinary citizens alike. During the Soviet era, the communist leadership tirelessly promoted the political myth that Marxism-Leninism enabled it to forecast the future. If Soviet citizens learned to discount this claim during the final decades of Soviet power, at least they experienced a large measure of predictability in their personal lives. The form of authoritarianism that evolved after Stalin's death in 1953 offered citizens a substantial measure of socioeconomic security despite heavy restrictions on political freedom. The collapse of the Soviet Union, however, exploded the predictability of daily life along with the ruling myth of communist infallibility. For some Russians, the end of the Soviet system brought freedom and economic opportunity; for others, it brought political disappointment and severe economic hardship. For virtually everyone, it brought great uncertainty and a desire for more stability.

The aftermath of the Soviet collapse also left ordinary Russians unsure of their country's international role (see box 7.1). Would Russia establish strong links with Europe, thereby expanding Europe's geographical extent and international influence? Or would it withdraw from Europe and "face east," seeking closer ties with Asian powers such as China in a bid to counterbalance the ascendancy of the United States and its allies in Europe? And what of its relations with the fourteen other former republics of the USSR? Would Moscow accept their gravitation toward Western groupings such as the European Union (EU) and NATO? Or would Moscow resist these trends, and with what consequences?

Box 7.1   From a Speech by Deputy Head of the Presidential Administration Vladislav Surkov to Workers of the United Russia Political Party, Moscow, February 7, 2006

[A]s President [Vladimir Putin] has indicated in his speeches, on the whole we have followed the same path as other European countries. . . . [A]bsolutism reached its apogee in Russia at about the same time as in France. . . . Russia abolished "dealing in people" [serfdom and slavery] . . . even earlier than . . . the United States of America. Our parliamentarism isn't much younger than that of other countries. As for the fact that we had quite a strange totalitarian state in the twentieth century, it's necessary to remember that we weren't alone, that Nazi Germany, Fascist Italy, and Francoist Spain existed in the same Europe . . . .

The big [Soviet] problem was . . . that such a closed society . . . produced an ineffective elite. . . . [A]t a time when people of the stature of Peter the Great were needed, a group of poorly educated and irresponsible comrades came to power. . . . [Former U.S.] Secretary of State Shultz writes in his memoirs that he was shocked by the incompetence of the Soviet leaders. . . . Rejection of such a society was unavoidable. . . .

[However,] the mass of the country was not prepared . . . for life in conditions of contemporary democracy. . . . [R]ather than move toward democracy, we got . . . an oligarchy. . . .In place of public discussion we got continual court intrigue. Instead of representation we got manipulation. . . . Competition was replaced by corruption. . . . If what I've described is democracy and a free and just society, then what is Sodom and what is Gomorrah? . . . [W]hen people try to convince us that someone [in Russia] is dismantling democracy, that is an absolute distortion. . . . The president is returning the real meaning of the word "democracy" to all democratic institutions. . . .

Russia, without a doubt, must remain in the ranks of the powers that make decisions about . . . the world order. . . .[F]or 500 years ethnic Russians and Russian citizens have been a state-bearing people . . . in contrast to many of our friends from the Soviet Union and many other countries. . . . It's clear that some countries that proclaim entry into the European Union to be their national idea are very happy countries; it is not necessary for them to think much. For them everything is very simple. The "Muscovites" . . . are guilty of everything, now we're running to Brussels and everything there will be all right. It's necessary to remember that these nations were not sovereign for one day of their history. . . . This is normal. They were the province of one country and will become the province of another. . . .

[In Russia] a psychology called "offshore aristocracy" has been established. . . . [Members of this group] see their future and the future of their children as outside Russia. . . . [S]uch people will not stand up for [Russia] or be concerned about it. . . . If our business community is not transformed into a national bourgeoisie, then, of course, we have no future. . . .

A second line of political restorationism . . . is . . . the isolationists. . . . These people are almost Nazis, people who spread the idea that the terrible West is threatening us, that . . . China is stepping on us . . . that Russia is for Russians, Tatarstan, apparently, is for Tatars, Yakutsk is for Yakuts, ... [I]f the national-isolationists come to power . . . [this] will lead the nation to a demographic catastrophe and a political crash. . . . [T]o provoke interethnic conflicts in our country is very dangerous. . . . [W]e must strongly oppose this. We stand for a Russia that is for ethnic Russians, Tatars, Mordvians, Ossetians, Chechens, for all of our peoples, for the entire Russia-wide nation.

Dimensions of Postcommunist Change

To succeed, the reform program for joining the West required fundamental changes in the traditional Soviet order. These included establishing a new territorial state in the heart of the former USSR, creating a democratic political system for choosing leaders and making policy, building a capitalist economy based on private ownership and competitive markets, stimulating civic activism, and creating a system of public administration that could uphold the rule of law in public life.

Considered individually, each of these objectives was daunting. Taken together, they represented a mammoth undertaking. Like individuals, governments have trouble dealing with more than one or two major problems at the same time, due to the limits on their resources and decision-making capacity. For example, the U.S. government struggled unsuccessfully for several decades to enact major health-care reform, and it remains unclear whether the reform passed under President Barack Obama will be successful. But reforming U.S. health care is a modest task compared to the sweeping political agenda that has confronted Russian leaders and citizens. The attempt to recast Russia's national identity, political structure, economic order, social life, and system of public administration—*all at the same time*—was bound to produce many unforeseeable consequences.

In deciding how to approach this complex political agenda, Russian leaders and officials have faced perplexing choices about which political tools to use. The consolidation of democracy is sometimes said to depend on a national consensus that "elections are the only game in town"—in other words, that no one can become a major government leader without winning a democratic election. Established democracies rest on the assumption that it is illegitimate to influence the outcome of an election by, for example, urging the armed forces to intervene or using government intelligence agencies to collect confidential information about opposition candidates. Mature democracies allow the leading candidates unfettered access to the news media. They also limit the electoral use of economic resources to, for example, buy votes or divert government funds to favor some candidates over others—although laws limiting the use of private economic resources in political campaigns raise vexing questions of free speech.

In postcommunist Russia, elections have certainly acquired heightened importance as a mechanism of elite selection and elite legitimation. However, Russia has inherited many undemocratic tools of coercion and manipulation from the Soviet era, and the competitors for power have frequently resorted to them—sometimes in order to preempt similar action by their political rivals. The tendency to change elections from a mechanism for selecting government leaders into a means of legitimizing leaders who have already gained power by nondemocratic means has become increasingly pronounced in the past dozen years.

The tumultuous attempt to democratize and marketize the public sphere has imposed severe strains on Russian society. Successful examples of capitalist democracy depend on the existence of a vigorous civil society able to foster participatory values in the citizenry and articulate the social interests that feed into government decision making. As used here, the term "civil society" denotes an extensive network of voluntary associations that are active, nonviolent, and autonomous from the government, and allow individuals to join or leave on their own initiative. The fact that these civic associations accept the legitimacy of one another's interests, even when those interests diverge, contributes to social pluralism and political compromise.[2]

In the USSR, the ruling elite, guided by a fundamental hostility to social pluralism, suppressed any tendency toward the development of a civil society. The elite forced society into a straitjacket, extending the party-state apparatus into every corner of daily life and creating a facade of monolithic popular support for communist rule. This Marxist-Leninist formula for state-society relations was boldly rejected by Gorbachev after he became the leader of the USSR. Seeking to tap the population's suppressed initiative and energy, Gorbachev slashed the power of the party-state apparatus and unleashed a surge of spontaneous sociopolitical activism that initially strengthened his campaign to revitalize the Soviet system. The vast upheaval he set in motion has continued in various guises for more than two decades, but its long-term social consequences remain uncertain. Has this torrent of change created the basis of a genuine civil society, or is Russian society destined once again to become a handmaiden of the state?

Turning Points in the Post-Soviet Era

Knowing a bit about the key turning points in Russia's recent development makes it easier to understand the interaction among these factors. One turning point, of course, was the dissolution of the USSR. The process of political liberalization launched by Gorbachev ultimately escaped his control and generated increasing polarization between anti-Marxist liberals and Leninist conservatives. In 1991, a radical democratic challenge from opponents of the Soviet regime and an unsuccessful last-ditch coup attempt by its supporters intensified the centrifugal forces undermining the Soviet Federation.[3] The outcome was Russia's emergence as an independent state with Boris Yeltsin as president, the promulgation of a program of radical economic reform known as "shock therapy," and a temporary ban on the Communist Party.

Another turning point came in 1993, when President Yeltsin's increasingly bitter political conflict with the Russian parliament finally prompted him to disband the parliament and use the army to crush the opponents who resisted. One result of this confrontation was the adoption of a new Russian constitution with government powers heavily skewed toward the presidency at the expense of the parliament.

A third turning point came in 1995–1996, when the severe economic hardships resulting from shock therapy made it seem likely that Yeltsin would be defeated by a communist candidate in the impending presidential election. Yeltsin seriously considered delaying the election, but in the end a group of new business tycoons who had acquired enormous wealth from the first stages of economic reform rallied around him, enabling him to mount an effective campaign and win the election. These tycoons, commonly known as "oligarchs," deeply feared a possible restoration of communist power.

A fourth turning point came in 1999–2000, when Yeltsin unexpectedly resigned a few months before the end of his term to smooth the way for Vladimir Putin, the politically untested prime minister, to become his successor. Feverish maneuvering in the run-up to the election enabled Putin to defeat better known presidential candidates who might have prosecuted Yeltsin and his close associates for corruption. Putin, who had spent most of his career in the Soviet security service, began to place security service "alumni" in other state agencies and took steps to rein in the most aggressive oligarchs.

A fifth turning point came in 2003–2005, when Putin's campaign to establish political order and tame the oligarchs culminated in the targeted destruction of Yukos, the country's largest and most efficient oil company. The Yukos affair redefined the relationship between wealth and power in Russia. It marked the ascendancy of political elites determined to reestablish the dominance of the Russian state, and it paved the way for further reductions of electoral competition and freedom in the political arena. These changes were manifested in Putin's landslide victory in the 2004 presidential election against a field of minor political personalities.

The most recent turning point occurred in 2010–2012. A few years earlier, Putin, in keeping with the constitutional requirement that no president serve more than two consecutive terms, had ceded de jure presidential powers to Dmitry Medvedev, his chosen successor, and had assumed the position of prime minister. In 2010, however, Putin declared unceremoniously that he would run for a third presidential term, and Medvedev obediently refrained from entering the race. Putin's cynical reassertion of his political primacy upset advocates of liberal reform, and widespread fraud in the parliamentary elections the following year provoked strong public protests in Moscow and St. Petersburg against the prospect of Putin's election to a third term as president. The protests, which drew some of the largest crowds since the end of the Soviet Union, rattled the Kremlin. In response, Putin adopted increasingly coercive policies and propagated xenophobic ideas to thwart meaningful mass participation in the presidential campaign and ensure his reelection in 2012.

National Identity and Statehood

Russia's postcommunist experience highlights the complex interaction among national identity, statehood, and democratization. Today, the view that every nation should have its own territorial state, or sovereign political structure, is widely accepted. However, the fit between existing nations and established states is anything but automatic. Most contemporary observers agree that nations are social groupings whose distinguishing characteristics can change over time; they also agree that in the absence of a common understanding about who belongs to a nation—and therefore to the corresponding state—democratization is extremely difficult. Democratic theory rests on the proposition that a nation or a people (the *demos* in the word "democracy") must govern itself.

But what if there is widespread disagreement about which individuals and territories belong to the nation? Democratic theory cannot answer this fundamental question. The problem cannot be resolved by invoking the principle of national self-determination, because conducting a national plebiscite or convening a representative national assembly requires prior agreement on which individuals are entitled to vote or be represented—the very question that the procedure is supposed to solve. Without a shared understanding of national identity, the inhabitants of a territory are likely to clash over whether they should have a single state or separate states. So, any historical situation that requires recasting a nation's identity or a state's structure to make them compatible hobbles the attempt to build democracy.

The Soviet breakup posed the question of which persons and lands belong to the Russian nation. This conundrum was somewhat mitigated by the fact that the Russian republic had been one of the constituent elements of the now-defunct Soviet Federation. Provisional Russian boundaries and a set of rudimentary political institutions already existed; indeed, these institutions were the mechanisms Yeltsin and his allies used to build up power on the eve of the Soviet collapse. Still, independent Russia's emergence from a larger state hampered the construction of a new political system. Many inhabitants of Russia remained ambivalent about the diminution of the state and the apparent shrinkage of the Russian nation.

One problem was whether to "unmix" the multinational populations inherited from the USSR—and, if so, how. Many ethnic Russians lived in other former Soviet republics, and many non–ethnic Russians (such as Ukrainians or Georgians) lived in Russia. Should all of these people become citizens of their "ethnic homeland" and "return" to it, even if they were born in another republic and had always lived there? Like most former Soviet republics, Russia dealt with this question by offering national citizenship to all its inhabitants (as well as to the inhabitants of other republics who requested it). Nevertheless, the issue of ethnic Russians living abroad has remained a sensitive topic in Russian domestic politics and foreign policy. This is especially true of Russia's relations with Estonia and Latvia, two former Soviet republics that refused to grant citizenship automatically to the ethnic Russians who put down roots there during the Soviet era. These countries have established stringent criteria for naturalization to emphasize that they were forcibly incorporated into Stalin's USSR and to fend off any new efforts by Moscow to control them through the local ethnic Russian population. For most ethnic Balts, as well as the non-Russian citizens of some other former Soviet republics such as Ukraine, the end of Moscow's domination represents a deeply satisfying national achievement that must be carefully safeguarded.

Most inhabitants of Russia view the Soviet collapse through a different lens. For many of them, the breakup of the Soviet state came to be perceived as a national loss. Even though the USSR was not a purely Russian state, Russian culture and language enjoyed a privileged position within it, and many Russians regarded the whole of the USSR as their homeland. Hence they regretted the independence of the other constituent republics, especially Belarus and Ukraine, whose main national groups have East Slavic origins in common with ethnic Russians.[4]

Although Moscow has gradually negotiated border agreements with most other former Soviet republics, the problem of ethnically mixed populations remains a source of political anxiety. This is especially true because contemporary Russia itself is a federation consisting partly of regional units that are the nominal homelands of non-Russian ethnic minorities such as the Tatars. The resulting fear that Russia might disintegrate just as the USSR did helps explain why during the past two decades Moscow has waged two destructive local wars to prevent Chechnya, a small region in Russia's southwest inhabited primarily by the Chechen ethnic minority, from becoming independent. The brutality of Moscow's military forces has been paralleled by numerous acts of terrorism that Chechen insurgents have committed in other parts of Russia, and Moscow's hold over Chechnya and other small southwestern territories remains uncertain.

Constitutions and Elections

Building reliable political institutions on these uncertain national-territorial foundations has been difficult. In the late 1980s, Gorbachev introduced media freedoms and contested elections as part of his campaign to democratize the Soviet system. But no stable set of democratic institutions crystallized across the USSR, and Russia's achievement of independence at the end of 1991 sharpened the basic contradictions among its own government organs. According to Russia's Soviet-era constitution, the Russian republic's government was parliamentary in form. However, as part of his struggle against Gorbachev, Yeltsin had used a popular referendum to create a new Russian presidency and had won the ensuing election. When the USSR disintegrated soon afterward, independent Russia emerged as an awkward political hybrid. The parliamentary powers enshrined in the constitution conflicted with the powers exercised by the president.

During the brief surge of national enthusiasm following the failed conservative coup and Russia's achievement of independence, the parliament granted Yeltsin authority to make a wide range of decisions by presidential decree, but tensions soon escalated as Yeltsin and his parliamentary critics argued over drafts of a new constitution and traded accusations over the mounting human price of shock therapy. Convinced that Yeltsin was driving the economy to ruin, these critics adopted increasingly confrontational tactics, including a serious threat to impeach the president. Yeltsin finally decided to dissolve the parliament; many of his parliamentary opponents barricaded themselves inside the parliament building and designated their own national president and minister of defense. Yeltsin ended the standoff by ordering the military to shell the parliament building and arrest his parliamentary opponents. Although he reneged on his promise to make early presidential elections part of a crisis settlement, suspicions that he harbored dictatorial ambitions were somewhat allayed by his decision to hold early elections for a new parliament and to conduct a referendum on his proposed new constitution.

The 1993 crisis has exercised a lasting influence on Russia's political development. Successful democratization requires the establishment of a constitutional structure that limits the government's capacity for arbitrary action, and the revamped constitutional structure that emerged from Yeltsin's victory over parliament gives too much power to the presidency. Under the Yeltsin constitution, the parliament lacks the authority to approve the president's selection of ministers for the government cabinet; it can reject his nominee for prime minister, but if it does so three times consecutively, he can dissolve the parliament and call new parliamentary elections. This situation has made it very difficult for the legislature to exercise effective oversight over ministerial behavior and the performance of government agencies, since cabinet ministers are beholden for their posts to the president rather than to the prime minister and other parliamentarians. With one brief exception, none of the prime ministers Yeltsin appointed during his eight years as president came from the party with the largest representation in the parliament.

Almost as serious has been the problem of creating an autonomous judiciary that can interpret the laws dispassionately and ensure that officials and citizens obey them. In 1993, the Constitutional Court was caught in the political crossfire between Yeltsin and the parliament, and Yeltsin showed his displeasure over the court's role by reducing its powers under the new constitution. The Soviet legacy of disdain for courts and the legal rights of individuals has made courts at the lower levels of the judicial system especially weak and susceptible to political pressures. Burdened with many judges selected during the Soviet era for their subservience, the courts must also contend with powerful government investigators and prosecutors who are accustomed to overriding legal safeguards and giving breaks to well-connected individuals. As a result, the judicial branch has generally been unable to counter corruption and other dysfunctional official behavior. In recent years, significant reforms have occurred within the court system, but political and bureaucratic obstacles continue to hinder the implementation of judicial decisions.

Together with a constitutional structure based on checks and balances, competitive elections are the bedrock of a functioning democracy. Although Russia has held national parliamentary and presidential elections at regular intervals since 1993, the conduct of these elections has increasingly fallen short of democratic standards. This is especially true of elections to the presidency, the most powerful institution in the political system.

On the eve of the 1996 presidential campaign, Yeltsin's single-digit public approval ratings seemed to guarantee that he would be defeated, perhaps by the candidate of the refurbished Communist Party of the Russian Federation (CPRF). Faced with this prospect, Yeltsin made preparations to declare a state of emergency and postpone the election, and some oligarchs signaled that they would favor this step. Significantly, Yeltsin's presidential campaign committee included the head of the Federal Security Service, Russia's main institutional successor of the Soviet Committee for State Security (KGB). It also included the head of the Presidential Security Service, part of a 20,000-strong leadership protection force that possessed substantial intelligence-gathering capabilities of its own.[5] The chief of the Presidential Security Service, a longtime Yeltsin confidant, repeatedly urged that the election be postponed, and only after he lost a political struggle with other campaign advisers did Yeltsin decide to hold it on time.

Measured by one key yardstick, the election marked the democratic high point of Russia's long political history. The intensity of contestation among the candidates and the closeness of the vote totals were unprecedented.[6] But the election also suffered from serious shortcomings. The media, which were dominated by a handful of new business tycoons who favored Yeltsin's reelection and journalists with a strong aversion to communism, devoted disproportionately large coverage to Yeltsin's campaign and very little to that of his CPRF opponent. Moreover, the media failed to reveal that between the two rounds of voting, Yeltsin suffered a heart attack that raised serious questions about his capacity to fulfill the duties of the presidency.

Four years later, the transfer of presidential power from Yeltsin to Putin was marred by more serious political machinations. In parliamentary elections held shortly before the presidential election was to occur, government-owned media outlets launched vicious personal attacks on the two prospective presidential candidates who had the greatest chance of winning the presidency. Deterred by their shrinking popularity ratings, these two candidates ultimately decided not to run, although the CPRF candidate and a few other nationally known politicians stayed in the race. Yeltsin then resigned a few months early, paving the way for Prime Minister Putin, his chosen successor, to become acting president and defeat this less threatening assortment of opponents in early presidential balloting. During the abbreviated electoral contest, Putin did not deign to present a campaign platform; his victory was already virtually certain. On taking office, Putin's first public act was to issue a decree that granted Yeltsin, as a former president, immunity from arrest or prosecution—thereby shielding him from any possible criminal charges connected with the corruption that had flourished during his time in the Kremlin.

Subsequent presidential elections marked a further retreat from democratic standards. Thanks to the Kremlin's tight control of the media, Putin's high public approval ratings, and the possibility of provoking personal retaliation, in 2004 no national politician with a serious political following was willing to enter the race. Instead, Putin faced a small group of second-rank candidates; the contest was like a series of Ralph Naders challenging an incumbent U.S. president.[7] Putin won in a landslide, racking up more than 70 percent of the vote. In 2008, Putin artfully arranged for Medvedev, the first-deputy prime minister he had designated to succeed him in the presidency, to chalk up an equally lopsided victory against a weak field of candidates from which the most serious contenders had been excluded on electoral technicalities. Finally, in 2012 Putin faced the same motley crew of unsuccessful presidential opponents along with one newcomer—the flamboyant billionaire Mikhail Prokhorov, who directed his appeals to the emerging "creative class" of younger voters. Despite a momentary surge of anti-Putin protests provoked by widespread fraud during the recent parliamentary elections, Putin won in the first round with 63 percent of the vote, proving once again that he was the master in the game of managed elections.

In addition to fair elections, successful democratization hinges on the creation of a system of political parties that enables voters to hold government leaders responsible for the government's conduct. So far, Russian parties have made little contribution to this democratic objective. During the first post-Soviet decade, they were generally weak and, with a few exceptions, short-lived. Most parties were Moscow-centered factions that lacked firm regional moorings.[8] At the grassroots level, party formation was hampered by widespread public suspicion that anyone who joined a party would face pressures for compulsory political participation and restrictions on personal autonomy like those long imposed on the members of the Communist Party of the Soviet Union (CPSU). Moreover, the rapid changes in new party labels were politically confusing. Many parties sprang up or disappeared, making it almost impossible for voters to hold party politicians responsible for government actions. In 1999, for example, three of the leading parties were all created between two and four months before the parliamentary balloting; in the parliamentary election four years later, 60 percent of the votes for the national party-list seats were cast for parties that had not competed in 1999. The main exception to this pattern was the CPRF, which inherited the grassroots structure and diehard adherents who previously belonged to the CPSU.

This pattern changed significantly after Putin became president. In 2003, United Russia, a new umbrella party, won slightly less than two-fifths of the party-list vote in the parliamentary elections, but it ultimately obtained control of more than two-thirds of the seats in the lower house of parliament when members elected as independents aligned themselves with the party. Two years later, the government changed the electoral system to make independent candidacies more difficult and to strengthen the party affiliations of legislators. Since then, United Russia has become the dominant party in the electoral landscape. In the 2007 parliamentary elections, it won almost two-thirds of the popular vote, while the CPRF trailed far behind with less than one-eighth of the ballots. Thanks to postelectoral switches of party affiliation by some legislators, United Russia ultimately commanded the loyalty of 70 percent of the lawmakers in the lower house.

These trends in party development have strengthened the Russian government, but their implications for Russian democracy are unfavorable. United Russia has developed a distinct party profile and a considerable public following among ordinary Russians, who accurately perceive it as a center-right party closely identified with Putin and Medvedev, and the party's electoral success has given the two leaders a strong lever for pushing legislation through the parliament.[9] However, there is no opposition party of comparable stature that can serve as an alternative channel for the expression of public dissatisfaction with government policies. Other parties, such as the CPRF and the left-leaning A Fair Russia, have won narrow slices of the popular vote and control only a small number of parliamentary seats; the liberal parties that championed radical reform in the Yeltsin era no longer have any parliamentary representatives.[10] The process of party building has been crippled not only by most parties' restricted access to media and financial resources, but also by numerous legal barriers designed to exclude small parties from parliament. Although some of these restrictions were relaxed during Medvedev's term as president, the vast disparities in available resources and the heightened risks associated with supporting the opposition have prevented alternative political parties from gaining ground.

Although United Russia maintained control over the majority of seats in the 2011 elections for the lower house of parliament, the balloting dealt a major blow to its reputation and public standing. Using online resources and regional media outlets, opposition activists organized an effective negative campaign against the ruling party under the slogan "Down with the party of swindlers and thieves!" They depicted United Russia as an elitist club for corrupt and opportunistic officeholders out of touch with the electorate. This message must have resonated among some of the party's voters since United Russia's share of the popular vote dropped sharply (from 64.3 percent in the previous election to only 49.3 percent in 2011). Several statistical analyses of the electoral results revealed large-scale fraud across regions and indicated that the party's actual support was much lower.[11] The risk that United Russia now faces is not unlike the fate that befell the CPSU in the post-Stalin years, when it became a mere vehicle for Soviet officialdom to maintain its privileges rather than a force acting in the interests of ordinary citizens. If Putin continues distancing himself from the party he had once created, United Russia may well lose its dominant position in the next round of parliamentary elections. The emergence of vibrant opposition parties with developed grassroots links and no corruption scandals in their past would add dynamism and competitiveness to Russia's stagnant party system. As in the case of the late Soviet years, renewed political competition would also pave the path to more substantive regime change further down the road.

Paths toward Capitalism

The trauma of shock therapy during the Yeltsin years starkly dramatized the complex relationship between democratization and capitalist economic reform. Although free markets are necessary for the survival of democracy, democracy is not always necessary for the creation of an effective market economy, and the relationship between the *processes* of democratization and marketization is especially problematic.

In Russia, where the government had controlled all enterprises as part of a centrally administered command economy, building capitalism required that reformers carry out three broad types of change: liberalization (paring back government intervention in price setting, distribution, foreign trade, etc.), stabilization (balancing government budgets and limiting the growth of the money supply to prevent runaway inflation), and privatization (distributing most state property to private owners subject to the economic discipline of competitive markets). In the Soviet era, attempts to introduce much more limited economic reforms in a gradual fashion had been defeated by the foot-dragging tactics of political and bureaucratic opponents. Together with the severity of the economic problems carried over from the final Soviet years, this may be one reason why the Yeltsin government tried to introduce its market reforms in a single "big bang."

The political consequences of attempting shock therapy turned out to be different from what many observers expected. The most enthusiastic proponents prophesied that rapid marketization under the auspices of a democratic government would create many "winners"—economic and social groups committed to institutionalizing capitalism and democratic political practices. By contrast, some pessimistic opponents warned that rapid marketization would create so many losers and so much suffering among ordinary citizens that it would trigger an authoritarian popular backlash against democratization as well as economic reform. The outcome fell midway between these forecasts. Attempts to implement shock therapy turned out to be far more difficult and painful than its proponents had anticipated, but the short-term effects were less damaging to electoral democracy than many of its opponents had feared. Nonetheless, shock therapy did damage the quality of Russian political life in ways that became much clearer in the Putin era.

Although some reformers tried to ensure that privatization would give ordinary Russians a material stake in shock therapy, the main beneficiaries were officials carried over from the Soviet elite and a significant number of ambitious newcomers willing to seize economic opportunities and exploit them ruthlessly. Bear in mind that the volume of economic resources waiting to be privatized was huge, and that there was no tested body of law and administrative procedure to regulate the scramble for ownership. It was as if the U.S. government owned hundreds of corporations such as Microsoft, Exxon Mobil, du Pont, U.S. Steel, and United Airlines and suddenly had to decide how to distribute them to the public in the midst of a paralyzing constitutional crisis over executive-legislative relations and relations between the federal government and the states. With economic stakes like these up for grabs, Russia's shaky governmental structures came under enormous pressure. To capture and hold these large new sources of wealth, ambitious individuals had compelling motives to manipulate the loose government privatization guidelines and, when necessary, to subvert basic democratic processes.

Paradoxically, the size of the economic stakes also made it harder to carry out shock therapy completely. Some aspiring members of the new economic elite had an interest in freezing economic reform at the halfway point—that is, at a stage where they had become owners but could exploit their personal connections with government officials and the loopholes in the many remaining forms of regulation to reap spectacular gains. [12] For the same reason, government officials in a position to extract bribes had little incentive to reduce or streamline the regulations. Take the example of oil exports. Attempting to avoid a further inflation spike, the government kept energy prices much lower at home than they were on the world market. This in turn required that it limit oil exports to keep adequate supplies inside the country. Hence, any businessman able to wangle a government license to export oil was guaranteed an extravagant profit, and any official with the power to grant a license—a power soon acquired by Yeltsin's Presidential Security Service—was in a position to extract a handsome bribe.

Because privatization was slanted toward individuals with inside connections, it created an economy with an exceptionally high concentration of ownership and a disproportionately large number of rich capitalists by international standards. Today, the Russian economy ranks sixth in the world by size of GDP. This puts it in the economic neighborhood of Germany, Britain, and Brazil. However, Russia ranks near the top of the worldwide list of countries with the most billionaires. It has more billionaires than any other country in Europe, and Moscow is the home of about twice as many billionaires as London. Some of these Russian tycoons not only keep their financial assets abroad, but live there as well. In 2013 one of them, Alisher Usmanov, topped the list of the wealthiest people in Great Britain. Russia's new rich have benefited from once-in-a-lifetime economic opportunities offered by the cut-rate privatization of state assets and other methods of manipulating government policies. Highly profitable export sectors, such as the oil and gas industries and steel and aluminum production, have become the focus of an especially bitter struggle for ownership and control among business and government elites.

The struggle to acquire valuable properties and economic favors from the state has been ruthless and sometimes deadly. The economic opportunities created by shock therapy were enormous, but so were the risks. In the 1990s criminal gangs quickly became involved in the quest for property and state favors, and the disputes were often settled by violence. In the "mob war" of the early 1990s, dozens of bankers were assassinated, mostly in Moscow.[13] The career of Boris Berezovsky exemplifies the dangers and opportunities of these years. During the 1990s, Berezovsky became one of the country's most powerful tycoons and wielded great influence over the policies and even the electoral survival of the Yeltsin government. However, achieving this status nearly cost him his life. In 1993, Berezovsky, still a minor economic player with ties to organized crime, fled for several months to Israel to avoid physical threats. The next year, after returning to Russia, he narrowly escaped being killed by a car bomb planted by rivals vying for control of the lucrative automobile market.

Faced with such physical dangers, the oligarchs sought to protect themselves by creating their own security forces. The Yeltsin government's continuing budgetary crisis led to drastic reductions in the funding of government agencies, including the military and the security police, and to sharp reductions in personnel. Under these conditions, the oligarchs used their new wealth to buy the services of individuals skilled in the arts of intelligence gathering and physical coercion. These individuals were recruited from the ranks of security agencies, the armed forces, and sports clubs. Take, for example, the holding company founded by Vladimir Gusinsky, a rising media tycoon during the early Yeltsin years. To protect its property and enforce its agreements with other firms, Gusinsky's company established a 1,000-man private security force. The force was headed by Filip Bobkov, a former deputy chairman of the KGB who had led the KGB department responsible for monitoring and repressing dissenters critical of the Soviet regime. Many freestanding private security concerns were set up by former government officials with similar backgrounds. By one count, half of these private firms were headed by retired KGB officers, one-quarter by retired officers from the Ministry of Internal Affairs, and the rest by retired officers from military intelligence and other agencies.[14] These trends show that the oligarchs' new wealth gave them the capacity to purchase coercive and intelligence resources that had previously been the sole prerogative of the state. They reflect the oligarchs' search for personal security and commercial advantage in the chaotic political and economic conditions of the 1990s.

During the Yeltsin era, security was much easier for rich businessmen to buy than for entrepreneurs of modest means. In the first two or three years of economic reform, many new businesses were started. Soon, however, the reported growth in the number of small businesses flattened out. There were two main causes of this change. One was a surge in the activities of organized crime, which viewed small businesses as easy targets for the extortion of "protection" payments. Another was the growth of predatory behavior by government officials, especially tax officials, who used their posts to squeeze bribes out of small business owners in exchange for allowing them to operate with fewer hindrances. To reduce such harassment, many small entrepreneurs switched their activities to the underground economy; in the late 1990s, government estimates indicated that at least one-quarter of the country's economic activity was in the unofficial sector. Although some of the reported slowdown in establishing new businesses was due to such evasive behavior, much of it was undoubtedly real. The Russian statistics present a striking contrast to other postcommunist countries such as

Poland and Hungary, where new businesses were about eight times as numerous in per capita terms and accounted for a substantial share of GDP.[15]

The obstacles to the creation and expansion of small businesses had political implications as well as economic ones. In most countries, the owners of small businesses are an important element of the middle class and one of its main economic underpinnings. In Russia, however, the conditions of shock therapy impeded the growth of this socioeconomic group. The Russian middle class has grown in the post-Soviet period, but it contains disproportionately large numbers of white-collar workers employed at various levels of government. Some evidence suggests that in Russia, small enterprise owners are the business group most favorably disposed toward the election of political leaders and the rule of law, probably because they lack the connections and resources used by big business owners to win special favors from the government.[16] On the other hand, white-collar government employees lack independent sources of legitimate income but do have opportunities for graft that may predispose them against reform. The stunted development of the small business sector has therefore narrowed the social foundation for the establishment of democracy in Russia.

During the past decade, the forms of elite competition over property have changed significantly. The recourse to physical violence to settle business disputes has declined markedly, but this does not signify that Russian business practices are converging with those of the advanced capitalist countries. By undercutting the resources of some oligarchs, the severe financial crisis of 1998 triggered a new round of struggle in which aggressive new claimants manipulated bankruptcy laws and local "pocket" jurisdictions to wrest holdings from their financially weakened competitors. In other words, a bitter struggle among business magnates continued even after a large amount of property had been transferred from state ownership to private hands. This raised the question of whether privatization had prompted Russian tycoons to put a new emphasis on productive entrepreneurship or had simply perpetuated their past preoccupation with amassing greater quantities of assets, and whether government reformers could promote such a shift by strengthening the curbs on illicit economic activities.[17] Although the answer remained uncertain, in 2006 the gangland-style murder of the deputy chairman of the Russian Central Bank, the leader of a government campaign to eliminate corruption from the commercial banking sector, underlined doubts that reformers could tame the all-out struggle for economic advantage. In any case, the harsh shakeout among Russian billionaires as a result of the global financial meltdown of 2008–2009 reminded them of their heavy dependence on the state in times of crisis.

Public Administration and Federalism

Successful democratization and marketization both depend on basic changes in the operation of government agencies. U.S. observers have often tended to regard good public administration as a natural by-product of political and economic liberalization, but in fact effective bureaucracies are an unusual modern achievement that should not be taken for granted. Under certain conditions, liberalization can actually worsen the functioning of government bureaucracies and heighten the administrative obstacles to successful reform. To achieve a transition to capitalist democracy, government agencies must give up many previous powers connected with the centralized control of society while taking on many new tasks connected with the operation of a market economy. Bureaucrats frequently have a strong incentive not to give up their old prerogatives, especially when these can be used to extract bribes. Moreover, they often lack the capacity to carry out their new responsibilities due to a shortage of the necessary technical skills or guidance from up-to-date laws.

These problems become especially severe when the territorial state is being recast. In the modern world, states are the master institutions of social life. The stability of nearly all other institutions—the worth of the national currency, the rules of property ownership and inheritance, business contracts, court verdicts, the validity of marriages, the certification of professional credentials, and the allocation of the electronic broadcast spectrum, to name just a few—hinges on the integrity of the state. When the state is weakened, other institutions are called into question, and effective governance becomes much more difficult.

Take, for example, the early efforts of the Yeltsin government to establish a modern central bank and manage the national currency (the ruble). When Russia declared independence, it had a central bank of sorts, but the bank had not yet established some key financial tools that are available to central bankers in developed capitalist countries, such as a market in government bonds. Moreover, the man who headed the bank in the mid-1990s believed that its main purpose was to keep industrial firms afloat with heavily subsidized loans, rather than to protect the value of the currency against inflation. This situation was compounded by the nature of the Soviet breakup, which gave the central banks of all the other former republics the authority to issue ruble credits—thereby preventing the Russian Central Bank from controlling the growth of the money supply. Within two or three years, the government solved this problem by abolishing the ruble zone that united most of the former Soviet republics, but not before great economic and human damage had been done in Russia.

Similar and longer lasting problems plagued the efforts to collect taxes and balance the budget. During the final stage of Yeltsin's political duel with Gorbachev, the government of the Russian republic waged an economic war against the Soviet central government for the control of fiscal resources and industrial enterprises. The aim was to cripple the central government by encouraging Russian banks and regional administrations to refuse to pay their customary taxes into the federal budget while continuing to draw their regular subsidies from the same budget. In addition, Yeltsin and his allies undermined the central government's control over enterprises located in Russia by offering the enterprise managers lower tax rates and enlarged subsidies if they would shift their allegiance to the Russian government. One effect of this political tactic was to show regional administrators and economic managers that they could avoid or reduce tax burdens by negotiating with higher level overseers and playing them off against each other.[18] This lesson, which persisted long after the Soviet breakup, contributed to the plunge in the Russian government's own tax receipts, which fell from about one-sixth of GDP in 1992 to less than one-tenth of GDP in 1996.

Russia's problems with public administration have been intensified by the country's geographic immensity and cultural diversity. Even without the rest of the USSR, the territory of the Russian Federation still encompasses eleven time zones and an ethnically diverse population. About one-quarter of Russia's eighty-three territorial units are so-called autonomous republics formally designated as the homelands of particular ethnic minorities such as the Tatars. This feature of Russia's federal structure bears a limited resemblance to the ethnofederal structure of the USSR (where all the constituent republics were designated as the homelands of particular ethnonational groups). As mentioned above, this structural resemblance has contributed to the fears of some observers and officials that Russia, too, might disintegrate, and it has played a role in Moscow's policies toward Chechnya and other parts of the increasingly volatile North Caucasus region.

During the Yeltsin years, relations between the federal government and the regions were marked by a dramatic "power deflation." Like the USSR as a whole, Soviet Russia had been a federation in name but a unitary state in fact, and during the 1990s, a large amount of administrative and economic power shifted from Moscow toward various regions. The specific allocation of power between Moscow and individual regions was decided through horse-trading and bilateral power-sharing deals whose terms were generally kept secret. As a result, Russia had no consistent national pattern of center-region relations arrived at through public discussion and legislative action—one of the key features of a genuine federation.[19] Playing on divisions and disorganization inside the federal government, the most assertive regions managed to wrest a great deal of power from Moscow and often ignored its wishes.[20]

For its part, the Yeltsin government needed regional governments to support it, especially by using their so-called administrative resources to mobilize the pro-Yeltsin vote during federal election campaigns. During the 1996 presidential campaign, for example, Yeltsin offered about a dozen regions new agreements that expanded their control over regional natural resources and finances. These circumstances spawned many legal and policy contradictions between the federal and regional governments. One analysis at the end of Yeltsin's presidency found that about one-quarter of regional laws and regulations were incompatible with the federal constitution.[21]

After becoming president, Putin worked hard to eliminate such inconsistencies and to reclaim power for the central government. His gradual consolidation of personal power in the presidency made it much more difficult for the regions to gain concessions by playing off political actors in Moscow against each other, especially during elections. In addition, soon after taking office, Putin established seven administrative "super regions" headed by presidential appointees. The leader of each super region is supposed to supervise about a dozen regional governments and ensure that their policies mesh with those approved in Moscow. Although this step eliminated many contradictions between regional and federal laws, the subsequent adoption of new regional laws generated fresh contradictions that will be difficult to iron out in the absence of an effective court system with the power to resolve jurisdictional conflicts.

This is probably one reason that in 2004–2005 Putin pushed through a federal law replacing the popular election of regional executives with appointment by the president (and pro forma approval by the regional legislature). Although rationalized as a response to a bloody school seizure by Chechen terrorists, the measure was actually an additional attempt to strengthen the leverage of the federal government in the country's far-flung regions. In narrow political terms the measure succeeded, because it helped the central government root out some deeply entrenched governors. However, it also increased the risk that the overcentralization of power in Moscow would make regional governments unresponsive to the needs of the local populations, thereby negating the main benefit of a federal system.[22] Amendments to the election law that were adopted in 2012 reinstated direct elections of regional executives but created additional barriers for participation. Individuals interested in running for the position must gain a nomination from a political party and obtain the endorsement of 5–10 percent of municipal legislators in order to be registered for the race. Another amendment adopted in the following year created a new loophole that gave regional assemblies the power to annul direct elections altogether and, instead, elect governors by a majority of assembly members. In this case, the assembly would have to choose among only three candidates nominated by the Russian president. The assemblies in Ingushetia and Dagestan—two conflict-ridden North Caucasian republics—became the first ones to use this loophole and regain the power to decide on the republics' governors, circumventing a popular vote.

The Depletion of Society

The past two decades of upheaval have taken Russian citizens on a dizzying rollercoaster ride from the heights of optimism to the depths of despair and partway back. Public optimism and political involvement peaked during Gorbachev's campaign for *glasnost* and *perestroika*. At the height of the campaign, the number of subscriptions to liberal newspapers containing real news skyrocketed, while subscriptions to orthodox newspapers stagnated or declined. There was a logical connection between *glasnost* and this surge in popular attention to political affairs, since open news media are a key mechanism through which potential members of civil-society groups learn about one another and articulate their common interests.

The level of direct public participation in politics also soared, even at moments when physical repression was a real danger. Near the climax of the struggle for political liberalization in the spring of 1991, pro-Yeltsin forces staged several Moscow protests that drew as many as 300,000 demonstrators. When Gorbachev declared a ban on public demonstrations and mobilized 50,000 troops to enforce it, Yeltsin countered by calling for another demonstration. Faced with a massive protest turnout on the streets of Moscow, Gorbachev pulled back from ordering a military assault, and Yeltsin and the demonstrators prevailed.

Since this high point of public enthusiasm and involvement, Russian society has undergone a marked political demobilization. In part, this demobilization was caused by shock therapy. The decision to free many prices caused a huge spike in inflation that wiped out the savings of many ordinary Russians. Although the depositors had banked these savings during the Soviet years partly because they could not find any goods they wanted to buy, slashing the apparent buying power of the accounts had a devastating emotional impact—especially because it was followed by a plunge in the real standard of living for many citizens. In the first three years of shock therapy, Russia's GDP fell by between one-third and one-half, and it continued to contract for most of the decade. Sustained growth did not resume for almost eight years, and then only after a severe new financial crisis that drove down real wages by one-third between 1997 and 1998. The plunge impoverished many white-collar employees, technical specialists, and skilled workers, especially those employed in the state sector—in other words, many people who had substantial educational and professional credentials.[23] This dire economic situation was compounded by mounting wage arrears, as cash-starved employers tried to bridge the financial gap by holding back the wages they owed their employees.

These socioeconomic shocks coincided with a broader demographic crisis in Russian society. Since independence, Russia's reported population has declined by about 4 percent, to about 143 million persons. In the 1990s, life expectancy dropped by 2 to 3 years, with the life expectancy of males lagging behind that of females by about thirteen years. Although overall life expectancy has increased significantly during the past decade, the Russian level remains below the worldwide average, which includes Third World countries.[24] The origins of this situation can be traced back to the final three or four decades of Soviet power, but the trauma of shock therapy has made it worse, and Russia's continuing population loss may speed up due to the influence of high levels of environmental pollution and other severe public health problems.[25]

Although Putin has publicly identified the demographic crisis as one of the most acute problems facing the country, his government's response has been weak, especially with respect to the mounting danger of an AIDS epidemic that could sharply accelerate the population decline. Other industrialized countries are also experiencing sharply reduced or negative rates of domestic population growth, but Russia is unique in that the population shrinkage stems largely from diminishing life expectancy due to bad health conditions rather than from declining birth rates. One careful outside analyst has even labeled Russia's situation "a humanitarian catastrophe."[26] Demographers project a total population of somewhere between 122 and 135 million inhabitants in 2030, compared with more than 140 million today.[27] Informed observers predict that the economy will soon be hamstrung by a severe shortage of workers and that the declining number of able-bodied men of draft age may cut the military to less than half its current size.[28] Nonetheless, Putin's budgetary plans put the needs of the armed forces and security services ahead of public health and other social programs.[29]

Trends in the educational and cultural makeup of the population are also worrisome. In the years after the Soviet collapse, Russia's traumatic liberalization and opening to the outside world triggered a dramatic outflow of highly educated professionals in search of better living conditions abroad, thereby depriving the country of many specialists who are needed to promote economic modernization and who generally cannot be replaced through immigration.[30] The situation with less skilled workers is somewhat different but no less troubling. As in North America and Europe, the Russian demand for labor has contributed to high levels of immigration by unskilled workers, much of it illegal, from Third World regions such as Central Asia. By one reckoning, Russia has one of the largest populations of illegal immigrants in the world—second only to that of the United States. The influx of these non-Slavic immigrants has sparked vigorous public controversy, but it has not been sizable enough to eliminate the negative economic consequences of population decline. Since the Soviet breakup, the inflow has compensated for about half of the contraction of the native-born population.

Russia's ethnic diversity has increasingly become a source of social tensions. About 80 percent of the population consists of ethnic Russians. Although this is a much higher level of ethnic homogeneity than the USSR had, some parts of Russia, such as the Northern Caucasus and the Middle Volga regions, have large concentrations of ethnic minorities. The marked increase in friction between ethnic Russians and ethnic groups from the Northern Caucasus has been reflected in a growing Russian tendency to view all inhabitants from the Caucasus as members of a single racial category of untrustworthy "blacks." Ethnic Russians are especially hostile to the Chechens—an attitude that has been reinforced by the wars in Chechnya and dramatic acts of terrorism by Chechen rebels. During Putin's years in power, Russian hate crimes directed against minorities have received widespread publicity, and popular sentiment favoring "Russia for the Russians" has gained ground. This outlook has received support from the highly conservative clerics who dominate the Russian Orthodox Church. Some of these churchmen contend that to be a Russian, an individual must have an Orthodox background—a narrow view that relegates the members of non-Orthodox minorities to second-class status.

These trends pose the question of whether Russia is becoming a society that is predominantly "uncivil." In any society, the uncivil and civil sectors have some features in common: both consist of active voluntary associations, and both are autonomous from the state. The key difference is that uncivil groups refuse to acknowledge that other groups' interests are legitimate and deal with them by illicit means that sometimes include violence. Organized crime, networks of corruption, and terrorist groups are all examples of uncivil social elements in Russia. Of course, even solidly democratic countries are home to some uncivil groups. The United States, for instance, has a long tradition of organized crime in big cities such as Chicago and New York, as well as a history of hate groups such as the Ku Klux Klan. The key issue is the relative weight of civil and uncivil groups in a given country.

In Russia, the balance between civil and uncivil groups is unfavorable. The level of citizen membership in voluntary associations is quite low. In postcommunist countries, the level of associational membership is generally lower than in countries emerging from noncommunist authoritarian systems. But Russia's level appears low even by comparison with most other postcommunist countries, and the professional and entrepreneurial elements of society have been slow to organize themselves and protect their interests as groups.[31] The level of membership in trade unions is a partial exception, but most unions were carried over from the Soviet era and have retained members largely because they still exercise control over social welfare benefits.

One barrier to the creation of more voluntary associations is a shortage of trust. Trust is an important part of life for ordinary Russians, but they tend to place their trust in individuals with whom they have long-standing personal ties, not in impersonal civic organizations. Although a substantial number of nongovernmental organizations (NGOs) have been created since the Soviet era, many have lacked broad-based support, and the weakness of domestic philanthropy has made them heavily reliant on foreign donors. The pursuit of outside funding distracts NGOs from developing strong grassroots connections and from focusing on the issues that concern ordinary Russians most; it also makes them vulnerable to the charge that they are the tools of foreign governments. Two thoughtful scholars have cautioned that Russian associational activity may be more extensive than this picture suggests, in part because civil-society initiatives are difficult to measure in the aggregate and are therefore easy to misinterpret.[32] However, even if this is true, civil society in Russia is developing from a low starting point and is encountering mounting pressure from the state.

On the "uncivil" side of the ledger, the level of criminal activity remains high, and corruption, particularly in the ruling elite, continues to expand. Opinion surveys show growing public skepticism about Putin's governing coalition; the share of respondents claiming it was motivated by personal material interests rather than national needs increased from 29 percent to 52 percent between 2008 and 2013.[33] Similarly, a majority of respondents (51 percent) agreed with the opposition's characterization of United Russia as "the party of swindlers and thieves." Despite some progress in the adoption of anticorruption legislation, many observers believe that the Russian authorities lack either the capacity or the will to implement it. As a result, Russia remains near the bottom of the list of states ranked according to the level of perceived corruption in their public sector, and surveys of businesspeople suggest that the incidence of corruption in commercial affairs has increased.[34]

The attitudes of the Russian public combine a positive disposition toward democracy with persisting cynicism and ambivalence. Russians recognize and prize the many new personal freedoms they have gained as a result of the end of Soviet power. High on the list are the freedom to start new businesses, to express their personal political views in conversation, and to travel abroad. However, they regard the Russian government as just as unresponsive to public opinion as the Soviet government was, despite the greater latitude for electoral competition. In fact, survey respondents believe the Russian government is less likely than the USSR was to treat them fairly, in part because they see it as far more corrupt. Although Russians respect Putin as a leader, they have very low opinions of the national parliament, the cabinet, the courts, and political parties—levels far lower than those typical of EU citizens.[35]

These feelings of dissatisfaction, however, have not translated into widespread public aversion to democracy. Surveys show that most Russians are opposed to major changes of political structure—such as a military dictatorship—that would amount to a formal repudiation of democratic principles. Moreover, a majority of respondents say that the present-day political system is not a democracy, and even those who think the country must be governed with "a strong hand" turn out mostly to want such rulers to be selected through free and competitive elections.[36] On the other hand, Russian respondents are much less ready to condemn arbitrary official acts, including violations of human rights and press freedoms that citizens in most European countries would regard as undemocratic. Moreover, they show little recognition of the Putin team's manipulation of recent national elections, and the financial meltdown of 2008–2009 did not directly undermine their confidence in the president.[37] Popular mobilization against fraud in the December 2011 election may have caught the authorities by surprise, but the rallies were mainly confined to Moscow and St. Petersburg. After Putin's reelection to the Presidency, protest participation dropped to just a few thousand people. By contrast, over two-thirds of respondents across the country have consistently refused to participate in any protests against fraudulent elections.[38] Overall, much of this skeptical and ambivalent worldview might be regarded as rational, given the tumult of the 1990s and the dramatic improvement of living standards under the increasingly undemocratic order of the past decade. Nonetheless, without a positive disposition toward civic and political action, ordinary Russians cannot be expected to exert a significant influence on the evolution of the political system.

The evolution of civil society is closely bound up with the fate of the media, which played a pivotal role in activating the public during the *glasnost* era. The Putin team's media policy bears some resemblance to Soviet practice but also differs from it in important respects. Government officials are acutely sensitive to the political impact of the media and work assiduously to shape it. But unlike the Soviet media watchdogs who searched for heresy in every corner of the intellectual world, today's media overseers focus narrowly on the segments of the media that have a large-scale impact on mass attitudes.[39] Above all, this requires close supervision of the political reportage broadcast by the principal television stations. These stations have become the main source of news for most Russians, and they regularly give uncritical image-enhancing coverage of top government officials and favored candidates for office. Media overseers pay less attention than their Soviet predecessors to print outlets, especially small-circulation publications, and the boldest publications still print direct criticism of the country's leaders. The most courageous newspapers also continue to sponsor muckraking investigations of particular cases of crime and corruption, even though this has led to the murder of a large number of journalists.[40]

Perhaps as important as the government's focus on political news is its relaxed attitude toward the media's nonpolitical content. Having abandoned the Soviet ideological commitment to transform citizens into morally superior human beings, the government allows television broadcasters free rein to develop nonpolitical shows that are slickly produced and entertaining. One example is a TV show called *The Star Factory*, which resembles *American Idol*. This kind of concession to popular tastes has enabled the Kremlin to avoid the dreariness that made the Soviet media uncommonly boring and contributed to the alienation of many Soviet citizens.

The Quest for a "Strong State"

When Putin became president in 2000, most Russians greeted him as a welcome change from the ailing and erratic Yeltsin. Methodical and low key, the new president spoke frankly about the country's problems and seemed determined to address them. He put a special emphasis on establishing order in Russian public life and strengthening the faltering economy. Putin promised to establish the "dictatorship of law" by requiring consistent compliance from the oligarchs as well as ordinary citizens and by working to make the laws and administrative decisions of various state organs consistent with one another.

Among Putin's early achievements were the introduction of simplified tax laws, which boosted the government's revenues and helped it pay down foreign debts, and an impressive economic revival sustained in large measure by a dramatic rise in the price of Russian oil on global markets. The enthusiastic public response to these changes was easy to understand. Between 2000 and 2005, the average real income of Russians increased by about 75 percent, halving the number of people below the official poverty line. Putin's public approval ratings consistently ranked above 70 percent and sometimes climbed to the low 80s.[41] Still, in recent years public support for his actions has dropped significantly, from 77 percent in 2008 to 52 percent in mid-2013.[42]

Although Putin regularly paid lip service to the goal of further democratization as well as economic liberalization, his acts increasingly belied his words. One straw in the wind was his heavy reliance on personnel with security service backgrounds to fill governmental posts having nothing to do with security issues. Putin had risen rapidly from relative political obscurity during the 1990s and lacked a wide circle of politicians he could trust. A belief that this narrow political base would limit his freedom of action may have been Yeltsin's main motive for choosing him to become the next president.

Putin coped with this paucity of tested political acquaintances by turning to individuals with backgrounds in the security police and the armed forces—the so-called *siloviki* or force wielders. Individuals with these backgrounds made up about one-third of the ministers and deputy ministers appointed in Putin's early years as president, plus about 70 percent of the staffs of the new super regions.[43] Within this pool, former members of the security services were politically more significant than ex-military men because the security services had traditionally penetrated all parts of Russian society and possessed an assortment of manipulative tools that extended well beyond the threat or use of violence.

These staffing decisions bolstered the tendency of the state to play an increasingly assertive role. The initial targets of state pressure were Berezovsky and Gusinsky, the two tycoons who had acquired dominant positions in the media and had used their media clout to advance their own narrow objectives. Under Kremlin-orchestrated harassment from the tax police, the courts, and compliant creditors such as the giant Gazprom energy corporation, the two were stripped of their media empires and driven into foreign exile.

The most important watershed in the Kremlin's relations with the oligarchs was the Khodorkovsky affair of 2003–2005. Mikhail Khodorkovsky, head of Yukos, the richest and best managed Russian oil company, rejected indirect signals from the government that he should follow these other oligarchs into exile. Instead, he plunged deeper into politics and began to underwrite opposition parties in the run-up to the 2003 parliamentary elections. He also worked to reduce the taxation of energy companies—taxation that was essential to maintaining Russia's newfound fiscal health—and challenged the government monopoly on the shipment of energy to foreign buyers.

The trial and imprisonment of Khodorkovsky and his business partners on charges of embezzlement and tax evasion were politically motivated. In the course of privatization, the defendants had undoubtedly engaged in many illegal and corrupt acts, but so had other tycoons who were not put on trial. Moreover, Khodorkovsky had recently taken his company in a new direction, upgrading its corporate governance and transparency in order to attract foreign investment. His real offense was to challenge the Kremlin's growing political dominance. The arrest was well timed to appeal to Russian voters, who had bitter memories of privatization and would soon have an opportunity to vote in the parliamentary and presidential elections. Around this time, one survey revealed that about 90 percent of the population felt that all large fortunes had been built up illegally, nearly 80 percent favored reviewing or revoking the results of the privatization process, and almost 60 percent advocated opening criminal investigations of the rich.[44]

The policies of Putin toward civil society have been more active and restrictive than Yeltsin's policy was. Harassment of civil society activists by the police and tax authorities has become more pronounced, and the government has begun to sponsor its own "in-house" organizations to compete against civil society groups perceived as too assertive.[45] For example, the Kremlin founded a youth group called Nashi ("Our Own") to channel the energy of young people into politically acceptable forms of activity. Suspended above this assortment of sponsored organizations is a new, quasi-autonomous "Public Chamber" created by the government. Ostensibly it was set up to facilitate government consultations with society, but critics understandably suspect that its unspoken purpose is to bleed off genuine grassroots energy and initiatives. The government has also put severe pressure on foreign-funded NGOs. It has introduced special registration and reporting requirements for those groups that receive financial support from abroad and engage in any activities aimed at changing state policies. It has also suggested rhetorically that these groups may be acting as conspiratorial agents of foreign powers. This step has crippled or closed several major organizations that previously played a crucial role in election monitoring and human rights advocacy. On the other hand, the government has underscored the need to increase domestic funding for voluntary associations, and it has prioritized channeling of financial support to groups engaged in offering social services and protection.[46] Compared to the previous year, the funding of state-sponsored grants available for nongovernmental organizations in 2013 more than doubled.[47] Time should clarify how much, or how little, these government measures resemble the state's treatment of society during the Soviet era. At present, they seem to indicate a deep suspicion of the unregulated expression of social interests, but still nothing like the absolute rejection of autonomous associational life in the Soviet years.

Russia and Europe

In the post-Soviet period, Russians who favor close ties with Europe have faced two fundamental problems that both stem from changes in Europe itself. First, the strategic imperatives that linked Russia to Europe at certain points in the past have disappeared. As long as the major European powers posed military threats to one another, they had a strong security motive to draw Russia into Europe as a counterweight, even when they found its internal politics distasteful. This is what motivated France and Britain to conclude a military alliance with Tsarist Russia against Germany before World War I and to pursue a similar alliance with the USSR on the eve of World War II. After World War II, however, the European powers laid aside their historic military rivalries, partly in order to counter the geopolitical threat from the USSR. Although post-Soviet Russia has changed dramatically and is far weaker militarily than the USSR, some Western observers continue to doubt that the changes have permanently altered Russia's international objectives. This is especially true of observers from Poland and other new EU members that were long trapped inside the Soviet bloc. Thus, to the degree that strategic calculations shape contemporary European attitudes toward Moscow, they make Russian integration into Europe less likely, not more.

Closely related changes within the European states have also made integration a far bigger challenge for Russia than in the past. Two and a half decades ago, Gorbachev evoked an enthusiastic response from Western Europe by proclaiming that the USSR was part of a "Common European Home" that bridged the continent's Cold War divide (see box 7.2). Today, however, postcommunist Russia seeks cooperation with a different Europe—one that has reached an unprecedented level of political and economic integration and therefore judges Russia by more exacting criteria. Candidates for EU membership must satisfy demanding EU standards for democratic governance, and under Putin, Russia has moved farther from those standards, not closer to them. The gap separating Russian capitalism from EU economic practices is just as large. To become a realistic EU candidate, Russia would first have to undergo a lengthy process of internal change, and even then the EU, whose appetite for enlargement seems exhausted by the protracted economic crisis that began in 2008, would probably refuse at the end of the day. Instead, Russia has been actively promoting economic integration projects among post-Soviet countries that the Kremlin believes would serve as an alternative to the EU. Membership in a Russia-led Customs Union, which now includes Belarus and Kazakhstan, is incompatible with any form of close economic association, such as participation in a free trade zone, with the EU member states. Putin's plan to establish an even more ambitious Eurasian Economic Union would create additional institutional barriers between the two sides.

On the Russian side, disenchantment with the idea of joining the West has also grown for several reasons. The Yeltsin government carried out shock therapy under the banner of Westernizing the Russian system. Since the reform effort was actively promoted by the United States and the European Union, the severe socioeconomic hardships that resulted gave many Russians second thoughts about the wisdom of Westernization. For a significant minority of Russians, the word "democracy" became identified with personal suffering, disorder, and extreme economic inequality. A small proportion of the population even came to believe that the Yeltsin reforms were part of a Western conspiracy to weaken Russia. These sentiments have increased some Russians' receptiveness to the idea that Russian cultural values are fundamentally different from those of the West.

Foreign policy disagreements have contributed to the more distrustful Russian outlook. NATO's decision to extend membership to several of Moscow's former allies in Eastern Europe upset members of the Russian foreign policy establishment, and a further round of NATO enlargement that included the Baltic states vexed them even

Box 7.2   Excerpts from Mikhail Gorbachev, *Perestroika: New Thinking for Our Country and the World* (1988, pp. 180–83, 190–91)

This metaphor [of a common European home] came to my mind in one of my discussions. . . . It did not come to me all of a sudden but after much thought and, notably, after meetings with many European leaders. . . . I could no longer accept in the old way the multi-colored, patchwork-quilt-like political map of Europe. The continent has known more than its share of wars and tears. It has had enough. Scanning the panorama of this long suffering land and pondering the common roots of such a multi-form but essentially common European civilization, I felt with growing acuteness the artificiality and temporariness of the bloc-to-bloc confrontation and the archaic nature of the iron curtain. . . .

Now, about the opportunities the Europeans have . . . to be able to live as dwellers in a "common home."

1. The nations of Europe have the most painful and bitter experience of the two world wars. The awareness of the inadmissibility of a new war has left the deepest of imprints on their historical memory. It is no coincidence that Europe has the largest and the most authoritative antiwar movement. . . .
2. European political tradition as regards the level of conduct in international affairs is the richest in the world. European states' notions of each other are more realistic than in any other region. Their political "acquaintance" is broader, longer, and hence closer.
3. No other continent taken as a whole has such a ramified system of bilateral and multilateral negotiations, consultations, treaties, and contacts at virtually every level. It has to its credit such a unique accomplishment in the history of international relations as the Helsinki process [the Conference on Security and Cooperation in Europe, subsequently renamed the Organization for Security and Cooperation in Europe]. . . . Then the torch was taken up by [an international conference in] Vienna where, we hope, a new step in the development of the Helsinki process will be made. So, the blueprints for the construction of a common European home are all but ready.
4. The economic, scientific, and technical potential of Europe is tremendous. It is dispersed, and the force of repulsion between the East and the West of the continent is greater than that of attraction. However, the . . . prospects are such as to enable some modus to be found for a combination of economic processes in both parts of Europe to the benefit of all. . . .

Europe "from the Atlantic to the Urals" [Russia's Ural Mountains] is a cultural-historical entity united by the common heritage of the Renaissance and the Enlightenment, of the great philosophical and social teachings of the nineteenth and twentieth centuries. . . . A tremendous potential for a policy of peace and neighborliness is inherent in the European cultural heritage. . . .

The building of the "European home" requires a material foundation—constructive cooperation in many different areas. We, in the Soviet Union, are prepared for . . . new forms of cooperation, such as the launching of joint ventures, the implementation of joint projects in third countries, etc. . . .

True, all of this would increase the European states' mutual interdependence, but this would be to the advantage of everyone and would make for greater responsibility and self-restraint.

> Acting in the spirit of cooperation, a great deal could be done in that vast area which is called "humanitarian" [and includes human rights]. A major landmark on this road would be an international conference on cooperation in the humanitarian field which the Soviet Union proposes for Moscow. At such a conference the sides could discuss all aspects of problems which are of concern to both East and West, including the intricate issue of human rights. That would give a strong new impetus to the Helsinki process.
>
> However, the . . . tangible prospects are such as to re-enable some modus [vivendi] to be found for a combination of economic processes in both parts of Europe to the benefit of all.

more. In the interim, NATO's decision to use force against Serbia over Kosovo without UN authorization made the alliance look like a potential threat to Russia, which feared secessionism inside its own borders, especially in Chechnya. Europe and the United States treated Moscow's first war in Chechnya with considerable diplomatic restraint, but they voiced stronger criticism when Moscow renewed the military conflict in the late 1990s and allowed its forces to commit rampant human rights violations against the local population. Many Russians, however, viewed the conflict quite differently. Moscow launched the war following a series of terrorist bombings in the heart of Russia that took several hundred lives and that the government blamed on the Chechens. In these circumstances, a significant proportion of Russians felt that the new war was justified—in contrast to widespread public condemnation of the earlier one.

In addition, during the past half-dozen years, Russia has become involved in a heightened competition with the West to influence the direction of change in several other former Soviet republics located on Russia's borders. Two prominent cases are the disputed presidential elections in Ukraine, where the "Orange Revolution" of 2004 sidetracked Moscow's favored candidate, and in Belarus, where Russia successfully backed the fraudulent reelection of the incumbent president. Russian policymakers have been especially determined to block any resumption of the U.S.-led campaign to win NATO membership for Ukraine. Whatever the causes of the 2008 war between Russia and Georgia—and the most detailed analysis suggests some responsibility on both sides—one result of the conflict was to reduce the prospect for any further NATO enlargement into the lands of the former USSR. These disagreements about Russia's so-called Near Abroad reflect a broader divergence of outlooks between Russia and the West. In the Yeltsin and early Putin eras, many Western and Russian leaders appeared to share the assumption that Russia and other former Soviet republics were converging with Western political and economic patterns. There was, in other words, broad-gauged agreement about what progress in the Soviet successor states should look like. Thanks to this shared outlook, leaders from across the continent declared their commitment to the political and human rights standards established under the auspices of the Organization for Security and Cooperation in Europe (OSCE).

However, after several years of Putin's presidency, a "values gap" started to appear between Russia and the West. In particular, the Russian government has begun to champion its own definitions of democracy and democratic practice. It has emphasized the theme of "sovereign democracy," by which it means that outside states should not try to tell Russia or nearby countries how to organize themselves internally

---

Box 7.3   From the Declaration on Human Rights and Dignity of the Tenth World Council of Russian People, Convened by the Russian Orthodox Church, Moscow, April 6, 2006

Aware that the world . . . is facing a threat of conflict between the civilizations with their different understanding of the human being and the human being's calling—the World Russian People's Council, on behalf of the unique Russian civilization, adopts this declaration:

Each person as image of God has singular unalienable worth, which must be respected by every one of us, the society and state. . . .

Rights and liberties are inseparable from human obligations and responsibilities. The individual in pursuit of personal interests is called to relate them to those of the neighbor, family, community, nation and all humanity.

There are values no smaller than human rights. These are faith, morality, the sacred, [and the] motherland. Whenever these values come into conflict with the implementation of human rights, the task of the society, state and law is to bring both to harmony. It is unacceptable, in pursuit of human rights, to oppress faith and moral tradition, insult religious and national feelings, cause harm to revered holy objects and sites, jeopardize the motherland. . . .

We reject the policy of double standards with regard to human rights, as well as attempts to use them for political, ideological, military and economic purposes, for imposition of a particular socio-political system.

We are willing to cooperate with the state and all benevolent forces in ensuring human rights. Particularly important for this cooperation are such endeavors as preserving the rights of nations and ethnic groups to their religion, language and culture, defending the freedom of conscience and the right of believers to their own way of life, combating ethnically and religiously motivated crime, [and] protecting against arbitrary actions by the authorities and employers. . . .

We seek dialog with people of diverse faiths and views on human rights and their place in the hierarchy of values. Like nothing else, this dialogue today will help avoid the conflict of civilizations and attain a **peaceful diversity of worldviews, cultures, legal and political systems on the globe.**

---

or how to behave abroad (see box 7.3). And it has worked to make these definitions stick—for example, by blocking efforts by the OSCE to monitor Russian elections and by sending Russian observers who have proclaimed that elections in former Soviet republics such as Belarus were free and fair even when OSCE observers condemned them. Recently it has also begun to promote negative depictions of Western countries designed to discredit Western democratic systems and shore up the Russian system's own uncertain stability through a process of "negative legitimation."

These controversies have spilled over into Russia's economic relations with Europe. By a wide margin, Europe is Russia's largest trade partner and biggest source of direct investment, but European-Russian energy relations have become a focus of tension. Toward the end of the Soviet era, Moscow gradually expanded trade with Europe and built a controversial pipeline to transport natural gas from Russia to Western Europe. The Soviet government took great pains to calm suspicions that it would manipulate the supply of natural gas for political purposes. Since that time, European dependence on Russian gas has grown dramatically, but Moscow's missteps have once again made the energy relationship a matter of Western political debate. In 2006, and again in 2008–2009, Russia, attempting to manipulate Ukraine's internal political alignments to suit its own preferences, cut off gas shipments to that country. Because the same pipeline carries gas to Western Europe, this measure caused economic disruptions there and provoked a public outcry, even though Russia quickly resumed full gas shipments.

This episode raised larger questions about the acceptable level of increased Russian investment in European energy distribution systems and the acceptability of Russian curbs on Western investment in energy production and pipelines inside Russia. These issues have become entangled with the concurrent European debate over the terms of ownership and competition among the EU members' own national energy corporations. Given the scope of Europe's energy needs and the importance of energy sales for Russia's economic prosperity, the Russo-European disagreements are likely to be resolved through compromises of some kind. But they show that even limited integration within one key economic sector faces significant obstacles.

Although Russia is highly unlikely to be formally integrated with Europe, it is more likely to remain engaged with Europe than with any other major country or group of countries outside the boundaries of the former USSR. At the elite level, Russian reformers continue to be interested in Europe. Within the citizenry as a whole, Europe enjoys a more favorable reputation and exercises a much stronger attraction than any other region, including the United States and China. A sizable proportion of Russians regard themselves as Europeans; none, of course, regard themselves as North Americans, and few see themselves as East Asians. From time to time, Moscow's leaders may make common diplomatic cause with China in cases of disagreement with the United States, and they will gradually increase their energy exports to booming Asian markets. But Russia's demographic and economic center of gravity remains west of the Ural Mountains, in European Russia, and a significant eastward shift of Russian trade will require two or three decades. Together with Moscow's apprehensions about the long-term security implications of Asia's unprecedented burst of economic dynamism, this structural factor nearly guarantees that Russia will not make a decisive geopolitical "turn" from Europe to Asia.

The Ukrainian Crisis and Relations with the West

Near the end of 2013, the outbreak of a major crisis over Ukraine caused a spike in tensions between Russia and the West. The trigger was the announced decision of Ukrainian President Viktor Yanukovych to finalize an Association Agreement with the European Union at the forthcoming EU-Ukraine summit in Vilnius. In past years Moscow had held a neutral view of EU enlargement—in contrast to its hostility toward NATO enlargement—but Putin concluded that the association agreement would undermine Moscow's influence over Ukraine by thwarting his efforts to integrate Ukraine into a Russia-led Customs Union. A major feature of the draft agreement was the goal of creating a Deep and Comprehensive Free Trade Area (DCFTA) between Ukraine and EU member-states to facilitate trade among them. Viewing the DCFTA as a geopolitical risk that would also injure its own economy, Russia threatened to revoke the trade privileges awarded to Ukrainian companies under the free trade arrangement between the two countries. This would have led to major short-term losses for many Ukrainian industrial producers, particularly those in the eastern region that depended heavily on continued access to the Russian market.

Putin's determination to keep Ukraine in Russia's sphere of influence became increasingly clear as the Vilnius summit approached. In August 2013, Moscow signaled its intention to impose major economic costs on Ukraine by temporarily tightening inspection procedures for all Ukrainian goods flowing into Russia. In addition to using sticks, it also offered carrots in the form of sizeable loans and a discount on the price of natural gas if Ukraine rejected the EU association agreement. In the end, the Yanukovych government succumbed to the pressure from Moscow. A week before the Vilnius summit, Yanukovych decided not to sign the agreement. Several weeks later Putin promised Ukraine $15 billion in financial aid and a thirty percent discount on gas supplies. The Kremlin's assertion of control over the country's foreign policy seemed nearly complete, but it was too early for Putin and his Russian supporters to celebrate.

Although the pressure from Moscow compelled Yanukovych to abandon the association agreement, it also helped accelerate the decline of Ukraine's corruption-ridden political regime. When Yanukovych's decision was announced, a wave of large-scale demonstrations protesting the turn away from the EU challenged the stability of Yanukovych's rule. The government's initial attempts to suppress the movement by force fueled broader discontent and revolutionized the protesters' demands. During the next two months, the movement spread beyond Kyiv (Kiev), engulfing most of Western and Central Ukraine in protests that called for the president's immediate resignation. Although Putin continued to back Yanukovych politically and financially, the EU and the US threatened sanctions against his government unless he made concessions to the opposition. Yanukovych responded by making a last-ditch attempt to intimidate protesters by mobilizing the military and special operation forces; when a bloody three-day stand-off in Kyiv's central square failed to end the protests, he finally agreed to withdraw the troops and surrender most of his powers to the legislature. Now alarmed for his own safety, Yanukovych fled the country, and an interim, opposition-led legislative coalition formally took charge. Putin, however, refused to recognize the coalition's authority, insisting that the replacement of Yanukovych amounted to a political coup.

The power vacuum in Kyiv and the country's dire economic condition gave Putin a brief window of opportunity to reclaim a part of Ukraine most Russians have long viewed as their own—the Crimean peninsula. For more than two centuries Crimea has been a home for Russia's Black Sea Fleet, and a new Ukrainian government was likely to contest the bilateral agreement negotiated by Yanukovych and Medvedev in April 2010 to allow continued basing of the fleet in Crimea until 2042. Meanwhile, official Russian media carried reports of an impending surge of Ukrainian nationalist paramilitary groups into the peninsula, heightening the fears of ethnic Russians in Crimea about the intentions of right-wing elements in the new Ukrainian government. On the pretext of protecting the locals against this danger, Moscow suddenly deployed Russian military units without official insignia across Crimea and around Ukraine's own Crimean military bases. The newly installed pro-Russian leadership of Crimea immediately called for secession from Ukraine, while the local parliament scheduled a snap referendum to give unification with Russia an aura of democratic legitimacy. The West, however, condemned the referendum as an illegitimate violation of Ukraine's territorial integrity and demanded that Russia pull back its troops or face sanctions. Putin ignored these warnings and invoked the lopsided Crimean popular vote in favor of annexation to justify his position. In March 2014 he signed a law finalizing Crimea's accession to the Russian Federation.

Although the long-term outcome of this crisis remains highly uncertain, it is likely to cast a shadow over Russia's relations with Europe for years to come. By violating a border that Russia previously recognized under bilateral treaties with Ukraine, Putin has raised the specter of a revisionist Russia bent on forcibly changing Europe's post–Cold War borders and threatening the continent's hard-earned security. Tellingly, Crimea's absorption was the first instance of forcible annexation on the continent since the World War II era. The resulting fears of Russia's continued expansion, especially among Eastern European states bordering Ukraine, have rejuvenated the waning significance of NATO as Europe's deterrent against incursions from the east. The crisis seems likely to deepen Russia's international isolation and set new limits on its interaction with the West, making it not only more insular but also less European. Moreover, the crisis has nudged Ukraine toward a European orbit, thus seemingly contributing to the very outcome Putin sought to avoid.

Ukraine's long-term geopolitical orientation will depend in part on future responses to the crisis from Russia, the EU, and the United States. But the country's future will also hinge on Ukrainians' ability to build a new political system capable of rooting out rampant domestic corruption, reconciling distinct interests of the country's diverse regions, and implementing the extremely painful economic reforms that closer economic ties with the EU would entail. Moscow will undoubtedly fight tenaciously to increase its leverage through economic pressures and "black" operations by its security services, especially in the eastern regions of Ukraine. Yet if Ukraine succeeds in its domestic transformation and moves decisively toward the West, Russia will either have to accept Kyiv's independent course or turn the Ukrainian question into a permanent irritant to its relations with the EU.

Conclusion: Russia's Futures

Russia's steady shift toward hypercentralization has given Putin unparalleled preeminence and Russians a renewed semblance of political order. The key question is whether the political structure they have built can deal with the grave problems of economic development and human welfare facing the country, as well as respond to the demands for greater accountability coming from the most assertive parts of the society. Historically, Russian leaders have often attempted to overcome crises by concentrating power and multiplying the state's administrative controls over societal activity. Under Putin, memories of the severe political conflicts and predatory economic behavior during the Yeltsin era have strengthened the impulse to follow this path. Aversion to the costs of elite conflict may have also facilitated a smooth return of presidential power from Medvedev to Putin in 2012. For the most part, ordinary Russians have accepted a formula of centralized state control, even though in principle many would prefer a more democratic political system. Thus far, relative financial security and political certainty have trumped the desire for greater political and economic freedoms.

The sustainability of this model, however, is clearly in question. To succeed in the contemporary world, states need high levels of active cooperation from their citizens and high levels of information about the internal workings of society. By relying increasingly on direct administrative control, the Russian government will almost certainly thwart essential socioeconomic initiative and shrink both the quality and quantity of information reaching policymakers. The typical result of such restrictive tactics is a state that tries to monopolize the initiative in policymaking but that also lacks the capacity to deal effectively with real societal issues—in other words, a state that combines the appearance of great power with the reality of substantive weakness.

Rather like the slogan of the "scientific technological revolution" endlessly mouthed by Gorbachev's predecessors, the modernization program advertised during Medvedev's brief presidential tenure remained no more than a vague promise. Apart from a grand but ill-conceived plan to build a Russian "Silicon Valley" in Moscow's suburbs, the program produced little substantive policy change. Over half of Russia's federal budget revenues in 2011—the last year of his presidency—came from the sale of oil and gas, while two-thirds of all of its exports were still based on hydrocarbons.[48] At the same time, the government gradually softened its earlier restrictions on spending windfall profits in order to subsidize priority economic sectors. Under these conditions, the international development of alternative energy resources combined with increasing extractive costs for domestic producers create serious risks for Russia's economic and political stability. Since the continued submissiveness of the public depends on maintaining the current level of social benefits, any prolonged external economic shocks will threaten the main source of the regime's legitimacy among ordinary Russians. To date, however, there is little evidence that Putin recognizes these long-term risks or is willing to initiate any sweeping economic restructuring to reduce them. Instead, since the start of his third term he has focused on eliminating immediate threats associated with revived opposition activity.

In pursuit of this goal, Putin has followed a policy of coercive demobilization of his most outspoken critics from nascent civil society groups. Criminal prosecution rather than simple administrative fines has become the default tool for curbing the growth of public protests in Moscow and other Russian cities. Overall, the Putin regime has exhibited the same pattern of defying any pressure from below and resisting calls for political liberalization or economic reform that the Soviet leadership showed in the decade preceding Gorbachev's *perestroika*. Excessive personalization of key political institutions and the high individual risks that Putin and his entourage would face in any genuine renewal of the elite have created strong incentives for them to prolong their rule for as long as possible. Therefore, the most likely scenario for Russia in the near term is institutional inertia combined with increasingly fragile elite unity and mounting doubts about the regime's long-term survival. But as the plentiful financial resources sustaining regime stability steadily diminish, Russia will face a developmental choice. It could either stick to its inefficient combination of quasi-Soviet politics and state capitalism or adopt more inclusive political institutions and liberalize the economy to enhance its global competitiveness.

The expansion and political orientation of the middle class will be crucial in the kind of choice Russia ultimately makes. Sustained pressure from an enlarged middle class could facilitate reform of the government bureaucracy and help strengthen the integrity of the judicial system. On the other hand, if the middle class fails to generate this kind of "demand for law," serious institutional overhaul is unlikely to succeed. Whether a shrinking society wracked by a severe health crisis can generate this kind of political pressure is uncertain. A dramatic increase in immigration might cushion the demographic decline, but it would probably intensify frictions between ethnic Russians and non-Russians. If a large number of the most talented Russian professionals choose to emigrate, that could also weaken the social support for liberal reform.

The crisis over Ukraine has damaged Russia's relations with Europe and unleased powerful anti-Western sentiments inside Russia. Even if Russia ultimately follows a liberal political path, many years are likely to pass before a positive new form of engagement with Europe becomes possible. Closer integration of energy networks may occur, but political and economic integration along a broader front faces much bigger obstacles. For many years to come, an ambivalent Russia is likely to remain on the periphery of an ambivalent Europe. Internationally as well as domestically, the uncertainty that has pervaded Russia's recent past is likely to shadow its future as well.

Notes

1. Martin E. Malia, *Russia under Western Eyes: From the Bronze Horseman to the Lenin Mausoleum* (Cambridge, MA: Belknap Press of Harvard University Press, 1999), 4–12, 43–60.

2. Ernest Gellner, *Conditions of Liberty: Civil Society and its Rivals* (New York: Allen Lane Penguin Press, 1994), 1–12, 88–96; and Richard Rose, "Toward a Civil Economy," *Journal of Democracy* 3, no. 2 (April 1992): 13–26.

3. The coup plotters were conservative leaders from the political police (KGB), the military, and the central organs of the Communist Party and the government. The state of emergency they declared soon collapsed due to their lack of political determination and paralyzing splits inside the military and police agencies. By discrediting the conservatives, the failed coup attempt boosted the centrifugal forces in the country. Equally important, it enabled Boris Yeltsin to eclipse Gorbachev. Yeltsin led public opposition to the coup, while the plotters held Gorbachev in seclusion until the attempt collapsed.

4. Vera Tolz, "Conflicting 'Homeland Myths' and Nation-State Building in Post-Communist Russia," *Slavic Review* 57, no. 2 (Summer 1998): 267–94.

5. Amy Knight, *The Security Services and the Decline of Democracy in Russia, 1996–1999*, Donald W. Treadgold Papers no. 23 (Seattle: University of Washington, 1999), 14–16.

6. Timothy J. Colton, "Putin and the Attenuation of Russian Democracy," in *Leading Russia: Putin in Perspective. Essays in Honour of Archie Brown*, ed. Alex Pravda (New York: Oxford University Press, 2005), 103–18.

7. This analogy is taken from Colton, "Putin and the Attenuation of Russian Democracy."

8. Richard Rose, "How Floating Parties Frustrate Democratic Accountability: A Supply-Side View of Russia's Elections," in *Contemporary Russian Politics: A Reader*, ed. Archie Brown (New York: Oxford University Press, 2001), 217; and Stephen White, "The Political Parties," in *Developments in Russian Politics*, 6th ed., ed. Stephen White, Zvi Gitelman, and Richard Sakwa (Durham, NC: Duke University Press, 2005), 90.

9. Henry E. Hale and Timothy J. Colton, "What Makes Dominant Parties Dominant in Hybrid Regimes? The Surprising Importance of Ideas in the Case of United Russia," revised version of a paper presented at the Annual Meeting of the American Association for the Advancement of Slavic Studies, Boston, MA, November 12–15, 2009.

10. After the 2007 election, the Communists controlled about 13 percent of the seats in the lower house; A Just Russia controlled about 8 percent.

11. Peter Klimek, Yuri Yegorov, Rudolf Hanel, and Stefan Thurner, "Statistical Detection of Systematic Election Irregularities," http://www.pnas.org/content/early/2012/09/20/1210722109.full.pdf (accessed January 15, 2014).

12. Joel S. Hellman, "Winners Take All: The Politics of Partial Reform in Postcommunist Transitions," *World Politics* 50, no. 2 (January 1998): 203–34.

13. Paul Klebnikov, *Godfather of the Kremlin: Boris Berezovsky and the Looting of Russia* (New York: Harcourt, 2000), 21, 31–32.

14. Vadim Volkov, *Violent Entrepreneurs: The Use of Force in the Making of Russian Capitalism* (Ithaca, NY: Cornell University Press, 2002), 77, 133.

15. Calculated from Harley Balzer, "Routinization of the New Russians?" *Russian Review* 62, no. 1 (January 2003): 23.

16. Timothy Frye, "Markets, Democracy, and New Private Business in Russia," *Post-Soviet Affairs* 19, no. 1 (January–March 2003): 24–45.

17. Andrew Barnes, *Owning Russia: The Struggle over Factories, Farms, and Power* (Ithaca, NY: Cornell University Press, 2006), 1–10.

18. Piroska Mohacsi Nagy, *The Meltdown of the Russian State: The Deformation and Collapse of the State in Russia* (Northampton, MA: Edward Elgar, 2000), 64–66.

19. Alfred Stepan, "Russian Federalism in Comparative Perspective," *Post-Soviet Affairs* 16, no. 2 (April–June 2000): 144.

20. Timothy Frye, "Corruption and Rule of Law," in *Russia after the Global Economic Crisis*, ed. Anders Åslund, S. M. Guriev, and Andrew Kuchins (Washington, DC: Peterson Institute for International Economics and Center for Strategic and International Studies, 2010), 66–68.

21. Cameron Ross, "Putin's Federal Reforms," in *Russian Politics under Putin*, ed. Cameron Ross (New York: Manchester University Press, 2004), 166.

22. Ekaterina Zhuravskaya, "Federalism in Russia," in Åslund, Guriev, and Kuchins, *Russia after the Global Economic Crisis*, 59–78.

23. Bertram Silverman and Murray Yanowitch, *New Rich, New Poor, New Russia: Winners and Losers on the Russian Road to Capitalism*, expanded ed. (Armonk, NY: M. E. Sharpe, 2000), 51–54, 153.

24. The demographic data in this paragraph are from the Population Reference Bureau, (http://www.prb.org) and the U.S. Census Bureau (http://www.census.gov). See, for example, Population Reference Bureau, "Russia: Highlights: Infant Mortality Rate," http://www.prb.org/DataFinder/Geography/ Data.aspx?loc=444#/map/population (accessed January 15, 2014). See also BBC, "Russia behind on Life Expectancy Compared to Neighbors" (in Russian), http://www.bbc.co.uk/russian/society/2013/03/130327_lancet_life_expectancy_russia.shtml (accessed January 15, 2014).

25. Murray Feshbach, "Russia's Population Meltdown," *Wilson Quarterly* 25, no. 1 (Winter 2001): 12–21; and Nicholas Eberstadt, "The Future of AIDS: Grim Toll in Russia, China, and India," *Foreign Affairs* 81, no. 6 (2002): 22–45.

26. Nicholas Eberstadt, *Russia's Peacetime Demographic Crisis: Dimensions, Causes, Implications* (Washington, DC: National Bureau of Asian Research, 2010), 2, 281–301.

27. Eberstadt, *Russia's Peacetime Demographic Crisis*, 30.

28. G. Ioffe and Z. Zayonchkovskaya, "Immigration to Russia: Inevitability and Prospective Inflows," *Eurasian Geography and Economics* 51, no. 1 (2010): 104–25.

29. Brian Taylor, "Kudrin's Complaint: Does Russia Face a Guns vs. Butter Dilemma?" PONARS Eurasia Policy Memo no. 254, June (Washington, DC: George Washington University, 2013).

30. Maria Repnikova and Harley Balzer, "Chinese Migration to Russia: Missed Opportunities," Eurasian Migration Paper no. 3 (Washington, DC: Kennan Institute, Woodrow Wilson International Center for Scholars, 2009).

31. Marc Morje Howard, *The Weakness of Civil Society in Postcommunist Europe* (New York: Cambridge University Press, 2003); Michael McFaul and Elina Treyger, "Civil Society," in *Between Dictatorship and Democracy: Russian Post-Communist Political Reform*, ed. Michael McFaul, Nikolai Petrov, and Andrei Ryabov (Washington, DC: Carnegie Endowment for International Peace, 2004), 140–41; and Balzer, "Routinization of the New Russians?" 25.

32. Debra Javeline and Sarah Lindemann-Komarova, "A Balanced Assessment of Russian Civil Society," *Journal of International Affairs* 63, no. 2 (2010): 171–88.

33. Levada Center, "More than Half of the Country Believes EP 'Party of Crooks and Thieves'" (in Russian), http://www.levada.ru/print/29-04-2013/svyshe-poloviny-strany-schitaet-er-partiei-zhulikov-i-vorov (accessed January 15, 2014).

34. Transparency International ranked Russia 133rd out of 176 states in 2013. See also Levada Center, (in Russian), http://www.levada.ru/files/1142009322.doc (accessed July 11, 2006); and Frye, "Corruption and Rule of Law," 83–86.

35. Stephen White, "Russia's Disempowered Electorate," in *Russian Politics under Putin*, ed. Cameron Ross (New York: Manchester University Press, 2004), 76–78.

36. Vladimir Petukhov and Andrei Ryabov, "Public Attitudes toward Democracy," in McFaul, Petrov, and Ryabov, *Between Dictatorship and Democracy*, 269, 290; and Henry E. Hale, "The Myth of Mass Russian Authoritarianism: Public Opinion Foundations of a Hybrid Regime," NCEEER Working Paper, September 8, 2009, http://www.ucis.pitt.edu/nceeer/2009_823-03_Hale.pdf (accessed January 15, 2014). A minority of respondents, young as well as old, also have ambivalent or positive feelings about Stalin as a leader; Sarah E. Mendelson and Theodore P. Gerber, "Soviet Nostalgia: An Impediment to Democratization," *Washington Quarterly* 29, no. 1 (Winter 2005–2006): 83–96.

37. Richard Rose and William Mishler, "How Do Electors Respond to an 'Unfair' Election? The Experience of Russians," *Post-Soviet Affairs* 25, no. 2 (2009): 118–36; and Richard Rose and William Mishler, "The Impact of Macro-Economic Shock on Russians," *Post-Soviet Affairs* 26, no. 1 (2010): 38–57.

38. Levada Center, "Support and Participation in Meetings Growing," press release (in Russian), http://www.levada.ru/29-01-2013/podderzhka-mitingov-i-zhelanie-uchastvovat-v-nikh-rastut (accessed January 15, 2014).

39. Scott Gehlbach, "Reflections on Putin and the Media," *Post-Soviet Affairs* 26, no. 1 (2010): 77–87.

40. Committee to Protect Journalists, "56 Journalists Killed in Russia since 1992," http://cpj.org/killed/europe/russia/ (accessed January 15, 2014).

41. Levada Center, http://www.levada.ru/prezident.html (accessed July 11, 2006).

42. Levada Center, "Vliianie, podderzhka i polozhytel'nye kachestva Vladimira Putina" (in Russian), June 10, 2013, http://www.levada.ru/10-06-2013/vliyanie-podderzhka-i-polozhitelnye-kachestva-vladimira-putina (accessed January 15, 2014).

43. Julie Anderson, "The Chekist Takeover of the Russian State," *International Journal of Intelligence and Counter Intelligence* 19, no. 2 (Summer 2006): 239–40; and Stephen White and Olga Kryshtanovskaya, "Putin's Militocracy," *Post-Soviet Affairs* 19, no. 4 (2003): 294.

44. Sergei Guriev and Andrei Rachinsky, "The Role of Oligarchs in Russian Capitalism," *Economic Perspectives* 19, no. 1 (2005): 140.

45. McFaul and Treyger, "Civil Society," 159–66.

46. Konstantin Kostin, "Kremlin Experts Suggested Support 'Socially Oriented' NGOs" (in Russian), March 28, 2013, http://lenta.ru/news/2013/03/28/nko/ (accessed January 15, 2014).

47. The amount rose from about $33 million to $77 million. Lilia Biriukova and Svetlana Bocharova, "NKO den'gami ne obidyat" (in Russian), *Vedomosti*, July 15, 2013, http://www.vedomosti.ru/newspaper/article/489941/nko-dengami-ne-obidyat (accessed January 15, 2014).

48. Thane Gustafson, "Putin's Petroleum Problem," *Foreign Affairs* 91, no. 6 (2012): 70–82.

Suggested Readings

Åslund, Anders, S. M. Guriev, and Andrew Kuchins, eds. *Russia after the Global Economic Crisis*. Washington, DC: Peterson Institute for International Economics and Center for Strategic and International Studies, 2010.

Barnes, Andrew. *Owning Russia: The Struggle over Factories, Farms, and Power*. Ithaca, NY: Cornell University Press, 2006.

Brown, Archie, ed. *Contemporary Russian Politics: A Reader*. New York: Oxford University Press, 2001.

Brown, Archie. *The Gorbachev Factor*. New York: Oxford University Press, 1996.

Brown, Archie. *The Rise and Fall of Communism*. New York: HarperCollins, 2009.

Colton, Timothy J. *Yeltsin: A Life*. New York: Basic Books, 2008.

Eberstadt, Nicholas. *Russia's Peacetime Demographic Crisis: Dimensions, Causes, Implications*. Washington, DC: National Bureau of Asian Research, 2010.

Fish, M. Steven. *Democracy Derailed in Russia: The Failure of Open Politics*. New York: Cambridge University Press, 2005.

Gustafson, Thane. *Wheel of Fortune: The Battle for Oil and Power in Russia*. Cambridge, MA: Belknap Press of Harvard University Press, 2012.

Hill, Fiona, and Clifford Gaddy. *Mr. Putin: Operative in the Kremlin*. Washington, DC: Brookings Institution, 2012.

Hoffman, David E. *The Oligarchs: Wealth and Power in the New Russia*. New York: Public Affairs, 2001.

Koesel, K. J., and Valerie J. Bunce. "Putin, Popular Protests, and Political Trajectories in Russia: A Comparative Perspective." *Post-Soviet Affairs* 28, no. 4 (2012): 403–3.

Lieven, Anatol, and Dmitri Trenin, eds. *Ambivalent Neighbors: The EU, NATO and the Price of Membership*. Washington, DC: Carnegie Endowment for International Peace, 2003.

Lipman, Mariia, and Nikolai Petrov, eds. *Russia in 2020: Scenarios for the Future*. Washington, DC: Carnegie Endowment for International Peace, 2011.

McFaul, Michael. *Russia's Unfinished Revolution: Political Change from Gorbachev to Putin*. Ithaca, NY: Cornell University Press, 2001.

McFaul, Michael, Nikolai Petrov, and Andrei Ryabov, eds. *Between Dictatorship and Democracy: Russian Postcommunist Political Reform*. Washington, DC: Carnegie Endowment for International Peace, 2004.

Reddaway, Peter, and Dmitri Glinski. *The Tragedy of Russia's Reforms: Market Bolshevism against Democracy*. Washington, DC: United States Institute of Peace Press, 2001.

"Rethinking Russia," *Journal of International Affairs* 63, no. 2 (special issue) (Spring–Summer 2010).

Taubman, William. *Khrushchev: The Man and His Era*. New York: Norton, 2003.

Taylor, Brian D. *State Building in Putin's Russia: Policing and Coercion after Communism*. New York: Cambridge University Press, 2011.

Tolz, Vera. *Russia: Inventing the Nation*. New York: Oxford University Press, 2001.

Volkov, Vadim. *Violent Entrepreneurs: The Use of Force in the Making of Russian Capitalism*. Ithaca, NY: Cornell University Press, 2002.

CHAPTER 8

Poland

THE LONG ARM OF TRANSITION

Ben Stanley

Poland

Population (million):	38.5
Area in Square Miles:	124,807
Population Density in Square Miles:	308
GDP (in billion dollars, 2012):	$814.1
GDP per Capita (PPP, 2012):	$20,900
Joined EC/EU	May 1, 2004

Performance of Key Political Parties in Parliamentary Elections of October 9, 2011

Citizens' Platform (PO)	39.2%
German Minority (MN)	0.2%
Law and Justice (PiS)	29.9%
Palikot's Movement (RP)	10.0%
Polish People's Party (PSL)	8.4%
Left and Democrats (LiD)	8.2%

Main officeholders: President: Bronislaw Komorowski, PO (2010); and Prime Minister: Donald Tusk, PO (2007)

A quarter of a century after the momentous events of 1989, Polish politics still remains dominated by the choices made in the wake of Poland's departure from communism, and governed by the political elites who realized those outcomes or stood in opposition to them. Although party politics initially reflected the divide between the outgoing communist regime and the dissidents who had forced it to the negotiating table, the second decade of transition saw a realignment of political competition around an increasingly potent distinction between the "winners" and "losers" of transition. This chapter argues that this "transition divide" came to supplant the "regime divide" of the first decade of transition as the "proto-cleavage" of Polish politics. While the party system remained only partially consolidated and many Poles were not mobilized by any parties, the "long arm" of transition was visible in the bifurcating effects of economic and social reforms.[1] When placed in the comparative context of similar processes of "integration" and "demarcation" under the aegis of globalization in Europe, it seemed plausible to expect that the divide over these reforms would deepen into a lasting political cleavage. However, the long arm of transition was manifested not only in the lasting consequences of policy choices made in the early 1990s, but also in the persistence of political actors from those years and the arcane webs of loyalty and enmity that sustained their relationships. In 2013, it remained an open question as to when they would exit the political scene, and whether existing political divides would survive their departure.

Extraordinary Politics

Whilst the ideology of liberalism inspired Poland's postcommunist reform after 1989, Polish liberals were in short supply. Liberal ideas only began to take root during communism, when the opposition movements of the 1970s pursued the development of a pluralistic civil society upholding human and civil rights.[2] These intellectual currents fed into the demands for autonomy and self-organization advanced by the Solidarity movement, which in 1980–1981 numbered some 10 million members. The suppression of Solidarity through the imposition of martial law in 1981 underlined the bankruptcy of communist legitimacy and the exhaustion of zeal for orthodox solutions. Yet the outlawing of the organization and internment of leading dissidents demonstrated that the coercive powers of the state remained insuperable. During the repressive years of the mid-1980s, opposition intellectuals increasingly turned away from civic, political freedoms and toward notions of freedom through economic liberalization.

After a decade of economic and ideological stagnation, reformers in the Polish United Workers' Party (PZPR) began to change their own attitudes toward the market. Laws on economic activity gave private businesses freedom to hire and promised equality of access to credits and inputs. The renewal of strike activity in the latter half of 1988 impressed on the authorities the need to co-opt Solidarity as a junior partner to ensure the maintenance of social peace.[3] This resulted in the convocation of a

Round Table from February to April 1989 that made significant concessions to political freedoms but maintained the principle that the PZPR would remain first among unequals, transferring its executive power to a strong presidency and dominating a legislature in which 65 percent of the seats were reserved for its members.

The semidemocratic elections of June 1989 equipped Poland with a set of bootstraps by which it would haul itself into democracy. Against all expectations, in the first round Solidarity won 160 of the 161 parliamentary seats they were permitted to contest and 99 out of the 100 freely contested seats in the new Senate. The PZPR and its minor satellite parties did badly in the first round. Their performance was cruelly reflected in the fortunes of prominent governing politicians who were placed on a "national list" of thirty-five seats to ensure their success. In only two cases did candidates achieve the necessary quota for election. This situation was only resolved through the embarrassing expedient of changing the electoral laws prior to the second round. Effectively, Solidarity won the election. It could not form a government, but after the defection of the satellite United Peasant Party (ZSL), neither could the communists. However, the continued existence of the Soviet Union in 1989 forced Solidarity to accept the communist leader General Wojciech Jaruzelski as president and "guardian" of the Round Table compromise.

In September, Solidarity intellectual Tadeusz Mazowiecki became prime minister of a Grand Coalition, dominated by Solidarity but including ministers from all parties. The rapid fall of communist regimes elsewhere turned thoughts from the selective application of remedial market reforms to the wholesale *transformation* of the economic system. The Balcerowicz Plan (named after Leszek Balcerowicz, Mazowiecki's finance minister), an economic package that came into force on January 1, 1990, simultaneously enacted "shock therapy" on the economy and laid the foundations of the new economic order. Balcerowicz emphasized swiftness of action, arguing that the window of opportunity for wholesale reform would rapidly give way to the party and interest-group sclerosis of politics as usual.[4]

In the new context of transition to democracy, the robust individualism advocated by enthusiasts of capitalism assumed a wider relevance. Just as the "proven model" of market capitalism seemed a panacea for economic problems, so the key postulates of liberalism promised remedies for the pathologies of political and cultural existence under communism. Liberalism appeared as "inverted Marxism," offering the opposite of all that was hated in the previous order.[5] As well as establishing a fully functioning capitalist economy, democracy had to be entrenched in accordance with liberal constitutionalist principles. The role of the state was to act as guarantor of the rights and freedoms of the individual and to ensure an open civil society in which free individuals could participate. This required legal protections for individual and minority rights and the decrease of direct state control over areas such as the media and the education system. Social and historical truth was no longer the province of the state but a product of the free market in ideas. Finally, openness in the domestic sphere was complemented by an open, nonantagonistic foreign policy, with an emphasis on cooperation and membership in international organizations.

Whose Poland Is It to Be? From the Round Table to the "War at the Top"

From the outset of transition, Polish liberals had feared a backlash against painful reforms. Many had witnessed firsthand the extraordinary political energies unleashed by Solidarity a decade before. Their concern was that in conditions of democratization, these might prove to be destabilizing tendencies. The 1989 elections took part largely in an atmosphere of optimism and goodwill on the part of both political elites and voters. Yet, as Balcerowicz had predicted, the period of popular assent was not to last long. The Round Table negotiations quickly became a focal point of resentment for radical opposition groups refusing all negotiation with the communists, a resentment exacerbated by the technocratic political style of the Mazowiecki government and its determination to avoid policies of revenge. The absence of public debate and the strict oversight of parliamentary discussion of the Balcerowicz Plan were easily construed as symptomatic of the unwillingness of the new elite to participate in a dialogue with society.

The deepening of democracy saw the deepening of the rift. Lech Wałęsa supported the drive for "acceleration" of democratic reform, insisting on early presidential elections in which he would run as the Solidarity candidate. Solidarity liberals perceived this stance as a threat to the gradual accretion of democratic gains, and they supported Mazowiecki's candidacy. Jaruzelski resigned to permit early presidential elections, but the resulting "war at the top" destroyed the unity of Solidarity in the bitter and destructive election campaign of November–December 1990. Liberal fears about the propensity of the electorate to be swayed by demagogic promises were compounded by the success of surprise candidate Stan Tymiński, a conspiracy theory–toting Polish émigré to Canada who attracted a quarter of the vote in the first round, pushing Mazowiecki into third place. Although liberal Solidarity temporarily swung behind Wałęsa to see off the threat of Tymiński, their support was laced with distaste for the lesser evil.

Wałęsa's victory sharpened the appetite for accelerated parliamentary elections, which took place in October 1991. With 29 parties—many of which barely warranted the name—entering the Sejm, the first democratic parliament was incoherent (see table 8.1). The two largest parties were the liberal Democratic Union (UD), built around Mazowiecki's milieu, and the successor to the Communist PZPR, the Democratic Left Alliance (SLD). Neither was able to form a coalition government: the SLD was politically untouchable and the UD bore responsibility for Poland's shock therapy. The exclusion of the latter from the eventual five-party minority coalition was testament to the depth of the divide in Solidarity.

As the first government of a fully democratic Poland, this coalition, under the Solidarity lawyer Jan Olszewski, regarded itself as mandated to accelerate transition. Refusing to acknowledge the Round Table compromise as the historical moment of departure from communism, it argued that "lustration" (the exposure of individuals' past collaboration with the communist secret police) was necessary to identify and remove the continuing influence of communists. The coalition's tenure was short and

Table 8.1 Genealogy and Ideology of Major Political Parties and Electoral Coalitions

Name	Origins	Period of Significance	Regime Divide	Economic	Cultural	Attitude to Transition
AWS *Solidarity Election Action*	Coalition of approximately 40 post-Solidarity parties	1996–2001	Post-Solidarity	Mixed—both anti- and promarket elements	Conservative, with Catholic-nationalist elements	Broadly positive
KLD *Liberal-Democratic Congress*	Post-Solidarity intellectuals and promarket pioneers	1990–1993	Post-Solidarity	Strongly promarket	Liberal	Positive
KPN *Confederation for an Independent Poland*	Non-Solidarity anticommunist movement (founded in 1979)	1989–1997	Anticommunist	Mixed, increasingly antimarket	Nationalist	Critical
LiD *Left and Democrats*	Coalition of SLD, SdPL, UP, and PD	2006–2008	Mixed	Centrist	Liberal	Positive
LPR *League of Polish Families*	Elements of ZChN, extraparliamentary Catholic nationalist parties	2001–2007	Neither	Mixed—some promarket elements but highly protectionist and autarchic	Strongly nationalist and clerical; moral traditionalism	Negative
PC / POC[1] *Centre Accord*	Christian Democratic and conservative Solidarity activists grouped around Jarosław Kaczyński	1990–1993	Post-Solidarity	Mixed—ostensibly promarket but critical of reforms	Moderately conservative	Critical
PiS *Law and Justice*	PC, elements of AWS	2001–present	Post-Solidarity	Increasingly statist and antiprivatization	Originally conservative; increasingly nationalist and clerical	Initially critical, then negative
PO *Civic Platform*	UW, KLD, elements of AWS	2001–present	Post-Solidarity	Originally very promarket, more moderately so in recent years	Mixed—both liberal and conservative elements	Positive, although initially critical of transition elites
PSL *Polish Peasant Party*	ZSL (communist-era satellite party)	1989–present	Postcommunist	Centrist	Moderately conservative	Positive
ROP *Movement for the Rebuilding of Poland*	Assorted conservative-nationalist post-Solidarity parties	1997–2001	Post-Solidarity	Mixed—ostensibly promarket but in practice interventionist	Conservative-nationalist	Negative

Party	Description	Years	Origin	Market orientation	Social/clerical orientation	Attitude to the past
RP *The Palikot Movement*	Predominantly new; some former PO and SLD members and assorted left-wing activists.	2011–present	Neither	Originally promarket and small-state but increasingly left-wing since mid-2011	Strongly anticlerical and liberal	Indifferent, tends to focus more on the politics of the present
SdPL *Polish Social Democrats*	Split from SLD	2003–present	Postcommunist	Moderately antimarket	Liberal, anticlerical	Positive
SLD *Democratic Left Alliance*	Successor to the communist PZPR. Originally a coalition based around *Social Democrats of the Polish Republic* (SdPR), formally constituted as a party in 1999	1990–present	Postcommunist	Moderately antimarket	Liberal, anticlerical	Positive
SO *Self-Defence*	Agrarian movement of the early 1990s; constituted as a party in 1992	1992–2007	Neither	Antimarket (especially privatization)	Ambiguous	Negative
UD *Democratic Union*	Liberal Solidarity intellectuals	1990–1994	Post-Solidarity	Strongly promarket	Liberal, but with a significant conservative faction	Positive
UW/PD *Freedom Union / Democratic Party*	Formed from the merger of UD and KLD	1994–2004 (UW) 2005–present (PD)	Post-Solidarity	Strongly promarket	Liberal, with conservative elements	Positive
UP *Labour Union*	Socialist groups from Solidarity; elements of reformist wing of PZPR	1992–present	Mixed	Moderately antimarket	Liberal, anticlerical	Positive
ZChN[2] *Christian National Union*	Clerical and nationalist elements of Solidarity	1989–2001	Post-Solidarity	Ambiguous	Strongly nationalist and clerical; moral traditionalism	Initially positive although increasingly critical

[1] In 1991, PC ran as the main party of the Civic Center Accord (POC).

[2] In 1991, ZChN ran as the main party in Catholic Election Action (WAK).

controversial, and its zeal for lustration led to its downfall after a clumsy attempt by Interior Minister Antoni Macierewicz to expose collaborators amongst the political elite, including Wałęsa himself.[6] In his outgoing speech, Olszewski posed a question that would resonate in the years to come:

> [F]rom today onwards the stake in this game is not simply the question of which government will be able to execute the budget to the end of the year; at stake is something more, a certain image of Poland: what sort of Poland it is to be. To put it another way, whose Poland is it to be?[7]

Olszewski's argument was that in the absence of a clean break with communism, both national identity and autonomy were under threat. However, at a time when many ordinary Poles were suffering the effects of economic reforms, it also raised the question: in whose interests was "shock therapy" working?

Most scholars assumed that politics would revolve around a key economic division between promarket and antimarket parties. This was supplemented by a variety of "cultural" divides such as "religiosity versus secularism," "liberalism versus cosmopolitanism," and "traditionalism versus libertarianism," all of which were in essence about differences between individualist and collectivist conceptions of society.[8] In the Polish case, a "triangle of values" was evident at an early stage: a group of liberal parties (UD and the Liberal-Democratic Congress [KLD]) advocated civic rights and rejected socioeconomic rights, the social democratic left (SLD and the Labour Union [UP]) supported both civic and socioeconomic rights, and the conservative-nationalist right (most prominently, the Christian-National Union [ZChN]) supported socioeconomic rights but argued for the primacy of the family and the nation over the individual.[9]

The fractious atmosphere of the Olszewski government carried over into the rest of the 1991–1993 term, amid growing social discontent at the effects of reforms. Waldemar Pawlak, leader of the agrarian Polish Peasant Party (PSL), failed to assemble a governing coalition, and Hanna Suchocka's post-Solidarity coalition proved too divided and fragile.[10] Both the SLD and the opposition right-wing post-Solidarity parties supported a motion of no confidence, leading to the dissolution of parliament and early elections in September 1993. The SLD won, forming a coalition with the PSL, the only coalition partner to regard them as acceptable. Whilst the UD put up a reasonable showing, the conservative-nationalist element of Solidarity was essentially eliminated from parliament. Around a third of the vote was "wasted" on parties of primarily nonliberal Solidarity provenance that failed to surmount the new 5 percent threshold.

The 1993–1997 Parliament was dominated by political forces associated with the negotiated transition. This is not to suggest that consensus reigned undisturbed. The postcommunist "regime divide" still governed popular perceptions of political opposition, and the SLD had campaigned on a platform strongly critical of liberal economic reforms. However, developments over this parliamentary term indicated a more complex ideological configuration underlying the regime divide.

Democratic in Form, Christian in Content? Constituting the New Poland

The early years of transition saw a piecemeal approach to institutional reforms. In April 1989, directly after the conclusion of the Round Table talks, the 1952 Constitution was amended to take account of the changes agreed upon at those talks. The lower house (*Sejm*) still retained its status as the supreme organ of state power, but the directly elected upper house (*Senat*) received limited powers to initiate, review, and delay legislation. The relationship between the two houses was broadly accepted, although periodically the case was made for liquidating the *Senat*.

Unsurprisingly, given the state of geopolitical uncertainty in mid-1989, the presidency was endowed with a number of political powers. As president, Jaruzelski retained many of the competencies associated with the communist-era Council of State: he could dissolve parliament and call early elections given certain conditions, initiate and veto legislation, and, aside from nominating the prime minister, was also empowered to give his views on ministerial candidates. It was unclear in some cases precisely where the prime minister's sphere of influence ended and that of the president began, with foreign and defense policy areas of particular ambiguity.[11] Jaruzelski displayed restraint in the exercise of his prerogatives, but Wałęsa's tenure was characterized by substantial conflict between the presidency and successive governments, who experienced unpredictable vetoes of legislation and the imposition of ideologically incompatible "presidential ministers" in key portfolios. Initially, it seemed that the presidency would remain strong: the "Little Constitution" of 1992 formalized the president's influence over key ministries, with prime ministers obliged to consult the president over the appointment of the foreign minister, defense minister, and interior minister. The idea of a strong president appealed to some political elites, for whom a powerful nonparliamentary executive could push through necessary reforms in relative freedom from the sectional interests of political parties.[12] However, the experience of the Wałęsa presidency gradually encouraged a mainstream consensus on a presidency set further apart from the day-to-day business of government.

The flourishing of democratic pluralism and President Wałęsa's creative approach to constitutional privilege significantly hindered the vital process of constitution building in the first years of transition. A change of pace occurred with the victory of Aleksander Kwaśniewski, leader of the parliamentary caucus of the SLD, in the presidential elections of November 1995. (See box 8.1 for a chronology of political events and box 8.2 for a list of major personalities.) The eventual promulgation of the 1997 Constitution resolved the issue of executive authority by diminishing the power of the president compared with that of the government. The president, who was no longer able to interfere in ministerial appointments, would be "guarantor of the continuity of state power" (Art. 126.1), and the prime minister and his cabinet charged with "carry[ing] out the domestic and foreign policies of the Polish Republic" (Art. 146). Overall, the Constitution increased the powers of the prime minister, notably with respect to government formation.[13] The structure of the dual executive rested most

Box 8.1   Chronology of Major Elections and Changes in Government

Election to the "Contract Sejm": June 4, 1989 (first round); June 18, 1989 (second round)
Turnout: 62.7 percent and 25 percent
Share of seats: PZPR (38 percent); ZSL (17 percent); SD (6 percent); Catholic (5 percent); Solidarity (35 percent)[1]

Government of Tadeusz Mazowiecki (September 12, 1989–December 14, 1990)[2]
Parties of the governing coalition: OKP; PZPR (SdRP); ZSL (PSL); SD[3]
Presidential election: November 25, 1990 (first round); December 9, 1990 (second round)
Turnout: 60.6 percent (first round); 53.4 percent (second round)
Results (first round): Lech Wałęsa (39.96 percent); Stanisław Tymiński (23.10 percent); Tadeusz Mazowiecki (18.08 percent).[4]
Results (second round): Lech Wałęsa (74.25 percent); Stanisław Tymiński (25.75 percent)

Government of Jan Krzysztof Bielecki (January 12, 1991–December 5, 1991)
Significant parties of the governing coalition: KLD; ZChN; PC[5]
Election to the Sejm: October 27, 1991
Turnout: 43.20 percent
Results: UD (12.32 percent); SLD (11.99 percent); WAK (8.74 percent); POC (8.71 percent); PSL (8.67 percent); KPN (7.5 percent); KLD (7.49 percent)

Government of Jan Olszewski (December 6, 1991–June 5, 1992)
Significant parties of the governing coalition: PC; ZChN

Government of Hanna Suchocka (July 8, 1992–October 26, 1993)
Significant parties of the governing coalition: UD; ZChN; KLD
Election to the Sejm: September 19, 1993
Turnout: 52.08 percent
Results: SLD (20.41 percent); PSL (15.4 percent); UD (10.59 percent); UP (7.28 percent); KPN (5.77 percent)

Government of Waldemar Pawlak (October 26, 1993–March 1, 1995)
Parties of the governing coalition: SLD; PSL

---

1. For the 1989 election, seat share is given instead of voter percentages, as Solidarity was only permitted to contest 35 percent of seats.

2. A change in government is registered when the prime minister changes, rather than when the party composition is altered. The endpoint of a government is defined in formal terms as the moment when the next government takes over, rather than the "effective" end that comes with the results of a general election.

3. OKP was the Civic Parliamentary Club, consisting of members of parliament from the election lists of Solidarity's Civic Committees. PZPR was the Polish United Workers' Party, the main party throughout the communist era. ZSL (United Peasant Party) and SD (Democratic Party) were satellite parties of the PZPR.

4. For the sake of relevance, only those presidential candidates gaining more than 10 percent of the vote are included.

5. "Significant parties" are those that proved of relevance to the development of the party "system." See box 8.2 for the full names and descriptions of parties.

Government of Józef Oleksy (March 6, 1995–January 24, 1996)
Parties of the governing coalition: SLD; PSL
Presidential election: November 5, 1995 (first round); November 19, 1995 (second round)
Turnout: 64.7 percent (first round); 68.23 percent (second round)
Results (first round): Aleksander Kwaśniewski (35.11 percent); Lech Wałęsa (33.11 percent)
Results (second round): Aleksander Kwaśniewski (51.72 percent); Lech Wałęsa (48.28 percent)

Government of Włodzimierz Cimoszewicz (February 7, 1996–October 31, 1997)
Parties of the governing coalition: SLD; PSL
Election to the Sejm: September 27, 1997
Turnout: 47.93 percent
Results: AWS (33.83 percent); SLD (27.13 percent); UW (13.37 percent); PSL (7.31 percent); ROP (5.56 percent)

Government of Jerzy Buzek (October 31, 1997–October 19, 2001)
Parties of the governing coalition: AWS; UW (until June 6, 2000)
Presidential election: Octber 8, 2000
Turnout: 61.08 percent
Results: Aleksander Kwaśniewski (53.9 percent); Marian Krzaklewski (17.3 percent); Andrzej Olechowski (15.57 percent)
Election to the Sejm: September 19, 2001
Turnout: 46.18 percent
Results: SLD-UP (41.04 percent); PO (12.68 percent); SO (10.2 percent); PiS (9.5 percent); PSL (8.98 percent); LPR (7.87 percent).

Government of Leszek Miller (October 19, 2001–May 2, 2004)
Parties of the governing coalition: SLD; PSL (until March 3, 2003); UP

Government of Marek Belka (May 5, 2004–October 31, 2005)
Parties of the governing coalition: SLD; UP; SdPL
Election to the European Parliament: June 13, 2004
Turnout: 20.87 percent
Results: PO (24.10 percent); LPR (15.92 percent); PiS (12.67 percent); SO (10.78 percent); SLD-UP (9.35 percent); UW (7.33 percent); PSL (6.34 percent); SdPL (5.33 percent)
Presidential election: October 9, 2005 (first round); October 23, 2005 (second round)
Turnout: 49.74 percent (first round); 50.99 percent (second round)
Results (first round): Donald Tusk (36.33 percent); Lech Kaczyński (33.10 percent); Andrzej Lepper (15.11 percent); Marek Borowski (10.33 percent)
Results (second round): Lech Kaczyński (54.04 percent); Donald Tusk (45.96 percent)
Election to the Sejm: September 25, 2005
Turnout: 40.57 percent
Results: PiS (26.99 percent); PO (24.14) percent); SO (11.41 percent); SLD (11.31 percent); LPR (7.97 percent); PSL (6.96 percent)

Government of Kazimierz Marcinkiewicz (October 31, 2005–July 14, 2006)
Parties of the governing coalition: PiS (plus SO and LPR from May 5, 2006 to July 14, 2006)

(continued)

Box 8.1   *(Continued)*

Government of Jarosław Kaczyński (July 14, 2006–November 16, 2007)
Parties of the governing coalition: PiS; SO (except September 21, 2006–October 16, 2006 and August 6, 2007–October 16, 2007); LPR (except October 22, 2007–November 16, 2007)
Election to the Sejm: October 21, 2007
Turnout: 53.88 percent
Results: PO (41.51 percent); PiS (32.11 percent); LiD (13.15 percent); PSL (8.91 percent)

Government of Donald Tusk: (November 16, 2007–November 18, 2011)
Parties of the governing coalition: PO; PSL
Election to the European Parliament: June 7, 2009
Turnout: 24.53 percent
Results: PO (44.43 percent); PiS (27.40 percent); SLD-UP (12.34 percent); PSL (7.01 percent)
Presidential election: June 20, 2010 (first round); July 4, 2010 (second round)
Turnout: 54.94 percent (first round); 55.31 percent (second round)
Results (first round): Bronisław Komorowski (41.54 percent); Jarosław Kaczyński (36.46 percent)
Results (second round): Bronisław Komorowski (53.01 percent); Jarosław Kaczyński (46.99 percent)
Election to the Sejm: October 9, 2011
Turnout: 48.92 percent
Results: PO (39.18 percent); PiS (29.89 percent); RP (10.02 percent); PSL (8.36 percent); SLD (8.24 percent)
Government of Donald Tusk: (November 18, 2011–)
Parties of the governing coalition: PO; PS

---

firmly on the parliamentary pillar. However, the president remained an important political player and far from the largely ceremonial figure preferred by some advocates of the parliamentary model. The ability to veto legislation and delay the countersigning of important documents, as well as wide-ranging competences to make appointments to important state posts, ensured that successive governments would have to take account of presidential opinion.

From the beginning of transition, judicial reform in accordance with liberal legal principles entailed the almost wholesale revision of existing legislation and the promulgation of new laws, establishing the judiciary as independent and separate, and setting up or adapting bodies of oversight. The Little Constitution restored the principle of the division of executive, legislative, and judicial powers: the *Sejm* was no longer the supreme organ of state power.[14] The Constitutional Court, which had been in operation since 1985, became genuinely independent during the first years of transition. The Constitution widened the competences of the Court, and most significantly removed the ability of the *Sejm* to overturn its rulings, which now became binding and final. The Constitution provided for independent and apolitical judges protected from political interference, and established a judicial system of courts and tribunals with a clear division of competences. A number of institutions of oversight and control were

Box 8.2   Major Personalities

Leszek Balcerowicz: Academic economist. Finance minister in the Mazowiecki government and architect of Poland's "shock therapy" economic reforms; leader of UW from 1995 to 2000.

Wójciech Jaruzelski: Army general and last communist leader of Poland; introduced martial law in December 1981 to suppress the Solidarity movement. First President of the Third Republic of Poland from 1989 to 1990.

Lech Kaczyński: President from 2005 until his death in the 2010 Smolensk tragedy. Previously a senator, member of parliament, president of the Supreme Chamber of Control, and mayor of Warsaw. Cofounded PiS with his twin brother, Jarosław.

Jarosław Kaczyński: Cofounder of PC and PiS. Member of parliament since 1991, except 1993–1997. Prime minister of the PiS-SO-LPR government; currently leader of PiS and chief opposition figure.

Aleksander Kwaśniewski: Reformist member of the PZPR and participant in the Round Table talks. Cofounder of SdPR and member of parliament from 1991 to 1995. President from 1995 to 2005.

Andrzej Lepper: Farmer, and founder and unquestioned leader of SO. Led controversial campaigns of direct action during the 1990s. Member of parliament between 2001 and 2007; Agriculture minister and deputy prime minister in the PiS-SO-LPR government.

Tadeusz Mazowiecki: Catholic intellectual, author, journalist, and member of parliament from 1961 to 1972 for *Znak*, a group representing Catholics. Subsequently a prominent Solidarity intellectual and key participant in the Round Table talks. First noncommunist prime minister, serving from 1989 to 1990. Member of parliament from 1991 to 2001, and leader of UD/UW from 1990 to 1995.

Leszek Miller: PZPR activist and participant in the Round Table talks. Cofounder of SdPR and member of parliament from 1991 to 2005. Prime Minister in the SLD-UP-PSL government from 2001 to 2004.

Jan Olszewski: Lawyer and Solidarity activist, first prime minister of the first fully democratically elected *Sejm* from 1991 to 1992. Member of parliament from 1991 to 1993 and from 1997 to 2005. Founder and leader of ROP from 1997 to 2001.

Janusz Palikot: Flamboyant, controversial, and outspoken leader of RP. A businessman during the 1990s and PO deputy between 2005 and 2010. Broke away from PO in 2010 to form RP, which he led to unexpected electoral success in 2011.

Waldemar Pawlak: Member of parliament since 1989. Leader of PSL between 1991 and 1997, and from 2005 to the present. Prime minister of the SLD-PSL government from 1993 to 1995. Deputy prime minister and economy minister in the PO-PSL government from 2007 to the present.

Tadeusz Rydzyk: Redemptorist Catholic priest, proprietor of *Radio Maryja*, and associated Catholic-fundamentalist media outlets.

Donald Tusk: Solidarity activist and cofounder of KLD. Member of parliament for KLD and subsequently UW from 1991 to 2001. Left UW to found PO; leader of PO since 2003. Currently prime minister of the PO-PSL government.

Lech Wałęsa: Shipyard worker who spearheaded the Solidarity movement. President of Poland from 1990 to 1995.

transformed from their communist-era precursors or brought into being, and their scope and competences outlined in and assured by constitutional articles.

One of the key aims of communist-era opposition movements was the return of real local government. Local government as a subject of legal regulation was liquidated in 1950 and remained so for the rest of the communist era, with local power structures merely instruments of the center, "geared only towards passing commands downwards and controlling their fulfilment."[15] Clean, accountable local government was regarded by the reformers as an important element of the establishment of the rule of law, and it would introduce mechanisms of representation more sensitive to local needs, acting as a counterbalance to central government. In 1990, the commune gained new functions as the basic element of local government, with the principle of administrative dualism revived and attempts made to define the division of competences between central and local government. However, full reform in this sphere was delayed for several years. Eventually, the Constitution articulated the fundamental principle of subsidiarity (that local government should carry out public tasks not reserved to other organs of state), extended legal person and protection to the commune as the basic unit of local government, and secured for local government "a share of public revenues in accordance with needs."[16] Provincial restructuring aroused much political and public conflict, but was completed at the beginning of 1999, with the restoration of the county tier of government and the introduction of regional parliaments.

Constitutions not only define institutions but also enshrine philosophies of the relationship between individuals and the state, and the process of promulgation brought fundamental ideological differences into conflict. Early in the transition period, the split in Solidarity exposed a significant divide amongst political elites over attitudes toward *Homo post-Sovieticus*. Unsurprisingly, given its close association with Solidarity and the strong identification of most Poles with Catholicism, the years after 1989 saw the reemergence of the Catholic Church as a political actor. Against the civic-individualistic vision espoused by the liberals and social democrats, the Church—and its political allies in the conservative-nationalist bloc—offered a comprehensive collectivist ethical model embracing personal morality, education, gender relations, minority rights, and attitudes to capitalism and Westernization.

The easy assumption of moral authority by the Church quickly came up against the anticlerical stance of the postcommunists and the determination of liberals to protect individual rights. Education and the media were prominent sites of conflict. Successive ombudsmen complained about violations of the separation of church and state, objecting to prayers and crucifixes in schools, and the insensitivity shown toward religious minorities and nonbelievers during the reintroduction of religious education. The Church left a clear imprint on the 1992 Broadcasting Law, with a clause requiring broadcasters to "respect the Christian value system," and at times enjoyed the indulgence of Catholic politicians in attempts to make media laws more restrictive. Its influence was also evident in the passing of an extremely restrictive abortion law in early 1993 and the subsequent signing of a concordat with the Vatican.

The constitutional debates stimulated a great many issues of controversy, but at the time, the most emotionally heated disagreements revolved around issues of cultural identity and national self-assertion. In debates over the Constitution, clerical input was substantial. The Church demanded that the preamble to the Constitution appeal to God and the principles of natural law and constitute "the Polish Nation," rejected the principle of separation of Church and state, and demanded the right to life "from conception to natural death." The eventual text attempted to accommodate these sentiments without thwarting the liberal character of the Constitution. The "separation" of church and state was not explicitly articulated, with the state bound instead by "impartiality." The preamble was a masterpiece of pick-and-mix fudging, with "law, justice, good and beauty" hailed as universal values whether derived from God or elsewhere, acknowledgment of the common culture of Poles "rooted in the Christian heritage of the nation and universal human values," and an invocation of "the Polish Nation—all citizens of the republic . . . responsible to God or to our own conscience." No explicit protection was extended to life "from conception to natural death." Instead, the Constitution referred to the "inborn and inalienable dignity of the individual" (Art. 30), which the Polish Republic was bound to defend by legal means (Art. 38).

The parliamentary draft document met with strong criticism from those representing the "Solidarity draft," a constitutional project submitted under the auspices of a citizens' initiative. The parliamentary spokesperson for the project echoed the views of other conservative, nationalist, and clerical critics in averring that the final version was "cut off from the values by which the Polish nation abides." In failing to pay tribute to God, legislating for a civic nationalism, and permitting the emergence of an extreme moral relativism, it spurned the "inheritance of history" and "Polish identity."[17] These sentiments reflected a substantial current in public attitudes. Those who favored the Solidarity draft were significantly more likely to agree that the Constitution should contain a preamble invoking God, be predicated on Catholic social teaching, contain clauses banning abortion and euthanasia, and explicitly define postcommunist Poland as the legal and historical continuation of the interwar Second Republic, symbolically cutting it off from the communist Polish People's Republic. Curiously, given the controversy surrounding the issue, both sides declared comparably strong support for an introductory reference to "we, the Polish Nation" rather than a more neutral, civic formulation.[18]

A Poland Richer, but Less Happy

The Polish economy was the first to emerge from recession in postcommunist Europe, and was regarded as one of the more successful examples of economic transition. GDP was 35 percent higher in 2005 than in 1989, a significantly greater increase than in neighboring countries.[19] Moreover, 37 percent of households declared in 2005 that their regular income was insufficient to satisfy current needs, compared to a figure of 70.6 percent in 1992.[20] However, such positive trends contrasted with the frequent observation that the average Pole was "richer, but unhappy."[21]

Economic policy presented parties with a dilemma. The average Pole was quite supportive of a strong role for the state in the economy. However, serious deviations from macroeconomic orthodoxy risked the wrath of the European Union and the suspicion of foreign investors. The SLD-PSL government of 1993–1997 made more concessions to trade unions than its predecessors but did not substantially depart from the path laid down in the first four years of transition. References to "positive" rights such as full employment and public health care were included in the Constitution at the insistence of the SLD, but these articles were essentially aspirational, with much of the substance relegated to ordinary statute.

Socioeconomic rights were also supported by many in the conservative-nationalist bloc of post-Solidarity parties. Nevertheless, the regime divide again transcended ideological divisions after the elections of September 1997. During the SLD-PSL term, the Solidarity trade union attempted to create a common opposition to the postcommunist resurgence in the form of Solidarity Election Action (AWS), an electoral coalition of some 40 parties of largely conservative-nationalist post-Solidarity provenance. The liberals of UD and KLD, meanwhile, banded together as the Freedom Union (UW). AWS and UW formed a post-Solidarity coalition government after the 1997 election, under the premiership of Jerzy Buzek.

The Buzek government faced substantial challenges in the sphere of the economy. If Poland's jump into the market was a swift technocratic exercise, the "deep reforms" of privatization, the restructuring of industries, agricultural reform, and the reforms of health care, pensions, and welfare proceeded unevenly. Small-scale privatization was a considerable success, but the privatization of large enterprises was still in an intermediate phase in the second decade of transition; the politically sensitive sectors of mining and energy remained dominated by the state.[22] Agriculture remained largely outside the ambit of the liberal reform process: in addition to tax relief, the state provided credits, financed pensions and welfare, and intervened in the market to purchase products and protect prices.[23] At first, restructuring of the relationship between the state and the individual was more a tale of cuts, with reductions in initially generous unemployment and housing benefits and tightening of eligibility rules, increases in prescription charges, and pensions capped.[24] As part of its program of "four reforms" (which also included education and the aforementioned changes to local government), the Buzek government attempted to enact significant structural changes to the systems of health care and social security provision, with the intention to inject an ethos of individual responsibility and choice into both systems.

The changes brought about by economic transition had a profound effect on a society hitherto accustomed to egalitarian ideals and—to a large extent—outcomes. Inequality was relatively low by the standards of Central and Eastern Europe, but significant enough in its own right. Educational capital increasingly mattered: in 1982 only 24 percentage points separated average incomes across the spectrum of educational attainment; in 1987 this stood at 41 percent, and in 2002 92 percent.[25] New mechanisms of distribution introduced an inegalitarian logic, with the cutting of subsidies having a differential effect on particular groups and the growth of the private sector seeing greater wage dispersion across professional groups and regions.[26] The liquidation of state-owned farms and factories, the decline of heavy industries, and knock-on effects led to long-term structural unemployment that was subject to significant regional differentiation on both a macro- and micro-scale. Increased inequality and unemployment brought poverty to the fore. This was characterized by greater physical and social concentration in regions characterized by a prevalence of rural and small-town conditions, and enclaves of poverty in the old centers of industrial cities and in former state farming collectives.[27] Perceptions of inequalities of opportunity and outcome were high and rising.[28]

Reaction to the health care and social security reforms reflected a generally increasing sense of apprehension that outweighed perceptions of personal economic improvement. People found it more difficult to gain access to a general practitioner, and confusion over the changes led to well-publicized incidents where individuals were refused medical aid.[29] Public opinion was strongly negative: in 2001, 62 percent of Poles viewed the health care system as functioning worse than prior to the reforms, with only 13 percent asserting that improvements had been made.[30] With social security reforms descending into administrative chaos, 40 percent were unable to say whether they thought it had been a success, and only 13 percent were willing to say that any improvement had occurred.[31]

The coalition, whose structure had lacked integrity from the outset, was shaken apart by these debacles. A frustrated UW departed the coalition in 2000. Whilst economic differences were not the only reason why the coalition and its constituent parties disintegrated, the failure of the post-Solidarity parties to cohere on this dimension had implications whose nature would gradually become apparent over the course of the next decade.

Poland's Political Earthquake: The Return of Transition Anxieties

Aleks Szczerbiak was not alone in opting for a seismic metaphor to describe the September 2001 election, dubbing it an "unexpected political earthquake."[32] One of the tectonic plates remained stable. The victory of the SLD-UP electoral coalition, which gained a hitherto unprecedented 41.04 percent of the vote, was widely expected for many months prior to the election, and a postcommunist government coalition was formed with the PSL under the premiership of Leszek Miller. However, on the opposition side, all other parties entered parliament for the first time. This does not mean that they were entirely new. The liberal Civic Platform (PO) was formed in large part by those who had deserted UW after its exit from the coalition, although it was not a continuation of that party. The core of Law and Justice (PiS), which capitalized on the popularity of hardline AWS Justice Minister Lech Kaczyński, consisted of politicians who had cut their teeth in the Olszewski administration. The populist Self-Defence (SO), and in particular its leader Andrzej Lepper, achieved increasing notoriety throughout the 1990s for protest actions, and had competed without success in every election from 1991. The League of Polish Families (LPR) represented the recrudescence of Catholic nationalists like ZChN, with whom it shared some personnel.

The success of SO and LPR was the epicenter of this seismic activity. Both parties offered abusive critiques of the politics of transition. The LPR gave parliamentary presence to the fundamentalist Catholic social movement centered around Radio Maryja and its charismatic proprietor, Father Tadeusz Rydzyk, whose tirades against atheist "Judeo-communism" implicated all transition elites in a conspiracy against "Poles-Catholics." SO, initially formed as an agrarian protest movement against the effects of economic reforms on small farmers, broadened its appeal to embrace small-town and urban "transition losers."

The radicalism of these parties reflected increasing uncertainty among sections of Polish society. The fraught public mood of the early years of transition gave way to a more optimistic attitude on a number of fronts during the middle years of the decade, but around the beginning of 1999 it clearly began to turn negative again. At the start of this year, approximately the same proportion of Poles viewed the "overall situation of the country" as good as considered it bad (40 percent); in mid-2001, with elections looming, some 75 percent considered it bad.[33] Almost exactly the same distributions were in evidence for assessments of the "economic situation." Whilst successive majorities remained "convinced of the superiority of the system of democracy over other forms of government," contentment with the way that democracy operated in Poland fluctuated in a 20 percent to 40 percent band. Persistent minorities remained skeptical of the significance of democracy in their own lives, with around 40 percent of respondents assenting to the statements "Sometimes non-democratic governments can be more desirable than democratic ones," and "For people like me, it has no real meaning whether governments are democratic or non-democratic."[34]

Although dissatisfaction with transition reforms and the democratic system was increasingly widespread in society, there was some evidence that these sentiments were increasingly concentrated in constituencies of "transition losers" whose economic and social position rendered them less able to take advantage of the new opportunities and who were more likely to be disturbed by the pace of change and the rise of challenges to traditional values. On the question of whether post-1989 reforms had succeeded or failed, a higher proportion of the following groups gave a negative answer: the old, those living in small towns and villages, those of lower educational attainment, those in the lower income quartile, the unemployed, the retired, and those receiving invalidity benefits. These patterns were repeated on the question of whether transition had made a positive impact on the life of the respondent, with these groups more likely to indicate that it had not.[35] Transition losers were also more likely to adopt more negative attitudes to democracy.[36]

SO and LPR swiftly exploited their newfound prominence to engage in bouts of direct action both within the *Sejm* and without. They were particularly active in their attacks on the process of Poland's accession to the European Union. Whilst no serious domestic opposition was raised to Poland's accession to NATO in 1999, EU accession proved more troublesome. Nearly ten years of hard negotiation and diminishing patience passed between formal submission to join the union and eventual accession in May 2004. The comprehensive system of monitoring and reporting that characterized the accession process dampened the pro-European ardor of some politicians and heightened fears of the effects that accession might have on Poland's agricultural sector and areas of industry such as mining and shipbuilding. Support for European integration always outweighed opposition, but from a high point of 80 percent in 1996 it declined to the mid-50s by the middle of 1999, rising fitfully and moderately to approximately 65 percent just prior to accession.[37] SO and LPR exploited the complicated accession process, aggressively criticizing the SLD-UP-PSL coalition for allegedly weak negotiation in areas such as the foreign purchase of Polish land and the level of agricultural subsidies offered to Polish farmers, and generally deploring the loss of sovereignty occasioned by accession. Whilst their efforts were ultimately thwarted by the success of the referendum on EU membership, the startling performance of LPR's candidates in the June 2004 European Parliament elections, gaining 10 of Poland's 54 seats and coming second to PO, gave notice that public attitudes remained ambiguous, as did the very low turnout of 20.9 percent.

These parties' blanket criticisms of the transition period drew in a number of other prominent areas of discontent, from SO's focus on irregularities in the privatization process to LPR's renewal of the assault on cultural liberalism. Lacking either post-Solidarity or postcommunist pedigrees, both parties claimed to be genuinely anti-establishment forces. However, whilst SO and LPR caused substantial problems for the ruling parties throughout the parliamentary term, the real challenge to the Third Republic was to emerge from a different source. In late 2002, Polish politics experienced another earthquake in the form of the Rywingate scandal, which centered around allegations that the government had attempted to extract a bribe from the owners of the prominent newspaper *Gazeta Wyborcza* in return for potentially lucrative amendments to a media bill. A controversial opposition report that suggested the existence of a shadowy, extragovernmental "group holding power" and implicated Premier Miller in the conspiracy was accepted by parliament as the official version of events. This, and subsequent *Sejm* investigative commissions on other allegations of corruption, nourished the narrative of "transition gone wrong."

The Miller administration never recovered from the blow of Rywingate, and Miller resigned in May 2004. His successor, phlegmatic social-liberal technocrat Marek Belka, attempted to drain a little of the color from politics. Yet the facts and rumors around Rywingate were conducive to the revival of arguments about the "afterlife" of communism. Law and Justice (PiS) was particularly active in this regard. The party's leader, Jarosław Kaczyński, had long advanced a theory of transition in which real power was held by a network composed of the old communist apparatus—the *nomenklatura*—and liberal elements of Solidarity. Having negotiated transition in protection of their mutual interests, these actors engaged in covert cooperation to ensure the stability of the new arrangement, systematically excluding patriotic and traditional values and seeing to delegitimize alternative political actors. The promulgation of the 1997 Constitution saw this system reach maturity, crystallizing unequal access to state institutions, the media, and the market and pushing dissenting political formations into more radical stances. The Miller administration witnessed the hubristic overstretching and collapse of the system.[38] Although EU accession in many respects marked the end of the "launch stage" of Polish transition and the economy began to return to health, the long campaign for the September 2005 elections was dominated by the question of whether there was not something seriously amiss with Polish democracy.

The Short "Fourth Republic":
Poland's Populist Moment

The decline of the SLD over its term in office was spectacular. In March 2004, a number of deputies broke away to form Polish Social Democracy (SdPL), citing the party's failure to get to grips with the questionable activities of some of its members. The party entered the dual presidential-parliamentary election campaign of September–October 2005 in a disoriented state, lacking experienced leadership and a clear political appeal. In contrast, both PiS and PO appeared to be credible advocates of the drive to clean up politics, and were expected to form a coalition government, the only question being which would be the major partner.

The concurrent presidential race was less clear-cut, and the manner in which its shifting dynamics intertwined with those of the parliamentary election had a strong influence on subsequent developments. With PiS's Lech Kaczyński and PO leader Donald Tusk emerging as the main contenders, PiS moved to recast both elections as a choice between the "liberal" ethos of PO and PiS's more "social" or "solidaristic" leanings. This socially sensitive rhetoric fed into a wider appeal to the losers of transition, and it sharpened PiS's electoral appeal against the background of all other parties at a crucial moment in the campaign. In the parliamentary election, PiS gained marginally more votes than PO. Both SO and LPR improved only slightly on their previous performance, and the SLD was humiliated. PiS's victory cast a shadow over the ongoing presidential campaign. With Tusk having a slight advantage in the first round, both sides escalated their rhetoric and with it their enmity. After the narrow victory of Lech Kaczyński in the second round, the PO-PiS coalition talks collapsed amid mutual distrust, with PiS left to form a minority government helmed by the largely unknown Kazimierz Marcinkiewicz.

This left PiS with a problem: they had clear ideas about what needed to be done and a president who would support them, but opportunities to effect substantial changes would be hugely inhibited by having to rule as a minority. The divide between PO and PiS being apparently insuperable, PiS cast around for different solutions. After tentative attempts at informal and then more formal cooperation, PiS invited SO and LPR to form a coalition government in May 2006. It was widely assumed that an unwritten taboo existed against coalition partnerships with these radicals, and the liberal elite were horrified at this "exotic threesome."[39] PiS depicted the coalition as a regrettable by-product of legislative mathematics, yet the short and turbulent period that followed saw the party absorb many of the features of its partners.

The term "Fourth Republic" was at first largely a metaphor for decommunization, but it swiftly assumed a more literal meaning. The overriding priority of PiS was the removal of the "network" from institutions it considered to be particularly afflicted by the blight of informal connections and corruption: the justice system, the civil service, military intelligence, and public media. The first major legislative act of the Marcinkiewicz government altered the powers, responsibilities, and personnel of the National Council of Radio and Television (KRRiT), transforming it from an institution in which the parliamentary opposition had representation into one peopled entirely by candidates of the ruling coalition. PiS vigorously pursued a new law on lustration that would significantly widen its scope—notably to embrace media owners, editors, journalists, and academics—and introduce sanctions for failure to submit affidavits. Justice Minister (and simultaneously Prosecutor General) Zbigniew Ziobro introduced a raft of reforms, increasing his oversight of the prosecution service and judges and attempting to break open the corporate structures of the legal profession. A Central Anticorruption Bureau (CBA) was set up with the specific remit of fighting corruption and with extensive, if ill defined, powers to detain and search. The Military Information Service (WSI) was liquidated.

Foreign policy was informed by deep-seated grievances about Poland's maltreatment by major European powers during the twentieth century. This stance resulted in tension between Poland and other EU member states and the Polish use or threat of the veto on a number of occasions, most notably over negotiations over the European Reform Treaty. For the national interest to be pursued, it needed to be defined and inculcated. A vital part of PiS's agenda, and one that chimed deeply with LPR's concerns, was the cultivation of a "politics of history" in which the state took a leading role in the dissemination of national, patriotic, and state traditions, with schools a particular site for the inculcation of such values. As minister of education, LPR leader Roman Giertych was tasked with implementing these policies. The party's flagship policy of "patriotic instruction" as a separate school subject never materialized, but the imprint of the coalition's moral traditionalism was evident throughout Giertych's controversial tenure.

Generally, the coalition trod warily in economic matters; such effects as it had were largely a product of inaction rather than action. The coalition's socially solidaristic rhetoric was tested by a wave of public sector strikes to which it responded in rather antagonistic fashion. Privatization slowed to a crawl as the government concentrated on consolidating state-held industries into strategic conglomerates, particularly in the energy sector. The ministries of Agriculture and Labour and Social Policy, headed by SO nominees, were stymied by incompetent administration and patronage.

The chief outcome of the period was not reform of the Third Republic, but realignment of the terms of political competition.[40] PiS's increasing radicalism saw it adopt and even transcend the populist rhetoric of its coalition partners. "Populism" is one of the most abused words in the political lexicon, but if it is understood as an ideology that is employed to cultivate an antagonistic relationship between an authentic, legitimate, and morally superior "people" against an illegitimate, usurping, and morally compromised elite, then the PiS-SO-LPR government was quintessentially populist. The language of political discourse reached new heights of aggression. PiS surpassed its coalition partners in the art of the damning epithet: Poland became a country in which "mendacious elites" and "pseudo-intellectuals" were arrayed against "ordinary" or "real" Poles. Politics was increasingly defined not as the clash of competing interests but as a battle of good versus evil.

This conflict came to a head in the tense and emotional public debate over the lustration law in the spring of 2007. The Constitutional Tribunal dealt a crushing verdict on the lustration law, ruling many of its provisions unconstitutional and rendering it inoperable. PiS viewed the outraged reaction of the Tribunal and its supporters to its accusations of political partiality as evidence that the "network" was defending itself, and as justification for redoubling the assault. This pattern was repeated in similar conflicts, such as that over PiS's confrontational approach to foreign policy, which at one point led all hitherto serving foreign ministers of the Third Republic to sign a public letter of rebuke. Political satire and media polemic flourished, but the most vivid expressions of the polarization of public life were the multiple acts of public protest—both against and in support of the government.

The turbulent internal life of the coalition increasingly militated against co-ordinated political action. SO's political and personal indiscipline was a persistent irritation to PiS, culminating in a "sex for jobs" scandal that implicated Lepper and seriously compromised the already shaky credibility of the coalition's claim to be engaged in "moral revolution." Attempting to regain lost ground on the radical right, LPR made virulent homophobia an ever more prominent feature of the party's public face. Fissures even emerged in PiS's hitherto impregnable inner sanctum over the lack of internal democracy. After a bizarre series of events in which the CBA attempted to entrap Lepper into accepting a bribe to reclassify agricultural land for development, the coalition crumbled over the summer of 2007. The hoped-for flow of SO and LPR deputies to PiS failed to materialize, and with both PO and SLD pressing hard for early elections, PiS had little choice but to support a vote to dissolve parliament.

The election of October 2007 was "a plebiscite on a polarising and controversial government."[41] This was as much a result of PiS's determination to defend its record as it was of the attacks conducted by the opposition. In contrast to 2005, PO found the appropriate response. Rowing back from its economic liberalism, it secured the support of many of those public sector workers that PiS had alienated, and landed effective blows on PiS's style of government. The role of SO and LPR in the election was minimal; neither party appeared to have much idea about how to retain their electorate, much less broaden it. With a high—by Polish standards—turnout of 53.8 percent, both major parties benefited. Exit poll figures showed that PO and PiS captured comparable percentages of newly mobilized voters as a proportion of their overall vote share.[42] However, PO's overall gains substantially exceeded those of PiS, and it won in convincing style, forming a coalition with the PSL, now firmly established as a centrist party of perennial coalitionability.

Short Steps and Sharp Shocks: The 2007–2011 Parliamentary Term

After the parliamentary elections of 2007, politics took place in a less frenetic register, with the new PO-PSL coalition government under PO leader Donald Tusk seeking to avoid the controversies of the past. Government strategists advocated the adoption of a "polarization and diffusion" model of growth, by which the development of Poland's metropolitan centers would result in associated benefits for the peripheral regions, and they stressed the need for more thoroughgoing reforms to the social security system and the rationalization of agriculture as elements of a comprehensive reform of public finances.[43] During the coalition's first term in office, this agenda was stymied by cohabitation with President Kaczyński, who vetoed key reform bills such as health care and public media and provided a strong negative incentive against further liberalizing measures in areas such as state funding for in vitro fertilization.

During the period of cohabitation, the presidency served as an alternative locus of opposition to the government, helping to keep the radical principles of the Fourth Republic reform program in the public eye. President Kaczyński sought to interpret his prerogatives as widely as possible and pursue a political agenda independently of the government, aided by the failure of the 1997 Constitution to specify adequately the division of competences between the two halves of the executive in foreign policy matters. President Kaczyński's foreign policy position was characterized by Euro-skepticism and distrust of Russian intentions toward Poland and other postcommunist states (particularly those of Eastern Europe), while the Tusk administration sought to establish a place for Poland as a constructive actor in European institutions—particularly as an ally of Germany—and attempted to improve relations with Russia. At best, this situation conveyed the impression of incoherence in foreign policy. At worst, it undermined the credibility of the Polish government abroad, as typified by the embarrassing contretemps over the Brussels summit of the European Council in October 2008. President Kaczyński attempted to assert his right to represent Poland as head of state at this summit, chartering a jet to fly him to Brussels after the prime minister's office excluded him from the official delegation, arguing that the Polish state should not be represented at such summits by two politicians with different opinions on foreign policy matters.[44]

The themes of the Brussels standoff returned in a tragic echo 18 months later. Exploiting the divisions between President Kaczyński and Prime Minister Tusk, Russian Premier Vladimir Putin invited the latter to a ceremony to commemorate the thousands of Polish nationals murdered in the Katyń massacre sixty years previously. In response to this snub, President Kaczyński organized his own delegation to Katyń, comprising the presidential couple and scores of military, political, and state dignitaries, along with representatives of the descendants of the victims of Katyń. On April 10, 2010, the entire delegation perished when the presidential plane crashed at the Smoleńsk airbase en route to the commemoration.

In the immediate aftermath of this disaster, the overwhelming emotion was one of desire for unity in the face of unimaginable tragedy. In moving ceremonies, politicians set aside the aggressive and antagonistic political culture of the Polish parliament to mourn the loss of colleagues from all points of the political spectrum. Journalists struggled to contain their emotions as they related the unfolding of events and attempted to comprehend their implications. A stunned public laid carpets of flowers and candles in scenes of national mourning reminiscent of the reaction to the death of Pope John Paul II almost exactly five years earlier. Yet the potential of the tragedy to deepen existing enmities was illustrated by the controversy over whether the presidential couple should be buried in the crypt of the Wawel Cathedral in Kraków. The erection of a large cross outside the presidential palace in the days following the crash also proved divisive, and the struggle of the authorities to remove the cross reenergized unresolved conflicts over the relationship between church and state, between Polishness and Catholicism, and between supporters of PO and supporters of PiS.

An early presidential election was held in June–July 2010. Acting President Bronisław Komorowski ran as the PO candidate, having already defeated Foreign Minister Radosław Sikorski in a primary election. A reluctant Jarosław Kaczyński ran as the PiS candidate: although he had hitherto been considered too divisive a figure to run for president, in the circumstances there were no credible alternatives. Kaczyński's candidacy ensured that the first round was decidedly restrained in comparison with previous presidential elections. The unexpectedly close nature of the first-round result prompted a more vigorous second-round campaign that again laid bare the emotional divide separating PO and PiS.

PiS refrained from exploiting the Smoleńsk tragedy during the presidential election campaign. However, it soon became a key feature of the party's political appeal after Kaczyński's defeat. Kaczyński blamed the "liberal" deputies who had run the election campaign for his failure to overhaul Komorowski in the second round, concluding that a harder line would have brought him victory. Setting its sights on the 2011 parliamentary election, PiS abandoned its moderate stance. Jarosław Kaczyński boycotted the presidential inauguration, averring that Komorowski's victory was the product of a "misunderstanding" by the electorate. Breaking his public silence on Smoleńsk, Kaczyński stated that Komorowski and Tusk were morally responsible for the disaster, and he explicitly connected PiS's strategy for the 2011 parliamentary elections to the need to uncover "the truth" about the crash.[45] The official Russian report and the PO-PSL government's own investigation merely accelerated PiS's embracing of a conspiracy-theory version of events according to which the tragedy was an assassination rather than an accident. The return to radicalism and Kaczyński's unyielding distaste for internal party democracy alienated some of the party's centrist deputies, who left to form a new party, Poland Comes First (Polska Jest Najważniejsza [PJN]).

For PO, the election of President Komorowski was something of a mixed blessing. Clearly, it would be significantly easier for the government to cooperate with a president from their own political camp. However, the timing of Komorowski's victory was less than optimal given the relative proximity of the next scheduled parliamentary elections. They would now be expected to make progress with the political agenda they had set out in 2007, much of which had fallen into abeyance as a result of President Kaczyński's blocking tactics. Seeking to move beyond the politics of transition, the Tusk administration outlined an ambitious long-term policy strategy dubbed "Poland 2030": a "civilisational project for Poland for the next two decades."[46] This project laid particular emphasis on significant reforms to the social security system and the rationalization of Poland's agricultural sector. While necessary in the long run, reforms in this area risked significant short-term political costs, particularly since PO relied on PSL—an agrarian party—for the passage of key government legislation that the opposition could be counted on to oppose regardless of its merits.

The Tusk administration's repeated excuses for caution irritated those who voted for PO in 2007 expecting bold liberal policy initiatives, and PO sympathizers in the media and business sector grew increasingly impatient. However, given the relatively buoyant performance of the Polish economy against a backdrop of European economic crisis, "government by small steps" was not unpopular with a general public still mindful of the experience of attempted radical reform in 2005–2007. As figure 8.1 shows, for the majority of the 2007–2011 term, supporters of the government outweighed its opponents. In late 2009, PO was hit by a potentially major scandal when a recording emerged that suggested that Zbigniew Chlebowski, leader of the party's parliamentary club, had sought to protect the interests of certain businessmen involved in the gambling industry. Yet, by dealing swiftly and decisively with the problem, Tusk ensured that the scandal did not inflict any lasting damage on his government or his party. For the first time since 1989, the prospect of an incumbent government returning to power looked possible, although it was not necessarily a foregone conclusion.

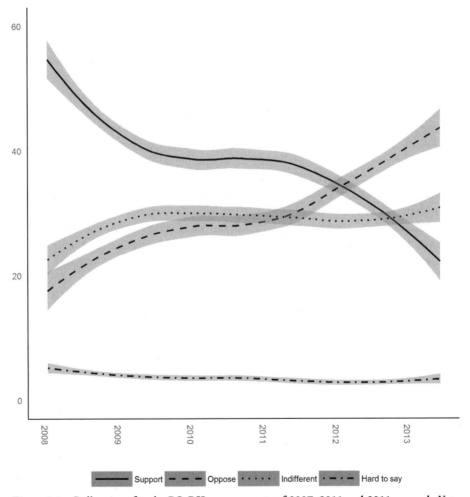

Figure 8.1   Poll ratings for the PO-PSL governments of 2007–2011 and 2011 onward. *Note*: The lines are loess smoothed curves derived from the raw polling data. *Data source*: Centrum Badania Opinii Społecznej (Warsaw).

Posttransition Politics? The 2011 Elections and After

The parliamentary elections of 2011 were paradoxical, in that they confirmed the essential stability of the new line of competition in Polish politics while simultaneously demonstrating the capacity of the party system to change in unexpected ways. Indeed, the party system—and the electoral system that structures it—were key topics of debate in the run-up to the parliamentary elections. In January 2011 a new election law came into force that—among other reforms—introduced a compulsory 35 percent gender quota for party lists and two-day elections. The latter of these reforms was ostensibly intended to increase Poland's notoriously low electoral turnout, but there were political considerations too. PO stood to benefit more from higher turnouts, while PiS—which had a more disciplined core electorate—tended to do better when fewer voters came to the polls. To PiS's relief, just prior to the start of the campaign the Constitutional Court ruled that two-day elections were in breach of the constitution.

The election campaign was a sterile affair. The governing parties had no incentive to depart from the politics of continuation. In spite of earlier intentions, PiS avoided making the Smoleńsk disaster central to their campaign. Kaczyński's refusal to meet Tusk in debate ensured that—in contrast to 2007—the campaign would not be defined by the confrontation between the main party leaders. With the SLD still moribund, a new party, the Palikot Movement (RP), came to the fore in the last month of campaigning. This party, founded and led by former PO deputy Janusz Palikot, stood out ideologically for its mixture of economic liberalism, cultural libertarianism, and anticlericalism. Initially, the party was not taken seriously by many, not least because of its lack of established candidates other than Palikot himself. However, it ran an effective "meta-political" campaign that centered on criticism of the "band of four" (*banda czworga*) established parties and the "frozen" (*zabetonowany*) party system in which they operated.

The election result gave a surprising margin of advantage to PO, which led PiS by nearly 10 percent. No challengers came close to the vote share achieved by the two largest parties, although RP's campaign paid off handsomely: they gathered 10.02 percent of the vote and became the third-largest party in parliament. If the main locus of political competition was preserved, the success of RP served as a reminder of the volatility that wracked Polish party politics during the first decade and a half of postcommunist democracy. RP stood out in the new parliament for its aggressive anticlericalism and the profile of its deputies, many of whom had no previous political experience, one of whom was Poland's first openly gay deputy, and one of whom was the only transgender deputy in parliament anywhere.

Once the initial excitement generated by the emergence of RP had died down, it became apparent that the party's success, however striking, had not altered the party system in ways that were immediately consequential. While RP's emergence testified—in contradiction to that same party's electoral message—to the openness of the party system, as third-placed party they held a share of votes some 3 percent lower than that of the LiD coalition in 2007. With the PSL merely retaining its share of votes and the once-mighty SLD reduced to the status of the smallest party in parliament, the elections left both minor parties unchallenged as the main competitors. Any of the three minor parties would have given PO the seats it needed to form a two-party coalition, but PO opted to renew the coalition with PSL, preferring a stable and relatively predictable partner over the mercurial RP or their former postcommunist rivals SLD.

Although unchallenged as the main party of opposition, PiS was shaken by its failure to mount a more robust challenge to PO. The party maintained a loyal core of support but was unable to build on it substantially. As in 2010, postelectoral disenchantment led to the departure of several deputies, who set up a new party, United Poland (SP), under the leadership of former Justice Minister and Member of the European Parliament Zbigniew Ziobro. Although PiS was weakened by the loss of several deputies, the departure of Ziobro—once thought of as successor-in-waiting—left Jarosław Kaczyński with no serious rivals to his preeminence as party leader. It soon became clear that SP posed no real threat to PiS's dominance, regularly polling beneath the electoral threshold and unable to lay its intended claim to "ownership" of the Catholic-nationalist right.

At the start of the new parliamentary term, the PO-PSL government set out a number of concrete proposals for reform, including cuts to tax relief, the raising of the retirement age, the phasing in of full taxation on agricultural incomes, and the liquidation of retirement privileges for certain professions.[47] These reforms were ambitious and likely to arouse controversy, particularly the proposed raising of the retirement age to 67 (for both sexes), which by its very nature affected society as a whole rather than distinct social groups. The coalition succeeded in passing this bill in the face of significant opposition from PiS and the Solidarity trade union. However, the political costs of this significant legislative achievement were substantial. At the beginning of 2012, the proportion of Poles opposing the government exceeded the proportion supporting it for the first time since PO-PSL took office in 2007 (see figure 8.1). The government's popularity decreased significantly over the course of 2012 amid the promulgation of unpopular reforms, the prospect of further ones, and the emergence of less propitious economic circumstances. In response to this drop in public support, Tusk called a vote of confidence in his government in October 2012. The government passed the vote, but without the backing of any opposition parties, and without arresting the decline in its popularity, which continued into 2013. While PiS remained distrusted by a majority of voters, through reining in its more extreme faction and concentrating on more substantive criticism of government policy, it began to make gains at PO's expense.

"Poland A versus Poland B": The Proto-Cleavage of Transition Politics

The postcommunist/post-Solidarity regime divide was a natural locus of competition for political elites in the immediate aftermath of transition, and during the first decade of transition it resonated with group identity and cultural attitudes, those of a nonreligious and anticlerical persuasion more likely to vote for postcommunists.[48] Yet it was premature to hail this as Central and Eastern Europe's contribution to the collection of classic cleavages. Some expected that class politics would grow in relevance as a result of the impact of further privatization and growing inequality;[49] others linked the emergence of economic differentiation to wider processes of Westernization, arguing that "[l]ogically, those who fear Western cultural and, particularly, economic dominance will assume a more protectionist, or even anti-market, position."[50]

After 2005, attitudes to the communist regime still constituted "a significant point of orientation for a substantial number of voters."[51] Yet the stances of political elites during and after the 2005–2007 parliamentary term suggested that these attitudes were no longer directly relevant to the postcommunist regime divide. Indeed, PiS proved inventive in adapting the symbolism of that divide to current political needs, repeatedly drawing equivalences between the actions of the liberal opposition and those of the communist regime and consciously effacing the difference between liberal Solidarity and the postcommunists. Deepening antagonisms within the post-Solidarity elite seemed to be more of a priority for PiS than maintaining the postcommunist divide. After the 2007 elections, PiS moderates made overtures to the SLD on the grounds of ideological compatibility in the economic dimension, a move unthinkable as recently as 2005.

With PO and PiS in the ascendancy, geographical divides became more salient to the main line of political competition. Regional voting patterns at the 2009 European Parliament elections, the 2010 presidential elections, and the 2011 parliamentary elections indicated that PO was increasingly popular in the western and northern regions of Poland, with PiS consolidating its lead in the regions of the southeast and along the eastern border (see figure 8.2). These patterns were strikingly congruent with the historical borders along which Poland was partitioned prior to 1918.[52] This divide tied the politics of the present to the inheritance of the past in plausible ways. In particular, culture and religiosity played a role. The southeast of Poland—which came under Austrian control—was most closely associated with the maintenance of the culture and religious identity of the Polish nation during its period of statelessness. In the 1990s, this historical legacy manifested itself in particularly high rates of support for anticommunist parties. With the passing of the regime divide, this region—and the east of Poland more generally—remained receptive to parties such as PiS, which placed a particular emphasis on national identity and Catholic values. PO benefited disproportionately from the support of voters in the formerly German partition, where cultural factors were less salient. To some extent, economic factors also played a role: the German partition left a legacy of greater economic development. While there are areas of significant poverty and unemployment in the regions of the former German partition—particularly in the north of Poland—the west of Poland is broadly more prosperous than the east.

The sense of a cultural and economic divide that mapped onto a geographical distinction found common expression as an individual-level distinction between a "Poland A" of transition winners and a "Poland B" of transition losers. This winner-loser divide encompassed an economic distinction between those who had materially benefited from transition versus those who had not, and a cultural distinction between

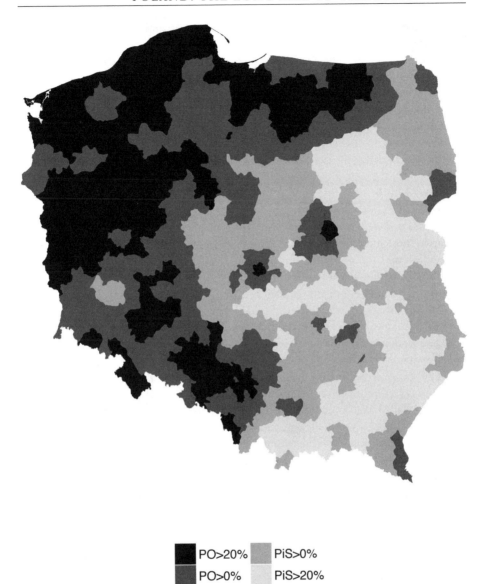

PO>20%   PiS>0%
PO>0%   PiS>20%

Figure 8.2   Regional dominance of PO and PiS at the county (*powiat*) level in the 2011 parliamentary elections. *Note*: The plot shows areas of dominance for PO and PiS, calculated by subtracting the percentage of the vote in that county achieved by PiS from the percentage achieved by PO. Areas where the difference was smaller than 20 percent are areas of moderate advantage; areas where the difference exceeded 20 percent are areas of strong advantage. *Source*: Author's own work, based on the official data of the Polish Electoral Commission.

those who embraced "Western" liberal values and norms and those who viewed them as deleterious to authentic Polish identity.

Studies of voting behavior sought to establish the extent to which this putative divide was reflected in both affinities for political parties and actual vote choice. Radoslaw Markowski identified a deepening sociodemographic divide between PO and PiS voters along the lines of the "transition winner-loser" dichotomy, and evidence of their increasing attitudinal differentiation—albeit in a relative sense—on the economic divide as well as the cultural one.[53] In 2007, flows of voters between parties reflected the division between those who supported and those who contested the politics of transition. PiS attracted disproportionally large numbers of those who previously voted for SO and LPR, while PO attracted in even greater disproportion those who voted for parties of the postcommunist left.[54] Sociodemographic variables and affinities for parties reflected clear divisions between, on the one hand, those preferring PiS and, on the other, those preferring PO, PSL, and LiD.[55] In 1997, political affinities were firmly oriented around the postcommunist divide and its attendant ideological correlates; by 2007, the main pattern of affinities clearly distinguished between PO and PiS and echoed the "politics of transition" divide.

Analyses of voting behavior at the 2011 parliamentary election largely confirmed that voting behavior mapped appropriately onto the divide between PO and PiS, in both sociodemographic and ideological terms. According to an exit poll that mirrored the overall results with striking accuracy, residence and education were particularly important. Half of the voters in large cities voted for PO, but only a quarter voted for PiS. By contrast, over a third of voters in rural areas voted for PiS, while just over a quarter voted for PO.[56] Nearly half of voters with primary education voted for PiS, but only one in five voted for PO; in the case of higher education, the proportions were reversed.[57] A major postelection survey found that religiosity was also significant: although many "ordinary believers" voted for both parties, the devout were more likely to vote for PiS, and those who attended church less than once a week were much more likely to vote for PO.[58] According to the same survey, ideological factors were also of significant importance: the more promarket on economic questions and the more liberal on cultural questions a voter was, the more likely he or she was to prefer PO over PiS. In contrast to sociodemographic factors, ideology was not a significant predictor of participation in elections.

By 2013, "Poland A and B" had overtaken the postcommunist divide as the proto-cleavage of Polish politics. Yet it remained too early to rule on the future electoral efficacy of this divide. "Leadership volatility, party volatility and electoral volatility created whirlpools of continuing uncertainty."[59] Greater attitudinal bifurcation, sociodemographic penetration, and voter mobilization were all required in order to entrench what remained an inchoate configuration of parties rather than a closed and predictable party system.

Conclusion

By 2013, Poland was firmly established as a member of the comity of liberal democratic states, with an economy that weathered the economic crisis rather better than many of its European contemporaries and with institutions that proved resistant to il-liberal backsliding. It still faced significant problems with corruption and the efficiency of the state, yet these were the problems of a young democracy, rather than factors that might imperil the continued existence of democracy in Poland. However, Polish politics had still not shaken off the legacy of the early years of transition, in terms of both personnel and policies. Whilst democracy was not contested, its liberal variant was, with the two major parties divided on economic and—to a lesser extent—cultural issues and on the meta-political divide of "imitative modernization" versus the pursuit of national-particularist paths of development.

In this respect, Poland was hardly an exception. After the entrenchment of democracy following the travails of Mečiarism, Slovakia experienced a similar political division between parties broadly accepting of the liberal orthodoxy and the idiosyncratic politics of the nationalist-populist coalition of 2006–2010. After its landslide victory in the 2010 Hungarian elections, Fidesz set about reshaping the Hungarian constitutional and political system in ways often inconsistent with liberal norms. These were not phenomena restricted to Central and Eastern Europe. A recent study of political change in six Western European democracies contends that processes of globalization have given rise to a bifurcation between the economic and cultural winners and losers of these processes, with the meta-politics of "integration" and "demarcation" becoming increasingly influential determinants of political appeals and voter mobilization.[60] Whilst the strength of traditional political divides has slowed the progress of this bifurcation in some Western European polities, there is potential for those Central and Eastern European countries whose transition models were imported from the West, who have become increasingly exposed to the same pressures of globalization, and whose "inherited" cleavage structures are comparatively weaker to be in the vanguard of these new cleavage alignments.

It is still too early to judge whether Poland's populist moment was a brief spasm of antiliberal discontent or the harbinger of more lasting divides. It is also unclear whether it has bequeathed to Poland a relatively stable party system or simply a temporary state of arrested instability. The divide between PO and PiS remains the central fact of Polish political life, and the concerns of both parties aptly reflect the divide between transition winners and losers. The assumption that this proto-cleavage will deepen into a more lasting divide is a justifiable one.

Nevertheless, there is still reason to remain cautious about drawing premature conclusions as to the future shape of Polish politics. In spite of the emergence of a genuinely new party and the rise of a generation of politicians for whom the early politics of transition are an abstraction rather than a lived experience, parties and governments are still largely dominated by the first generation of postcommunist politicians: those whose political experiences and personal rivalries were forged in the context of the politics of transition. The ability of the two main parties to survive the departure of their founders has not yet been put to the test. If one of the hallmarks of a genuine political cleavage is its independence from particular political actors, the test of Poland's transition divide must come from a generational change in political elites.

Notes

1. Frances Millard, "Poland's Politics and the Travails of Transition after 2001: The 2005 Elections," *Europe-Asia Studies* 58, no. 7 (2006): 1007.

2. Jerzy Szacki, *Liberalism after Communism* (Budapest: Central European University Press, 1995), 100.

3. Anthony Kemp-Welch, *Poland under Communism: A Cold War History* (Cambridge: Cambridge University Press, 2008), 395–96.

4. Leszek Balcerowicz, *Socialism, Capitalism, Transformation* (Budapest: Central European University Press, 1995), 311–12.

5. Ackerman, cited in Jerzy Szacki, *Liberalism after Communism* (Budapest: Central European University Press, 1995), 6.

6. For an account of this event, see Frances Millard, *The Anatomy of the New Poland: Post-Communist Politics in Its First Phase* (Aldershot: Edward Elgar, 1994), 99–104.

7. J. Olszewski, stenographic transcript from the session of the *Sejm*, June 4, 1992, http://orka2.sejm.gov.pl (accessed January 14, 2014).

8. Tomáš Kostelecky, *Political Parties after Communism* (Baltimore, MD: The Johns Hopkins University Press, 2002), 171–72.

9. Jacek Kurczewski, *Ścieżki emancypacji: Osobista teoria transformacji ustrojowej w Polsce* (Warsaw: Trio, 2009), 85–88.

10. This government was separated from that of Olszewski by a brief interlude in which Waldemar Pawlak, leader of the PSL, tried and failed to form a government.

11. Millard, *The Anatomy of the New Poland*, 149.

12. J. Dzwończyk, *Populistyczne tendencje w społeczeństwie postsocjalistycznym (na przykładzie Polski)* (Torun: Wydawnictwo Adam Marszałek, 2000), 82.

13. Marian Kallas, *Historia ustroju Polski* (Warsaw: Wydawnictwo Naukowe PWN, 2005), 372.

14. Kallas, *Historia ustroju Polski*, 363.

15. J. Regulski, *Samorządna Polska* (Warsaw: Rosner i Wspólnicy, 2005), 18.

16. Kallas, *Historia ustroju Polski*, 400.

17. A. Grześkowiak, stenographic transcript from the session of the National Assembly, February 24, 1997, http://orka2.sejm.gov.pl (accessed January 9, 2014).

18. OBOP, "Tresc przyszlej konstytucji w opinii Polaków," 1997, tables 4 and 5, http://www.obop.com.pl (accessed January 9, 2014).

19. J. G. Otto, "Polak bogatszy, ale nieszczęśliwy—portret obywatela po 16 latach transformacji," in *Studia Politologiczne 10* (Warsaw: Instytut Nauk Politycznych Uniwersytetu Warszawskiego, 2006), 236.

20. T. Panek, J. Czapiński, and I. E. Kotowska, "Strategie radzenia sobie z trudnościami finansowymi, pomoc społeczna i dopłaty bezpośrednie dla rolników," in *Diagnoza Społeczna 2005: warunki i jakość życia Polaków*, ed. J. Czapiński and T. Panek (Warsaw: Wyższa Szkoła Finansów i Zarządzania w Warszawie, 2006), 48.

21. J. G. Otto, "Polak bogatszy, ale nieszczęśliwy—portret obywatela po 16 latach transformacji," in *Studia Politologiczne 10* (Warsaw: Instytut Nauk Politycznych Uniwersytetu Warszawskiego, 2006).

22. M. Bałtowski and Maciej Miszewski, *Transformacja gospodarcza w Polsce* (Warsaw: Wydawnictwo Naukowe PAN, 2006), 252.

23. Frances Millard, *Polish Politics and Society* (London: Routledge, 1999), 175.

24. Millard, *Polish Politics and Society*, 150.

25. Henryk Domański, "Jedna struktura społeczna," in *Polska jedna czy wiele?* (Warsaw: Wydawnictwo TRIO, 2005), 23.

26. Grzegorz Kolodko, *From Shock to Therapy: The Political Economy of Postsocialist Transformation* (Oxford: Oxford University Press, 2000), 208.

27. E. Tarkowska, "Ubóstwo i wykluczenie społeczne. Koncepcje i polskie problemy," in *Współczesne społeczeństwo polskie: dynamika zmian*, ed. J. Wasilewski (Warsaw: Wydawnictwo Naukowe Scholar, 2006), 352.

28. See B. Badora, W. Derczyński, and M. Falkowska, "Nierównosci społeczne," in *Polska, Europa, Świat: opinia publiczna w okresie integracji*, ed. K. Zagorski and M. Strzeszewski (Warsaw: Wydawnictwo Naukowe Scholar, 2005), 202; and B. Wciórka and M. Wenzel, "Bezrobocie i bezrobotni," in Zagorski and Strzeszewski, *Polska, Europa, Świat.*

29. A. Dudek, *Historia Polityczna Polski 1989–2005* (Kraków: Wydawnictwo ARCANA, 2007), 368.

30. Centrum Badania Opinii Społecznej, "Cztery reformy w opinii społecznej," BS/14/2001 (Warsaw: Centrum Badania Opinii Społecznej, 2001), table 1.

31. Centrum Badania Opinii Społecznej, "Cztery reformy w opinii społecznej," table 1.

32. Aleks Szczerbiak, "Poland's Unexpected Political Earthquake: The September 2001 Parliamentary Election," *Journal of Communist Studies and Transition Politics* 18, no. 3 (2002): 41–76.

33. See Centrum Badania Opinii Społecznej, "Trendy," http://www.cbos.pl/PL/trendy/ trendy.php (accessed January 14, 2014), for the trends cited here.

34. Centrum Badania Opinii Społecznej, "Krytyczni demokraci: akceptacja demokracji a ocena jej funkcjonowania w Polsce," BS/7/2007 (Warsaw: Centrum Badania Opinii Społecznej, 2007), tables 1, 3, 4.

35. Janusz Czapiński, "Stosunek do przemian systemowych i ocena ich wpływu na życie badanych," in *Diagnoza Społeczna 2005: warunki i jakość życia Polaków*, ed. Janusz Czapiński and Tomasz Panek (Warsaw: Wyższa Szkoła Finansów i Zarządzania w Warszawie, 2006).

36. A. Paczynska, "Inequality, Political Participation, and Democratic Deepening in Poland," *East European Politics and Societies*, 19, no. 4 (2005): 598–600.

37. See trend data at Centrum Badania Opinii Społecznej, http://www.cbos.pl/EN/trends/ trends.php (accessed February 2, 2014).

38. Jaroslaw Kaczyński, "The Fall of Post-Communism: Transformation in Central and Eastern Europe," speech delivered at the Heritage Foundation, September 14, 2006.

39. Janina Paradowska, "Tercet egzotyczny," *Polityka* 19, no. 2553 (2006).

40. Two-thirds of the legislative proposals of the coalition agreement were not realized, either as the result of the failure of the coalition to address these policies in the time available or because legislation had been struck down by the Constitutional Tribunal. See Krzysztof Burnetko and Mariusz Janicki, "Raport specjalny: Duże wierzby, małe gruszki, czyli rozliczamy PiS z jego obietnic," *Polityka* 42, no. 2625 (2007).

41. Aleks Szczerbiak, "The Birth of a Bi-polar Party System or a Referendum on a Polarising Government? The October 2007 Polish Parliamentary Election," SEI Working Paper no. 100 (Sussex, UK: University of Sussex, Sussex European Institute, 2008), 27.

42. Radoslaw Markowski, "The 2007 Polish Parliamentary Election: Some Structuring, Still a Lot of Chaos," *West European Politics* 31, no. 5 (2008): figure 1.

43. Board of Strategic Advisers to the Prime Minister of Poland, *Polska 2030: Development Challenges. Introduction and Final Recommendations* (Warsaw: Office of the Prime Minister, 2009), 30, 35.

44. Dudek, *Historia Polityczna Polski 1989–2013*, 603.

45. Andrzej Stankiewicz and Piotr Śmiłowicz, "Chcę Być Premierem [interview with Jarosław Kaczyński]," *Newsweek* (September 27, 2010), http://polska.newsweek.pl/jaroslaw-kaczynski-chce-byc-premierem,65296,1,1.html (accessed February 3, 2014).

46. Board of Strategic Advisers to the Prime Minister of Poland, *Polska 2030*.

47. Donald Tusk, *Sejm* stenographic transcript, November 18, 2011.

48. M. Grabowska, *Podział postkomunistyczny: Społeczne podstawy polityki w Polsce po 1989 roku* (Warsaw: Wydawnictwo Naukowe Scholar, 2004), 358–60.

49. Kazimierz M. Slomczynski and Goldie Shabad, "Systemic Transformation and the Salience of Class Structure in East Central Europe," *East European Politics & Societies* 11, no. 1 (1996): 155–89. doi:10.1177/0888325497011001005.

50. T. Zarycki, "Politics in the Periphery: Political Cleavages in Poland Interpreted in Their Historical and International Context," *Europe-Asia Studies* 52, no. 5 (2000): 864–65.

51. Aleks Szczerbiak, "'Social Poland' Defeats 'Liberal Poland'? The September–October 2005 Polish Parliamentary and Presidential Elections," *Journal of Communist Studies and Transition Politics* 23, no. 2 (2007): 207.

52. K. Jasiewicz, "The Past Is Never Dead: Identity, Class, and Voting Behavior in Contemporary Poland," *East European Politics and Societies* 23, no. 4 (2009): 508.

53. Radoslaw Markowski, "The Polish Elections of 2005: Pure Chaos or a Restructuring of the Party System?" *West European Politics*, 29, no. 4 (2006): 826–29; and Radoslaw Markowski, "The 2007 Polish Parliamentary Election: Some Structuring, Still a Lot of Chaos," *West European Politics* 31, no. 5 (2008): 1065.

54. Markowski, "The 2007 Polish Parliamentary Election," 1060.

55. K. Jasiewicz, "The Past Is Never Dead: Identity, Class, and Voting Behavior in Contemporary Poland," *East European Politics and Societies* 23, no. 4 (2009): 491–508.

56. Gazeta.pl, "Triumf PiS wśród słabiej wykształconych. PO 'partią inteligencką'?" 2011, http://wiadomosci.gazeta.pl/wiadomosci/1,114873,10440851,Triumf_PiS_wsrod_slabiej_wyksztalconych__PO__partia.html (accessed January 14, 2014).

57. Gazeta.pl "Wybory 2011. Mieszkańcy wsi głosują na PSL i PiS, dużych miast—na PO," 2011, http://wiadomosci.gazeta.pl/wiadomosci/1,114873,10440877,Wybory_2011__Miesz kancy_wsi_glosuja_na_PSL_i_PiS_.html (accessed January 14, 2014).

58. These conclusions are based on the author's analysis of data from the Polish National Election Survey of 2011, which remain under embargo.

59. Frances Millard, "Poland: Parties without a Party System, 1991–2008," *Politics & Policy* 37, no. 4 (2009): 795.

60. Hanspeter Kriesi et al., *West European Politics in the Age of Globalization* (Cambridge: Cambridge University Press, 2008), 4.

Suggested Readings

Balcerowicz, Leszek. *Socialism, Capitalism, Transformation*. Budapest: Central European University Press, 1995.

Kemp-Welch, Anthony. *Poland under Communism: A Cold War History*. Cambridge: Cambridge University Press, 2008.

Kolodko, Grzegorz. *From Shock to Therapy: The Political Economy of Postsocialist Transformation*. Oxford: Oxford University Press, 2000.

Kolodko, Grzegorz, and Jacek Tomkiewicz. *Twenty Years of Transformation: Achievements, Problems and Perspectives*. London: Nova Science, 2011.

Kostelecky, Tomáš. *Political Parties after Communism.* Baltimore, MD: The Johns Hopkins University Press, 2002.

Millard, Frances. *Democratic Elections in Poland, 1991–2007.* London: Routledge, 2012.

Millard, Frances. *Polish Politics and Society.* London: Routledge, 1999.

Szczerbiak, Aleks. *Poland within the European Union: New Awkward Partner or New Heart of Europe?* London: Routledge, 2012.

Szczerbiak, Aleks. "'Social Poland' Defeats 'Liberal Poland'? The September–October 2005 Polish Parliamentary and Presidential Elections." *Journal of Communist Studies and Transition Politics* 23, no. 2 (2007): 203–32.

PART TWO

THEMATIC CHAPTERS

CHAPTER 9

European Integration

AN UNCERTAIN PROSPECT

John Van Oudenaren

On October 12, 2012, the Norwegian Nobel Committee, meeting in Oslo, Norway, announced that it would award that year's Nobel Peace Prize to the European Union (EU). In explaining its decision, the committee declared that the union and its forerunners "have for over six decades contributed to the advancement of peace and reconciliation, democracy and human rights in Europe" and specifically credited the EU with having achieved reconciliation between France and Germany, brought peace and stability to southern and Eastern Europe, and contributed to stability in southeastern Europe by holding out the promise of membership to the countries of the region. The committee acknowledged that the "EU is currently undergoing grave economic difficulties and considerable social unrest," but it went on to emphasize that it saw "the EU's most important result" as political.

The following month, Herman von Rompuy, president of the European Council, and José Manuel Barroso, president of the European Commission, gratefully accepted the prize on behalf of the union. In their jointly delivered Nobel lecture, von Rompuy and Barroso echoed many of the points made by the Nobel Committee: political achievement against the background of economic and social adversity. While the award of the prize was a morale booster for the somewhat beleaguered union, the rhetoric emanating from Norway if anything understated the challenges facing the European project, which had become particularly acute since the global financial crisis of 2008. By 2013, unemployment in the 27 member states of the EU had climbed to 11.0 percent, up from about 7.0 percent at the end of 2007. In the euro zone, the 17 countries of the EU that use the euro as their currency, unemployment was even higher at 12.2 percent.

Equally striking were the great disparities among the member states. Unemployment rates ranged from around 5 percent in Germany and Austria to 27 percent in Greece and Spain. Unemployment among youth (persons under 25) was a staggering 62.5 percent in Greece and 56.4 percent in Spain, compared to just 7.5 percent in Germany. For a union that had spent decades of effort and many billions of euros on "cohesion" policies aimed at evening out differences in wealth and levels of development between the more and less affluent parts of the bloc, such stark disparities were bad news. They also constituted a major challenge for the euro, as creation of the common currency always had been premised on the establishment of an *economic* and monetary union, a continental economic entity in which performance with reference to key economic indicators would converge over time, which clearly was not happening.

Most ominously of all, the economic difficulties of the union were, in the view of many, beginning to call into question the very political achievements lauded by the Norwegian Nobel Committee. Greeks (and others in southern Europe) were bitter at the prosperous Germans, who they saw as selfish and unwilling to help a fellow EU country coping with grave economic challenges and deepening poverty in its population. The Germans saw the Greeks as responsible for their own problems—the result of too many vacation days, too much government spending, and excessive pension costs. In Britain, traditional Euro-skepticism was on the rise, as the government of Prime Minister David Cameron was pressured by his own Conservative Party to agree to renegotiate the terms of Britain's EU membership and hold a national referendum in 2017 on whether or not to remain in the union. France and Germany, the traditional "motors" of European integration, had increasing difficulty agreeing on economic policies, as the austerity-minded government of Chancellor Angela Merkel clashed with the government of Socialist François Hollande, which favored more expansionist policies.

Establishing the European Community

The political mission of building a united Europe goes back to the 1940s and the decision by European leaders to pursue integration as a means to recover from the material and spiritual devastation brought about by World War II. Their goal was to knit Europe together in such a way as to preclude such a destructive intra-European war from ever recurring. In 1948, Belgium, the Netherlands, and Luxembourg formed the Benelux Customs Union. That same year, France, Britain, and the three Benelux countries concluded the Treaty of Brussels in which they pledged to come to each other's defense in the event of external attack, hold regular consultations among their foreign ministers, and cooperate in the economic, social, and cultural spheres.

Early steps toward European integration received a boost from the U.S.-backed Marshall Plan, which Secretary of State George C. Marshall proposed in a speech at Harvard University in June 1947. Concerned about the danger of communist subversion in a postwar Europe still wracked by shortages of food and fuel, Marshall proposed a program in which the United States would provide Europe with money and goods, on the condition that the Europeans came up with a joint program for using this aid effectively. In April 1948, sixteen European states founded the Organization for European Economic Cooperation (OEEC), a Paris-based body that helped to administer U.S. aid and provided a forum in which the member states negotiated arrangements to lower intra-European trade and currency barriers.

The Brussels Pact and the OEEC were modest steps toward European cooperation, but they fell far short of a United States of Europe, the ambitious objective then being advocated by political activists known as federalists. Looking to the United States as a model, they believed that integration had to move beyond treaties among governments and be based directly on the will of the people. The federalists called for the convening of a European assembly, whose members would not be chosen or controlled by national governments. Instead, it would constitute a new organization to unite the peoples of Europe. The federalists convinced the five signatories of the Brussels Pact to convene a ten-power conference in London in early 1949 to discuss their ideas. The conference led to the creation of the Council of Europe, a Strasbourg-based organization charged with harmonizing laws and promoting human rights. Although useful in its own way, the Council of Europe was not a truly federal institution. Governments in key countries retained their sovereign powers, setting strict political and legal limits to how far integration could proceed.

The other major development of this period was the creation of the North Atlantic Alliance. In April 1949, the United States, Canada, and nine European states signed the North Atlantic Treaty, in which they pledged to come to each other's assistance in the event of external attack. The treaty was followed by the creation of the North Atlantic Treaty Organization (NATO). Like the Marshall Plan, NATO was an important U.S. contribution to the postwar revival of Europe. It allowed the European countries to concentrate on economic cooperation, leaving sensitive and contentious matters of defense to the Atlantic organization.

The lineal precursor to today's EU, the European Coal and Steel Community (ECSC), was established in 1952. It went beyond these initial efforts at integration by putting into effect for the first time the principle of supranationalism—the idea that the European nation-states would permanently give up at least a part of their sovereignty to a new entity, the Community, which at least in limited spheres could issue orders to the nation-states that they would be required to follow. The ECSC was the brainchild of Jean Monnet, a French businessman who had spent the war years in the United States and who had devoted much thought to the problem of bringing about European unity. Like the federalists, Monnet believed that European integration had to go beyond the traditional methods of diplomacy in which governments agreed to cooperate with each other. Governments could easily renege on such commitments and return to old patterns of isolation and mutual hostility. But Monnet also believed that it was naïve to think that Europe could form a federation by a simple act of political will. Too much tradition, too many vested national interests, and direct opposition from Britain, which had no interest in losing its identity in a continental federation, stood in the way.

Monnet concluded that the way to start the process of integration was to achieve concrete results in specific sectors, establish permanent institutions to consolidate those results, and then achieve new results that would generate additional political support for a united Europe. As a first step, Monnet conceived a plan for France and Germany to combine their coal and steel industries under a joint authority. This authority was to be independent of the governments of the two countries and would guarantee each country full and equal access to a common pool of resources. The significance of this proposal was both political and economic. With the production of coal and steel—the very sinews of modern military capability—subject to a joint authority, war between these two traditional enemies would become unthinkable.

On May 9, 1950, French Foreign Minister Robert Schuman formally proposed Monnet's plan to the French Cabinet. France, West Germany, Belgium, Luxembourg, the Netherlands, and Italy all agreed to join the new Community. The treaty establishing the ECSC was negotiated in the months following Schuman's dramatic declaration and was signed in Paris in April 1951. For the commodities covered—coal, coke, iron ore, steel, and scrap—the ECSC created a common market in which all tariff barriers and restrictions on trade among the six member countries were banned. The treaty provided for the establishment of four institutions, roughly corresponding to the executive, legislative, and judicial branches of government, with extensive legal and administrative powers.

The High Authority was established as a nine-member commission with executive powers to administer the market in coal and steel. The members of the authority (two each from France, Germany, and Italy; and one each from Belgium, Luxembourg, and the Netherlands) were to be "completely independent in the performance of their duties." They were to decide what was best for the ECSC as a whole, rather than represent the views of the member countries. The High Authority was empowered to issue decisions, recommendations, and opinions prohibiting subsidies and aids to industry that distorted trade; to block mergers and acquisitions; and under certain circumstances to control prices. It could impose fines to ensure compliance with its decisions. Monnet was named the first head of the High Authority.

The Council of Ministers consisted of ministers from the governments of the member states, with each state represented by one minister. For some policy actions, the Council of Ministers had to endorse the decisions of the High Authority. Some decisions were taken by unanimity, and others by majority voting. The Common Assembly introduced an element of legislative participation in the ECSC. Its members were not directly elected by the people but were chosen by the national legislatures. Its power, moreover, was to advise rather than to pass legislation. Still, the principle of parliamentary participation was established, and the powers of what later was to become the European Parliament were to expand greatly in subsequent decades. The European Court of Justice (ECJ) was set up to settle conflicts between member states of the Community or between member states and the ECSC itself.

THE EUROPEAN ECONOMIC COMMUNITY

The ECSC's scope of activity was by definition quite limited. Seeking to build upon the successes of the ECSC, the six member states began looking for ways to broaden the scope of integration. They turned initially to defense. In May 1952, the six ECSC countries signed a treaty establishing a European Defense Community (EDC) in which decisions over defense and a jointly commanded European army were to be made by supranational institutions patterned on those of the ECSC. However, in August 1954, the French National Assembly rejected the EDC treaty. Whereas national governments and parliaments were willing to surrender sovereignty in some key economic areas, the EDC experience showed that defense was too sensitive—too close to core issues of national identity—to be treated the same way. The emphasis thus shifted back to economics.

Following the EDC setback, the foreign ministers of the six ECSC states met in Messina, Italy, in June 1955 to consider ways to energize the integration process. Two courses of action were discussed: a further stage of sectoral integration based on a proposed atomic energy community, and a plan for market integration through the elimination of barriers to trade and the eventual creation of a common market. The ministers agreed to establish a committee to study these options and to formulate proposals. The Spaak Committee (named for its chairman, Belgian Foreign Minister Paul-Henri Spaak) presented its report to the May 1956 Venice meeting of foreign ministers. It struck a balance between the two approaches to integration and proposed that the ECSC states create both a European Atomic Energy Agency (Euratom) and a European Economic Community (EEC). Following arduous negotiations, leaders of the six countries met in Rome on March 25, 1957, to sign two treaties creating these new entities.

Of the two institutions created in 1957, the EEC—or Common Market, as it was widely known—was by far the more important. The agreement establishing the EEC became known as the Treaty of Rome and remains in many ways the core constitutional document of today's EU. The basic objective of the EEC was simple in principle but sweeping in its implications: to create an internal market characterized by the free movement of goods, services, persons, and capital. Initially, the emphasis was on eliminating obstacles to trade in goods. The treaty provided for the phasing out, in stages, of all tariffs and quantitative restrictions on trade among the member states. The common internal market also necessitated the establishment of a common external tariff and a common commercial policy. Since goods that entered one member state could travel freely throughout the EEC, member countries needed to adopt the same tariffs toward third countries, lest goods simply be diverted to ports in countries with the lowest tariff for a given import. The EEC thus was empowered to speak with one voice in international negotiations within the framework of the General Agreement on Tariffs and Trade (GATT).

The Treaty of Rome used the basic institutional framework established for the ECSC. The High Authority for the EEC, called simply the European Commission, was endowed with broad executive powers, including the sole right to initiate Community legislation. The member states were responsible for selecting the commissioners, who were chosen for four-year terms (five-year terms since 1979). The European Commission president, also provided for under the treaty and selected by the member states, soon emerged as the most visible champion of and spokesperson for the Community.

A Council of Ministers was to be the main decision-making body of the EEC, in which representatives of the member states would vote on proposals put forward by the European Commission. Votes could be made on the basis of unanimity or by qualified majority—a weighted system that assigns votes in rough proportion to the population sizes of the member states and that requires a certain critical mass of votes to pass a measure. France, Italy, and West Germany each had four votes; Belgium and the Netherlands two; and Luxembourg one. Twelve of the seventeen votes were considered a qualified majority. In practice, qualified majority voting was disliked by some member state political leaders, especially in France, as too supranational, and it was little used until the 1980s. The chairmanship of the council rotated, with each member state serving as council president for a six-month period.

In addition, the member states agreed that the three communities—the ECSC, Euratom, and the EEC—would share the same Common Assembly and Court of Justice. The ECSC High Authority remained in Luxembourg, but the new European Commission was established in Brussels, which became the de facto capital of uniting Europe. The Common Assembly was situated in Strasbourg, France. The treaty also provided for the establishment of two other institutions, the Economic and Social Committee and the European Investment Bank, that were to play much lesser roles in Community decision making.

Operating under a concept that became known as "functionalism," promoters of European federalism believed that the gradual expansion of economic ties and of cooperation in various practical spheres such as atomic energy eventually would "spill over" into the political realm, as governments, parliaments, and national electorates yielded sovereignty in small but politically manageable steps. This aspiration to go beyond economic cooperation was expressed in the very first sentence of the Treaty of Rome, in which the signatories declared their determination "to lay the foundations of an ever closer union among the peoples of Europe."[1]

Although the focus of the EEC was on the creation of a common market through the elimination of barriers, the Treaty of Rome also provided for the establishment of common policies in other areas. Agriculture was the most important, but others included transport, competition (antitrust), and policies toward colonies and former colonies in Africa and the Caribbean. Over time, the EEC was to assume a role in a growing range of policy areas, some, like telecommunications and industry, closely linked to the internal market, but others, such as the environment, much broader in scope.

Completion of the common market for goods took place between 1958 and 1968, a period of rapid economic growth and rising prosperity. Businesses became more efficient and productive as they were able to sell to a larger market and were forced to invest to meet competition from firms in other countries. The Common Agricultural Policy (CAP) was established in 1962 in accordance with general goals laid down in the Treaty of Rome based on a system of subsidies and protective tariffs designed to benefit European farmers. This system worked in sustaining farmers' incomes and ensuring the stability of supplies, but it also led to higher food prices for consumers, overproduction, and disputes with trading partners who were being progressively squeezed out of the protected EEC market.

Despite its initial successes, the EEC went through a crisis in the mid-1960s. President Charles de Gaulle of France was suspicious of what he saw as a power grab by unelected bureaucrats in Brussels that threatened French sovereignty. He thus resisted efforts to strengthen the Community's central institutions and insisted that all decisions be made on the basis of unanimity among the member states, even though this was not the intent of the Treaty of Rome. De Gaulle also vetoed Britain's application to join the EEC. Britain had been a founding member of the WEU (an outgrowth of the 1947 Brussels Treaty), the OEEC, NATO, and the Council of Europe, but it had declined to join the ECSC and the Common Market, which British politicians believed went too far in limiting Britain's national sovereignty. The British economy at that time was still larger than those of the continental European powers, and Britain retained strong links with its colonies, the Commonwealth, and the United States, with which it had a "special relationship" growing out of World War II. It thus was unwilling to surrender sovereignty to a fledgling enterprise based in Brussels.

By the 1960s, however, the empire was dissolving, and Britain's ties with the Commonwealth and the United States were diminishing in importance. British economic growth was lagging that in continental Europe, where British industry saw new and growing markets. Thus, in the summer of 1961, Britain, joined by Denmark and Ireland, applied to become an EEC member.[2] The British government received a rude shock when, at a news conference in January 1963, de Gaulle announced that he would veto Britain's application. This decision was rooted in de Gaulle's distrust of the "Anglo-Saxon powers" and his view that Britain would be a stalking horse for the United States, whose influence in Europe he wanted to diminish.

Despite these many problems, by the end of the 1960s the Common Market was largely complete, and the economic results were positive. Franco-German reconciliation was a reality. De Gaulle relinquished his post in April 1969 to his successor, Georges Pompidou, who was more open to European integration. Pompidou announced, in July 1969, that France no longer would oppose Britain's admission to the Community. The time thus seemed right for bold new initiatives. At the Hague summit in December 1969, the leaders of the six member states agreed to explore ways to strengthen the EEC's institutions, to establish an "economic and monetary union" by 1980, and to begin cooperation in the foreign policy sphere.

DEVELOPMENTS IN THE 1970s

The 1970s saw a number of milestones in European integration. Cooperation in foreign policy, or European Political Cooperation (EPC), was launched in 1970. The member states agreed to "consult on all questions of foreign policy" and where possible to undertake "common actions" on international problems. EPC was to take place outside the federal structures of the Community. The European Commission and the European Court of Justice did not have competence or jurisdiction in foreign policy matters, making EPC a much weaker form of cooperation than that established in the economic sphere by the Treaty of Rome.

On January 1, 1973, the first enlargement of the Community took place, as Denmark, Ireland, and Britain became members. At the December 1974 Paris summit, the leaders of the member states agreed to hold summit meetings three times (later changed to twice) each year. These regular gatherings constituted a new institution, the European Council. Unlike the Council of Ministers, which was assigned extensive legislative responsibilities under the Treaty of Rome, the European Council was to operate more informally. It was a forum in which leaders could gather behind closed doors for discussion and bargaining and to launch new initiatives relating to the future of the Community.

The Community also began accession negotiations with three Mediterranean countries, Greece, Portugal, and Spain. These countries were much poorer than the EEC average, and all three were emerging from authoritarian rule and were attempting to establish democratic systems. While many in Europe questioned whether the Community could afford to absorb these applicants, European leaders saw an overriding political imperative for Mediterranean enlargement. The Community thus began accession negotiations in 1976–1979, although membership was achieved for Greece only in 1981 and Portugal and Spain in 1986.

The first direct elections to the European Parliament took place in June 1979, bringing to Strasbourg a popularly elected body of men and women who could claim to speak for Europe on behalf of the electorate. The Community took its first major step toward monetary union with the establishment, in March 1979, of the European Monetary System (EMS), a system of fixed but adjustable currency rates built around a central unit of account, the European Currency Unit (ECU). The latter was an artificial currency whose value was set by a weighted basket of EEC member country currencies. In the EMS, each national currency had a fixed rate against the ECU. The central rates in ECUs then were used to establish a grid of bilateral exchange rates. Countries were responsible for ensuring that this rate fluctuated by no more than 2.25 percent (6 percent in the case of Italy). The central rates could be changed only with the consent of the other members of the EMS. The EMS thus provided a high degree of intra-European monetary stability and paved the way for a still more ambitious project, Economic and Monetary Union (EMU), at the end of the decade.

These developments all took place against a very challenging external economic and political environment that included the problems of the U.S. dollar and the breakdown of the Bretton Woods monetary system in August 1971, the October 1973 Arab-Israeli War and the cutoff of oil exports by Arab countries that followed, and the deep economic recession of 1974–1975 and the ensuing years of "stagflation," a devastating combination of low growth and high inflation. These external shocks all put strains on the Community and made the process of integration more difficult—even if more essential. Foreign policy coordination became more rather than less difficult, the EPC notwithstanding, as the member states made separate approaches to the Arab countries and Soviet Union. The hard-won gains of economic integration were also threatened, as national governments looked to national solutions to combat rising unemployment. The Treaty of Rome prohibited the reimposition of tariffs and import quotas, but governments increased many open and hidden subsidies to industry, imposing nontariff barriers to trade that undermined the single market.

These many difficulties notwithstanding, by the end of the 1970s the Community had set in motion four long-term processes that were to mark the European integration process for the next several decades: (1) ongoing enlargement from the original core in northwestern Europe to the other parts of Europe; (2) efforts to develop a coordinated European foreign policy and a stronger and more autonomous international identity for Europe; (3) an ambitious effort to move beyond an initial customs union with a few common policies to a full-fledged economic union and common currency; and (4) the continuous search for improved political mechanisms able to manage all of these complex processes, to engage the loyalty of Europe's citizens, and to do so in ways consistent with the democratic values and traditions of the member states.

RELAUNCHING THE COMMUNITY: THE SINGLE EUROPEAN ACT

While EPC, EMS, direct elections to the European Parliament, and enlargement all were stirrings of a new dynamism in European integration, the fact remained that the EEC of the early 1980s was bogged down by economic and political problems, suffering from a huge gap between the ambitious long-term goals of the European project and the problems of slow growth and unemployment. The 1979 revolution in Iran produced a second oil shock and another deep recession. The terms "Euro-pessimism" and "Euro-sclerosis" were coined to sum up a sense that Europe's internal structures—businesses, the welfare state, and the educational system—were resistant to change and were unable to respond to increased competition from Japan, the United States, and the newly industrializing countries.

The Community also faced, in British Prime Minister Margaret Thatcher, its most determined political critic since de Gaulle. Elected in 1979, Thatcher was known for her skepticism about European integration and was determined to redress what she saw as a fundamentally unjust financial relationship between Britain and the EEC.[3] Britain imported large amounts of food and industrial goods from outside the EEC on which it paid customs duties and agricultural levies to Brussels, while it received far less back from the CAP, owing to the small size of its farming sector relative to those in other Community countries. The result was an imbalance between what the UK paid into and what it received from Brussels that by 1979 was well over $1 billion per year. For five years, Thatcher pressed her counterparts in the European Council for a rebate, all but crippling political decision making in the Community.

The British budgetary question finally was resolved at the Fontainebleau summit in June 1984, where the heads of government agreed to cut Britain's contribution as well as to undertake a wider budgetary reform. At the same meeting, the European Council responded to widespread concerns about the seeming inability of the Community to face its economic and political problems by accepting a proposal by French President François Mitterrand to establish a committee to explore ways to improve the functioning of the Community and of EPC. Much of the discussion about reform and revitalization centered on the internal market, in many ways the core area of European integration going back to 1950.

The EEC was supposed to be an internal market characterized by the free flow of goods, services, persons, and capital. As a practical matter, only a free market in goods had been established, and even this was riddled with exceptions. Differing national standards and technical regulations hindered the import of products from other EEC countries. Paperwork at the borders and disparate national policies on taxation, health and safety, company law, and subsidies to industry all fragmented the market. Businesses had limited ability to compete across borders in industries such as banking, insurance, and construction. Governments and central banks retained controls on capital, making it difficult, for example, for savers to deposit funds in banks outside their country of residence. And citizens of one EEC country seeking to work in another were hampered by rules on residency and work permits and by national pension and insurance schemes.

Jacques Delors, a former French minister of finance, became European Commission president on January 1, 1985, and immediately launched a program to complete the single market. The European Commission drafted a detailed plan with approximately three hundred proposals to be turned into Community law to complete the internal market. Each proposal was assigned a target date so that the whole program would be implemented by December 31, 1992. The report identified physical, technical, and fiscal barriers to the internal market, all of which it proposed to dismantle. Physical barriers included customs posts and paperwork and inspections at borders. Technical barriers included national standards and regulations that had the effect of impeding commerce among EEC member states. Fiscal barriers included types and levels of taxation that varied from one EEC country to another.

Delors realized that many of the plan's specific measures would be difficult to turn into law. Much Community legislation takes the form of directives, which lay out general guidelines as to "the result to be achieved" but leave it to the member states to enact appropriate national legislation. With each of several hundred proposed measures requiring unanimous approval by twelve governments, there was little chance that the ambitious single-market program could be implemented. Institutional reform, meaning change in the way the Community made decisions, thus was needed. The committee on institutional reform established at Fontainebleau presented its final report to the Brussels summit in March 1985. The report called for institutional reforms that would strengthen the Community and speed up decision making. It recommended convening an Intergovernmental Conference (IGC) among the member states that would draw up a new treaty of European Union. The general thrust of the report was toward significant changes in the Treaty of Rome as a way of restarting the integration process and ensuring that the single-market program was implemented.

The IGC began in September 1985 and culminated in an intense round of bargaining among the Community leaders at the December 1985 Luxembourg summit. The result was a new treaty, the Single European Act (SEA), which was formally signed on February 17, 1986, and came into effect on July 1, 1987, after all of the member states had ratified it. The SEA broadened the Community's areas of responsibility and made changes in Community decision-making processes. New policy areas added to Community competence included the environment, research and technology, and "economic and social cohesion" (meaning the regional policy aimed at narrowing income disparities between different parts of the Community).

The SEA also inserted a new article in the Treaty of Rome that mandated completion of the internal market by the end of 1992. The SEA specified that for certain policy areas, the Council was empowered to take decisions by a qualified majority vote. These areas included some social policy matters, the implementation of decisions relating to regional funds and Community research and development programs, and, most importantly, most measures "which have as their object the establishment and functioning of the internal market." This last amendment was the crucial change that allowed the completion of the single-market program by the deadline.

The act also increased the power of the European Parliament. Whereas the Treaty of Rome required only that the Parliament be consulted on legislation before its adoption or rejection by the Council of Ministers, the SEA introduced a cooperation procedure under which the Parliament could demand from the Council an explanation as to why its proposed amendments had not been adopted. The treaty also introduced an assent procedure under which the Parliament was required to approve certain legislative actions, including the Community budget and association agreements with countries outside the EEC. These changes expanded the power of the European Parliament and marked a new stage in its transition from a consultative to a genuinely legislative body.

Finally, the SEA introduced an important change in the foreign policy sphere by creating a legal basis for EPC. Under the terms of the act, the signatories henceforth were bound by legal agreement, rather than just a political commitment, to consult and cooperate with each other in foreign policy. However, the EPC itself was not (unlike, e.g., such new policy areas as the environment or regional policy) incorporated into the Treaty of Rome. There thus was no such thing as a Community foreign policy, but rather only an agreement among the member states that they would forge a common foreign policy. This meant that foreign policy would remain a matter for intergovernmental cooperation rather than supranational coordination. Community institutions such as the European Commission would not have a role in EPC, and foreign policy decisions would not be subject to the jurisdiction of the European Court of Justice.

The SEA was a compromise between those in Europe who wanted progress toward political union and those, like the British and the Danes, who preferred a community with more limited responsibilities, focused mainly on the single market. It introduced important reforms in the Community's founding treaty and demonstrated that the member states could use the mechanism of an intergovernmental conference to push the integration process forward. Above all, it elevated to the level of a legal principle the key goal—a single market by the end of 1992—that was to become synonymous with the "relaunch" that Delors had sought to achieve and provided the means to achieve that goal through expanded use of qualified majority voting.

The Treaty on European Union

The SEA was followed within a few years by an even more ambitious agreement, the Treaty on European Union (TEU), signed in the Dutch city of Maastricht in early 1992. The Maastricht Treaty, as it was commonly known, did three main things: (1) it transformed the European Community into a "European Union," with expansive political responsibilities and ambitions; (2) it made the common currency—later called the euro—a centerpiece of the EU and established a process whereby the member states (with a few exceptions) were to surrender their national currencies and adopt the new EU money; and (3) it extended European competence to a range of new policy areas, for example social policy and citizenship and justice and home affairs, as would befit a political union rather than a mere economic bloc.

The push for economic and monetary union (EMU) was in some respects a logical outgrowth of the single-market program. The EMS had been operating for nearly
a decade, and had succeeded in its original goal of insulating intra-European trade
from turbulence in global currency markets. As the EMS evolved toward a de facto
fixed-rate regime, a growing number of economists and political leaders argued that
Europe should take the next logical step and move to full EMU. Proponents of monetary union argued that there was an inconsistency between the single market and
the maintenance of separate currencies, since changes in the value of these currencies affected the prices of goods and services traded in the internal market and thus
constituted a barrier to trade. National currencies also imposed transaction costs on
businesses and consumers. The elimination, under the single-market program, of
all national controls on capital also meant that it would be difficult to sustain the
EMS—a system that retained different national currencies but that tightly regulated
variations in the value of these currencies relative to each other—in circumstances
in which investors were free to move money across borders to seek the highest rate
of return. The choice, some economists warned, was either to regress to pre-EMS
instability or move forward to full-fledged EMU.

At the June 1988 Hanover summit, the European Council agreed to establish,
under the chairmanship of Delors, a committee to propose steps leading to economic
and monetary union. Composed mainly of the central bank heads from the member
states, the Delors Committee developed a detailed three-stage plan for the establishment of EMU. It proposed that in stage 3, exchange rate parities be "irrevocably fixed"
and full authority for determining economic and monetary policy be transferred to
EEC institutions. At the June 1989 summit, the European Council approved the
Delors Committee's approach and declared that stage 1 of EMU should begin on
July 1, 1990, with the closer coordination of member state economic policies and the
completion of plans to free the movement of capital. European leaders further agreed
that another IGC would be held to consider moving to stages 2 and 3, which unlike
stage 1 required amendment of the EEC treaty.

EMU most likely would have gone ahead in any case, but developments in Eastern and Central Europe lent new urgency to this project. The fall of the Berlin Wall
in November 1989 led to the virtual collapse of the East German communist regime
and a fast-moving set of negotiations involving the governments of the two German
states, along with the Soviet Union, Britain, France, and the United States (the four
victor powers of World War II), that resulted in the reunification of Germany in
October 1990. The five states of the former East Germany, with some 16 million
inhabitants, automatically became part of the Community. Although leaders such
as Mitterrand accepted German reunification as inevitable, they were concerned
that the creation of a larger and more eastward-oriented Germany could damage the
process of European integration. Mitterrand was determined to push forward with
plans to "deepen" the Community, and thereby to ensure that the new Germany
remained firmly anchored in the West. He was strongly supported in this by Chancellor Helmut Kohl of Germany.

In December 1989, the European Council agreed to convene an IGC on EMU
by the end of 1990 and to adopt a social charter—a Community-wide agreement on

labor standards that the trade unions had pressed for as a concomitant to the single European market. Alongside these developments in the economic sphere, the changing international situation gave new momentum to the old project for political union. In April 1990, Kohl and Mitterrand jointly called for steps to realize the aspirations toward political union expressed in the SEA. The Kohl-Mitterrand proposal set the agenda for an extraordinary session of the European Council in Dublin in April 1990, at which the twelve leaders reaffirmed their commitment to political union. Meeting in the same city two months later, the European Council agreed to convene an IGC on political union to begin at the same time as the IGC on EMU and to run in parallel with it. Both IGCs formally opened at the Rome summit in December 1990. Thus, after not holding a single such conference in the three decades after 1955, the Community was to have three IGCs in five years, two of which would run concurrently. This extraordinary situation reflected the extent to which, as Delors had phrased it, history was "accelerating," forcing the Community to respond.

NEGOTIATING THE MAASTRICHT TREATY

The focus of the IGCs was on strengthening the decision-making process in areas in which the EEC already had competence and on extending the range of issues subject to common policymaking. The negotiations lasted a year and concluded at the December 1991 European Council with agreement on the TEU, which was finalized after last-minute negotiations in which Britain and Denmark secured the right to "opt out" of certain of the treaty's provisions. The treaty was signed in Maastricht in February 1992.

As its official name indicated, the treaty brought into being a new entity called the European Union—a complicated structure of three "pillars" dealing with different policy areas using different decision-making processes. The first pillar consisted of the three existing communities—the EEC (renamed the European Community [EC] to reflect its broadened and no longer strictly economic areas of responsibility), the ECSC, and Euratom—in which the member states pooled sovereignty and transferred decision-making powers to the European Commission, the Council of Ministers, the European Parliament, and the European Court of Justice, with a powerful guiding role also assigned to the European Council.

The second pillar, the Common Foreign and Security Policy (CFSP), replaced and was based upon EPC. Decisions in the second pillar were to remain largely intergovernmental, with only a limited role for Community institutions. Such decisions would not be subject to the jurisdiction of the Court of Justice. The European Commission could suggest actions under CFSP, but it was not given the sole right of initiative in this area, as the member states could also initiate policy actions under CFSP. The Maastricht Treaty specified certain foreign policy goals that were to be pursued under CFSP, such as safeguarding the common values, fundamental interests, and independence of the EU; strengthening its security; and promoting peace and respect for human rights. These objectives were to be pursued through "common positions" and "joint actions" by the member states, with decisions taken primarily by unanimity. CFSP also provided for the "eventual framing of a common defense policy."

The third pillar consisted of cooperation in the fields of Justice and Home Affairs (JHA), including asylum policy, control of external borders and immigration from outside the EU, and combating drug addiction and international crime. The completion of the single European market and the abolition of controls on the movement of people and capital had made EU-level cooperation on cross-border problems increasingly necessary, but the member states with their different legal traditions and approaches to such sensitive internal matters were reluctant to surrender sovereignty to Brussels in these areas. The twelve thus agreed to establish the third pillar on an intergovernmental basis, with decision-making procedures similar to those used in CFSP. The treaty also established a European citizenship, to supplement rather than replace national citizenship, which brings with it certain rights, such as the right of an EU citizen to be represented by the consulate of another member state while overseas or to vote in local elections while resident in another member state.

The Maastricht Treaty strengthened the European Parliament by adding a new procedure, co-decision, under which the Parliament for the first time could block legislation introduced by the Commission and passed by the Council of Ministers. Co-decision was prescribed only for a limited number of policy areas, although one of these—the internal market—was quite important. The Parliament was also given a say in the appointment of the Commission and the Commission president, hitherto a matter of exclusive concern for the Council of Ministers. The treaty also established a new institution, the Committee of the Regions, to provide a means whereby regional entities in Europe (the provinces) can give direct input to policymaking in Brussels.

The most significant achievement of the Maastricht Treaty was EMU. Building on the Delors Committee report and the experience of EMS, the treaty established a detailed timetable and institutional provisions for the phasing out of national currencies and the introduction of a European currency, initially called the ECU and later renamed the euro. Stage 2 of EMU was to begin on January 1, 1994. The member states were to meet certain economic convergence criteria relating to inflation, national debt and deficits, currency stability in the EMS, and long-term interest rates to ensure that the economies entering the economic and monetary union would have broadly similar performance.

Stage 3 would begin no later than January 1, 1999, and would entail the "irrevocable locking" of the value of the European currencies against each other and their phasing out by July 2002. The treaty provided for the establishment of a European Central Bank and a European System of Central Banks responsible for conducting monetary policy at the EU level. Britain and Denmark, both traditional skeptics of EMU, secured "opt-outs" from the main provisions of EMU and were not required to surrender their national currencies if they chose not to do so.

BEYOND MAASTRICHT: AMSTERDAM AND NICE

Ratification of the Maastricht Treaty proved unexpectedly difficult. In June 1992, voters in Denmark narrowly rejected the treaty in the referendum that was required under the Danish Constitution. In September, French voters approved the treaty, but only by the narrow margin of 51 to 49 percent. In Germany, the treaty was challenged in the Supreme Court, where opponents argued that it contravened the German Constitution by transferring powers of the German states to Brussels. In all these countries, there was increased uncertainty about the speed and ultimate destination of the integration process. In the end, the treaty was ratified. The European Council negotiated additional opt-outs for Denmark, and in May 1993, the Danish voters approved the treaty by a healthy margin in a second referendum. Legislatures in the other countries approved the treaty, as did the German federal court. Maastricht thus went into effect on November 1, 1993, some ten months later than originally planned.

On January 1, 1995, the membership of the European Union expanded to fifteen, with the accession of Austria, Finland, and Sweden. This was a mere prelude to the more extensive enlargement that had been placed on the agenda following the collapse of communism in Central and Eastern Europe in 1989–1991. The leaders of these newly democratic countries pressed for admission to the EU and NATO. Many in Western Europe had doubts about the feasibility of absorbing a relatively poor region with over 100 million inhabitants, but EU leaders soon concluded that they had little choice but to welcome these new democracies into the fold. At the June 1993 Copenhagen summit, the European Council agreed that these countries could become members provided they went through a period of transition in which they prepared their economies and established working democracies.

The prospect of enlargement drew heightened attention to what many observers saw as the shortcomings and unfinished business of the Maastricht Treaty. In many areas, disagreements among the member states had led to vague compromises and statements of intent that could be interpreted in different ways. For example, the article that introduced defense into the EU structure stated, "The common foreign and security policy shall include all questions related to the security of the Union, including the eventual framing of a common defense policy, which might in time lead to a common defense." But how were terms like "eventual" and "might in time" to be interpreted and translated into action? Many of the decision-making procedures provided for in the treaty were slow and cumbersome, and they threatened to become more so with the addition of ten or more new member states.

Recognizing that the treaty would need to be revised at some point, the twelve had agreed, in the Maastricht Treaty, to hold another IGC in 1996 to review the workings of the treaty and to introduce such amendments as were necessary. The scheduled IGC convened in Turin in March 1996 and concluded in June 1997 with the adoption of a treaty amending the Maastricht arrangements. Called the Treaty of Amsterdam after the city in which it was signed, the agreement provided for some strengthening of CFSP, for example by creating the post of a high representative for CFSP and by introducing the mechanism of "common strategies" toward third countries and regions. It also mandated closer cooperation in third-pillar matters such as immigration and asylum policies, in large part through a phased shift of these responsibilities from the third to the first pillar. As in past revisions, the powers of the European Parliament were expanded.

Meanwhile, the two ambitious projects of the 1990s—the euro and enlargement—steadily advanced. The euro was introduced as scheduled on January 1, 1999, with eleven EU members (all but the United Kingdom, Denmark, Sweden, and Greece) adopting the common currency and forming their own grouping of economic and financial ministers to coordinate euro-related policy matters. The technical switchover to the euro over the long New Year's holiday went surprisingly well, without computer crashes or increased volatility in financial markets. The European Council had already decided that accession negotiations with six leading candidate countries—the Czech Republic, Cyprus, Estonia, Hungary, Poland, and Slovenia—could begin in March 1998. At Helsinki in December 1999, the member states further declared that all of the Central and Eastern European candidate countries and Malta (although not yet Turkey) had made sufficient progress in bringing their political and economic situations up to EU levels to begin accession negotiations.

In March 2000, the member states launched yet another IGC, the fourth to take place in less than a decade. With enlargement to another ten countries looming, the focus was on streamlining and strengthening EU decision making, goals that were to have been pursued in the previous IGC but that the member states, focused on the transition to the euro, had not seriously tackled. The overriding need was to ensure that an organization with an institutional setup originally designed for six relatively homogeneous members could function with a more diverse membership of twenty-five or more members. As a practical matter, it was also necessary to decide the relative weight—in terms of votes in the Council of Ministers, representatives in the European Parliament, and so forth—each member state of the enlarged union would have.

The most sensitive issue was the reweighting of votes in the Council of Ministers. Qualified majority voting was designed to ensure efficiency through use of majority voting but to preserve some of the safeguards associated with the unanimity procedure. Legislation could not be blocked by one or two recalcitrant member states, but neither could it be passed, as in most national parliamentary systems, by a narrow numerical majority. This system generally had worked quite well. However, as many more small countries joined the EU, France and the other large member states were increasingly concerned about the declining relative weight of the bigger countries. Whereas the original Community of the 1950s had had three large and three small member states, an enlarged EU would have only six large member states (France, Germany, Italy, Poland, Spain, and the UK) and eventually more than twenty smaller members. Concerned about the diminution of its relative influence, France pressed for a reweighting of votes in favor of the large member countries (although not, somewhat inconsistently, an increase in Germany's weight relative to France to reflect its increased post-reunification population).

In the end, the fifteen approved, at the December 2000 European Council, a new agreement that became known as the Treaty of Nice. The treaty decided how many seats in the European Parliament and weighted votes in the Council of Ministers each current and projected member would have after enlargement. To reduce the size and thereby preserve the cohesion and effectiveness of the Commission, the "big five" gave up their second commissioner. The treaty further stipulated that after membership reached twenty-seven, the EU would shift to a rotation system in which the number of commissioners would be less than the number of member states. The relative weighting of the big states was increased, but France (along with Italy and the UK) continued to have the same number of votes in the Council of Ministers as Germany. To give somewhat greater weight to population and to defuse German complaints of unfairness, a complex "triple majority" was put in place, under which a qualified majority vote had to not only have the required number of Council votes but also be formed by countries representing at least 62 percent of the EU's population.

Although Nice technically cleared the way to enlargement by deciding the distribution of decision-making power in an enlarged European Union, the treaty was hardly the simplification and streamlining that many European commentators thought were essential. Its provisions were more complicated than ever. At the insistence of the member states, policy decisions in such key areas as taxation, social policy, cohesion policy, asylum, and immigration, and above all such constitutional issues as reform of the treaties, remained subject to unanimity rather than qualified majority voting. Most tellingly, the treaty was long, complicated, and difficult for the average citizen to understand and support, a circumstance that was underscored dramatically in June 2001 when the traditionally pro-Europe Irish electorate voted down the treaty. Nice finally went into effect after the Irish voters approved the treaty in a second referendum in October 2002.

ENLARGEMENT AND THE CONSTITUTION

Even before the Treaty of Nice had been concluded, a number of political leaders were calling for a debate about the envisioned endpoint of the integration process ("finality") and the need for radical reforms going beyond institutional tinkering. A key theme to emerge from this debate was the call for a European Constitution—a set of definitive rules, like the U.S. Constitution, that would last for a long time, that would be understood and respected by the citizenry, and that would be amended infrequently and with difficulty. Adoption of a constitution would end the constant series of IGCs that had been underway since the 1980s and the political and institutional tinkering that they entailed.

Thus, in December 2001, the European Council agreed to launch a European Convention to draw up a European Constitution. Chaired by former French President Valéry Giscard d'Estaing, the convention was to be composed of representatives of member state governments, members of national parliaments, European Commission representatives, and representatives of the European Parliament. The convention began in March 2002 with great enthusiasm, its members conscious that they were embarking on an exercise that in some ways paralleled the one that had taken place in the United States in the 1780s. After sixteen months of intense deliberations, the European Convention adopted a draft constitutional treaty and forwarded it to the European Council for consideration by the member states. The treaty was to supersede the 1957 Treaty of Rome and all subsequent amendments and additions to the EU's founding treaties. The three-pillar structure was to be abolished and replaced by a single European Union that would have legal personality and the ability to conclude binding agreements with other countries and international organizations. The treaty would preserve the five key EU institutions, but make changes in how they operated, including by providing for a European Council president to be elected by the member states for a two-and-a-half-year term and a new EU foreign minister. The powers of the European Parliament were to be extended to new (although still not all) policy areas, and the complicated triple-majority system enshrined in the Nice Treaty was to be abolished. In place of the system of national weights used since qualified majority voting was established in the Treaty of Rome, the new system would require that for legislation to be adopted, it must be supported by a majority of member states representing at least 60 percent of the EU population.

Led by France and Germany, most member states favored rapid approval of the constitutional treaty without significant amendment. However, Spain and Poland (the latter already participating in the reform discussions as a prospective member state) were unhappy with the diminution from the Nice formula of their relative voting power in the new treaty and blocked its adoption at the European Council. The member states finally approved the treaty in June 2004, after adjustments were made in the formula for qualified majority voting to satisfy the two holdouts. Under the new compromise, passage of legislation would require the support of at least 55 percent of the member states representing 65 percent of the EU's population; in cases where states representing 35 percent or more of the EU population chose to block legislation, at least four member states had to comprise the blocking group. Ratification by the member states was to take place in 2004 and 2005, and the treaty was to go into effect by 2006.

Amid the endless haggling over institutional reform, the EU managed to complete both EMU and enlargement. Euro notes and coins came into circulation in January 2002, successfully completing the transition to EMU and giving the European Union tangible proof of its cohesion and its ability to accomplish ambitious, long-term goals. On May 1, 2004, ten new member states were admitted to the EU. Bulgaria and Romania were making slower progress in meeting the criteria for membership, and their accession was put off to 2007.

As with Maastricht more than a decade earlier, the drive to establish the Constitution encountered unexpected difficulties, as the people in various EU countries questioned the wisdom of the predominantly pro-EU political elites and expressed their doubts about the headlong rush to a united Europe. In May 2005, voters in France rejected the constitutional treaty by a stunning margin of 55 percent "no" and 45 percent "yes." A few days later, voters in the Netherlands delivered a similar verdict. The rejection of the treaty in two founding member states of the EU came as a shock to political leaders across the continent and reflected the degree to which public perceptions of the integration project had diverged from the views of the pro-integration elites. Whereas the latter saw a larger and more cohesive EU as the key to enhancing Europe's role in the world and to solving the economic and political challenges raised by globalization, the former were no longer so sure about the benefits that integration offered to the average citizen.

Following the votes in France and the Netherlands, European leaders declared a "pause for reflection" while they figured out what to do about the constitutional treaty and the by-now perennial question of institutional reform.[4] This pause lasted until July 2007, when representatives of the member states, meeting in Lisbon, opened yet another IGC to amend the EU treaties. The plan was to abandon the constitutional treaty as too ambitious and too controversial, and instead to follow the tested path of making incremental changes to the existing treaties, but to try to preserve as much of the substance of the institutional changes that had been agreed in the constitutional treaty. This was in fact achieved over the summer and fall of 2007, with the adoption and signature on December 13, 2007, of the Lisbon Treaty.

The treaty strengthened the powers of the European Parliament and provided for greater involvement by national parliaments in EU affairs, both measures intended to address the widely perceived "democratic deficit" in the EU. On the thorny question of balancing the rights of large and small states in EU decision making, the treaty established a new system of qualified majority voting in the Council of Ministers. From 2014, the passage of legislation is to require a new double majority, which will be achieved when 55 percent of member states representing at least 65 percent of the EU's population vote for a measure. The treaty also established two new posts—a president of the European Council, to be elected to a two-and-a-half-year term, and a high representative for the Union in Foreign Affairs and Security Policy (a de facto EU foreign minister)—both of which were intended to raise the external profile of the EU. To assist the high representative, a new European External Action Service, or diplomatic corps, was established. In addition, the Lisbon Treaty conferred legal personality on the EU, so that it can now conclude treaties and negotiate directly with third parties on the international stage.

The Lisbon Treaty entered into force on December 1, 2009, after one more unanticipated delay caused by the rejection of the treaty by voters in Ireland in June 2008, which was reversed by a second referendum approving the treaty in October 2009. The member states elected former Belgian Prime Minister Herman Van Rompuy to the post of European Council president, and selected British politician and trade commissioner Catherine Ashton as high representative. The fact that both individuals were rather low-key figures suggested to many observers that the member states, while they in principle favored giving the EU a higher international profile and a means to speak with a single voice, were wary of turning over power and the spotlight to a higher profile figure such as former British Prime Minister Tony Blair.

Crisis and Drift

The scaling back of the ambitious plan to adopt a European constitution in many ways reflected the more difficult economic and political environment confronting Europe in the twenty-first century. Voters were worried about further expansion of the EU, especially to Turkey, which was pressing to become a member. The Iraq war in early 2003 badly split the EU, as France and Germany took the lead in opposing the U.S. effort to topple Saddam Hussein, while leaders in other member states—especially Britain but also Spain, Italy, and the accession countries—were more supportive of U.S. policy. Europe itself was caught up in the post–September 11 conflict between Islamic radicalism and the West, as was seen most dramatically in the March 2004 bombings in Madrid that killed almost two hundred people.

Amid the vast amount of attention that the EU member states devoted to institutional reform, the EU struggled to make itself relevant to a number of pressing domestic and international policy problems. Turkey was still formally a candidate for EU membership and was engaged in membership negotiations, but governments in key countries, France and Germany in particular, were opposed to full membership for Turkey, preferring instead a "privileged partnership" with Ankara. The domestic sensitivity with regard to membership for Turkey reflected both the complex state of Europe's relationship with the Muslim world and rising fears among EU voters concerning the problems of immigration, unemployment, and loss of national identity in a globalizing world.

Since the early 2000s, the EU had promulgated "effective multilateralism" as the guiding light of EU foreign policy. As articulated in the European Security Strategy of 2003, this concept meant that the EU would lead the way in building a system of global governance, more or less patterned after intra-EU norms of adherence to law and sharing of sovereignty, in which the international community would collectively address such problems as climate change, international terrorism, and the proliferation of weapons of mass destruction. Effective multilateralism was an implicit rebuke to the United States under the Bush administration, which the EU accused of taking a "unilateral" approach to addressing international problems, and an invitation to powers such as China, India, and Russia to follow the EU's lead in addressing shared problems.

By the second half of the decade, however, it was becoming increasingly clear that rising, assertive powers elsewhere in the world were more interested in pursuing their own narrow economic and political interests than in following the EU's lead in building a new system of global governance. Russia re-imposed authoritarian rule at home, invaded neighboring Georgia in 2008, and ignored many trade and other agreements it had signed. China clamped down on dissidents at home, sought to lock up natural resources in Africa, and manipulated the value of its currency to maintain a competitive advantage. Iran showed few signs of abandoning its drive toward possession of nuclear weapons.

Amid all this uncertainty, the euro, along with enlargement, seemed to confirm the success of Europe's more than 60-year experiment with integration. In 2008–2009, four new member states—Slovenia, Cyprus, Malta, and Slovakia— adopted the euro, which was already well established as the world's second most widely used reserve currency, after the dollar. But the worldwide financial crisis that erupted in September 2008 cast shadows over Europe's financial stability and, as it lingered and deepened, raised questions about Europe's bet on the euro and the wisdom of this ambitious project that had absorbed so much political energy and that was seen as so decisive for the future of the continent.

At first the EU seemed to weather the crisis rather better than the United States, where crisis had originated in the subprime mortgage bust of 2008. But as the recession dragged on, it exposed deep economic disparities within the EU and the narrower euro zone, which both reflected and reinforced differences in policy and political outlooks. Since the introduction of the common currency in 1999, Germany had improved its competitiveness, both within the EU and globally, and enjoyed rising exports and generally sound national finances. However, in Eastern and southern Europe, as well as in Ireland, the situation was far different. These countries were running large fiscal and current account deficits, and their industries had lost competitiveness over the past decade, raising questions about how they would repay their international debts and produce economic recovery. The situation was particularly acute in Greece, where investors feared that the government, unable to restore its finances by sufficiently raising taxes and cutting expenditures (a large part of which were accounted for by wages and benefits to public sector employees, who were resisting cuts), might be forced to default on its bonds.

The EU eventually came to Greece's rescue with a financial support package, and in May 2010 set up a new European Financial Stability Facility intended to provide financing to indebted EU member states no longer able to raise funds on private markets. But the fact that support for Greece was strongly opposed by voters and politicians in Germany and other more affluent member states raised doubts about the future of EU cohesion and solidarity. The German government also insisted that the International Monetary Fund (IMF) be brought into the potential rescue packages for EU member countries and provide both economic advice and additional financing. IMF involvement in Europe's internal affairs was an especially bitter pill for federalists such as Delors, who had always argued that the whole point of the euro was to increase the EU's international power and autonomy.

In July 2011, the euro-zone countries signed a treaty creating a European Stability Mechanism, able to lend up to €500 billion to euro-area countries in crisis. In January 2012, the European Council reached agreement on a new Treaty on Stability, Coordination and Governance in the Economic and Monetary Union (popularly known as the "fiscal compact") that would tighten fiscal discipline through automatic sanctions and stricter surveillance and require member states to achieve balance in their budgets. The treaty went into effect on January 1, 2013.

But none of these measures served to revitalize the European economy, which remained bogged down by its own internal imbalances and hampered by a worsening global economic outlook. The IMF projected that the euro-zone economy would remain in recession in 2013, contracting by 0.6 percent, and that growth would be restored in 2014, but only to an anemic 0.9 percent. Unemployment, particularly among young people, remained stubbornly high, leading to deepening poverty and social crises in some parts of Europe. There were still occasional successes and flashes of dynamism. The Nobel Peace Prize was, of course, one. Croatia became the twenty-eighth member of the EU on July 1, 2013, the first expansion of the union since 2007. Negotiations on a transatlantic free trade agreement aimed at stimulating growth and investment began with the United States in the summer of 2013.

Overall, however, there was no denying that the European experiment, underway since the early 1950s, was in trouble. While catastrophic outcomes such as the collapse of the euro or the exit of Great Britain from the union still were regarded as unlikely, they were impossible to rule out and they rendered all but irrelevant the once-soaring rhetoric about achieving full political and economic union, promoting the European social model on a worldwide basis, and having Europe take the lead in promoting "effective multilateralism" as a solution to global problems. The best that could be hoped for, at least for the next several years, was that Europe would continue to muddle along, probably without risk of falling back into the national enmities that it had managed to overcome in the aftermath of World War II, but still falling far short of the ambitious vision for a united Europe once entertained by federalists such as Monnet.

Notes

1. European Commission, *European Union: Selected Instruments from the Treaties* (Luxembourg: Office for Official Publications of the European Communities, 1995). The treaties also can be found on http://europa.eu.int (accessed January 15, 2014).

2. Hugo Young, *This Blessed Plot: Britain and Europe from Churchill to Blair* (Woodstock, NY: Overlook Press, 1999).

3. For Thatcher's views on Europe, see her memoirs, *Downing Street Years* (New York: HarperCollins, 1993).

4. For a more detailed analysis of the issues, see Youri Devuyst, *The European Union at the Crossroads: An Introduction to the EU's Institutional Evolution*, Brussels: PIE-Peter Lang, 2002.

5. Brussels European Council, *June 15–16, 2006: Presidency Conclusions*, June 16 (Brussels: Council of the European Union, 2006).

Suggested Readings

Cini, Michelle, and Nieves Perez-Solorzano Borragon. *European Union Politics*, 4th ed. Oxford: Oxford University Press, 2013.

Dinan, Desmond. *Ever Closer Union: An Introduction to European Integration*, 4th ed. New York: Palgrave Macmillan, 2010.

Gilbert, Mark. *European Integration: A Concise History*. Lanham, MD: Rowman & Littlefield, 2011.

Grant, Charles. *Delors: Inside the House That Jacques Built*. London: Nicholas Brealey, 1994.

Jones, Erik, Anand Menon, and Stephen Weatherill, eds. *The Oxford Handbook of the European Union*. Oxford: Oxford University Press, 2012.

Moravcsik, Andrew. *The Choice for Europe: Social Purpose and State Power from Messina to Maastricht*. Ithaca, NY: Cornell University Press, 1998.

Nugent, Neill. *The Government and Politics of the European Union*, 7th ed. New York: Palgrave Macmillan, 2010.

Peterson, John, and Michael Shackleton, eds. *The Institutions of the European Union*, 3rd ed. Oxford: Oxford University Press, 2012.

Tiersky, Ronald, and John Van Oudenaren, eds. *European Foreign Policies: Does Europe Still Matter?* Lanham, MD: Rowman & Littlefield, 2010.

Van Oudenaren, John. *Uniting Europe: An Introduction to the European Union*. Lanham, MD: Rowman & Littlefield, 2004.

CHAPTER 10

Economic Governance and Varieties of Capitalism

Benedicta Marzinotto

The global financial and economic crisis sparked a vast debate about the relative merits of different models of capitalism, defined as "ways of organizing a market economy." The initial reaction to the crisis was to blame the Anglo-Saxon model for allowing excessive liberty in financial markets. According to this view, the subprime crisis was in fact largely due to excessive financial innovations, poor regulation, and insufficient supervision of financial markets. Despite its U.S. origins, however, it did not take long for the crisis to affect the euro zone as well, where there was less financial innovation and stronger reliance on bank credit (which is normally more regulated). There was nevertheless an important difference between developments in the United States and in Europe. In the euro zone, unlike in the United States, the crisis translated into a sovereign debt crisis where it affected a range of different countries—like Greece, Ireland, Portugal, Spain, and Italy—although each to different degrees and for slightly different reasons.

The purpose of this chapter is to analyze the process of European economic integration and the crisis phenomenon in light of the debate on different varieties of capitalism. Chapter 11 provides a narrative overview of the crisis itself. The goal here is more analytical. It deals with the contentions about member state predominance and national distinctiveness but does not fail to recognize that European integration has forced adjustment from within its numerous member states, especially following the completion of the Single European Market (SEM) and the introduction of the single currency. At the same time, the crisis that started in 2007 raises questions about the notion that one model of capitalism is superior to another and calls for a rethinking of the borders as well as the distribution of competences and responsibilities between European Union (EU) institutions and national governments.

The discussion builds on four contentions. First, the United States and Europe represent two distinct models of capitalism. They mainly differ in the level of competition on products, labor, and financial markets, and over time their macroeconomic performances have also diverged. However, it is probably inappropriate to compare such distinct ways of organizing a market economy. Any recipe that works well for the United States may be unable to solve the same problem in Europe, and any change to the organization of production in Europe that simply mimics the U.S. model is deemed to compromise the region's strong record in the delivery and preservation of some degree of income equality.

Second, in Europe itself, there are different models of capitalism. European integration inevitably poses a challenge to national forms of capitalism, their organization of production, and their management of aggregate demand through monetary and fiscal policy tools. Still, economic integration in Europe and the protection of national specificities and institutions have not always been in contraposition. The postwar period is considered to be the heyday of European integration, not least because greater trade liberalization served the purpose of sustaining the growth of national economies. The contrast emerged thereafter, when full economic integration and Economic and Monetary Union (EMU) membership required that member governments lost portions of power over product market regulation, monetary policy, and fiscal policy. Moreover, under EMU, the devolution of sovereignty to the EU level remained incomplete, as members of the euro area lost control over aggregate demand management via monetary and fiscal instruments, but retained sovereignty, for example, over the quality and organization of social expenditures and banking supervision; the latter came also with the obligation to rescue domestic banks under stress.

Third, the constant tension between the EU and national prerogatives since the 1980s is responsible for the complex structure of EU economic governance, in which member states lost control of some instruments but not others and multiple state and nonstate actors are simultaneously involved with shared or at times confusingly overlapping competences.

Fourth, the crisis that started in 2007 raised questions about the need to impose one single model of capitalism, while also highlighting weaknesses in the structures of European economic governance. Some adjustments to the EMU architecture have been introduced as a result; they are based on the idea that stronger economic policy coordination is needed in the euro area but in a framework that allows for a more long-term view of countries' problems and for the preservation of some diversity, especially concerning social preferences. The resulting EMU governance architecture does not necessarily offer a conclusive alternative to the complex multilevel governance structure we have been seeing so far, which only a more ambitious project of a political union would bring about.

This chapter has five sections. The first sketches both the strengths and the limitations of any argument that builds on the notion of varieties of capitalism. The second describes key institutional differences between the Anglo-Saxon model, as epitomized by the United States, and the European continental model of capitalism, explaining the extent to which differences in institutional settings between these two regions have led to differences in economic performance at different points in time. The third probes more deeply into the varieties of capitalism that have been identified in the literature along selected institutional domains, namely skills regimes, labor markets, financial systems, and macroeconomic regimes. The fourth links this discussion to the broader structure of EU economic governance, and by doing so, it looks at the areas in which the impact of the European integration process was mostly felt. The fifth focuses on the new challenges posed by the 2007 crisis to the notion of a single successful model of capitalism and to the management of newly emerged EMU-related problems. Crisis-related institutional reforms at the EU level are described and briefly assessed.

What's on the Menu?

The crisis that started in 2007 reopened the old debate about which of the two models of capitalism is superior—the Anglo-Saxon model practiced in Great Britain and the United States or the European model practiced on the Continent. But it should be obvious to everyone that there is no single superior model of capitalism. Free markets in the Anglo-Saxon world may have been responsible for the financial exuberance that led to the subprime crisis, but more bank-based systems in Europe did not perform any better; they, too, relied on relatively lax monetary policy and favorable long-term interest rates during the previous years, which resulted in a vast expansion of credit, including a high volume of nonperforming loans at the outbreak of the crisis, eventually forcing disrupted banks to cut lending or increase lending spreads for customers. In some instances, the national financial sector in European countries not only had liquidity problems but also was explicitly considered insolvent, as in the case of Ireland, where the government had to step in to bail out the country's largest banks, with the result that Ireland's deficit and debt jumped to historically unprecedented levels almost overnight.

Not only is there no single superior model, but also it is misleading to compare different varieties of capitalism, especially those of the United States and Europe, which differ substantially in their institutions and in the institutional frameworks under which they operate. Hence, despite the stimulus package passed by the Obama administration in the early months of 2009, the crisis in the United States never created a realistic concern that the federal government would go bankrupt (unless politicians chose not to pay the government's debts—which is a different matter). On the contrary, many economists believed the stimulus package was too small and the Obama administration too timid. In Europe, by contrast, financial markets started betting in favor of a default by one or the other troubled member states because it was clear that the European Union did not have the means to intervene systematically in support of member countries under stress by means of top-down transfers comparable in size to the U.S. federal budget, especially when the fate of large countries such as Spain and Italy was at stake. At the very last minute, the EU had to decide in favor of a one-off loan to Greece, a small country, and put together an emergency rescue package to support possible future victims, with Ireland and Portugal calling for financial assistance soon thereafter. This instrument evolved over time into a permanent crisis management mechanism under the name of the European Stabilization Mechanism (ESM). These solutions to the problem of government default raised a number of questions that are unique to the euro area, such as the role and efficacy of fiscal policy coordination, the role of the independent European Central Bank (ECB), the relationship between government debts and banks, and the desirability of a banking union.

Despite these more idiosyncratic differences, however, there are some patterns that suggest the need for comparison. For example, the crisis caused more unemployment in the United States, initially, than it did among those countries that use the euro as their currency (the euro zone). Nevertheless, as the North American labor market started to recover together with more benign growth rates in the gross domestic product (GDP), unemployment rose in Europe, particularly in countries like Italy or Spain, which already had a history of high levels of long-term unemployment. The reason why the U.S. unemployment rate increased disproportionally during the crisis but had a shorter duration has to do with the way in which their market economy is organized. The U.S. labor market is more flexible in the sense that workers move freely from one part of the country to the next, and wages are often determined individually rather than through collective bargaining, so they end up reflecting the characteristics of individual workers, such as their level of education and training, seniority, and so forth. This is what makes U.S. wages competitive from an economic perspective. It implies that employers will increase demand for labor whenever in need, as when the economic cycle is improving, and it implies that the wage that employers will have to pay new employees is fair from their perspective, meaning that it reflects the worker's relative productivity and so is unlikely to generate losses that could push the firm out of the market. Moreover, relatively weak employment protection legislation allows employers to hire new workers in good times and to eliminate redundancies whenever the cycle turns negative. In a nutshell, labor demand in the United States is very much dependent on economic cycles so that negative shocks increase unemployment, and positive shocks decrease it. As the U.S. economy started growing again, more employment has been created, limiting the need for the government to rely on fiscal policy to create jobs.

The European labor market, with the possible exception of the UK, is much less flexible than in the United States. Labor mobility has increased in Europe over the last decade, but it remains relatively low. In addition, it is common in Europe for wages to be agreed collectively by trade unions and employers and then extended to all workers in one particular sector, or even to the entire economy in some cases. This implies that wages do not always reflect the specific characteristics of individual workers. They might be too high or too low relative to actual productivity. Employers are careful when it comes to hiring because they worry that worker productivity will be too low to cover the cost of collectively agreed wages. They also worry that strict employment protection legislation will make it difficult or expensive to lay off workers should economic conditions take a turn for the worse. Unemployment in Europe has surged in the crisis, even if not to the same extent across all European countries and in any case with a lag relative to the United States. This is because strict employment protection legislation allows employers to lay off groups of workers only in extreme economic conditions, which allegedly materialized only after a few years. In the end, unemployment rates in some European member states have reached levels that have never been seen in the United States, not even at the deepest point of the economic cycle, particularly in countries like Greece and Spain.

Most worryingly, the same kind of stickiness will operate on the upside as well. Market forces alone are unlikely to offer a substantial contribution to employment creation in the recovery, and so governments will come under pressure to create jobs. This is the debate about supply-side reform in Europe: it concerns how quickly and how comprehensively governments should pass legislation to make labor markets more flexible through individual wage bargaining and weaker employment protection. At the same time, supply-side structural reforms take time to deliver so that more short-term measures like reducing fiscal pressures on labor income and introducing tax incentives in favor of employers that hire new workers are likely to become important components of European governments' policies to fight unemployment and support the otherwise slow recovery.

Such patterns in labor market performance do lend themselves to analysis using the notion of varieties of capitalism. The comparative political economy literature distinguishes between two ideal types: liberal market economies (LMEs) or the Anglo-Saxon model, and coordinated market economies (CMEs) coinciding closely with the continental European model.[1] Crucial to the distinction is the level and role of market competition. LMEs are characterized by strong competition on goods, labor, and financial markets. Price mechanisms allow the efficient allocation of resources; namely, prices of whatever type—be it goods' prices, wages, or asset prices—send signals about what products, employees, or financial investments are worthwhile. The key feature of CMEs is, by contrast, the high level of protection on goods, labor, and financial markets and the fact that it is up to institutional actors such as organized employers, employees, or management boards to allocate resources (i.e., raw materials, labor, and capital) in a strategically efficient fashion.

The theoretical framework is helpful, but it should be used with caution. In this debate, the United States and Europe are often portrayed as the ideal types of a liberal and a coordinated market economy, respectively, even though Europe is in fact a group of very heterogeneous countries, and all the more so after the enlargement of the European Union to Central and Eastern European countries. Put simply, there are important differences in the ways the national economic systems are organized. Germany is closest to the ideal type for a CME. Government regulation in Germany imposes important barriers to entry on product markets; unions negotiate wages with their employers for the entire sector, with the result that there is limited wage differentiation across types of workers and almost no differentiation at all across firms in the same sector; firms rely on patient long-term credit from banks and are less dependent on equities and thus on external pressures about their short-run sales and profits performance. By contrast, the UK is clearly more liberal than coordinated. British product markets are intensely competitive, wages are negotiated individually in many sectors of the economy, and large firms get their finances not from banks but directly from the markets. However, Germany and the UK are hardly the only alternatives. The Mediterranean countries represent a third category characterized by high product market regulation and bank-based financial systems, as in CMEs, but less centralized wage setting than in Germany or the Scandinavian countries. Finally, the new member states of Central and Eastern Europe went from being transition economies to LMEs, but they still have features distinct from the rest of the European Union.

While there is no easy way to determine whether one model is superior to the others in guaranteeing long-term economic growth, there are certainly differences concerning other dimensions of performance, particularly in terms of the distribution of income; patterns of innovation—whether radical or incremental; and, for some, the relative efficiency with which they use scarce resources (like labor, but also energy and other inputs to production). Hence, for example, Belgian economist André Sapir classifies models of capitalism along the dimensions of efficiency and equity.[2] In Sapir's classification, efficient economic systems are those in which labor markets are flexible and quick, meaning that it is easy both to find a job and to switch from one job to the other, mainly because employment protection legislation is not so strict that it would hinder labor mobility. The opposite holds for inefficient economic systems, where strict employment legislation is the main reason that it is difficult for outsiders to access the labor market and why insiders, in contrast, can preserve their position over time. The contrast here is similar to the one made between liberal economies and coordinated economies, but the emphasis is much more on outcomes than on institutions per se. Sapir defines equity in terms of the distribution of income and the level of poverty in each system. More equitable systems have a more even distribution of income and a low incidence of poverty; less equitable systems have a skewed distribution of income—meaning the rich have much more than anyone else—and a high incidence of poverty.

European countries can be found to illustrate any possible combination of efficiency and equity as Sapir describes those traits. The extremes are easy to identify. The Scandinavian countries score high on both dimensions. They tend to have very high rates of employment, low unemployment, an even distribution of income, and very few people below the poverty line. The Mediterranean countries underperform in terms of both efficiency and equity. Employment is low, unemployment is high, income is unevenly distributed, and many people are poor. The mixed types are also present. For example, the UK is more efficient than equitable. It has relatively high employment and low unemployment, but income is distributed inequitably and many are poor. Meanwhile, the continental countries such as France and Germany are more equitable than efficient. They have equitably distributed income and a low incidence of poverty, but employment rates are low and unemployment is persistently high.

The fact that all these countries participate in the same European Union does not eliminate the importance of the differences between them. On the contrary, given the diversity across European countries, it is hardly surprising that different member states would at times perceive the process of European integration as a threat to their own economic well-being or autonomy. This was not so evident in the early days after World War II when European integration was mainly about the liberalization of trade, an objective that was largely consistent with the preservation of national specificities. However, as the EU progressed to ever deeper levels of economic integration, from the further liberalization of goods, services, capital, and labor movements in the late 1980s to the creation of the EMU in the late 1990s, virtually every country was forced to adapt. Repeated stops and starts in the process of European integration and member state oscillation between the desire for integration and the will to preserve national sovereignty have also had an effect. Hence, the more Europe has grown to resemble the United States as a large integrated economy, the less the European Union has come to resemble anything like the U.S. government. Today the EU is a complex system of governance in which some decisions are sponsored by the EU Commission and then voted by a majority of the member countries, while others are fully initiated by the national governments and voted by unanimity only.

The U.S. versus the European Model and Their Performance

Having worked through the necessary qualifications, it is necessary to admit that the contrast between Europe and the United States nevertheless frames much of the contemporary debate. Indeed, the United States and Europe are often portrayed as the ideal types of an LME (U.S.) and a CME (EU), respectively. The contrast between the two models became especially prominent in the 1980s. The United States was perceived as flourishing under the influence of Reaganomics and, compared to Europe, had freer product markets; American labor markets were weakly regulated, with trade unions having very limited bargaining power; and equity markets were efficient in punishing underperforming firms and rewarding profitable ones. In the same period, in Western European economies, product market regulation was intense and public ownership of enterprises was widespread; labor markets remained very rigid and equity markets were not sufficiently developed; in addition, EU economies were showing signs of fatigue, suffering from significant fiscal imbalances, high interest rates, and accelerating inflation; and welfare states had clearly reached the limits of their expansion and were believed to operate as a constraint on potential growth.

It did not take long for observers to conclude that the Anglo-Saxon model was more successful in terms of macroeconomic performance than the European model. This situation created the myth of a superior model of capitalism, that of the United States, to which the old continental Europe should have aspired. An important contribution to this debate came from the economics profession, where the consensus had shifted from Keynesianism and its strong focus on the role of the state in the economy toward the new orthodoxy and its appreciation of monetary and fiscal discipline as means to liberate resources that had been captured by the state, allowing for the full operation of private markets.

The 1980s were an era in which European economies went through important transformations under different pressures ranging from the example of the successful U.S. economy, to the changed ideational context in which policy decisions were taken, to the parallel strength of autonomous global forces. It is no coincidence that the European project for the full liberalization of trade and the free movement of capital and labor took root in these years. Starting with the late 1980s, European economies entered a period of strong liberalization. Soon after, in the early 1990s, candidates for Europe's EMU had to start preparing for accession into the new single currency. The reform process in the run-up to EMU was extensive for most candidates, with the possible exception of Germany, which had but to deal with the process of reunification that equally required transformation, albeit for a different reason. Especially the Mediterranean countries had to go through a vast macroeconomic stabilization program to bring interest rates, inflation, deficit, and debt down to levels comparable to those of the other EU countries, most notably Germany. The so-called Maastricht fiscal criteria required, for example, that candidate countries' deficit and debt levels not exceed 3 and 60 percent of gross domestic product (GDP), respectively. Such a requirement implied that the large majority of EU countries had to implement massive fiscal consolidation measures, either by raising taxes or by cutting expenditures. It was often not sufficient to opt for one-off tax increases or expenditure restraints, but instead it became necessary to put in place structural measures to reform the welfare state, and the public pension system in particular, so as to make it sustainable over time.

The reform process initiated in the late 1980s and in the run-up to EMU was viewed by many as an effort to impose a more liberal economy. In particular, product market reform and the privatization of numerous state-owned companies enhanced product market competition in all European countries. But any convergence toward a common model of capitalism probably stops there. Notwithstanding the project for the completion of the internal market, progress in the liberalization of the service sector—from insurance and general financial services to the liberal professions, like law, medicine, or architecture—has been much more modest than in the goods sector, held back by the persistence of protectionist national regulations. Labor markets have not reached levels of flexibility comparable to those of the United States. In some cases, employment protection legislation has been softened, but there was no evident movement toward greater decentralization in wage bargaining, which is normally associated with greater wage flexibility. If anything, the trend toward the decentralization of wage bargaining that started in the 1980s in many European countries was reversed. With the emergence of a few social pacts across the EU from 1991 to 1997 (e.g., in Belgium, the Netherlands, Ireland, and Italy), collective wage bargaining became more and more centralized, with trade unions preferring national wages over firm-level negotiations. The reason why centralization in wage bargaining was so popular at the time also had to do with how the process of convergence in preparation for monetary union was organized. The Maastricht Treaty required that EMU candidates fulfill a series of criteria in addition to the fiscal consolidation mentioned earlier in order to qualify for participation in the single currency.

One of the most important of these criteria was the requirement to achieve a moderate rate of price inflation—within 1.5 percent of the three best performers in Europe. By negotiating wages at the national level, trade unions were better able to offer a direct and tangible contribution to controlling inflation while obtaining in return some social benefits or at least the preservation of the status quo. The new social pacts of the 1990s were thus political exchanges between unions and governments, in which the former offered their help to control inflation and the latter limited welfare retrenchment or at least accepted that any labor market reform was collectively discussed.

Europe continued to disappoint expectations in the 1990s and 2000s when compared to the United States in terms of macroeconomic performance, and that despite any putative progress toward American-style liberalization. Just before the onset of the global economic and financial crisis, output per capita was still much higher in the United States than in Europe. Measured in dollars and corrected for relative purchasing power, output per capita was about $30,000 on average in 2007 across the twenty-seven member countries of the European Union (EU-27)—which means including the original member states as well as Central and Eastern European countries—and it was just above $34,000 in Germany. Meanwhile, output per capita was $45,500 in the United States. Remarkable differences stand out also in labor markets. The unemployment rate in EU-27 was 7.1 percent of the active labor population in 2007 and 8.4 percent in Germany, while the corresponding U.S. figure was only 4.6 percent. In the same year, the employment rate in EU-27 was 65.4 percent and 71.8 percent in the United States. Again, even a newly invigorated German labor market—with 69 percent of working-age people holding a job—could not match American performance. Differences in the average participation rate were mostly driven by the modest employment activities of women in Europe, with only 58.3 percent of working-age females having a job in EU-27, against a much higher percentage of 65.9 in the United States.[3]

Differences in macroeconomic outcomes were also evident during the crisis. True, the detonator was the subprime mortgage market in the United States, and North America was the first region to be hit by lower growth and higher unemployment, but the signs of recovery starting in 2010 were more evident there than in Europe. Indeed, much of Europe fell back into recession in 2011 and 2012.

The explanation for this difference in performance across the Atlantic is threefold. First, Europe is still affected by labor market rigidities. Where the crisis forced employers to lay off workers, these are unlikely to find a job in the short term because tight employment protection legislation discourages firms from employing new people in times of uncertainty. They may well remain unemployed for a while, and the long-term unfavorable scenario is that their unused skills will gradually deteriorate or, worse, become obsolete. Second, U.S. businesses were relatively quicker than European ones in declaring their inability to pay back their debt. The so-called process of private deleveraging took place quite early on, acting as a cleansing mechanism through which banks and financial markets could achieve clarity on which firms were worth lending to and which were not. By contrast, slow private deleveraging in Europe together with a greater sense of uncertainty about the future of the European single currency left lending institutions relatively reluctant to make credit available to industry, with the result that high lending spreads on customers acted as a break on investment and overall economic recovery.

A third and accompanying factor that contributed to different rebound dynamics across the Atlantic is the size of the fiscal stimulus packages conceived in reaction to the crisis. The U.S. government injected resources into the system at an amount that was about three times the sum of the fiscal efforts by individual European governments. If the U.S. stimulus package was too timid for many economists, the European version hardly had an impact. At the same time, however, and linked to the relative size of the stimulus packages, the fiscal position of the United States is worse than that of the euro zone taken as a whole. The United States is unlikely to go bankrupt—and some euro-zone countries may well face default—but on average it has gone considerably deeper into debt. Moreover, that difference looks set to widen. The U.S. fiscal deficit is higher than the euro area average, and the U.S. debt is expected to grow more than in Europe over the next twenty years. Against this scenario, it is paradoxical that, in the aftermath of the crisis, Europe has been more explicit about the need to go back to fiscal rigor than the United States.

Overall, it is difficult to establish what accounts for Europe's incapacity to mimic the macroeconomic performance of North America, especially in terms of productivity and hence long-term economic growth. The reform process Europe went through in the late 1980s and 1990s is not yet complete. But, then, should it be? The United States and Europe represent very different models of capitalism, and it is not necessarily true that full liberalization in Europe will succeed in delivering a macroeconomic performance similar to that of the United States. Also, European countries have a much better record in guaranteeing and preserving income equality, and any dramatic reform process risks jeopardizing this dimension of performance. The "The Varieties of Capitalism" section looks specifically at the institutional domains along which varieties of capitalism differ from each other.

The Varieties of Capitalism

The varieties of capitalism (VoC) literature provides indicators for grouping national economies into distinct models of capitalism. There are two ideas behind this literature. First, it is possible to classify economies into distinct varieties with regard to the degree of regulation in product markets, labor markets, welfare regimes, and financial and corporate governance. Second, the institutions of one variety of capitalism are complementary to each other, meaning that one institution works better if the other one is present, or only the two together can lead to efficient economic outcomes. This notion of "institutional complementarity" is at the heart of the VoC approach.

In their book *Varieties of Capitalism*, Peter Hall and David Soskice set out the characteristic features of LMEs and CMEs.[4] Product market competition is pivotal to their distinction between the two ideal types. The core idea is that LMEs mimic the functioning of perfectly competitive markets in which equilibrium outcomes are dictated by relative prices and market signals, as in neoclassical economic models. They are thus characterized by deregulated product and financial markets, flexible labor markets, and systems of corporate governance that encourage firms to pay almost exclusive attention to actual earnings and to the price of their shares. A typical example is that of the UK in Europe or of the United States. By contrast, CMEs are governed by imperfectly competitive markets in which coordination between all the relevant economic agents is of a nonmarket nature. In the CMEs, product and credit markets are highly regulated, labor markets are fairly rigid, and systems of corporate governance are such that companies are not necessarily dependent upon current returns but can rely on patient capital from banks, as in the case of Germany.

Table 10.1 provides a description of the most exploited institutional domains along which varieties of capitalism have been defined and highlights key differences between the two ideal types. The VoC approach is originally an institutional theory of the supply side. Its most original feature is, in fact, the orientation of the firm at the center of the analysis. Firms are socializing agencies, centers of power and institutions that build sanctions and incentives that generate other actions. By exploiting these

Table 10.1   Institutional Features of Liberal Market Economies (LMEs) and Coordinated Market Economies (CMEs)

		LMEs	CMEs
Supply side	*Content of skills*	General	Sector or firm specific
	Level of skills	Low and high	Average and high
	Wage bargaining	Individual (decentralization)	Collective (centralization)
	Labor markets	Low EPL	High EPL
	Financial systems	Market based	Bank based
Demand side	*Macroeconomic regime*	Flexible and discretionary	Rigid and rule based

potentials, they affect a country's macroeconomic performance in important ways. It follows that the institutional domains that have been identified by the literature concern supply conditions in one way or another and include the availability of certain types of skills (i.e., whether general or specific), their cost (i.e., wage levels), outside options (i.e., employment protection legislation), and the availability of credit (i.e., whether coming from banks or equity markets). Only recently has the VoC literature been enriched with an explicit account of the demand side, having incorporated a reference to the fact that LMEs and CMEs also have distinct macroeconomic regimes, as will be explained below.

Labor is a key input to production. The availability and the quality of labor importantly direct production decisions by firms. The VoC literature has been mainly concerned with the contents of the skills of one country's labor force and has distinguished between general and specific skills. The reference framework is Nobel Prize winner Gary Becker's theory of human capital. General skills are portable in the sense that they are useful with other employers. A worker who has general skills can move quite easily from one job to another. Specific skills are not portable and can be used with one employer only. Hall and Soskice further distinguish between firm- and sector-specific assets, where the firm-specific assets are useful in one company only and sector-specific assets are useful across a whole sector. A worker that has long worked in a very specialized firm and has accumulated knowledge of both the products and the organizational structure of that particular firm would find it difficult to move to a different company while being equally productive. Similarly, workers who have been trained to work in the automotive industry can probably use their skills in any company of the same sector but are unlikely to need the same skills should they have to move to the service sector, for example.

The literature associates LMEs with general skills and CMEs with sector- or firm-specific skills. Why would freer markets be associated with general skills, and more regulated ones with specific skills? The impressionistic argument developed by David Soskice, both independently and in collaboration with Peter Hall, is that neither employers nor employees have an incentive to invest in specific nonportable skills in highly competitive product markets, where in fact the firm survival probability is low. Specific training is an investment that employers are unlikely to recoup, while employees would be left unemployed if the firm is indeed pushed out of the market. For the same reason, employers and employees have an incentive to develop firm-specific skills in the presence of tight regulatory regimes. Employers can afford to invest in training because limited competition in product markets implies that they have high chances of remaining in the market, thus having sufficient time to benefit from the returns of their investment. Employees themselves feel protected from highly volatile market dynamics and are guaranteed that they will make use of their skills as long as the firm that employs them is not pushed out of the market. In CMEs, strong vocational training institutions contribute to the supply of firm- or sector-specific skills.

Besides the effect of product market competition on the content of skills, skill levels are also affected. When markets are competitive, as they are in LMEs, the worker's wage equals her productivity so that there is no incentive for employers to invest in skill formation, of whatever type, because workers are still paid proportionally with their skills, and employers do not get a profit from paying workers less than they should.[5] Under these premises, the key investor is the employee only. Whether she obtains high-level skills or not depends on her capacity to pay for it. In turn, two distinct equilibriums can emerge depending on the relative efficiency of credit markets. If workers are credit constrained, they will give up investing in their own education. However, in the presence of efficient loan markets, employees are expected to have a strong interest in funding their own education, considering that their wage rises proportionally with their productivity.[6]

The situation is reversed in CMEs. Product markets are not fully competitive. There are high-to-average entry costs for firms, and employers can exercise power by controlling positions of employment, implying that they are the only ones or among the few that demand labor in the markets. Under these circumstances, the very few employers that are in the market will be able to extract rents out of the employment relationship and to use these rents to support on-the-job training. They do have an interest in doing so, as stronger skills will further increase the size of rents to employers, if wage levels remain unchanged. The end result is the high-skill equilibrium that has been detected, for example, in the case of Germany.[7]

Another important dimension of labor markets is the way wages are determined. Wage bargaining in liberal market economies is decentralized, meaning that wages are negotiated individually by the employee and the employer. This results in high levels of wage flexibility. In the case of a boom, full flexibility means that individual wage earners can easily ask and obtain higher wages since labor is scarce in good times by definition. By the same token, they are also more likely to accept wage cuts in bad times because LMEs tend to be less unionized.

As noted above, an important notion in the VoC literature is that institutions complement one another. For example, wage determination modes are complementary to the existing skill regime. Decentralized wage bargaining is the preferred option in LMEs. Here, as skills tend to be general and their level is determined by the amount of private investment each individual puts into her own education, highly educated workers will be able to arbitrage between different employers to obtain individual wages that maximize returns on their private investment in education. Employers themselves embrace decentralization as a mechanism that allows them to acquire educated employees. In CMEs, by contrast, wages are determined collectively by industrial unions and then are extended to all employees in the same sector or even in the entire economy, as happened in some Scandinavian countries until the 1980s (e.g., Sweden). This form of wage bargaining is called "centralized," meaning that wage formation takes place at the sectoral or even at the national level. Employers in CMEs have a strong interest in centralized wage bargaining because equal wages across the same sector prevent poaching of highly skilled workers by other firms in the same sector. Indeed, a worker with sector-specific skills could move freely from one firm to the other but is unlikely to do so unless she is promised a higher wage. Again, there is an important and visible complementary relationship between wage and skill formation institutions.

An additional feature of labor markets is the level of employment protection legislation—which is to say, the extent to which it is easy to access or exit the labor market. LMEs typically have low levels of employment protection. Easy access to and exit from labor markets imply that job tenure is generally short, with employees moving freely from one job to another. This also enhances the cyclical component of unemployment, meaning that in bad times employers will have no institutional constraint that prevents them from firing unnecessary workers. Unemployment will rise in recession but also fall in good times, when employers are easy about hiring new employees because they can lay them off at any time.

In CMEs, labor markets are highly regulated, and strong employment protection creates a divide between labor market insiders (those who have a permanent job) and outsiders (those who are seeking work or who are employed part-time or in temporary contracts). The insiders are likely to stay where they are, resulting in long job tenure and incentivizing the development of sector- or firm-specific skills. On the other hand, outsiders will find it very difficult to find a permanent place in the labor market and may remain long-term unemployed.

One factor that affects the level and quality of production by firms is access to credit. Financial systems are classified into market-based and bank-based systems.[8] Market-based systems are typical of most LMEs, where companies are financed through equity markets and are thus obliged to keep a firm eye on short-term returns and profitability. Bank-based systems prevail in CMEs. Here, banks have responsibility for mobilizing savings, allocating capital, and monitoring decisions made by corporate managers. Firms in CMEs are thus mainly financed through bank credit, and it is access to patient capital of this kind that allows them to focus on long-term objectives, such as investment in research and development and incremental innovation.

The explicit interest of the VoC literature in macroeconomics and in demand-side conditions started in the early 2000s. In a comprehensive overview of the relationship between varieties of capitalism and aggregate demand management, David Soskice observes that LMEs tend to be characterized by flexible and discretionary macroeconomic regimes, while CMEs are more rigid and mostly rule based.[9]

Monetary and fiscal policies make a macroeconomic regime. They both determine demand conditions in one economic system. Historically, central banks have been responsible for monetary policy, either in association with governments or autonomously (i.e., central bank independence). Practically, this means that central banks set official interest rates for the economy as a whole. By fixing the price of money, they impact on aggregate demand and, more precisely, on two components of aggregate demand, investment in machinery and equipment, which is very much sensitive to interest rate levels and changes, and consumption in all those cases in which consumers need to borrow money in order to buy goods (i.e., credit consumption). This is how monetary policy determines aggregate demand.

The channels through which fiscal policy operates are different, but fiscal policy also conditions aggregate demand. Fiscal policy is a government's responsibility and concerns all the decisions about tax systems and public expenditures. National governments influence the level of disposable income, for example, to the extent that they decide on income taxes. They also determine the spending capacity of specific social groups such as pensioners or the unemployed when they make decisions on how to distribute public resources across spending programs like pensions and unemployment benefits.

Saying that LMEs are characterized by flexible and discretionary macroeconomic regimes is much the same as saying that national monetary and fiscal authorities react flexibly when it comes to offsetting unfavorable cyclical fluctuations and do so with full discretion. The evidence is that, in the case of a recession, the central banks of Anglo-Saxon countries are prompt in reducing interest rates to support investment and (credit) consumption. Similarly, fiscal authorities allow for some deficit spending until the business cycle turns favorable. In CMEs, macroeconomic regimes are instead rigid and are founded on rules rather than discretion. Monetary and fiscal authorities typically refrain from responding to exogenous shocks by using, respectively, monetary or fiscal leverage. Central banks are often independent and are subjected to an inflation-targeting regime. Historically, they have reduced interest rates only moderately and progressively to boost demand in a recession and immediately reacted to inflationary booms by raising interest rates.

Most CMEs also have formal or informal fiscal rules that limit their room to maneuver in the management of business cycles. Successive German governments have been historically devoted to the objective of fiscal discipline, for example. The Merkel government has recently agreed to introduce a constitutional rule that requires the government to achieve a balanced fiscal position over the medium term. The sovereign debt crisis has also forced other EU member states to adopt fiscal rules as a means of strengthening their national fiscal frameworks.

The LMEs and CMEs responded differently to the crisis, and in line with expectations for the two different types of regime. The average fiscal effort over 2009–2010 was 1.7 percent of GDP in Europe, if one takes as a reference the policies of the three largest euro-zone countries, Germany, France, and Italy, but it was a much more generous 4.7 percent of GDP in the United States, confirming that LMEs react more flexibly to poor demand conditions than CMEs do.[10]

EU Economic Governance Structure and Varieties of Capitalism over Time

Throughout the history of European integration, it has been clear that a unified Europe could only be governed by a multiplicity of actors, national (the member state governments) and supranational (the European Commission), state (the Council of Ministers of the EU) and nonstate (the Economic and Social Committee and the ECB). The end result is a complex structure of multilevel governance in which hard and soft forms of power are shared among EU institutions, national governments, parliaments, regions, and social partners. At present, all of these actors are involved in one way or another in the legislative process at the EU level. The standard procedure, known as the "Community" method, prescribes that the supranational EU Commission initiates a piece of legislation. This then is passed on to the Council of Ministers, which gathers all the national ministers of the EU member states and is asked to vote on the proposal by majority voting and in co-decision with the European Parliament. In most instances, the Economic and Social Committee and the Committee of the Regions are consulted in the process but do not have veto power.

While the Community method is the standard procedure, it is not the only one. Moreover, the Community method applies only to specific policy sectors, most notably all the regulations concerning the main aspects of the single European market and the liberalization of product markets in Europe. In other policy areas, however, the Council of Ministers becomes de facto the only body with decision-making powers, the EU Commission plays no role, and the European Parliament is merely consulted. This is notably the case when at stake are discussions regarding the Common Foreign and Security Policy (CFSP) and Justice and Home Affairs (JHA). The euro-zone crisis forced the EU to conceive of alternative intermediate forms of decision making. Starting in particular with the euro-area debt crisis of 2010 following the 2007 financial crisis, national governments occupied the driving seat under the coordination of Herman Van Rompuy, president of the European Council, an institution responsible for setting the EU's political agenda and priorities, whose existence was formalized by the Lisbon Treaty of 2009. As a matter of fact, the decisions to provide financial assistance to crisis countries were inevitably political and needed to be taken over short periods of time. Against this background, the Community method failed to be a viable option.

The main reason for the complex multilevel governance that is now in place is that, over time, national governments have been differently inclined to devolve portions of national sovereignty so that the current governance architecture is the result of successive stratifications of decisions taken by governments with different attitudes toward European integration. The EU moved from relatively soft forms of economic integration in the postwar period to ever deeper ones, culminating in the adoption of the single currency in 1999. Initially the process of economic integration posed little challenge to national models of capitalism, but over time the EU has become progressively more intrusive, forcing governments to adjust their ways of organizing the national market economy to the new EU rules.

When the heads of government and state gathered to discuss European integration at the end of World War II, the strong message that came through and that seemed to be acceptable to most of them was that full political integration of Europe would have been too ambitious for a start, but economic integration—mainly through the removal of barriers to trade—would serve the same purpose if the desire for further integration spilled over to other policy areas and levels. So, in the early days from the Treaty of Rome (1957) to the actual completion of the common market (1968), the members of the European Economic Community (EEC) accepted the abolition of tariffs, quotas, and other tangible barriers to trade as the first step toward a future common political union. The process at the time foresaw the creation of a customs union, which implied the abolition of internal barriers to trade but also the adoption of a common external tariff vis-à-vis third countries that the EEC would trade with. This was as far as the loss of sovereignty was going, and it explains, for example, the initial refusal by the United Kingdom to take part in the foundation of the EEC due to the fear that it would in fact lose preferential trade agreements with Commonwealth countries.

The six founding member states, Germany, France, Italy, Belgium, the Netherlands, and Luxembourg, in fact did not perceive the project as a threat to their national authority. Stronger international competition following the elimination of barriers to trade supported industrial exports and, indirectly, the growth of national economies. This form of European integration is what theorists call "negative integration," which consists of the elimination of existing obstacles to integration but does not require large adjustment efforts from within, let alone the devolution of key policy competences and the creation of new institutions.

Still, the convergence of national interests and European integration was only a fortunate coincidence and thus was deemed to be short lived. The 1970s marked a weakening of integrationist forces in the midst of the collapse of the Bretton Woods system and the two successive oil shocks. The Bretton Woods system was a mechanism for allowing international payments by making international currencies convertible with each other. It implied that national governments and central banks in Europe had to make monetary policy decisions with an eye to the impact that changes in money supply would exercise on the declared parity between the national currency and other European currencies. It became unsustainable at a time when national economic interests started diverging and the first oil shock shifted policy priorities away from the preservation of the exchange rate parity toward the fight against inflation and poor growth, albeit with diversified priorities from one member state to the other because some of them were concerned with inflation and some others with poor growth.

The creation of the European Monetary System (EMS) in 1979 relaunched the European project. The EMS was meant to replace the collapsed Bretton Woods system. It was a currency regime in which bilateral parities were fixed between European currencies. Exchange rates were thus fixed, but they were adjustable. Participation in the EMS implied some loss of control over monetary policy because any change in the official interest rate by national central banks also had to serve the purpose of respecting the parity declared within the EMS agreement, but the fact that the fixed exchange rate could actually be changed under some circumstances gave national governments the impression that autonomy in monetary policymaking could have been taken back at any time.

Starting in the 1980s, it became evident that any progress in European integration would have forced individual member states to devolve portions of their national sovereignty and to adapt their distinct models of capitalism to ever-developing new challenges. This was a time in which economic integration stopped being an instrument and started being considered an end in itself, not least because full political integration was not a realistic target anymore. Projects such as the completion of the European internal market and EMU in the 1990s fall under this category. They both represent examples of what theorists call "positive integration." Neither project was about the elimination of existing constraints on integration. Instead, they required the devolution of sovereignty in the areas of product market regulation and monetary policy, respectively, and they culminated, in the case of monetary union, in the creation of the new independent European Central Bank. They nonetheless came about without an explicit discussion about political union, a topic around which the EU continued to act in a benign-neglect mode.

The project launched in 1985 to complete the internal market thus marked a structural break from the past. It extended liberalization to nontariff barriers to trade in goods and services and devised measures to allow the free movement of capital and people. It was more than just eliminating taxes on imports, which had been the very first objective of the EEC. By imposing stronger competition on product markets and by improving the efficiency of European financial markets through capital mobility, the internal market required that changes be made to the national organization of production. Producers in the export-oriented sectors were forced to cut profit margins to preserve market shares. It required changing national regulatory frameworks and recognizing other member states' regulations, for example, in the area of technical standards. In this respect, the completion of the internal market implied a deeper level of economic integration than was ever achieved with the customs union of the 1960s.

At the same time, the internal market project granted the European Commission exclusive responsibility over competition policy, meaning that it is now the responsibility of that institution to monitor the functioning of the internal market and make sure that the European market does not suffer from anticompetitive practices, whether these take the form of state aid, international mergers that generate dominant positions, cartels, or monopolies. In the area of finance, consumers and investors in Germany, Austria, and France continued to use bank credit more than any other financing tool (such as equities and bonds), but capital markets certainly did gain greater importance, also increasing managers' sensitivity to short-term returns and performances. As a result, all European countries were under much less regulation on financial markets than in the past, a development that to some extent brought typical CMEs such as Germany much closer to the Anglo-Saxon financial model.

The monetary union, whose operations started officially in 1999, represented the final step toward the completion of the internal market and full economic integration. Not only can goods, services, capital, and people currently move freely within the internal market, but also a common currency further facilitates trade and free movement by allowing cost and price comparability. Seen this way, EMU is about the supply side, much like the completion of the internal market. It fosters the mobility of production inputs and promotes the fight against anticompetitive practices. Its impact falls largely on producers and the conditions under which they operate, whether these concern the cost of their inputs or the factors they need to take into account when determining output prices (such as the role of competitors). But the supply side is only one dimension of EMU; more precisely, it is the microeconomic dimension of EMU. In fact, the most revolutionary change that came about with the introduction of the euro concerns the demand side: EMU indeed represents a new macroeconomic regime for Europe.

Monetary unification involved more than just the creation of a single European currency. It also depended on fiscal policy coordination between the member states through a collection of rules and procedures called the "Stability and Growth Pact" (SGP). As part of this pact, euro-zone member states have accepted limits on the conduct of their fiscal policies by committing not to run budget deficits greater than 3 percent of GDP or to maintain public debts greater than 60 percent of GDP. Thus, in the case of fiscal policy, national governments continue to be responsible for qualitative decisions on tax systems and welfare spending, but they are constrained in their aggregate figures. Such coordination challenges the organization of individual forms of capitalism to a much greater extent than previous forms of European integration.

Monetary policy is now an exclusive competence of the European Central Bank. The common central bank is in charge of setting official interest rates for the monetary union as a whole and is fully independent in the exercise of this policy function. The ECB operates in a so-called inflation targeting regime. This means that it has committed to an average inflation of 2 percent and manages monetary policy, in full independence from the member states, with the final objective of preserving price stability. So, in boom periods, when prices start growing excessively under demand pressures until they risk overshooting the formal inflation target, the ECB would intervene by increasing interest rates. In periods of recession, the common central bank would do the opposite, but with caution. During the crisis, for example, the ECB reacted much later than the U.S. Federal Reserve did to lower interest rates.

Overall, EMU is a relatively rigid macroeconomic regime with an unaccommodating central bank and a relatively strong emphasis on fiscal rigor that largely resembles the German macroeconomic regime before the introduction of the single currency. The success of this new regime has been mixed. The introduction of a single currency for such a vast and diverse regional area is by all means a political success; in practice, EMU was also able to deliver price stability and some convergence in real growth. Yet two important challenges remain and would have been visible even if the crisis had not happened. First, the monetary union remains politically incomplete; economic policy coordination through the SGP, for example, is promoted and supported by strong institutions and rules, but policy preferences vary from one country to the other not least because each country represents its own special variety of capitalism. The divergence is at times fundamental in that key member states may even have a different perception of what economic policy coordination is about and what purpose it should serve.[11] Second, the ECB is conducting a single monetary policy for a group of seventeen different countries. It is not an easy task when the member states find themselves in different positions in the business cycle. By way of example, countries in deep recession would need a lower interest rate than countries that are not in recession, as low interest rates would help stimulate demand for consumption and investment. By contrast, they risk producing inflation where economic growth is already sustained. If euro-zone member countries find themselves in relatively different business cycle positions, as has happened over the last few years and indeed even before the inception of the euro-area debt crisis, then the ECB cannot be optimal for each of them.

But economic policy coordination in Europe is not only about the demand side. It can also concern structural reform on the supply side. The need to combine the creation of the new aggregate demand management regime of EMU with supply-side measures had emerged already in the 1990s. At the time, EMU candidates were preparing for access into the monetary union with draconian measures that aimed to control inflation and cut public deficits and debts. There was a risk that the rigid and severe macroeconomic regime that was coming into place was detrimental to growth. Fiscal consolidation in particular required candidate countries to either increase fiscal pressure to improve budget positions, to cut spending, or both. In this climate, the attention of EU institutions shifted to the need to counterbalance possible negative growth effects with measures that, on the supply side, would support employment creation. The renewed interest in the supply side took the form of the so-called Lisbon strategy, a policy initiative launched in 2000 whose primary objective was to make of Europe "the most competitive and dynamic knowledge-based economy in the world capable of sustainable economic growth with more and better jobs and greater social cohesion" by 2010.[12] At the time, the focus was on the need to promote spending in research and development and to support innovation, skill formation, and education. The Lisbon strategy disappointed expectations and was relaunched in 2005 with the more clearly defined objective of achieving "more and better jobs."

The governance of such initiatives is different from the type of policy coordination the Stability Pact imposes. Policy guidance by the EU is not mandatory, legally speaking; failure by the member states to follow recommendations is not punishable with fines, even if that possibility in the case of the SGP remains on paper more than anything else. By contrast, the EU uses supply-side policy recommendations to exercise moral suasion and push through structural reforms that are deemed necessary to improve each country's growth potential and in turn that of the euro zone as a whole. While the very first Lisbon Strategy may have failed because it was not sufficiently focused, doubt remains that little effectiveness is related to the fact that the recommendations are nonbinding.

Moreover, it is difficult to say whether the streamlining of objectives under the 2005 Lisbon Strategy had a positive outcome, as success was eventually compromised by the outbreak of the financial and economic crisis in 2007. In 2010, Europe's leaders replaced the Lisbon Strategy with "EU2020," which is a policy initiative that places greater emphasis on human capital accumulation, skills and long-term sustainability of public finances, and less emphasis on technology and innovation. The Brussels European Council summit conclusion of June 17, 2010, indicates that "the new strategy responds to the challenges of reorienting policies away from crisis management towards the introduction of medium-term to longer term reforms that promote growth and employment and ensure the sustainability of public finances, *inter alia* through the reform of pension systems."[13] EU2020 imposes new headline targets regarding employment, the conditions for innovation, research and development, climate change and energy objectives, education and social inclusion, and poverty. As for the governance of the new strategy, there is a much stronger emphasis on national ownership of the reform process compared to in the past, and extraordinary weight is given to the long-term national reform plans that each EU member state is obliged to submit to EU institutions.

The European Commission is explicit about the fact that member states must implement these policy priorities at the national level. They should, in close dialogue with the Commission, finalize their national targets, taking account of their relative starting positions and national circumstances, and according to their national decision-making procedures. They should also identify the main bottlenecks to growth and indicate, in their National Reform Programs, how they intend to tackle them. Progress toward the headline targets is regularly reviewed and, following the crisis, monitoring by the EU is taking place within a more integrated framework.[14]

The Crisis and the Reform of EU Economic Governance

European integration is an ambitious project, with important political and economic elements to it. Still, no one can deny that the economic dimension has prevailed at many points in time, either as the primary instrument for integration or as the final objective of an integrationist project, or as the signal of profound weaknesses in the governance structure of the EU and an expedient for rethinking the EU architecture, as demonstrated in the financial and economic crisis of 2007. Indeed, the crisis further strengthened the perception that the EU is primarily an economic project that is both fragile and resilient at the same time. On the one hand, the economic and the ensuing sovereign debt crisis revealed a number of shortcomings such as the failure of fiscal surveillance; the limitations of having banking systems that are fragmented along national lines, with domestic authorities retaining the final word over financial supervision; the lack of attention devoted to other macroeconomic imbalances (such as private sector debt); and the absence of any previously defined crisis management system. On the other hand, however, the political response was prompt—all considered—and some of the reform proposals were sufficiently innovative to calm financial markets for some time, even if the response was mainly reactive in addressing the different problems that emerged over the period 2010–2013.

The financial and debt crisis unveiled weaknesses in the structure of European economic governance beyond the lack of a political union and the difficulty of managing monetary policy for a group of countries finding themselves in relatively different cyclical positions, both of which had been previously recognized. Chapter 11 surveys the crisis. For the present argument, four things are important to note.

First, the SGP requires fiscal policy coordination across the monetary union in the sense that all member states need to have similarly low deficit levels. Nevertheless, the effectiveness of fiscal surveillance and its enforcement are not always guaranteed. The Greek case shows how public budgets can easily go out of order even in the presence of a formally binding commitment such as the SGP. Greece accumulated excessive deficits and debts over a long period of time, and its fiscal problems well preceded the economic crisis. In the European scenario, it represents a special case, one of weak budget institutions and maybe of technical incompetence. Still, the existing SGP was insufficient to induce successive reforms. As the crisis dragged on, financial markets began to worry about the prospect of a Greek default. They also began to consider whether other economies were on shaky foundations. The costs of servicing public debt also rose for Spain, Portugal, and Ireland, even if they did not have the same severe fiscal problems that Greece had.

Second, cases like Spain and Ireland show how quickly fiscal positions can deteriorate, even starting from apparently sound footing, once the government is obliged to step in either to support the national economy in recession or, more specifically, to rescue the financial sector. This is proof of tight interlinkages between banks and sovereigns. Banking supervision after 1999 remained in the hands of national authorities. This implied that each national authority could make a discretionary assessment of the health and resilience of the national banking system, but also that governments were bearing the costs of bank failures in the attempt to limit damage to the credit system and the domestic real economy as a whole. Against this background, the euro debt crisis posed an additional strain on domestic banks holding own government bonds in their coffers because rising yields would reduce the value of the financial assets that banks held. Observers have thus often referred to a negative feedback loop between banks and sovereigns.

Third, the EU had been playing little attention to imbalances other than fiscal ones until the crisis broke out in 2007. Spain, for example, did not have the same severe fiscal problems that Greece had. However, the country had been accumulating high private debts over the previous decade. Both consumption and investment were buoyant, but national savings were not sufficient to finance them. They were eventually financed by foreigners in the form of capital inflows, which turned into a growing current account deficit—low saving equals, in fact, high consumption and thus a strong demand for imports. Market participants generally feared that the Spanish government would intervene to rescue debtors, thus transforming large private liabilities into public ones. This explains why confidence on financial markets was low for Spain as it was, albeit with differences in magnitudes, for Greece in spite of the fact that Spain was more fiscally prudent than Greece. Whereas surveillance on fiscal positions was weak in EMU, surveillance on private sector imbalances was completely missing.[15]

Fourth, the crisis caught Europe by surprise in that no crisis management mechanism was put in place when EMU started. It was not carelessness, but there was the firm belief that countries sharing the same currency would not be subject to balance-of-payment crises. These types of crisis have been frequent in the postwar regime of fixed exchange rates under Bretton Woods. They normally occur when a speculative attack on a country, whatever the motivation for it, increases doubts about the country's capacity to stick to the declared exchange rate parity, generating massive capital outflows and thus forcing a collapse of the fixed exchange rate system. Such a scenario was well anticipated at the 1944 Bretton Woods conference, when the International Monetary Fund (IMF) was indeed created with the aim of providing financial support to the participant countries that would be subject to this type of shock.

The possibility that euro-area countries would suffer from financial shocks of this sort did not receive much attention. Balance-of-payment crises are associated with fixed but adjustable exchange rate regimes and not monetary union. Hence the architects of the euro believed a single currency would preempt the possibility of balance-of-payment crises in the euro zone. And yet, with capital moving freely in the EU since 1990 following the completion of the single market, countries in the periphery of Europe that seemed at risk of default were soon subject to massive capital outflows. In turn, rising government bond yields made it prohibitive for them to finance maturing public debt on the market and, in the extreme case of Greece, the financial market was simply not an available creditor. As Chapter 11 explains in greater detail, the minute that market access was cut off for Greece, Ireland, and Portugal and the public debt had to be refinanced, the EU was induced to intervene by providing financial assistance to these countries in the extreme attempt to avoid default.

The response of the EU to the fundamental weaknesses in the architecture of the single currency and to the need for additional financial assistance materialized relatively promptly. The March European Council in 2010 oversaw the creation of the "Van Rompuy Task Force" with the responsibility of producing recommendations to enhance governance. In May 2010, the EU Commission conceived a series of proposals to strengthen surveillance on fiscal positions as well as to extend it to other macroeconomic imbalances, such as high levels of private debt and large trade deficits, a proposal later endorsed by the European Council in June. In September 2010, the EU Commission officially published a set of recommendations to tackle weaknesses in EMU economic governance. The Commission proposed to strengthen the Stability and Growth Pact by encouraging euro-zone members to maintain fiscal discipline in good times, creating buffers that would be useful in bad times. The proposal makes the Stability and Growth Pact even more stringent by tightening the constraints on the debt level, which should not exceed 60 percent of GDP, and by strengthening the application of sanctions in the case of noncompliance.

More needs to be done at the national level too. Not all member states have efficient national fiscal frameworks. Not all of them have a practice of medium- to long-term financial planning; many of them still concede to parliament's extensive amendment powers on government budget proposals, which inevitably end up altering the aggregates of public finance. Moreover, for private sector imbalances, the EU Commission proposes a strict monitoring exercise of countries' current accounts, competitiveness developments, and financial sector indicators as a means of controlling the buildup of macroeconomic imbalances other than fiscal ones. Where these imbalances have been identified but not corrected, the EU foresees a system of sanctions similar to that of the SGP.[16] The final text of the proposals was eventually approved with some amendments put forward by the European Parliament in December 2011 under the name of "six-pack," as it consists in fact of six new pieces of law.

One additional overarching reform that was adopted in reaction to the crisis was the so-called European Semester. This aims at enhanced economic policy coordination across countries and is a monitoring exercise by the EU, in which finance ministers of the EU would meet to anticipate the main contents of their budget law proposals and structural reform plans every spring. A successive piece of law adopted in early 2013 under the name of "two-pack" requires that countries that have excessive fiscal deficits submit their budget laws to the EU also a later stage in the fall when the legislation is going through national parliaments as a way of reinforcing scrutiny by EU institutions close to the actual adoption of reforms.

As to crisis management, the idea of some euro area countries providing assistance to others was institutionalized after the ad hoc packages initially offered to Greece, Ireland, and Portugal. The new European Stabilization Mechanism (ESM) that was finally adopted in September 2012 is a permanent crisis management and resolution system with a maximum lending capacity of €500 billion. The ESM, which mimics to a large extent the IMF, provides assistance to countries that apply for it either to refinance public debt or with the purpose of recapitalizing domestic banks in distress. Loans through the ESM include conditionality because recipient countries need to submit to a detailed program of reforms in exchange for assistance.[17] Moreover, assistance is open only to euro-area countries that have ratified the Treaty on Stability, Coordination and Governance (TSCG), often referred to as the Fiscal Compact. The TSCG is an intergovernmental treaty that came into force on January 1, 2013, through which member states commit to fiscal discipline in a credible way by including into their constitutions or similar laws a balanced budget rule. The Treaty was agreed to reinforce the six-pack against the principle that reforms are successful only if "nationally owned."

Finally, at a later stage, the EU Commission put forward a proposal to further integrate banking systems through the creation of a European banking union. The project aims to put a halt to the negative feedback loop between banks and sovereigns that made the euro debt crisis a financial crisis, as explained above, contributing to the credit crunch and the disappointing pace of economic recovery. The idea of a banking union, which continues to raise some opposition in its full form, consists of taking responsibility for financial supervision away from national central banks and financial authorities in favor of the ECB through the creation of a Single Supervisory Mechanism (SSM), providing for a common deposit insurance so that there is no risk of discrimination across bank deposits in different countries, and creating a common resolution fund that would be used to rescue banks at risk of default in any euro-zone country.

The European Council under the Presidency of Herman Van Rompuy officially presented in December 2012 a roadmap for completing EMU under the suggestive title "Towards a Genuine Economic and Monetary Union" that provides for a detailed description and sequencing of the reforms that are still necessary to improve the functioning of the monetary union. It contains references to the reinforced fiscal framework—through the six-pack, the Fiscal Compact, and the two-pack—and further stronger economic policy coordination under the European Semester, the banking union, and, possibly, some form of fiscal union made by a common EU budget that allows for fiscal resources to be transferred to countries going through financial difficulties (see box 10.1).

But whatever shape of EU economic governance at the end of this long reform process, there is no reason to believe that the resulting EU will be different from the complex multilevel governance that characterizes it at present, mainly because there is no appetite for any change that would move Europe toward a closer political union.

Box 10.1   Toward a Genuine Economic and Monetary Union, December 5, 2012

Overview of Sequencing

The process could rest on the following three stages:

Stage 1 (End 2012–2013): Ensuring Fiscal Sustainability and Breaking the Link between Banks and Sovereigns

The completion of the first stage should ensure sound management of public finances and break the link between banks and sovereigns, which has been one of the root causes of the sovereign debt crisis. This stage would include five essential elements:

- The completion and thorough implementation of a stronger framework for fiscal governance (Six-Pack; Treaty on Stability, Coordination and Governance; and Two-Pack).
- Establishment of a framework for systematic *ex ante* coordination of major economic policy reforms, as envisaged in Article 11 of the Treaty on Stability, Coordination and Governance (TSCG).
- The establishment of an effective Single Supervisory Mechanism (SSM) for the banking sector and the entry into force of the Capital Requirements Regulation and Directive (CRR/CRDIV).
- Agreement on the harmonization of national resolution and deposit guarantee frameworks, ensuring appropriate funding from the financial industry.
- Setting up of the operational framework for direct bank recapitalization through the European Stability Mechanism (ESM).

Stage 2 (2013–2014): Completing the Integrated Financial Framework and Promoting Sound Structural Policies

This stage would consist of two essential elements:

- The completion of an integrated financial framework through the setting up of a common resolution authority and an appropriate backstop to ensure that bank resolution decisions are taken swiftly, impartially, and in the best interest of all.
- The setting up of a mechanism for stronger coordination, convergence, and enforcement of structural policies based on arrangements of a contractual nature between member states and EU institutions on the policies that countries commit to undertake and on their implementation. On a case-by-case basis, they could be supported with temporary, targeted, and flexible financial support. As this financial support would be temporary in nature, it should be treated separately from the multiannual financial framework.

Stage 3 (Post 2014): Improving the Resilience of EMU through the Creation
of a Shock Absorption Function at the Central Level

This stage would mark the culmination of the process. Stage 3 would consist of the following:

- Establishing a well-defined and limited fiscal capacity to improve the absorption of country-specific economic shocks, through an insurance system set up at the central level. This would improve the resilience of the euro area as a whole and would complement the contractual arrangements developed under Stage 2. A built-in incentives-based system would encourage euro-area member states eligible for participation in the shock absorption function to continue to pursue sound fiscal and structural policies in accordance with their contractual obligations. Thereby, the two objectives of asymmetric shock absorption and the promotion of sound economic policies would remain intrinsically linked, complementary, and mutually reinforcing.
- This stage could also build on an increasing degree of common decision making on national budgets and an enhanced coordination of economic policies, in particular in the fields of taxation and employment, building on the member states' National Job Plans. More generally, as the EMU evolves toward deeper integration, a number of other important issues will need to be further examined. In this respect, this report and the Commission's "Blueprint" offer a basis for debate.

Notes

1. See Peter A. Hall and David Soskice, eds., *Varieties of Capitalism: the Institutional Foundations of Comparative Advantage* (Oxford: Oxford University Press, 2001).

2. See Andre Sapir, "Globalization and the Reform of European Social Models," *Journal of Common Market Studies* 44, no. 2 (1996): 369–90.

3. Unless otherwise stated, the data are taken from the OECD *Factbook*, which is available online at http://www.oecd.org.

4. Hall and Soskice, *Varieties of Capitalism*.

5. See Daron Acemoglu and Jorn Steffen Pischke, "Beyond Becker: Training in Imperfect Labor Markets," *Economic Policy* 109 (1999): 112–42.

6. See Benedicta Marzinotto, "Assessing Complementarities between Product and Labor Markets," paper presented at the SASE Annual Conference, Paris, mimeo, 2009.

7. See Pepper D. Culpepper, "The Future of the High-Skill Equilibrium in Germany," *Oxford Review of Economic Policy* 15 (1999): 43–59.

8. Franklin Allen and Douglas Gale, *Comparing Financial Systems* (Cambridge, MA: MIT Press, 2000).

9. See David Soskice, "Macroeconomics and Varieties of Capitalism," in *Beyond Varieties of Capitalism*, ed. R. Hanckè (Oxford: Oxford University Press, 2007), 86–125.

10. These data are taken from International Monetary Fund, "Fiscal Monitor: Navigating the Fiscal Challenges Ahead," May 14 (Washington, DC: International Monetary Fund, 2010), 54–55.

11. See Jean Pisani-Ferry, "Only One Bed for Two Dreams: A Critical Retrospective on the Debate over the Economic Governance of the Euro Area," *Journal of Common Market Studies* 44, no. 4 (2006): 823–44.

12. See Lisbon European Council Presidency Conclusions, March 23 and 24, 2000. The full text of the European Council Conclusions can be downloaded from http://www.consilium .europa.eu/uedocs/cms_data/docs/pressdata/en/ec/115346.pdf (accessed January 17, 2014).

13. The full text of the European Council Conclusions can be downloaded from http:// www.consilium.europa.eu/uedocs/cms_data/docs/pressdata/en/ec/115346.pdf (accessed January 17, 2014).

14. The full text of the European Council Conclusions can be downloaded from http:// www.consilium.europa.eu/uedocs/cms_data/docs/pressdata/en/ec/115346.pdf (accessed January 17, 2014).

15. For an early discussion of the different facets of the crisis in Europe, see Benedicta Marzinotto, Jean Pisani-Ferry, and Andre Sapir, "Two Crises, Two Responses," *Bruegel Policy Brief*, March 2010. http://www.bruegel.org/publications/publication-detail/publication/392 -two-crises-two-responses/ (accessed January 18, 2014).

16. See Carlo Altomonte and Benedicta Marzinotto, "Monitoring Macroeconomic Imbalances: Proposal for a Refined Analytical Framework" (Brussels: Monetary and Economic Affairs Committee, European Parliament, 2010).

17. See Benedicta Marzinotto, André Sapir, and Guntram Wolff, "What Kind of Fiscal Union?" *Bruegel Policy Brief*, November 2011. http://www.bruegel.org/publications/publication -detail/publication/646-what-kind-of-fiscal-union/ (accessed January 18, 2014).

Suggested Readings

Acemoglu, Daron, and Jorn Steffen Pischke. "Beyond Becker: Training in Imperfect Labor Markets." *Economic Policy* 109 (1999): 112–42.

Allen, Franklin, and Douglas Gale. *Comparing Financial Systems*. Cambridge, MA: MIT Press, 2000.

Altomonte, Carlo, and Benedicta Marzinotto. "Monitoring Macroeconomic Imbalances: Proposal for a Refined Analytical Framework." Brussels: Monetary and Economic Affairs Committee, European Parliament, 2010.

Culpepper, Pepper D. "The Future of the High-Skill Equilibrium in Germany." *Oxford Review of Economic Policy* 15 (1999): 43–59.

Hall, Peter A., and David Soskice, eds. *Varieties of Capitalism: The Institutional Foundations of Comparative Advantage*. Oxford: Oxford University Press, 2001.

International Monetary Fund. "Fiscal Monitor: Navigating the Fiscal Challenges Ahead." May 14. Washington, DC: International Monetary Fund, 2010.

Marzinotto, Benedicta, Jean Pisani-Ferry, and André Sapir. "Two Crises, Two Responses." *Bruegel Policy Brief*, March 2010. http://www.bruegel.org/publications/publication-detail/ publication/392-two-crises-two-responses/ (accessed January 18, 2014).

Marzinotto, Benedicta, André Sapir, and Guntram Wolff, "What Kind of Fiscal Union?" *Bruegel Policy Brief*, November 2011. http://www.bruegel.org/publications/publication-detail/ publication/646-what-kind-of-fiscal-union/ (accessed January 18, 2014).

Pisani-Ferry, Jean. "Only One Bed for Two Dreams: A Critical Retrospective on the Debate over the Economic Governance of the Euro Area." *Journal of Common Market Studies* 44, no. 4 (2006): 823–44.

Sapir, André. "Globalization and the Reform of European Social Models." *Journal of Common Market Studies* 44, no. 2 (2006): 369–90.

Soskice, David. "Macroeconomics and Varieties of Capitalism." In *Beyond Varieties of Capitalism*, ed. R. Hanckè. Oxford: Oxford University Press, 2007, pp. 86–125.

CHAPTER 11

Europe and the Global Economic Crisis

Erik Jones and Gregory W. Fuller

On February 24–25, 2013, Italian voters went to the polls to register strong disapproval of their government's navigation of Europe's troubled economic waters. Outgoing Prime Minister Mario Monti, the unelected technocrat favored by both Brussels and Berlin for his commitment to putting Italy's public finances back in order, barely garnered 10 percent of the vote in the Chamber of Deputies. Comedian Beppe Grillo's Five Star Movement—which had openly spoken of the possibility of leaving the euro zone—emerged as the single largest party in the new parliament with over a quarter of the vote. Silvio Berlusconi's increasingly Euro-skeptic rightist bloc took nearly 30 percent. The election made two things abundantly clear: first, it demonstrated that Italy had become nearly ungovernable, with three ideologically opposed blocs all polling around 25–30 percent. Second, it was further proof that public commitment to the austerity measures seen as necessary in northern European capitals was weakening, generating uncertainty across Europe.

The purpose of this chapter is to explain how the EU got into such a dire situation—one that many have described as the most important challenge yet to the stability of the single European currency. In this sense, the chapter is a narrative companion to the more analytic treatment of the interaction between varieties of capitalism offered in Chapter 10. The story is broken into eight sections that proceed more or less chronologically. The first looks at how the crisis began with concern over Greek public indebtedness. The second then explains how the problem at the core of the Greek crisis—unbalanced capital flows across the euro zone—was much bigger than just Greece. The third sketches Europe's halting attempts to address the situation in Greece before it metastasized into something bigger, while the fourth section describes how these efforts failed, with the crisis jumping to Ireland and then Portugal. The fifth section turns to an analysis of why stopping the crisis in its earlier phases had proven so hard, focusing on the political opposition to solutions in both creditor and debtor countries. The sixth section picks the story of contagion back up, narrating how financial markets punished European policymakers' enduring paralysis, particularly threatening the stability of large euro-zone economies in Spain and Italy. The seventh section presents a somewhat pessimistic assessment of Europe's efforts to ensure that the present crisis never repeats itself. The conclusion suggests that the immediate threat of crisis has passed and yet European leaders still have much to do.

Greek Public Finances

For much of the world, the crisis in European sovereign debt markets traces back to the Greek national parliamentary elections that were held on October 4, 2009. The elections were called early due to a combination of social unrest and corruption scandals—the previous elections were held only in 2007—and they were fought primarily along economic lines. The incumbent New Democracy (ND) party sought a mandate for austerity. Although the government reported only a relatively modest fiscal deficit—estimated at 3.7 percent of gross domestic product (GDP) for 2009—the party leadership was well aware of the need to rebalance government finances in light of the global economic downturn. The opposition Pan-Hellenic Socialist (Pasok) Party took the opposite view and campaigned on a platform of increased government spending to restart the economy. Given these alternatives, the voters opted for a Keynesian-style reflation; ND's vote share fell by more than 8.3 percentage points, Pasok's increased by 5.8 percentage points, and Pasok leader George Papandreou was allowed to form the government with control of over 160 out of 300 seats.[1]

Almost immediately following the elections, however, it became clear that Greece's financial situation was far worse than it had been portrayed during the campaign. On October 21, the newly formed government informed the euro zone's statistical agency, Eurostat, that their 2008 deficit had been 7.7 percent of GDP (instead of 5 percent)[2] and that their 2009 estimate was being revised from 3.7 percent up to 12.5 percent—a figure that would eventually climb to 15.4 percent.[3] Moreover, most of this difference was due to a misreporting of the fiscal data rather than a mistaken estimation of the underlying GDP. When Eurostat announced this to the financial community the following day, it included a footnote in the press release signaling its reservations "due to significant uncertainties over the figures notified by Greek statistical authorities."[4]

The new Pasok government may have hoped that the announcement would demonstrate that it had more integrity than its predecessor; instead, what it underscored was the scope of the country's statistical and fiscal mismanagement. With each successive news story, confidence in Greek self-reported data diminished and concern about the country's "true" fiscal situation grew. German chancellor Angela Merkel emerged from the December 2009 European Council meeting making it clear that assistance for Greece was not on the table. Instead, she insisted, the Greek government would have to accept its responsibility for making sweeping structural reforms.[5] Within days, Papandreou announced a host of austerity-minded reforms on December 14, but markets failed to react positively, jumping more than six-tenths of 1 percent (64 basis points) in the span of a week. In short, the markets had very little faith in Greece's ability to help itself.[6]

That Greece had misstated its financial data was something akin to the "shocked, *shocked*" moment in the classic Humphrey Bogart film *Casablanca*: Greece has a long history of poor accounting practices dating back at least to the mid-1990s, if not earlier. Eurostat has always had difficulties getting reliable data from the Greek government, and it was an ND government that first conducted a major restatement of public accounts in

2004.[7] Well before Pasok won the October elections, the International Monetary Fund (IMF) published the results of its annual Article IV consultations—which made it very clear not only that "Greece needs a coherent fiscal adjustment path, based on durable measures," but also that "staff is concerned that large and growing data discrepancies ... could harbor a worse underlying deficit than currently reported."[8] All Pasok did with its data revision was underscore that such IMF concerns were justified.

However, if Greece had always been so untrustworthy, the movement of Greek interest rates becomes something of a puzzle. European bond traders hoped that participation in the euro zone would create both the opportunity and the incentive for Greece to get its fiscal house in order—a hope that compressed the difference between Greek and German bond yields to less than 50 basis points, or half of 1 percent, from early 2003 until March 2008.[9] Amid the financial crisis, the spread between German and Greek bonds peaked at over three percentage points on February 17, 2009. This speculation only calmed down in February 2009 when the then–German Finance Minister Peer Steinbrück made it clear that his country would not stand by and allow another euro-zone member state to go into default.[10] Greece's interest rates then converged back on German norms—despite the IMF's warning on Greece's fiscal situation. Markets then reacted slowly to Pasok's announcement in October: Greek ten-year government bonds yielded an average of 4.56 percent in September 2009 and only 4.84 in November. It was only in December that market movements became more severe.

What this longer story indicates is that interest rate differentials between Greece and Germany tended to track with the market's perception of the likelihood that Germany and the rest of the euro zone would ultimately prevent a Greek default. The fact that markets responded to Steinbrück and Merkel but not to Papandreou indicated that it was Berlin—and not Athens—that the markets were looking to for a solution. See figure 11.1.

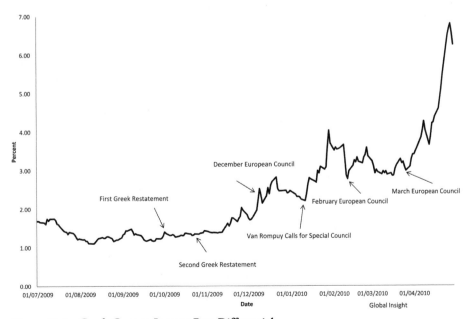

Figure 11.1   Greek-German Interest Rate Differential

Macroeconomic Imbalances

To understand why the markets took such a sanguine view of the Pasok government's Greek deficit revisions—and was largely willing to turn a blind eye to the poor state of Greek fiscal accounting more generally—it is necessary to step back and consider the impact of the single currency on Europe's already-interdependent economies. To begin with, countries that share a common currency are no longer constrained by international payments requirements—only the monetary union as a whole must worry about matching its assets and liabilities in relation to the rest of the world. Hence, if Greece or any other country wants to import more than it exports, it can always borrow the money—in euros—from other countries in the euro zone. Similarly, if Germany or any other country wants to export more than it imports, it can always lend the excess money it receives—again, in euros—to other countries in the euro zone.

This notion of "excess money" is the only confusing part. It is easy to see that a country that wants to consume more than it makes must borrow from abroad. If a country's income is limited to its output and yet it wants to consume more than it produces, it obviously does not have the income, and so the money to purchase that excess consumption must come from somewhere else. The idea of "excess money" on the net exporting side of the relationship comes from looking at things the other way around. If a country wants to export some of its output, then it must consume less than what it produces and therefore also less than what it earns. Indeed, that only makes sense because it must be earning money on those goods that it produces and yet sells abroad (rather than at home). The problem is that this money cannot be used at home; otherwise, it would raise consumption (or physical investment) to match the level of output and so eventually would eliminate the trade surplus. Therefore, that money must be sent (i.e., invested or lent) abroad.

Suppose German firms or individuals decide to lend some of their savings—such as retained earnings or financial investments to be used later for education, health care, pensions, and so forth—abroad. The motivation for doing this is simply that they know they can get a higher rate of interest in other countries than they can get at home. Moreover, they believe that the excess rate of return more than exceeds the risk of putting their money in another country. This seems a particularly reasonable assumption when the other country uses the same currency as Germans do, so no matter what the rate of inflation over there, Germans know they will get the money back in euros that they can use at face value, without any exchange rate risk, for domestic consumption in their own low-inflation market (where the value of the currency has been protected). This kind of thinking explains why the gap between German and peripheral European economies' interest rates on long-term government debt collapsed from more than twenty percentage points in the early 1990s to less than one-half of one percentage point in the early 2000s.

A consequence of this type of investment behavior—where Germans send some of their savings to chase higher interest rates in Greece or Portugal or Spain—is that these same Germans are going to have to look for export markets to absorb some of their excess output. The reason they have to export more than they import is that the money they sent abroad was earned by generating output at home that was never actually consumed or invested by Germans. Germany ran current account deficits in the 1990s when the gap between German and Greek interest rates was very high, and Germany ran current account surpluses in the 2000s after changing investment patterns, with Germans investing in assets in the European periphery, thereby pushing interest rates in smaller euro-zone economies to very low levels. Meanwhile, firms and individuals in countries like Greece were willing to pay higher rates of interest than in Germany because they have historically had much less access to credit and because they paid more in terms of premiums to cover the cost of inflation or exchange rate risk associated with their domestic currency. But once firms and individuals in the periphery began to borrow from abroad above and beyond their income, they also needed to buy goods from abroad: all the new borrowed money had to be spent on something that they themselves did not produce.

The argument about capital markets and goods markets is best illustrated through the data. The crucial data concern the nominal interest rate on long-term government bonds and the balance on current transactions (meaning the trade in goods and services, but also net transfers and the income from net lending). The argument is that bond investors abroad began to put their money in the bonds of peripheral economies like Greece, Portugal, Spain, and Ireland. This not only meant that the interest rate on those bonds declined as the EU approached adoption of the euro, but also it ensured that more money would be available for lending and investment within those peripheral economies: interest rates declined for Greek, Irish, and Portuguese private sector borrowers as well.

The influence of these decisions about where to save money and where to invest it can also be seen in the data for gross fixed capital formation. This data offer a very crude measure of the level of physical investment in the economy. During the 1990s, for example, the German economy grew in real (meaning price-deflated) terms by about 16 percent—not annually, but over the whole period. Real gross fixed capital formation accounted for just over 22 percent of that real growth, or 3.6 percentage points in the total headline figure. The story in Greece during the same period is slightly more impressive because the Greek economy is less developed and so has to invest and grow at a higher level in order to catch up. Hence the Greek economy grew in real terms in the 1990s by just over 20 percent, of which real gross fixed capital formation accounted for 31 percent, or 6.3 percentage points of the total. Once the two countries joined in the same currency, the difference became much more striking. From 2000 to 2007, German growth collapsed to just 9 percent (again, not annually but over the whole of the period), and gross fixed capital formation accounted for only 3 percent of that growth, or 0.3 percentage points of the total. In other words, investment in Germany increased very little, if at all. Meanwhile, the Greek economy expanded by more than 20 percent in real terms over the same period, and gross fixed capital formation accounted for 27 percent (or 7.7 percentage points) of that expansion. Germans sent their savings to Greece, and the Greeks borrowed that money to invest in the growth of their domestic economy.[11]

Actually, the story is not entirely complete. Some of the money borrowed at lower interest rates—meaning some of the excess credit available to peripheral European borrowers by savers in the European core (particularly Germany)—was used to purchase services that cannot be traded internationally. As the demand for these services increased beyond the periphery's ability to supply them, inflation in the periphery accelerated as well. The reverse is true for Germany. Money sent abroad could not be used at home, and so demand for everything—not just tradable manufactured goods but also services—declined. Inflation in Germany slowed down as a result. The price effects here are perhaps only marginal. Nevertheless, an increase in one year adds to the base level for the next, and so the implications are cumulatively important. The longer these divergent patterns of relative inflation rates continue, the more prices in Greece and Germany will appear to diverge.

For the present argument, though, the important point is that monetary integration brought German lenders and peripheral European borrowers together by lowering the risk associated with Germans lending to the euro-zone periphery: in replacing national currencies like the drachma with the euro, there was no longer any risk that the peripheral countries' currencies would lose value, wiping out German investments. At the same time, this lowered the cost associated with these peripheral economies borrowing from the core. The trend holds across the euro zone, with the consequence that numerous Austrian, Belgian, Dutch, German, and French banks ended up lending vast amounts of money to governments, firms, and individuals in Greece, Ireland, Italy, Spain, and Portugal. Some of that money went to firms and individuals directly in the form of corporate borrowing or interbank lending; some went indirectly in the form of sovereign debts to finance government expenditures that otherwise would have to be paid for out of tax receipts.

The symptoms of this exchange showed up in the form of current account balances and relative inflation rates. The borrowing countries had relatively large current account deficits and high rates of inflation (because domestic demand outstripped domestic supply); the lending countries showed relatively large current account surpluses and low rates of inflation (because domestic supply exceeded domestic demand). The effects here can be seen in figure 11.2, which shows the dispersion (or standard

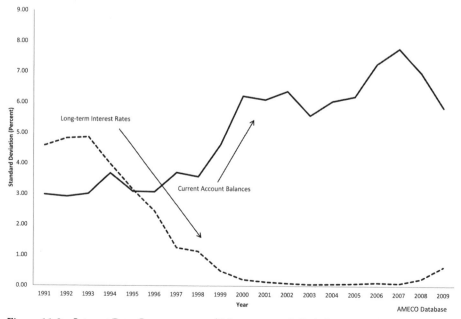

Figure 11.2   **Interest Rate Convergence and Macroeconomic Imbalances**

deviation) of interest rates and current account performance across major euro-zone economies. The downward movement in the dispersion of interest rates represents a convergence of borrowing costs across the euro zone as a whole. At the end of the story, there is essentially only one interest rate within the single currency, plus or minus about one-half of 1 percent. The upward movement in the dispersion of current account performance represents a divergence in positions from one country to the next. Some countries, like Greece and Ireland, run significant deficits; others, like Germany and the Netherlands, run surpluses.

In this sense, the lenders and borrowers in the euro zone were two sides of the same coin. To give a sense of the symmetry, consider the respective current account positions of Germany, on the one hand, and Greece, Spain, Italy, Ireland, and Portugal on the other hand. In 2007, Germany recorded a surplus of €192.1 billion; taken together, the smaller and more peripheral euro-zone economies showed a deficit of €192.8 billion. The point here is not to suggest that there is a strict bilateral relationship between Germany and the rest. Rather, it is to suggest that both sides are out of balance. The relative exposure is more complicated because there are many more actors involved in European bond markets than just the Europeans themselves, and many European countries in addition to those highlighted in this analysis. Nevertheless, the level of exposure is significant, as the Bank for International Settlements made clear in its June 2010 quarterly review:

> As of 31 December 2009 as events in Greece began their downward spiral, banks headquartered in the eurozone accounted for almost two thirds (62 percent) of all internationally active banks' exposures to the residents of the euro area countries facing market pressures (Greece, Ireland, Portugal and Spain). Together, they had $727 billion of exposures to Spain, $402 billion to Ireland, $244 billion to Portugal and $206 billion to Greece. French and German banks were particularly exposed to the residents of Greece, Ireland, Portugal and Spain. At the end of 2009, they had $958 billion of combined exposures ($493 billion and $465 billion, respectively) to the residents of these countries. This amounted to 61 percent of all reported euro area banks' exposures to those economies.[12]

No wonder the lenders would expect the borrowers to be bailed out. If Greek borrowers defaulted on their debts, German lenders would suffer the losses. It only stands to reason, therefore, that the German government would have an interest in ensuring that did not happen. So long as everyone participated in the system and everyone continued to benefit, everyone had a reason to keep the system intact.

Halting Responses

The problem with this logic is that the response of the euro-zone governments to the Greek crisis failed to live up to market expectations. Greece was evidently unable to solve its own problems, and the expectations that wealthier and highly exposed euro-zone countries—Germany above all—would ultimately backstop Greek debt suddenly appeared in doubt. As mentioned, Steinbrück had originally described a euro-zone default as unimaginable.[13] Financial market participants took this statement as a pledge that

Germany would step in to prevent such a default from taking place. Despite this rhetorical commitment, though, Germany and much of the rest of northern Europe expressed dismay that the debt situation had gotten so out of hand. They criticized the Greeks for failing to abide by the rules for fiscal stability in the euro zone and even more so for having failed to reorganize and rationalize control over their national statistics.

Confusion over how much the other countries of the euro zone were willing to do to help Greece simmered through February and into March 2010, although the stabilization of bond prices during this period suggests that, on balance, bondholders were still confident in Germany's willingness to backstop Greece. Whenever the Greek government went into the markets to issue new debt as part of its regular refinancing operations, it found much more demand than it expected. Yet Merkel's line toughened in March 2010 as she made it clear that Germany was not willing to borrow from private markets—and then only if the IMF also became involved. These statements, particularly the invocation of the IMF, sent alarm bells through bond markets.[14]

Following Merkel's statements, the yield on Greek debt started to grow faster through March and April, jumping to 8.64 percent by April 22, 2010. This was nearly double the 4.4 percent that Greece had paid the day of Papandreou's election just seven months prior. The sharp rise in borrowing costs compelled Papandreou to request assistance on April 23. The ratings agencies responded immediately, cutting Greek sovereign debt to "junk" status. By the end of April, it was clear that the uneven rhetorical solidarity expressed by Germany had failed: the situation could not continue without some sort of EU intervention. On May 2, the finance ministers of euro-zone countries agreed to provide €110 billion to Greece over three years, supported by €30 billion IMF funds.

The European Central Bank (ECB) supported the stabilization operations, announcing that it would continue to accept Greek government debt as collateral despite the fact that its junk rating would ordinarily not have satisfied ECB requirements. This was intended to ensure that secondary markets for Greek debt would retain some liquidity despite the official assistance. The financial package did not come free: Greece agreed to stringent conditions that, the country's new euro-zone creditors hoped, would bring about longer term financial stability.

While the Greek bailout temporarily solved the Greek situation, a wider problem was already spreading through the rest of the euro-zone periphery. While much of the public attention in early 2010 had been focused on the "Greek" crisis, the underlying macroeconomic imbalances were not limited to Greece alone. Other states had found themselves similarly indebted—either due to public or private borrowing—and by mid-2010, the cost of Portuguese and Irish borrowing had begun to rise as well. A week after the agreement of the interim solution to the Greek problem, euro-zone members agreed that some sort of more permanent arrangement was needed to avoid the sort of uncertainty that had plagued the early response to the Greece crisis.

Two interim institutions were set up with the capacity to provide €500 billion to countries that were using the euro but could no longer sustainably borrow from open markets. The resources were spread across two entities: the €440 billion European Financial Stability Facility (EFSF), which was secured by subscribed capital paid by euro-zone members, and the European Financial Stability Mechanism (EFSM), which could borrow €60 billion secured against the EU's budget. In both cases, the new institutions would raise funds on international capital markets at the relatively low rates permitted for more creditworthy borrowers and then offer those funds to distressed euro-zone countries in exchange for negotiated conditions. These European funds were then supplemented by an additional €250 billion facility provided by the IMF.

The overall support was worth just over $968 billion, meaning $200 billion more than the "troubled asset relief funds" requested by the outgoing George W. Bush administration and authorized by Congress in 2008 during the market turmoil that followed the failure of the Lehman Brothers investment bank.[15] Meanwhile, the Governing Council of the ECB decided over the same weekend to intervene directly in "dysfunctional" public and private debt security markets in order to ensure that they remain both liquid and deep, buying up distressed bonds and holding them on its own balance sheet.[16] After months of dithering, it had finally seemed by the late spring of 2010 that the EU had arrived at a robust response.

The Crisis Spreads

While Greece seemed manageable and the EFSF and EFSM were in place to provide a framework for containing future outbreaks, the situation was far from completely under control. The problem was that the crisis had never been limited to Greece. Every part of the euro zone played a role in the destabilizing capital flows at the heart of the crisis. Greece was heavily indebted in its fiscal accounts, but Spain and Ireland were indebted in the private sector. Hence few actors in the financial markets viewed the European solution to the Greeks' fiscal crisis as a credible solution for the system as a whole. And as they worried about precisely which institutions were going to lose financially because of the wider implications, they began to panic. In this sense, Greece was very much like a European "Lehman Brothers"—it was small in the greater scheme of things but yet still "too big to fail."

Sure enough, soon after the Greek situation was temporarily resolved, the state of Ireland's private and public finances began to deteriorate. Ireland was particularly troublesome because it looked so different from Greece: whereas the Greek crisis was unquestionably brought on by fiscal irresponsibility and creative accounting, the Irish government had long been relatively frugal. The country rarely ran deficits in the 2000s and had sovereign debt amounting to only 25.1 percent of GDP as late as 2007. In Ireland, the culprit was overleveraging in the private and household sectors, not with the government. Unlike in Greece, the capital that had flooded into Ireland had largely fueled an expansion of credit within the Irish banking sector that led to a boom in consumption and property values. It is difficult to put these numbers in perspective: the liabilities of the Irish financial sector jumped from over 900 percent of GDP in 2001 to over 2000 percent by 2009—higher than any other European economy but Luxembourg's. The expansion of household debt was less, but in many ways just as remarkable, jumping from 50 percent to 125 percent over the same time period.[17]

As a result of such large private debt burdens, the Irish economy was particularly exposed to the sort of financial crisis which struck in 2007–2008. The freezing of international credit markets, combined with a subsequent wider economic downturn both deprived banks and households of new funding sources while also depressing ordinary income: the credit spigot was off and the country was facing a recession to boot. In fact, Ireland slipped into recession faster than any other euro-zone economy. By September 2008, the Irish government was forced to choose between a massive bailout of its oversized financial sector and utter financial chaos.

In the end, the Irish government chose to bail out its troubled financial system, issuing a blanked deposit guarantee, guaranteeing all bank-issued debt, injecting capital into its largest banks or renationalizing them outright, and creating a "bad bank" that could concentrate and eventually dispose of the toxic assets polluting the system. In 2010 alone, the package cost around €40 billion—or roughly 25 percent of Irish GDP.[18] This cost was compounded by the fact that the recession had dented tax receipts, pushing the Irish national deficit from zero in 2007 to over 32 percent of GDP by 2010, the largest in the world.[19] The country's sovereign debt quadrupled in just a handful of years.

Ireland began with a fair share of market goodwill: despite the catastrophic collapse of their public finances, the bond markets did not react particularly severely due to the strong recent history of the Irish state as a borrower. Though rates did creep up during the acute phase of the Greek crisis, they stabilized again with the establishment of the EFSF and EFSM. The situation changed on October 18, 2010, with the summit between Angela Merkel and Nicolas Sarkozy at Deauville, France. Emerging from the summit, Merkel made two announcements: first, that new macroeconomic rules were needed; and, second, that private sector investors would have to share in the cost of any future debt restructuring. The text of this announcement is reproduced in box 11.1. From the wording of the text, it is clear that Merkel's interests in avoiding moral hazard and punishing fiscal profligacy were paramount. Her strong conviction that German taxpayers should not have to pay for irresponsible borrowing elsewhere features prominently as well.

Unfortunately, Merkel's actions showed a poor understanding of how traders in the bond market discount future events. Even if it is true that the cost to the private sector will be borne only from 2013 onward, that is no reason why the cost of those future expected losses cannot be priced into government bond purchases today. The principal victim was not Greece—by this time, almost entirely out of public markets—but Ireland. Once Merkel and Sarkozy made their Deauville declaration, the Irish bond market went into a rout. The day of the summit, Ireland only had to pay 6.02 percent on its borrowing. That figure had leapt to 8.92 percent in just one month. The effect was not unlike what happened to Greek bonds after the March 2010 European Council summit. The consequences were similar as well. Within weeks of the Deauville declaration, the Irish government became the second in the single currency to make a formal request for financial help, receiving a package worth €85 billion.[20]

From Greece and Ireland, the crisis then metastasized to Portugal. While it was eventually the third country to request help from the EFSF and EFSM, its problems were also deeply rooted. Its situation could be described as a less severe version of Greece's; however, because Portugal's debt-to-GDP ratio in 2007 was 68.3 percent (as compared to Greece's 105.4 percent level), it simply took longer for the situation

Box 11.1   Franco-German Declaration: Statement for the France-Germany-Russia Summit, Deauville, Monday, October 18, 2010

France and Germany agree that the economic governance needs to be reinforced. To this aim, they have agreed on the following points:

1) France and Germany emphasize that budgetary surveillance and economic policy coordination procedures should be strengthened and accelerated. This includes the following issues:

   a. *A wider range of sanctions should be applied* progressively in both the preventive and corrective arm of the Pact. *These sanctions should be more automatic,* while respecting the role of the different institutions and the institutional balance. In enforcing the preventive arm of the Pact, the Council should be empowered to decide, acting by QMV to impose progressively sanctions in the form of interest-bearing deposits on any Member State whose fiscal consolidation path deviates particularly significantly from the adjustment path foreseen in the Stability and Growth Pact.

   b. As to the corrective arm, *whenever the Council decides to open an excessive deficit procedure, there should be automatic sanctions for any Member States found by the Council, acting by QMV, to have failed to implement the necessary corrective measures within a 6-month time limit.*

   c. Complementing the new legislative framework for the surveillance of economic imbalances, the case of any Member State with persistent imbalances under surveillance by the Council will be referred to the European Council for discussion.

2) France and Germany consider that an amendment of the Treaties is needed and that the President of the European Council should be asked to present, in close contact with the Members of the European Council, concrete options allowing the establishment of a robust crisis resolution framework before its meeting in March 2011. The amendment of the Treaties will be restricted to the following issues:

   a. The establishment of a permanent and robust framework to ensure orderly crisis management in the future, *providing the necessary arrangements for an adequate participation of private creditors* and allowing Member States to take appropriate coordinated measures to safeguard financial stability of the Euro area as a whole.

   b. In case of a serious violation of basic principles of Economic and Monetary Union, and following appropriate procedures, *suspension of the voting rights* of the Member State concerned. The necessary amendment to the Treaties should be adopted and ratified by Member States in accordance with their respective constitutional requirements in due time before 2013.

---

to reach the crisis point. Despite this general similarity, however, the Portuguese case remains somewhat puzzling. Its debt burdens were not initially outrageous, and the impact of the financial crisis on the country was muted. Instead, Portugal's problem was long-standing lackluster economic performance, coupled with lingering worries over the state's flexibility, competitiveness, and ultimate need for reform.[21]

Yet, like Greece, Portugal was forced to make upward revisions to its deficit figures in 2009—from 5.9 percent of GDP to 8 percent. This led to an eighteen-month slow-burn crisis as Jose Socrates' Socialist government repeatedly attempted to impress ratings agencies with reform plans, only to see their debt ratings cut and their borrowing costs continue to climb. The most extreme moves came in early 2010, with the state announcing a raft of pay freezes, tax hikes, public sector cuts, and privatizations. Despite their efforts, the government was compelled to revise its deficit figures upward again—this time to 9.4 percent of GDP. Another round of downgrades pushed the yields on Portuguese long-term bonds from 3.85 percent to 7.80 percent between October 2009 and March 2011.

The slowly moving crisis finally came to a head when Socrates failed to secure the needed votes for additional austerity measures on March 23, 2011. Portuguese debt was immediately dropped to "junk" status, pushing interest rates up ten basis points a day thereafter. With few other options, the government was compelled to turn to the EFSF and EFSM on April 6, 2011. The assistance would total €78 billion over three years. While Portugal is sometimes the least studied of the peripheral European crisis, the rejection of Socrates' plans underscored that politics—often subsumed by technical details in the early phases of the crisis—was returning to center stage.

Political Constraints

The lack of political support for adjustment plans in Europe came from two sides: on one hand, the countries footing the bill for peripheral countries' adjustment plans were steadily losing patience with sending their "hard-earned" currency to countries widely seen as irresponsible. On the other hand, from the perspective of the countries asked to make such severe adjustments, it was clear that the conditions placed on them by wealthier external actors were manifestly harming their economies over the short term.

It is worth considering why politicians in the euro-zone core were not more forthcoming in their commitment to come to the aid of Greece. This is particularly true considering that much of the debt issued by Greece was held by other countries' banks, France and Germany foremost among them. There are many good arguments to explain the situation. Four of the most commonly held positions concern trade competitiveness, moral hazard, populist politics, and constitutional courts.

The competitiveness argument builds on the relative price movements that have been described above. Put simply, price inflation was higher in the periphery than it was in Germany. As a result—so the argument runs—countries like Greece effectively priced themselves out of foreign markets. Hence any correction of current account balances in the periphery should come as a result of efforts to slow down (and even reverse) the inflation of prices and wages. Attempts to create comprehensive bailouts might not solve the underlying competitiveness problem and could even make it worse. So long as Greeks or the Irish were able to borrow money in order to live beyond their means, they would have little incentive to accept the austerity measures necessary to bring their trade accounts back into balance.

This competitiveness issue is a serious one that has attracted a lot of attention from important economists (particularly in the United States) who believe that countries like Greece, in particular, were wrong to enter into a monetary union with Germany in the first place—or, more generally, that European monetary integration was a folly. These economists claim they also knew that two such different economies could not survive the discipline of having a common monetary policy, that some countries would experience competitiveness problems that would impose long-term adjustment costs on the society as a whole, and that only a devaluation of the currency—supported by fiscal austerity measures and effective wage restraints—can bring the pain of that adjustment down to acceptable levels.[22]

The problem with this competitiveness argument is that it does not fit the data very well. While it is true that inflation rates have differed between Germany and Greece, there is little sign that this has had a negative impact on exports from the European periphery. Indeed, Greece's external market share is roughly unchanged throughout its participation in Europe's economic and monetary union. Much the same is true for countries like Italy, Ireland, Spain, and Portugal as well. Indeed, if we look across the whole period of monetary unification—starting with the 1991 Maastricht Treaty and ending with the onset of the global economic crisis in 2007—the combined export market shares of these five peripheral countries hold up better than the market share for Germany itself. Manufacturing employment in the peripheral countries has done better still. Both Germany, on the one hand, and the peripheral countries, on the other hand, had about 10 million manufacturing workers at the start of the 1990s. By 2007, the peripheral countries still had about 10 million manufacturing workers, and Germany had about 7.6 million. If Greece and the other countries were suffering from competitiveness problems before the onset of the crisis, this level of manufacturing employment should not be sustainable alongside a relatively constant export market share. Something just does not add up.

The problems with the competitiveness argument get even worse when we compare Greece's situation within the euro zone with its situation before monetary integration. The simple fact of the matter is that Greece lost more competitiveness under the fixed but adjustable exchange rate regime embedded in the European Monetary System (EMS) than it lost while in the single currency—at least when we measure competitiveness in terms of relative movements in the relative real effective exchange rate. Meanwhile, the cumulative deficit on Greece's current account was almost four times worse under the euro than during the EMS period that preceded it. Again, something just does not add up here. If relative movements in competitiveness were behind Greece's foreign indebtedness, we would expect the situation to be the other way around and the EMS period would show more Greek borrowing than took place under the euro.[23]

The moral hazard argument is more straightforward. If Germany bails out countries for becoming so heavily indebted this time, what is to prevent those countries receiving bailouts from doing it again? Worse, as more and more countries take advantage of Germany's largesse, the result will be to increase government expenditures across the euro zone as a whole and so run the risk of accelerating price inflation. This is why the European Union included a no-bailout clause in its provisions for economic and monetary union in the first place. It is also why it included a prohibition against excessive deficits, to which Germany insisted that the EU member states add a Stability and Growth Pact (SGP). Of course, the fact that Germany itself was responsible for suspending the excessive deficit procedure in 2003 and reforming the SGP in 2005 does create some confusion. The perils of moral hazard are not limited to the Greeks. Nevertheless, it is clear that some rules need to be in place (and enforced) if the Greek crisis is not to be a harbinger of more widespread profligacy in the future. The precise wording of the no-bailout clause in the Treaty on the Functioning of the European Union is reproduced in box 11.2. The point to note is that while the treaty does provide for exceptional circumstances, it also sets out fairly starkly worded restrictions.

The populist argument is unambiguous as well. Like it or not, there is much prejudice among northern Europeans toward southern Europeans, particularly toward the Greeks. According to this prejudice, the south is lazy and corrupt while the north is hardworking and virtuous. Hence, any northern European politician seen to be bailing out the South risks being portrayed as rewarding indolence and abetting corruption. Examples of this tendency are not limited to the German tabloid *Bild-Zeitung* but can be found across euro-zone member states from the Netherlands to Slovakia and all points in between. Again, there is a problem with the data. If we stick to a comparison between Greece and Germany, it is easy to show that the Greeks work longer hours on an annual basis and that they tend to work longer during their lifetimes as well. Of course, the data for these comparisons are hardly perfect. Nevertheless, two factors stand out. One is the magnitude of the difference in average annual hours worked. In 2008, for example, the average Greek worked 2,120 hours, while the average German worked just 1,432. The other feature that stands out is the fact that while Greeks tend to work beyond their statutory retirement age, Germans tend to retire before they even qualify for full benefits.[24]

These data never entered into the popular debate in Germany, and it is unlikely they would have been accepted had anyone tried to introduce them. Instead, the public embraced stereotypes about lazy southern Europeans and so moved staunchly against any spending of their hard-earned tax receipts to bail them out. According to this line of argument, Chancellor Merkel was most concerned about the consequences of aiding Greece for her party's performance in the regional election held on May 9 in North-Rhine Westphalia. This election was crucial to her control over the upper house of the German federal parliament; any bailout of Greece was wildly unpopular with the voters, so the chancellor had to appear tough on the Greeks to stand a chance at the polls. There is, no doubt, some truth to this argument—not least because the 2005 elections in that same region signaled the demise of the previous German chancellor on the center-left—but it is hard to see it as the principal factor.[25] In any event, when the votes were cast on May 9, the German chancellor's Christian Democrats lost more than ten percentage points in support.

The constitutional argument is arguably more important.[26] In October 1993 and March 1998, the German high court rendered decisions about the constitutionality of Germany's participation in the euro zone. The first decision made it clear that the European Union is a union of states—not of peoples—and so established that German constitutional law has priority over European treaty obligations (including those related to monetary union). That decision also underscored that any international monetary union must guarantee the same level of protection as the German currency. By implication, the euro must be as solid as the deutschmark that it replaced. The 1998 decision reinforced these performance considerations. Germany could enter the euro zone, the court ruled, but only because strong guarantees for the price stability of the euro remain in place. The prohibition of excessive deficits and the no-bailout

Box 11.2   Treaty Provisions Pertaining to the "No-Bailout Clause," Consolidated Version of the Treaty on the Functioning of the European Union, May 9, 2008

Article 122 (ex. Article 100 TEC)

1. Without prejudice to any other procedures provided for in the Treaties, the Council, on a proposal from the Commission, may decide, in a spirit of solidarity between Member States, upon the measures appropriate to the economic situation, in particular if severe difficulties arise in the supply of certain products, notably in the area of energy.

2. *Where a Member State is in difficulties or is seriously threatened with severe difficulties caused by natural disasters or exceptional occurrences beyond its control, the Council, on a proposal from the Commission, may grant, under certain conditions, Union financial assistance to the Member State concerned.* The President of the Council shall inform the European Parliament of the decision taken.

Article 123 (ex. Article 101 TEC)

1. *Overdraft facilities or any other type of credit facility with the European Central Bank* or with the central banks of the Member States (hereinafter referred to as 'national central banks') in favour of Union institutions, bodies, offices or agencies, central governments, regional, local or other public authorities, other bodies governed by public law, or public undertakings of Member States *shall be prohibited, as shall the purchase directly from them by the European Central Bank or national central banks of debt instruments.*

2. Paragraph 1 shall not apply to publicly owned credit institutions which, in the context of the supply of reserves by central banks, shall be given the same treatment by national central banks and the European Central Bank as private credit institutions.

Article 124 (ex. Article 102 TEC)

Any measure, not based on prudential considerations, *establishing privileged access* by Union institutions, bodies, offices or agencies, central governments, regional, local or other public authorities, other bodies governed by public law, or public undertakings of Member States *to financial institutions, shall be prohibited.*

Article 125 (ex. Article 103 TEC)

1. *The Union shall not be liable for or assume the commitments of central governments,* regional, local or other public authorities, other bodies governed by public law, or public undertakings of any Member State, without prejudice to mutual financial guarantees for the joint execution of a specific project. *A Member State shall not be liable for or assume the commitments of central governments,* regional, local or other public authorities, other bodies governed by public law, or public undertakings *of another Member State,* without prejudice to mutual financial guarantees for the joint execution of a specific project.

2. The Council, on a proposal from the Commission and after consulting the European Parliament, may, as required, specify definitions for the application of the prohibitions referred to in Articles 123 and 124 and in this Article.

clause are among the most important of those guarantees. Should Chancellor Merkel show little regard for these restrictions by bailing out a profligate Greece, she would invite a challenge in the high court—and there were many people queued up, including prominent economists, petitioning to make the case against her. An unfavorable decision by the German high court would cast the euro zone into turmoil. Chancellor Merkel's decision to set firm conditions for supporting Greece was designed to ensure that would not take place.

This constitutional threat is debatable because it is reasonable to believe that the German high court would be very reluctant to pass a ruling with such wide implications. Moreover, it would be even more reluctant to be seen as usurping the sovereignty of the German parliament and, by implication, of the people who elected those representatives in the first place. To understand why this is so, it is worth considering the bases upon which plaintiffs have argued against Germany's participation in the euro. Essentially, they claim that a weak international currency would undermine the value of their property, which the German constitution promises to defend. They argue that a weak currency would interfere with their personal freedom in the marketplace because it would complicate relationships between buyers and sellers. And they argue that a weak multinational currency would violate the sanctity of the relationship between representatives and voters because the German parliament would have no recourse through which it could make the currency strong again.

Of these arguments, the German high court has only given serious consideration to the sanctity of parliament. That is why the court refused to accept an automatic entry into the euro in its 1993 ruling—because the German parliament should retain the right to decide. That is also why it placed such emphasis on institutional guarantees in its 1998 ruling—because these guarantees were an important part of what the German parliament accepted to join. The implication of this line of argument is clear. The German high court is unlikely to interfere with the single currency so long as the German government maintains parliamentary support for its actions. If Merkel was slow to respond to the Greek crisis, it was most likely because she doubted whether she could maintain that support.

Not only was political support for further bailouts in the core fragile, but also it became evident by 2011 that the countries receiving the bailouts were chafing over the adjustment costs imposed by their benefactors. Austerity increasingly became seen as pain imposed by Brussels eurocrats and the Germans, not a necessary process of macroeconomic adjustment. The first major crisis of popular support struck in Greece. By June 2011, Papandreou's government was almost entirely dependent on its euro-zone partners for averting default—private debt markets would have charged an entirely unrealistic 16 percent on new Greek debt—and he was in the position of asking for further assistance. Papandreou was stuck between a rock and a hard place: the adjustments called for by the Greek bailout were causing widespread dissent at home and appeared to be nearing the limits of measures they were willing to accept. The political situation on the streets of Greece was rapidly deteriorating. By June 5, several hundred thousand protesters had descended on Athens' Syntagma square to protest Pasok's austerity plans and the opposition New Democracy (ND) party had opportunistically taken the position that it would oppose any further capitulation by Pasok to Brussels or Berlin.[27] As Socrates had found several months earlier in Portugal, public patience for further austerity was in short supply.

Yet it was equally clear that the Greek state would require significantly more assistance than was provided in the first assistance package. From the perspective of lender countries, it was politically imperative that any further financing for Greece be subject to further strict conditionality. As creditor countries debated the merits of further support for the Greek government, tensions came to a head during a meeting of European leaders on June 23–24. The European Council officially agreed to release the final tranche of Greece's original bailout—and to negotiate a further €120 billion to be released in the future—but solely on the condition that the Greek government pass further draconian cuts within the week. Despite a general strike and protests which turned violent, Papandreou barely pushed the new measures through the Greek parliament.

The new temporary success could not hide the fact that a new, more difficult dynamic had emerged. While the euro zone did come through with a new €130 billion package for Greece, major parties in the Netherlands, Finland, and Slovakia voiced strong opposition. Within Greece itself, Papandreou's control of the situation collapsed. After briefly announcing that further cuts would be subject to a referendum (which would be almost certain to fail), he was compelled to resign. In his place, a technocratic government was formed with the mandate for continuing the Brussels-guided reform process. What the political opposition to the second Greek bailout from both Greece and its euro-area benefactors made apparent was that additional assistance packages would face stiffer opposition, both from debtor countries balking at further austerity and from creditors losing patience with profligate peripheral economies. The risk of uncontrolled default was again rearing its ugly head.

Further Contagion

The second Greek bailout signaled the beginning of a new, more dangerous period of the crisis. At least since the creation of the EFSF and EFSM, there had been some certainty that the euro zone could contain default risk for smaller countries like Portugal, Ireland, and Greece (and, as of early 2013, Cyprus). But what about a crisis somewhere larger, like Spain or Italy? While Europe's political leaders sought to use their stabilization resources sparingly, they also needed to head off new uncertainty in an attempt to prevent instability in those larger states. Unfortunately, the clock was already ticking: the uncertainty over the second Greek bailout contributed to the spread of the crisis to Italy in the summer of 2011. Furthermore, a July 15 European Banking Authority's stress test found that sixteen of the ninety-one banks tested still had insufficient capital bases, many of them in Spain.[28]

The increased risk of new systemic instability was particularly dangerous for Italy. In many respects, Italy's inclusion in the infamous "PIIGS" acronym was unfortunate: while the country had relatively large outstanding sovereign debts, much of the debt was held by Italy's very active domestic savers. Moreover, Italy had successfully managed its heavy debt burdens for decades and had quite conscientiously kept deficits low during the financial crisis and ensuing global downturn. The problem for Italy was that any major weakness in the European financial system might compromise the system's capacity to roll over Italian debt.

This concern set in motion a series of events that led to the collapse of Silvio Berlusconi's government and the ascendance of a second Brussels-backed technocrat to the head of a troubled European government. In August, ECB President Jean-Claude Trichet and Bank of Italy Governor Mario Draghi wrote to Berlusconi, pressing him to push forward with the IMF's recommended set of reforms for the country.[29] These were politically difficult to achieve: pension reform, seen as necessary by the IMF, faced stiff opposition from Berlusconi's Lega Nord coalition partners, and a proposal to raise Italy's value-added tax was overshadowed by cabinet infighting between Berlusconi and his economic minister, Giulio Tremonti.[30]

The paralysis of the Italian political elite caused the cost of Italian borrowing to continue rising. Berlusconi was unable to assemble a package that could be put into law, and his personal relationship with Tremonti devolved publicly.[31] In September, citing the "fragile" government situation, Standard & Poor's downgraded Italian debt.[32] After an attempt to auction new Italian debt on October went undersubscribed, a rout was on once again: selling of Italian debt caused yields to rise to 7.42 percent. Berlusconi, rendered politically impotent in the face of these challenges, was forced to resign on November 12. The new technocratic government under Monti briefly restored a degree of faith in the Italian government's ability to close its fiscal holes, though—as the final section of this chapter will detail—his tenure was relatively short-lived and he resigned from office in December 2012, a few months before the end of his parliamentary mandate.

Meanwhile, it was Spain and not Italy that was the source of trouble. The Spanish economy had borrowed excessively during the period of relatively low interest rates in the late 1990s and early 2000s. However, much of that debt was used to finance construction rather than government borrowing. As a result, the Spanish economy experienced bubbles in both commercial and residential property markets. Once interest rates started to rise during the crisis, those bubbles burst. This meant not only that borrowers found themselves holding loans worth more than the property they purchased but also that the huge population involved in construction was suddenly without work. Incomes were squeeze by the rising cost of indebtedness, and government expenditures increased on the back of rising social welfare payments.

The Spanish government nevertheless retained the confidence of the markets. In part, this was due to the relatively low weight of government indebtedness at the start of the crisis and in part it resulted from the solidity of the country's three largest banks. To a large extent, however, it was the result of the belief that the Spanish government would pull itself together. Center-left Prime Minister Jose Luis Zapatero called for early elections in July 2011 just as the Italian crisis was starting; center-right Prime Minister Mariano Rajoy was elected just before Italian Prime Minister Silvio Berlusconi was forced out of office. Throughout this political alternation, Spanish borrowing costs rose along with Italy's but then quickly settled back down.

The situation changed again in the early months of 2012. The problem was two-fold. First, the newly installed Rajoy government was struggling with fiscal consolidation. The European Union wanted Spain to reduce its fiscal deficit, and yet the Rajoy government could not do much against the arithmetic of declining revenues and rising expenditures. Instead, Rajoy told the European Commission to mind its own business. Soon thereafter, the smaller regional banks buckled under the weight of their nonperforming loans. Rajoy was forced to nationalize the largest of these—Bankia, which was the fusion of seven smaller banks that collectively became Spain's third largest domestic lender. He then had to bail Bankia out.

The combination of high fiscal deficits and new capital requirements for Bankia was too much for Spanish sovereign debt markets, and international investors started to pull their money out of the country. Rajoy had to appeal to his European counterparts to provide resources for the Spanish banks. He also called upon them to do something to change the wider institutional framework. The result was a European commitment to provide the Spanish government with a €100 billion credit line to be used for banking recapitalization. Europe's leaders also began to look for ways to build a banking union that would provide permanent European resources to supervise and backstop systemically important banks. This marked a sea change in how Europe's political leaders sought to respond to the crisis. Nevertheless, for the markets it proved to be too late.

July 2012 was Europe's worst month. Sovereign debt yields for Spain and Italy skyrocketed, and borrowers on the periphery of the euro zone found themselves cut off from most forms of bank credit. For the ECB, this was a major problem. If borrowers on the periphery cannot borrow at any cost, then efforts to lower interest rates further will not translate into new activity and investment. In other words, the mechanism that transmits monetary policy across the euro zone was broken. For ECB President Mario Draghi, it was the last straw. On July 26, 2012, he gave a historic speech to the London finance community. In that speech he promised to do whatever it takes to safeguard the euro. He also reassured his audience that it would be enough. (See box 11.3.)

What followed was a period of unprecedented monetary activism. The ECB effectively committed itself to shore up sovereign debt markets with the unlimited firepower of its balance sheet through what Draghi referred to as "outright monetary transactions." Investors in sovereign debt markets were suitably cowed. Bond prices for Italy and Spain rose accordingly, and the yield differential between those countries and Germany fell. For many participants, the most acute phase of the crisis was over. Europe's economies would continue to suffer under the weight of the recession, but European sovereign debt markets would not experience another rout. The only question is whether this state of affairs is temporary or permanent. The answer is unknowable until the ECB's new firepower is tested. If it is found wanting, then the crisis could return even more quickly than it dissipated in the winter of 2012–2013.

Box 11.3   Speech by Mario Draghi, President of the European Central Bank, at the Global Investment Conference in London, July 26, 2012

I asked myself what sort of message I want to give to you; I wouldn't use the word "sell," but actually I think the best thing I could do, is to give you a candid assessment of how we view the euro situation from Frankfurt. . . .

The first message I would like to send, is that the euro is much, much stronger, the euro area is much, much stronger than people acknowledge today. Not only if you look over the last 10 years but also if you look at it now, you see that as far as inflation, employment, productivity, the euro area has done either like or better than US or Japan. . . .

The second point, the second message I would like to send today, is that progress has been extraordinary in the last six months. If you compare today the euro area member states with six months ago, you will see that the world is entirely different today, and for the better. . . .

But the third point I want to make is in a sense more political. When people talk about the fragility of the euro and the increasing fragility of the euro, and perhaps the crisis of the euro, very often non-euro area member states or leaders, underestimate the amount of political capital that is being invested in the euro. And so we view this, and I do not think we are unbiased observers, we think the euro is irreversible. And it's not an empty word now, because I preceded saying exactly what actions have been made, are being made to make it irreversible.

But there is another message I want to tell you. Within our mandate, the ECB is ready to do whatever it takes to preserve the euro. And believe me, it will be enough.

Solving the Next Crisis?

This chapter has largely been the story of responses to emergent situations. At the same time, European policymakers have attempted to take steps to prevent history from repeating. Several efforts are either complete or in the implementation phases, some of which are more promising than others. Unfortunately, the lions' share of resulting reform efforts has been focused on fixing the wrong problem. As this chapter has pointed out, Europe's fundamental problem stemmed from large and unbalanced capital flows. The most developed reform efforts underway—the so-called six-pack and two-pack of new EU rules and a new intergovernmental Treaty on Stability, Coordination, and Governance (TSCG, or more commonly, the "fiscal compact")—deal less with this problem than with the perceived danger of excessive government spending. Each of these agreements—backed with particular strength by Germany and the other more fiscally sound economies—seek to put in place rules that would theoretically prevent euro-zone members from incurring large sovereign debts.

The TCSG and much of the six-pack are focused on imposing binding rules on sovereign deficits and debts—limiting debt to 60 percent of GDP, observed deficits to 3 percent of GDP, and structural deficits to 0.5 percent of GDP. If these rules sound somewhat familiar, it is because they are essentially a resurrection of the original excessive deficit procedure set out in the 1992 Maastricht Treaty and strengthened in the

1997 Stability and Growth Pact. The irony here is that despite Germany's insistence on strict rules, it was Germany itself that had effectively eviscerated the original rules by breaching its deficit limit and then exempting itself from the excessive deficit procedure in the early 2000s. Merkel has made it clear that her country's actions had been a mistake; her efforts to strengthen fiscal discipline within the euro zone by adding harsher penalties and automatic sanctions have been an attempt to redress the balance.

The more pertinent question is whether a re-imposition of a stricter fiscal pact between euro-zone members could have prevented the outbreak of the current crisis. This was almost certainly not the case in Ireland or Spain—where fiscal irresponsibility played virtually no part in their troubles—or Italy, which has generally stayed within the original Maastricht rules. The cases of Portugal and Greece are more questionable. Portugal had been one of the few states successfully subjected to the excessive deficit procedure in its original form, reforming its public finances in the process. It presents perhaps the best case for a resumption of the old regime.

It is difficult to address Greece, not least because of clear evidence that the country actively hid the extent of its overindebtedness. It sold off (or hypothecated) future income streams from user fees and other forms of taxation. It systematically understated its expenditures and overestimated its revenues. And it was able to do all this while under special supervisory regimes that were in many ways more intrusive than for any other country in the euro zone. While the six-pack does call for stiff penalties for misstating fiscal statistics, there is little in this story to suggest that either a more intrusive regime or a more credible threat of sanctions would have made much of a difference. Unless there is a clear positive incentive to comply with European requirements for statistical collection and budgetary reporting, some circumvention is almost sure to occur. While the two-pack would allow the EU even more intrusive inspection of troubled states economies, it generally only does so once countries are already subject to ESM assistance—which already entails strict oversight. In other words, those new rules generally codify the status quo more than create new regulatory regimes.

Arguably the most promising of the EU's new effort to ensure future stability is the provision within the six-pack that allows the European Commission to maintain surveillance on broader macroeconomic imbalances—moving beyond a simple focus on fiscal problems. After all, countries like Spain and Portugal did not have obvious fiscal problems on the scale of Greece, and yet nevertheless they fell into difficulty. Meanwhile, countries like Belgium and Italy were much more heavily indebted in their public accounts than Spain and Portugal, yet they fared better once the financial market turmoil hit. The explanation lies in the macroeconomic balance between savings and investment rather than in the level of public indebtedness per se. Private savings in Belgium and Italy offset much of the borrowing on the public side in those countries; public savings in Spain and Portugal comes nowhere close to offsetting private sector indebtedness.

However, problems remain with this approach, too. It would be difficult for the EU to carry out the level of surveillance planned: the system currently envisions tracking a "scoreboard" of macroeconomic indicators such as asset and credit markets, unemployment, and the balance of payments, triggering alarms when a country's data exceed certain reference targets. Keeping track of such data in real time will be a challenge, as will sorting out different interpretations of the same figures.

Perhaps even more difficult, though, it is unclear where blame will be placed for intra-euro-zone imbalances. The problem is that these imbalances are symmetrical; German current account surpluses are offset by southern deficits just as German excess savings is paired with southern indebtedness. Constraints on fiscal deficits only address one small part of the larger issue. Even efforts to ensure competitiveness among the deficit countries will do little to address the imbalances generated by those countries that run persistent surpluses.

A more promising line of attack in preventing a repeat of the present crisis would target the unbalanced capital flows at the heart of Europe's current difficulties. It would also focus on the financial institutions that were most at risk when European financial markets began to break apart. This line of reform was suggested at the June 2012 European Council summit and accompanying meeting of the euro-area governments. They argued initially for the power to use European bailout funds to inject capital directly into troubled banks. They also called for the ECB to play the leading role in the supervision of financial institutions. Over time, European leaders called for common efforts (and funds) to wind up troubled banks and to insure their deposits.

This collection of financial market proposals became known collectively as the "banking union." Together, they represented the best chance to bring an end to the crisis and also to ensure that it would not be repeated. Unfortunately, however, the political will to carry through with such reforms has been limited. There was some enthusiasm for a banking union during the summer of 2012 when the euro area was in the depths of the crisis, but that enthusiasm waned increasingly as monetary activism on the part of the ECB calmed the markets. This is unfortunate because the ECB can only address the symptoms and not the causes of the problem. Without major structural reform of European financial markets like that promised by the banking union proposals, there is always the chance that the ECB's commitment to stability could be tested by market participants or national electorates—and found wanting.

The Primacy of Politics

Twice already—in Greece and Italy—popularly elected governments were set aside in favor of technocrats that were viewed by other European capitals as better economic stewards. In both cases, the ensuing popular elections yielded troubling results for the EU.

In May 2012, the Pasok government that had presided over the crisis for three years went from 160 of the 300 seats in the Hellenic Parliament to only forty-one. The ND, which had ultimately shifted away from anti-austerity rhetoric, moved up to 108 seats. The big winner, however, was the radical left Syriza bloc, which had campaigned on a platform of renegotiating Athens' deal with the EU, which they saw as regressive. With the vote dispersed so widely, no party was able to assemble a working government, forcing a second election in June. The results were similar, but with a slight boost in support for the ND, it was able to join with Pasok and a smaller party to narrowly establish a new government broadly committed to maintaining past commitments with its European members. Yet the closeness of the vote—and the fact that the Greeks were forced to vote twice in two months—indicated how divided the state had become, particularly over how committed the people were to further austerity.

The February 2013 European elections in Italy proved to be nearly as inconclusive as the May 2012 elections in Greece. The only stanchly pro-euro, pro-austerity candidate, Monti, got trounced. The parties and coalitions led by the other three major players—Berlusconi, Grillo, and Pier Luigi Bersani—have expressed opinions ranging from lukewarm to outright hostility toward Europe. Bersani, trying to cobble together a governing coalition of his own party, Monti's supporters, and defectors from Grillo's movement, made it clear that he saw the election as a "thermometer" on Euroskepticism, one reflecting a lack of enthusiasm for further economic pain in order to support the wider European project.[33] Ultimately, what happens next in the euro crisis may have far less to do with what Brussels, Berlin, and Frankfurt want than what is politically palatable in the capitals of those countries taking the blame for what has gone wrong.

Notes

Parts of this chapter were published in preliminary form as briefing notes on the website of the University of North Carolina at Chapel Hill's European Union Center of Excellence and are reproduced here with permission. For more briefings on related subjects, please go to: http://www.unc.edu/depts/europe/business_media/business.htm.

1. The electoral and seat allocation data come from Adam Carr's electoral archive: http://psephos.adam-carr.net/countries/g/greece/greece2009.txt (accessed January 23, 2014).

2. Eurostat, "Provision of Deficit and Debt Data for 2008: Second Notification," Eurostat Newsrelease, Euroindicators, October 22, 2009, http://epp.eurostat.ec.europa.eu/cache/ITY_PUBLIC/2-22102009-AP/EN/2-22102009-AP-EN.PDF (accessed January 23, 2014).

3. Charles Forelle, "EU Sees Wider Greek Deficit, Roiling Markets," *Wall Street Journal*, April 23, 2010, http://online.wsj.com/article/SB10001424052748703876404575199520197362174.html (accessed January 23, 2014); and Eurostat, "Euro Area and EU27 Government Deficit at 6.0% and 6.4% of GDP Respectively," Eurostat Newsrelease, Euroindicators, April 26, 2011, http://epp.eurostat.ec.europa.eu/cache/ITY_PUBLIC/2-26042011-AP/EN/2-26042011-AP-EN.PDF (accessed January 23, 2014).

4. Eurostat, "Provision of Deficit and Debt Data for 2008—Second Notification," Eurostat Newsrelease: Euroindicators 149/2009 (October 22, 2009).

5. "Pressekonferenz der Bundeskanzlerin nach dem Europäischen Rat," December 11, 2009, http://www.bundesregierung.de/ContentArchiv/DE/Archiv17/Mitschrift/Pressekonferenzen/2009/12/2009-12-12-pk-bk-bruessel.html (accessed February 2, 2014).

6. Helena Smith, "Papandreou Unveils Radical Reforms to Salvage Greece's Public Finances," *The Guardian*, December 14, 2009, http://www.guardian.co.uk/world/2009/dec/14/greece-unveils-reforms-to-public-finances (accessed January 23, 2014).

7. European Commission, "Report on Greek Government Statistics," January 8 (Brussels: European Commission, 2010).

8. International Monetary Fund, "Greece: Staff Report for the 2009 Article IV Consultation," June 30 (Washington, DC: International Monetary Fund, 2009), 1, 20.

9. The bond yield data in this and the following paragraph are based on ten-year bid rates taken from Global Insight.

10. Bertrand Benoit and Tony Barber, "Germany Ready to Help Eurozone Members," *Financial Times*, February 19, 2009.

11. These data are taken from the AMECO database of the European Commission. The relevant data lines are OVGD (for real gross domestic product [GDP]) and CVGD2 (for the contribution of gross fixed capital formation to real GDP growth). The spreadsheets are easy to compile using the online AMECO database but can also be had on request from the author.

12. Bank for International Settlements, *BIS Quarterly Review*, June 2010, 18–19.

13. Bertrand Benoit and Tony Barber, "Germany Ready to Help Eurozone Members," *Financial Times*, February 19, 2009, http://www.ft.com/intl/cms/s/0/825af89a-fe02-11dd-932e -000077b07658.html#axzz1t5GRRr5M (accessed January 23, 2014).

14. Angela Merkel, "Pressekonferenz Der Bundeskanzlerin Nach Dem Europäischen Rat," March 26, 2010, http://www.bundeskanzlerin.de/nn_683698/Content/DE/Mitschrift/ Pressekonferenzen/2010/03/2010-03-26-pk-bk-bruessel.html (accessed January 23, 2014).

15. This is calculated at interbank exchange rates on the first market day after the policy was announced, May 11. The exchange rate data are taken from http://www.oanda.com for May 11. The euro strengthened against the dollar that day by two cents, only to fall back once questions began to arise about the details of the rescue package.

16. European Central Bank, "ECB Decides on Measures to Address Severe Tensions in Financial Markets," press release, May 10, 2010, http://www.ecb.int/press/pr/date/2010/html/ pr100510.en.html (accessed January 23, 2014).

17. Eurostat Financial Balance Sheets.

18. "Cost of Ireland's Bank Bail-out to Hit €40 Bn," *The Telegraph*, September 30, 2010, http://www.telegraph.co.uk/finance/financialcrisis/8034070/Cost-of-Irelands-bank-bail-out -to-hit-40-bn.html (accessed January 23, 2014).

19. "Best Countries for Business: #4 Ireland," *Forbes*, June 2011.

20. Bank for International Settlements, *BIS Quarterly Review*, December 2010, 11–12.

21. Robert Fishman, "Portugal's Unncessary Bailout," April 12, 2011, http://www.nytimes .com/2011/04/13/opinion/13fishman.html?pagewanted=all (accessed January 23, 2014).

22. For a recent review of this literature, see Lars Jonung and Eoin Drea, "It Can't Happen, It's a Bad Idea, It Won't Last: U.S. Economists on the EMU and the Euro, 1989–2002," *Econ Journal Watch* 7, no. 1 (January 2010): 4–52. That article drew consideration criticism from many quarters. The authors' reply to their critics was published as Lars Jonung and Eoin Drea, "The Euro: It Happened, It's Not Reversible, So . . . Make It Work," *Econ Journal Watch* 7, no. 2 (May 2010): 113–18.

23. These data on relative movements in real effective exchange rates and cumulative current account balances are available from the AMECO database of the European Commission. A copy of our calculations is available upon request.

24. Erik Jones, "Merkel's Folly," *Survival* 52, no. 3 (June–July 2010): 29–30.

25. Klaus-Jürgen Nagel, "North Rhine Westphalia: The *Land* Election That Dismissed a Federal Government," *Regional and Federal Studies* 16, no. 3 (September 2006): 347–54.

26. This paragraph is adapted from Peter Ludlow, "In the Last Resort: The European Council and the Euro Crisis, Spring 2010," *Eurocomment Briefing Note* 7, nos. 7–8 (June 2010).

27. Rachel Donadio and Niki Kitsantonis, "Two-Day Strike in Greece Ahead of Austerity Vote," *New York Times*, June 28, 2011, http://www.nytimes.com/2011/06/29/world/europe/ 29greece.html (accessed January 23, 2014).

28. European Banking Authority, *2011 EU-Wide Stress Test Aggregate Report*, July 15, 2011, http://stress-test.eba.europa.eu/pdf/EBA_ST_2011_Summary_Report_v6.pdf (accessed January 23, 2014).

29. Mario Draghi and Jean-Claude Trichet, Letter published by Italian newspaper Corriere Della Serra, August 5, 2011, http://www.corriere.it/economia/11_settembre_29/trichet _draghi_inglese_304a5f1e-ea59-11e0-ae06-4da866778017.shtml (accessed January 23, 2014).

30. For a fuller discussion, see Erik Jones, "Italy's Sovereign Debt Crisis," *Survival* 54, no. 1 (March 2012): 83–110.

31. Again, for further discussion, refer to Erik Jones, "Italy's Sovereign Debt Crisis," *Survival* 54, no. 1 (March 2012): 83–110.

32. Drew Fitzgerald and Stacy Meichtry, "S&P Cuts Italy's Sovereign-Debt Rating," *Wall Street Journal*, September 20, 2011, http://online.wsj.com/article/SB10001424053111904106 704576581301721363640.html (accessed January 23, 2014).

33. Christopher Emsden, "Italy's Bersani Set on Forming Government, Asks Grillo to be Clear," *Wall Street Journal*, March 6, 2013.

Suggested Readings

Blanchard, Olivier, and Francesco Giavazzi. "Current Account Deficits in the Euro Area: The End of the Feldstein-Horioka Puzzle?" *Brookings Papers on Economic Activity*, 2002, 147–209.

Caballero, Ricardo J., Emmanuel Farhi, and Pierre-Olivier Gourinchas. "Financial Crash, Commodity Prices, and Global Imbalances." *Brookings Papers on Economic Activity*, 2008, 1–55.

Decressin, Jörg, and Emil Stavrev. "Current Accounts in a Currency Union," IMF Working Paper WP/09/127, June. Washington, DC: IMF, 2009.

Fagan, Gabriel, and V. Gaspar. "Macroeconomic Adjustment to Monetary Union." ECB Working Paper No. 946, October. Frankfurt: European Central Bank, 2008.

Hardie, Iain, and David Howarth, eds. *Market-Based Banking and the International Financial Crisis*. Oxford: Oxford University Press, 2013.

Royo, Sebastián. *Lessons from the Economic Crisis in Spain*. Basingstoke: Palgrave.

Shmidt, Vivien A., and Mark Thatcher, eds. *Resilient Liberalism in Europe's Political Economy*. Cambridge: Cambridge University Press.

Wolf, Martin. *Fixing Global Finance*. New Haven, CT: Yale University Press, 2009.

CHAPTER 12

European Law and Politics

R. Daniel Kelemen

Since the end of World War II, across Europe the power of courts has expanded dramatically. Many scholars refer to this trend as the "judicialization of politics." The judicialization of politics in Europe takes many forms—national constitutional courts declaring acts of parliaments unconstitutional, administrative courts challenging state actions, aggressive prosecutors using the courts to stamp out corruption and topple politicians at the highest levels of government, the European Court of Justice (ECJ) asserting legal doctrines that erode national sovereignty, or the European Court of Human Rights (ECHR) issuing rulings that challenge national practices on highly controversial social and cultural issues. In the broadest sense, the judicialization of politics involves "[greater] reliance on courts and judicial means for addressing core moral predicaments, public policy questions and political controversies."[1]

While the judicialization of politics is a global phenomenon, it is nowhere more pronounced than in Europe.[2] In Europe, judicialization has occurred at both the national level and the regional or supranational level. At the national level, constitutional courts have increasingly asserted the power of judicial review and other courts have become more significant actors in a variety of policy processes. Above the level of the nation-state, the ECJ and the ECHR have emerged as the most powerful supranational courts in world history. Developments at these two levels have been tightly linked, with supranational and national courts often relying on one another as allies in expanding judicial power.

This chapter examines the causes, the scope, and the consequences of the judicialization of politics in Europe. First, we explore why courts have gained so much power in recent decades. Next, we survey the reach of judicial power. What fields of politics and policy do national and supranational courts influence at the moment? Finally, we ask, "What difference does judicialization make?" If democratically elected Parliaments have lost power relative to courts, does this mean that judicialization has undermined democracy? Or are courts providing vital safeguards for individual rights? Ultimately, is judicialization a positive development to be celebrated or a worrying trend that needs to be reined in?

Causes of Judicialization

The growth of judicial power in Europe cannot be attributed to a single explanation. A confluence of trends at the national, supranational, and global levels has led courts to take on an unprecedented degree of political power.

THE AGE OF RIGHTS

The aftermath of World War II saw the spread of a rights discourse and a rights ideology across advanced industrialized countries. With the United Nations' adoption of the Universal Declaration of Human Rights in 1948 and the near-universal acceptance of the idea of human rights in subsequent decades, we entered what Louis Henkin termed "the age of rights."[3] Across Europe and the world, democracies placed greater emphasis on the protection of individual human rights. In part, this was a reaction to the crimes committed by the Nazis and other fascist regimes in Europe. The rise of fascism at least partially discredited the model of unrestricted parliamentary democracy that had prevailed in most European democracies. Unlike in the United States, where the doctrine of separation of powers and the practice of judicial review were already deeply entrenched, most European democracies had been based on the concept of parliamentary sovereignty. Parliamentary sovereignty suggests that the parliament, as the elected body representing the will of the people, is sovereign and has supremacy over all other organs of government. However, in the run-up to World War II, fascist parties in Germany and elsewhere had used their control of parliamentary power to extinguish individual rights. The lesson drawn by many postwar leaders—particularly those in countries that had been ruled by fascist regimes—was that the power to govern could not simply be left to parliamentary majorities. Government power would need to be checked by powerful courts that could protect individual rights, even against the wishes of powerful parliamentary majorities. Thus, it is no surprise that some of the most powerful constitutional courts in Europe were created in countries with some of the darkest wartime legacies.

The postwar architects of democracy in West Germany, Italy, and Austria all opted to create powerful constitutional courts, dedicated to the protection of individual rights.[4] After the collapse of their authoritarian regimes in the 1970s, Spain and Portugal followed suit. These courts were given extraordinary powers of judicial review. In Germany, individuals were guaranteed direct access to the constitutional court (the *Bundesverfassungsgericht*). In Italy, any court that doubted the constitutionality of a statute at issue in a case before it was given the power to refer the case to the Italian Constitutional Court (*Corte costituzionale*) for an opinion on the constitutionality of the statute. By contrast, support for the model of parliamentary supremacy persisted to a greater extent in the UK and in Nordic countries, which helps explain the resistance to domestic and supranational judicial review in these countries.[5]

In expanding protection of fundamental human rights, national constitutional courts were not acting alone. They received a significant encouragement from the supranational level, through the work of the European Court of Human Rights. The

European Court of Human Rights (not to be confused with the European Court of Justice, which we discuss below) is a judicial body attached to the Council of Europe. Established in 1949, the Council of Europe aimed to promote democracy, human rights, the rule of law, and European integration. A year later, the Council of Europe drafted a European Convention on Human Rights, a treaty that required all Council of Europe member countries to protect the human rights of their citizens and that established a court (the European Court of Human Rights) to hear cases brought by citizens who claimed that their rights had been violated. As Andrew Moravcsik has argued, the European Convention on Human Rights served as a kind of commitment device, enabling governments to credibly signal their commitment to human rights norms and to assure neighbors that they could not abandon liberal democracy.[6] By submitting themselves to the jurisdiction of the supranational European Court of Human Rights, European governments put an external check on themselves, tying their own hands.

ECONOMIC LIBERALIZATION AND THE CHANGING ROLE OF THE STATE

Over the past thirty years, European countries have profoundly liberalized their economies. To a large extent, this process of economic liberalization has been linked to the process of European integration and the construction of a common market, as we discuss below. But even if we leave aside for a moment the EU dimension, it is clear that at the national level the state has retreated from many of its traditional roles in economic management and many governments have opened up competition in markets that were previously sheltered from it. This economic liberalization has encouraged judicialization across a wide range of areas of economic regulation.

The connection between economic liberalization and judicialization is not self-evident. Economic liberalization is widely understood as a process that relies on deregulation—the removal of legal restrictions on free enterprise. In fact, scholars from Karl Polanyi to Steven Vogel have explained that deregulation of one kind is often followed by reregulation of another and the establishment of freer markets may paradoxically require the adoption of even more rules.[7] Why? In part, the explanation is political, as the public demand new rules to add a social component to the process of market making and to protect them against the vagaries of free markets. In part, the explanation is functional. When economic liberalization lifts restrictions on entry into economic markets, it allows a far greater number of economic actors to enter the marketplace. In these circumstances, policymakers tasked with pursuing public policy goals—such as protecting consumer safety or policing fraud of various sorts—cannot easily rely on the sorts of informal, flexible approaches to regulation that are effective in relatively closed markets with a limited number of familiar players. Instead, they find it more effective to rely on more formal, transparent and "juridical" rules that assure that all market players are treated equally.

One related aspect of this phenomenon concerns privatization of state-owned enterprises. When governments privatize state-owned monopolies in areas such as transportation, energy, and telecommunications (as European countries did throughout the 1980s and 1990s), they set up systems of regulation to ensure fair competition in the new markets and to ensure that providers meet minimal safety standards and public service obligations. While the enterprises were state owned, the government could achieve most of its policy aims by informally pressuring management. Once enterprises are privatized, governments lose this direct control; to compensate, they put in place regulatory regimes that dictate the rules that enterprises (former state monopolies and new entrants alike) must follow, and they invite the courts to enforce these rules.

EUROPEAN INTEGRATION

The process of "European integration"—the term scholars use for the ongoing transfer of authority from national governments to the European Union—has played a major role in encouraging the judicialization of politics across all the EU's member states. Courts have both helped to drive forward the process of European integration while they also have been empowered by European integration. The European Union's legal system is unprecedented in world history. Over time, the European Court of Justice has emerged as the supreme court of the European Union, with jurisdiction—and supremacy—over the many areas of law in which the EU is active. It is the EU's legal system more than anything that distinguishes the EU from other international organizations and gives it the character of a quasi-federal political system.

European integration has encouraged judicialization for two main reasons. First, it is the very political structure of the EU that encourages the process. The EU has a weak and highly fragmented institutional structure that stimulates lawmakers to rely on courts to pursue their policy objectives. With little more than 25,000 civil servants working for EU institutions, the EU has extremely limited capacities to administer its own policies. The EU adopts policies that affect nearly half a billion citizens, but they must attempt to do so with the same number of employees as a typical midsized European city. Instead of implementing its own policies, the EU relies primarily on national governments for implementation. But EU lawmakers do not trust national governments to implement EU laws faithfully. They have good reasons to be skeptical, as many EU rules impose substantial costs on national governments and industries. Not only do policymakers in the European Commission and European Parliament distrust member states, but also the governments represented in the EU's Council of Ministers may distrust one another's commitment to implementing EU law.

Given the EU's weakness and the desire of EU lawmakers to ensure that EU laws are implemented in all member states, lawmakers draft laws in a way that invites the European Court of Justice and national courts to play an active role in monitoring implementation. Lawmakers do this by framing many policies in terms of rights, such as rights for employees, rights for shareholders, rights for consumers, rights for women, and economic rights for firms. The EU's strategy is to encourage the individuals and companies that enjoy these rights to enforce them before national and EU courts. Moreover, despite the fact that national leaders frequently protest that the ECJ is engaging in judicial activism and illegitimately extending its own powers, leaders have nevertheless repeatedly introduced institutional reforms designed to strengthen the ECJ. For instance, in the 1992 Maastricht Treaty, member governments gave the ECJ the authority to impose penalty payments on member states that fail to comply with previous ECJ rulings. Through a series of treaty revisions over the past thirty years, the member states have steadily expanded the ECJ's jurisdiction. Most recently, with the Lisbon Treaty, they extended the jurisdiction of the ECJ to all EU matters except for foreign policy.

While EU policy makers in the Council of Ministers, the European Parliament, and the European Commission clearly play an important role in encouraging judicialization, the European Court of Justice has hardly been a passive player in this process. (See box 12.1.)

The ECJ has not simply accepted policymakers' invitation to become involved in the policy process; the Court has played an indispensable role in extending its own power far beyond what many EU lawmakers had envisioned. Over the years, the ECJ's expansive interpretations of Community law transformed a set of international treaties into a constitution in all but name. In landmark rulings in the early 1960s, the ECJ asserted the revolutionary legal doctrines of direct effect (*Van Gend en Loos*[8]) and supremacy (*Costa v. ENEL*[9]), establishing the bedrock of the Community legal order. (See box 12.2.)

The combination of direct effect and supremacy created a situation in which individuals could go before their national courts and invoke their rights under European Community law, even where these conflicted with national law. Certainly, these highly controversial doctrines were not accepted overnight, and there are still considerable

---

Box 12.1   The European Court of Justice

The European Court of Justice is the supreme court of the European Union. Located in Luxembourg City, the Court is composed of twenty-seven judges, one appointed by each member state for a six-year, renewable term. The plenary of twenty-seven judges very rarely hears a case together. Rather, the ECJ organizes itself into a system of chambers, and chambers of three or five judges hear most cases. Very significant cases are heard by the Grand Chamber of thirteen judges. Though various combinations of judges decide cases, the decisions are always published and treated as the consensus ruling of the ECJ. No minority opinions are drafted, and no records of internal deliberations are published. To protect the independence of individual judges—for instance, to shield them from pressure from their home government—the deliberations of the court are kept secret.

To help the ECJ cope with its burgeoning case load, the 1986 Single European Act called for the establishment of a lower court beneath the ECJ. This "Court of First Instance" commenced operations in 1989, and with the adoption of the Lisbon Treaty in 2010 its name changed to "The General Court." Like the ECJ, the General Court is composed of twenty-seven judges, who divide themselves into chambers, deliberate in secret, and issue their opinions as the consensus of the court. Much of the General Court's jurisdiction focuses on cases brought directly by private parties—such as firms—that claim they have been harmed by actions or omissions by the European Commission or other EU institutions. The General Court's rulings can be appealed to the ECJ.

Box 12.2   Direct Effect and Supremacy

The principle of direct effect held that European Community law was, under some conditions, capable of conferring rights on individuals, which those individuals could invoke in legal proceedings before national courts. This marked a profound departure from traditional approaches to international law. Normally, international law is binding upon states: the states that sign treaties are obliged (at least in principle) to fulfill their treaty obligations. But international treaties do not confer rights directly on individuals. However, in *Van Gend* the ECJ ruled that the Treaty of Rome was not an ordinary treaty between states, but instead that the treaty established a Community that comprised both the states and their citizens. Thus, as the Court explained, "the Community constitutes a new legal order of international law for the benefit of which the states have limited their sovereign rights, albeit within limited fields, and the subjects of which comprise not only Member States but also their nationals. Independently of the legislation of member States, Community law therefore not only imposes obligations on individuals but is also intended to confer upon them rights which become part of their legal heritage."[1]

In its 1964 *Costa v. ENEL* ruling, the ECJ took the next landmark step by asserting the principle of supremacy. Supremacy means that in cases where national law and Community law conflict, Community law must take supremacy. Again, this was a radical doctrine that departed from traditional norms of international law and certainly from what many governments had in mind when they signed the Treaty of Rome in 1957. As it clarified and developed the concept of supremacy in subsequent rulings, the ECJ asserted that national courts were legally bound to set aside any provisions of national law that were incompatible with requirements of European Community law.

---

1. *Van Gend en Loos*, (1963) ECR 13.

tensions between the ECJ and national courts over who holds the ultimate supremacy in cases of conflict between European and national law.[10] But over the course of the next two decades, national courts and national governments across Europe did come, in practice, to accept direct effect and supremacy—along with a variety of other bold ECJ doctrines.[11] The puzzling question is how the ECJ managed to assert these bold doctrines and strip so much away from national sovereignty without national governments slapping the Court down. In other words, how did the ECJ defy the laws of political gravity and lift itself by its own bootstraps to a position of supremacy?

One key to the ECJ's success has been its ability to build partnerships with and attract the support of judges across Europe. The ECJ did not cloister itself away in Luxembourg, but actively reached out to judges in the EU member states, encouraging them to embrace Community law and to refer cases to the ECJ through the preliminary ruling procedure. If national courts have been the ECJ's indispensable partners in contracting the EU's legal order, then the preliminary ruling procedure has been the key channel of communication through which they developed their relationship.

The preliminary ruling procedure had a modest birth, as a clause of little note included in the Treaty of Rome with little thought given to its potential consequences. The procedure was included in the treaty as a way to allow individuals to challenge European law and to help national courts interpret it. But this little procedure took

Box 12.3 The Preliminary Ruling Procedure

Article 267 of the Treaty on the Functioning of the European Union ("The Lisbon Treaty")

The Court of Justice of the European Union shall have jurisdiction to give preliminary rulings concerning:

(a) the interpretation of the Treaties;
(b) the validity and interpretation of acts of the institutions, bodies, offices or agencies of the Union;

Where such a question is raised before any court or tribunal of a Member State, that court or tribunal may, if it considers that a decision on the question is necessary to enable it to give judgment, request the Court to give a ruling thereon.

Where any such question is raised in a case pending before a court or tribunal of a Member State against whose decisions there is no judicial remedy under national law, that court or tribunal shall bring the matter before the Court.

If such a question is raised in a case pending before a court or tribunal of a Member State with regard to a person in custody, the Court of Justice of the European Union shall act with the minimum of delay.

on a big life as it enabled national courts—not just courts but even the most obscure tribunals—that were faced with cases that hinged on questions of Community law to send references to the ECJ to ask for its interpretation of Community law. In other words, national courts could order a stay in their proceedings and send a reference to the ECJ asking for its interpretation of the legal questions of European Community law that would determine the outcome of the case. The ECJ did not simply wait for the cases to arrive in its mailbox. The Court actively cultivated and trained a network of national judges committed to European law who might send them cases through the preliminary ruling procedure.[12] (See box 12.3.)

This procedure had a number of profound effects. First, it established a channel for direct dialogue between the ECJ and national courts, not mediated by national governments. This eventually allowed the ECJ to enlist national courts as its partners in the construction of the European legal order in a way that national governments could scarcely impede. When a national court used a ruling from the ECJ as the basis for its own domestic judgment, this ruling became part of domestic law that governments could only resist by ignoring their own courts. In the 1960s and 1970s, national governments did attempt to pressure their courts to ignore the ECJ's supremacy claims.[13] However, given the value placed on judicial independence and the rule of law in European democracies, governments were loath to defy their own courts when—as became increasingly common—those courts relied on ECJ jurisprudence.

Second, the preliminary ruling procedure helped trigger a dynamic of intercourt competition, whereby many judges at lower level courts within national judicial systems saw references to the ECJ as a way to circumvent superior courts or rival courts within their own judicial hierarchy.[14] Lower court judges who feared having their rulings quashed by higher courts in their national judicial hierarchies could skip over these higher courts and request a preliminary ruling directly from the European Court of Justice. In other words, the ECJ became the judicial trump card in national inter-court disputes. More generally, many courts across Europe came to see the ECJ as their ally in the cause of empowering the judiciary vis-à-vis other branches of government.[15]

Finally, by opening up a channel for cases brought by private litigants to reach the ECJ, the preliminary ruling procedure democratized European law and dramatically increased the potential volume of cases the ECJ could hear. To be vibrant and powerful, courts need cases. A steady volume of cases unleashes a self-reinforcing cycle of institutionalization in which rulings establish legal doctrines that then provide the legal basis for judging subsequent disputes. A steady volume of cases also enhances the legitimacy of a court as the authoritative forum in which disputes are resolved within a political system. The European Commission did (and still does) bring many enforcement cases (so-called infringement proceedings) before the ECJ. However, given the Commission's limited capacities, it was vital to open up the legal system to private parties.

The combination of doctrines such as direct effect and supremacy with the channel afforded by the preliminary ruling procedure meant that private actors with an interest in enforcing their EU rights could at least have indirect access to the ECJ through their national courts. And a variety of litigants took advantage of that channel, mobilizing to enforce their rights under European law.[16] That being said, the system has shortcomings and faces a number of challenges. Access to EU justice is uneven, with privileged litigants (such as large corporations) enjoying better access than individuals or small organizations of modest means and with significant variations in rates of litigation enforcing European law across policy areas and across countries.[17] Individuals contemplating litigation to enforce their rights under European law face extremely high hurdles, in terms of the cost and time involved in the legal process. For all but the most privileged litigants, litigation support structures such as legal aid services are crucial for making access to justice a reality.[18] Moreover, courts in some new Eastern European states and in the EU's Nordic member states are reluctant to use the preliminary ruling procedure, effectively cutting off many citizens in those countries from access to the EU legal system.[19] Recent challenges to the independence of the judiciary in Hungary, Bulgaria, and Romania have raised new questions about the EU's ability to rely on national courts in those countries to enforce European law and, more generally, about the EU's ability to ensure respect for the rule of law in an increasingly sometimes unreliable network of thousands of national courts.

The fragmentation of political power in the EU that we discussed above also opened up space for ECJ activism. Many ECJ decisions have sparked denunciations from the individual national governments directly touched by those decisions. Some ECJ decisions have proven controversial enough to spark outcries from multiple member state governments. But very few decisions have ever led member states to act collectively to rein in the ECJ.[20] To overturn ECJ interpretations of European law, the member states either have to pass new laws (which typically involves supermajority voting and the support of the European Parliament) or revise the treaties (which requires unanimous agreement of all member states). Given the diversity of preferences among member state governments, they will rarely take the same view of controversial ECJ decisions or be able to agree on how to respond. This political division allows the ECJ to assert its interpretations of EU law with little fear of political backlash. Moreover, there is considerable evidence that the ECJ tends to engage in what Miguel Maduro has called "majoritarian activism," meaning that they make rulings that strike down national laws and practices differing from those that prevail in the majority of member states.[21] In other words, many ECJ decisions essentially impose the will of the majority of member states, which clearly makes it unlikely that that majority would seek to reverse those decisions.

Thus far we have focused on how the institutional structure of the EU and the activism of the ECJ encouraged judicialization, but European integration has encouraged judicialization through another pathway as well—by promoting economic liberalization. Above we discussed, in general terms, how economic liberalization tends to enhance judicialization. The EU has played in driving forward this dynamic in recent decades. Since its founding, one of the EU's central aims has been to construct a single European market in which goods, services, capital, and labor could move freely. The project gained new momentum in the mid-1980s when Commission President Jacques Delors relaunched the stalled effort to complete the single market. One might assume (and many have) that creating a single market simply requires lawmakers to eliminate tariffs and dismantle nontariff barriers to trade (such as national regulations that discriminate against foreign products, services, and workers) through deregulation. But in fact completing Europe's single market has also required reregulation.

In areas where national rules that distorted trade were dismantled, new EU level regulations were put in place to create a level playing field for economic actors. For example, in many areas where national consumer safety and environmental protection standards distorted trade, these have been replaced with uniform EU regulations. Or likewise in the field of financial regulation, many traditional national regulations were dismantled and replaced with EU regulations that aimed to establish an integrated European financial market. Compared to the national regulatory systems that they replaced, new EU regulations rely far more on courts and litigation. So the creation of a single market has sparked a cycle of deregulation and judicialized reregulation.[22]

The Scope of Judicialization

Just how far has judicialization in Europe gone? Which areas of policy are affected by the growing power of courts? The judicialization of politics in Europe has led courts to become involved in nearly every sort of major political and policy dispute imaginable. The words of Aharon Barak, former chief justice of the Supreme Court of Israel and noted legal scholar, capture the broad scope of law's impact in contemporary Europe: "Nothing falls beyond the purview of judicial review; the world is filled with law; anything and everything is justiciable."[23] Commenting on the distinctive features of the American legal system and legal culture in the 1830s, Alexis de Tocqueville wrote, "Scarcely any political question arises in the United States which is not resolved, sooner or later, into a judicial question."[24] Much the same could be said of Europe today.

At the national level, constitutional courts across Europe have intervened decisively in most major areas of political life. From governing the economy, to determining the relations between different branches and levels of government, to setting the terms of immigration, asylum, and citizenship policies, to combating discrimination, to setting the terms of church-state relations, to protecting civil liberties in the context of the struggle against terrorism, again and again we can observe national high courts asserting themselves in the midst of some of the most heated political controversies.

Germany's constitution (the Basic Law or *Grundgesetz*) enables citizens who allege that public authorities have violated their fundamental rights to file a constitutional complaint directly with the Constitutional Court. Thousands of such individual complaints are filed every year, generating the main source of the Constitutional Court's caseload and the basis on which it has issued many of its most significant judgments. The Constitutional Court has declared hundreds of federal and state statues to be unconstitutional, and its rulings have shaped German policy on major issues including abortion, criminal sentencing, education, nuclear power, divorce, and taxation.[25] As a result, German lawmakers take into account the anticipated reactions of the Constitutional Court when crafting legislation.[26]

The Italian constitutional court has shaped policy in areas as diverse as pensions, divorce, sexual identity, executive-legislative relations, civil liberties, and church-state relations.[27] Beyond the impact of the Constitutional Court, the judiciary has transformed politics in even more fundamental ways. Aggressive public prosecutors worked through the courts in the *mani pulite* (clean hands) investigations to expose the *Tangentopoli* (Bribeville) scandal that helped to topple the Italian political establishment.[28]

France too has experienced a dramatic expansion of judicial power in recent decades.[29] Under the constitution of France's Fifth Republic introduced in 1958 (and reforms introduced in 1974), a group of lawmakers from the legislative minority (a minimum of sixty deputies in the National Assembly or sixty senators) can challenge the constitutionality of a statute before it goes into effect. Through this "abstract review" procedure, minority lawmakers can and do use the Constitutional Council (*Conseil Constitutionnel*) to place a check on the legislative majority, striking down unconstitutional laws before they ever go into effect. As Alec Stone explains, "Since the late 1970s, virtually every major bill, and every budget since 1974, has been referred [to the Constitutional Council] by parliamentary minorities. Their efforts have been rewarded: since 1981 more than half of all referrals have resulted in annulments." In 1982, the Constitutional Council blocked the centerpiece of the new Socialist government's economic plan. The Council ruled that a bill to nationalize major industrial conglomerates, banks, and financial services firms was unconstitutional because it failed to provide adequate compensation to those whose property (shareholders) was nationalized. To satisfy the Constitutional Council, the Socialist government later passed a new version of the bill that provided for more compensation to shareholders, and which substantially increased the cost of the privatization program. As Alec Stone (later Stone Sweet) has demonstrated, as a result of such assertions of judicial power, French lawmakers regularly shape their legislative proposals in order to guard against censure by the Constitutional Council.[30] Nevertheless, rulings by the Constitutional Council annulling government bills have decisively shaped policy in a host of areas, including media pluralism, electoral rules, and education.

In the United Kingdom, this process has been driven to a significant degree by the introduction of the Human Rights Act in 1998. The Human Rights Act sought to strengthen British compliance with the European Convention on Human Rights. It did so by enabling individuals to invoke rights contained in the European Convention on Human Rights before British courts and by demanding that those courts seek to interpret UK law in a manner compatible with the Charter. Where UK law clearly violates the Charter, British courts can issue a "declaration of incompatibility," which, while not formally voiding the legislation, places immense pressure on Parliament to amend the legislation such that it will comply with the Charter.[31]

In the UK, the Appellate Committee of the House of Lords (until recently the highest judicial authority in the UK) declared the UK's post-9/11 state-of-emergency legislation unconstitutional (*Belmarsh*[32]) and ruled on whether the government had to take action on behalf of Guantanamo detainees who might be tortured by U.S. authorities (*Al Rawi*[33]). Even more dramatically, the UK dramatically reorganized its judiciary by establishing a new Supreme Court in October 2009. The Supreme Court replaced the Appellate Committee of the House of Lords as the highest court in the United Kingdom. The fact that the highest court of the UK had in fact been an organ of its (undemocratic) upper legislative chamber (the House of Lords), and that the Lord Chancellor was in fact a member of the Cabinet (in other words, the executive) violated prevailing norms concerning judicial independence across Europe—and potentially violated the European Convention on Human Rights' (Article 6) requirement that states provide for a fair trial before an "independent" court. The establishment of an independent Supreme Court sets the stage for an even greater judicialization of British politics in the future.

At the European level, the EU and the ECJ have encouraged judicialization across a broad spectrum of policy areas. European law has had a profound impact on the fight against discrimination in Europe. The judicialization of antidiscrimination policy arose first in the field of gender equality. The Treaty of Rome included a provision that prohibited discrimination in employment on the basis of sex. This provision was included not due to a deep commitment to gender equality on the part of the EU's founders, but rather because some member states feared that others would gain a competitive advantage by relying on lower wage female workers. Nevertheless, on the basis of this treaty article and subsequent directives on gender equality enacted by EU lawmakers, the ECJ dramatically expanded gender equality rights in Europe.

The process began in the 1970s, when a Belgian labor lawyer, Elaine Vogel-Polsky, working together with a Belgian flight attendant, Gabrielle Defrenne, brought a series of test cases asserting that the Treaty of Rome's prohibition on sex discrimination in employment (in what was then Article 141) constituted an individual right with direct effect. The Court agreed that the sex equality rule did have direct effect, setting the stage for other women's organizations and activists to wage strategic litigation campaigns based on European rights in later years. Proponents of gender equality in a number of member states leveraged women's rights under European law in order to generate pressure for policy reform in their countries.[34] Over the years, the ECJ has extended the prohibition on gender discrimination to protect against discrimination on the basis of pregnancy, to demand gender equality in pensions and to declare that unequal treatment of part-time workers (in terms of not offering them the same benefits as full-time workers) amounted to indirect sex discrimination, since the majority of part-time workers were women.

More recently, the EU's adoption of the Employment Equality and Racial Equality Directives (Directives 2000/78/EC and 2000/43/EC) in 2000 has set the stage for extending the model developed in the gender discrimination field to fight other forms of discrimination. The Racial Equality Directive prohibits discrimination on the basis of race in employment, education, social protection, and access to goods and services. The Employment Equality Directive prohibits discrimination in employment on the basis of age, disability, religion, and sexual orientation. Already national courts have experienced an upsurge of discrimination claims in some fields, such as age discrimination, and important cases have reached the ECJ.[35] With the adoption of the Lisbon Treaty, which gives legal force to the EU's Charter of Fundamental Rights, more rights-based litigation can be expected.

We can observe significant judicialization in a wide range of areas of economic policy making. The field of antitrust (or, as it is known in Europe, "competition policy") has become thoroughly juridified. Traditionally, European approaches to competition policy were based on an approach that granted regulators great flexibility and involved little litigation or judicial review. Government regulators had the flexibility to balance the promotion of competition against other policy goals such as maintaining employment or encouraging industrial cooperation to foster technological innovation. However, over the past twenty years, as the European Commission became more aggressive in enforcing competition policy and penalizing violators, the European Court of Justice and the Court of First Instance (now called the General Court) have pressed European regulators to adhere to strict procedures and to provide legally defensible justifications for its actions. The Commission now regularly imposes multimillion-euro fines on companies, only to see these fines challenged by the firms before European courts. Since 2004, as part of the so-called modernization of competition policy, the EU has pushed to encourage private parties to play a more active role in enforcing competition policy by taking legal action before national courts against competitors who violate EU competition law.[36]

In the field of securities regulation, EU legislation has established a host of shareholders rights that have provided a legal basis for the emergence of shareholder litigation in countries across the EU—a phenomenon that had been almost unheard of before the EU became involved in the field. Before the mid-1980s, across Europe stock exchanges were largely self-regulating. Generally, governments imposed few disclosure requirements and did little to protect investors; instead, they relied on the notion that the established, trusted players in their sheltered financial markets would self-regulate in the interest of maintaining their reputations. But as the EU has worked to open up national markets and create a truly pan-European market for trading stocks, bonds, and other financial instruments, it has simultaneously encouraged the judicialization of regulation. The EU has established an enormous body of law that establishes legally enforceable disclosure rules and various investor rights.[37] This in turn has triggered the emergence of forms of shareholder litigation that were previously unknown in Europe, as investors seek to enforce their EU rights (and recoup their losses) in court.

The ECJ has developed a body of jurisprudence that significantly influences national health care systems.[38] The health care sector was long thought to be immune to the influence of European law. However, in recent years, ECJ rulings have affected patients, doctors, and other major players in the health care sector. The ECJ has applied the Working Time Directive to health care, issuing rulings on maximum allowable working hours for doctors. Beginning with its 1998 *Kohll*[39] and *Decker*[40] decisions, the Court has issued a string of judgments on patients' rights, in particular the right to seek nonemergency medical care across borders.

One landmark decision involved the case of a British woman who was suffering extreme pain while lingering on a National Health Service (NHS) waiting list for hip replacement surgery. She decided to go to France to have the hip replacement surgery done and then asked her local NHS health care trust to reimburse her for the costs— which they refused to do. She challenged that decision in the British courts and the case was eventually referred to the ECJ through the preliminary ruling procedure. In its *Watts*[41] judgment, the ECJ ruled that the NHS must reimburse patients for treatments in other member states if the waiting time for treatment in the UK exceeds "the period which is acceptable in the light of an objective medical assessment of the clinical needs of the person concerned" (para. 68 and 149(4)). The Court said that the NHS must allow clinical experts to assess the acceptable waiting time for the individual—depending on their case and their level of pain—and patients must be able to challenge refusals to grant authorization for treatment abroad in "judicial or quasi-judicial proceedings" (para. 116–17). Beyond patients and doctors, other economic actors in the health care sector, such as health service providers and insurers, have been affected as the Court has extended EU rules on competition, state aid, and public procurement to the health sector in some instances.[42]

The ECJ's highly controversial rulings in *Viking*,[43] *Laval*,[44] Rüffert,[45] and *Luxembourg*[46] demonstrate the significant—and potentially destabilizing—impact that European law is having on systems of industrial relations. These rulings center on the conflict between the right to free movement of services in the common market, on the one hand, and national systems of industrial relations, on the other. The details of each case differ, though in essence the conflicts pit service providers (in fields such as construction) against workers from lower wage jurisdictions that wish to provide their services in higher wage member states.

Should firms from lower wage countries who win contracts in higher wage countries be able to pay the workers that they send there to do the work with the lower wages that prevail in their home country, or the higher wages that prevail in the country where the job is being done? Should unions in the host country be able to strike to block the lower wage workers from completing the job? The ECJ has held that where national law provides for a legal minimum wage, foreign workers must be paid that wage. However, where wages and other working conditions are set through collective bargaining between employers and unions—rather than through statutes—the terms of those collective bargains cannot be applied to foreign companies. In other words, the ECJ rulings could force countries that wish to defend their minimum wages and working conditions to transform their systems of industrial relations—setting minimum wages and working conditions by statute rather than through collective bargaining if they want to apply them to foreign operators.

While this might sound like a technicality, it would actually involve a profound transformation of systems of industrial relations which are deeply rooted in the distinctive national "styles of capitalism" that prevail in each EU member country.[47] So far, the ECJ has held that while unions have a right to take collective action, this can only interfere with the freedom to provide services where it is "justified, proportionate and necessary." The ECJ's rulings in this field have sparked an outcry from trade unions across Europe that argue that the ECJ will encourage a race to the bottom in wages and working conditions.

In the context of the euro-zone crisis, EU lawmakers have even sought to judicialize the field of fiscal policy. The Maastricht Treaty, which created the legal framework for the euro-zone common currency area, had established limits on the deficit and debt levels for euro-zone states, but had left the enforcement of these limits mostly up to political actors in the Commission and Council. This approach proved unsuccessful and member states managed to violate the deficit and debt rules with impunity from the mid-2000s onward. Finally, in February 2012, after the euro-zone sovereign debt crisis revealed the shortcomings of the existing system, twenty-five of the member states signed the Fiscal Compact Treaty that required them to enshrine a balanced budget rule and a so-called debt brake into domestic law and to enforce these rules through their national courts. In other words, as EU leaders reform euro-zone governance, they are seeking to reduce political discretion and to judicialize fiscal policy by empowering courts to enforce deficit and debt limits on governments.[48]

Historically, the ECJ's role in the field of protecting fundamental human rights has been more limited, as human rights protection fell to the jurisdiction of the European Court of Human Rights, which as we mentioned above is a judicial body attached to an entirely separate international organization—the Council of Europe. The division in jurisdiction between the ECJ and the ECHR has its roots in the early postwar decades and the distinct approaches to European integration taken by the European Economic Community (the predecessor of today's EU) and the Council of Europe. As its name suggests, the European Economic Community (EEC) focused on economic integration—aiming to create a common market. While many of its founders hoped the EEC would eventually encourage far reaching political integration of Europe, initially the scope of the EEC's activities was limited to matters of economic regulation relevant to the construction of a common market. In this context, questions of human rights did not seem particularly relevant, and the ECJ initially ruled that it did not have the power to review acts of the Community institutions to ensure respect for fundamental human rights.[49] Though the ECJ later affirmed that it would uphold fundamental human rights as general principles of Community law,[50] international human rights adjudication remained for the most part in the jurisdiction of the European Court of Human Rights.

The power of the ECHR has developed more slowly and inconsistently than that of the ECJ. Nevertheless, the ECHR has had a profound impact in many areas. The ECHR has impacted national practices in highly sensitive areas such as rights of prisoners, gay rights, the display of religious symbols, and abortion. In an early land-mark ruling, the ECHR ruled that a number of interrogation techniques practiced by the United Kingdom in the context of the conflict in Northern Ireland amounted to "inhuman and degrading treatment" prohibited by the Convention.[51] In a 1981 judgment, the ECHR ruled that the criminalization of homosexuality in Northern Ireland violated the convention.[52]

The ECHR has heard a series of cases challenging national restrictions on the wearing of Islamic veils in various contexts. Generally, the court has upheld governments' right—under certain conditions—to impose such restrictions.[53] In 2009, a panel of the ECHR ruled on a case, *Lautsi v. Italy*,[54] in which a parent argued that her right under the Convention to educate her children in keeping with her convictions and her children's right to freedom of religion were violated by Italy's practice of af-fixing crucifixes in Italian public schools. A chamber of the ECHR ruled unanimously that her rights had been violated and ordered Italy to pay her €5,000 in damages. The Italian government denounced the decision, and more than twenty other governments joined the Italian government in opposing it. The case was referred to the ECHR's Grand Chamber on appeal, and in 2001 the Grand Chamber overturned the cham-ber's ruling, holding that the display of crucifixes in classrooms did not violate the Convention. In December 2009, the ECHR heard yet another highly controversial case, *A. B. and C. v. Ireland*,[55] as three Irish women challenged the legality under the Convention of Ireland's ban on abortion.

Not only has the ECHR also worked to empower national courts directly, but Ar-ticle Six of the European Convention on Human Rights guarantees a right to a fair trial, which entails a hearing before an independent tribunal in a reasonable time. Article Six has been, by far, the most frequent basis for legal action before the ECHR. Thousands of litigants dissatisfied with the pace of domestic civil, criminal, and administrative pro-ceedings; their rights of defense; or their access to courts more generally have challenged the deficiencies of their domestic justice systems before the ECHR.

Stepping back from individual cases and looking at aggregate trends in litigation before the ECHR, we can observe a judicial body that is clearly gaining momentum—in some ways, too much for its own good. Prior to 1998, cases brought to the ECHR by individuals were screened by a gatekeeping body (the European Commission on Human Rights), which severely restricted the flow of cases to the ECHR. However, the structure of the ECHR was transformed in 1998. Reforms instituted that year abolished the European Commission on Human Rights and opened up direct access to the court for residents of all forty-seven member states of the Council of Europe—ap-proximately 800 million people.

The result of this opening has been a flood of cases; in recent years, the ECHR has regularly faced a backlog of roughly 100,000 cases. And while the court declares many cases inadmissible on various technical grounds, it has issued rulings on thousands of cases in recent years, finding states to be in violation of the European Convention on Human Rights in approximately 70 percent of the cases.[56] Though the ECHR has clearly gained strength over the years and had remarkable success in securing compliance with its rulings, today the court is having difficulty coping with the huge volume of cases it receives every year, despite recent reforms intended to limit the flood of cases.

Normative Implications of Judicialization

How should we assess the implications of the judicialization of politics in Europe? Is it a destructive trend or a healthy development? Some critics argue that judicialization leads to "government by judges," which undermines democracy.[57] Other critics warn of the spread of an "American disease" of excessive reliance on lawyers and litigation in the policy process. Defenders of judicialization may argue that the trend brings with it greater legal certainty, transparency, and access to justice for European citizens. Let us examine these views.

How much government or governance by judges should we accept in a democracy? Does the fact that courts regularly annul the legislative acts and administrative decisions of democratically elected officials threaten democracy? Is it legitimate for courts to block elected representatives from enacting laws pursuant to their electoral mandate? Is it legitimate for courts tasked with interpreting and applying the law to interpret it in an expansive way—creating new rights and effectively "legislating from the bench"? To evaluate such activities, we must begin by recalling, as we mentioned earlier in this chapter, that after World War II many European democracies discarded the concept of unlimited parliamentary sovereignty. The UK and some Nordic countries were exceptions in this regard, but even the venerable Parliament in Westminster has to a large extent bowed to the supremacy of the European courts in Strasbourg and Luxembourg City. Contemporary European democracies are liberal democracies under the rule of law: in other words, they are democracies in which elected majorities are restrained by the requirement that their actions respect individual rights—even the rights of unpopular minorities. And it is courts that protect those rights. National constitutional courts—and even more so the European Court of Justice and the European Court of Human Rights—have surely extended their powers further than their founders intended, but in a broader sense courts in Europe are doing what the political systems in which they are embedded have asked them to do.

In assessing the impact of judicialization on democracy, we must not ignore the democratic dimensions of courts and legal processes. The fact that judges are not elected does not make courts and the judicial process entirely undemocratic. First, while national constitutional courts and European courts (the ECJ and ECHR) may be a step removed from the democratic process, they are formed with democratic input. Democratically elected national governments appoint the judges who sit on the ECJ and ECHR. The processes for appointing judges to national constitutional courts vary, but in all cases democratically elected officials play a central role. Second, the judicial process itself creates opportunities for democratic participation. The process of judicialization has brought with it new opportunities for "access to justice" as the expansion of rights and the reform of legal procedures to encourage enforcement of those rights has created new opportunities for previously marginalized groups to influence policy through the courts.[58] More generally, courts can serve as a powerful tool that citizens can use to hold their governments accountable, thus ultimately enhancing the quality of democracy in Europe.

The judicialization of politics encourages policy makers to frame policies in the language of rights. By framing policies as rights, policy makers can essentially privatize some of the work of governance—encouraging individuals to enforce their own rights in court so that the state does not have to. Framing policies in the language of rights also has strong rhetorical appeal, as the defense of individual rights is a fundamental value of all modern European democracies. For the EU, developing a "rights-based" model of citizenship is particularly appealing, given that the EU cannot ground its citizenship on any unifying sense of national identity. But, in another sense, framing policies in terms of rights and engaging in rights discourse create tensions with central aspects of the prevailing models of democracy in Europe. As Arend Lijphart has explained, most European democracies are based on a consensus model of democracy that emphasizes not simply following the will of the majority but also building consensus and compromise among a broad range of stakeholders.[59] The increasing focus on the judicial enforcement of individual rights may undermine the political culture of compromise and the emphasis on policies that serve general public interests that is central to European democracies.[60]

Finally, it is important to recognize that judicialization will bring with it certain economic costs. The judicialization of politics has encouraged a dramatic increase in the number of lawyers in Europe and in the size of the legal services industry.[61] Compared to the more flexible, informal approaches to regulation that traditionally prevailed in Europe, the highly judicialized approaches that are taking root in many fields today often operate more slowly and are far more costly. In many economic sectors affected by the rise of judicialization, business groups have warned against the dangers of moving toward American-style litigiousness.

The judicialization of politics in Europe entails costs and benefits. Regulatory processes may become slower and more expensive—while providing ample employment opportunities for lawyers. Unelected judges may substitute their decisions for those taken by elected representatives. At the same time, these trends will enhance the transparency and accountability of government and ensure greater access to justice and the protection of individual rights.

Notes

1. Ran Hirschl, "The Judicialization of Politics," in *The Oxford Handbook of Law and Politics*, ed. K. Whittington and G. Calderia (Oxford: Oxford University Press, 2008), 119.

2. C. Neal Tate and Torbjörn Vallinder, eds., *The Global Expansion of Judicial Power* (New York: New York University Press, 1997).

3. Louis Henkin, *The Age of Rights* (New York: Columbia University Press, 1990).

4. It is important to note that the constitutional courts that have become so powerful in postwar Europe were not modeled on the U.S. Supreme Court. Many observers assume that since the judicial review was so well established in the United States, the U.S. model must have guided the construction of the judiciaries in postwar European democracies. However, the courts established in Europe followed the Kelsenian model, which had been established in Austria after World War I; see Alec Stone Sweet, *Governing with Judges: Constitutional Politics in Europe* (Oxford: Oxford University Press, 2000). In the U.S. system, ordinary judges can declare legislative acts to be unconstitutional, and these decisions can then be appealed up to the U.S. Supreme Court. In the Kelsenian model, developed by Austrian legal theorist (and

later University of California, Berkeley Professor) Hans Kelsen, constitutional review could not be exercised by ordinary courts but was the exclusive task of a specialized constitutional court. These Kelsenian constitutional courts were separated from the rest of the judicial system.

5. Marlene Wind, "The Nordics, the EU and the Reluctance towards Supranational Judicial Review," *Journal of Common Market Studies* 48, no. 4 (2010): 1039–63.

6. Andrew Moravcsik, "The Origins of Human Rights Regimes: Democratic Delegation in Postwar Europe," *International Organization* 45, no. 2 (2000): 217–52.

7. Steven Vogel, *Freer Markets, More Rules: Regulatory Reform in Advanced Industrialized Countries* (Ithaca, NY: Cornell University Press, 1996); and Steven Vogel, "Why Freer Markets Need More Rules," in *Creating Competitive Markets: The Politics of Regulatory Reform*, ed. Mark Landy, Martin Levin, and Martin Shapiro (Washington, DC: Brookings Institution Press, 2007), 25–42.

8. Case 26/62, *Van Gend en Loos v. Nederlandse Administratie der Belastingen* (1963), ECR 1.

9. Case 6/64, *Flaminio Costa v. Ente Nationale per L'Energia Elettrica (ENEL)* (1964), ECR 585,593.

10. Arthur Dyevre, "The German Federal Constitutional Court and European Judicial Politics," *West European Politics* 34, no. 2 (2011): 346–61; and Arthur Dyevre, "Judicial Non-Compliance in a Non-Hierarchical Legal Order: Isolated Accident or Omen of Judicial Armageddon?" Working paper, January (Hamburg: Max Planck Institute for International and Comparative Law, 2012).

11. Anne-Marie Slaughter, Alec Stone Sweet, and Joseph Weiler, eds., *The European Courts and National Courts: Doctrine and Jurisprudence* (Oxford: Hart Publishing, 1998); Karen Alter, *Establishing the Supremacy of European Law: The Making of an International Rule of Law in Europe* (Oxford: Oxford University Press, 2001); and Stone Sweet, *Governing with Judges*.

12. Anne-Marie Burley and Walter Mattli, "Europe before the Court: A Political Theory of Legal Integration," *International Organization* 47 (1993): 41–76.

13. Karen Alter, "The European Court's Political Power," *West European Politics* 19, no. 3 (1996): 458–87; and Karen Alter, *Establishing the Supremacy of European Law: The Making of an International Rule of Law in Europe* (Oxford: Oxford University Press, 2001).

14. Alter, *Establishing the Supremacy of European Law*.

15. Stone Sweet, *Governing with Judges*, 165; Joseph H. H. Weiler, "The Transformation of Europe," *Yale Law Journal* 100 (1991): 2403–83; and Eric Stein, "Lawyers, Judges and he Making of a Transnational Constitution," *American Journal of International Law* 75 (1981): 1–27. However, as noted above, there are countries, such as Denmark, in which these dynamics seem not to have come into play. See Wind, "The Nordics, the EU and the Reluctance towards Supranational Judicial Review."

16. Anne-Marie Burley and Walter Mattli, "Europe before the Court: A Political Theory of Legal Integration," *International Organization* 47 (1993): 41–76; Stone Sweet, *Governing with Judges*; Alec Stone Sweet and Thomas Brunell, "Constructing a Supranational Constitution," *American Political Science Review* 92 (1998): 63–81; and Rachel Cichowski, *The European Court and Civil Society* (New York: Cambridge University Press, 2007).

17. Damian Chalmers and Mariana Chaves, "The Reference Points of EU Judicial Politics," *Journal of European Public Policy* 19, no. 1 (2012): 25–42.

18. Lisa Conant, *Justice Contained: Law and Politics in the European Union* (Ithaca, NY: Cornell University Press, 2002).

19. Wind, "The Nordics, the EU and the Reluctance towards Supranational Judicial Review"; and Michal Bobek, "Learning to Talk: Preliminary Rulings, the Courts of the New Member States and the Court of Justice," *Common Market Law Review*, 45, no. 6 (2008): 1611–43.

20. Geoffrey Garrett, R. Daniel Kelemen, and Heiner Schulz, "The European Court of Justice, National Governments and Legal Integration in the European Union," *International Organization* 52, no. 1 (1998): 149–76; and Mark Pollack, *The Engines of European Integration* (Oxford: Oxford University Press, 2003).

21. Miguel Maduro, *We, the Court: The European Court of Justice and the European Economic Constitution* (Oxford: Hart Publishing, 1998).

22. Vogel, "Why Freer Markets Need More Rules"; and R. Daniel Kelemen, "Suing for Europe: Adversarial Legalism and European Governance," *Comparative Political Studies* 39, no. 1 (2006): 101–27.

23. Ran Hirschl, *Towards Juristocracy: The Origins and Consequences of the New Constitutionalism* (Cambridge, MA: Harvard University Press, 2004), 169.

24. Alexis De Tocqueville, *Democracy in America*, ed. and abridged by Richard Heffner (New York: Mentor Books, 1835/1984), 126.

25. Donald Kommers, *The Constitutional Jurisprudence of the Federal Republic of Germany*, 2nd ed. (Durham, NC: Duke University Press, 1997); and Stone Sweet, *Governing with Judges*.

26. C. Landfried, "Judicial Policy-making in Germany: The Federal Constitutional Court," *West European Politics* 15 (1992): 50–67.

27. Mary Volcansek, "Political Power and Judicial Review in Italy," *Comparative Political Studies* 26, no. 4 (1994): 492–509; Mary Volcansek, *Constitutional Politics in Italy: The Constitutional Court* (New York: St. Martin's Press, 1999); Mary Volcansek, "Constitutional Courts as Veto Players: Divorce and Decrees in Italy," *European Journal of Political Research* 39 (2001): 347–72; Maria Elisabetta De Franciscis and Rosella Zannini, "Judicial Policy-making in Italy," *West European Politics* 15, no. 3 (1992): 68–79; and Stone Sweet, *Governing with Judges*.

28. Patricia Pederzoli and Carlo Guarnieri, "The Judicialization of Politics, Italian Style," *Journal of Modern Italian Studies* 2, no. 3 (1997): 321–36; and Carlo Guarnieri and Patrizia Pederzoli, *The Power of Judges: A Comparative Study of Courts and Democracy* (Oxford: Oxford University Press, 2001).

29. Alec Stone Sweet, *The Birth of Judicial Politics in France* (New York: Oxford University Press, 1992).

30. Stone Sweet, *The Birth of Judicial Politics in France*.

31. In 2013, concerns over the limits to British sovereignty imposed by the Charter and by rulings of the European Court of Human Rights led British Home Secretary Theresa May and other senior Conservatives to suggest that the UK should consider withdrawing from the European Convention on Human Rights.

32. *A (FC) and others (FC) v. Secretary of State for the Home Department* (2004), UKHL 56.

33. *R (Al Rawi) v. Secretary of State for Foreign and Commonwealth Affairs* (2006), EWCA Civ 1279.

34. Karen Alter and Jeannette Vargas, "Explaining Variation in the Use of European Litigation Strategies," *Comparative Political Studies* 33, no. 4 (2002): 452–82; and Cichowski, *The European Court and Civil Society*.

35. See, for instance, Case C-144/04, *Werner Mangold v. Rüdiger Helm* (2005), ECR I-9981; Case C 411/05, *Félix Palacios de la Villa v. Cortefiel Servicios SA* (2007) ECR I-8531; Case C-13/05 *Chacón Navas v. Eurest Colectividades SA* (2006) ECR I-6467; and *Coleman v. Attridge Law* (2008) ECR I-5603.

36. Alan Riley, "EC Antitrust Modernisation: The Commission Does Very Nicely—Thank You! Part 1: Regulation 1 and the Notification Burden; Part 2: Between the Idea and the Reality: Decentralisation under Regulation 1," *European Competition Law Review* 24, nos. 604–15 (2003): 57–72; Angela Wigger and Andreas Nölke, "Enhanced Roles of Private Actors in the EU Business Regulation and the Erosion of the Rhenish Model of Capitalism: The Case of

Antitrust Enforcement," *Journal of Common Market Studies* 45, no. 2 (2007): 487–513; and R. Daniel Kelemen, *Eurolegalism: The Transformation of Law and Regulation in the European Union* (Cambridge, MA: Harvard University Press, 2011).

37. R. D. Kelemen and E. C. Sibbitt, "The Globalization of American Law," *International Organization* 58, no. 1 (2004): 103–36; and Kelemen, *Eurolegalism*.

38. Tamara K. Hervey and Jean Vanessa McHale, *Health Law and the European Union* (New York: Cambridge University Press, 2004); and Scott Greer, *The Politics of European Union Health Policies* (Berkshire, UK: Open University Press, 2009).

39. Case C-158/96, *Kohll v. Union des Caisses de Maladie* (1998) ECR I-1931.

40. Case C-120/95, *Decker v. Caissede Maladie des Employés Privés* (1998) ECR I-1831.

41. Case C-372/04, *Yvonne Watts v. Bedford Primary Care Trust, Secretary of State for Health* (2006) ECR I-4325.

42. Kelemen, *Eurolegalism*.

43. Case C-438/05, *International Transport Workers' Federation and Finnish Seamen's Union v. Viking Line ABP and OÜ Viking Line Eesti (Viking)* (2007) ECR I-10779.

44. Case C-341/05, *Laval un Partneri Ltd v. Svenska Byggnadsarbetareförbundet, Svenska Byggnadsarbetareförbundets avdelning 1, Byggettan and Svenska Elektrikerförbundet (Laval)* (2007) ECR I-11767.

45. Case C-346/06, *Rüffert v. Land Niedersachsen* (2008) ECR I-1989.

46. Case C-319/06, *Commission v. Luxembourg* (2008) ECR I-4323.

47. See chapter 10 by Benedicta Marzinotto, this volume.

48. R. Daniel Kelemen and Terence Teo, "Law and the Eurozone Crisis," paper presented at the Annual Meeting of the American Political Science Association, September 2012, http://papers.ssrn.com/sol3/papers.cfm?abstract_id=2107426 (accessed January 17, 2014).

49. Case 1/58, *Stork v. High Authority*, ECR 1959, 43.

50. For overviews, see Paul Craig and Gráinne De Búrca, *EU Law: Text, Cases and Materials*, 4th ed. (Oxford: Oxford University Press, 2008), 379–89. Early landmark cases include, for instance, Case 29/69 *Stauder v. City of Ulm* (1969) ECR 419; and Case 11/70, *Internationale Handelsgesellschaft* (1970) ECR 1125.

51. *Ireland v. United Kingdom* (1978) ECHR (5310/71).

52. *Dudgeon v. United Kindgom* (1981) ECHR (7525/76).

53. See, for instance, *Leyla Şahin v. Turkey* (2005) ECHR (4474/98); *Dogru v. France* (2008) ECHR (27058/05); *Kervanci v. France* (2008) ECHR (31645/04); and *Dahlab v. Switzerland* (2001) ECHR (42393/98).

54. *Lautsi v. Italy* (2009) ECHR (30814/06), referral to the Grand Chamber on March 1, 2010.

55. *A. B. and C. v. Ireland* (application no. 25579/05).

56. Rachel Cichowski, "Courts, Rights and Democratic Participation," *Comparative Political Studies* 39 (2006): 50–75, 62.

57. See, for instance, Richard Bellamy, "The Democratic Constitution: Why Europeans Should Avoid American Style Constitutional Judicial Review," *European Political Science* 7 (2008): 9–20; and Fritz Scharpf, "Legitimacy in the Multilevel European Polity," MPIfG working paper, no. 09/1 (Frankfurt: Max Planck Institute for the Study of Societies, 2009).

58. Cichowski, "Courts, Rights, and Democratic Participation"; and Cichowski, *The European Court and Civil Society*.

59. Arend Lijphart, *Patterns of Democracy: Government Forms and Performance in Thirty-Six Countries* (New Haven, CT: Yale University Press, 1999).

60. Stuart Scheingold, *The Politics of Rights: Lawyers, Public Policy and Political Change* (New Haven, CT: Yale University Press, 1974); and Mary Ann Glendon, *Rights Talk* (New York: Free Press, 1991).

61. Kelemen, *Eurolegalism*; and Kelemen and Sibbitt, "The Globalization of American Law."

Suggested Readings

Alter, Karen. *The Europe Court's Political Power: Selected Essays*. Oxford: Oxford University Press, 2010.

Cichowski, Rachel. *The European Court and Civil Society*. New York: Cambridge University Press, 2007.

Conant, Lisa. *Justice Contained: Law and Politics in the European Union*. Ithaca, NY: Cornell University Press, 2002.

Kelemen, R. Daniel. *Eurolegalism: The Transformation of Law and Regulation in the European Union*. Cambridge, MA: Harvard University Press, 2011.

Maduro, Miguel, and Loic Azoulai, eds. *The Past and Future of EU Law: The Classics of EU Law Revisited on the 50th Anniversary of the Rome Treaty*. Oxford: Hart Publishing, 2010.

Slaughter, Anne-Marie, Alec Stone Sweet, and Joseph Weiler, eds. *The European Courts and National Courts: Doctrine and Jurisprudence*. Oxford: Hart Publishing, 1998.

Stone Sweet, Alec. 2004. *The Judicial Construction of Europe*. Oxford: Oxford University Press.

CHAPTER 13

Migration in Europe

Jonathon W. Moses

The history of Europe is one of massive movements of people: either across Europe, beyond Europe, and into Europe. While these long-term trends provide an important backdrop, this chapter focuses on the nature of these flows today and on some of their most evident consequences.

To do this, we need to untangle the complex political and institutional weave that influences migration patterns in Europe today. In the process, we can learn of the two important roles that migration plays in the larger European project. The first of these is functional, in that free labor mobility plays a central role in the establishment of a common European market. The second role is more ideational, in that migration facilitates the creation of a common European identity. When German workers move to France, they gain perspective on their own national identities; they begin to see themselves less as Germans, and more as Europeans.

But there is a backside to the face of European identity, one more visible in recent years. Europe is scarred by a growing xenophobia, and many Europeans see their own identities and communities being threatened by foreigners. This fear is reflected in the rise of Europe's radical right and its calls to restrict immigration, and is fueled by economic crisis. In short, the European project both depends upon and is threatened by the foreigner at its doorstep.

This chapter aims to shine some light on Europe's inconvenient truth. It begins with a short introduction to the history of European migration patterns, before offering a brief description of the nature of contemporary migration trends in Europe. The bulk of the chapter is then used to describe the complex and overlapping political geometry that regulates and channels these diverse flows. In this depiction, the European Union is just one of several relevant actors—but it is one that is playing an increasingly visible and important role. The third section considers the difficulty of integrating Europe's sundry faces into a common identity, while the fourth section concludes.

Europeans on the Move

We begin by sketching out a historical backdrop. This backdrop can help us see how Europe's relationship to migration has changed over time, and how that relationship is not particularly unique or special. In fact, when we manage to wrestle a little distance between ourselves and the current context, we can see that the history of European migration follows a familiar pattern: over the course of 150 years, Europe has gone from a region that experienced net emigration to one that is now characterized by net immigration.

The history of Europe is full of migrant stories. From the middle of the sixteenth century until the French Revolution, Europe experienced a number of major population shifts: whether it was the repopulation of the German territories after the Thirty Years' War, the flow of migrants that followed the retreat of the Ottomans under Hapsburg rule, the opening up of the Southern Russian plains for settlement, or the Baltic migration system that followed in the wake of the Hanseatic League.

The continent was also animated by more temporary migration flows, as rural populations moved around in search of better farmland, to follow the harvests, or to settle in towns and cities. Merchants and skilled artisans moved from town to town selling their wares and skills—or they were tempted to settle in new areas following the incentives offered by enterprising political elites. To give you an idea of the size of these flows, consider the growth of a major European city. From 1600 to 1650, Amsterdam is said to have grown from 60,000 to 175,000 people! This expansion could not have occurred by natural population growth alone—the town was being filling up with the likes of German workers, Norwegian sailors, French refugees, and Spanish traders. With industrialization, the opportunity for temporary migration increased along with the ease of transport. Large industrial projects—such as the digging of canals or the construction of railway and road networks—required workers to travel, often to faraway places.

With time, these local and regional migration patterns became increasingly intercontinental. In the last quarter of the nineteenth century, and before World War I, millions of Europeans left the continent in search of a better life. As a percentage of population, the Irish, Norwegians, and Italians were most prone to intercontinental emigration, but their examples were followed by many across Europe. In the century after 1820, it is estimated that about 55 million people left Europe to settle in the New World.

This story of Europe, as a source of emigration, is well told and understood—but this period of the Great Atlantic Migration tells another story that is less often heard. While large numbers of Europeans left to the New World, even larger numbers stayed in Europe, but moved within the continent. Small landowners moved into towns, skilled artisans and workers moved to markets that still appreciated their skills, and unskilled workers of all sorts moved to Europe's growing industrial centers in search of employment. Given the nature of this emigration, its size is more difficult to trace: the migrants were not collected in large, oceangoing vessels, with clear and explicit destinations. But we know that intra-European migration was large and varied: England attracted workers from Ireland, Switzerland from Italy, Germany from Poland

and Italy, and France from wherever it could find them. Indeed, France was already a major importer of labor before World War I, and was a country of immigration when the rest of Europe was experiencing net emigration. Whatever the reason, we find it convenient to remember the exodus from Europe to the New World, while forgetting about the even larger migration streams that crisscrossed Europe at the same time.

After World War II, the same sort of bias in perspective is evident: our attention is drawn to the immigrant experience in Europe. We know that Europe has turned from exporting to importing its workers—and this transition introduces significant challenges. But we must not forget that Europe maintains a heavy ballast of internal migrants—of Europeans moving from one state or region to another. While the external balance may have changed over time, pan-European migration has remained an important and relatively constant feature on the face of European politics. In the midst of a Great Recession, Europe's internal movements are becoming more necessary and pronounced.

State of the Union

Before exploring the tricky politics of European migration, we can begin with a simple demographic snapshot. This picture gives us a glimpse of the nature and scope of migration in Europe, lending a backdrop for the discussion that follows.

In the midst of Europe's current economic hardship, overall immigration into Europe has fallen significantly. At the start of the millennium, net migration into the EU-27 was about 2,000,000 people. This figure includes migration between EU member states, as well as migration from beyond the EU-27. In 2011, net immigration dropped by more than half, to less than 890,000 (figure 13.1). More precisely, 3.2 million people (that constitutes 6.4 immigrants per 1,000 residents, or 6.4‰) immigrated into, and 2.3

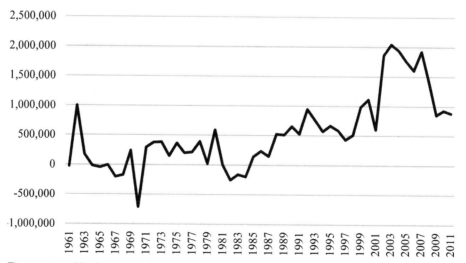

Figure 13.1   Net Migration, EU-27. *Note*: **Net migration plus statistical adjustment.** *Source*: **Eurostat [demo_gind].**

million people emigrated out of, an EU-27 member state in that year. Of these, roughly 1.7 million immigrants (or 3.4‰) came from beyond the EU-27.[1]

While the overall number of immigrants is falling, the Great Recession is forcing more Europeans to move away from their homes in search of a livelihood. The design of Europe's common monetary area forces the burden of economic transition onto the backs of workers: rising unemployment levels are fueling emigration from states hardest hit by the euro-zone crisis. This is clearly evident in figure 13.2: Greeks, Spaniards, Portuguese, Latvians, and the Irish are now fleeing economic conditions at home. In the near future, we can expect Cyprus to join this unfortunate club.

In 2011, most of these (net) immigrants ended up entering Germany (281,784), Italy (241,064), and the United Kingdom (218,615). But the heaviest hit states (in terms of the size of the immigrant flow, relative to the population) were in Luxembourg and Cyprus, or beyond the EU (Norway and Switzerland), as seen in figure 13.3. Like the previous figures, this picture has changed rather markedly with the Great Recession. As recently as 2009, most EU member states were experiencing net in-migration; now many states are experiencing net outflows: overall EU net in-immigration was then 3.9‰, while today it has fallen to 1.8‰.

The figures thus far capture the foreigner's most common means of entry into European states: worker migration, family reunion, and students. These figures reveal a very broad measure of immigration, but there are two additional categories of migrants that fall outside these statistics: refugees and irregular migrants.

A refugee is someone who has been granted a right to live in a country because the authorities suspect that he or she will suffer persecution at home (e.g., on account of race, relation, nationality, membership in a particular class, group, or even political opinion). This right is granted under the 1951 UN Convention Relating to the Status of Refugees. States that have signed that Convention—including all states in Europe—are obliged to take in refugees: this is not something they are allowed to

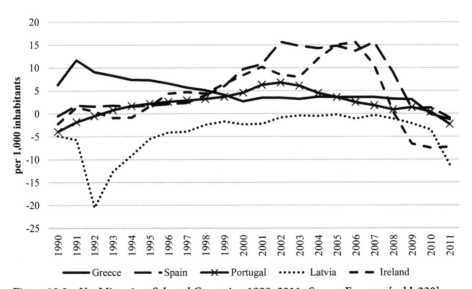

Figure 13.2   Net Migration, Selected Countries, 1990–2011. *Source:* Eurostat [tsdde230].

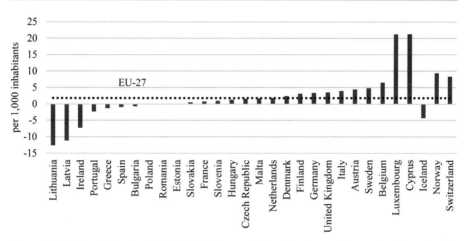

Figure 13.3   Net Migration in 2011, by Country. *Note*: Crude rate of net migration plus adjustment. *Source*: Eurostat [tsdde230].

steer for political gain. But signatory states do evaluate asylum claims to see whether they are legitimate. To gain access, then, a person must first apply for asylum, and the host state is obliged to grant asylum if the applicant can show that he or she meets the Convention's criteria. As a result of this process, there is a wide spectrum of different types of immigrant status that fall under the refugee rubric.[2]

The size of the asylum stream into Europe is surprisingly small, when compared to the more general migration figures shown in the figures above. In 2011, the EU-27 received about 258,950 asylum applicants (down from 424,200 in 2001!), with France, Germany, Sweden, Belgium, and the UK receiving the largest numbers.[3] This compares to the EU's 3.2 million total immigrants (or roughly 890,000 net immigrants). On top of this, about 76 percent of asylum applications are rejected by EU-27 member states! Thus, while the number of asylum seekers is relatively small to start with, an even smaller number of them makes it through the verification process: only 59,560 refugees were granted protection by all EU member states in 2011 (by contrast, two puny countries on the margins of the EU—Switzerland and Norway—together admitted 10,460!). This is a remarkably small number of refugees, from a world mired in political conflict, for an area whose total population exceeds 500 million people! Nonetheless, as refugees tend to receive much critical media attention, the public's perception of their numbers is almost always larger than they actually are.

The third remaining source of foreigners is more difficult to measure: this is the stream of undocumented immigrants to Europe. While some rough flow counts are available, attempts at measuring irregular migrant stocks are somewhat more reliable. One commonly cited estimate holds that there were between 1.9 and 3.8 million irregular foreigners living in the EU-27 in 2008, compared with about 11 million in the United States that year.[4] This number is probably smaller today, on account of the economic crisis, yet it only represents somewhere between 0.39 and 0.77 percent of the total population. To get a feel for the size of this irregular stock, Eurostat's estimate of the share of the (regular) foreign-born population in the EU-27 was about 8 percent in that year.

When we combine these three different sources of immigration, we realize that a lot of people are moving around Europe today. A very rough count (including both regular and irregular immigrants and refugees) puts the total (gross) number at around 4.2 million people a year. Roughly 1.3 million of these are people moving within Europe: from one European country to another. This means that a substantial number of foreigners has been arriving in Europe for some time, and we can expect their numbers to accumulate. For this reason, it is important to be familiar with the size of Europe's foreign population stock.

Figure 13.4 presents that share of foreign residents, by state, across Europe in 2011. In total, there were 33.3 million foreign citizens living in the EU-27 in 2011—or about 5.6% of the total population. Most of these (20.5 million, or 62%) were from beyond the EU (only 12.8 million were citizens from other EU member states).

On average, foreigners make up less than 6 percent of the total European population. This average was spread across Europe, with small states such as Luxembourg, Latvia, Cyprus, and Estonia (and non-EU member Switzerland) reaping the largest shares. This handful of states at the deep end of integration suggests that the distribution of the share of foreigners across Europe reflects the history (the foreign populations of Latvia and Estonia are predominantly Russian) and size of these countries, as much as any evidence of a move toward greater labor market harmonization.

In fact, Europe's share of foreigners is not all that large by international standards. Compared to other world regions, such as North America and Oceania, the broader European migrant stock was relatively small, at 9.5 percent of the population (see table 13.1). This level is especially low when one realizes that the European figures include migrants from other member states of the European Union. On the other hand, compared to Africa, Asia, and Latin America, Europeans do host many foreigners.

There is a substantial amount of migration within and across Europe. The "Levels of Difference" section seeks to unravel the complex political constellations that channel these migration flows in, and around, Europe.

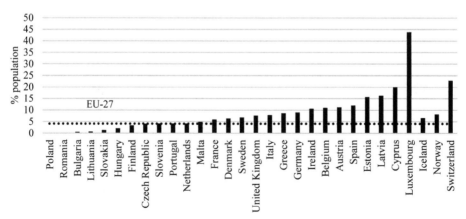

Figure 13.4   Share of Foreign Population, by State, 2012. *Note*: Foreigners, as a percentage of population. *Source*: Eurostat [migr_pop1ctz].

Table 13.1   International Migration Stocks, by World Region (2010)

	Number of Migrants	Migrant Share (% of Population)
Latin America and Caribbean	7,480,267	1.3
Asia	61,323,979	1.5
Africa	19,263,183	1.9
Europe	69,819,282	9.5
North America	50,042,408	14.2
Oceania	6,014,693	16.8

Source: United Nations, Department of Economic and Social Affairs, Population Division, *Trends in International Migrant Stock: The 2008 Revision*, POP/DB/MIG/Stock/Rev.2008 (New York: United Nations, 2009), http://esa.un.org/migration/index.asp?panel=1 (accessed January 30, 2014).

Levels of Difference

The challenge of understanding European migration patterns lies in the fact that there is no one political authority, or no single set of rules, that applies to each type of migrant. Thus, the rules affecting migration between EU member states are different than the rules affecting migration between nonmember states and member states. Worse, those rules can change from member state to member state, and from one type of migration to another. For this reason, it is rather optimistic, even misleading, to speak of an EU migration regime. What we have is a complex, multilevel geometry of political authority governing European migration. The task of this section is to make sense of this mess.

The easiest way to do this is to break the migrant stream down into three component types: European migration, international migration, and asylum. At this level of generality, one can begin to see the different rules, and constellations of power, that are relevant for understanding the size and nature of the component flows.

EUROPEAN MIGRATION

European migration refers to migrant streams within Europe, but across national borders.[5] This realm is usually seen as the domain of EU politics, as it was one of the fundamental rights secured in the 1957 Treaty of Rome. As such, worker mobility is understood to be an integral part of the logic of Europe's market integration: workers need to be able to move across national borders as freely as do capital, goods, and services.

But this interpretation privileges the European Community. Mobility is a right that is also enjoyed by other workers, whether they originate in nonmember EU states or from further abroad. Already in 1953, the Organization for European Economic Cooperation (OEEC, subsequently the OECD) adopted a rule that facilitated movement across member states: when a job opened up, native workers were given priority for a specified period of time (usually four weeks), after which foreign workers were allowed to compete on an equal footing with native workers. In the following year (1954), the Nordic countries entered into a formal agreement that secured a common labor market across signatory states (Denmark, Finland, Iceland, Norway, and Sweden). Also, several individual states in Europe had remarkably liberal immigration laws in the immediate postwar period (e.g., Switzerland and the UK). In short, worker mobility is not some sort of gift from the European Union—it is an ambition that precedes the Treaty of Rome and one that has found a home in several multinational organizations across Europe.

Still, the Treaty of Rome is often used as a road sign to mark the advent of a European common labor market—and the EU is clearly the most important political mover on this front today. The 1957 Treaty embraced the free movement of labor within Europe and—just as importantly—the Treaty provided mobility rights for workers from other member states.

Immediately after WWII, the Treaty of Rome and the OEEC agreement proved insufficient for meeting the labor needs of Europe's growing economy. For this reason, member states found it necessary to open their labor markets by way of a number of bilateral guest worker agreements, which extended these mobility rights to workers from other countries. Individual states in Europe signed agreements with other states (both within Europe and across the Maghreb) to facilitate temporary migration.

Since then, there has been much progress (and resistance!) in securing a borderless labor market for European workers, and a more secure and fortified border for keeping low-skilled foreign workers at bay. (As we shall soon see, these are two sides to the same coin.) Today, European legislation grants all EU citizens the right to move and settle with their family to any other member state, so long as they are able to support themselves.

The problem is that this EU-wide system applies to more than just EU-member states. Actually, when speaking about European-wide labor markets, it is more accurate to refer to the European Economic Area (EEA), created in 1994, which includes EU-member states plus European Free Trade Association (EFTA) member states (Iceland, Liechtenstein, and Norway).[6] Add to this the fact that Swiss voters passed a referendum in 2005 that allowed them to participate in this common labor market (effective December 2008). Finally, several non-EU microstates (such as Monaco, Lichtenstein, San Marino, and the Vatican City) participate de facto in the European labor market, as they enjoy open borders with neighboring states that are already integrated into the broader EEA area. Thus, when we speak about a European migration regime, we refer to the mobility rights that exist between most of the EU member states (more on this later), plus the EFTA states, plus Switzerland and the microstates. For this reason, it is more accurate to refer to this area as the EEA+.

Locating the political center of gravity for this variable geometry of European migration issues is anything but straightforward. It tends to shift with the issue space: sometimes it is located in the EU, sometimes it is not. The heterogeneity and institutional rigidities of the EU make it difficult to secure consensus on contentious issues—even when they reflect the core values agreed to in the Treaty of Rome. For this reason, EU member states sometimes find it more convenient to work outside the union's political framework.

This sort of difficulty is clearly evident in the history of the Schengen Agreement—the original pilot project for today's borderless Europe. In the mid-1980s, the EC's ten member states could not agree among themselves about how to further liberalize the borders that separated them. Five of these states—Belgium, France, Luxembourg, the Netherlands, and West Germany—became impatient with the lack of progress and set out on their own path to a borderless Europe. In 1985, these states met to sign an agreement on a river boat in Schengen, Luxembourg—an agreement that would remove physical border controls among signatory states. In 1990, this agreement was made into a Convention, and other states (both EU member states and not) began to join the club. In 1991, Italy signed the Convention, followed by Spain (1992), Portugal (1992), Greece (1995), Austria (1995), and in 1996 the Nordic countries—including the nonmember states, Iceland and Norway. It was only with the Amsterdam Treaty in 1999—fourteen years later—that the Schengen Convention was integrated into the EU framework, introducing the Schengen-Acquis.

Since 1999, most of the remaining EU member states have embraced the Schengen idea, if not all its glory. Indeed, most of the subsequent signatory states have only agreed to certain aspects of the larger dream. The original Schengen Agreement was about abolishing border controls and checks among signatory states, and creating a unified external border—where common rules of entry into the Schengen Area were to be carried out. To facilitate this common border control, signatory states needed to pool and share information, in what is now known as the Schengen Information System (SIS) and its supporting network of Supplementary Information Request at the National Entry (SIRENE) offices. (EU bureaucrats have an odd affinity for unwieldy names, so long as they produce sexy acronyms.) This framework, in effect, instituted a system for sharing relevant political and legal information among signatory states.

After the Amsterdam Treaty, most new signatory states to Schengen have only agreed to the police- and judicial-cooperation elements of the treaty—they have not yet agreed to drop their border guards. In other words, one could argue that the police forces of new member states have gained more than their ordinary workers. This is true of the UK (2000), Ireland (2002), and each of the ten new member states in 2004. Since the Amsterdam Treaty, only Switzerland (a non-EU member state), has agreed to full membership in the Schengen Agreement (in 2004, pulling Lichtenstein in with it).[7]

Neither does this area of free mobility apply to workers in all states equally. Old members of the European club have always treated new members with equal doses of caution and suspicion; and the EU has allowed states to employ restrictions on migrants coming from new member states. Thus, workers from Greece, Spain, and Portugal were not allowed access to the whole of the European labor market until six years after joining (i.e., Greece in 1987, and Spain and Portugal in 1992). The argument for limiting these member state rights was the need to ensure that labor migration from poorer states didn't have a sudden and inverse impact on older member state economies. In practice, these concerns proved to be overblown, but it hasn't stopped today's member states from exploiting their precedence.

Two of the new member states in 2004 managed to avoid this fate. Malta and Cyprus secured immediate access for their workers in the European labor market.

But the other eight new members, the A8,[8] met a colder reception (like Greece, Spain, and Portugal before them). A number of protectionist measures were allowed by the EU, as it did not require existing member states to open their labor markets to A8 workers until seven years after their joining (i.e., 2011). In effect, the new member states were not granted full access to EEA+ labor markets unless individual member states granted them dispensation.

Several EEA+ states have done just that. Ireland, Norway, Sweden, and the UK allowed immediate access to workers from the ten new member states. Other states agreed to a variable timeline: some member states agreed to a two-year moratorium (Finland, Greece, Portugal, Spain, and Italy); others to three years (the Netherlands and Luxembourg), four years (France), or five years (Belgium and Denmark); and still others chose to protect their domestic labor markets until the entire grace period had expired (Germany and Austria). Thus, EU membership for these eight countries did not offer immediate or full access for their workers, only the promise to secure that access over time.

In theory, worker mobility rights in the EEA+ are impressive. And it is important not to belittle this remarkable and admirable achievement: the opportunities available to millions of workers and their families have been expanded significantly. In practice, however, these rights are too often curtailed by a number of factors. Migrants must be able to prove that they have sufficient means to support themselves (and their families), and member states retain the prerogative to determine nationality and citizenship laws. These constraints, in addition to the barriers of culture and bureaucratic/legal entanglement, mean that the European labor market remains very rigid.

To understand the nature of these constraints, we might look at them from the perspective of a fictional worker. Imagine you are an unemployed real estate agent from Portugal, in search of work in Germany. As an EEA+ citizen, you have a right to enter any other EEA+ member state (including Germany) on presenting a valid form of identification. You can then stay there for six months. At the end of this period, you will need to apply for permission to stay, and that permission will depend on your ability to show one of the following four things, that you are (1) working or self-employed; (2) that you are not a drain on Germany's resources (i.e., that you have enough resources, including health insurance); (3) that you are enrolled in a vocational school (and have the financial support necessary to continue); and/or (4) that you are a family member of someone who meets one of the three previous requirements. If you meet these criteria and stay for five years, you can then gain a right to permanent residency.

But the constraints do not end here. There are a whole slew of informal constraints that are difficult to overcome. The most striking of these is the formidable language barrier that separates Portuguese from German. And before you move, you will need to check to see if your Portuguese realtors' license is valid in Germany, and you'll have to learn the very different ways that the German real estate market works, compared to the Portuguese market. You will need to consider the difficulty of transferring your pension credits and social security benefits, and the very different tax regimes in both countries.

To put this in a comparative perspective, I'll make this personal. Many years ago I moved from Seattle to Los Angeles to pursue my graduate career. I found the move difficult, not only because I missed the rain. Everything from the traffic rules to the local tax code seemed to be different in these two states. Despite these challenges, I was still speaking the same language, still paying taxes to the same federal government, and I didn't even need to change my television news provider (or, more importantly, my brewer). The nature of the constraints facing a Portuguese migrant to Germany is of a whole different order of magnitude.

The European Union is completely aware of these difficulties and how they limit the options available to workers (and the degree of mobility that they can hope to entice). Europe cannot expect to experience the same level of mobility found in the United States—not to mention the degree of mobility we find for capital, goods, and services. But the EU has worked hard, for several years (if not decades), to try to minimize these barriers. Already in 1996, the Commission set up a High-Level Panel on the Free Movement of Persons, which identified a number of barriers to mobility and produced eighty (!) recommendations, many of which were included in the Commission's 1997 Action Plan for the Free Movement of Workers. This Action Plan has been succeeded by others, but the barriers to free mobility across the EEA+ area—although shrinking—remain formidable.

But the level of migration across European states remains remarkably low. This is especially problematic for a region where many of these states share a common currency, the euro, as labor mobility and wage flexibility are important means for regional economic adjustment within a common currency area. Indeed, this is very evident in the postcrisis rise of emigration evident in figure 13.2. Still, the amount of mobility is insufficient to clear local labor markets, and we can expect it to increase even more. Compared to the United States, for example, EU citizens are about half as mobile: over the last ten years, 38 percent of EU citizens changed residence, but only about 4 percent of these moved to another member state.[9]

As mentioned briefly in the introduction, the creation of a common labor market plays an important role in the larger European project. The lack of real mobility in Europe is a symbol of the difficulty in creating a common sense of identity and trust across nation states with deep and conflict-filled histories. While much progress has been made, we still refer to Polish and Portuguese workers—not to European workers—even in an increasingly integrated European labor market.

NON-EUROPEAN IMMIGRATION

Europe's regulatory attitude toward immigrants from beyond the EEA+, so-called Third Country Nationals (or TCNs), is even more chaotic. One reason for this is that the Treaty of Rome failed to mention external border controls. Another reason is that member states have long histories, some of which include colonialist pasts, and have several good reasons for maintaining special relationships with some TCNs. Not to be left out is the recognition that states are often leery of seceding political authority, and physical control of the border is seen by many as a core sovereign right.

It is for these reasons that the regulation of TCN immigration has been located mostly outside of the EU's legal framework: member states jealously guard this area of authority. But it is to this area—the effort to create a common immigration, asylum, and family-reunion policy with respect to TCNs—that the EU is devoting much of its current attention.

Despite these intentions and much supporting rhetoric, there remains remarkable variation across states in Europe with respect to their TCN immigration policies. To illustrate this variation, consider the immigration policies of two neighboring countries in northern Europe, both of whom are EU member states: Sweden and Denmark.

Sweden has a remarkably liberal immigration policy with respect to TCNs. Indeed, as we saw in the discussion about labor market integration, Sweden has embraced immigrant labor from the new member states as well. In December 2008, the Swedish government introduced new laws and regulations that allow Swedish employers to hire TCN workers directly, if they are not able to find suitable workers in the EEA+ labor pool.

In effect, the Swedish government is giving its employers a free hand to decide which workers are best qualified to do the required work. These employers—not the state—are then put in charge of processing the necessary residence and work permits, based on their own assessment of needs. The Swedish Migration Board then ensures that the terms being offered (e.g. salary, insurance protection, and other terms of employment) are in accordance with the rules and standards applied to employees who are already in Sweden. As part of the reform, it has become easier to attend job interviews in Sweden, and permit periods are more easily extended to help match the supply and demand for labor in Sweden.

Just a stone's throw away, across the Kattegat, sits a state whose immigration policy has a much more colored reputation: Denmark. In practice, Danish immigration policy, with respect to skilled TCN workers, is not as restrictive as its reputation would have it. Indeed, the Danish authorities are very active in trying to attract highly skilled workers from outside of Europe, so long as they meet a number of specific criteria, collected under three rubrics: the Danish Green Card system (which allocates temporary permits on the basis of age, education, work experience, and language skills), a "Positive List" (where certain occupations are fast tracked), and a "Pay Limit Scheme" (which provides access to high-salaried foreign employees). But, in contrast to Sweden, the state is a very central actor (and gatekeeper) in this heavily regulated system.

Denmark's isolationist reputation is earned not from its attitude toward foreign (and skilled) workers, but for its restrictive position with respect to family reunification. In particular, Danish immigration laws block family reunification for non-EU citizens residing illegally and in cases where one of the spouses is under the age of twenty-four. Denmark also requires that family reunion applicants have to sign a declaration of integration before they are granted a right of entry.

In fact, a 2008 ruling of the European Court of Justice (ECJ) challenged this law, to the annoyance of Denmark's authorities. The Court's decision prompted Danish Prime Minister Anders Fogh Rasmussen to declare, "Denmark determines its own immigration policy and it remains unchanged. . . . The government will not tolerate having its family reunification rules hijacked."[10] Fogh Rasmussen's rebuttal to the ECJ illustrates the challenges facing European Union authorities as they try to streamline and coordinate member-state immigration policies. Immigration is a very high-profile and sensitive political issue, and elected national officials are hesitant to secede authority to the European Union, unless this secession brings with it a more restrictive policy that they can defend in front of skeptical constituents.

Despite the resistance of many member state governments, the EU has made much progress in coordinating member state policies and assuming greater authority over wider areas of immigration policy. This evolving role is traced in table 13.2, where we can see immigration and asylum issues being increasingly consolidated under the EU's political mandate.

Given this rapidly changing distribution of authority and responsibility, it makes little sense to focus on the particular institutions involved in forming and implementing Europe's immigration policy. Needless to say, there is a dense network of committees, permanent representatives, and working groups—most of which are associated with the Justice and Home Affairs (JHA) Council—producing a series of five-year action plans: Tampere (1999–2004), The Hague (2005–2009), and Stockholm (2010–2014).

For most Europeans, however, the authority of the European Union in these matters is most evident in its issuing of regulations, directives, decisions, and recommendations. It is important to note that these actions apply to both EU and EFTA states, even if the latter do not have any formal say as to how they are formulated. To illustrate the breadth of this reach and its controversial nature, we can take a brief glimpse at three important directives, each on an important source of migration: European migration, family reunification, and irregular migration.

- *The Services Directive (2004)* is one of the most controversial directives to come down the European pipeline. The biggest magnet of controversy was a reference in the original draft to the so-called country-of-origin principle, under which companies registered in any member state could provide services abroad, but under the laws and regulations of the country in which they are registered. This destined the directive to become a focal point in a larger debate about social dumping in Europe. While the "country-of-origin" reference was dropped from the text of the revised directive, its political sting lingered, as it provoked intense debate and mass protests in several countries, including France, Belgium, Sweden, and Denmark. Indeed, the directive became a flashpoint for European integration; it was perceived as a critical test for the Commission's (liberalizing) agenda and a threat to the power of organized labor in Europe.
- *The Directive on Family Reunion (2003)* came to life only after a rather lengthy and controversial period of negotiation, as it concerns the right to family reunification for TCNs who reside lawfully in the EEA+. The directive sets out the conditions for entry and residence in the EEA+ area, the sort of demands that these states can make on TCNs, and the specific rights that family members have once reunification is granted (e.g., with respect to education and training). The controversial nature of the directive is underscored by the fact that it doesn't apply to all EEA states: Denmark, Ireland, the UK, and Switzerland are not subject to its provisions.
- *The Returns Directive (2008)* underwent three years of negotiations following the original Commission proposal, before final adoption by the European Parliament. Its purpose is to lay down EU-wide rules and procedures on the return of irregular

Table 13.2   Evolving EU Control over Immigration Issues

1976	Council of Ministers' Resolution encouraging member states to develop common immigration policies, in consultation with the Commission.
1985	The Commission issues a series of "Guidelines for a Common Policy on Migration." ➢ But emphasis is on free mobility for EU citizens and equal treatment for all migrants (EU citizen or not). Commission decision requiring member states to signal in advance future decisions relating to TNCs. ➢ But member states challenged the decision in the ECJ, which delivers a compromise opinion.
1986	With the introduction of the Single European Act and its four freedoms, the Commission interprets "freedom of persons" to mean legally resident people. ➢ But member states issue a declaration affirming their right to control immigration policy.
1992	The Maastricht Treaty attempts to introduce a common migration policy, based on a common asylum and immigration policy and control over a common external border (Art. K.1 EUV). ➢ But the resulting institutional setup, with a third (intergovernmental) "pillar" to deal with Justice and Home Affairs (JHA), effectively prevented this. Decisions needed to be unanimous, and were largely made outside EU institutions.
1999	The Amsterdam Treaty pushes immigration cooperation back to center stage by incorporating the Schengen Agreement into the EU framework, and taking migration and asylum out of the JHA pillar (and away from intergovernmental cooperation) and into a new Title IV TEC* (concerning visas, asylum, immigration, and other policies related to the free movement of persons). The explicit competencies were laid out in Articles 62–64, and included things like: responsibility for assessing asylum claims; action against undocumented migrants; procedures for granting and withdrawing refugee status, and so on. The ECJ was given jurisdiction over immigration issues (but only on referrals from high courts). ➢ But the UK, Ireland, and Denmark opt out.
2001	The Nice Treaty places visa, asylum, and immigration policy under the co-decision principle (where the Commission presents proposals and the text is adopted if it secures the approval of the European Parliament and the Council, where member states vote by qualified majority [QMV]). In particular, Article 61 was amended to put a deadline on adopting measures aimed at ensuring free movement within Europe and flanking measures with respect to external borders controls, asylum, and immigration. ➢ But the right of member states to determine access to their labor markets by (and integration of) TCNs remains unaffected by the Treaty.
2004	FRONTEX, or the Agency for the Management of Operational Cooperation at the External Borders of the Member States of the EU, is created by a Council Regulation to coordinate the border security measures of member states.
2005	Commission Green Paper on the "EU Approach to Managing Economic Migration" aims to establish a common framework for economic immigration. For example, it proposes to adopt common admission criteria for TCNs, simplify entry procedures, and clarify the rights and legal status of the different types of migrants. It also emphasizes the importance of accompanying measures for ensuring the control of immigration.
2008	Commission creates a European Border Surveillance System (EUROSUR) to prevent unauthorized border crossings, to reduce the number of deaths associated with irregular immigration, and to prevent cross-border crime.

2009   The Lisbon Treaty further increases consolidation: migration and asylum become, in effect, "normal" EU issues, with QMV in the Council and co-decision with the European Parliament; and the ECJ is given complete jurisdiction (with referrals now from any level of court). In relation to specific measures, Articles 77–80 set out provisions on borders, asylum, and migration.

    ➢ But member states maintain an exclusive right to determine the number of foreign nationals admitted to their territory. Also, cooperation on integration is supplementary and not about the harmonization of laws.

The EU Blue Card is introduced. The Council adopts a directive to facilitate the entry and residence of TNCs with desired skills for employment in Europe. In effect, it introduces a fast-track procedure for issuing a special residence and work permit.

    ➢ But the UK, Ireland, and Denmark opt out.

---

*TEC refers to the Consolidated Treaty establishing the European Community (i.e., the revised Treaty of Rome).

immigrants. It covers periods of custody, reentry bans, and a number of legal safeguards. EEA+ states are banned from applying harsher rules to irregular immigrants, but they are allowed to keep or adopt more generous rules. In any case, this legislation applies only after a decision has been taken by the national authorities to deport an illegal immigrant (i.e., each state retains the authority to decide whether it wishes to regularize or deport the immigrant).

As in the realm of European migration, considerable progress has been made toward establishing a legislative foundation and the institutions necessary to formulate and implement a common immigration policy for TCNs. Immigration and asylum issues have been taken out of an institutional setting that allowed states a veto over sensitive outcomes, and moved into a new institutional setting that is determined mostly by qualified majority voting. While substantial areas of national policy autonomy remain, and national politicians loathe ceding any more authority, the institutional framework now in place will ensure that the EU can advance its common immigration policy.

ASYLUM

Europe believes that it must erect imposing and common barriers toward the outside world if its internal market is to work as planned. A common internal market implies a common external front. Given the political history of Europe's component states, it has proven quite difficult to secure consensus over the rules governing family reunion and immigration from TCNs. These sorts of constraints do not hinder Europe's common asylum policy, at least not to the same degree. It is for this reason that we see most progress on developing a common front in the area of Europe's asylum policy.

The willingness of states to cooperate has resulted in an ambitious attempt to standardize national approaches, processes, applications, and recognition of status for protection. The end result of this collaboration has been a generally more restrictive policy with respect to asylum across Europe—if only because the number of potential asylum havens has diminished, thereby limiting the opportunities available to asylum seekers.

Since the Amsterdam Treaty, one European agreement after the other has signaled an interest in creating a common European asylum policy. In particular, the Nice Treaty moved asylum issues from the third to the first pillar of European governance, allowing asylum decisions to be carried out by majority voting. This means that member states lost their right to veto policies that they oppose, accelerating the development of a common policy in this area. In short, the EU intends to create a common EEA-wide asylum system. This system would rely on a single procedure, mutual recognition of member state decisions, and the creation of an institutional hub at the European Asylum Support Office. So far, a European-wide asylum system rests on four important components:

- The first of these is known as the Dublin Regulation from 2003, the objective of which is to identify (as quickly as possible) the member state responsible for examining an asylum application, to establish reasonable time limits for each of the phases of determining the member state responsible, and to prevent abuse of asylum procedures in the form of multiple applications. In effect, this regulation creates a one-stop asylum procedure, where asylum applicants are forced to make a claim in the first EEA+ state that the applicant enters or passes through. The system is designed to prevent "asylum shopping" and, at the same time, to ensure that each asylum applicant's case is processed by only one member state. Thus, if you enter the EEA+ space through Italy but settle in Denmark, your application for asylum needs to be filed in Italy—and Italy alone.
- The second component of a European-wide asylum system is anchored in the Reception Conditions Directive (2003), which introduced minimum standards for reception and detention (e.g., access to information, labor markets, and health care). The motivation behind the directive was to ensure that asylum applicants received a dignified standard of living, wherever they settled in the EEA+ area. This is especially important now that asylum seekers have lost their ability to choose the state that will examine their application (due to the Dublin Regulation, discussed above).
- The third component lies in the Asylum Procedures Directive of 2005, where states are obliged to agree on minimum standards for processing asylum claims. In particular, the directive grants certain basic procedural guarantees (e.g., the right to a lawyer and interpreter, access to the United Nations High Commissioner for Refugees, and the right to appeal).
- Finally, the Qualifications Directive (2004) establishes minimum standards for granting and withdrawing refugee status. The objective of this directive is to establish common criteria for identifying persons who need international protection (and to ensure they are granted a minimum level of benefits). In particular, the directive provides minimum standards for protection from refoulement (the forced return of a person to a country where he or she faces persecution), maintaining family unity, and access to employment, education, health care, and so on.

These four legislative steps have brought the European Union much closer to a common asylum policy, and the future will surely bring even more harmonization and streamlining. But there is still a very long way to go before Europe's asylum policies and practices are completely harmonized. National governments continue to wield significant power, and national practices are remarkably diverse.

This diversity can be seen in the different rates by which member states still reject (or, inversely, recognize) asylum claims. For example, in 2011, the rejection rate ranged from 43 percent in Portugal to 98 percent in Greece. National differences are also evident in the very different ways that member states responded to recent asylum streams from Afghanistan, Iraq, Chechnya, Syria, and so on. In short, states interpret common regulations in different ways, and they employ derogation clauses that allow them to maintain national policies and interests. The end result is a lack of harmonization, in terms of both recognition and reception conditions.

Shades of Difference

Thus far, I have aimed to paint a face of European immigration that is varied, but not threateningly different. As we have seen, European immigration levels are not especially high in a global perspective, Europeans have been on the move for centuries, and a significant share of European migration comes from other European states.

My intent with this depiction is to temper a more common perception of Europe—a picture of Europe full to the gills with foreigners (mostly draped in burqas and turbans) and going quickly to hell in a hand-basket. Foreigners are seen as a growing threat to romanticized images of the European polity, bringing with them values and social practices that threaten the essence of European traditions. This picture is familiar to anybody following European politics in recent years, and I would like to close this chapter by reflecting on some of the integration challenges facing Europe today.

THE RISE OF THE RIGHT

In recent decades, the radical right has gained significant political support in Europe. In almost every European country, it is possible to find a nationalist party that is poised to exploit voter dissatisfaction and alienation. The radical right has gained enough support to enter government coalitions in Austria, Denmark, Italy, the Netherlands, and Switzerland. Vehement national parties can also be found in other countries, and their support appears to rise in inverse proportion to the surrounding economic conditions.

This political landscape is marked by a number of important and influential political figures, whose political successes have rippled across Europe. In France, Jean-Marie Le Pen's Front National has been the third-largest party for most of the millennium, and he was runner-up in the 2002 French presidential elections. In 2000, Jörg Haider—then leader of the FPÖ (Freedom Party of Austria)—joined a coalition government that sent the European Union into a political frenzy. In the Austrian elections of 2008, far-right parties captured 30 percent of the vote, and in the Netherlands, Geert Wilders' Partij voor de Vrijheid (Party for Freedom [PVV]) finished as the third-biggest party in the country's 2010 elections.

The nationalist right is rising at the European level as well. In the June 2009 European Parliament (EP) elections, almost a million Brits voted for the British National Party (BNP), giving the party its first two seats in the EP. In the Netherlands, Geert Wilders' PVV won second place. Similar parties managed to gain around 15 percent of the European vote in Austria, Denmark, Hungary, and Slovakia.

These are complex and varied political movements, responding mostly to local conditions in each country. This makes it difficult to generalize about them. But they do share some common features, the most common of which are a very critical view of the current state of affairs, and a strong and explicit distrust of foreigners, especially Muslims.

From an outsider's perspective, Europeans seem intent to provoke conflict. Danish newspaper editors gloated in their stubborn determination to publish offensive caricatures of the Prophet Mohammed in 2005. Voters in a 2009 referendum in Switzerland accepted a constitutional amendment banning the construction of new minarets. Across Europe, politicians debate whether and how to regulate the religious attire of their increasingly diverse populations (in an effort to liberate women from what they see as the tyranny of the veil). Clearly, something is amiss in Europe—and its problems seem to be connected to immigration.

WHERE'S THE BEEF?

The rhetoric of the radical right links its rise to an increase in immigrants to Europe. The net numbers lend some credence to this claim. As we saw in figure 13.1, net immigration to the EU-27 countries increased dramatically, more than doubling, at the turn of the millennium (although it has since dropped off precipitously). It could be that the intensity and the pace of that immigration surge were driving European xenophobia. But this interpretation should be tempered by the realization that Europe's

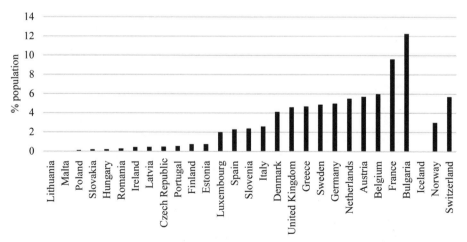

Figure 13.5   Muslim Population Share, 2011. *Source*: **http://www.muslimpopulation.com/Europe/**

share of foreigners, as a percentage of population, is not particularly high from a global perspective, as we saw in table 13.1.

Neither is the size of Europe's Muslim population particularly high. Figure 13.5 ranks European countries by the share of their Muslim population. Here we see a very significant variation separating Lithuania and Malta (practically none) from France (9.6 percent) or Bulgaria (12.3 percent). On average, however, the percentage of the EEA+ population that is Muslim is only about 2.2 percent. This is very close to the 2.19 percent we find in North America, and is not especially high or threatening in its own right. Given the remarkably small size of the Muslim population in Europe (2.2 percent!), it draws an inordinate amount of critical attention.

Whatever the reason, foreigners in Europe are treated differently. Evidence of this is seen in the variance in unemployment levels between foreigners and nationals across European labor markets (see figure 13.6). The first thing to note is the astronomically high unemployment rates for foreigners in Europe (e.g., almost 40 percent in Spain!). In addition, there is a large spread between native and foreigner unemployment rates in Europe. On average, foreigners in the EU-27 suffer under an unemployment rate that is more than double that of EU-27 nationals (21.3 percent compared to 10 percent for nationals). This spread differs remarkably across Europe, with Sweden and Belgium hosting the largest spreads, whereas foreigners in Cyprus enjoyed a lower unemployment rate than the natives!

In short, it would seem that Europeans have a difficult time integrating their foreigners—even in the labor market, where most of the EU's legal and political attention has been focused. To understand this difficulty, we need to glance back on the history of nationalism in Europe, and the competing perceptions of how to control membership in Europe's national communities.

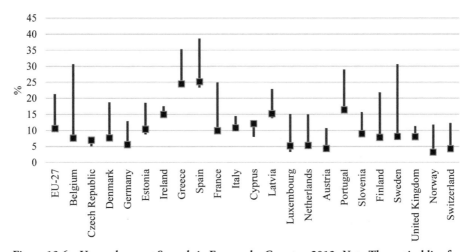

Figure 13.6 Unemployment Spreads in Europe, by Country, 2012. *Note*: **The vertical line for each country stretches from the unemployment level for foreigners (top) to the unemployment level for natives (bottom), while the box marks the country's total unemployment level. The larger the spread, the larger the unemployment difference between foreigners and natives (e.g., contrast Sweden with the UK).** *Source*: **EUROSTAT [lfsa_urgan].**

NATIONALISM AND INTEGRATION

Immigration has a long history of challenging traditional conceptions of community. This history is complicated, in that its effect works in two, opposing, directions. On the one hand, migrants provide a convenient benchmark for defining "the other." On the other hand, immigration forces communities to consider ways by which newcomers can (or cannot) be incorporated into that community.

The first lesson is clearly seen in the long history of European migration, as briefly traced in the introduction to this chapter. It is a history that has always brought communities into contact with foreigners—whether they are from across the valley, the continent, or the globe.

Today we think of the foreigner in terms of religion or skin color, but differences can be spun out of almost anything (or nothing at all). Indeed, during earlier periods of (intra-European) migration, the migrant in question did not look or act any differently from his or her host: they often shared the same religion, diets, music, and traditions—but host communities still excluded the migrants as outsiders, as foreign. We have a remarkable capacity to find (and to generate) the differences we use to separate ourselves.

This primitive sentiment was exacerbated by a system of nation states built on national myths. The modern nation-state system was born in northern Europe, with the Treaty of Westphalia in 1648. Its modern forms of citizenship were the result of a very European debate about the source of nationhood (and membership in the national community) and competing conceptions of how new members should be integrated into those national communities.

While these traditions are slowly eroding, they continue to influence the way that many Europeans think about membership and inclusion in the political community. These attitudes also hamper attempts by Europe's political elites to create a new common identity for all Europeans.

- *Citizenship*: There have been two main traditions by which membership in the political community was determined in Europe: *jus sanguinis* and *jus soli*. *Jus sanguinis* grants citizenship on the basis of ethnicity (Latin, meaning "right of blood"), so that a person gains access to citizenship by being born of parents who are already citizens of the state. Traditionally, this has been the most common means of allocating citizenship in continental Europe, and Germany is usually seen as the archetype. The alternative source of citizenship, *jus soli* ("right of soil"), provides citizenship to any individual born in the territory of the state, even if the child's parents were ethnically foreign. The archetype for this source of citizenship is Republican France.

  As it becomes easier to migrate and settle across Europe, we might expect Europeans to abandon *sanguini* traditions of citizenship. After all, the birthright (*soli*) tradition of citizenship facilitates immigrant inclusion (as immigrants cannot choose the ethnicity of their parents). Instead, we find a convergence of citizenship traditions in Europe, as states such as Germany soften up their *sanguini* positions, while countries such as France have scuttled important *soli* components.

- *Integration*: On top of these competing conceptions of citizenship lies another relevant cleavage. States in Europe have maintained different traditions for incorporating or integrating new members into the political community. While the first (citizenship) cleavage concerns an individual's access to rights, obligations and privileges, the second cleavage concerns the character or nature of the resulting community. Here too we can distinguish between two main variants: assimilationist and multiculturalist integration strategies.

Assimilationists believe that immigrants benefit most if they become part and parcel of the new community. In effect, immigrants are expected to grow into the host culture, adopting its norms and values. This assimilation is directed by a number of host culture institutions (e.g., schools, local communities, and state officials), and also by families and civic-society organizations. In Europe, the archetypical state in this tradition is France, where immigrants are not encouraged to embrace their ethnic or national background or to describe themselves as Algerian-French (as, e.g., Norwegian-Americans do in the United States). Rather, a Frenchman is a Frenchman is a Frenchman.

Multiculturalists, by contrast, celebrate difference; they are less concerned about the need to fuse immigrant and host communities together. Instead, the emphasis is on encouraging tolerance and pluralism, so that different immigrant communities can coexist with, and without feeling threatened by, the host community. In this approach, the host community's efforts are directed at ensuring that immigrant groups are not disadvantaged with respect to established groups, and to create social conditions that encourage tolerance. From the EU's perspective, it makes sense to encourage member states to embrace multiculturalist approaches: the creation of a common European identity cannot be facilitated by a mushrooming of twenty-eight competing assimilationist responses!

Some of Europe's growing xenophobia may be explained by the way that increased integration challenges attitudes borne of these competing conceptions of citizenship and integration. More to the point, these competing conceptions represent a serious challenge to the effort by Europe's political elites to create a new, and common, *European* identity.

This challenge is particularly difficult in Europe, if only because the modern nation-state was born there, and the concept of (and debate about) nationhood has deep roots in European soil. It is, after all, this strong sense of nationalism that is often blamed for Europe's affinity for war and conflict; and it is this sort of nationalist history that the European Union is designed to overcome. The point of creating a pan-European identity is not just to create a common European market, so producers can sell more products. One of the driving logics of the European project has been to create a common sense of identity—to overcome national identities that have too often led to war and conflict. Unfortunately, the evident failures of the euro-zone are now driving Europeans apart, pitting poor member states against rich ones.

To bridge these competing conceptions of nationhood, citizenship, and integration, Europe needs to create a common political space where different nationalities can meet and meld. (At the same time, Europe needs to build a market that can bring together rather than further divide the denizens of its member states.) Somehow, Europe needs to navigate the treacherous waters that separate *jus soli* from *jus sanguinis*, and assimilationists from multiculturalists. It is this tricky navigational task that the next section considers.

POLITICAL EFFORTS AT INTEGRATION

Like everything else in Europe, competing integration policies can be seen at different levels of government. At the member state level, vestiges of earlier traditions continue to linger, but more European states seem to be embracing assimilationist strategies.

In particular, a growing number of European states now require potential TCN immigrants to take an exam that tests their capacity to integrate. The best known of these, perhaps, is the "Civic Integration Examination Abroad" given to non-EU immigrants to the Netherlands at the Dutch embassy of the sending country in question. This examination consists of a half-hour-long film, some questions (in Dutch) about the film, and a more general test of the potential immigrant's Dutch language skills. But there is nothing unique about the Netherlands in this regard: other countries conduct similar tests (including the UK, Denmark, France, and Germany).

Increasingly, European states expect TCN immigrants to assimilate into the distinct national cultures of the host country. These states expect immigrants to bear the costs of integration; by implication, they do not see a need to facilitate integration by changing national attitudes or institutions. At the national level, the effort of integration is aimed to minimize the original distance separating the foreigner (on arrival) from the host culture.

The strategy at the European level is somewhat different, if not fully developed. The EU is obviously concerned about the problem, but it can hardly support twenty-eight different assimilation policies, where each new TCN immigrant is turned into a new mini-nationalist! Instead, the EU's legislative efforts have aimed to secure equal treatment and protection from discrimination for immigrants after they arrive. While member states lean in the direction of more assimilationist policies, the EU's thrust has been in a more multiculturalist direction.

In particular, the EU's focus is trained on deterring abuses and discrimination in member states. By implication, the problem of integration lies in national frameworks that require correction. This concern is long-lasting, and we can see it early on in the EC's desire to make jobs available to foreign workers from other EU states, or by TCNs already working in Europe.

Indeed, the treatment of TCNs has been a hot-potato issue for several years between the EU and its member states. Already in 1986, with the SEA's commitment to the four freedoms, the Commission was anxious to interpret the freedom of persons to include legally resident TCNs—but member states wanted this freedom to be restricted to EU citizens only. In 1999, the Tampere European Council emphasized the need to harmonize national legislation on the conditions for admission and residence of TCNs.

In 2003, the Commission introduced a directive (2003/109/EC) that created a single status for long-term TNC residents to ensure their equal treatment, across the union, regardless of state residence. While the original ambitions were admirable, the resulting legislation was watered down by a number of national requirements, including a German demand for favoring the treatments of nationals over TCNs. Member states were also allowed to set numerical quotas on TNCs and to require them to comply with integration measures (e.g., taking the sort of language classes referenced above).

On a parallel front, Europe is developing a common antidiscrimination policy. The seeds to this policy were planted in the 1997 Treaty of Amsterdam, where the Community gained new powers in Article 13 to combat discrimination. These seeds have begun to bear fruit in the form of three directives. The first two of these were enacted in 2000. The Race Discrimination Directive (2000/43) guarantees equal treatment of people, irrespective of racial or ethnic origin; and the Equal Treatment Framework Directive (2000/78) provides a framework for equal treatment at the job (and training) site. As these directives were limited to the sphere of employment, the Commission has more recently (July 2, 2008) issued a new draft directive on anti-discrimination, which is intended to extend antidiscrimination protections into areas that extend beyond employment. Ever since, the bill has been stuck at the first reading stage in the member states' secretariat, the EU Council, in Brussels.

Mostly, the EU has talked about the need for action, but accomplished very little. Since 2002, the EU has issued annual reports on migration and integration (which basically review trends in member state integration policies, and identify common barriers); it has published a (2004) handbook on integration, which lists a number of best practices; and EU leaders have adopted several (mostly commonsense) principles for immigrant integration policy. It has established the European Union Agency for Fundamental Rights (FRA) and the European Commission against Racism and Intolerance (ECRI) to document and advise on these sorts of issues. In the same year (2004), the Commission proposed a "Common Agenda for Integration," which included some very concrete proposals (e.g., boosting participation of immigrant women in the work place and promoting interfaith dialogue), but—like all the measures noted in this paragraph—none of its proposals were binding.

More promising is the European Fund for the Integration of TCNs—an €825 million fund (covering the 2007–2013 period) to help member states enable TCNs in their attempt to integrate into their host countries. Tellingly, Denmark is the only member state to have opted out.

Conclusion

Even though Europe has a long relationship and much experience with migration, it has not been able to develop a coordinated response to the challenges of migration, whether the migrants are workers from other member states or TCNs from abroad. Europe's difficulty is evident in the relatively low levels of internal (European) migration and the frighteningly high levels of support for the xenophobic parties of the radical right.

The European Union has worked hard to try to overcome these difficulties, and recent developments have clearly shifted more responsibility for migration issues from member states up to the EU level. But the unwillingness of member states to consistently adopt European policies that apply to issues of mobility, immigration, and integration has meant that the European policy space with respect to migration issues is remarkably complex.

Worse, design failures in Europe's internal market are exacerbating nationalist tensions in Europe. The need to defend the euro zone has generated rescue packages that pit debtor member states in the South against their creditors to the North. The result of these packages has been massive unemployment, and a flight from poverty that has further undermined the legitimacy of the broader European project and deepened the nationalist fissures that the EU was supposed to resolve.

To provide some order to these overlapping ambitions, policies, and outcomes, I have divided immigration issues into three main areas: European migration, international immigration, and asylum. Within each of these areas, I have shown how different states interpret and respond to EU proposals, and this variance makes it difficult to refer to any common EU policy platform with respect to migration issues.

This variance is also evident in the ways in which member states and the EU respond to the growing challenges of integration. With the growth of nationalist sentiment and the radical right, we see a plethora of attempts to require foreigners to assimilate into diverse national political cultures. The EU's response to this development has been a rather feeble attempt to discourage discrimination.

Notes

1. Unless otherwise noted, all figures come from the Eurostat homepage, http://epp.euro stat.ec.europa.eu (accessed January 17, 2014).

2. For example, one region in the United Kingdom (Yorkshire and Humber) lists thirteen distinct categories of refugees and asylum seekers under three broad headings: Refugee (includes refugee status; humanitarian protection; discretionary leave; exception leave to remain; and indefinite leave to remain), Asylum Seeker (includes induction asylum seeker; dispersed asylum seeker; subs' only asylum seeker; unsupported asylum seeker; and detained asylum seeker), and Refused Asylum Seeker (which includes section 4 refused asylum seeker; destitute refused asylum seeker; and detained refused asylum seeker).

3. These figures come from the *Eurostat Yearbook 2012*, 151–52, http://epp.eurostat .ec.europa.eu/portal/page/portal/publications/eurostat_yearbook_2012 (accessed January 17, 2014).

4. See Christal Morehouse and Michael Blomfield, "Irregular Migration in Europe," Migration Policy Institute, 2011, http://www.migrationpolicy.org/pubs/tcmirregularmigration.pdf (accessed January 17, 2014).

5. European Union officials like to refer to these streams as "mobility," in contrast to the "migration" that comes from outside Europe. But it is very difficult to use this politicized terminology in any consistent fashion, so I will leave it to the politicians.

6. The EEA is based on the same freedoms of mobility as agreed to in the Treaty of Rome (free movement of goods, persons, services, and capital), and EEA member states enjoy free trade with the European Union, in return for adopting parts of European law and contributing significant sums of money to the larger project (in the form of "EEA and Norway Grants").

7. In 2008, the Czech Republic, Poland, Slovenia, Slovakia, Hungary, Lithuania, Latvia, Estonia, and Malta agreed to lift internal air border controls.

8. The A8 countries are Poland, Lithuania, Estonia, Latvia, Slovakia, Slovenia, Hungary, and the Czech Republic.

9. European Commission, "High Level Task Force on Skills and Mobility: Final Report," Directorate-General for Employment and Social Affairs, Unit EMPL/A.3, December (Brussels: European Commission, 2001).

10. "EU Court Ruling Threatens Denmark's Immigration Policy," *EUbusiness*, September 1, 2008.

Suggested Readings

Bauböck, Rainer, ed. *Migration and Citizenship: Legal Status, Rights and Political Participation.* Amsterdam: Amsterdam University Press, 2006.

Boswell, Christina, and Andrew Geddes. *Migration and Mobility in the European Union.* Basingstoke: Palgrave, 2011.

Eurostat. *Migrants in Europe: A Statistical Portrait of the First and Second Generation.* Luxembourg: Publications Office of the European Union, 2011.

Papademetrious, Demetrios. *Coming Together or Pulling Apart? The European Union's Struggle with Immigration and Asylum.* Washington, DC: Carnegie Endowment for International Peace, 1996.

CHAPTER 14

A Reassessment of Transatlantic Security

EUROPE, THE UNITED STATES, AND NATO

Simon Duke and Roberta Haar

When NATO adopted its New Strategic Concept on November 19, 2010, transatlantic security relations, especially those between NATO and the European Union (EU), were "still at the crossroads."[1] The question is whether they have changed decisively in the interim. While NATO has remained in Afghanistan, unlike in 2010 the conclusion of combat operations heralds a far smaller presence. Whatever the outcome of future stability in Afghanistan, NATO's diminishing presence poses awkward questions for the Alliance since being there has been linked to NATO's nominal raison d'être for much of the post–Cold War era, although, for some, Russia's territorial grab on the Crimea has revived NATO and underlined its continuing relevance.[2] Additionally, during these years, the EU and its members continued to develop the Common Security and Defense Policy (CSDP) and undertake new missions, both civilian and military, many of them in Africa (Somalia, the Horn of Africa, South Sudan, Niger, and Mali). Appreciable effort was also invested in the implementation of the 2009 Lisbon Treaty, including the attempt to persuade EU members to spend their strained defense budgets more wisely, for example by more joint research, development, procurement, and production.

The general context of transatlantic security relations also changed since 2010. From an American perspective, considerable attention in geopolitical and security terms shifted to the Asia-Pacific region, which until recently was considered more dynamic but less stable than the Euro-Atlantic area. The vibrancy of the region brings opportunities for both Europe and the United States, but growth in the region is matched by higher defense expenditure and saber rattling over long-held territorial disputes, like those between China and Japan over the Diaoyu or Senkaku Islands. The ongoing global economic crisis has exerted enduring downward pressure on the defense expenditures of NATO allies and, as a consequence, the slippage of security-related issues down many national agendas. Even before the financial crisis, numerous European allies maintained static or negative defense budgets in real terms, preferring to prioritize the funding of their social welfare models, which are integral to much of Western Europe's postwar character and to the EU's distinct role in global politics. This has led some in Washington to question the extent to which the European allies can be counted on, an impression exacerbated by the many conditions attached to the use of many national forces in Afghanistan.

The EU and NATO are therefore still at a crossroads, but the nature of this juncture is different from that in 2010. It is dissimilar in two main senses. First, the EU and NATO have found a *modus vivendi* with formal and informal cooperation evident both at the headquarters and in the field.[3] The handwringing, at both the political and academic levels, about the mutual exclusivity of the EU and NATO in security terms, or the possibility of NATO withering away as the result of benign neglect, has largely stopped. It has also been pointed out that the EU and NATO are, in many ways, complementary in the sense that they share a significant degree of "normative overlap" with the exception of the use of force, the range and type of missions, and the resources required to execute them.[4] The two actors are also beset by common challenges, especially those resulting from stagnant or declining defense expenditure. Stereotypes about NATO being responsible for hard security, while the EU dabbles in soft security, have also been revised.[5] The military operation in Libya, whilst nominally a NATO undertaking, was mainly advocated and conducted by France and the United Kingdom with the United States playing a critical backseat role (removing much of Libya's air defense system and providing much of the intelligence, reconnaissance, and refueling capabilities). This led to the memorable, but controversial, phrase that the United States was "leading from behind."[6]

The second dissimilarity regards the complexity of their current crossroads. Rather than being a simple intersection, the junction looks more like a node with multiple routes—not unlike NATO's symbol. The choices are no longer about either NATO or the EU, or any other European security body for that matter, but rather a question of when one or the other, or a combination thereof, will be useful. Consequently, the selection of an institution to meet the needs of a particular concern will be influenced by a number of interlinked factors, the first being the question of *leadership*. The United States, the traditional leader in transatlantic security relations, has realized through painful experience in Afghanistan and Iraq that it is often unable to solve problems alone. This calls for the ability to form and sustain allied support for common aims. However, the leadership task of the United States has become all the more difficult because publics in both the United States and Europe are preoccupied by sagging economies. If, indeed, the strategic gaze of the United States will increasingly be drawn to the Pacific and less to the Atlantic, the allies that America will be courting will be Australia, India, Japan, and South Korea in a bid to balance a rising Chinese power. The informal networks of alliances in the Pacific may do far more to shape the twenty-first century than the formal alliance structures of old. Any reinvention of NATO, with a more global vocation in mind, must nevertheless nurture the underlying transatlantic cohesion, which has always been the bedrock of the Alliance.

Although Europe is not the customary leader in transatlantic security relations, Europe too is certainly focused on the Asia-Pacific region, largely for economic reasons. There are also important cultural ties that play a role in the European context, especially when former colonies are concerned. In security terms, though, it is more apparent that the European allies remain preoccupied with the longer term effects of the euro-zone crisis, which has resulted in a growing bifurcation of Europe into north and south. In the case of the former, a slowdown in growth, possibly recession, and some level of austerity are likely, but this cannot be compared to the prospects of years of austerity in Bulgaria, Cyprus, Greece, Portugal, Romania, and Spain. The suggestion is not that instability will lead to a 1930s situation with the prospect of war, but instead that it will make the identification and pursuit of common security agendas that much more challenging. It is also quite possible that internal security concerns, like migration from North Africa to southern Europe and then on to the north, will further divide EU members. Associated issues, such as organized crime, trafficking, and terrorism, will also place demands upon security services and militaries (i.e., to provide intelligence assets, or possible riot control and/or disorder avoidance). The danger therefore is one of rifts across the Atlantic, between a traditionally outward looking United States, while Europe looks to internal security challenges emanating from its littoral.

The leadership dilemma is linked to a second overarching question, already referred to briefly above: the hollowing out of *defense budgets*. Most of the European allies have systematically cut or failed to maintain end-of-Cold-War levels of defense expenditure so that in most instances defense outlays are well below the intended 2 percent of gross domestic product. Further cuts may be put into effect if any post-Afghanistan peace dividend is anticipated. This has led a number of American commentators to pose the same questions voiced by Robert Gates in June 2011 when he noted (with reference to Libya) that "every alliance member voted for the Libya mission, less than half have participated at all, and fewer than a third have been willing to participate in the strike mission. Frankly, many of those allies sitting on the sidelines do so not because they do not want to participate, but simply because they can't. The military capabilities simply aren't there."[7] For Gates, this presages "collective military irrelevance" for the Alliance. Over time, much of the allies' slack was picked up by the United States, which gradually increased its portion of NATO's overall spending from 50 to almost 75 percent. However, with the advent of sequestration this is no longer feasible—prompting one commentator to ask whether NATO was being condemned "to slow death by a thousand spending cuts." And if such an ignoble end were in store for the Alliance, "the more honest thing to do would simply be to shut it down."[8]

The third (related) problem is that of *solidarity*. NATO's engagement in Afghanistan has profoundly challenged the Three Musketeers principle with the frequent advocacy of caveats and exceptions on the use of combat forces. Solidarity was again challenged in Libya, joined in this instance by the United States itself becoming a caveat country. But solidarity is not only an issue across the Atlantic; it also reflects different perspectives among the European allies. Most recently equivocation was evident among the European allies to the Russian annexation of Crimea in March 2014, although eventual agreement was secured on sanctions against key individuals in the Russian leadership. These three overarching themes—leadership, defense budgets, and solidarity—will structure this chapter.[9] But before embarking upon our examination of these three principal themes, some background is necessary for those unfamiliar with the evolution of postwar transatlantic relations and structures. The next part considers the origins of NATO, followed by a section looking at the advent of the EU as a security actor with an increasing hard edge added to its traditional soft-power image.

The North Atlantic Treaty Organization

NATO is a product of the early Cold War period, and so the Alliance's formation must be understood within the overall postwar goals of securing and integrating Europe. Postwar security concerns first centered on the Soviet-communist threat that became apparent not long after the Soviet Union refused to observe its election promises in Eastern Europe while at the same time it supported subversive communist groups in Greece and Turkey and put pressure on Iran. A communist coup in Czechoslovakia and the Berlin blockade in 1948 reinforced the realization that the Soviet Union was a potent physical threat to Europe. The Western response to this threat was to form NATO with the signing of the Washington Treaty on April 4, 1949. The preamble to the treaty sets forth the general aims of membership of the Alliance as being to "promote stability and well-being in the North Atlantic area. [The members] are resolved to unite their efforts for collective defense and for the preservation of peace and security."[10] The danger of the emerging Cold War turning hot was considered the greatest threat in the early 1950s in the aftermath of North Korea's invasion of South Korea. The first chancellor of the Federal Republic of Germany, Konrad Adenauer, reflected this fear when he recorded in his memoirs that "Stalin was planning the same procedure for West Germany as had been used for Korea."[11]

Throughout the Cold War, NATO was the cornerstone of the Western Alliance. The protection offered by NATO allowed some of the European allies to move ahead with various types of economic and, eventually, political integration. During the evolution of the European Coal and Steel Community (ECSC), to the creation of the European Economic Community (EEC) in 1957, to the attachment of the foreign and security aspects of the newly formed union at the tail end of the Cold War, NATO provided the framework for high-level foreign and security policy discussions to take place. In essence, NATO and its close ties to the United States provided a security environment in which the EEC, the European Community, and then the European Union could take shape. The Western European Union (WEU), created in 1954, extended an existing self-defense treaty, signed by Belgium, France, the Netherlands, Luxembourg, and the United Kingdom, to include Italy and the Federal Republic of Germany.[12] The WEU would spend much of its life in the shadow first of NATO and later of the EU as it handed over its collection of defense-related tasks, known as the Petersberg tasks after the picturesque German town where they were agreed upon, to the EU. (See table 14.1.)

The overwhelming military and political weight of the United States during this period, symbolized by 326,000 American military personnel based in various European countries, meant that it was an American-dominated Alliance. As such, NATO was often subject to buffeting by variations in political barometric pressures within the Alliance. Indeed, each decade starting in the 1950s had an Alliance crisis, with NATO often acting as the conduit for the expression of transatlantic discontent. The Suez crisis of 1956 saw Britain and France at variance with the United States, followed, a mere decade later, by the demands of General Charles de Gaulle for all U.S. installations to be withdrawn from French soil. Other debates, such as those surrounding the controversial placement of Pershing II or Ground-Launched Cruise Missiles in Europe

Table 14.1   Timeline of the North Atlantic Treaty Organization (NATO), the European Union (EU), and the West European Union (WEU)

Year	NATO	European Community/EU	WEU
1948–1949	Washington Treaty		Brussels Treaty
1954–1955	Warsaw Pact created	European Defense Community fails	Modified Brussels Treaty
1957		Rome Treaty (European Economic Community)	
1966	France withdraws from integrated military command		
1970		European Political Cooperation	
1986		Single European Act	
1989	Warsaw Pact Dissolves		
1992–1993	First Gulf War	Maastricht Treaty (Common Foreign and Security Policy)	Petersberg Tasks
1997		Amsterdam Treaty	
2001	New Strategic Concept	Nice Treaty	Marseilles Declaration
2003		European Security Strategy	
2009		Lisbon Treaty	
2010	New Strategic Concept		Treaty Terminated

in the 1980s, also proved highly disruptive across the Atlantic as well as within the member states themselves. Some of the winds came the other way across the Atlantic, such as the divisive burden-sharing debates, sparked by U.S. Senator Mike Mansfield in the 1970s, which alleged free riding by the allies. NATO was therefore no stranger to differences between its members but, in the context of the Cold War, there was always the glue of the common external threat posed by the Soviet Union and the Warsaw Pact to keep any centrifugal forces in check.

The end of the Cold War and the lack of any obvious enemy against whom NATO could concentrate its energies gave rise to fundamental questions about the direction and the utility of the Alliance. Doctrinally, NATO was quick to adapt to the changing circumstances of the post–Cold War world. In practice, however, NATO was slower to adjust and there are diverging opinions on the extent to which it has really adapted at all. Moreover, post–Cold War operations, such as Operation Deliberate Force in Bosnia-Herzegovina in 1995 or Operation Allied Force against the Federal Republic of Yugoslavia in 1999, whilst nominally successful, raised as many questions about the future of the Alliance as they apparently answered.

In particular, two different lessons were learned from the operations in Bosnia and Yugoslavia that would have the overall effect of weakening the standing of the Alliance. First, the obvious reliance upon not only American military power but also diplomatic influence spurred the ambitions of some European allies for more foreign and security policy autonomy as an integral part of wider European integration. Second, the technical, logistical, and even political inability (as well as a measure of unwillingness) of a number of the European allies to work with American forces strengthened Washington's determination to avoid planning and running operations through the North Atlantic Council (NAC), NATO's highest civilian-level body. Instead, Washington's preference would be for handpicked allies, or "coalitions of the willing," to collaborate in geostrategic locations with the United States as the dominant partner. This preference explains why when the European members of NATO invoked for the first (and only) time the collective defense commitment (in Article 5) of the North Atlantic Treaty in the immediate aftermath of the 9/11 attacks, the Pentagon rebuffed them.[13] This snub would subsequently have influence on European political debates about the desirable level of association with or autonomy from NATO and the United States.

Arguably, the growing American preference to work with coalitions of the willing under President George W. Bush's first administration undermined the utility of the Alliance as a discussion forum for the security issues of the day and as a base upon which future consensual action could be built. Nowhere was this more true than in the case of the multinational force (MNF) in Iraq, one of the biggest foreign and security policy actions of the decade and one in which both NATO and the EU were essentially bypassed. The net result of the successive use of coalitions is that NATO has become less of an alliance and more of a toolbox out of which the necessary coalitions can be assembled.

The NATO Response Force (NRF), first suggested by U.S. Secretary of Defense Donald Rumsfeld in 2002, was designed in part to allay the growing concerns about reliance on coalitions of the willing. The NRF is intended for worldwide missions addressing many different types of scenarios but with the primary purpose of acting as a short-term stabilization or bridgehead force preparing the way, if need be, for larger follow-on missions. The NRF is composed of land, sea, and air components made available by NATO members on a rotating six-month basis. The NRF can number up to twenty-five thousand troops, can commence deployment after five days' notice, and can be sustained for up to thirty days or longer.

In spite of the potential of the NRF on paper, it has been activated for duties that were perhaps not envisaged as core missions. In August 2004, the NRF was used for protection duties at the summer Olympics in Athens, and from September to October 2005 it was deployed to assist in Hurricane Katrina disaster relief. From October 2005 until February 2006, the NRF was deployed in earthquake relief in Pakistan. Despite the police and humanitarian nature of these deployments, the NRF remains, according to NATO's own website, "the driving engine of NATO's military transformation."[14] Such statements add to the confusion concerning the direction of the Alliance as well as its relations with the EU, which has also created a more modest version of the NRF under the Battlegroup concept, with a similarly broad range of missions in mind.[15]

Alongside the creation of the NRF, various attempts have been made to prove the relevance of NATO to the post–Cold War world. Ivo Daalder and James Goldgeier argued for an alliance of liberal democracies constructed around NATO, but not confined to the transatlantic area. The idea of global NATO, built around shared liberal values rather than a set regional membership, appeared to gain some traction within NATO with the formation of the International Security Assistance Force (ISAF), whose membership went beyond European NATO members. Daalder and Goldgeier argued that a "shared commitment to shared values should be a more relevant determinant of membership than geography."[16] Daalder, who later became the U.S. ambassador to NATO, also spoke of the European NATO allies as crucial partners in "trying to defeat the terrible trinity of terrorists, tyrants and technologies of mass destruction." But, in an important caveat, Daalder also emphasized that in the wake of 9/11, Washington viewed Europe as a partner only when it supported "the fundamental course that Washington is embarked upon."[17] This was precisely one of the concerns felt by the European allies—that any "global NATO" would primarily exist to serve American interests and possible military adventurism of the type that had severely divided European publics over Afghanistan and Iraq.

American advocacy for some form of a "concert of democracies," based on a revitalized NATO, not only barely registered, but also was not taken seriously in Europe.[18] The lack of any equivalent intellectual agonizing on the part of the European allies can to some extent be accounted for by the profound differences and unpopularity of the first George W. Bush administration among many European publics, but was largely due to the energy being expended by members of the EU on building up the European Security and Defense Policy (ESDP). Although created in 1998, at least on paper, it did not become operational until 2003, and thereafter, considerable effort was made to refine and improve this important policy area. ESDP was not created as a conscious alternative to NATO, with a number of stalwart Atlanticist EU members, notably the United Kingdom, taking great care to avoid the EU being portrayed as an alternative.

The arrival of the Barack Obama administration in January 2009 was greeted with considerable enthusiasm in Europe, as it was viewed as a chance to repair some of the damage inflicted to the transatlantic relationship during the first administration of the previous president. Alas, in 2014, it is evident that much of the shine has rubbed off. Public perceptions of the state of transatlantic relations were already mixed in 2012, with a slight plurality (44 percent) of American respondents feeling that relations were good (a response 10 percentage points down from 2010) and 43 percent opining that relations were mixed.[19] European respondents were almost equally divided between those who thought relations were good (46 percent) or mixed (45 percent). Rather surprisingly, since they are often viewed as two of the staunchest Atlanticist countries, the lowest favorable ratings were in the United Kingdom (35 percent) and Poland (34 percent).

A new, and possibly uncomfortable, truth is emerging in which European and American priorities and perspectives are changing, perhaps with longer term implications for NATO. The "pivot to Asia" is often mentioned in this context. However, it is worth noting that a turn to Asia should be seen not only as a geopolitical calculation by Washington, but also as a reaction to the inevitable demands from smaller countries in Southeast Asia for strong ties with both Beijing and Washington. The pivot is, in part, a rebalancing of America's traditional focus on East Asia toward the southeast, whereas for Europe the tools with which to engage East Asia generally are exceedingly limited, aside from trade ties.

The unveiling of the Alliance's New Strategic Concept (its third) at its summit in Lisbon on November 19–20, 2010, reflected the dispositions of its members at that time. The Strategic Concept noted that "the Euro-Atlantic area is at peace and the threat of a conventional attack against NATO territory is low."[20] Ironically, highlighting this peaceable state (which many would attribute at least in part to NATO) makes it even more difficult for European Alliance members to divert scarce resources into military budgets. Remaining threats ranged from the "proliferation of ballistic missiles" and "nuclear weapons and other weapons of mass destruction, and their means of delivery," to "cyber attacks" and "key environmental and resource constraints, including health risks, climate change, water scarcity and increasing energy needs." The identification of possible proliferation risks stemming from the spread of nuclear weapons and the means of their delivery made the lack of any mention about the role of nuclear weapons in the NATO context all the more notable.[21] This was later addressed in the form of a Deterrence and Defense Posture Review (DDPR), which was unveiled at NATO's 2012 Chicago summit.

The challenges identified in NATO's New Strategic Concept were not exactly new or unique to the Alliance. The version of "globalism" traditionally preferred by the NATO allies took the form of a wider multilateral engagement with international partners, like the EU and the United Nations, while at the same time trying to develop relations with Central Europe and Russia through the Euro Atlantic Partnership Council (EAPC), which was established in 1997. Critically, on relations with Russia the Strategic Concept pledged to "seek cooperation on missile defense with Russia and other Euro-Atlantic partners," in spite of the fact that it was quite evident that the topic of missile defense was a severe impediment to the development of reciprocal relations. It is clear that the Strategic Concept reflected the tensions within the Alliance over its future purpose and role and, as such, represents the lowest common denominator, an aspect not unlike its 1999 predecessor. The biggest question left in the air by the Strategic Concept was how, after all of the good words, the allies were going to live up to their commitments or risk revealing that the emperor was threadbare, at best.

In spite of a lack of a compelling strategic dialogue and even the ongoing questions about its purpose since the end of the Cold War, NATO has managed to attract new members. Since it was founded in 1949, NATO has enlarged seven times. The last two members, Albania and Croatia, joined in NATO's sixtieth year. There are currently twenty-eight members with another twenty-two engaged in the Partnership for Peace (PfP). The latter enables countries to enter into an individually tailored partnership program (IPAP) that, in some cases, will be the precursor to a Membership Action Plan (MAP) with eventual membership. The value of the PfP lies in its ability to extend military integration and interoperability beyond current NATO members that, in turn, can serve as the basis for NATO's adaptability to its political and military nonthreat security missions.[22] However, NATO's enlargement has not brought much to the table in terms of resources or strategic clout and is unlikely to change the outcome of the three big challenges facing transatlantic security that are examined in more detail later on in this chapter.

Any further expansion of membership is most likely to come from the south. Three countries in the Western Balkans have embarked upon a MAP (Bosnia-Herzegovina, the Former Yugoslav Republic of Macedonia, and Montenegro). Although the conditionality that goes along with preparing for membership, in terms of agreement on norms and basic standards of behavior, is to be welcomed, none of the aspirant members will make a significant difference to the underlying equipment and defense expenditure issues outlined above. An expansion of membership to the east must also take into account NATO/U.S.-Russia relations as well as those with the European allies. In spite of an American-backed political commitment to eastern enlargement, European (especially Franco-German) resistance to Ukrainian membership has meant that to date no plans have been offered. European opposition is based on a reluctance to further antagonize relations with Russia, which were already strained by plans to install a missile defense system in Poland and the Czech Republic. The official position on Ukraine and Georgia, reiterated at the Strasbourg-Kehl summit of April 2009, is that the two states will at some (indeterminate) point become NATO members.[23] In light of the forced Russian annexation of Crimea it remains unlikely that NATO membership will be in the cards for Ukraine, partly for fear of antagonizing an already delicate situation. Indeed, Ukraine's interim prime minister, Arseniy Yatsenuk, has given pledges that Ukraine will not join NATO.

What is more likely is far greater security cooperation between NATO members and Ukraine, including military support, training, intelligence exchange, and assistance with border monitoring. Other non-NATO European countries, such as Azerbaijan, Georgia, and Moldova, are watching closely to ascertain NATO (and EU) reactions to Russia's actions in Ukraine. This could lead to demands for similar forms of security assistance, if not actual membership of NATO. Paradoxically, the Crimean crisis has shifted the geopolitical focus in security terms back to Europe at the very time when many allies were fretting over the consequences of America's ostensible shift in focus towards Asia.

The European Union

For much of its life, the EU has not been considered a security actor per se. During the Cold War the European Community, as it was then called, concentrated largely on building its internal market (demolishing barriers to the free movement of goods, capital, services, and people). Its external interests were primarily confined to external trade, development, and assistance. In time, these external dimensions demanded some form of rudimentary foreign policy at the European level, which commenced in 1970 through regular but informal meetings of the foreign ministers known as European Political Cooperation (EPC). It was only in 1986, with the Single European Act, that EPC was cautiously extended to "the political and economic dimensions of security" based upon the observation that "closer co-operation on questions of European security would contribute in an essential way to the development of a European identity in external relations."[24]

With the advent of the European Union in 1992, following the amendment to the founding treaty, the original Community gave way to the Union, which included a Common Foreign and Security Policy (CFSP) and an area for Police and Judicial Cooperation on Criminal Matters, two new areas supplementing the original economic dimensions (the internal market) of the Community. This so-called three pillar structure was in place until the Lisbon Treaty in 2007. The creation of CFSP coincided with the disintegration of Federal Yugoslavia, which soon saw the outbreak of war and thousands of refugees fleeing into the EU itself. Although the original logic behind the creation of the security component of CFSP, known as the

ESDP, was to respond to the changing security environment of the post–Cold War world following the collapse of the Soviet Union, it soon became apparent that the fledgling EU had a far more pressing reason to develop ESDP. This need was made all the more stark since in response to the expression of European concerns about the deteriorating situation in the Western Balkans, James A. Baker III, then U.S. secretary of state, declared in his folksy way in 1991 that "we don't have a dog in that fight." Although this position was later reversed with the result that the United States played a vital role in reaching a diplomatic solution in Bosnia-Herzegovina and Kosovo, providing the initial military wherewithal to bring the necessary security stability for such an agreement to take place, this did not undermine the rationale for the EU to develop as a security actor in its own right.

The first important turning point in the EU-NATO relationship took place in December 1998 at Saint Malo, France, where a meeting between French and British leaders produced a clear intent to develop EU capacities. The St. Malo declaration states that the Union shall have "the capacity for autonomous action, backed up by credible military forces, the means to decide to use them and a readiness to do so, in order to respond to international crises."[25] Nevertheless, it left sufficient latitude to interpret the precise relationship with NATO in a number of ways. The declaration includes the following stipulations:

> In order for the European Union to take decisions and approve military action where the Alliance as a whole is not engaged, the Union must be given appropriate structures and a capacity for analysis of situations, sources of intelligence and a capability for relevant strategic planning, without unnecessary duplication, taking account of the existing assets of the WEU and the evolution of its relations with the EU. In this regard, the European Union will also need to have recourse to suitable military means (European capabilities pre-designated within NATO's European pillar or national or multinational European means outside the NATO framework).

Five notable factors emerge from these provisions. First, although the "capacity for autonomous action" is mentioned, it is conditioned by the caveat that "the Alliance [NATO] as a whole is not engaged" in the possible operation. This qualification satisfied French concerns about overreliance on NATO, whilst also safeguarding British fears that the statement should not be misinterpreted in Washington (which was not entirely successful). This stipulation also created divergent opinions on whether or not NATO enjoyed a right of first refusal.

The second factor relates to the WEU, which at that time was responsible for the defense-related aspects of the EU's work. The WEU's role and mandate made it difficult for the EU itself to assume the full gamut of security and defense responsibilities. Indeed, it was not long before the development of military crisis management tools in the EU context, and the lack of any overt territorial threat, presented the WEU with a stark choice: either transform or transfer responsibilities. The decision to hand over crisis management responsibilities to the EU was made in the 2000 Marseille Declaration,[26] which in effect condemned the WEU to a minor role in regional security. The entering into force of the Lisbon Treaty in December 2009 spelled the end of the road for the WEU, since Article 42(7) of the treaty states, "If a Member State is the victim of armed aggression on its territory, the other Member States shall have towards it an obligation of aid and assistance by all the means in their power, in accordance with Article 51 of the United Nations Charter." Since this clause effectively ended the need for the WEU, a decision was made to cease its activities by June 2011.

Figure 14.1 illustrates the largely overlapping membership of the EU and NATO (and the now-defunct WEU). The overlap of membership is extensive save for the EU, including six members that are not NATO members and that are classified as neutral or nonaligned. The disappearance of the WEU had the generally underappreciated effect of making any debate about defense in the EU, which previously was left to the WEU and NATO, much more difficult. In fact, the sensitive nature of defense as an issue for some member states impacted the ratification of the Lisbon Treaty, as it was one of the factors behind the negative outcome of the first Irish referendum on the treaty (the second was, obviously, successful). Figure 14.1 also shows that the EU and NATO are not exclusively responsible for European security since the Organization for Cooperation in Europe (OSCE) also has an important role to play. However, the OSCE's responsibilities primarily relate to observation and to human and minority rights, and, unlike the EU and NATO, its members may not call upon military support from each other.

The third factor raised by the provisions in the St. Malo declaration concerns what capacities the EU should build, all the while being mindful to avoid U.S. Secretary of State Madeleine Albright's infamous three "D's"—the duplication of NATO assets, the decoupling of the transatlantic Alliance, and the discrimination against non-EU members. But avoiding the three D's proved difficult, and serious clashes were provoked by an April 2003 proposal by Belgium, France, Germany, and Luxembourg to create a permanent and autonomous Operations Headquarters within shouting distance of the

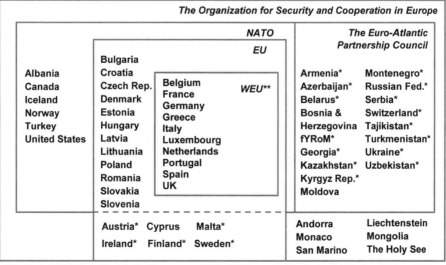

Figure 14.1   European Security Organizations

official residence of the U.S. ambassador to NATO. The United States and the United Kingdom reacted disapprovingly, with a U.S. State Department spokesman making a derogatory reference to the "chocolate summit."[27] Interestingly, this incident paved the way for the eventual creation of a civilian/military cell in the EU Military Staff as well as an Operations Center, both announced with a minimum of fanfare or reaction.

The fourth factor of note is that there are many links between the EU and NATO, in terms of both agreements and personnel. The NATO-EU Declaration on ESDP, agreed on December 16, 2002, sets forth the political parameters for cooperation between the two organizations, while the March 17, 2003, Berlin Plus arrangements specify the basis for NATO-EU cooperation in crisis management. The documents contain framework agreements for several areas of cooperation, including mutual crisis consultation, security and exchange of information, assured access to NATO planning, the availability of NATO assets and capabilities, and a NATO European command option for those operations using NATO assets under the EU's aegis. The importance of the Berlin Plus arrangements is further emphasized by their rather grand portrayal as establishing a "framework for permanent relations."[28]

These agreements have been invoked on a number of occasions. Operation Concordia (2003) in the Former Yugoslav Republic of Macedonia is one example in which NATO assets were used and where the EU Operations Commander was the Deputy Supreme Allied Commander Europe (DSACEUR). In December 2004 the EU launched Operation Althea, taking over from NATO's Stabilization Force (SFOR) in Bosnia-Herzegovina. Operation Althea drew upon NATO planning assets and DSACEUR again assumed command of the operation. EU-NATO cooperation is also close in Kosovo, where the EU's Rule of Law Mission (EULEX), which deployed fully in December 2008, and NATO's peacekeeping force (KFOR) work hand in hand. On the personnel side, there are formal links between the respective civilian and military bodies within the EU and NATO. At the highest civilian level, discussions take place between the North Atlantic Council and, on the EU side, the Political and Security Committee. A NATO Permanent Liaison Team has also been operating at the EU Military Staff since November 2005, and an EU Cell was set up in March 2006 at SHAPE (Supreme Headquarters Allied Powers Europe, NATO's strategic command for operations in Mons, Belgium).

Finally, the fifth feature to take notice of concerns the doubts about the military capacity of NATO's European members. The EU, like NATO, has no "army" as such. Both draw upon military and civilian resources from their member states. Since both have a largely overlapping membership, any lack of capacity is a matter of common concern. A number of initiatives on the EU side have been taken to wrestle with the shortcomings. The European Defense Agency (EDA) was created in 2004 with the objective of developing defense capabilities, promoting defense research and technology, encouraging armaments cooperation, and creating a competitive European defense equipment market.[29] NATO has also made efforts to address the military capacity problem. In the Prague summit of November 2002 a "Prague Capabilities Commitment" (PCC) was approved, which represented a more ambitious and focused version of the earlier 1999 Defense Capabilities Initiative (DCI).

In the context of ESDP, the EU has also developed substantial civilian capabilities for crisis management. These include a 5,000-strong police force available for international missions (of which 1,000 should be deployable within 30 days). The creation of this police force is a significant step since most of the EU's twenty-three missions to date have been police missions. There are also 200 national rule-of-law experts who may be called upon (including a rapid response team capable of deployment within a month). National civilian administrators can also be summoned, as can 2–3 national civil protection assessment teams and up to 2,000 civilian protection intervention personnel. A European Gendarmerie Force (EGF), agreed upon in September 2004 by France, Italy, Portugal, the Netherlands, and Spain, is also available to the EU and other international organizations, including NATO. The EGF consists of 900 police officers that can be deployed within 30 days.

EU efforts to establish military and civilian capabilities led to its eventual engagement in crisis management operations. The first ESDP operation was held in the Democratic Republic of the Congo in 2003, the same moment in time when the EU member states were disagreeing so disastrously over Iraq. Since then, the EU has launched over twenty missions on three continents, most being civilian crisis management missions.[30] It should be pointed out that the creation of ESDP was never intended to compete with NATO—as, indeed, was jealously ensured by a number of stalwart NATO members that are also EU members, like Denmark and the United Kingdom. It is equally important to point out that neutral or nonaligned members of the EU did not want the Union to be seen as a proxy for NATO.[31] Under the Lisbon Treaty, ESDP became the Common Security and Defense Policy (CSDP)—presumably because it sounded somewhat strange to keep discussing a *common* foreign policy and a *European* security and defense policy.

The Lisbon Treaty also introduced a "European Capabilities Action Plan" and "permanent structured cooperation" to address the issue of capacity (or lack thereof). Article 42(6) of the treaty states, "Those Member States whose military capabilities fulfill higher criteria and which have made more binding commitments to one another in this area with a view to the most demanding missions shall establish permanent structured cooperation within the Union framework."[32] The latter can be viewed primarily as an incentive mechanism to encourage members to fulfill the "higher criteria" as well as to introduce an element of flexibility for those that wish to move faster and further. Perhaps most interesting of all, the treaty provides for "the progressive framing of a common defense policy. This will lead to a common defense, when the European Council, acting unanimously, so decides."[33] This provision initially appeared to many Irish as an assault on their neutrality, and to others like an attempt to usurp NATO. A more careful reader would have noted that below the defense proviso the treaty declared, "The policy of the Union in accordance with this Section shall not prejudice the specific character of the security and defense policy of certain Member States and shall respect the obligations of certain Member States, which see their common defense realized in the North Atlantic Treaty Organization (NATO), under the North Atlantic Treaty and be compatible with the common security and defense policy established within that framework."

It may, in other words, be the eventual desire of some EU members to be responsible for their own defense but, for most, no such aspiration is evident. Should NATO disappear, that will be a different matter with a whole host of practical issues to boot.

Just who and what is responsible for European defense is for the heads of state and government of the EU members (the European Council) to decide upon at some point in the far future. The organizations are, however, at risk of competing in precisely the areas that NATO has adapted to and where the EU is building up capacity and experience. This involves primarily crisis prevention, crisis management, and postconflict stabilization. While NATO will remain a serious player due to the military clout of the United States, the EU is developing into an inherently deeper actor in terms of its increasing ability to address different stages of the conflict cycle, especially those associated with postconflict stabilization. NATO may have the troops and widgets, largely courtesy of the United States, but the EU has the financial reserves and expertise for conflict stabilization that NATO lacks.

Undoubtedly, NATO has influenced the development of the EU's crisis management capabilities. Indeed, the histories of the two organizations should not be regarded as distinct. As Steven Blockmans observed, "NATO laid the foundations of a European military culture and the norm of multinational cooperation, which in effect provided the EU with a vital head start for the development of its own military missions and multinational schemes."[34] It is equally true that the preferences and choices of EU leaders will have a decisive impact on the future of NATO. As was suggested at the outset, the issues that will determine the selection of an institution and also shape outcomes revolve around leadership, capacity, and solidarity—subjects that the chapter now addresses.

Leadership and Transatlantic Security

One of the core challenges facing transatlantic security is the diffusion of leadership. This is an important distinction since the issue is not an absence of leadership per se, but the absence of a clear direction for that leadership. What is more, notions of leadership differ. For Americans the idea of leadership has come naturally, almost as an assumption. The 2010 U.S. *National Security Strategy* mentions "U.S. leadership" no less than five times in a relatively short document. Indeed, at one point, the document modestly claims the goal of "An international order advanced by U.S. leadership that promoted peace, security, and opportunity through stronger cooperation to meet global challenges."[35] It is precisely this concept of leadership that explains why the United States continues to station two brigade combat teams in Europe. Until recently, their presence has had little to do with the security of their allies, and everything to do with providing "out-of-area" support for potential military operations in the Middle East, Central Asia, or even East Asia. The actuality of two brigades of U.S. soldiers in Europe is also part of the reason that relations with Russia remain complicated since, however many times Washington tries to reassure Russia about its military presence in Europe or the role of U.S. missile defense systems in the region, the reality to Moscow must often "seem that the Cold War is only half over."[36]

Europeans often like to dismiss U.S. statements on its own leadership role as a further example of American hubris. Yet Europeans have their leadership pretensions as well. For many EU members, leadership is the promotion of the Union as an exemplar to third parties. The implicit argument that a third party would want to be like, act like, enjoy life like, or have the prosperity of Europeans is fundamental to the Union's external relations. Beyond providing models, few individual EU members have any leadership pretensions, based on the awareness that they remain twenty-seven medium- to small-sized countries in a part of the world that is unlikely to decisively influence geopolitics in the twenty-first century in the manner that it did in the previous century.

American and European assumptions underpinning leadership are also remarkably different, as are their perceptions of each other. This was (and still is) encapsulated in two books that appeared in the same year (2003) and that both made reference to one another. This particular year was an *annus horribilis* for solidarity across the Atlantic as well as between Europeans. The first book, by Robert Kagan, argues,

> It is time to stop pretending that Europeans and Americans share a common view of the world, or even that they occupy the same world. On the all-important question of power—the utility of power, the morality of power—they have parted ways. Europeans believe they are moving beyond power into a self-contained world of laws and rules and transnational negotiation and cooperation. Europe itself has entered a post-historical paradise, the realization of Immanuel Kant's "Perpetual Peace." The United States, meanwhile, remains mired in history, exercising power in the anarchic Hobbesian world where international rules are unreliable and where security and the promotion of a liberal order still depend on the possession and use of military might. This is why, on major strategic and international questions today, Americans are from Mars and Europeans are from Venus: They agree on little and understand one another less and less.[37]

Robert Cooper, a British diplomat turned EU official, became one of Kagan's sparring partners in the debate about divergent worldviews. In his book, *The Breaking of Nations*, Cooper points out that a "post modern" Europe faces the same dangers as the United States, but the way in which threats are perceived and the subsequent responses differ. Cooper writes, "The U.S. approach is based on hegemony: control—by military means if necessary—of the foreign policies of all potentially threatening states. The weakness of this approach is that the task may be too great even for the United States. . . . The postmodern, European answer to threats is to extend the system of cooperative empire ever wider."[38]

The Kagan and Cooper respective theses have been thoroughly debated, and there is no need to reiterate the pros and cons of either argument here. There is, however, the need to underline the fact that, with some nuances, the European allies continue to have a fundamentally different concept of leadership from their American counterparts. Much of the EU's external relations are about appealing to states and regional entities using the power of attraction (i.e., the idea that third parties will wish to emulate the stability and prosperity of the members of the Union). The most obvious example of this is in the enlargement context, where any candidate has to look, behave, and act like any other EU member prior to entry. The magnetism of the appeal becomes less potent with distance, however. In order to counter this, the EU relies upon "essential elements" and other forms of normative conditionality in agreements with third parties in an attempt to, at least, propagate the values and principles that guide the Union.

In addition to the potency of their attraction becoming weaker, other limitations are apparent in the postmodern European leadership model. When it comes to security, CFSP (of which CSDP is an integral part) is resolutely intergovernmental—meaning that it can only operate on the basis of agreement by the EU's members. It is also worth noting that notwithstanding the normative pretensions of the EU's external policy, actual courses of action occasionally crumble in the face of *realpolitik* when human rights entreaties are largely ignored, for example in favor of stable energy imports from Russia or good trade relations with China. There are also, as mentioned, nuances within the EU whereby France and the United Kingdom, its two largest military powers and arguably the only powers with global foreign policy aspirations, often pursue a dual-track diplomacy promoting the EU but also pursuing national interests that may sometimes be at variance with the former.

American ideas about leadership are further linked to the modern notion of the "West" built upon shared values, a concept that the United States created and encouraged. The United States also shaped much of the latter half of the twentieth century by dint of its military power, buttressed by a ring of worldwide military bases that remain unsurpassed. The challenge for contemporary NATO, as noted by Goldgeier, is that it must "accept a global role" and, if it fails to do so, "the United States will lose interest in investing in the alliance's future."[39] Yet, it is precisely American leadership "beyond Europe" that has made so many Europeans skeptical, especially when following the United States might involve them in dangerous security situations like those in Iraq and Afghanistan, notwithstanding the enormous human and capital costs such missions might entail. Differences in perspective on relations with key common partners, like Russia, also create reservations about any possible joint leadership. For the United States, even after Obama's "reset" in relations with Russia, security issues loom high up the agenda. For the European allies, especially Germany, Russia is seen primarily in terms of trade, in particular energy, where mutual dependency keeps gas and oil flowing to Western European markets that are highly dependent upon energy imports. The crisis in Ukraine, the subsequent Russian annexation of Crimea, and Russian militarism towards the Baltics may shift German and European perspectives in the long-term (with the possible help of American shale-gas exports to Europe). However, in the short term, given the magnitude of EU-Russian trade, the European allies will be more cautious than the United States in their dealings with Russia. There is also a notable absence of a common leadership perspective toward the rising powers, particularly with regard to China and India, where the EU members and the United States have pursued quite different approaches.

The hazards of a diffusion of leadership were clearly exposed in the 2011 NATO operations in Libya, where the Alliance was used as a shell to propagate a mission with an ambiguous mandate while the EU was left on the sidelines. As Kurt Volker, a former U.S. ambassador to NATO, observed, after having played a significant initial role, the United States "abruptly pulled back from the mission, saying—in the words of President Obama—that Washington was 'handing over to NATO' the operational lead."[40] This refusal to lead and the referral of NATO as a separate entity from the United States—as if it was not a member of the alliance—is new for American policy makers. Volker points out that "the tendency to think of NATO as 'them' has long been the pattern in Europe, where NATO is often synonymous with 'the Americans.' So when both the United States and Europe think of NATO as 'them,' who exactly takes ownership of the Alliance?"[41] The lack of leadership led in turn to a lack of consensus among NATO's members about the robustness of the mission. While France, Italy, and the United Kingdom put Special Forces advisors on the ground (with American support), Germany withdrew four warships from the Mediterranean in order to avoid that it might become involved in the mission.

None of this means that the United States will not continue to try to exert global leadership, even despite the results of the November 2010 congressional elections and the economic crisis. To start with, there is no other serious contender for global leadership aside from the United States (with the support of the EU) on a variety of security- and non-security-related issues. China has certainly shown no desire to assume global responsibilities other than protecting and developing its trade interests. Unlike the EU and the United States, one of the features of Chinese foreign policy has been an absence of most normative dimensions and a preference for economic diplomacy. Brazil, for its part, remains very much a regional power. Perhaps more telling, efforts by Brazil to develop a global role generated disquiet. Brazilian attempts, accompanied by leaders from Turkey, to broker a nuclear deal with Iran just when the Obama administration was pushing a UN Security Council resolution on sanctions created consternation in Washington. Russia too is hardly a compelling candidate, with President Vladimir Putin facing his own internal legitimacy challenge as long as his stewardship is based on repression and enforcement.

It may not be the willingness to lead that is the most important issue, but rather that the United States must become more comfortable with leading together with others, such as its allies in Europe. Contrary to the (somewhat dated) Mars versus Venus analogies, all is not lost. The United States has learned in Iraq and Afghanistan that the use of military power has its limitations and that state building is a long, tedious, expensive, and often frustrating process. The economic crisis further generates fiscal reasons for joint leadership. In the United States, the introduction of sequestration will probably encourage more calls for fairer burden sharing within NATO. However, in order to persuade like-minded countries to make the necessary sacrifices, the rationales made for leading or for following must be compelling. The degree to which forceful leadership and direction of NATO will emerge is mainly a matter of political will, but it will also be shaped by important practical considerations and, above all, defense budgets.

Defense Budgets—The Emperor's Clothes

The "Leadership and Transatlantic Security" section above considered the political dynamics of leadership; this one will turn to the economic dimensions. In simple terms, defense-related expenditure accounts for around 20 percent of the U.S. federal budget and around 60 percent of all nondiscretionary spending (i.e., expenditure that is not allocated to social entitlement programs like Medicaid, Medicare, and Social Security). The United States provides around 75 percent of all NATO defense expenditure and together with the spending by the European allies represents around 70 percent of global defense expenditure. U.S. military expenditure actually declined in constant terms from the end of the Cold War (1988–1989) until roughly 2003 and the beginning of American involvement in Iraq. Since then, it has increased. In terms of gross domestic product (GDP), defense expenditure accounted for around 5.75 percent of U.S. GDP in 1988 and declined steadily until the first George W. Bush administration, when it stood at 3.0 percent.[42] Since then, it has increased both in terms of constant dollar expenditure, due largely to military involvement in Iraq and Afghanistan, and as a percentage of GDP, in which it has increased from 3.0 percent in 2002 to 4.8 percent in 2010.

The United Kingdom showed broadly similar trends with declining defense expenditure from 1988 to 2002 (as a percentage of GDP, defense expenditure dropped from 4.1 percent to 2.5 percent over the same period). From 2003 to 2011, British defense expenditure grew, largely as a result of its commitments in Afghanistan. But it was only in 2004 that the United Kingdom regained, in constant terms, comparable levels of defense expenditure to levels in 1988. By 2011, defense expenditure as a percentage of GDP stood at 2.6 percent. Similar patterns are evident with France but with a less dramatic overall decline in defense expenditure from 1988 until 2003. Unlike the United Kingdom, French defense expenditure did not increase as dramatically after 2003 and only peaked in 2009 before declining to comparable levels with the beginning of that decade. When expressed in GDP terms, French defense expenditure stood at 2.3 percent in 2011 (compared to 3.6 percent in 1988). In an effort to offset the rising costs, in particular those related to advanced weaponry, Britain and France signed a defense pact in November 2010 to share research costs and the operation of aircraft carriers as well as to develop a joint expeditionary force.[43] Together, the two still account for nearly half of Europe's defense spending and more than two-thirds of Europe's total military research and development spending.

German defense expenditure has declined more or less steadily since 1988, notwithstanding its involvement in Afghanistan, while its defense expenditure as a percentage of GDP stood at 1.4 percent in 2011. Midsized countries like Poland have seen a gradual increase in defense expenditure, notably over the last decade (presumably due to both NATO and EU membership), although Polish spending registered at just under 2.0 percent of GDP in 2011. The Netherlands also has seen a steady increase in defense expenditure, with a slightly sharper increase in 2002–2011, but this still represented 1.4 percent of Dutch GDP. Spain's defense spending fluctuated until 2002–2003 and then increased perceptibly until a peak in 2008, when it slid back to levels seen earlier that decade, representing 1.0 percent of GDP by 2011.

What do these numbers suggest? Aside from the obvious—that the United States outspends all of the other allies by a considerable margin—the figures suggest that all members of NATO and the EU are struggling with diverse economic pressures that are negatively affecting defense budgets. Although defense expenditure as a percentage of GDP is only one indicator, and a rough one at that, most of the allies spend under 2 percent on defense, with some states realizing real-term declines exceeding 10 percent. In March 2012, the International Institute of Strategic Studies (IISS) noted that, for the first time in modern history, Asian defense spending was likely to surpass European expenditures.[44] The NATO operation in Libya made clear that such spending levels have consequences. American military assets were crucial from the start of the operation, in particular for providing air-to-air refueling and identifying targets. As the conflict continued, European NATO members ran out of munitions, forcing the Americans to up their contribution. U.S. Secretary of Defense Robert Gates commented, "The mightiest military alliance in history is only 11 weeks into an operation against a poorly armed regime in a sparsely populated country—yet many allies are beginning to run short of munitions, requiring the U.S., once more, to make up the difference."[45] Part of the Europeans' problem is that current defense expenditures are uncoordinated and fragmented among many armies, navies, and air forces. Despite capacity shortfalls, future trends strongly suggest continued downward pressure on defense budgets, not necessarily due to changing strategic perceptions but mainly due to the opportunity cost considerations that accompany every dollar, pound, or euro tagged for defense-related expenditure. These competing demands are especially evident and troublesome in the American case and may have profound implications for leadership and the future of NATO.

Pressure on the U.S. defense budget emerges out of the fact that the Obama administration inherited a massive deficit and a rapidly growing public debt in part because the Bush administration's military interventions had ignored costs. The costs associated with over a decade of military engagement in Iraq and Afghanistan, combined with the crippling expenditures of the social entitlements that accompany these military operations, alongside other non-defense-related factors like the soaring costs of medical treatment for the poor or elderly, led many to conclude that the "United States is on an unsustainable path under the current federal tax and entitlement regimes."[46] A graying population will make further huge demands upon Medicare and Social Security in particular. The clear danger is that rising debt will pose a challenge to U.S. national security and that mandatory social spending will squeeze defense-related programs out.

In his first term, Obama clearly indicated that he would not follow in Bush's footsteps when he stated that he refused to set foreign policy goals that exceeded the United States' means. Additionally, Obama and his then–Secretary of Defense Leon Panetta proposed to cut the U.S. defense budget by $487 billion over ten years.[47] This was the situation when, on March 1, 2013, automatic budget reductions, or sequestration, went into effect. In simple terms, sequestration was introduced as the result of the Budget Control Act of 2011, which attempted to balance a $2.1 trillion increase in government borrowing capacity with matching deficit reductions. The first $1 trillion of the latter were to come about as a result of cuts in discretionary spending, while the second part, $1.2 trillion, was supposed to have been agreed upon by Congress by January 2013. Having missed the deadline, sequestration came into effect on March 1 by default. The implementation of cuts in defense and nondefense budgets will be divided equally over a period of eight years. This implies that the Pentagon's base funding faces a reduction of $500 billion. Fiscal year 2013 was treated somewhat differently with $46 billion in spending reductions but, unlike other years, this has to be spread proportionately across all individual discretionary defense programs—in other words, *each* budget item faces a 9 percent reduction, whether a toilet seat or an aircraft carrier. The immediate effect was the furloughing (i.e., leave without pay) of most of the Pentagon's 800,000 civilian personnel.

However, it is the long-term effects of the cuts that will be profound. At the most general, cutbacks will slow down economic growth in an economy that is already sluggish. The private sector will inevitably face redundancies as a result of reduced orders or requests that cannot be completed (e.g., it is not possible to cancel 9 percent of an aircraft carrier). The local effect will be uneven, hitting those states with heavy concentrations of defense industries and military installations the hardest (like California, Florida, New York, Texas, and Virginia). Of most interest to the subject at hand is an assessment by Jonathan Masters of the Council on Foreign Relations, who noted, "The longer the Pentagon is made to operate with reduced resources, the greater the impact on its ability to project power abroad, protect U.S. interests, safeguard the global commons, and provide humanitarian aid. Protracted budget uncertainty, defense analysts say, inhibits the department's ability to make the investment decisions, such as for R&D and procurement, needed in a security environment that requires long-term strategic thinking."[48]

Although sequestration has put much of the focus, temporarily, on the United States, the picture is hardly any more cheering in Europe. The United States and Europe share some common general challenges. One of the most urgent is posed by the burgeoning costs of care for the elderly. The "graying" phenomenon is even more apparent in Europe than in the United States. Much of the initial impetus for growth in the developed world stemmed from demographics. North America, the United Kingdom, and Ireland will probably see slight population growth in the coming decades. For much of Europe, though, the problem looks quite different, with a combination of static or negative population growth rates; and, as a consequence, most of the EU members will experience falling working populations, rising debt, and fewer taxpayers. In this scenario, it becomes "hard to get the arithmetic to add up."[49]

The costs of the wars in Afghanistan and Iraq have also been staggering. The initial cost of operations in Afghanistan in fiscal year 2001–2002 was around $20.8 billion, reaching a peak of $122 billion in 2011 and $111.1 billion in 2012. The figures for Iraq range from $53 billion in the initial year of engagement, 2003, to a high of $142.1 billion in 2008 and $10.1 billion in 2012.[50] Brown University's "Costs of War Report 2011" calculated that the expenditures since 2001 in Afghanistan and Iraq amounted to $2.3 trillion and over 6,000 American lives.[51] The end of mission in both cases does not, however, imply the end of financial commitments. The funding involved will continue to be in substantial amounts for Iraq as well as Afghanistan, although the budget lines will shift from the Department of Defense to the Department of State (for reconstruction, stabilization, training, etc.). History has shown that underresourced commitments, like those in Lebanon or Somalia, tend to end prematurely with the fundamental security goals unachieved. There is an apparent danger of the same happening in Afghanistan and Iraq, notwithstanding the political rhetoric. Less directly, the costs of both wars will be borne by U.S. taxpayers as the full economic implications of those injured, both physically and psychologically, or retired from the armed forces become apparent. Nearly half of the 1.6 million soldiers who served in Iraq and Afghanistan have asked for disability benefits from the U.S. government, while new regulations on eligibility expanded the number of claimants from earlier conflicts.[52] Entitlements are difficult (and perhaps unwise politically) to cut.

As a complement to his vow not to set foreign policy goals that exceeded America's means, Obama pledged to focus on renewing America's core strengths. The U.S. National Security Strategy, quoted above, notes that restoring American leadership will depend upon the "commitment to renew our economy, which serves as the wellspring of American power."[53] Obama believes that Europe is essential to America's economic renewal. In the summer of 2012, Obama explicitly said that he was worried about Europe's recovery from its own debt crisis. He made his remarks soon after a dismal U.S. jobs report heightened concerns about the impact of Europe's predicament on U.S. growth. Obama emphasized that pro-growth policies need to be part of Europe's plan to deal with its crisis in addition to austerity tactics. Obama said that if Europe goes into a recession, it "means we're selling fewer goods, fewer services, and that is going to have some impact on the pace of our recovery."[54] He urged EU member states to keep Greece in the euro zone and sent his then–Secretary of the Treasury Tim Geithner to meet with European leaders seventeen times. In particular, Obama focused attention on Germany's Chancellor Angela Merkel, who has been less flexible on relaxing austerity approaches, and the UK's David Cameron, who is weighing up the pros and cons of remaining in the EU. Obama clearly sees a fragmenting European Union as a threat to international economic security as a whole and that a well-functioning European internal market is beneficial to American interests.

Unfortunately, the immediate picture does not look encouraging in terms of any substantial economic rejuvenation. This means that the United States is unlikely to be able to afford two simultaneous wars in the future, especially since the longer term costs of Afghanistan and Iraq are not yet evident. The Strategic Guidance released on January 5, 2012, in which Obama proposed to cut nearly $500 billion over ten years, also acknowledged America's limitations by abandoning the two-war strategy, which had been policy for more than two decades.[55] American strategy is also based upon the recognition that "Our relationship with our European allies remains the cornerstone for U.S. engagement with the world, and a catalyst for international action."[56] Yet there are few signs that any of the allies are in a position to, or willing to, pick up any slack. The question of transatlantic security and leadership is thus intimately bound up with economics. The path to growth is no longer to rely upon the affluence of the American marketplace but, as Obama is aware, to stimulate domestic demand and output with global partners, most especially with European partners. The main economic platforms of American leadership that made the Marshall Plan possible and that underpinned the postwar international financial structures are crumbling, making the case for leadership more difficult, even for allies. The possible lack of leadership has a mirror in the form of the lack of followers or, as will be argued below, obvious solidarity between NATO members.

Solidarity and Transatlantic Security

European involvement in Libya in 2011 exposed dissension, most notably between France and Germany—in the case of the former due to its go-it-alone posture on military intervention and, in the case of the latter, its abstention on the Libya resolution in the UN Security Council. This display of discord was humiliating for all involved and mocked any ideas of European solidarity meeting global crises. What sort of solidarity did Europe have if it disintegrated when faced with managing a crisis on Europe's doorstep? The positioning of six NATO Patriot missile batteries in Turkey in the following year (to deter Syria from launching missiles on Turkey) appeared to offer a chance to demonstrate an *esprit de corps* notably absent over Libya. The takeover of half of Mali by Islamists presented another opportunity. However, what transpired in Mali in January 2013 was a largely French military operation with little European support (and, in some cases, little interest) and even less support from African countries. The French operation followed an extraordinary meeting of foreign ministers in the middle of the month (where many were not present). The much-vaunted EU Battlegroups (units of around 1,500 composed of national or combinations of national forces with two on standby for a six-month period) were not even mentioned, and the EU's comprehensive approach to security, in place on paper since 2003, appeared to be fictive. The eventual EU response, in the form of a European Training Mission to Mali, was also slow in coming.

The Mali case illustrates a number of general points about the nature of solidarity. First, it is not just a matter of transatlantic solidarity that is at issue. It is also, crucially, about solidarity within Europe, whether in the EU or NATO context. The second aspect is that any new implicit division of responsibilities, with the European allies taking a leading role in Africa, is probably an illusion—especially since many EU and NATO members had little interest or experience in Africa. Third, the United States could conclude from Europe's inexperience and disinterest that it is best to deal bilaterally with its closest and most capable allies on security issues (i.e., primarily France and the United Kingdom; Germany can be dealt with bilaterally for other things), rather than through any multilateral frameworks. Each of these points will now be explored in more detail.

The issue of transatlantic solidarity must start with the question of who the "Europeans" are. It could be argued that they represent the combined membership of the EU and NATO and, if we include NATO's PfP, this further means most of the membership of the Organization for Cooperation and Security in Europe (OSCE). The OSCE has its own role to play in European security but, due to its large membership and different mandate, it is unlikely to evolve into a primary security partner for the United States, although Russia has been trying to promote exactly this role for the organization in its security relations with Europe since 2008.[57] But if membership is limited to just the EU and NATO, one still encounters problems. The danger of lumping together the combined members of the EU and NATO is that this also includes the six neutral or nonaligned EU members. These states have specific reservations (including constitutional ones, in the case of Austria) regarding involvement in defense organizations while general peacekeeping activities are permissible. Other non-

EU but NATO members, like Norway and Turkey, bring their own problems, despite the fact that they actually have legitimate security contributions to make and, in the case of the latter, the largest armed forces in NATO after America. Unfortunately, including such non-EU members in any mission cannot get around the *realpolitik* of relations between the EU and NATO, which are still largely paralyzed by differences over Cyprus. Practical cooperation between the EU and NATO is hindered by the fact that Turkey, a NATO member, refuses to provide equipment or resources under the Berlin Plus arrangements (agreed to in 2002 by which the EU could draw upon NATO assets for its own peacekeeping operations) to any EU member that is not a NATO member or part of the PfP (which applies only to Cyprus). This *realpolitik* behavior has also stymied the exchange of classified information between the two organizations. Although there is day-to-day cooperation, and meetings at the highest civilian and military levels, any meaningful development of relations between NATO and the EU is unlikely to make headway until the Cyprus issue is resolved. To date, and for the foreseeable future, such a resolution is unlikely, especially since Turkish prospects of joining the EU seem to be ever more distant with a distinct lack of enthusiasm among some EU member states and, more worryingly, growing disinterest and an increasingly independent foreign policy on the part of Turkey.

The second issue with solidarity is whether the allies are able to decide on geographical or even thematic areas of responsibility so that tasks are sensibly divided and resources are used most appropriately. Alas, the possibility of a geographical division of responsibilities is illusory since it would assume that the European allies and the United States have distinct interests. Since U.S. interests tend to be global, it is unlikely that there will be specific areas where the Europeans have interests and the Americans do not. In fact, for many EU members independence is still a relatively new concept meaning that the idea of an independent foreign policy is a fairly new experience too. Most of the members that joined in 2004 (the central Europeans plus Cyprus and Malta) and 2007 (Bulgaria and Romania) are still in the process of formulating their strategic interests. This means that the notion of, for example, European "experience" in Africa is mainly confined to a small number of former colonialist countries (primarily France, Germany, Italy, the Netherlands, Portugal, and the United Kingdom). In each case, it can be asked if former colonial overlords are the most desirable strategic partners for African countries. Current British relations with India point to the likelihood that former colonial ties might actually complicate as much as facilitate mutual relations.

The obvious exception to the geographical argument is the Western Balkans, which as an area is very much a European creation and which has benefited from European resources. For instance, all countries in the Western Balkans have been offered the prospect of EU membership status. This is also an area where the EU is actively engaged in a variety of security missions (the largest being the rule-of-law mission in Kosovo). Notwithstanding these accomplishments, detractors could argue, with some justification, that European achievements were largely made possible by American diplomatic intercession and military brawn to bring about a settlement so that the slow and difficult process of state (re)building could take place. The Western Balkans is also the area where the EU's soft power is at its most potent, precisely because the benefits of EU membership are most evident to those on the EU's direct borders. The same logic does not, however, apply to the east, where Georgia, Moldova, and Ukraine have all demanded a membership prospect. Giving these countries such a chance would be politically risky and would mark a European "reset" of its own relations with Russia. But, since interactions are becoming increasingly strained under Putin, such a bold throw of the dice may be what is required to demonstrate EU seriousness and leadership.

The possibility of more thematic specializations has surfaced from time to time, but they normally evoke the negative analogy of America as the cook while Europe is the dishwasher. It is precisely the nervousness about relying exclusively on the United States that has underpinned much of the development of doctrine and forces in Europe—the French independent nuclear deterrent being a striking example. Conversely, it is unlikely that the United States would wish to be subject to potential vetoes by any ally for lack of critical equipment or skills. The idea of pooling or sharing has also been mooted, although from the European side this is normally to gain access to exclusive American assets. Beyond possible access to common provisions and assets (there are actually very few in NATO, with a number of Advanced Warning and Control aircraft being the only obvious example), other leasing arrangements have been explored in the NATO and EU contexts. The loan of equipment, like the United States C-17 Globemaster transport aircraft that flew troops and equipment from Istres, France, to Bamako, Mali, suggests an interesting potential direction for transatlantic security. The possibility of the United States providing equipment or specialist services (notably intelligence) so that its closest allies can address common security concerns may, as outgoing Secretary of Defense Panetta observed, be "the kind of model that you're going to see in the future."[58]

The final issue will be whether the United States will tire of trying to work with the EU and its security components and whether bilateral approaches to close (and more capable) allies might be preferable. This is certainly one of the conclusions that could be reached if the EU members fail to convince their external partners that they are serious about security and have the wherewithal to play harder security roles when appropriate. In this context, the United States may well prefer to work with tried and tested partners, like France and the United Kingdom, as well as others that may have excellent niche capabilities (like Poland and its special forces). It would, however, be a short-term strategy, and the negative results of relying upon coalitions of the willing under President George W. Bush are evident. The undesirable outcomes could range from undermining attempts at solidarity in the multilateral setting (whether NATO or the EU) to sending out damaging signals about the importance of multilateralism in international relations at a time of global change when both the United States and the EU are trying to persuade China, Russia, and others to play by "the Western world's" rules.

Picking and choosing your allies may also be unwise because even the most capable states face challenges from time to time that they are unable to address alone. For example, the European allies have recognized (at least on paper) the logic of pooling resources, joint development and procurement, and the construction of common or shared platforms in order to stretch dwindling defense budgets and to cut unnecessary waste. As the full effects of the global financial crisis become more evident, this logic may become far more compelling. Such an approach will demand solidarity, common perspectives, and shared mindsets. The arguments above suggest a certain degree of skepticism, but by the same token there is also hope that shared economic shocks across the Atlantic will jolt all with a healthy dose of realism.

NATO, the EU, and the Crimea

The results of the crisis in Ukraine and the subsequent Russian annexation of Crimea are hard to estimate. From a Russian perspective, former President Viktor Yanukovich was ousted by a Western coup d'etat, in violation of a 1994 security agreement where Ukraine's sovereignty and independence were guaranteed. The situation was further compounded by the demotion of the Russian language from its official status, as well as the alleged underrepresentation of politicians from the eastern parts of Ukraine (who are more likely to be pro-Russian) in the new transitional government and parliament. All of these factors contributed to Russian threat perceptions and ultimately led to the annexation of the Crimea in March 2014, ostensibly to protect Russian passport holders from hostile acts perpetrated by alleged fascists. Whatever the rights or wrongs of the Russian perceptions, it was not an entirely one-sided crisis, since fundamental mistakes were made on the Ukrainian side that, in retrospect, could have been avoided.

The immediate crisis over Crimea is over, in the sense that it is a fait accompli. Since Ukraine is not a NATO member, there is little that the Alliance can do to alter the facts on the ground. Nor is it entirely obvious that NATO's members would have been uniformly enthusiastic about coming to Ukraine's assistance, since, if it were a member, this would have implied a military showdown with Russia. The longer-term implications of the crisis for NATO, the EU, and their members are only just beginning to be understood. The first and more obvious legacy of the Crimean annexation is the atmosphere of uncertainty and fear, especially due to the presence of Russian passport holders in other parts of Europe—such as Transnistria, which broke away from Moldova after a brief war in 1992—and the concern that they will be used as the pretext for further military "protection" and annexation. Such concerns are palpable within NATO, notably by Poland and the Baltic states, which have invoked Article 4 of NATO's founding treaty that promises consultation whenever any member feels "their territorial integrity, political independence or security" is threatened.

For NATO, Russia's behavior is popularly portrayed as positive, in the sense that it gives the Alliance a sense of purpose at a time when it was casting around for a post-Afghanistan raison d'être. A more nuanced view is that it is mixed news. If the crisis revives NATO, it also has important implications for NATO's future. First, it shifts the geopolitical focus away from "global NATO" back to Europe. This is not entirely good news for Washington, which was in the midst of refocusing its security attention towards Asia, based on the common but erroneous assumption that there were few grave security threats in Europe. This will pose not only awkward questions for the administration about focus and leadership but also economic questions concerning America's overseas military presence, force posture, and any associated expenditure at a time when the defense budget is being reduced. For the European allies, the immediate questions concern thinking more seriously about security, including capabilities and expenditure, and their role in contributing to a credible deterrence for Europe—whether in the NATO or EU guise.

The second implication for NATO is more emphasis on deterrence. Since the potential danger zones lie predominantly beyond NATO (with the obvious exceptions of Poland and the Baltic states), the main emphasis is not going to be on Article 5 type contingencies but on providing a credible deterrence to dissuade any further territorial annexation on NATO's borders. In practical terms this will imply more arms sales (with generous loans if necessary), technical assistance, training, joint exercises with NATO members, aerial and border observation assistance, and intelligence exchanges. Naturally, this also means the indefinite suspension of Russia-NATO relations and arms sales from NATO members to Russia—although diplomatic space will have to be left to engage in discussions.

Conclusions

Many of the points raised in this chapter concerning leadership, defense budgets, and solidarity are subject to interpretation and, we hope, debate. If the points above had to be distilled into a succinct debating motion, it would be as follows: the United States faces a Gordian knot of unaffordable aspirations to global leadership, while many of the European allies are as concerned about the results of American leadership as they are about nonleadership. Both recognize that many of the contemporary security challenges are beyond any one country's ability to address. With a few quibbles here and there, both see the world around them in the same manner and attempt to propagate the same values. Above all, neither has an obvious alternative partner. The challenge for any alliance worth preserving is whether it can foster the conditions to bring about the required changes in mindset so that all parties can learn to work together. The crisis in the Ukraine serves, at the very least, to concentrate minds. The lessons to come out of this crisis require further reflection, but the initial message is clear. Whatever the differences across the Atlantic, the interests of the United States and its European allies are inextricably linked. So too are the EU and NATO in the obvious sense that their memberships largely overlap but also due to the strong political and economic interdependence across the Atlantic. This continues to have profound implications for mutual security, where both organizations and all of their respective members have compelling interests in promoting shared interests and values. Sometimes it takes a crisis to remind us of the obvious.

Notes

1. See Steven Erlanger, "Russian Aggression puts NATO in Spotlight," *New York Times*, March 18, 2014.

2. See Simon Duke and Roberta Haar, "Still at the Crossroads: Europe, the United States and NATO," in *Europe Today*, 4th ed. (Plymouth, UK: Rowman & Littlefield), 399–432.

3. See Simon John Smith, "EU-NATO Cooperation: A Case of Institutional Fatigue?" *European Security* 20, no. 2 (2011): 243–64.

4. See Benjamin Zyla, "Overlap or Opposition? EU and NATO's Strategic (Sub) Culture," *Contemporary Security Policy* 32, no. 3 (2011): 667–87.

5. Trine Flockhart, "Me Tarzan—You Jane: The EU and NATO and the Reversal of Roles," *Perspectives on European Politics and Society* 12, no. 3 (2011): 263–82.

6. See Ryan Lizza, "The Consequentialist: How the Arab Spring Remade Obama's Foreign Policy," *The New Yorker*, May 2, 2011, http://www.newyorker.com/reporting/2011/05/02/110502fa_fact_lizza?currentPage=1 (accessed January 26, 2014).

7. Speech by U.S. Secretary of Defense Robert M. Gates, "The Security and Defense Agenda of NATO," Belgium, June 10, 2011, http://www.defense.gov/speeches/speech.aspx?speechid=1581 (accessed January 26, 2014).

8. Philip Stevens, "Pay Up for NATO or Shut It Down," *Financial Times*, March 7, 2013.

9. See Kurt Volker, "Don't Call It a Comeback," *Foreign Policy*, August 23, 2011, http://www.foreignpolicy.com/articles/2011/08/23/dont_call_it_a_comeback (accessed January 26, 2014); and Kurt Volker, "Libya Not NATO comeback," *New Atlanticist*, August 23, 2011, http://www.atlanticcouncil.org/blogs/new-atlanticist/libya-not-nato-comeback (accessed January 26, 2014).

10. The North Atlantic Treaty, Washington, DC, April 4, 1949, http://www.nato.int/cps/en/natolive/official_texts_17120.htm (accessed January 26, 2014).

11. Konrad Adenauer, *Memoirs 1945–1953* (Chicago: Henry Regnery, 1966), 273.

12. The Western European Union (WEU) was created in 1954, when the 1948 Brussels Treaty was modified. It was a collective self-defense organization that until recently had ten EU members among its full members and, if all forms of membership were included, twenty-eight. Like NATO, the WEU also had article 5 commitments, although in the case of the latter the actual commitment to come to one another's assistance was stronger than in the NATO variant (which only commits the members to take such action as is deemed necessary).

13. Although, in a largely symbolic gesture, NATO AWACs surveillance aircraft were deployed to the United States in order to provide air cover.

14. At NATO, "The NATO Response Force," http://www.nato.int/cps/en/natolive/topics_49755.htm (accessed January 26, 2014).

15. The EU's far more modest and younger version of the NRF, the so-called Battlegroups of around 1,500 combat personnel, has never been deployed since it reached full operational capacity in January 2007.

16. Ivo Daalder and James M. Goldgeier, "Global NATO," *Foreign Affairs* 85, no. 5 (September–October 2006): 11.

17. Ivo Daalder, "The End of Atlanticism," *Survival* 45, no. 2 (Summer 2003): 150.

18. Tobias Bunde and Timo Noetzel, "Unavoidable Tensions: The Liberal Path to Global NATO," *Contemporary Security* 31, no. 2 (August 2010): 298.

19. *Transatlantic Trends: Key Findings 2012*, German Marshall Fund of the United States, 7.

20. NATO, *Strategic Concept for the Defence and Security of the Members of the North Atlantic Treaty Organization*, adopted by the Heads of State and Government at the NATO summit in Lisbon, November 19–20, 2010, para. 7.

21. See Christos Katsioulis, "The New NATO Strategy: A Temporary Compromise," *International Policy Analysis*, Friedrich Ebert Stiftung, January 2011.

22. Celeste Wallender, "Institutional Assets and Adaptability: NATO after the Cold War," *International Organization* 54, no. 4 (Autumn 2000): 729.

23. *Strasbourg / Kehl Summit Declaration*, issued by the Heads of State and Government participating in the meeting of the North Atlantic Council in Strasbourg (France) / Kehl (Germany), April 4, 2009, press release no. (2009) 044, para. 29.

24. Single European Act, February 17, 1986, Luxembourg, Title III, art. 30, 69(a).

25. Franco-British Summit, Joint Declaration on European Defence, Saint Malo, December 4, 1998.

26. Western European Union, *Marseilles Declaration*, November 13 (Marseilles, France: WEU Council of Ministers, 2000).

27. François Heisbourg, "The French-German Duo and the Search for a New European Security Model," *International Spectator* 3 (2004): 62.

28. Council of the European Union, "EU-NATO: The Framework for Permanent Relations and Berlin Plus," November 2003, http://www.consilium.europa.eu/uedocs/cmsUpload/78414%20-%20EU-NATO%20Consultation,%20Planning%20and%20Operations.pdf (accessed January 26, 2014).

29. See European Defence Agency, http://www.eda.europa.eu/Aboutus/Whatwedo/Mission andfunctions (accessed January 26, 2014).

30. See http://consilium.europa.eu/eeas/security-defence/eu-operations?amp;lang=en (accessed January 26, 2014) for details and locations of missions.

31. At the time this consisted of Ireland, which was then joined by Austria, Finland, and Sweden in 1995 and by Cyprus and Malta in 2004.

32. Treaty on European Union (as amended in the Lisbon Treaty), art. 42.

33. Treaty on European Union, art. 42.

34. Steven Blockmans, "The Influence of NATO on the Development of the EU's Common Security and Defence Policy," in *Between Autonomy and Dependence: The EU Legal Order under the Influence of International Organisations*, ed. Ramses A. Wessel and Steven Blockmans (The Hague: TMC Asser Press, 2013), 251.

35. *National Security Strategy*, May 2010, 7.

36. Richard K. Betts, "The Lost Logic of Deterrence: What the Strategy That Won the Cold War Can—and Can't—Do Now," *Foreign Affairs* 92, no. 3 (March–April 2013): 88.

37. See Robert Kagan, "The U.S.-Europe Divide," *Washington Post*, May 26, 2002; and Robert Kagan, *Of Paradise and Power: America and Europe in the New World Order* (New York: Knopf, 2003).

38. Robert Cooper, *The Breaking of Nations: Order and Chaos in the Twenty-First Century* (New York: Atlantic Monthly Press, 1982), 77–78.

39. James Godgeier, *The Future of NATO*, Council on Foreign Relations Special Report no. 51, February (New York: Council on Foreign Relations, 2010), 4.

40. Volker "Don't Call It a Comeback"; and Volker, "Libya Not NATO Comeback."

41. Volker "Don't Call It a Comeback"; and Volker, "Libya Not NATO Comeback."

42. Figures from *SIPRI Yearbook 2012: Armaments, Disarmament and International Security* (Stockholm: SIPRI, 2012), 200; online data available from SIPRI, "The SIPRI Military Expenditure Database," http://milexdata.sipri.org/result.php4 (accessed January 26, 2014).

43. Information on the 2010 Anglo-French defense treaty can be found at "UK and France Open 'New Chapter' on Defence Cooperation," November 2, 2010, http://www.number10 .gov (accessed January 26, 2014).

44. Remarks by Dr. John Chipman, director-general and chief executive, The International Institute for Strategic Studies, London, March 7, 2012, http://www.iiss.org/en/about%20us/press%20room/press%20releases/press%20releases/archive/2012-ebe1/march-1290/military -balance-2012-press-statement-b956 (accessed January 26, 2014).

45. Thom Shanker, "Defense Secretary Warns NATO of 'Dim' Future," *New York Times*, June 10, 2011.

46. Jonathan Masters, "Debt, Deficits, and the Defence Budget," Council on Foreign Relations, February 22, 2013, http://www.cfr.org/us-strategy-and-politics/debt-deficits-defense-budget/p27318 (accessed January 26, 2014).

47. U.S. Department of Defense, "Defense Budget Priorities and Choices," January 2012, http://www.defense.gov.

48. Masters, "Debt, Deficits, and the Defence Budget."

49. See HSBC Global Research, *The World in 2050: From the Top 30 to the Top 100*, January 2012, 13.

50. Data from National Priorities Project, "Annualized Costs of the Wars in Iraq and Afghanistan," http://nationalpriorities.org/cost-of/notes-sources/?redirect=cow (accessed January 26, 2014).

51. Eisenhower Study Group, Brown University, "Costs of War Report," June 2011, http://www.costsofwar.org (accessed January 26, 2014).

52. Statement of Daniel Bertoni, "Veterans' Disability Benefits: Challenges to Timely Processing Persist," Testimony before the Committee on Veterans' Affairs, U.S. Senate, and U.S. Government Accountability Office, March 13, 2013.

53. *United States National Security Strategy*, May 2010, 2.

54. "Remarks by the President," June 8, 2012, http://www.whitehouse.gov (accessed January 26, 2014).

55. U.S. Department of Defense, "Sustaining U.S. Global Leadership: Priorities for 21st Century Defense," strategic guidance, January 3, 2012, http://www.defense.gov/news/Defense_Strategic_Guidance.pdf (accessed January 26, 2014).

56. *United States National Security Strategy*, May 2010, 41.

57. On June 5, 2008, former Russian President Dimitri Medvedev first unveiled the idea of developing a pan-European security treaty: see President of Russia, "The Draft of the European Security Treaty Has Been Published," http://archive.kremlin.ru/eng/text/themes/2009/11/291600_223080.shtml (accessed January 26, 2014).

58. Luis Martinez, "U.S. Assistance to French in Mali Could Serve as Model," *ABC News*, January 21, 2013, http://abcnews.go.com/blogs/politics/2013/01/panetta-u-s-assistance-to-french-in-mali-could-serve-as-model/ (accessed January 26, 2014).

Suggested Readings

Aybet, Gulnur, and Rebecca R. Moore, eds. *NATO: In Search of a Vision*. Washington, DC: Georgetown University Press, 2010.

Bindi, Federiga, ed. *The Foreign Policy of the European Union: Assessing Europe's Role*. Washington, DC: The Brookings Institution, 2010.

Braun, Aurel. *NATO-Russia Relations in the Twenty-First Century*. Abingdon: Routledge, 2008.

Defence Committee, House of Commons. *The Future of NATO and European Defence*. Ninth Report of Session 2007–8. London: House of Commons, 2008.

Deni, John R. *Alliance Management and Maintenance: Restructuring NATO for the 21st Century*. Aldershot: Ashgate, 2007.

Douglas, Frank R. *The United States, NATO, and a New Multilateral Relationship*. Westport, CT: Praeger, 2008.

Goldgeier, James M. *The Future of NATO*. New York: Council on Foreign Relations Press, 2010.

Herd, Graeme P., and John Kriendler, eds. *Understanding NATO in the 21st Century: Alliance Strategies, Security and Global Governance*. Abingdon: Routledge, 2013.

Kaplan, Lawrence. *NATO 1948: The Birth of the Transatlantic Alliance*. Lanham, MD: Rowman & Littlefield, 2007.

Larrabee, F. Stephen. *Turkey as a U.S. Security Partner*. Santa Monica, CA: RAND Corporation, 2008.

Lindley-French, Julian, and Neil Macfarlane. *The North Atlantic Treaty Organization: The Enduring Alliance*. Abingdon, Oxon: Routledge, 2007.

Morelli, Vincent, and Paul Belkin. *NATO in Afghanistan: A Test of the Transatlantic Alliance*. Washington, DC: Congressional Research Service, 2009.

Orfy, Mohammed Moustafa. *NATO and the Middle East: The Geopolitical Context Post-9/11*. Oxford: Routledge, 2011.

Pouliot, Vincent. *International Security in Practice: The Politics of NATO-Russia*. Cambridge: Cambridge University Press, 2010.

Reichard, Martin. *The EU-NATO Relationship: A Legal and Political Perspective*. Burlington, VT: Ashgate, 2006.

Sloan, Stanley R. *Permanent Alliance? NATO and the Transatlantic Bargain from Truman to Obama*. London: Continuum, 2010.

Smith, Julianne. *The NATO-Russia Relationship: Defining Moment or Déjà Vu?* Washington, DC: Center for Strategic and International Studies, 2008.

Smith, Martin J., ed. *Where Is NATO Going?* Abingdon, Oxon: Routledge, 2006.

Thies, Wallace J. *Why NATO Endures*. New York: Cambridge University Press, 2009.

Toje, Asle. *America, the EU and Strategic Culture: Renegotiating the Transatlantic Bargain*. Abingdon, Oxon: Routledge, 2008.

Williams, Michael J. "Enduring but irrelevant? Britain, NATO and the Future of the Atlantic Alliance." *International Politics* 50 (2013): 360–86.

Glossary

acquis communautaire: A French term denoting the sum total of EU treaties, regulations, and laws developed since the 1950s; must be accepted by new member states as it exists at the time of accession.

Barcelona Process: Initial framework to manage bilateral and regional relations between the EU member states and 14 partners in the greater Middle East. Its key goals are to establish an area of peace and security in the Mediterranean, to implement a free-trade agreement, and to bolster institutional contacts between the EU and Middle Eastern countries. It was negotiated in 1995, is currently known as the Euro-Mediterranean Partnership, and was relaunched as the Union for the Mediterranean in 2008. *See also* European Neighborhood Policy.

Bretton Woods system: The international monetary system created at the end of World War II in Bretton Woods, New Hampshire. It was designed to establish international management of the global economy and to provide for the cross-convertibility of national currencies through a fixed exchange rate with gold or with currencies backed by gold (such as the U.S. dollar at that time). The exchange rate system was terminated in 1973, but other key foundations remained in place: the General Agreement on Tariffs and Trade, the International Monetary Fund, and the International Bank for Reconstruction and Development, which in 1956 was merged with other institutions to form the World Bank.

Common Agricultural Policy (CAP): A controversial subsidy and price support system established under the Treaty of Rome to increase agricultural productivity and sustain farm incomes in the European Community. For long it represented more than half of the EU budget. That share has declined through successive revisions, and in 2013 the CAP accounted for only about 30 percent of EU outlays, with another 10 percent going to rural development and fisheries. The main criticism is that such outlays benefit wealthy European farmers and damages developing countries' agricultural exports.

Common Assembly: The parliamentary arm of the European Coal and Steel Community (ECSC). It is the precursor to the European Parliament and existed between 1952 and 1958.

Common Foreign and Security Policy (CFSP): From the Maastricht Treaty to the Lisbon Treaty, this is the "second pillar" of the European Union. In 1991 it replaced the European Political Cooperation. It establishes the broad foreign policy objectives of the EU and requires member states and the EU institutions to cooperate in promoting these objectives. The Lisbon Treaty created a High Representative of the Union for Foreign Affairs and Security Policy as well as an EU diplomatic corps, the European External Action Service.

Common Security and Defence Policy (CSDP): Since the Lisbon Treaty, the successor of the European Security and Defence Policy (ESDP) and part of the Common Foreign and Security Policy. *See also* European Security and Defense Identity (ESDI).

Conference on Security and Cooperation in Europe (CSCE): A process designed to promote European cooperation on trade and human rights. Its members include the United States, Canada, Russia, the former Soviet republics, and all of Europe—adding up to 56 member states. It was renamed the Organization for Security and Cooperation in Europe (OSCE) in 1995.

constitutional monarchy: A monarchy in which the monarch accepts limits on his or her power imposed by a constitution, often keeping mainly ceremonial roles and retaining a safety net for when national politics break down entirely.

consumer price inflation: The rate of increase of the prices for goods and services weighted according to their share in a standard consumption bundle.

Copenhagen criteria: The rules that define whether a nation is eligible to join the European Union. The criteria require a state to have the institutions to preserve democratic governance and human rights, to have a functioning market economy, and to accept the *acquis communautaire* (*see acquis communautaire*). These membership criteria were laid down at the June 1993 European Council in Copenhagen, Denmark.

corporatism: Democratic corporatism provides for the representation of organized economic interest groups in the policymaking process. Most often, such interests include business, labor, agriculture, and so on. In practice representation may be formal, such as in the EU Economic and Social Council and in many national commissions (health, environmental protection, etc.), but most often it is informal through lobby groups that have access to the policymaking process.

Council for Mutual Economic Assistance (CMEA): Economic organization established by the Soviet Union in 1949 to coordinate trade among the communist countries of Central and Eastern Europe. Disbanded in 1991 after the breakup of the Soviet Union.

Council of Europe: Organization established in 1949 to promote European stability through democracy, human rights, and the rule of law. It currently has 47 members, operates the European Court of Human Rights, and is located in Strasbourg. Not to be confused with the European Council. *See* European Council.

Council of Ministers: The decision-making institution of the EU comprising ministerial-level representatives from each of the member states. Differs according to policy field. In cooperation with the European Parliament, it has the power to adopt or reject EU legislation, but it remains subordinate to the European Council's (Heads of State or Government) overall authority.

debt-to-GDP ratio: The ratio of gross public debt to gross domestic product (GDP) across all levels of government. The EU threshold for sustainability is formally put at 60 percent and as such is incorporated in the Stability and Growth Pact.

euro: The single European currency. Introduced in financial market accounting in 1999. Coins and banknotes replaced national currencies in circulation on January 1, 2002.

EUROCORPS: A multinational military corps composed of troops from France, Germany, Spain, Belgium, and Italy. Operated within the framework of the Western European Union.

Eurogroup: The ministers of finance of the euro-zone member states.

European Atomic Energy Agency (Euratom): One of the three European communities set up in the 1950s, established simultaneously with the European Economic Community (EEC) in 1958 to promote the peaceful use of atomic energy. Since 1967, Euratom has shared common institutions with the EEC and the European Coal and Steel Community.

European Bank for Reconstruction and Development (EBRD): A London-based international development bank established in 1991 to promote economic development and political reform in Central and Eastern Europe. Its main shareholders are the EU member states and the EU institutions, along with the United States and Japan.

European Central Bank (ECB): The European Central Bank is located in Frankfurt, Germany, and is responsible for control over—and the stability of—the euro. It sets the interstate monetary policy for the whole of Europe's Economic and Monetary Union, though it has, different from the U.S. Federal Reserve, no outspoken mandate for economic targets other than currency stability.

European Coal and Steel Community (ECSC): The first institution attempting European integration, created under the 1951 Treaty of Paris. Established a common pool for coal and steel products and strong institutions to regulate the coal and steel industries on a supranational basis, especially to make Germany's and France's economies more interdependent.

European Commission: The executive body of the European Union. Initiates legislation, executes EU policies, negotiates on behalf of the EU in international trade forums, and monitors compliance with EU law and treaties by member states.

European Community (EC): Term used informally before 1993 for what the Maastricht Treaty named the European Union (EU).

European Constitution: Also known as the Treaty Establishing a Constitution for Europe; was agreed by the European Council in October 2004. It was designed to provide a constitution for the EU that would allow the institution to function effectively with twenty-seven members following the enlargement that included Central and Eastern European countries. The treaty was rejected by the French and Dutch electorates in national referenda held in 2005. In 2007, negotiations were relaunched and resulted in the adoption of the Lisbon Treaty, the text of which was only slightly different.

European Convention: Also known as the Convention on the Future of Europe. The body was established by the European Council in December 2001 following the Laeken Declaration. Headed by Valery Giscard d'Estaing, it produced a draft EU constitution. The Convention finished its work in July 2003. The draft treaty, establishing a constitution for Europe, later failed ratification.

European Council: The EU institution comprising the Heads of State or Government of the member states and the president of the European Commission. It meets at least twice each year and sets broad guidelines and directions for the development of the EU, as worked out in the Council of Ministers. The Lisbon Treaty provided the Council with a more permanent presidency (a 2.5-year mandate)—next to the rotating one.

European Court of Justice (ECJ): The judicial arm of the European Union, which may decide cases brought by EU member states, institutions, companies, and, in some cases, individuals. It ensures uniform interpretation of EU law by decisions that are binding upon the member states.

European Currency Unit (ECU): Artificial unit of account established to operate the exchange rate mechanism of the European Monetary System; consisted of a basket of member states' currencies. Replaced by the euro on January 1, 1999.

European Economic Area (EEA): Members of the EEA have full access to the European Union's single market in most areas of trade (agriculture and fisheries are exceptions) but do not have influence on the policy decisions of the European Union. The European Economic Area comprises the EU countries and Iceland, Norway, and Liechtenstein.

European Economic Community (EEC): The most important of the original European communities, set up under the 1957 Treaty of Rome to promote an "ever closer union" among the peoples of Europe through the development of a common market, a common external tariff, and common policies in agriculture, transport, and other fields. It was renamed the European Community (EC) in the Maastricht Treaty.

European External Action Service (EEAS): The diplomatic corps of the European Union. It has been created by the Lisbon Treaty, and will report to the High Representative for Foreign Affairs and Security Policy. Its staff comes from the European Commission, the European Council, and the national diplomatic corps.

European Free Trade Association (EFTA): Organization formed in 1960 under British leadership to promote economic cooperation among European states not wishing to become members of the EC. Unlike the EC, it did not have strong supranational institutions or a mandate to promote political union. Lost importance as most of its members decided to join the EC.

European Monetary System (EMS): Exchange rate regime, established in 1979, to limit currency fluctuations within the European Community. Operated an exchange rate mechanism (ERM) under which member states are required to maintain the value of their currencies relative to those of other member states. It laid the groundwork for monetary union and the single currency (euro), established in January 1999.

European Neighborhood Policy (ENP): Policy aimed at providing Europe with stable and peaceful borders and neighbors. The vision is that of a ring of countries, drawn into further integration, but without necessarily becoming full members of the European Union. The policy was first outlined by the European Commission on March 2003 and adopted in 2004. The countries covered include the Mediterranean coastal states of Africa and Asia, as well as the European members of the Commonwealth of Independent States (with the exception of Russia and Kazakhstan) in the Caucasus and Eastern Europe.

European Political Cooperation (EPC): Foreign policy cooperation among the member states of the European Economic Community, established in 1970 and conducted on an intergovernmental basis by foreign ministries. It was officially included in the Single European Act (1986) and replaced by the Common Foreign and Security Policy in the Maastricht Treaty.

European Rapid Reaction Force (ERRF): The European Union Rapid Reaction Force is a transnational military force of 60,000 soldiers available to EU missions. Formal agreement to found the ERRF was reached in November 2004.

European Security and Defense Identity (ESDI): The ESDI was first established by the Western European Union as a means of creating a European pillar within NATO that could fulfill the "Petersberg tasks": rescue and relief, peacekeeping, and peacemaking. Following the Anglo-French meeting at St. Malo in December 1998, responsibility for ESDI was transferred to the EU and it was renamed the ESDP. With the Lisbon Treaty, it was renamed once again to Common Security and Defence Policy (CSDP). It is supported by a number of institutional bodies, including the Political and Security Committee (PSC) of the European Council, an EU Military Committee (EUMC), an EU Military Staff (EUMS), and a European Defence Agency (EDA).

European Security Strategy (ESS): Entitled "A Secure Europe in a Better World," the ESS was drafted by Javier Solana in response to the controversial 2002 National Security Strategy of the United States. Approved by the European Council in December 2003, the ESS identifies a string of key threats that Europe needs to deal with: terrorism, the proliferation of weapons of mass destruction, regional conflict, failed states, and organized crime. The 2008 report "Providing Security in a Changing World" reinforces the ESS.

European Stability Mechanism (ESM): Created in 2011, the ESM is an organization comprising all states that use the euro that provides conditional loan assistance to financially distressed countries in the euro-zone. Direct proportional contributions from the member states provide the collateral for the ESM to borrow money from financial markets.

euro-zone: The group of countries having adopted the euro; also known as the "euro area."

exchange rate mechanism (ERM): A multilateral framework for the joint management of exchange rate movements between participating countries to within set tolerance margins.

General Agreement on Tariffs and Trade (GATT): Multilateral trade treaty signed in 1947 and establishing rules for international trade. Forum for eight rounds of tariff reductions culminating in the 1994 Uruguay Round agreements and the establishment of the World Trade Organization (WTO) as successor to the GATT.

gross domestic product (GDP): Annual value of goods and services produced in a country.

High Authority: The executive body of the European Coal and Steel Community (ECSC). Ceased to exist in July 1967 with the entering into effect of the merger treaty establishing a single commission for the ECSC, Euratom, and the European Economic Community.

intergovernmentalism: Approach to integration in which national governments retain their sovereign powers and cooperate with each other by interstate bargaining and agreement. Opposed to federalism and supranationalism.

Lisbon strategy: Also known as the Lisbon agenda, this is an EU action and development plan adopted for a ten-year period in 2000 in Lisbon, Portugal, by the European Council. The Lisbon strategy intends to deal with the low productivity and stagnation of economic growth in the EU through the formulation of various policy initiatives to be taken by all EU member states. The long-term goal is to make the EU "the world's most dynamic and competitive knowledge-based economy" by 2010. In June 2010, the strategy was replaced by the Europe 2020 strategy.

Lisbon Treaty: Treaty signed in December 2007 but, due to a difficult ratification process, entered into force only in December 2009. Lisbon became the Plan B after the Constitutional Treaty had failed ratification in 2005. Lisbon provides, among other things, for an EU Council president, a diplomatic corps, and a "High Representative of Foreign Affairs and Security Policy." It also boosted the European Parliament with more powers and emphasized the practice of subsidiarity.

Maastricht Treaty: The Treaty on European Union (TEU), known as the Maastricht Treaty, was signed at Maastricht, the Netherlands, on February 7, 1992. It constituted by far the most sweeping revision of European Community treaties ever attempted. The TEU created the entity called the European Union (EU), a complicated structure of three pillars profoundly redefining European economic and political governance and the start of a more organized common foreign policy.

Marshall Plan: Officially known as the European Recovery Program, this plan was proposed in 1947 by U.S. Secretary of State George C. Marshall to foster postwar European economic revival through extensive U.S. aid. It is seen as the economic arm of the Truman doctrine.

nominal long-term interest rate: The rate of return on benchmark government bonds of a set maturity (usually equal to or greater than ten years).

North Atlantic Cooperation Council (NACC): Created by NATO at the Rome summit in November 1991. A U.S. initiative, the NACC was a new institutional relationship of consultation and cooperation on political and security issues open to all of the former, newly independent members of the Warsaw Pact. In July 1997, it was replaced by the Euro-Atlantic Partnership Council (EAPC).

North Atlantic Council: NATO's decision-making body.

North Atlantic Treaty Organization (NATO): A political-military institution founded in 1949 for the collective defense of its member states, which include the United States, Canada, and fourteen European countries. Initially designed against the Soviet threat, the end of the Cold War made NATO enlarge to include Central and Eastern European countries and redefine its mission.

Organization for Economic Cooperation and Development (OECD): An international organization established in 1961 and comprising mainly the industrialized market economy countries of North America, Western Europe, Japan, Australia, and New Zealand. Successor to the OEEC and based in Paris.

Organization for European Economic Cooperation (OEEC): Organization of European Marshall Plan aid recipients, created at the behest of the United States to administer the aid and serve as a forum to negotiate reductions in intra-European barriers to trade.

Organization for Security and Cooperation in Europe (OSCE): See *Conference on Security and Cooperation in Europe.*

parliamentary democracy: The form of democracy in which the composition of the executive branch is determined by the legislative majority, which may also dismiss the executive. The legislative branch of government is elected by the people.

Partnership for Peace (PFP): Framework agreements for non-NATO states to have a military relationship with the alliance.

purchasing power parity (PPP): Adjusts foreign currencies for dollar equivalents in purchasing power.

Schengen Agreement: The 1985 Schengen Agreement is an agreement among European states harmonizing visa requirements and external border controls. Includes all EU states except the Republic of Ireland and the United Kingdom, and includes non-EU members Iceland, Norway, and Switzerland. Border posts and checks have been removed between Schengen countries, and a common "Schengen visa" allows tourist or visitor access to the area.

Single European Act (SEA): First major revision of the founding treaties of the European Community; went into effect in 1987. Increased the powers of the European Parliament, broadened the policy responsibilities of the EC, and, above all, scheduled the completion of a single economic market by December 31, 1992, as a member state treaty commitment.

Stability and Growth Pact (SGP): Adopted in 1997; with this pact, member states promised to maintain certain fiscal statistics so as to support the stability of the euro zone. These include limits to inflation differentials, budget deficits, and debt-to-GDP ratios. The SGP lacks a punishment mechanism.

Stability Pact for South Eastern Europe: The Stability Pact was created by the EU on June 10, 1999, to provide a comprehensive, long-term conflict prevention and peace-building strategy for the Balkans. The Stability Pact is not an organization itself; rather, it offers a political commitment and a framework agreement to develop a shared international approach to enhance stability and growth in the region.

subsidiarity: The practice of handling and deciding issues at the lowest level possible. Through applying subsidiarity, a clearer division of labor between the European and the national levels is envisioned.

supranationalism: Approach to integration in which participating states transfer sovereign powers and policymaking responsibilities to transnational institutions whose decisions are binding on those states. This is, for example, the case regarding the common market of the EU.

Treaty on European Union (TEU): See *Maastricht Treaty.*

Treaty on Stability, Coordination, and Governance (TSCG): Adopted by all member states except the UK and Czech Republic in 2012, the TSCG reduced the level of acceptable structural deficits, required the adoption of a fiscal "golden rule" in national law, and strengthened the oversight of national budgets by the EU Commission and independent national bodies.

unicameral parliament: A legislative body consisting of a single house.

unitary government: The form of government in which the national government is the only repository of sovereign power and in which the powers of subordinate levels of government are determined by the national government.

Warsaw Pact: A military alliance founded by the Soviet Union in 1955 in response to West Germany's entry into NATO. Its membership included the USSR and the countries of Central and Eastern Europe.

Western European Union (WEU): An exclusively Western European mutual defense organization established in 1954. It was moribund through much of the Cold War, revived in 1984 as a vehicle to develop European defense cooperation, and designated the defense arm of the EU in the Maastricht Treaty.

Index

About the Contributors

Gianfranco Baldini is associate professor of political science at the University of Bologna.

Simon Duke is professor at the European Institute for Public Administration (EIPA) in Maastricht.

Eric S. Einhorn is professor emeritus at the University of Massachusetts, Amherst.

Gregory W. Fuller is professorial lecturer at the School of International Service at the American University.

Gabriel Goodliffe is professor of international relations at the Instituto Tecnologico Autonomo de Mexico.

Roberta Haar teaches international relations at Maastricht University.

Jonathan Hopkin is reader in comparative politics at the London School of Economics.

Erik Jones is director of European and Eurasian studies at the Paul H. Nitze School of Advanced International Studies of the Johns Hopkins University.

R. Daniel Kelemen is professor of political science at Rutgers University.

Serhiy Kudelia is assistant professor of political science at Baylor University.

Benedicta Marzinotto is lecturer in political economy at the University of Udine and a visiting professor at the College of Europe.

Jonathon W. Moses is professor of political science at the Norwegian University of Science and Technology, Trondheim.

Bruce Parrott is professor of Russian and Eurasian studies at the Paul H. Nitze School of Advanced International Studies of the Johns Hopkins University.

Sebastián Royo is vice provost and professor of government at Suffolk University in Boston.

Kate Alexander Shaw is a doctoral candidate at the London School of Economics.

Ben Stanley is Marie Curie Post-Doctoral Fellow at the Institute for Public Affairs, Bratislava.

Ronald Tiersky is the Joseph B. Eastman Professor of Political Science at Amherst College.

John Van Oudenaren is director of the World Digital Library (www.wdl.org).

Helga A. Welsh is professor of political science at Wake Forest University.